Christian-Muslim Relations
A Bibliographical History

History of Christian-Muslim Relations

Editorial Board

Jon Hoover (*University of Nottingham*)
Sandra Toenies Keating (*Providence College*)
Tarif Khalidi (*American University of Beirut*)
Suleiman Mourad (*Smith College*)
Gabriel Said Reynolds (*University of Notre Dame*)
Mark Swanson (*Lutheran School of Theology at Chicago*)
David Thomas (*University of Birmingham*)

VOLUME 40

Christians and Muslims have been involved in exchanges over matters of faith and morality since the founding of Islam. Attitudes between the faiths today are deeply coloured by the legacy of past encounters, and often preserve centuries-old negative views.

The History of Christian-Muslim Relations, Texts and Studies presents the surviving record of past encounters in a variety of forms: authoritative, text editions and annotated translations, studies of authors and their works and collections of essays on particular themes and historical periods. It illustrates the development in mutual perceptions as these are contained in surviving Christian and Muslim writings, and makes available the arguments and rhetorical strategies that, for good or for ill, have left their mark on attitudes today. The series casts light on a history marked by intellectual creativity and occasional breakthroughs in communication, although, on the whole beset by misunderstanding and misrepresentation. By making this history better known, the series seeks to contribute to improved recognition between Christians and Muslims in the future.

A number of volumes of the *History of Christian-Muslim Relations* series are published within the subseries *Christian-Muslim Relations. A Bibliographical History.*

The titles published in this series are listed at *brill.com/hcmr*

Christian-Muslim Relations
A Bibliographical History

Volume 15. Thematic Essays
(600-1600)

Edited by
Douglas Pratt and Charles Tieszen

with David Thomas and John Chesworth

TUTA SUB AEGIDE PALLAS · 1683 ·

BRILL

LEIDEN · BOSTON
2020

Arts & Humanities Research Council

Cover illustration: Mosaic showing Sultan Mehmed II (r. 1444-6, 1451-81) officially recognising Gennadios II (r. 1454-64) as Ecumenical Patriarch. Alamy stock image, HX1K1X

The Library of Congress Cataloging-in-Publication Data is available online at http://lccn.loc.gov/2009029184

Typeface for the Latin, Greek, and Cyrillic scripts: "Brill". See and download: brill.com/brill-typeface.

ISSN 1570-7350
ISBN 978-90-04-42319-0 (hardback)
ISBN 978-90-04-42370-1 (e-book)

Koninklijke Brill NV incorporates the imprints Brill, Brill Hes & De Graaf, Brill Nijhoff, Brill Rodopi, Brill Sense, Hotei Publishing, mentis Verlag, Verlag Ferdinand Schöningh and Wilhelm Fink Verlag.

This book is printed on acid-free paper and produced in a sustainable manner.

CONTENTS

Foreword vii

Editors' Preface xii

Abbreviations xiv

Contributor Notes xv

1 Introduction. *Douglas Pratt and Charles Tieszen* 1

2 Relational dynamics in the first millennium. A thematic analysis. *Douglas Pratt* 23

3 Encounter and inquiry. Trajectories of interaction. *David Bertaina* 53

4 Christians, Muslims and the True Religion. *Mark N. Swanson* 73

5 Debating the concept of God. *I. Mark Beaumont* 99

6 Muslim perceptions of Jesus. *Mourad Takawi and Gabriel Said Reynolds* 123

7 Christian perceptions of Muḥammad. *Clinton Bennett* 153

8 Defending the faith. Lines of apology. *Sandra Toenies Keating* 181

9 Muslims engaging the Bible. *Ayşe İçöz* 207

10 Latin Christianity engaging with the Qur'an. *Ulisse Cecini* 227

11 'Our Friendly Strife'. Eastern Christianity engaging the Qur'an. *Gordon Nickel* 255

12 The crusades to the eastern Mediterranean, 1095-1291. *Nicholas Morton* 281

13 Conduits of interaction. The Andalusi experience. *Juan Pedro Monferrer Sala* 307

14 Interactions in the early Ottoman period (1299-1518). *Tom Papademetriou* 331

15 Muslim rulers, Christian subjects. *Luke Yarbrough* 359

16 Martyrdom and conversion. *Christian C. Sahner* 389

17 Muslim and Christian apocalypticism. Playing off each other. *David Bryan Cook* 413

18 Conflict, conquest and reconquest. Arabian and Iberian experience. *James Harry Morris* 435

19 Christian missions to Muslims. *Martha T. Frederiks* 461

20 Discussing religious practices. *Charles Tieszen* 489

Bibliography 515

Index of *CMR* References 559

Index 571

FOREWORD

David Thomas

The aim of the *Christian-Muslim relations, a bibliographical history* (herein, *CMRBH*) project is to provide a complete history of works written by Christians and Muslims, or authors writing in Christian and Islamic contexts, about or for the other and against them in the period 600-1914. It includes expositions of the beliefs of the other, encompassing their scriptural teachings, doctrines and religious practices; polemical works that set out to expose flaws in their religious claims; and apologetic works that respond to accusations. Alongside these, it includes travelogues that describe the other and in the process invariably divulge the attitude of the author to their religion and culture, and histories of the other, nearly always in the form of Christian accounts of the life of Muḥammad and the first generation of Muslims, together with histories of Islamic regimes.

The works included contain a broad variety of reactions to the other faith and its followers. On the Muslim side, there are arguments that God is not multiple and Jesus was no more than a human prophet, aimed against the doctrines of the Trinity and Incarnation and supporting the qur'anic teaching that God is one and does not share divinity. There are also historical explanations of how the original *Tawrāt* and *Injīl*, which as revealed books would originally have agreed in essence with the Qur'an, were corrupted and resulted in the impaired historical Torah and Gospels. To match these there are Christian accounts of how a fraudulent Muḥammad attracted a following and grew in political power, sometimes through demonic assistance, and how the Qur'an is no more than a rough and inaccurate paraphrase of the Bible.

A particular feature of Christian works in the earlier part of this period, when the majority who knew about Islam and were concerned to counter it were living as clients under Muslim rule, is the strategies they employed to resist the other faith. There are a few uncompromisingly savage attacks on the moral probity of Muḥammad, and on the inconsistencies and confusions in the Qur'an, written by prudently anonymous authors, stories of converts to Islam who reverted to their original Christianity and then, to demonstrate the truth of the faith to which they had returned, actively sought martyrdom from Muslims, and a series of apocalypses that situated the current sufferings of the Christians in the wider sweep of divinely willed history and predicted the eventual triumph of the faith. These were some of the main means by which Christian authors attempted to staunch the flow of Christians to Islam and to make clear that Christianity was the true, God-given faith.

Of course, this kind of apologetic literature is not matched among Muslim works, because vastly fewer Muslims were tempted to convert to Christianity (though there were some). The main reason for this is that for most of this period Christians and Muslims encountered one another in situations where Muslims were in the political ascendant, and had tangible proof in the form of the victorious Islamic state to support their claim that theirs was the faith blessed by God. The rule of Islam was quickly established in the 7th and early 8th centuries, embracing substantial populations of Christians in the Middle East, North Africa and the Iberian Peninsula. Christians living within the Islamic Empires were compelled to accommodate their personal and communal lives to Muslim expectations, and to the Pact of ʿUmar that, among other things, required them to show deference to Muslims and to keep themselves separate from them. Even though this pact, which was in existence in some form by about 800 (it was usually linked with the second caliph ʿUmar ibn al-Khaṭṭāb, in order to lend it authority), was rarely applied systematically by Muslim authorities, it must always have been in the background as a disincentive to frank expression by Christians of what they thought about their rulers' faith. Hence the anonymous diatribes, testimonies of martyrdom, and apocalypses.

The period from 600 to 1600 was one of great variety in the ways that followers of the two faiths interacted, not to speak of the underlying motivations. All this is traced in the first seven volumes of the series (*CMR* 1-7), each collecting together entries on known works, and focusing on the information or hints in these works about what the followers of one faith wrote about the other and the attitudes they developed as they reflected on the implications of what they knew. If anyone were to read through these entries as they are set out in the chronological order followed in the volumes of *CMRBH*, they would find these attitudes surprisingly consistent, though extremely varied in detail, pointing to the likelihood that as time went on authors both Christian and Muslim turned to earlier comments in written and oral form. While it is rarely easy to substantiate this for the first centuries of encounter, it becomes easier as surviving works increase in number. Thus, what can be called an informal motif tradition towards the other came into being, and there are signs that for many polemicists reference to this was preferred to direct encounter with followers of the other religion. Attitudes on both sides thus tended to become set and stereotypical, and perceptions were perpetuated without reference to what the other actually taught or believed.

A clear example on the Christian side is the suspicion that Muḥammad was assisted in the compilation of his scripture and the development of his teachings by a disaffected Christian, who was the source of what for Christians were the incomplete and inaccurate versions of Bible stories and denials of their fundamental doctrines to be found in the Qur'an. From a very early date a tradition existed among Muslims that while he was on a journey the young Muḥammad met a Christian hermit who recognised him as the prophet who was foretold in the hermit's Christian books. Christians came to know of this, and recast the hermit first as a heretic who was the teacher of the relatively naïve Arab and supplied him with ideas intended to correct misguided church teachings, and then gradually as a disaffected church leader who used Muḥammad as his instrument for revenge, or even a demon who decanted heresies into Muḥammad's ear. All these manifestations served the purpose of showing why Muḥammad could present himself as a prophet, and how he acquired a scripture that vaguely approximated to the Bible. This explanation gained widespread popularity, not only among Christians in the Islamic world, where it originated, but also throughout Europe.

An equally vivid example on the Muslim side is the explanation of how the historical Torah and Gospels deviated from the Qur'an on crucial issues. Based on statements in the Qur'an, Muslim belief was that the original *Tawrāt* and *Injīl* were revelations from God and agreed in essentials with it. The Qur'an also hinted that the communities to which these two revelations had been given had hidden parts of them, and also substituted and altered parts. On this basis, Muslims widely repudiated the Torah and Gospels as unreliable, while some authors attempted to explain the historical processes by which corruption of the original *Tawrāt* and *Injīl* and distortion of their doctrines had occurred. One of the earliest versions, from around 800, was that the Apostle Paul, who was a scoundrel, had persuaded three of his followers, who were named Yaʿqūb, Nasṭūr and Malkūn, that Jesus was divine (thus creating the three Christian denominations most prevalent in the Islamic world, the *Yaʿqūbiyya*, the *Nasṭūriyya* and the *Malkiyya*), though he failed with a fourth, al-Mu'min (the believer), who maintained his pure monotheism in the wilderness of Arabia and passed it on to his followers, who would be the predecessors of the Muslims. Another version, from the mid-9th century, is that when Christ was taken away from the disciples and they were scattered the *Injīl* was lost, and then a short time later four Christians volunteered to make reconstructions of it and produced only partially accurate Gospels. Other versions give equally tantalising accounts that appear to play with known facts in order to arrive at results that both concur with truths acknowledged by Christians and also support Muslim beliefs about the Bible.

Explanations such as these, built up and elaborated over time, became accepted among Christians and Muslims as authentic, despite being no more than speculations based in inferences and unfounded interpretations. They feature regularly in the works left by the many authors recorded in the entries in the seven volumes of *CMRBH*, although finding them presents a formidable challenge, for while the entries in each volume follow a chronological sequence they cannot easily be linked together into a smooth narrative. Hence the importance of a thematic history of Christian-Muslim relations as sketched in this volume of essays (*CMRTE*).

This is the first of two volumes that accompany the bibliographical history volumes (the second, covering the years 1600-1914, will appear among the final volumes in the *CMR* series). The essays of thematic history take up main topics that arise in the works analysed in the entries in *CMRBH* and link together their individual treatments into broad accounts that show when the motif traditions first appeared and developed over time, and how they appeared in the different regions of the Christian and Islamic worlds. Sometimes the vehicle of transmission was explicitly named, but more often it was not. Of course, this is not to say that the process by which a tradition came into existence and was accepted as a normative account or interpretation involved conscious choice on the part of the individuals who passed on arguments or narrative accounts. It is more likely that a particular apologetic or polemical element, or indeed a book written by a respected master, was recognised for its intrinsic worth and was repeated until it was taken as normative without question.

The essays in this volume also constitute a first attempt to gauge how attitudes towards the religious others gradually came to form a context in which encounters between Christians and Muslims, both live and literary, took place. They begin to explain how, for example, without explanation or justification, Christians could call Muḥammad a fraud, wicked, lascivious and inspired by the devil, and how Muslims could reject Christian belief in God as tritheism or even polytheism, and dismiss the Bible as corrupt.

It should be made clear that this volume is not an attempt to order the variegated history of Christian-Muslim relations into a tidy plan or chart in which all the records of encounters could be located and placed in relation to one another. The history is far too diverse and intricate for that. Neither is it an attempt to present a comprehensive account of the full range of relations. Too much remains unrecorded or no longer extant, and too many elements that made up relations lie beyond the limits of documentation in the form of personal friendships and loves, and the relatively stable communal living that must have continued for years in towns and villages.

This first *CMRTE* volume represents an attempt to give some shape to the records of encounter in the first millennium of relations between Christians and Muslims. Its interpretations may be held up to question and in time they may be reshaped, refined or overturned. But that is welcome, because this volume constitutes an invitation to a conversation about how impressions and guesses turned into perceptions that gradually gained hold as the motif traditions came into being, and both Christians and Muslims absorbed them without full consideration for their potential to stain and taint relationships.

Any communications regarding the views expressed here (which are those of each contributor) can be sent to David Thomas at d.r.thomas.1@bham.ac.uk

EDITORS' PREFACE

Christians and Muslims have encountered, engaged and interacted with each other, whether directly or indirectly, since early in the 7th century of the Common Era. In the process, works pertaining to Muslim-Christian relations were written 'by individuals seeking to gain a picture of the nature of the other faith, or to persuade others to adopt particular attitudes towards it, or else to defend their own faith from accusations that by comparison with the other it was incoherent or is some other way deficient' (D. Thomas, 'Introduction', in D. Thomas (ed.), *Routledge handbook on Christian–Muslim relations*, Abingdon, 2018, 1-6, p. 2). The bibliographical history (*CMRBH*) project has yielded multiple volumes (denoted *CMR*), also published online, of entries on works that together bear testimony to the record of that interaction. This volume of essays (*CMRTE*) comprising a thematic history attempts to draw out the content, to provide an indication of what has been the substance, the agenda, of the interaction during the period 600 to 1600. A second volume, taking the coverage up to 1914, will eventually follow. A measure of chronological overlap is to be expected, as the second volume continues to explore themes that are found in the first. However, some themes and topics appear to fade out toward the end of the first millennium, while yet other new ones may well emerge.

The division that defines the two volumes is largely arbitrary, although it does reflect two distinctions. The first is geographical. Due entirely to the locations in which Christians and Muslims interacted during the first millennium and, concomitantly, the origins of the texts they produced that constitute our principal material evidence, this volume is necessarily restricted to western Asia, northern Africa, and south-western Europe. The next *CMRTE* volume will have a much broader geographical scope in direct correlation to the period on which it concentrates.

The second distinction is between classical and early-modern eras on the one hand and, on the other, the emergence of what, in the West at least, is regarded as the 'modern era' with all the developments of communications' technologies, travel, exploration, and globalisation trajectories that went with it. This latter era is premised on what went before, varyingly modifying, developing or simply striving to maintain the traditions of the past. It would appear some themes and topics emerge more toward the end of the first 1000-year period traversed by the *CMRBH* project, and these may be expected to be reflected in regards to their development within the purview of the second volume of thematic history. In short, the first millennium of Christian-Muslim engagement sets the scene for the modern era and, together, the two volumes should provide the backdrop for what is often referred to as the post-modernity of the 20th and 21st centuries.

As with the bibliographical history project (*CMRBH*), this volume of thematic essays is conceived and designed especially as a means of assisting scholars, as well as others, to grapple not only with historical matters but also with contemporary issues of Christian–Muslim relations. Discerning the themes was premised on the bibliographical history project. Accordingly, the contributors of the essays in this volume were asked to consult and use relevant entries in the *CMR* volumes. As chapters 1 and 2 will show, some preliminary sieving of arguments, stories and records into thematic groups had already been undertaken in order to determine the themes to be included.

The editors of this volume are grateful for the readiness of contributors to take on the task of checking through the many pages of *CMR* in order to find the examples they needed, and to link and discuss these within the essays in this volume. They are also grateful to David Thomas who entrusted this task to them, to Carol Rowe for her meticulous copy editing, to the attention and work of the Brill production team, and to John Chesworth for his sterling support and his maintaining communication with the publisher in bringing this volume to fruition.

Douglas Pratt & Charles Tieszen
March 2020

ABBREVIATIONS

AH
Anno Hegira

BSOAS
Bulletin of the School of Oriental and African Studies

CMR
Christian-Muslim Relations, a Bibliographical History (600-1600), vols 1-7, Leiden, 2009-15

CMRBH
Christian-Muslim Relations, a bibliographical history (research project)

CMRTE
Christian-Muslim Relations, Thematic Essays

ICMR
Islam and Christian – Muslim Relations

*EI*1
Encyclopaedia of Islam

*EI*2
Encyclopaedia of Islam, 2nd edition

*EI*3
Encyclopaedia of Islam Three

EQ
Encyclopaedia of the Qur'an

Q
Qur'an

CONTRIBUTOR NOTES

I. Mark Beaumont is a Research Associate at the London School of Theology. He completed an Open University PhD through the Oxford Centre for Mission Studies in 2003. He has published articles and monographs focusing on theological issues in Christian-Muslim debate and recently edited a collection of essays, *Arab Christians and the Qur'an from the Origins of Islam to the Medieval Period* (Leiden, 2018). He has also recently published the monograph *Jesus in Muslim-Christian Conversation* (Eugene OR, 2018).

Clinton Bennett has taught Religious Studies at the State University of New York at New Paltz since 2008. He earned his PhD (Islamic Studies) from the University of Birmingham in 1990. He is also a graduate of Manchester and Oxford Universities. His most recent publication, *Sufism, Democracy and Pluralism* (Sheffield, 2017) was co-edited with Sarwar Alam. Dr Bennett is Western Europe Team leader with the Christian-Muslim Relations: a bibliographical history, 1500-1900, project.

David Bertaina PhD (Catholic University of America, 2007) is Associate Professor of History at the University of Illinois at Springfield. He teaches on religion in Late Antiquity and the Medieval Middle East. His research focuses on the history of Christian-Muslim encounters and he is co-editor of *Heirs of the Apostles. Studies on Arabic Christianity in Honor of Sidney H. Griffith* (Leiden, 2019).

Ulisse Cecini, a philologist, is a postdoctoral researcher at the Universitat Autònoma de Barcelona. His main field of expertise is Latin. He obtained his PhD (2010) at the University of Erlangen-Nuremberg with a thesis on Latin Qur'ān translations in the 12th and 13th centuries. Dr Cecini is also competent in Greek, Arabic, Hebrew, Aramaic and Sanskrit. In 2018 he published in the *Corpus Christianorum* series the critical edition of the Latin translation of the Talmud (1245). With an orientation toward the study of cross-cultural relationships through textual analysis, his research interests are with relations between Christians, Muslims and Jews in the Middle Ages; translations from Arabic and Hebrew into Latin; translation theories and interreligious cultural transfer in the Middle Ages.

David Bryan Cook PhD (University of Chicago, 2001) is professor of Religion at Rice University, Houston, Texas specialising in Muslim apocalyptic literature and movements, both classical and contemporary. He gained his doctorate with a thesis entitled 'Beginnings of Islam in Umayyad Syria'. His most recent publications include *Top of Form 'The Book of Tribulations. The Syrian Muslim Apocalyptic Tradition'. An Annotated Translation by Nu'aym b. Ḥammād al-Marwazī* Bottom of Form (Edinburgh, 2018). He is currently the co-editor of the series *Edinburgh Studies in Muslim Apocalypticism and Eschatology*.

Martha T. Frederiks PhD (Utrecht, 2003) holds the Chair for the Study of World Christianity at Utrecht University (the Netherlands). She is team leader for Africa and the Americas with the CMR1900 bibliographical history project. Together with Lucien van Liere she is the managing editor of *Exchange: Journal for Contemporary Christianities in Context*. Her research interests include the study of Christianity and Christian-Muslim relations in Africa.

Ayşe İçöz is a Research Assistant at Marmara University in Istanbul. She obtained her PhD from the University of Birmingham (2017) with a thesis entitled *Christian Morality in the Language of Islam. The Case of al-Maṣābīḥ Chapter in the Kitāb al-Majdal*. Currently, she is interested in exploring the development of moral theories in Christian Arabic sources and the ways in which Arabic language was adopted and used by Medieval Christian authors as an apologetic tool.

Sandra Toenies Keating PhD (Catholic University of America, 2001) is Associate Professor of Theology at Providence College. She is a graduate of the Pontifical Institute of Arabic and Islamic Studies (PISAI, 1995) and has published numerous articles in the area of early Christian-Muslim relations. She is the author of *Defending the "People of Truth" in the Early Islamic Period. The Christian Apologies of Abū Rā'iṭah* (Leiden, 2006). She is an editor of HCMR, and is most recently a co-editor of *Heirs of the Apostles. Studies on Arabic Christianity in Honor of Sidney H. Griffith* (Leiden, 2019).

Juan Pedro Monferrer Sala PhD (University of Granada, 1996) is currently Full Professor of Arabic and Islamic Studies at the University of Córdoba. His research interests include Arabic literature (Jewish, Christian and Muslim); manuscript editing, textual criticism, literary criticism, and comparative Semitics. His most recent publications include *De Córdoba a Toledo. Tathlīth al-Waḥdāniyyah ('La Trinidad de la Unidad'). Fragmentos teológicos de un judeoconverso arabizado*, in collaboration with Pedro Mantas (Madrid, 2018); '"You brood of vipers!" Translations and revisions in the Andalusi Arabic version of the Gospels', *Le Muséon* 131/1-2 (2018) 187-215; and 'Qur'ānic Textual Archaeology. Rebuilding the Story of the Destruction of Sodom and Gomorra', in I.M. Beaumont (ed.), *Arab Christians and the Qur'an from the Origins of Islam to the Medieval Period*, Leiden, 2018, 20-49.

James Harry Morris FRAS, completed his PhD (University of St Andrews, Scotland, 2018) with a thesis on conversion to Christianity in Japan. He is presently an Assistant Professor in the Center for Education of Global Communication at the University of Tsukuba, Japan. A member of the Northeast Asia sub-team of the CMR bibliographical history project, he has published on Christian-Muslim Relations in China and Japan, and on Syriac Christianity in East Asia. Dr Morris is an Associate Researcher with the Centre for the Study of Religion and Politics at the University of St Andrews and the Japan Studies' editor of *The Digital Orientalist.*

Nicholas Morton is a lecturer in History at Nottingham Trent University, UK. He is the author and/or editor of several books covering themes of crusading and Christian–Islamic relations during the medieval period. His most recent book, *The Field of Blood. The Battle for Aleppo and the Remaking of the Medieval Middle East* was published by Basic Books (New York, 2018). He is also an editor of two Routledge book series: *Rulers of the Latin East* and *The Military Religious Orders*. At present he is working on a general military and political history of the Near East.

Gordon Nickel PhD (University of Calgary, 2004), has taught on Islam and the Qur'an at Associated Canadian Theological Schools, the University of Calgary, Trinity Evangelical Divinity School, and the University of British Columbia. He recently completed an assignment as director of the Centre for Islamic Studies at the South Asia Institute of Advanced Christian Studies in Bangalore. He is a member of the South Asia team for *Christian-Muslim Relations: A Bibliographical History*. Gordon is author of *Narratives of Tampering in the Earliest Commentaries on the Quran* (Leiden, 2011), *The Gentle Answer to the Muslim Accusation of Biblical Falsification* (Calgary, 2015), and *The Quran with Christian Commentary* (New York, 2019).

Tom Papademetriou PhD (Princeton University, 2001) is Professor of Historical Studies at Stockton University, Galloway, New Jersey. His research focuses on the history of non-Muslims under Ottoman rule, especially the relations of the Greek Orthodox Church and state in the early Ottoman centuries which is the subject of his book, *Render unto the sultan. Power, authority, and the Greek Orthodox church in the early Ottoman centuries* (Oxford, 2015).

Douglas Pratt FRAS, FRHistS, PhD (1984, St Andrews, Scotland) DTheol (2009, Melbourne College of Divinity), taught Religious Studies at the University of Waikato, New Zealand, for 30 years. Now retired, he is currently Honorary Professor, *Theological and Religious Studies* (University of Auckland, NZ); Adjunct Professor, *Theology and Interreligious Studies* (University of Bern, Switzerland;) Adjunct Professor, *Law and Religion* (The University of Fiji); Senior Research Fellow, *School of Philosophy, Theology and Religion* (University of Birmingham, UK) and Associate Researcher, *Centre for the Study of Religion and Politics* (University of St Andrews, UK). He has researched and written on contemporary religious issues and Christian-Muslim relations, including *Christian Engagement with Islam: Ecumenical Journeys since 1910* (Leiden, 2017) and *The Challenge of Islam. Encounters in Interfaith Dialogue* (Abingdon, 2017). Professor Pratt is leader of the Asia research team (1500-1900) and a member of the 19th century editorial team on the CMR bibliographical history project.

Gabriel Said Reynolds PhD (Yale University, 2003) is Professor of Islamic Studies and Theology at the University of Notre Dame. He is Chair, Board of Directors of the International Qur'anic Studies Association and the author of *The Qur'an and the Bible. Text and Commentary* (Yale, 2018), among other works.

Christian C. Sahner PhD (Princeton University, 2015), is an associate professor of Islamic History at the Oriental Institute, University of Oxford, and a fellow of St Cross College. His research deals with the transition from Late Antiquity to the early Islamic period, relations between Muslims and Christians, and the history of Syria and Iran. His most recent book is *Christian Martyrs under Islam. Religious Violence and the Making of the Muslim World* (Princeton NJ, 2018).

Mark N. Swanson is the Harold S. Vogelaar Professor of Christian-Muslim Studies and Interfaith Relations at the Lutheran School of Theology at Chicago. His doctorate is from the Pontifical Institute of Arabic and Islamic Studies (PISAI, 1992) in Rome. He is the author of *The Coptic Papacy in Islamic Egypt (641-1517)* (Cairo and New York, 2010). He was the Christian Arabic section editor for *Christian-Muslims Relations. A Bibliographical History* (vols. 1-5).

Mourad Takawi earned his PhD from the University of Notre Dame (2019), where he is currently a postdoctoral fellow. His research focuses on the reception of the Qur'an and Christian-Muslim encounters in the Medieval Islamic World.

Charles Tieszen FRHistS, PhD (2010, University of Birmingham), is an Adjunct Professor for Islamic studies and Christian-Muslim relations at Fuller Theological Seminary. He was made a Fellow of the Royal Historical Society in 2019. His recent monograph is *Cross Veneration in the Medieval Islamic World* (London, 2017) and has edited *Theological Issues in Christian-Muslim Dialogue* (Eugene OR, 2018). He is currently writing a book on Christian assessments of the Prophet Muḥammad. Dr Tieszen is a member of the 19th century editorial team on the CMR bibliographical history project.

Luke Yarbrough PhD (Princeton University, 2012) is Assistant Professor in the Department of Near Eastern Languages and Cultures at the University of California Los Angeles. His research focuses on interreligious relations and contacts in the premodern Islamic world. He is author of *Friends of the Emir. Non-Muslim State Officials in Premodern Islamic Thought* (Cambridge, 2019) and editor-translator of *The Sword of Ambition: Bureaucratic Rivalry in Medieval Egypt* (New York, 2016).

Chapter 1
Introduction

Douglas Pratt and Charles Tieszen

As the term suggests, Christian-Muslim relations is about the ebb and flow of interactive encounter between the two faiths, whether immediate, face-to-face and interpersonal, or mediated across time, space and different languages. Paradoxically, it can also be about the lack of relationship or even about 'anti-relationship', in that there is either no direct engagement of any sort, but rather only prejudicial perceptions or assumptions about each other, or at times an attitude of rejection and resistance to the idea of acknowledging the other as a relational partner in any sense. Certainly, as a field of human engagement, Christian-Muslim relations is about people and ideas, both of self and of others. It is people who interact, who stand in some kind of relation one to another, whether positive, negative, neutral, indifferent, or otherwise. People bring to the context of relationship a perspective of the other with whom they are engaging. Moreover, this perspective is shaped varyingly by predisposition, presupposition and prejudice. Much depends on background knowledge and assumptions, on the one hand, and the context of any given relational interaction, on the other. People interact, and in the interaction, ideas of one another may be confirmed, challenged or changed. Whether the result is positive or negative largely depends on the complex matrix of what is brought into the encounter (in terms of ideas), the context of the encounter (social, political and/or religious setting) and the quality and aims of the interlocutors of the encounter (including intellectual acumen, educational level, self-perception in relation to the other, as in, e.g., a sense of superiority versus a sense of relative equality).

'Christians and Muslims have approached each other throughout history in multiple ways', notes Mona Siddiqui, adding that this has been 'often without meeting one another but in written responses to the polemics against their faith'.[1] Yet the historical inception and early development of Islam certainly took place, to a large degree, 'in dialogue

---

[1] M. Siddiqui, 'Introduction', in M. Siddiqui (ed.), *The Routledge reader in Christian-Muslim relations*, London, 2013, 1-17, p. 1.

with Christianity' with the result that 'the engagement of Muslims and Christians [has ever been] a most particular dialogue'.[2] Direct and immediate relationship has always been present, although by no means universally so, down through the centuries. Furthermore, 'dialogue' or relational engagement, whether direct or indirect, has taken many forms – not all of them suggestive of mutually positive or appreciative relationship. Yet alongside the testimony to negative interaction, there are also indications of positive and relatively neutral forms of engagement and perception. In this regard, Asma Afsaruddin suggests that the 'spirit of inclusiveness that prevailed in the early [Muslim] community toward Jews and Christians' may provide a reference point for today.[3] Her comment throws up an underlying reason for a volume of thematic history such as this: to quarry the past in order to understand better the present and discern options for the future. History is alive; the past impacts the present in multiple ways. For, indeed,

> [...] relations between the two faiths and their perceptions of one another are undeniable influences behind many current conflicts, declarations of mutual recognition and peace negotiations, not to speak of the brooding hatred of religious extremists.[...] The re-emergence of questions about relations between Christians and Muslims in the last few decades is only the latest phase in a history that goes back to the early seventh century.[4]

Christianity and Islam have a shared history of theological dynamics: each experienced 'internal schisms brought about by theological and political conflicts'.[5] Further, Islam, as a historical reality, emerged and developed 'in both confrontation and conversation with Christians', with the result that 'certain themes have continued to recur as prevailing points of debate and polemic over the centuries'.[6] Whilst, to be sure, there are some points of apparent commonality, differences – of belief, perception, worldview understanding and so forth – are deep and wide-ranging. Philosophical and theological debates have ranged over many subjects, including the concept of God, the Incarnation and crucifixion of Jesus, the prophethood of Muḥammad, the afterlife, and many others. 'Theological issues are crucially important in the relationships between

---

[2] D. Madigan, 'Christian-Muslim dialogue', in C. Cornille (ed.), *The Wiley-Blackwell companion to inter-religious dialogue*, Oxford, 2013, 244-60, p. 245

[3] A. Afsaruddin, *The first Muslims. History and memory*, Oxford, 2008, p. 198.

[4] D. Thomas, 'Introduction', in D. Thomas (ed.), *Routledge handbook on Christian-Muslim relations*, Abingdon, 2018, 1-5, p. 1.

[5] Siddiqui, *Routledge reader in Christian-Muslim relations*, p. 1.

[6] Siddiqui, *Routledge reader in Christian-Muslim relations*, p. 1.

Christians and Muslims, not least because they have been central throughout that dialogical history.'[7] Interestingly, Dan Madigan identifies the underlying issue of 'the proximate other' as critical in the outworking of relations between Christians and Muslims, for each is 'the other who is problematic because [of being] too-much-like-us, or perhaps even claiming-to-be-us'.[8] Theological issues are certainly at the heart of dissension and tension in much of the history of interaction between Muslims and Christians, and several of these are directly addressed in this volume.[9]

However, theology and overtly religious topics do not tell the whole story for, as has also been rightly observed, 'the Islamic and Christian civilisations have had a long history of civilisational cross-pollination without which our present (post-) modern world would not have been possible'.[10] And it is equally true, as Richard Bulliet points out, that the 'past and future of the West cannot be fully comprehended without appreciation of the twinned relationship it has had with Islam over some fourteen centuries', and he adds that this is equally so with respect to the Islamic world.[11] Although issues of the relationship between the world of Islam and the West – indeed, the whole non-Islamic world – is itself of pressing concern and interest, this wider – and more modern – relationship is not our focal concern here. Rather this volume, and the project of which it is a part, is concerned with the history of interaction that has taken place between Christianity and Islam. It is a history that has been enacted, engaged in and experienced by the followers of these faiths and testimony to it is found in the extant records that the CMR bibliographical history (*CMRBH*) project references.

There is, of course, 'no one dominant account of Christian-Muslim encounter nor is there one authoritative voice. Both these religions are lived religions with complex histories of conflict and coexistence which have influenced mutual perceptions and understandings over centuries.'[12] In fact, this history 'is replete with examples of cooperation and cross-fertilization, of examples where adherents of one community received

---

[7] M. Accad, *Sacred misinterpretation. Reaching across the Christian-Muslim divide*, Grand Rapids MI, 2019, p. xxiv.

[8] Madigan, 'Christian-Muslim dialogue', p. 244.

[9] I.M. Beaumont, 'Debating the concept of God' (ch. 5); M. Takawi and G.S. Reynolds, 'Muslim perceptions of Jesus' (ch. 6); C. Bennett, 'Christian perceptions of Muḥammad' (ch. 7).

[10] A. Duderija and H. Rane, *Islam and Muslims in the West*, Cham, Switzerland, 2019, p. 11.

[11] R. Bulliet, *The case for Islamo-Christian civilization*, New York, 2004, p. 10.

[12] Siddiqui, 'Introduction', *Routledge reader*, p. 1.

care, inspiration, or companionship from adherents of the other', and yet there are also many 'examples of antagonism, dominance, and even violence between the two communities'.[13] Indeed, as has been noted, any attempt to navigate 'one's way through the ambiguities of this history [...] can be daunting.'[14] The CMR project, underway since 2005, is producing the sort of resources that will help in this navigation. As at the end of 2019, 14 volumes of bibliographical entries, spanning the 6th to the 18th centuries of Christian-Muslim relations, have been produced.[15] However, it is the first seven volumes, spanning the first millennium (600-1600), that undergird the work and production of this volume of thematic essays on Christian-Muslim relations (*CMRTE*).

A key criterion is that the thematic history needs to connect closely to, and reflect, the bibliographical history (*CMRBH*). *CMRTE* thus engages relevant texts from this history with a view to discerning the development and transmission of themes reflected in them. The focus is on what reflects and reveals something of the relational dynamics that have engaged these two faiths. Contributing essays trace trajectories of development with respect to tropes of perception, image and judgement, and so forth, which are held by each with regard to the other; or otherwise discuss relational dynamics and issues that have obtained between Christians and Muslims. Selected themes aim to strike a balance of perception and experience, for both Christians and Muslims. These include the diversity of relational interaction (positive, negative, neutral) to which *CMRBH* bears witness; some of the key recurring theological themes; differences in reaction (Christian responses to Islam; Muslim responses to Christianity); broad common motifs (repetitive patterns); and local, specific elements that illustrate, counter or challenge the broad repetitive patterns of interaction.

By the end of the first millennium, a transitional phase (15th-16th centuries, broadly speaking) incorporating developments that feature heavily in later centuries (e.g. the impact on the West of the Ottoman Empire; the incursion of Christianity and Islam into West Africa) is clearly discernible. In some cases, certain themes – e.g. Christian apocalyptic responses to Islam – appear prominent for a time, and maybe more in some places than others, then fade out. In other cases – e.g. martyrdom – there is an ebb and flow, with a particular Armenian development, for example,

---

13 C. Tieszen (ed.), *Theological issues in Christian-Muslim dialogue*, Eugene OR, 2018, p. xiv.

14 Tieszen, *Theological issues*, p. xiv.

15 *Christian-Muslim relations. A bibliographical history*, Leiden, 2009-19.

which very much suggests a geographical focus, at least in part, within a wider historical narrative. A thematic history is not a sequential narrative work as such. The aim of this volume is not simply to tell the story of the first thousand years, to be followed by the second volume at the point where the first ends. Rather, the thematic history we here pursue is an exercise that dips into, and draws out from, the many themes and topics that span the history of Christian-Muslim relations, so enabling us to discern the key dynamics that have been at play during the first millennium of Christian-Muslim encounter.

In preparing for the task of designing and commissioning this volume, a preliminary analysis was made of the first seven volumes of *CMRBH*, covering the years 600-1600. This yielded four categories of relationship, that arguably encompass much of Christian-Muslim interaction. These relational categories provided an underlying orientation to this thematic volume. In Chapter 2, Douglas Pratt outlines and illustrates these, in the process highlighting the immense possibilities for further research into the many dimensions and facets of relations between Muslims and Christians. These four are named as 'antipathy', 'affinity', 'appeal', and 'accommodation'. Each of these categories yields a greater or lesser number of themes and topics, all of which are evidenced by texts that are referenced in *CMRBH*. Emerging early in the encounter of Christians and Muslims, these relational categories include themes that have predominated at some times and faded out at others; some have had greater prominence in particular quarters, while others have been relatively constant and consistent across time and geography. Furthermore, these categories are not to be regarded as mutually exclusive; they can often be found intermingled. There are some texts whose themes, or topics, range over two or more of the relational dynamics, and there are topics that do not fit readily into this four-fold structure. It would be a grave error to presume these four categories are all encompassing. Nevertheless, they do arguably provide a useful guide to an exploration of the sheer diversity and complexity of the history of Christian-Muslim relations. Chapters of this thematic history volume varyingly refer to, or are guided by, these relational categories.

David Bertaina, in Chapter 3, undertakes an engaging exploration of some main trajectories of relational interaction with a focus on some 'of the centres where the major encounters and exchanges between Muslims and Christians took place'.[16] Christians were by no means all of

[16] See below, D. Bertaina, Chapter 3. 'Encounter and inquiry: trajectories of interaction', 53-71.

the same ilk. There were three major groups living under Islamic rule, each quite different from the others. These included the Chalcedonian Orthodox, known as Melkites, or 'royalists' – as this was the group closely aligned with the Byzantine Eastern Roman Empire; the West Syrian Orthodox, sometimes referred to as the Syriac Orthodox and also known as Jacobites; and the East Syrians, or simply 'The Church of the East', also known as Nestorians. As well, there were Coptic, Armenian and Maronite Christians, all of whom interacted with Muslims in one way or another. The contexts and trajectories of interaction were nothing if not multifarious. Multiple modalities were utilised in the task of each side seeking 'to learn about one another and to explain the other's religion to their communities in preparation for both polemical and apologetic activities'.[17] As thinkers on either side responded to the other, particularly with to matters of doctrine or belief, so were significant treatises written, and letters of argumentation, apologia and entreaty exchanged.

In some cases, it appears such exchanges may have been the work of an author or authors from one side only, endeavouring to pursue a quasi-Socratic dialogue as a literary device with some underlying purpose in mind. In the process, there were Muslims who gained a very clear grasp of Christianity, or at least of one of its then current variants; and on the Christian side there were some who dug deep into the Qur'an and had a good grasp of Islamic thought. Yet there were also cases of misunderstanding and even misrepresentation. Nevertheless, the realm of scholarly engagement, even in a cooperative context, especially with regard to language studies and the translation of texts, enabled a quite positive relational dynamic. For often the subject matter was not so much directly religious as it was an engagement in a range of sciences, including medicine, philosophy and mathematics. Bertaina also notes that events and places – festivals and holy sites – proved to be 'key places of inquiry and encounter well into the medieval era'.[18] This reflected a much later truism that it is in inquiring about the practices and performances of religion, as much as the professed belief system, that one can learn deeply about the faith it represents. Bertaina concludes by observing that although 'their aim was often to engage in apologetics or polemics, Christians and Muslims sometimes imitated, esteemed and adapted alternative models of thought via inquiries into the other religious tradition in order to express

[17] See below, Bertaina, 'Encounter and inquiry', p. 54.
[18] See below, Bertaina, 'Encounter and inquiry', p. 64.

their own religious claims'.[19] This is not to suggest balanced reciprocity, rather that there is evidence of this sort of interaction found to varying degrees in the textual record.

Mark Swanson's Chapter 4, on Christians, Muslims and the True Religion, discusses various categories that Christians have used in order to find a comprehensible place for Islam. Following a survey of such categories, derived mainly from the Bible and the experience of the early Church, Swanson alights on one in particular that became prominent in Christian Arabic writing about Islam, namely 'the notion of Islam as a *dīn* among the *adyān*, or as we would say today, a religion among the religions'.[20] Furthermore, this early pluralistic notion had the effect of spurring a quest to discern criteria for determining which one is the true religion. Any acknowledgement of religious diversity is not a concession to any perception of relative equality or validity; rather the fact of religious diversity begged the question of true religion: which one fitted the bill? In addition, how was 'the bill' of true religion to be defined? Swanson highlights that, in and through the resources found within the *CMRBH* there may be found 'stories of the ebb and flow, the rise and fall, of particular forms of inter-religious discourse'.[21] Within this record there can be traced the rise and fall of the true religion apology that occupied both Muslim and Christian scholars for a time.

The concept of God is a fundamental element in the theological dialogue between Christians and Muslims. Each religion declares itself monotheistic. However, the Trinitarian monotheism of Christianity contrasts with the singularity monotheism of Islam, at least *prima facie*, and certainly enough to have provoked and promoted much debate, confusion and rejection between the two. In Chapter 5, Mark Beaumont carefully explicates how, at the very beginning of interaction, thinkers in each religion looked not only at their own scriptural heritage, but also into the scripture of the other in order to discern confirmation of their own unique monotheistic concept. For example, Christians looked to the Qur'an (e.g. Q 4:171) to support their belief in the Trinity and Muslims 'turned to the Christian Gospels to show that Jesus did not claim to be

---

19 See below, Bertaina, 'Encounter and inquiry', p. 71.
20 See below, M.N. Swanson, Chapter 4. 'Christians, Muslims and the True Religion', 73-97, p. 73.
21 See below, Swanson, 'Christians, Muslims and the True Religion', p. 73.

equal to God, or to be the second person of the Trinity'.[22] On the one hand, Muslims argued that 'Jesus taught that his relationship to God as a son to a father could be experienced by his followers'. On the other, Christians argued that the Gospels implied an equality of divine status between God the Father and God the Son (Jesus) that required the doctrine of the Trinity to explicate. Indeed, they argued that 'attributes of fatherhood, sonship and spirit were unlike the other attributes in alone being essential' to the very being of God. Nevertheless, and in effect ever since, the Trinitarian doctrine from a Muslim perspective failed 'the test of the absolute unity of God'.[23] This theme is perennial in the realm of theological dialogue between Christians and Muslims.

Mourad Takawi and Gabriel Said Reynolds traverse Muslim perceptions of Jesus in Chapter 6. Islam sees Jesus as a prophet, albeit standing out in some way from other prophets. Indeed, 'the figure of Jesus' has been developed 'in distinct ways' in Islamic thought, both from remarks and comments about him in the Qur'an and with respect to 'asceticism and wisdom sayings, elements that do not appear in the Qur'an'.[24] Noting that he is 'distinguished by the name ʿĪsā given to him in the Qur'an', our two authors review the many qur'anic references to Jesus and then examine the Islamic tradition about Jesus that subsequently emerged. Inscriptions containing comment and perspective on Jesus and written on rocks, monuments – such as the Dome of the Rock – and other prominent places, form one of the genres in which the figure of Jesus receives attention. Historiographical reports and polemical writings form other significant genres of text with respect to discussion about him. As well, there is the phenomenon of a Muslim 'thematic' study or explication of Jesus, beginning even in Hadith. For 'the prophet Jesus has a special place as the prophet who immediately precedes Muḥammad'.[25] Muslim topics about Jesus include simple descriptions; his being the subject of miracles, and the performer of them; wisdom and asceticism as they pertain to the person of Jesus; and eschatological motifs. Whilst rooted in the Qur'an, 'richly diverse accounts of Jesus in the Islamic tradition' are found in many quarters and genres of Muslim literature, for 'the qur'anic

22 See below, I.M. Beaumont, Chapter 5. 'Debating the concept of God', 99-121, p. 99.

23 See below, Beaumont, 'Debating the concept of God', p. 121.

24 See below, M. Takawi and G.S. Reynolds, Chapter 6. 'Muslim perceptions of Jesus', 123-51, p. 123.

25 See below, Takawi and Reynolds, 'Muslim perceptions of Jesus', p. 135.

account at once draws the broad contours that the diverse portrayals of Jesus fill and effectively acts as their underlying unifying principle'.[26] The textual record indicates that, polemical motives notwithstanding, there is evidence of considerable Muslim interest in, and no small attraction to, the figure of Jesus, who, it seems, is both a recognisable prophet and something of an enigma.

Christian perceptions of Muḥammad have been quite varied, substantially negative, and always a lead item in theological assessments and the formation of attitudes, images and perceptions of Islam more generally. One only has to consider the various strands and expressions of 21st-century Islamophobia to realise that, today, there are Christians and others who are simply recycling ancient negative and prejudicial tropes of Muḥammad as a charlatan, and Islam as a false religion. Clinton Bennett begins Chapter 7 with a scene-setting orientation, noting that 'Christian writings about Muḥammad during the first thousand years of Christian-Muslim encounter were almost all negative and hostile, presenting an attitude of virtually unrelieved antipathy'.[27] Nevertheless, there were some who 'did express affinity with Islam by writing more sympathetically about Muḥammad', and others who 'attempted to accommodate Muḥammad within a Christian theological view that recognised some legitimacy regarding his status as a prophet'.[28] One significant factor has to do with the proximity of Christians to Muslims – a factor as relevant today as it was during the first millennium of encounter. Bennett notes that, on the one hand, Christian writers 'living among or in proximity to Muslims often wrote to reassure their own constituency that, despite the political ascendancy of Islam, it was illegitimate and could not survive'.[29] On the other hand, there were Christians 'who lived at a distance and had no contact with Muslims, [and] simply set out to demonise and dehumanise a potential enemy'.[30] Here, we find an early pattern that, in many quarters today, is so easily discernible. Bennett's treatment of this theme is wide-ranging and highly instructive, and he concludes that what was largely missed in any Christian assessment of Muḥammad 'was the place

26 See below, Takawi and Reynolds, 'Muslim perceptions of Jesus', p. 149.
27 See below, C. Bennett, Chapter 7. 'Christian perceptions of Muḥammad', 153-79, p. 153.
28 See below, Bennett, 'Christian perceptions of Muḥammad', p. 153.
29 See below, Bennett, 'Christian perceptions of Muḥammad', p. 153.
30 See below, Bennett, 'Christian perceptions of Muḥammad', p. 153.

Muḥammad occupied devotionally and spiritually in Muslim life'.[31] It is still largely missing in much of the Christian community today.

Apologetics, the art of defending one's faith and endeavouring, thereby, to present it in a favourable light, is another perennial theme of theological intercourse between Muslims and Christians. Sandra Tonies Keating, in Chapter 8, tackles this element of relational history, noting the 'mixed reactions' and, indeed, highly fluid patterns and developments of interreligious interaction between the two faith communities – or, rather, between various emerging Muslim communities and the already well-established diversity of Christian denominations, perceived by Muslims most usually as 'sects'. Theological differences were reflected in politics: with the sudden rise of an Arab Muslim polity, there were Christians for whom, having 'rejected the conclusions of the Council of Chalcedon (in 451), the promise of an alternative to Melkite Byzantine rule was attractive'.[32] However, for others, Muslim 'conquest signalled the expected end times, setting in motion the final conflict with the armies of the Antichrist'.[33] Realpolitik contrasted with apocalyptic assessment – and, in some ways, perhaps, this has been the case to a greater or lesser degree down subsequent centuries. As a theme, it is not only historically significant, but also shows strong contemporary resonance. Keating also notes that, with the emergence of the dynastic era in Islam, instances of early Christian indifference gave way to 'the beginning of the flowering of intellectual engagement between Muslims and Christians, as well as the start of significant religious apologetical writing'.[34] And she concludes that the literary record 'reflects the long and often painful relationship between Muslims and Christians as they worked to articulate common beliefs and differences'.[35] The foundation of serious theological encounter between Muslims and Christians was laid early, and continues to form a focus for dialogue.

One of the avenues by which Christians and Muslims engaged with each other's religious beliefs and perspectives was by attending to the scriptural text of the other. In Chapter 9, Ayşe İçöz tackles Muslim engagement with the Bible, for which the primary lens was, and for most

[31] See below, Bennett, 'Christian perceptions of Muḥammad', p. 179.

[32] See below, S. Toenies Keating, Chapter 8. 'Defending the faith: lines of apology', 181-205, p. 181.

[33] See below, Keating, 'Defending the faith', p. 181.

[34] See below, Keating, 'Defending the faith', p. 182.

[35] See below, Keating, 'Defending the faith', p. 205.

arguably still is, the Qur'an. What it says is largely determinative. Therefore, for this theme, İçöz examines pertinent suras that indicate that 'the Qur'an understands itself as continuing the earlier divine message that was revealed in the Bible'.[36] She notes that, with respect to differences between the Bible and the Qur'an, 'in the early Islamic era the issue of the corruption of the Bible (*taḥrīf*) constituted one of the major topics in Muslim refutations of Christianity'.[37] And yet, it was also the case that 'at the same time many Muslim polemicists used verses from the Bible to support their arguments against Christians (and also Jews)'.[38] The Bible, although perceived as essentially inferior to the Qur'an, was nevertheless a repository of revelation that Muslims could yet draw upon. It is some of this early Muslim usage that İçöz usefully traverses, beginning with the 9th-century Christian convert to Islam, Abū l-Ḥasan ʿAlī ibn Sahl Rabbān al-Ṭabarī. A variety of representative Muslim perspectives are examined from the 10th century, and İçöz remarks that the selected works and their authors regard the Bible throughout 'as a reliable source' and claim that it is Christians who have by and large misinterpreted it.[39] By contrast, Muslim scholars in the 11th century regarded the biblical text itself as having been corrupted by both Jews and Christians. It is no longer the pristine revealed Word that it was proclaimed to be by these forebears of Islam. This presumption of textual corruption certainly became embedded in normative Islamic assessments of the Bible, yet there were other 'novel' Muslim approaches that indicate something of 'how vibrant and diverse were the attitudes of Muslim authors towards Bible'.[40]

Christian engagement with the Qur'an has been variable and multifaceted. Ulisse Cecini, in Chapter 10, delves deeply into the theme of Latin Christianity engaging the Qur'an. He explores how the Qur'an 'entered gradually into the argumentation of Christian authors who dealt with Islam, moving from mere mentions to become more and more the centre of attention and an object of discussion', and shows how Christian use of the Qur'an has been to engage Islam, whether positively or, more usually, negatively. However, it was also used to attack Christian opponents. For example, in the 16th century, 'both Catholics and Lutherans used the Qur'an in order to accuse the doctrines of their Christian opponents of

36 See below, A. İçöz, Chapter 9. 'Muslims engaging the Bible', 207-26, p. 207.
37 See below, İçöz, 'Muslims engaging the Bible', p. 207.
38 See below, İçöz, 'Muslims engaging the Bible', p. 207.
39 See below, İçöz, 'Muslims engaging the Bible', pp. 207, 214.
40 See below, İçöz, 'Muslims engaging the Bible', p. 217.

being even more deviant than the Qur'an'.[41] Commencing with a discussion of the first appearances of the Qur'an in Latin Christian works, Cecini focusses on the examples of the so-called *Istoria de Mahomet*, a variety of influences that came into the West from the emerging Eastern Christian polemical tradition, and the works of the Iberian Christians Eulogius and Albarus of Cordova. Whereas the Qur'an was relatively marginalised in the 9th to 11th centuries, during the 12th to 14th centuries Qur'an translations, and treatises upon it, were much more prominent. Key figures such as Petrus Alfonsi, Peter the Venerable, Robert of Ketton, William of Tripoli and Ramon Llull feature in Cecini's discussion, along with an exploration of the developments in the work of translation that led to polemics. The 15th and 16th centuries are a time of relative reflection upon the former periods, together with the activity of new translations of, and new perspectives on, the Qur'an. Thus, by the close of the first millennium of engagement, 'Latin Christianity had built a large repository of resources on the Qur'an: translations, treatises, dialogues and epistles'.[42] Over time, the Qur'an, for Western Christianity, 'gradually came into focus, concerning first its nature and origin (revealed or not, demonic, human or divine), later its contents, and eventually its underlying message, which was supposedly common to every religion'.[43]

Gordon Nickel's Chapter 11 addresses the complex dynamics involved in Eastern Christian engagement with the Qur'an. In the early days of Arab Islamic expansion, Eastern Christianity found itself now existing within *dār al-Islām* and so directly encountering Muslims and Islamic life, thought and practice. In consequence, new and challenging circumstances required from 'Eastern Christians new ways of thinking about and expressing their own faith, as well as responding to the claims of a conquering Arab power'.[44] The building of the Dome of the Rock in Jerusalem was Islam's stake in the ground, declaring its presence, assertions and claims. In a context in which dialogical interlocutors represent a 'victor' on the one side and the 'vanquished' on the other, the playing field of interaction is by no means level. As a *dhimmī* people, the condition and

41 See below, U. Cecini, Chapter 10. 'Latin Christianity engaging with the Qur'an', 227-53, p. 227.

42 See below, Cecini, 'Latin Christianity engaging with the Qur'an', p. 247.

43 See below, Cecini, 'Latin Christianity engaging with the Qur'an', p. 253.

44 See below, G. Nickel, Chapter 11. '"Our Friendly Strife": Eastern Christianity engaging the Qur'an', 255-79, p. 255.

interaction of Christians within *dār al-Islām* was always subject to the mood and outlook of the caliph or prevailing Muslim authority. Unlike Western Christians, Eastern Christians trod a different – more cautious, perhaps – path. Nickel draws upon a wide variety of documents from the early centuries of engagement and notes the range of languages involved – Greek, Syriac, Coptic, Armenian and Arabic – and the resultant 'striking differences in how directly they write or speak as well as in the extent of their knowledge about the Qur'an'.[45] Nickel makes use of the *Risāla* of al-Kindī as 'it shows the most extensive range and depth of engagement with the Qur'an of all existing records from early Eastern Christianity'.[46] Eastern Christians invoked a number of approaches and strategies in assessing and responding to Islam and, in particular, the Qur'an. A number of key themes tended to be at the forefront of discussion, including the deity and death of Jesus; Muslim accusations, derived from the Qur'an, against the Bible; assessment of the Qur'an with respect to miracle, morality and prophecy; and Muslim claims for and about the Qur'an, its characterisation and legacy.

The epoch of the ostensibly Christian crusades to the Holy Land is one of the most significant periods in the history of Christian-Muslim relations. Nicholas Morton, in Chapter 12, explores some of the main features of Christian-Muslim relations in this period, highlighting something of the diversity and 'complexity of cross-cultural interactions', while at the same time 'demonstrating how the tides of war, faith, trade, and realpolitik could create some fascinating and – at times – bizarre relationships across ethnic and religious boundaries'.[47] Neither side was a monolithic singularity, despite any appearance or pretension to the contrary. Threads of cultural, ethnic and religious diversity are to be found in each, leading Morton to aver that 'any simplistic notion of a monolithic "Christianity" fighting a monolithic "Islam" quickly falls apart'.[48] For all the energy and resources spent on trying to assert Christian hegemony both militarily and politically, in the end, the crusades failed in their goal of wresting the Holy land out of the control of Islam. On one hand, the crusades mark a nadir in the relationship between

---

45 See below, Nickel, '"Our Friendly Strife": Eastern Christianity engaging the Qur'an', p. 257.

46 See below, Nickel, '"Our Friendly Strife": Eastern Christianity engaging the Qur'an', p. 257.

47 See below, N. Morton, Chapter 12. 'The crusades to the eastern Mediterranean, 1095-1291', 281-306, p. 282.

48 See below, Morton, 'The crusades to the eastern Mediterranean, 1095-1291', p. 286.

Islam and Christianity, cementing the trope of inherent opposition of one to the other and embedding further the presumption of necessary mutual antipathy. It is a wonder that any sort of positive engagement might ever have been possible as a result. Yet, on the other hand, for all the mutual destruction that this period wrought, there were some intriguing instances of positive interaction. Morton concludes that the 'resulting picture is one of diversity, encompassing moments of friendship, technological exchange, tolerance and inter-faith interest, alongside times of violence, hatred and aggressive propaganda. The sum of these components is to render the crusading period a fascinating and confused moment in Middle Eastern history'.[49]

Juan Pedro Monferrer Sala, in Chapter 13, explores the dynamics of Christian-Muslim interaction in Andalusia in the period 700-1500. Works from this period 'reveal a complex and varied picture' and 'can be described as providing a socio-religious architecture of communities from the two faiths'.[50] Whilst there were many instances of misunderstanding, there was also a considerable degree of collaboration, which paved the way for 'extensive intellectual interaction' over time. Following a context-setting discussion of land, peoples and faiths, the phenomena of Arabisation, Islamisation and acculturation are examined with reference to selected texts. This leads to a section on 'sensing the other', which explores the field of diverse perceptions of one by the other: there was, indeed, a 'universe of perceptions held by the Christians and Muslims of al-Andalus',[51] and Monferrer Sala takes the reader into this complex and rich world of idea and image, the stuff of perception. He concludes with a reflection on the 'expulsion of the Christians from al-Andalus in the mid-12th century and of the Muslims in 1492' as well as 'the exiling of the Moriscos in 1609-13', none of which brought to an end 'the complex and challenging socio-religious and intellectual situation shared through the centuries by Christians and Muslims in the Iberian Peninsula'.[52] Mutual interest in each other, spanning inquiry, apologetics and polemics, and much beside, contributed to an intellectual environment in which 'Christians and Muslims – though ideologically opposed

---

49 See below, Morton, 'The crusades to the eastern Mediterranean, 1095-1291', p. 306.

50 See below, J.P. Monferrer Sala, Chapter 13. 'Conduits of interaction. The Andalusi experience', 307-29, p. 307.

51 See below, Monferrer Sala, 'Conduits of interaction. The Andalusi experience', p. 319.

52 See below, Monferrer Sala, 'Conduits of interaction. The Andalusi experience', p. 328.

– found a common space that enabled peaceful coexistence for some time', which was, indeed, a 'coexistence of knowledge' that obtained in a context of 'competing prejudices and vested interests of all kinds'.[53]

The early Ottoman period is replete with many dimensions and, in Chapter 14, Tom Papademetriou provides a detailed context to understanding Christian-Muslim relations at this time. Although military prowess and the religious ideology of holy war played a part in Ottoman success, it was rather 'a practical approach to conquest and governance that integrated the local populations into their emerging state' and which thus played the more significant part.[54] Nevertheless, and somewhat paradoxically, 'local populations were both victims and agents of the great transformation that took place'.[55] A first task is to understand the nature of interaction between the Ottomans and Christian communities living within the caliphate. Papademetriou thus commences with the context of Asia Minor in the 13th century and the origins of the Ottomans in Anatolia. He then discusses 'the role of Christian *Timariots*, the competing motifs of *gaza* (holy war) and *istimalet* (accommodation through *dhimmī* regulations), the phenomenon of Christian boys taken into Ottoman service through the *Devshirme*, cultural transformations, and the "holy man" motif'.[56] In addition, the topics of bishops and the emirs, Byzantine observers of Ottoman conquest, and the 1453 conquest of Constantinople are also touched on. The motif of 'accommodation', of both Christian communities to Ottoman governance, and of the Ottomans to the presence of such communities, could be said to be the underlying relational dynamic of the first two centuries or so that mark the early period. Many issues and questions flowed from this. They form much of the substance of interaction between the two sides. At the close of this period, the Ottomans made a greater turn towards more overt 'Islamic principles', in the process 'jettisoning the previous accommodationist practices, thus shaping the way in which Christians would be treated for the next three centuries'.[57]

---

53 See below, Monferrer Sala, 'Conduits of interaction. The Andalusi experience', p. 328.

54 See below, T. Papademetriou, Chapter 14. 'Interactions in the early Ottoman period (1299-1518)', 331-58, p. 331.

55 See below, Papademetriou, 'Interactions in the early Ottoman period (1299-1518)', p. 331.

56 See below, Papademetriou, 'Interactions in the early Ottoman period (1299-1518)', p. 331.

57 See below, Papademetriou, 'Interactions in the early Ottoman period (1299-1518)', p. 358.

In Chapter 15, Luke Yarbrough tackles a socio-political dimension of Christian-Muslim relations, where Muslims were rulers and Christians their subjects. Two key elements are examined, namely the *dhimma* system, and demographic decline. The former encompasses a 'body of legal theory that Muslim jurists devised in order to rationalise and regulate the permanent presence of non-Muslim populations in Muslim-ruled territories', although enforcement was by no means uniform, with Muslim rulers in different times and places acting with considerable variability towards their non-Muslim *dhimmī* populations.[58] By contrast, in areas where Christians may once have been in the majority, for example in Egypt, Syria or Anatolia, 'the eventual reduction of Christians and other non-Muslims to a position of demographic minority in Muslim-ruled lands' became a distinct feature of Muslim political engagement with, in particular, Christians.[59] Interest in the history and concept of the *dhimma* system(s) has been considerable in modern times, and for a variety of reasons, and especially where there is a perception on the part of present-day Christians that Muslim rulers have treated fellow Christians badly at other times and in other places. This plays into a contemporary trope of Muslim persecution of Christians, and often elides the great variety in tone, context and nature of the relationship between Christians and Muslims throughout the first millennium of interaction. As Yarbrough remarks: 'The motif of Muslim persecution doubles as a convenient aetiology for Christian decline "under Islam". It is intuitively attractive, for example, as an explanation for why Christians converted to Islam in substantial numbers and in numerous milieus.'[60]

Yarbrough focusses his analysis and discussion by addressing themes of accommodation, affinity and antipathy across four periods of Islamic history. These include the period of the Prophet and the first caliphs (c. 610-61); the time of the Umayyads and major ʿAbbasids (661-945); the period of empire fragmentation (945-1250); and the phase of crisis and reconsolidation, 'when the Islamic world was split into regional states, with no central symbol of political unity (1250-1600)'.[61] He also notes that it is simply a fact that a variety of Christian communities found themselves living under Muslim rule during the first millennium of encounter,

58 See below, L. Yarbrough, Chapter 15. 'Muslim rulers, Christian subjects', 359-87, p. 359.
59 See below, Yarbrough, 'Muslim rulers, Christian subjects', p. 359.
60 See below, Yarbrough, 'Muslim rulers, Christian subjects', p. 360.
61 See below, Yarbrough, 'Muslim rulers, Christian subjects', p. 362.

but there was no comparable phenomenon of Muslim communities living under Christian rule. 'The reasons for this asymmetry are, of course, complex. One difference is that, until the 18th century, there was no Christian-led military expansion into large parts of the Islamic world that compares with the 7th-century Arab conquests in the Christian world.'[62]

In Chapter 16, Christian Sahner adroitly traverses the thorny dual themes of martyrdom and conversion. The Islamisation of former Christian-majority lands proceeded at a steady pace in the early centuries of Islam as a socio-political as well as religious reality. Sahner notes 'the conversion of the Christian population was not inevitable, especially at the beginning' and that, in fact, there are 'numerous examples of the process unfolding in reverse, in which instead of conversion to Islam, we find Muslim conversion to Christianity'.[63] Furthermore, there are 'examples of Christians challenging the Islamic social and political order through acts of blasphemy', and it is these events that could, and did, lead to instances of martyrdom, which were recorded in the form of 'stylised hagiographical accounts of violence, often but not exclusively at the hands of Muslim officials'.[64] Martyrs soon became 'revered as saints, with annual feasts and pilgrimages held and churches built in their honour'.[65] Martyrdom was often construed as an act not just of faithfulness but of imitation of the sacrifice of Jesus himself: 'Jesus served as the prototype of finding strength through weakness and achieving victory through defeat.'[66] The violent deaths of many early followers and all but one of the Apostles reinforced martyrdom as a holy, almost necessary, expectation, at least for some. Death for a martyr was something not to be feared or avoided, but rather willingly embraced. In the Roman Empire, martyrdom effectively ended with the Constantinian promotion of Christianity in the early 4th century. However, there were places and times when it subsequently flared up in the context of intra-Christian disputes, such as with Donatism, and re-emerged more overtly with the 7th-century advent of Islam. Viewed as a parallel to the suffering experienced by the early Church, now, instead of pagans, it was Muslims who were 'portrayed as forcing Christians to choose between life and death; between converting

62 See below, Yarbrough, 'Muslim rulers, Christian subjects', p. 386.
63 See below, C.C. Sahner, Chapter 16. 'Martyrdom and conversion', 389-412, p. 389.
64 See below, Sahner, 'Martyrdom and conversion', pp. 389-90.
65 See below, Sahner, 'Martyrdom and conversion', p. 390.
66 See below, Sahner, 'Martyrdom and conversion', p. 390.

to Islam – for Christians, effectively "heathenism" – and preserving their Christian faith'.[67] The phenomena of martyrdom and conversion are complexly intertwined.

In Chapter 17 David Cook delves into 'the genre of apocalyptic literature [which] has been an important one for the communication of group fears, for the creation of group solidarity, and for the promulgation of polemics against the other religious group'.[68] Cook here focusses on Islamic apocalyptic motifs and some of the responses and reactions of Christians. Muslim apocalyptic beliefs and traditions are traced in terms of origin, most notably the 'failure of the cataclysmic apocalypse that is foreseen in the Qur'an (see Q 54:1, 87:1-2, etc.) to appear', and the traditions recorded in Hadiths that reference dramatic eschatological motifs.[69] Muslim apocalypticism in general and the Islamic messianism fomented by Shīʿa Muslims are supported by a substantial literary heritage. Christian responses included the trope of regarding the success of Islam as a sign of Christian failing. 'God's allowing the Muslims to rise up so suddenly and dominate Christians in some of their most venerable holy cities' became quite widespread; indeed, this Christian 'apocalyptic framework for interpreting the appearance of Islam, and the place of Muslims in the divine plan, proved to be enduring and influential'.[70] Apocalypticism and, with it, messianism played a significant role in both the development of Islam and the interaction between Muslims and Christians. Renewal, or revival, and the motif of restoration form recurring contexts that interlink with both messianism and apocalypticism within the Muslim world. Cook examines a number of significant examples, concluding that the 'apocalyptic and messianic heritage of Islam, in both its Sunnī and Shīʿī versions, is considerable' and to a large extent 'focused against the Other, often Christians and Jews', with apocalyptic predictions 'full of polemical themes against Christianity, and to a lesser extent, against Judaism'.[71]

The motif of antipathy, so undoubtedly prominent in the history of Christian-Muslim relations, has many dimensions. In Chapter 18, James Harry Morris tackles the vexing theme of conflict, focussing on the

---

67 See below, Sahner, 'Martyrdom and conversion', p. 390.

68 See below, D.B. Cook, Chapter 17. 'Muslim and Christian apocalypticism: playing off each other', 413-33, p. 413.

69 See below, Cook, 'Muslim and Christian apocalypticism', p. 413.

70 See below, Cook, 'Muslim and Christian apocalypticism', p. 420.

71 See below, Cook, 'Muslim and Christian apocalypticism', p. 433.

dynamic of conquest and re-conquest with reference to the early Arabian and, more particularly, the Iberian contexts. Given that tropes of past conflict resurface either directly or indirectly, this element of antipathic relation is an important theme to address. Morris touches on a range of texts 'pertaining to conflictual and hostile relations reflecting Christian-Muslim antipathy during the first millennium of encounter'.[72] They represent a particular concern for 'Christian and Muslim responses to violence, and explanations and justifications of it, as these are encapsulated in writings from both sides, as well as in the authors' practices of "othering" their religious counterparts through polemical and apologetic texts'.[73] Following an exploration of Christian reaction to Arab conquests, Morris pays close attention to texts reflecting Christian-Muslim encounter in the Iberian context. These are pertinent 'not only to Muslim and Christian conquest of the region, but also to attitudes of antipathy towards religious "others" encapsulated in the work of some contemporary commentators.'[74] Morris notes that 'reactions of Eastern Christians to the Arab conquests bear a thematic similarity to later Western Christian responses to the Muslim conquest of the Iberian Peninsula, and this suggests that some overarching trends may be perceived by exploring both period and geographical dimensions'.[75] Authors from each side sought to describe, explain and reflect upon the presence and viewpoints of their religious counterparts. Both polemical and apologetic texts were composed, to a large degree contributing to the burgeoning narrative of mutual opposition. Nevertheless, Morris notes that in general terms, 'whereas Christian writers tended to take an uncompromisingly anti-Muslim view, Muslim writers provided more "balanced" visions of Christian-Muslim relations by focusing on Christian-Muslim cooperation and coexistence, even within texts that focused on conflict'.[76]

As the centuries passed, and Christians and Muslims developed strategies of coping with the fact of the other, the idea that the other posed some sort of religious challenge underwent change. For Christianity, this meant the emergence of the idea and activity of seeking the conversion of Muslims by way of intentional missionary endeavour. Martha

72 See below, J.H. Morris, Chapter 18. 'Conflict, conquest & reconquest. Arabian and Iberian experience', 435-60, p. 435.
73 See below, Morris, 'Conflict, conquest & reconquest', p. 436.
74 See below, Morris, 'Conflict, conquest & reconquest', p, 436.
75 See below, Morris, 'Conflict, conquest & reconquest', p, 436.
76 See below, Morris, 'Conflict, conquest & reconquest', p, 436.

Frederiks, in Chapter 19, notes that for the first half of the first millennium of engagement one with the other, Christian mission to Muslims, as an evangelical activity, was effectively absent. The historical record suggests, indeed, that it was not until well into the second half of this millennium, the 13th century, that there was any organised Christian missionary outreach towards Muslims, namely 'when the Latin Church encountered substantial communities of Muslims in the reconquered territories on the Iberian Peninsula and in the Crusader states'.[77] Nevertheless, from the 11th century on, in the context of the crusades, and then later the Spanish *Reconquista*, there is clearly reference to the idea, if not the direct activity, of missions to Muslims. Certainly, by the mid-12th century, 'conversion (including enforced) of Muslims seems to have become widely accepted as a central goal of the crusades'.[78] Frederiks makes it clear that, in exploring the theme of Christian missions to Muslims, the intentional effort is to bring about conversion, to effect the radical change in identity from 'being Muslim' to 'being Christian', that is in the frame. This was 'part of a larger project in the context of Islam and part of a larger reform movement that simultaneously promoted the spiritual renewal of Western Europe's Christianity and the evangelisation of non-Christians'.[79] A notable example of an early 13th-century missionary endeavour towards Muslims is, of course, that of St Francis of Assisi. Franciscan missionary outreach was perhaps the first example of such mission as an inherent element in the life and work of a Christian religious order. For Francis, 'mission to Muslims was part of an all-encompassing mission project'.[80] The Dominican Order also had Islam in its sights, but took a different, more intellectual and discursive approach to mission to Muslims than did the Franciscans. The story of Christian missions to Muslims is a vast and complex one, with many twists and turns, to which the historical record bears clear testimony. Marked more by failure than success, nevertheless it is a theme that reflects an embedded imperative within much of Christianity.

Charles Tieszen, in the final chapter, engages in a discussion of religious practices, and points out that the encounter between Christians and Muslims was not restricted to civic or political life or even philosophical

---

[77] See below, M.T. Frederiks, Chapter 19. 'Christian missions to Muslims', 461-87, pp. 461-2.

[78] See below, Frederiks, 'Christian missions to Muslims', p. 469.

[79] See below, Frederiks, 'Christian missions to Muslims', p. 462.

[80] See below, Frederiks, 'Christian missions to Muslims', p. 473.

or dogmatic debates. 'Muslims and Christians were observing the ways one another worshipped God and making commentary and even accusation based on their observations.'[81] These discussions functioned as the means by which authors defended their acts of piety against accusations of idolatry and explained their meaning. Perhaps more importantly, they also served a catechetical function: in multi-religious contexts, religious practices could help to distinguish one religionist from another. Reminding Christian readers, for example, why they venerated icons and why they should maintain the practice highlighted a signpost that delineated Christianity from Islam and explained the practice as much to the Christians who performed the act as to the Muslims who might be bemused by it.

Noting that a wide variety of religious practices appear in the relevant literature, Tieszen concentrates on five practices: icon veneration, cross veneration (and the frequently corresponding practices of venerating the Qur'an and the Kaʿba), the Eucharist, baptism, and prayer, in particular the direction faced in prayer. One of the intriguing features the *CMRBH* project helps to bear out is that these five practices are mentioned frequently and consistently in apologetic and disputational texts, such that they constitute a topos of Christian-Muslim literature. Indeed, it seems clear that some authors take up the religious practices theme not necessarily in response to a felt need of a specific community in which a religious practice was in dispute, but rather in order to make their texts conform to the literary conventions that had come to be expected of apologetic or disputational texts. Although aspects of Muslim piety are discussed, Christian practices tend to predominate, with commentary coming from both Muslim and Christian authors. In turn, many of the presentations also constitute repositories for Christian strategies of explaining their devotion, so many of which are drawn from early Christian literature and the discussions those authors had with pagan and Jewish interlocutors. What is intriguing, then, is to see how arguments were drawn into Islamic milieus where they were copied or reshaped; at other times, completely fresh arguments developed as a result of a new interreligious environment.

---

81 See below, C. Tieszen, Chapter 20. 'Discussing religious practices', 489-513, p. 490.

History is ever the teacher of the present and mentor to the future. As the saying goes: if we do not learn from our history, we shall be doomed to repeat it. The past has much to teach the present, if the present cares to take notice. As editors, we hope this volume will not only shed light on the past but also illuminate the present and offer a beacon for the future of Christian-Muslim relations.

Chapter 2
Relational dynamics in the first millennium. A thematic analysis

Douglas Pratt

Introduction

As noted in Chapter 1 above, this thematic history project began with the question: based on the bibliographical evidence, what does the history of Christian-Muslim relations reveal of the underlying dynamics of the relationship? By working through the first seven volumes of *CMRBH*, paying attention to the Significance section of entries and then the Description section, a sense or 'feel' for the substance of Christian-Muslim relations throughout the first millennium of encounter could be gleaned. This was very much a preliminary exploration; an initial analytical foray. As such, it was necessarily provisional and somewhat general and suggestive, opening up possibilities and further questions and lines of potential research inquiry. Nevertheless, despite these limitations, it enabled a scholar whose primary focus is on modern events and history, especially 20th- and 21st-century Christian-Muslim relations activities,[1] to gain some sort of reasonable grasp of the reality of a much longer history. It provided the clue and direction for proceeding in the development of this volume.

As a result of this preliminary research, four terms emerged that seem to draw together a wide range of interactions denoting key underlying dynamics of the relationship as it has been lived and experienced and, importantly, expressed in texts that are recorded within the *CMRBH* volumes.

Antipathy flags the rather dominant feature of – by and large – mutual rejection; that sense of asserting superiority one over the other, of exposing the other as false, devilish, and much besides. Antipathy is expressed through texts of polemics. Within this category of relational dynamics,

---

[1] D. Pratt, *Christian engagement with Islam. Ecumenical journeys since 1910*, Leiden, 2017; D. Pratt, *The challenge of Islam. Encounters in interfaith dialogue*, Farnham, 2005 (Abingdon, 2017).

some nine themes or topic areas have been discerned. As we shall see, antipathy is made up of many elements, many ways in which misrepresentation and distortion have been advanced and embedded.

Affinity, by contrast, refers to the motif of sensing commonality, of an open inquiry with respect to the other premised on a sense of 'sameness', more or less. Within this category, issues and instances of inquiry, theological debate, and other aspects of relatively positive relational engagement may be identified. Four specific themes or topics will illustrate this relational category.

The third term, *Appeal*, refers to the arena of apologetics, with six topic themes here identified. Appeal is a relational dynamic indicating an approach made by one to the other, either with respect to the consequence of a perception of affinity ('We are nearly the same, so come on over and become one of us'), or as an alternative to the outright rejection of antipathy ('You are clearly in the wrong – but we don't attack you; rather, here is why you should come on over to us').

Our fourth category, *accommodation*, with four topic themes, reflects a measure of tolerance and coexistence, whether relatively harmonious or as a reflection of acquiescence and acceptance, by one side of the other. It is certainly a long-standing dynamic, whether seen in the Muslim *dhimmī* institution that locates and regulates Christian existence within *dār al-Islām* as a 'People of the Book', or in Christian attitudes towards Muslims framed in terms of law or socio-cultural realpolitik.

The scope for discerning themes and topics within the four relational dynamic categories is really quite large. Certainly, this chapter does not claim to have identified them all, far from it. The analysis undertaken is no more than a start. While individual texts might range over two or more relational categories and themes, many can be seen to have a predominant theme and to sit primarily within one relational category.

Although Christianity and Islam share a common heritage and points of connection, there are also considerable differences between them. In consequence of both heritage and difference, instances of tension, hostility and direct conflict have been manifest throughout the history of relationship, and are still found today. Yet there is also a trajectory of 'considerable positive interaction', where mere tolerance can and does give way to 'peaceful coexistence' even though, to be sure, 'mistrust, misunderstanding and mutual antipathy' do tend to denote the predominant relational dynamic throughout.[2] The relational dynamic of antipathy has run very deep – and in many ways, continues to do so. Polemics has undoubtedly been a dominant arena of engagement, with each side endeavouring to discount and dismiss the other. Misunderstanding, misrepresentation, and prejudicial attitudes have been all too prominent and persistent. As William Montgomery Watt has observed,

> (whenever) a misrepresentation or distorted image has become firmly rooted in the general outlook of a whole cultural community, it is difficult to change it. New generations of scholars are taught by those who accept the old perception, and when they themselves find new facts, these are still fitted into that perception. Only when the discrepancies have become serious do scholars begin to think of correcting the old perception.[3]

It is to this all-too predominating negative dynamic in Christian-Muslim relations that we now turn.

Antipathy – *polemics*

From the outset, a predominant element in the attitude Muslims and Christians have had towards each other has been one of suspicion, if not outright rejection. For a long time, Muslims and Christians

> [...] tended to regard one another as defective versions of themselves, Muslims looking on Christians as errant monotheists who had abandoned their pristine revelation and in consequence had slipped into irrational and unviable beliefs about God, and Christians seeing Muslims as deniers of the true forms of belief because they had adopted the deceptive versions given in the Qur'an.[4]

Antipathy finds expression primarily in polemical works, which in terms of their content can present as wide-ranging and general, or as more focussed and specific. An analysis of many entries pertaining to antipathy suggests, alongside a broad general group, at least the following eight sub-category thematic areas or topics:

---

[2] C. Kimball, *Striving together. A way forward in Christian-Muslim relations*, Maryknoll NY, 1991, p. 37.

[3] W.M. Watt, *Muslim-Christian encounters. Perceptions and misperceptions*, London, 1991, p. 111.

[4] D. Thomas, 'Introduction', in D. Thomas (ed.), *The Routledge handbook on Christian-Muslim relations*, Abingdon, 2018, 1-6, p. 4.

- perceptions of the Bible and the Qur'an
- Christian perceptions of Muḥammad and Islam *and*
- Christian anti-Muslim polemics, especially refutations of Islam
- Islam as punishment for Christian sin
- martyrdom
- the crusades
- Muslim refutations of Christianity
- Muslim perceptions of Christians as inherently inferior

This list is by no means exhaustive, and many texts will involve more than one of these themes or topics. Nevertheless, it is possible to discern leading motifs within many texts, and some representative works have identified within each sub-category. However, before examining those, we begin with some examples of the overarching and broad general category.

A reconstructed letter (there are two documents from which it has come), purportedly by the Caliph 'Umar II to the Byzantine Emperor Leo III, is an early example of a wide-ranging general polemic expressing antipathy towards Christianity from a variety of perspectives.[5] A classic example of the Muslim 'technique of holding the Bible against Christianity', and advancing certain Islamic practices and perceptions as, indeed, found and endorsed in the biblical text, this letter forcefully argues against the divinity of Christ with clear and logical *reductio ad absurdum* lines of reasoning. For example, it argues that Christians had corrupted the original biblical text, asking questions such as 'who ruled the world when Christ was in the womb'.[6] It contains precursors to later Muslim 'proofs of prophethood' arguments as well as, in conjunction with its Christian reply, giving 'evidence of the fact that certain Muslim and Christian apologetical arguments were conceived in direct response to criticisms from the other party'.[7] Another example is an early 10th-century *vita*, *The Life of Elias the Younger*, written in 'the literary style of hagiography', which describes various conflicts – attacks, sieges and other destructions – wrought by Muslims invading Byzantine Christian lands; it refers to the Arab invaders 'as infidel barbarians whose faith should be resisted by Chalcedonian Christianity'.[8] It also 'provides a valuable

5 See B. Roggema, '*Pseudo- 'Umar II's letter to Leo III*', in *CMR* 1, 381-85.
6 Roggema, '*Pseudo-'Umar II's letter*', p. 382.
7 Roggema, '*Pseudo-'Umar II's letter*', p. 384.
8 B. Krönung, '*The Life of Elias the Younger*', in *CMR* 2, 246-50, p. 248.

insight into the response of the Muslim threat by Byzantine orthodoxy: using the strategy of constructing the concept of "the enemy" in order to maintain its own identity'.[9]

A good 12th-century example of the polemical genre from the Muslim side exemplifies 'the kind of arguments that have been used throughout the history of Christian-Muslim relations'.[10] And a 14th-century work echoes earlier polemical themes, 'notably the contention that Christianity is a distorted form of Jesus' original teaching [...] and that the Bible preserves some of his true teachings and also predictions of the coming of Islam, despite being corrupt and written by human authors'.[11] Another 14th-century text is reckoned to be 'one of the longest polemical works against Christianity and Judaism', and has found renewed popularity with several new editions appearing since 1978.[12] General polemical literature is effectively ubiquitous throughout the history of Christian-Muslim relations in the millennium period of our study with, as we shall now see, a good number of focused themes and topics. All are illustrative of antipathy.

Bible and Qur'an

Antipathy is to the fore with examples of negative perceptions and rejections of the Bible and the Qur'an.[13] An early 11th-century Muslim text that 'shows startling originality in its reading of the New Testament books, and its aggressive proof that they cannot be authentic because they repeatedly disagree with one another' is a good example of this genre.[14] The author, Abū Muḥammad ʿAlī ibn Ḥazm, may be regarded 'as possibly the most adamant proponent of the view that it was the actual text of Christian scripture that had been corrupted, rather than that it was wrongly interpreted by Christians'.[15] Another example is an 11th-century text by the Ashʿarī and Shāfiʿī scholar Abū l-Maʿālī l-Juwaynī, which 'is one of the few Muslim works from the early centuries that investigates the issue of textual alteration in any detail, as opposed to stating it in

---

9 Krönung, '*Life of Elias the Younger*', pp. 248-9.
10 See M. Iskenderoglu, 'Fakhr al-Dīn al Rāzī', in *CMR* 4, 61-5, p. 65.
11 D. Thomas, 'Al-Qaysī', in *CMR* 4, 732-6, p. 735.
12 J. Hoover, 'Ibn Qayyim al-Jawziyya', in *CMR* 4, 989-1002, p. 999.
13 See also chs 9, 10 and 11 below.
14 J.P. Monferrer Sala, '*Kitāb al-fiṣal fī l-milal wa-l-ahwāʾ wa-l-niḥal*', in *CMR* 3, 141-3, p. 142.
15 Monferrer Sala, '*Kitāb al-fiṣal*', p. 142.

principle'.[16] This author uncompromisingly asserts that the biblical text must have been altered so as to remove reference to the foretelling of Muḥammad that otherwise should be there.

A further example of Muslim negation of Christian scripture is the 12th-century redaction of an eclectic mix of texts 'partly based on the biblical Psalms' but consisting 'mostly of Islamic materials [...] and traditions about David from the *Tales of the prophets* literature'.[17] Containing 'predictions of Muḥammad, scattered polemics about Christ's divinity and the corruption of the Bible' along with other material, it was written to promote among Muslims 'a repentant and ascetic piety like that associated with David'.[18] Nevertheless, it reflects the fact that Jews, Christians and Muslims shared and drew upon a common scriptural source and shared values and stories, thus forming a 'common symbolic repertoire', though at the same time reinforcing 'the polemical claim that the Jewish and Christian scriptures are corrupt'.[19] An example from the Christian side is a translation and paraphrase of the Arabic Qur'an into Latin, the first of its kind, undertaken in the mid-12th century by Robert of Ketton. This proved to be a key source and reference for many 'Latin polemical and apologetic works directed at Islam [...] (and) [...] a good deal of Latin Christendom's hostile approach to Islam'; indeed, this work 'was by far the most widely read to the end of the 17th century'.[20]

Christian perceptions of Muḥammad and Islam

Christian perceptions of Islam, and especially Muḥammad,[21] form another theme within polemical texts of antipathy. A polemical poem in Arabic, written by a Christian, typifies a common trope of disdain that expresses 'the confident belief that while the other side is in error one's own side follows the true faith from God'.[22] A Latin text from around the end of the 9th century provides an example of a life of Muḥammad written from a dismissive Christian perspective, aiming 'to discredit Muslim claims for the legitimacy of Muḥammad's revelation' by affirming he was duped by a false angel.[23] And an early 11th-century historical work, the

16 D. Thomas, 'Al-Juwaynī', in *CMR* 3, 121-6, p. 123.
17 See D.R. Vishanoff, 'Islamic "Psalms of David"', in *CMR* 3, 724-30, p. 724.
18 Vishanoff, 'Islamic "Psalms of David"', pp. 724, 726.
19 Vishanoff, 'Islamic "Psalms of David"', p. 727.
20 O. de la Cruz Palma and C.F. Hernandez, 'Robert of Ketton', in *CMR* 3, 508-19, p. 511.
21 See also chs 4 and 7 below.
22 D. Thomas, 'Representative of Nicephorus Phocas', in *CMR* 2, 367-9, p. 368.
23 J. Tolan, '*Tultusceptru de libro domni Metobii*', in *CMR* 2, 83-4, p. 84.

Chronicon of Adémar of Chabannes, which references episodes of conflict between Muslims and Christians, 'provides important insights into Christian attitudes toward Islam in the early 11th century' and displays an 'aggressive attitude toward Islam and increasingly hostile depiction of Muslims'. In effect, this is a foretaste of 'similar attitudes held at the time of the First Crusade'.[24]

A 12th-century Latin text on the life of Muḥammad in verse form represents a well-established legendary tradition of denigration of the Prophet, which nonetheless gives evidence of 'a rising interest in Islam and its prophet', together with 'a need to relegate the faith to the level of a ridiculous and despicable heresy'.[25] Indeed, one early 12th-century 'life of Muḥammad' represents him 'as the most recent and scurrilous example of a long line of oriental heresiarchs'.[26] The image of Muḥammad as 'a 4th-century Libyan heresiarch, driven by lust and worldly ambition to lead his people into a depraved cult', was by no means uncommon.[27] And the late 12th-century Old French epic *La Chanson de Roland* became a 'standard representation' of Islam, construed by Christians as no more than 'pagan idolatry'.[28] Anti-Muḥammad attitudes included portraying him as 'as a poor man suffering from epilepsy who was hired by a rich woman to take care of her camels and trade with the Arabs in Egypt and Palestine, where he became acquainted with Jewish and Christian teaching'.[29] This text reflects completely hostile sentiments towards 'the Arabs and their religion', which compares with similar sentiments expressed 'by other Byzantine authors'.[30]

Christian anti-Muslim polemics

Christian attitudes towards Islam tended to harden as antipathy towards this religious rival intensified. Anti-Muslim polemics became something of a flourishing industry. A short anti-Muslim polemic appended to an East Syrian recension of the *Legend of Sergius Baḥīrā* portrays Islam 'as a continuation of the paganism found among the pre-Islamic Arabs'.[31]

---

24 M. Frassetto, 'Ademar of Charbannes', in *CMR* 2, 648-56, p. 651.
25 J. Tolan, 'Gautier de Compiègne', in *CMR* 3, 601-3, p. 602.
26 See J. Tolan, 'Adelphus', in *CMR* 3, 572-3, p, 573.
27 See J. Tolan, 'Embrico of Mainz', in *CMR* 3, 592-5, p. 593.
28 S. Kinoshita, '*La Chanson de Roland*', in *CMR* 3, 648-52, p. 649.
29 See S. Efthymiadis, 'George the Monk', in *CMR* 1, 729-33, p. 730.
30 Efthymiadis, 'George the Monk', p. 732.
31 B. Roggema, '*The Confession which Kaʿb al-Aḥbār handed down to the Ishmaelites*', in *CMR* 1, 403-5, p. 403.

Even so, its vehemence contrasts sharply with East Syrian texts 'which maintain that Muḥammad is to be praised for converting his people to the one god, even if Muslims do not recognize the Trinity'.[32] Here, we find a reminder that antipathy, whilst dominant, is by no means the only relational dynamic at play in the encounter between Christians and Muslims. Nevertheless, antipathy was writ large, especially in attempts to refute Islam. *Liber denudationis sive ostensionis aut patefaciens*, a late 11th- or early 12th-century Latin translation of an Arabic text, comprises 'a Christian polemical and apologetic treatise against Islam very typical of the genre and clearly based heavily on earlier eastern Arab Christian models'.[33]

It was perhaps Peter of Cluny, known as Peter the Venerable, Abbot of the monastery at Cluny, who in the 12th century produced some of the more distinctive, and certainly better known in later years, Christian anti-Muslim polemics. A scholar and prolific author, his concern was to defend the Christian faith and Church from its enemies, who included heretics, Jews and 'Saracens'.[34] It was he who commissioned Robert of Ketton to make the first Latin translation of the Qur'an, and he was instrumental in commissioning and promoting other works, with a view to providing a Christian intellectual armoury with which to combat Islam. Peter himself wrote two polemical anti-Muslim works.[35] He regarded Islam as the repository of all known Christian heresies, although Muslims themselves are more likely to be viewed simply as pagans, rather than heretics *per se*. The teachings of Muḥammad vis-à-vis Christianity are clearly denounced and refuted. In his *Summa totius haeresis Saracenorum*, he 'seeks to furnish a basis of a polemical vision of Islam',[36] while, in *Liber contra sectam sive hearesim Saracenorum*, he 'attempts to combat Islam through a close examination of what constitutes prophecy'.[37]

A Muslim work from the mid-12th century, *Maqāmiʿ al-ṣulbān* ('Mallets for crosses'), has preserved a letter from a Christian priest that includes 'an attack on the Islamic version of paradise and against the spread of Islam by force, ending with a call for the conversion of Muslims to Christianity'.[38] And a Syrian Christian theologian of the 12th century,

---

32 Roggema, '*Confession which Kaʿb al-Aḥbār handed down*', p. 404.
33 T.E. Burman, '*Liber denudationis*', in *CMR* 3, 414-17, p. 415.
34 See D. Iogna-Prat and J. Tolan, 'Peter of Cluny', in *CMR* 3, 604-10.
35 *Summa totius haeresis ac diabolicae sectae Saracenorum siue Hismahelitarum*, and *Contra sectam Saracenorum*, see Iogna-Prat and Tolan, 'Peter of Cluny', pp. 606-7, 608-10.
36 Iogna-Prat and Tolan, 'Peter of Cluny', p. 606.
37 Iogna-Prat and Tolan, 'Peter of Cluny', p. 608.
38 J.P. Monferrer Sala, 'Al-Khazrajī', in *CMR* 3, 526-8, p. 527.

Dionysius bar Ṣalibi, took up the pen to refute not only Muslims but also non-Jacobite Christian communities (Nestorians, Chalcedonians, Armenians) and others, as well as Jews.[39] However, whereas the critique of Armenian and Chalcedonian Christianity is highly polemical, the 'refutation of the Muslims is by comparison more balanced and detached'.[40] Nevertheless, it comprises 'the most comprehensive refutation of Islam written in Syriac', and reflects the 'traditional themes found in the Syriac and Christian Arabic refutation literature'.[41]

Islam as punishment for Christian sin

Another trope of antipathy has to do with Christian responses to violent interaction with Muslims. For instance, in a sermon that reflects on the capture of Thessaloniki in the early 10th century, the preacher blames the disaster on the 'lack of faith among the people and sees it as divine punishment that compels sincere repentance'.[42] The sermon 'does not attempt to chronicle events but to draw a moral and religious lesson', specifically that the event was brutal in both its inhumanity and the resultant suffering of Christians, causally attributed to their sinfulness.[43] The trope of Islam as a divine punishment for Christian sin may be found elsewhere as, for example, in an early Syriac chronicle written in the mid-9th century by Dionysius of Tell-Maḥrē. This expresses 'a certain vision about the power of Islam, which is seen as a chastisement for the sins of the Christians in general or of particular groups of Christians'.[44] This work is also echoed in the mid-12th century by William of Malmesbury, for whom 'God has allowed the Turks and Saracens to dominate the lands of God's birth and passion as a punishment for the people's mores'.[45] And apocalyptic reactions to, or perspectives on, Islam at times found expression in Christian acts of martyrdom, or else the post-facto interpretation of violent death of Christians at the hands of Muslims as the making of martyrs.

---

39 See H.G.B. Teule, 'Dionysius bar Ṣalibi', in *CMR* 3, 665-70.
40 Teule, 'Dionysius bar Ṣalibi', p. 667.
41 Teule, 'Dionysius bar Ṣalibi', p. 669.
42 M. Vaiou, 'Nicolas Mysticus', in *CMR* 2, 169-83, p. 172.
43 Vaiou, 'Nicolas Mysticus', p. 173.
44 Cf. H.G.B. Teule, 'Dionysius of Tell-Maḥrē', in *CMR* 1, 622-6, p. 625.
45 J. Tolan, 'William of Malmesbury', in *CMR* 3, 483-7, p. 487.

Martyrdom

Texts that record violence both reinforce a negative image and provide a reference for the promotion of martyrdom as a holy response.[46] An example of the former is an account from the 9th or 10th century of the refusal by the young Christian Elias of Helioupolis to renounce his faith under pressure from his employer, a former Syrian Christian who had converted to Islam. The young man was eventually martyred for his refusal to become a Muslim.[47] On another occasion, two 9th-century Christian women of Córdoba, 'imprisoned for apostasy from Islam', were exhorted to remain steadfast in their newfound faith, 'and to endure persecution and martyrdom', the oppressive Muslim captor being described in lurid terms as 'lusting after innocent Christian virgins'.[48] And in her account of the 10th-century martyrdom of 'Pelagius', the German canoness Hrotsvit of Gandersheim depicts Muslims and Islam as 'a clear and present danger to Western Christendom', although 'God continues to support and defend (the Christian) community with the blood of virgin martyrs – a most powerful weapon'.[49] And in a much later account from the 16th century, attributed to the Russian monk Nifont Kormilitsin, its point and significance is 'as an encouragement to the faithful who read and heard it' even as far as martyrdom.[50]

In a Georgian text 'that contains clear, polemical, theological arguments against Islam', there is a record of the martyrdom of Abo, a perfumer from Baghdad, who converted from Islam to Christianity after moving to Georgia in the late 8th century.[51] Another work from Georgia, a martyrdom written in the early 10th century, a time when Muslim power was posing an increasing threat, provides an account of 'refusal to convert to Islam, preferring death to apostasy' that 'would have served as an example to Georgian Christians and provided an encouragement to remain true to their faith'.[52] Finally, an account of a bishop's death in the crusade of 1101, given in an early 12th-century Latin text, 'presents a vivid example, in the wake of the First Crusade, of the stereotypical image of Saracens as pagan idolaters' in the context of celebrating the bishop's

46 See also ch. 16 below.

47 See S. Efthymiadis, '*The martyrdom of Elias of Helioupolis* (*Elias of Damascus*)', in *CMR* 1, 916-18.

48 See J. Tolan, 'Eulogius of Cordova', in *CMR* 1, 679-83, p. 682.

49 L.A. McMillin, 'Hrotsvit of Gandersheim', in *CMR* 2, 293-7, p. 296.

50 See C. Soldat, 'Nifont Kormilitsin', in *CMR* 7, 372-8, p. 374.

51 G. Shurgaia, 'Ioane Sabanisdze', in *CMR* 1, 334-7, p. 336.

52 See M.D. Abashidze, 'Stepane of Tbeti', in *CMR* 2, 141-4, p. 143.

elevation as a martyr.[53] A Christian valuing of martyrs can be seen as an influencing factor in the way the bishop's death was both perceived and received. Having a bishop proclaimed a martyr was a high prize: it brought spiritual prestige to his church, often accompanied by economic benefit through pilgrimages. Certain religio-cultural norms and prejudices coloured polemical and hagiographical writings in order to achieve an ulterior purpose. This is a comment on, not a denigration of, the motif of martyrdom.

The crusades

If Christians found themselves on the receiving end of Muslim violence, there is no lack of examples of Christians in turn meting out violence to Muslims. Antipathy is very much a two-way street. The crusades, Western Christendom's holy war against Islam, is a lead contender.[54] A late 11th-century poem, written shortly before the First Crusade (1095-9), expresses 'a vision of holy war against Muslims' in which Muslims are regarded as heretics (and not idolators), 'and Muḥammad as a heresiarch (rather than a false god)'.[55] Written at the beginning of the 12th century, the *Historia Francorum qui ceperunt Iherusalem* 'provides an early example of theological development in crusade ideology and the justification for Holy War', with Muslims viewed 'as the pagan enemies of God's people', which 'thereby justifies crusader aggression against them'.[56] Indeed, for this author the crusade is regarded 'as a divine punishment for Muslims, whom he portrays as pagans, for their sacrilege of holy places and atrocities against Christians'.[57] And another text, from the early 12th century, but some time 'after the First Crusade and the foundation of the crusader states', upholds the view 'that the Crusade was a unique, monumental event in history, in which the diverse people of the West came together to overthrow the Muslims, who are presented as an eschatological force'.[58] Oceans of ink have been expended in analysing and discussing the Crusades, and a first port of call for any serious work is the texts, such as those noted above, that appear within the bibliographical history.

---

53 J. Tolan, *'Martyrdom of Bishop Thiemo'*, in *CMR* 3, 555-7, p. 556.
54 See also ch. 12 below.
55 J. Tolan, *'Carmen in victoriam Pisanorum'*, in *CMR* 3, 223-5, p. 224.
56 See B. Packard, 'Raymond of Aguilers', in *CMR* 3, 297-300, p. 299.
57 Packard, 'Raymond of Aguilers', p. 299.
58 See A. Mallett, 'Orderic Vitalis', in *CMR* 3, 490-6, p. 493.

Muslim refutations of Christianity

On a more theological level, we find significant examples of Muslim refutations of Christianity.[59] One of the 'longest and most detailed' assaults on the doctrines of Incarnation and Trinity, from the pen of the mid-9th-century scholar Abū 'Īsā l-Warrāq, is of considerable importance as it is 'the longest extant pre-14th-century anti-Christian polemic'.[60] Another significant text is Abū Yūsuf al Kindī's 'Refutation of the Christians', also from the 9th century, which makes use of Greek philosophical concepts that would have been familiar to educated Christians at the time and holds that 'the doctrine of the Trinity makes the Godhead into a plurality'.[61] In addition, an early 10th-century work, Abū Manṣūr al-Māturīdī's *Kitāb al-tawḥīd*, 'is the earliest surviving Muslim work that can be regarded as a systematic theology, in that it brings together individual questions debated among theological specialists into a structured whole'.[62] It combines 'the presentation of positive theological teachings with refutations of opposing views' that include 'a brief examination of Christian claims for the divinity of Christ'.[63] The result is an argument ruling out the divinity of Jesus on the basis of his manifest human traits, meaning that 'Christian teachings about Jesus are logically unsustainable, with the obvious implication that the teachings of Islam about him are correct', and so, typically, Christianity is disproved and Islam is vindicated.[64]

It seems clear that, by the mid-10th century, 'a set procedure of anti-Christian polemic in Islam was fast developing'; indeed, it was quite well advanced.[65] A 9th-century work by al-Nāshi' al-Akbar that discusses various religions and philosophies contains a significant section on Christianity, which displays a sound knowledge of key Christian theological doctrines and issues. An accompanying refutation focuses 'entirely on the doctrines of the Trinity and the Incarnation' using scripture and rational arguments, together with a critique of contemporary Christians.[66] Although representative of a great number of works of refutation,[67]

---

59 See also chs 5 and 6 below.
60 D. Thomas, 'Abū 'Īsā l-Warrāq', in *CMR* 1, 695-701, p. 698.
61 D. Thomas, 'Al-Kindī', in *CMR* 1, 746-50, p. 747.
62 D. Thomas, 'Al-Māturīdī', in *CMR* 2, 251-4, p. 253.
63 Thomas, 'Al-Māturīdī', p. 253.
64 Thomas, 'Al-Māturīdī', p. 253.
65 D. Thomas, 'Al-Bāqillānī', in *CMR* 2, 446-50, p. 449.
66 D. Thomas, 'Al-Nāshi' al-Akbar', in *CMR* 2, 85-8, p. 87.
67 See, for example, D. Thomas, 'Ibn Bābawayh', in *CMR* 2, 514-18; G.S. Reynolds, '*Al-mughnī fī abwāb al-tawḥīd wa-l-'adl*', in *CMR* 2, 597-602; G.S. Reynolds, '*Tathbīt dalā' il*

this particular text also gives evidence of 'an extremely lively dialogue between Muslims and Christians, in which both sides were able to employ the same concepts and logic'.[68]

Alongside refutation can be found the trope of distortion, that is, the Muslim charge of Christian distortion of true belief and scripture, and not only with regard to textual corruption or misinterpretation. An exemplary text in this respect is the mid-11th-century *Kitāb al-milal wa-l-niḥal* by Abū l-Fatḥ al-Shahrastānī, the significance of which lies not only in the accuracy of its description and understanding of Christianity, but also in 'its evaluation of Christianity as a distortion of true monotheistic beliefs'.[69] This particular text 'provides a typically Muslim appraisal of Christianity, stemming from the assumption that the true faith was anticipating the coming of Muḥammad and his revelation, and its historical forms have thus clearly neglected this original purity and degenerated into error'.[70] Another example is a mid-12th-century historical work in which four entries, on Jesus, Mary, John and the disciples, pertain to a discussion of Christianity in which relations between Christians and Muslims are portrayed negatively. Christians are seen 'as having deserted the true message of Jesus' in response to which 'Jesus stands against his historical followers, and will help Islam and the Muslims defeat them'.[71] This takes us to the last of the themes identified as coming within the relational dynamic category of antipathy.

Muslim perceptions of Christians as inherently inferior

A perhaps 'softer' form or expression of antipathy can be found in the trope of Muslim perception and presumption of Christian inferiority. It can be expressed even in a context that might otherwise suggest appreciative inquiry, or a measure of acceptance and accommodation. For example, a late 10th-century text, *Kitāb al-diyārāt* ('The book of monasteries') by Abū l-Ḥasan al-Shābushtī, is a compilation of poetic and narrative passages from earlier Arab Muslim writers penned in order to 'convey the image of monasteries as celebrated by poets and perceived by cultured court circles. The presence of Christians and monasteries is accepted as a fact

al-nubuwwa', in *CMR* 2, 604-9; D Thomas, '*Kitāb al-Shāmil fī uṣūl al-dīn*', in *CMR* 3, 124-6; L. Demiri, 'Naṣr ibn Yaḥyā', in *CMR* 3, 750-4.

68 Thomas, 'Al-Nāshi' al-Akbar', p. 87.

69 D. Thomas, 'Al-Shahrastānī', in *CMR* 3, 549-54, p. 552.

70 Thomas, 'Al-Shahrastānī', p. 552.

71 S.A. Mourad, 'Ibn 'Asākir', in *CMR* 3, 683-9, p. 688.

of life; religious polemic is absent.' However, these Christians were perceived as belonging 'to a socially inferior community'.[72] Another example is an early 12th-century Arabic text by the Andalusian Ibn ʿAbdūn al-Ishbīlī, which 'refers to Jews and Christians as socially and religiously inferior to Muslims' and favours 'separation between them and Muslim society'.[73] Directives for interaction are issued governing the manner of relations between Muslims and Christians, as well as with Jews.

We pass now from the dynamic of antipathy to that of affinity.

Affinity – *inquiry*

A thread 'of mutual recognition and respect' suggestive of a degree of affinity and a measure of inquiry one of the other is certainly present in the textual heritage but, importantly, this element 'is admittedly minor and it remains to be more fully explored alongside the dominant strain of misperception and reproach.'[74] In what follows, the possibility of such exploration can, hopefully, be more readily seen and acknowledged. For it is certainly the case that, threaded among the many texts expressing antipathy, there are those that express elements of both affinity and inquiry. These can be grouped into at least the following four sub-categories:

- Common values and appreciation
- Interreligious cooperation (e.g. translation of the scriptures)
- Christian inquiry of Muslims
- Muslim inquiry of Christians

Common values and appreciation

The Chronicle of Khuzistan, a mid-late 7th-century Syriac text, most likely of East Syrian provenance, interprets Muslim success theologically, 'explaining that their victory comes from God. Muslims are seen as the descendants of Abraham, based on their tradition of worship at the Dome (*qubtā*, Kaʿba) of Abraham.'[75] And the correspondence of the 7th-century East Syrian Catholicos Ishoʿyab III of Adiabene indicates

[72] H. Kilpatrick, 'Al-Shābushtī', in *CMR* 2, 565-9, p. 567.

[73] C. de la Puente, 'Ibn ʿAbdūn al-Ishbīlī', in *CMR* 3, 397-400, p. 398.

[74] D. Thomas, 'Introduction', in D. Thomas (ed.), *The Routledge handbook on Christian–Muslim relations*, Abingdon, 2018, 1-5, p. 4.

[75] H.G.B. Teule, '*The Chronicle of Khuzistan*', in *CMR* 1, 130-2, p. 131.

that he regarded Nestorian Christology as 'more compatible with Muslim views on Christ' than the Christologies of other denominations, and ascribed Arab Muslim predominance to the providence of God.[76] Along with a positive disposition toward the Arabs, he 'denounces the weakness of some Christians who convert to Islam, not under Muslim pressure, but for financial reasons'.[77]

In a late 7th-century work that outlines a history of the world, John bar Penkāyē, a monk of the Church of the East, refers to the rise of Islam as 'God's providential relationship with the Muslim conquerors' which is 'evidenced by their monotheism and their ability to conquer almost the entire world'.[78] Likewise, a 9th-century East Syrian theologian by the name of Moses bar Kephā wrote on a range of topics, including free will and predestination, in which he acknowledged 'the Muslim theological and cultural context', and reflected a measure of 'Muslim technical theological concepts'.[79] Another, most likely late 9th-century work, while denying Muḥammad was a true prophet, nevertheless affirms God as being pleased with Muḥammad, 'in and by whom God has fulfilled his promise to Abraham in Ishmael'.[80] It could be said that this early perception of Muḥammad 'anticipates modern Christian attempts to move towards a positive evaluation'.[81]

Around the mid-10th century an Iranian Ismāʿīlī, Abū Yaʿqūb al-Sijistānī, wrote the *Kitāb al-yanābīʿ* ('Wellsprings').[82] This is notable for its lack of animosity towards Christians and Christianity; indeed, it reveals a degree of respect, even drawing on Matthew's Gospel (25:35-46) in support of a more philosophical argument pertinent to both faiths. In his knowledge and positive use of Christian scripture and beliefs, al-Sijistānī accords to Christianity 'a measure of validity that few others Muslims did'; however, in a form of Muslim fulfilment theology, he holds 'only Islam can give these Christian elements their true meaning'.[83] Similarly, a 12th-century Christian monk, William of Malmesbury, took a fresh, relatively objective and open approach to understanding Islam and the figure of Muḥammad. Apparently, he was 'less interested in polemicizing than

76 H.G.B. Teule, 'Ishoʿyahb III of Adiabene', in *CMR* 1, 133-6, p. 135.
77 Teule, 'Ishoʿyahb III of Adiabene', p. 135.
78 L. Greisiger, 'John bar Penkāyē', in *CMR* 1, 176-81, p. 177.
79 H.G.B. Teule, 'Moses bar Kephā', in *CMR* 2, 98-101, p. 101.
80 M.N. Swanson, '*The Disputation of the monk Ibrāhīm al-Ṭabarānī*', in *CMR* 1, 876-81, p. 879.
81 Swanson, '*Disputation of the monk Ibrāhīm al-Ṭabarānī*', p. 879.
82 D. Thomas, 'Abū Yaʿqūb al-Sijistānī', in *CMR* 2, 381-5.
83 Thomas, 'Abū Yaʿqūb al-Sijistānī', p. 384.

in trying to understand how and why Muḥammad came to be revered as a prophet and continued to his own day to be seen as prophet by many nations'.[84] Indeed, William notes that Jews and Saracens, while disagreeing with Christians about the figure of Jesus, 'all believe in God the Father in their hearts and proclaim him in their words', and so he 'affirms the monotheism of Muslims and asserts that Jews and Muslims worship the same God as Christians'.[85] Likewise, a 12th-century Muslim exposition of the 113 names of God 'makes frequent use of biblical quotations, showing no apparent unease at using either the Old or New Testaments'.[86]

Interreligious cooperation

Cooperation in the scholarly work of translating ancient texts, mainly from Greek to Arabic, together with mutual inquiry into philosophical and other fields where there were overlapping and common interests, forms the core of the 'interreligious cooperation' affinity theme. Although indicative of the search for proofs of the absolute truth of Islam that was generated in the early Abbasid period, a 9th-century Muslim text, together with two Christian responses, forms 'an example of a truly historical interreligious encounter [...] the product of amicable encounters of Muslims and Christians who lived and worked in the same scholarly and cultural milieu'.[87] And an early 10th-century Andalusian work of translation and revision of a pre-existing Latin text by two scholars, one Christian and the other Muslim, is another clear example of cooperative inquiry.[88] Albeit rather rare at the time, it nevertheless prefigures such cooperation in centuries to come. Indeed, this work 'was very influential on later Muslim histories [...] as late as the 15th century'.[89]

Another example comes from Yaḥya ibn 'Adī, a 10th-century Jacobite theologian and philosopher,[90] who lived mostly in Baghdad. He reflects in his work a considerable degree of mutual engagement and inquiry by Christian and Muslim thinkers in the area of philosophical theology, engaging questions such as divine foreknowledge and human free will. In addition, a universal history written by the Christian Maḥbūb

---

84 J. Tolan, 'William of Malmesbury', in *CMR* 3, 483-7, p. 485.
85 Tolan, 'William of Malmesbury', p. 487.
86 J.P. Monferrer Sala, 'Ibn Barrajān', in *CMR* 3, 488-9, p. 489.
87 B. Roggema, "Alī ibn Yaḥyā ibn al Munajjim', in *CMR* 1, 762-7, p. 766.
88 J.P. Monferrer Sala, 'Ibn Albar al-Qūṭī', in *CMR* 2, 281-4.
89 Monferrer Sala, 'Ibn Albar al-Qūṭī', p. 283.
90 See E. Platti, 'Yaḥya ibn 'Adī', in *CMR* 2, 390-438.

ibn Qusṭanṭīn al-Manbijī in the late 10th century has significance 'both by virtue of its preservation of an early witness to the rise of Islam [...] and by its contributions to a joint historiographical enterprise, in which Christians and Muslims shared texts and techniques'.[91] Such cooperative activity certainly contrasts with the ubiquitous polemical interactions that otherwise mark much of Christian-Muslim relations at the time. In addition, it indicates that negative interaction does not tell the full story of Christian-Muslim relations.

Christian inquiry of Muslims

A work written by Rodulfus Glaber, a monk of the Abbey of Cluny, in the second quarter of the 11th century is most informative concerning Christian attitudes toward Islam and Muslims that reflect a measure of inquisitiveness and curiosity. 'Glaber reveals an interest in the rival faith that would grow in the generations to come, and he sought to develop some understanding of Islam. His work reveals the awareness among some Latin Christians that Muslims honored the Bible and its prophets.'[92] In the East, ʿAbd Allāh ibn al-Faḍl al-Anṭākī, a prolific 11th-century Melkite theologian, produced several works on Christian-Muslim relations that demonstrate a considerable depth of inquiry and grasp of Muslim sources by a Christian. For example, his *Kitāb al-manfaʿa* draws heavily on Muslim philosophical works, which is something of 'an indication of surprisingly deep ties between Christian Arab intellectuals living in Antioch under Byzantine rule, and Muslim philosophical circles'.[93] However, such inquiries were not necessarily benign, in this case having an underlying polemical purpose with a number of classical polemical arguments against Islam advanced, and Muslim positions opposed to Christian doctrines decisively countered on philosophical grounds.

The late 11th-century chronicle written by Hugh of Flavigny 'illustrates how Islam and Muḥammad were perceived in Christian, West-European historiography' at that time, reflecting 'the common Christian view [...] that Muḥammad received some religious training at a Christian school and was seduced into founding the religion of Islam by the devil in the guise of the Archangel Gabriel'.[94] Inquiry is not necessarily for benign or purely disinterested academic purposes. Yet William of Tyre, writing in

91 M.N. Swanson, 'Maḥbūb ibn Qusṭanṭīn al-Manbijī', in *CMR* 2, 241-5, p. 243.
92 M. Frassetto, 'Rodolfus Glaber', in *CMR* 2, 721-6, p. 722.
93 A. Trieger, "Abdallāh ibn al-Faḍl al-Anṭākī', in *CMR* 3, 89-113, p. 95.
94 P. Healy, 'Hugh of Flavigny', in *CMR* 3, 301-6, p. 305.

the late 12th century, 'demonstrates that, to some extent at least, there was a real [on behalf of Christians] effort to understand' Muslims and Islam during the time of the crusades.[95] Similarly, a late 12th-century travel narrative, written by Burchard of Strasbourg, provides a surprisingly rare non-judgemental description and evaluation that gives a 'non-polemical presentation of doctrinal differences between Christianity and Islam'.[96] However, its tendency towards a glowing 'portrayal of idyllic harmony between Egyptian and Syriac Christians and Muslims' rather suggests this irenic account had more to do with serving a diplomatic purpose than with making an objective assessment of Christian-Muslim relations as such.[97] Nevertheless, there had to be some justification for such a view.

Muslim inquiry of Christians

In his late 9th-century universal history, the Muslim scholar Abū l-ʿAbbās al-Yaʿqūbī gives an atypical 'full and more or less objective treatment of the biblical Jesus' that results in 'an account of the life of Jesus that readers familiar with the Christian tradition would recognize as largely true to what they know'.[98] The early 10th-century Ismāʿīlī Abū Ḥātim al-Rāzī, in *Aʿlām al-nubuwwa* ('Signs of prophethood') argues for deep agreement between the revealed religions, and insists that disagreement in terms of differing narratives can be reconciled. Indeed, in making its point, his work is 'one of only a few texts that recognize that Jesus died on the cross, even if only physically'.[99] The inclusion of several biblical passages reinforces the observation that this is indeed 'a rare example from this time of a detached, objective attitude towards Christianity and its scripture'.[100]

Abū l-Ḥusayn al-Miṣrī's mid-10th-century work of refutation reveals the depth of knowledge about intra-Christian theological debates and differences that this Muslim author had acquired. This is a veritable case of 'a rare knowledge of the detailed teachings of one faith by a follower of another', thus suggesting 'some intellectual curiosity', which, at the time, and in preceding centuries, was very rare indeed.[101] And a substantial

95 A. Mallett, 'William of Tyre', in *CMR* 3, 769-77, p. 772.
96 J. Tolan, 'Burchard of Strasbourg', in *CMR* 3, 679-82, p. 681.
97 Tolan, 'Burchard of Strasbourg', p. 681.
98 D. Thomas, 'Al-Yaʿqūbī', in *CMR* 2, 75-8, p. 77.
99 S. Nomoto and D. Thomas, 'Abū Ḥātim al-Rāzī', in *CMR* 2, 200-9, p. 205.
100 Nomoto and Thomas, 'Abū Ḥātim al-Rāzī', p. 206.
101 D. Thomas, 'Abū l-Ḥusayn al-Miṣrī', in *CMR* 2, 373-6, p. 376.

multi-authored 10th-century Ismāʿīlī work advocates 'the universality of the Gospels and the message of Jesus', and reinterprets the qur'anic verse concerning the crucifixion, Q 4:157, to assert 'acceptance of the actual historical death of Jesus'.[102] The key is, of course, the application of an appropriate philosophy (including epistemology and metaphysics especially) and hermeneutic. And the pseudonymous *Al-radd al-jamīl li-ilā hi yyat ʿIsābi- ṣarīḥ al-Injīl*, attributed to al-Ghazālī, presents

> some of the most detailed and complete discussions of biblical texts that are known from the medieval Islamic period [...] [The author] accepts the authenticity of the text itself, while he disputes the interpretation given by Christians. Even more strikingly, he accepts that Jesus was united with God, though he interprets this as a unique form of mystical experience [...] and argues that it is possible for a human to have union with God, although it is logically impossible to become God.[103]

Evidently, significant interest in other religions and a willingness to learn, rather than simply judge and condemn, was not unknown within the ancient Muslim world.[104]

Appeal – *apologetics*

The category of 'appeal', which embraces apologetic texts, yields some six thematic sets:

- General Muslim apologetics
- General Christian apologetics
- Christian defences of the faith
- Muslim proofs of the prophethood of Muḥammad
- The superiority of Islam
- Christian missions to Muslims

General Muslim apologetics

The 10th-century Muslim thinker Abū l-Ḥasan al-ʿĀmirī was very interested in 'the intersection of Aristotelian-Neoplatonic metaphysics and religion', particularly as this related to Islam.[105] He was also interested

102 O. Ali-de-Unzaga, 'Ikhwān al-Ṣafā'', in *CMR* 2, 306-11, p. 310.
103 M. El Kaisy-Friemuth, 'Al-Ghazālī', in *CMR* 3, 363-9, p. 368.
104 Cf. A. Mallett, 'Abū l-Maʿālī', in *CMR* 3, 214-16.
105 E.K. Rowson, 'Al-ʿĀmirī', in *CMR* 2, 485-90, p 485.

in what today would be termed comparative religion, albeit loaded in the direction of seeking to prove the necessary superiority of Islam over all others. Nevertheless, his work is largely dispassionate and irenic; he eschews polemics. His *Al-iʿlām bi-manāqib al-Islām* ('Information about the virtues of Islam'), in which Islam is favourably compared with Judaism, Christianity, Zoroastrianism, Greek astral religion and pagan idol worship, with particular attention paid to Christianity, suggests that he had a Christian audience in mind. The debunking of Christian beliefs was the necessary counterpoint to asserting an appeal for the veracity and superiority of Islam. Another example of a more general apologetics, the mid-13th-century *Al-risāla l-nāṣiriyya* ('Treatise of assistance') by the Ḥanafī jurist Abū l-Rajā l-Zāhidī, is notable for its 'awareness of Christian concerns and also some experience in responding to them'.[106] Al-Zāhidī attempts to answer a raft of questions, both scholarly and populist, that Christians have about Islam. The work is 'a valuable witness to a tradition of inter-religious encounter on a popular level at a time when Islam was in the ascendancy and Christian confidence was unsteady'.[107]

General Christian apologetics

On the Christian side, Job of Edessa, a philosopher and physician belonging to the Church of the East, sought in the early 9th century 'a philosophical language that was universally acceptable and by means of which he could confirm the truth of Christianity to Christians and demonstrate it to non-Christians'.[108] He shows that Syrian Christians could, and did, reformulate Christian apologetics 'in the light of Islamic doctrine', distinguishing 'between what should be accepted by faith and what should be accepted through rational inquiry of the physical world' as a line of thinking 'emblematic of the apologetical trend of the time'.[109] The mid-9th-century Syrian apologetic treatise by Nonnus of Nisibis defends miaphysite (sole-nature) Christology and offers a wide-ranging defence of Christianity more generally, whilst still according sympathetic recognition to Muslim positions and perspectives.[110] And another 9th-century Arabic work, the anonymous *Al-jāmiʿ wujūh al-īmān* ('The compendium of aspects of faith'), presents a broad theological apology

106 D. Thomas, 'Al-Zāhidī', in *CMR* 4, 397-9, p. 399.
107 Thomas, 'Al-Zāhidī', p. 399.
108 B. Roggema, 'Job of Edessa', in *CMR* 1, 502-9, p. 505.
109 Roggema, 'Job of Edessa', p. 508.
110 H.G.B. Teule, 'Nonnus of Nisibis', in *CMR* 1, 743-5.

for Christianity, including the Trinity and the unity of God, and the understanding of Christ (Christology and Incarnation), and responds to arguments against the divinity of Christ.[111] A particular thread is the rebuffing of any Christian accommodation to Muslim sensibilities, urging instead a *modus vivendi* of clear witness and theological positioning. This work is a significant 'compendium of apologetically formulated explanations of Christian doctrines and practices', providing an insight into a perceived 'crisis' for the Church and Christian identity as a result of Arabic-speaking Christians adopting and adapting to 'Islamic modes of speech and thought' so as not to cause offence to their rulers.[112] Finally, in this brief review, mention should be made of the Melkite bishop Theodore Abū Qurra, a major Christian theologian in the late 8th and early 9th centuries, who wrote in Arabic and Greek, and was himself a prolific scholar who tackled theological and philosophical themes.[113] These included theological epistemology with specific reference to the challenge posed by Islam,[114] a defence of the doctrine of the Trinity,[115] and a defence of soteriology.[116]

Christian defences of the faith

Many apologetic treatises attempt to explain, or argue for, belief in specific Christian doctrines, such as the Trinity and the Incarnation (among Eastern Christians expressed as the uniting of the divine and human natures in Christ), using philosophical terms familiar to Muslims as well as Christians. These often contain multiple thematic elements, among which is a strong defence of the Christian faith. One Syriac text, probably from the early 8th century, *Testimonies of the prophets about the dispensation of Christ*, while it argues against Islam, also includes arguments that exhort Syrian Christians 'to prove that they are the true children and heirs of Abraham', and 'seeks to show that the Christians are the new chosen people' over against both Jews and Muslims.[117] Another 8th-century text, *The disputation between a monk of Bēt Ḥālē and an Arab notable*, arguably 'one of the oldest surviving examples of the disputation

111 M.N. Swanson, '*Al-Jāmiʿ wujūh al-īmān*', in *CMR* 1, 791-8.
112 Swanson, '*Al-Jāmiʿ wujūh al-īmān*', p. 794.
113 J.C. Lamoreaux, 'Theodore Abū Qurra', in *CMR* 1, 439-91.
114 See Lamoreaux, 'Theodore Abū Qurra', pp. 448-50.
115 See Lamoreaux, 'Theodore Abū Qurra', pp. 453-4, 478-9
116 See Lamoreaux, 'Theodore Abū Qurra', p. 485.
117 M. Debie, '*Testimonies of the prophets about the dispensation of Christ*', in *CMR* 1, 242-4, p. 243.

genre of Christian apologetics vis-à-vis Islam', is also 'the earliest Christian text to show familiarity with the existence of the Qur'an, its contents and its importance as a source of law for Muslims'.[118] This work references some of the major areas of contention and disputations between Muslims and Christians, namely 'the [apparent] worship of icons and relics, the direction of prayer, the validity of the laws of the Torah, the Trinity, the Incarnation, the crucifixion of Christ, and the authority of scriptural proofs'.[119]

A famous defence of the Christian faith with respect to Islam is found in *The apology of al-Kindī*, which was probably composed by a Christian and takes the form of a dialogical disputation narrative. Comprised of two letters, ostensibly one by a Muslim and one by a Christian, in which the former invites the other into his faith and the latter advances a number of reasons not to accept, the Christian letter is both 'a refutation of Islam and an apology for Christianity'.[120] The result is that this work as a whole is 'the best-known Christian Arabic apology in both east and west' (it was translated into Latin in the 12th century), in which 'the discussion aims to prove the internal coherence of the Christian revelation and the contradictory nature of Islamic revelation'.[121] It has frequently been referred to and cited down the centuries. More theologically, the East Christian 'Ammār al-Baṣrī's early 9th-century *Masā'il wa-ajwiba* ('Questions and answers') 'presents the most thorough defense of a number of Christian teachings, especially the authenticity of the Gospels and the reality of the Incarnation', displaying considerable 'capacity to provide answers to well-understood Muslim objections'.[122] Another of his works, *Kitāb al-burhān* ('The book of the proof'), is an early 'apology for Christianity in Arabic that deals systematically with the major beliefs and practices that gave rise to Muslim criticism of Christians'.[123] Its topics include 'proofs for the existence of God', 'criteria for determining the true religion', 'the truth of Christianity' and 'the authenticity of Christian scripture', as well as accounts of the Trinity, Christology, the Incarnation and crucifixion, baptism, Eucharist, 'the symbol of the cross', and 'eating and drinking in the afterlife'.[124]

118 B. Roggema, '*The Disputation between a monk of BētḤālē and an Arab notable*', in *CMR* 1, 268-73, pp. 268 and 271.

119 Roggema, '*Disputation*', p. 270.

120 L. Bottini, '*The Apology of al-Kindī*', in *CMR* 1, 585-94, p. 588.

121 Bottini, '*Apology of al-Kindī*', p. 589.

122 M. Beaumont, "Ammār al-Baṣrī', in *CMR* 1, 604-10, p. 606.

123 Beaumont, "Ammār al-Baṣrī', p. 609.

124 Beaumont, "Ammār al-Baṣrī', p. 607-8.

A further significant example is that of Sāwīrus ibn al-Muqaffaʿ, a 10th-century Coptic Orthodox theologian. He composed theological doctrinal defences, utilising Muslim Arabic terminology as he sought 'to engage Islamic challenges to Christian theology directly, in terminology comprehensible to practitioners of the Islamic *kalām*', and drawing, in particular, on Muʿtazilī theological discourse.[125] His important *Kitāb miṣbāḥ al-ʿaql* ('The lamp of understanding') reads as a summary of Christian faith using a 'template provided by the faith and practice of Muslims'.[126] A final example is a mid-12th-century anonymous work, known as *Apologetic commentary on the Creed*, which presents a substantial and systematic defence of Christian beliefs and doctrines, including the Trinity, Christology, soteriology and ecclesiology. As well as drawing on biblical texts, it also makes use of qur'anic texts 'in support of the Christian author's arguments', which marks this out as a significant work of Christian apologetic defence of faith with a Muslim audience in mind.[127]

Muslim proofs of the prophethood of Muḥammad

Among the genre of proofs of prophethood texts, one 9th-century work by the theologian Abū ʿUthmān al-Jāḥiẓ is notable as 'a rare surviving example of a very popular genre in early Islam'.[128] In it, al-Jāḥiẓ duly acknowledges that the miracles performed by Jesus and Paul came from God, though he 'argues that just as Jesus' miracles and healing were intended for a time when medical ability was esteemed, so Muḥammad's miracle of the Qur'an was intended for a time when rhetoric was valued'.[129] Another (early 10th- or possibly late 9th-century) work, seeking to confirm or prove the prophethood of Muḥammad, was 'written in the context of inter-religious debate'.[130] The author, the Zaydī Imām al-Hādī ilā l-Ḥaqq, addresses Jewish and Christian refutations of, or incredulity towards, Islam. The work is representative, yet 'recourse to traditional miracle stories marks a stark contrast to the *kalām*-minded anti-Christian polemics' that otherwise abounded.[131] A lost early

125 M.N. Swanson, 'Sāwīrus ibn al-Muqaffaʿ', in *CMR* 2, 491-509, p. 495. Note: ʿAmmar al-Basri (see above), also did this in his *Kitāb al-burhān*, employing Muslim concepts of the attributes of God to explain the Trinity.

126 Swanson, 'Sāwīrus ibn al-Muqaffaʿ', p. 502.

127 P. Masri and M.N. Swanson, 'Apologetic commentary on the Creed', in *CMR* 3, 671-5, p. 674.

128 D. Thomas, 'Al-Jāḥiẓ', in *CMR* 1, 706-12, p. 708.

129 Thomas, 'Al-Jāḥiẓ', pp. 707-8.

130 G.S. Reynolds, 'Al-Hādī ilā l-Ḥaqq', in *CMR* 2, 125-9, p. 127.

131 Reynolds, 'Al-Hādī ilā l-Ḥaqq', p. 129.

10th-century work, known simply as *Dalāʾil al-nubuwwa* ('Proofs of prophethood'), by Abū ʿAbd Allāh al-Wāṣitī, noted as a significant example of the 'proofs of prophethood' field, reinforces 'how firmly established this kind of work had become [...] and also how it was able to draw upon a tradition of arguments in defense of Muḥammad'.[132] And another lost mid-12th-century example of the genre, *Khayr al-bishar bi-khayr al-bashar* ('The best of tidings concerning the best of humankind') by Abū ʿAbd Allāh ibn Ẓafar, whose principle aim was 'to establish the authenticity of Muḥammad's prophetic mission', is particularly significant for the sheer 'variety of Arabic versions of the biblical texts quoted in it'.[133]

The superiority of Islam

Asserting superiority is arguably a standard trope within apologetics; it accompanies argumentation seeking to appeal to the religious 'other' to capitulate and convert, but it can also serve an internal aim of bolstering the faithful. Thus, a late 15th-century work that discusses the figure of Jesus from a Muslim perspective, *Nuzūl ʿĪsā ibn Maryam ākhir al-zamān* ('The descent of Jesus son of Mary at the end of time') by Jalāl al-Dīn al-Suyūṭī, is aimed primarily at reinforcing Islamic belief, rather than engaging Christians directly.[134] An exemplary 16th-century work, the *Breve compendio de nuestra ley y sunna* by 'the young man of Arévalo', although mainly of instruction for Aragonese Moriscos and clearly asserting the superiority of Islam, 'is never aggressively polemical against Jews and Christians'.[135] Rather, whilst errors of these others are pointed out, recourse is made to Jewish and Christian scripture in support of Islam, setting out the superiority of the faith more to Muslims themselves than to outsiders. Furthermore, the work 'demonstrates that not all Morisco thought in the 16th century was limited to mechanical repetition of earlier Islamic rituals and teachings'.[136] Where one side makes an assertion of superiority, such as a Christian affirmation of 'the

---

132 D. Thomas, 'Al-Wāsiṭī', in *CMR* 2, 145-6, p. 146. Cf. D. Thomas, 'Abū l-Ḥasan ibn al-Munajjim', in *CMR* 2, 234-6, pp. 235-6; D. Thomas, 'Al-Zuhayrī', in *CMR* 2, 522-3.

133 L. Demiri, 'Ibn Ẓafar', in *CMR* 3, 625-31, pp. 629, 630.

134 S. Burge, 'Jalāl al-Dīn al-Suyūṭī', in *CMR* 7, 556-64, pp. 559-61.

135 J. Chesworth and L.F. Bernabé Pons, 'The young man of Arévalo', in *CMR* 6, 159-68, p. 163.

136 Chesworth and Bernabé Pons, 'Young man of Arévalo', p. 163.

superiority of Jesus over Muḥammad', a counter assertion is forthcoming from the Muslim side.[137]

Christian missions to Muslims

The theme of Christian missions to Muslims emerges late in the first millennium of encounter.[138] Three 13th-century works will suffice to demonstrate it within the umbrella relational dynamic of Appeal. Oliver of Paderborn's *Epistola salutaris doctoribus Egipti transmissa* ('Letter of greeting to the learned men of Egypt') demonstrates a good degree of Christian understanding of Islam, as it 'attempts to missionize via debate and the shared authorities of scripture, reason, and Aristotelian philosophy'.[139] Another document, 'current among mendicant missionaries', which is known as *The Gregorian report*, 'shaped' the arguments of missionaries 'as they sought to evangelize Muslims'.[140] Lastly, the late 13th-century Catalan-language *Llibre del gentil i dels tres savis* ('The book of the Gentile and the three wise men') by Ramon Llull 'presents a cordial debate between a Jew, a Christian, and a Muslim before a Gentile who seeks the truth'.[141] Although it is often cited as an early example of a tolerant exchange, the work's tolerance was actually in the cause of enabling 'the conversion of the infidel, which was [Llull's] ultimate goal'; nevertheless, the tone is exceptionally irenic, and 'presents a remarkably fair and accurate portrayal of each of the three religions'.[142] But the underlying assumption, understood to be held by all three interlocutors, is that of the three religions only one can be right and true – 'and the adherents of the two erroneous religions are bound for hell'.[143] It becomes clear that Llull regards Islam as irrational. Mission, after all, is usually premised on the assumption of superiority or even exclusivity of religious truth, with the concomitant motivation to both assert this and have it confirmed by attracting converts.

137 L. Demiri and M. Kuzey, 'Ibn Kemal', in *CMR* 7, 622-38, pp. 631-4. Cf. J. Allen, 'Birgivî Mehmed Efendi', in *CMR* 7, 705-14, for Ottoman works arguing the superiority of Islam.

138 See also ch. 19 below.

139 See J. Bird, 'Oliver of Padderborn', in *CMR* 4, 212-29, p. 222.

140 L. Gimalva, 'The Gregorian report', in *CMR* 4, 259-63, p. 261.

141 See H. Hames, 'Ramon Llull', in *CMR* 4, 702-13, p. 709.

142 Hames, 'Ramon Llull', p. 710.

143 Hames, 'Ramon Llull', p. 710.

Accommodation – *tolerance*

The fourth and final relational dynamic category may be termed 'accommodation'. It is marked by measures of tolerance, more or less, with four thematic sets identified, although others could be discerned (to reiterate an early point, this foray is both initial and provisional). These four are:

- Policies and strategies
- *Dhimmī* communities
- Diplomacy
- Pragmatic coexistence

Policies and strategies

Government official policies and strategies concerning faith communities emerged very early in the life of the Muslim community as, from the outset, the new Islamic political reality closely related to, and soon needed to incorporate within its polity, the presence of other faiths, especially communities of Christians and Jews. In Egypt, sometime around the year 700, George the Archdeacon wrote a collection of Lives of Coptic Orthodox patriarchs in which he provides a picture of the realities of the life of the Christian community living under Muslim rule. This was only some six decades after the ascendancy of Islam. George demonstrates 'a picture of the ideal relationship between governor and patriarch that speaks of mutual acceptance, support and recognition'.[144] In another early work, a biography of the Coptic Archbishop Isaac by the monk Mēna of Nikiou, relations between Christians and Muslims, including in particular those between the archbishop and the Muslim governor of Egypt, gives an insight into the mutual accommodation and respect that obtained, albeit not without moments of tension.[145] And a later text from Georgia, giving a history of Queen Tʿamar, demonstrates 'the vitality of political relations that existed between Georgia and its Islamic neighbors, and the reciprocal flow of information and ideas between them'.[146] Texts, or references within texts, dealing with this theme are likely to be scattered throughout the *CMRBH* corpus.

---

144 M.N. Swanson, 'George the Archdeacon', in *CMR* 1, 234-8, p. 236.
145 See H. Suermann, 'Mēna of Nikiou', in *CMR* 1, 219-21.
146 M.D. Abashidze, 'Historians of Tʿamar Queen of Queens', in *CMR* 4, 1003-7, p. 1005.

Dhimmī *communities*

The principal Muslim mode of dealing with non-Muslim 'People of the Book' has been by way of incorporating them as *dhimmī* communities. One of the earliest texts pertaining to this is known as the *Pact of ʿUmar*, which 'is the name given to the canonical text that defines the status of non-Muslims under Muslim rule and the restrictions imposed upon them'.[147] It moved in the direction of greater constraint and control. Although 'not always systematically or strictly enforced in early times, it seems to have progressively become the accepted norm in later centuries'.[148] Relations in the context of the *dhimmī* community construct are reflected in many texts. For example, in *Kitāb al-kharāj* ('The book of property tax'), the 8th-century jurist Abū Yūsuf 'provides a rare glimpse into the legal and social position of Christians and other client communities in Islamic society in the late 8th century', which spells out some of the features and issues of *dhimmī* status.[149] And a North African Mālikī jurist, Abū Jaʿfar al-Dāwūdi, addresses various legal matters specifying 'the rights and duties of Christians and Jews, who as "protected people" are given the freedom to follow their own beliefs and rituals, though not allowed full political rights and sovereign status'.[150]

Diplomacy

Eventually, as the socio-political reality of Islam consolidated, new forms of relations emerged. If the context of *dhimmī* communities led to forms of relationship with non-Muslim communities within *dār-al-Islām*, the geo-political context of empires and kingdoms resulted in patterns of interaction across borders, whether for commerce, trade or other modalities of international relationship. This is the realm of diplomatic relations and it is found within the wider ambit of Christian-Muslim relationships. For example, in the wake of the July 904 assault on Thessaloniki, a request for an exchange of prisoners was made to the Muslim ruler. 'As a diplomatic message intended to make a request of its recipients, the letter is constructive in tone', employing polite obsequies and terms of respect.[151] There is no criticism of, or negativity expressed

[147] M. Levy-Rubin, '*The Pact of ʿUmar*', in *CMR* 1, 360-4, p. 360.
[148] Levy-Rubin, '*The Pact of ʿUmar*', p. 362.
[149] D. Thomas, 'Abū Yūsuf Yaʿqūb', in *CMR* 1, 354-9, p. 357.
[150] J.P. Monferrer Sala, 'Al-Dāwudī', in *CMR* 2, 637-9, p. 638. See also ch. 15 below.
[151] M. Vaiou, 'Nicolas Mysticus', in *CMR* 2, 169-83, p. 176.

towards, Islam and Muslim sensibilities. Similarly, in other diplomatic documents, what is revealed is that 'relations between Byzantines and Muslims at the highest level were not always polemical and aggressive', and that such letters 'express no less than respect of the other's religious practices even though they differ and rival one's own'.[152]

Pragmatic coexistence

The theme of community coexistence where there was a measure of mutual cooperation or at least tolerant acceptance at a pragmatic level is arguably a topic in its own right, though overlapping with others in the accommodation category, and perhaps discernible elsewhere. Examples of texts referenced in *CMRBH* would seem to support this view. For instance, one Christian text, *Jāmiʿ wujūh al-īmān*, encountered above, also provides 'an intriguing witness to processes of assimilation and differentiation in the encounter of religious communities'.[153] And an early 16th-century work, Gabriel of Mt Athos's life of St Nēphōn, indicates 'that relatively soon after the Ottoman conquest of the Balkans the higher Orthodox authorities considered Ottoman rule over Christians to be fully legitimate'.[154] The mid-12th-century *Assizes of Roger* comprises laws for Norman Italy issued by the new ruler, Roger II of Sicily. Significantly, these 'demonstrate that the Muslims under Norman rule were generally left to live under Islamic law, as long as this did not conflict with the law of the Normans. This was much like the position of Christians under Islamic rule, and may point to the Normans borrowing such ideas from Muslims.'[155] This is a theme or topic within the accommodation dynamic that would appear to be worthy of fuller exploration.

Conclusion

My own conclusion, arising from the above preliminary and broad-brush analysis, is that the history of Christian-Muslim relations is marked, perhaps even defined, by dynamic complexity. It is not the case that the relationship, whether in real or potential terms, is necessarily and unremittingly negative. To be sure, we see affinity and inquiry struggling with

152 Vaiou, 'Nicolas Mysticus', p. 179.
153 Swanson, '*Al-Jāmiʿ wujūh al-īmān*', p. 794.
154 R.G. Păun, 'Gabriel, Superior of Mount Athos', in *CMR* 7, 76-84, p. 81.
155 A. Mallett, 'Roger II of Sicily', in *CMR* 5, 671-4, p. 673.

antipathy, and apologetics and accommodation mingling together with polemics and rejection. This very struggling and mingling of dimensions of relationship is reflective of the deep dynamics that embrace a range of positive and negative elements. Charles Tieszen has rightly observed that the history of relationship between Muslims and Christians 'is a story of great complexity and nuance. It resists just one interpretation and forces those who wish to accurately understand the history to consult a variety of sources and perspectives' – my point exactly.[156] As ever, context plays a vital part in the shaping and transmission of idea and image, presupposition and prejudice. The foregoing, as noted, is a scoping exercise; a taster not only of what follows in this volume of essays, but also of what lies beyond it, inviting fresh scholarly consideration.

---

156 C. Tieszen, *A textual history of Christian-Muslim relations, seventh-fifteenth centuries*, Minneapolis MN, 2015, p. 1.

Chapter 3
Encounter and inquiry. Trajectories of interaction

David Bertaina

Introduction

In the 9th century, a prominent Muslim scholar from Baghdad named Ibn Abī l-Dunyā (d. 894/5) edited and published a work containing 24 aphorisms that recounted Muslim inquiries addressed to Christian monks regarding the spiritual life. In one report, a group of Muslims noticed a monk walking on a mountain. They asked him where he was going, to which he replied that he was searching for the good life. The Muslim party suggested that he had left behind the good life in the city, with its fine food, clothing and pleasures. To which the monk replied, 'It is not like this with us. Verily, a good life for us is when you summon your senses to the obedience of God and they answer you.'[1] This story hints that the formation of Islam during the period of Late Antiquity was shaped, at least in part, by the interactive processes of encounter between its followers and Christians.

Within the developing Islamic Empire in the first centuries after its founding, Damascus and later Baghdad were centres where the major encounters and exchanges between Muslims and Christians took place. On the Muslim side, it was theologians belonging to the rationalist group known as the Muʿtazila who appear to have most often participated in explorations, while on the Christian side, it was theologians belonging to the three major communities within the Islamic Empire. The Melkites, or 'royalists', were Chalcedonian Orthodox Christians faithful to the Byzantine Church and its liturgical traditions and theology. The Syrian Orthodox or West Syrians, also known as Jacobites, were loyal to the miaphysite teaching of the Alexandrian Coptic Patriarchate. The Church of the East, or East Syrians, or Nestorians, primarily resided in the regions of Mesopotamia and Iraq. In addition, the Copts, Armenians

---

[1] See the quotation in MS Rampur, Uttar Pradesh, Raza Library - 565 *al-Muntaqā min Kitāb al-ruhbān*, fol. 190b, lines 9-13; D. Thomas, 'Ibn Abī l-Dunyā', in *CMR* 1, 829-31.

and Maronites also exerted some influence on Christian-Muslim discussions because of their presence in Egypt, Cilicia and Lebanon.[2] These Christian churches had had long traditions of interacting with Jews, Manicheans and Zoroastrians before the arrival of Islam, and patterns of intellectual exchange established in the pre-Islamic period set the tone for many subsequent discussions with Muslims.

There were a number of avenues for mutual discovery among Christians and Muslims in the medieval Middle East, including scriptural, legal, linguistic, social and cultural, theological and doctrinal, historical, literary and poetic, philosophical, political, and festal. Christians and Muslims made use of these conduits in their attempts to learn about one another and to explain the other's religion to their communities in preparation for both polemical and apologetic activities. Christians and Muslims interacted in varied contexts and domains, and at different levels. Each was, in a sense, sizing up and framing perspectives on the other, and this required tasks of inquiry and taking, or making, opportunities to engage.

Association with the other

The Qur'an is the first witness to encounter between Christians and Muslims. Within the text are recollections and retellings of biblical stories about a number of prophets as well as Jesus Christ,[3] which usually appear in different forms or with different details. For instance, the Qur'an retells the birth of Jesus by recollecting Christian lore that appears in such non-canonical infancy narratives as *The Proto-Gospel of James*, *The Infancy Gospel of Thomas*, and *The Infancy Gospel of Pseudo-Matthew*.[4] Thus, we might think of the Qur'an as a commentary on the biblical narrative of salvation that connects itself with earlier revelations.[5] Later, biographies of Muḥammad also reconstructed his life within biblical frameworks, with the intent to recount faithfully the signs that indicated the appearance of a prophet. The inquiry into biblical accounts of prophethood

[2] On these communities and their literature, see S. Griffith, *The church in the shadow of the mosque. Christians and Muslims in the world of Islam*, Princeton NJ, 2008.

[3] J. Kaltner and Y. Mirza, *The Bible and the Qur'an. Biblical figures in the Islamic tradition*, London, 2018.

[4] See S. Mourad, 'On the qur'anic stories about Mary and Jesus', *Bulletin of the Royal Institute for Inter-Faith Studies* 1 (1999) 13-24.

[5] See the introduction in G.S. Reynolds, *The Qur'ān & the Bible. Text and commentary*, New Haven CT, 2018, 1-25; S. Griffith, *The Bible in Arabic. The scriptures of the 'People of the Book' in the language of Islam*, Princeton NJ, 2013.

were meant to connect Muḥammad organically with earlier scriptural figures.[6]

Within a decade of Muḥammad's death, Arab victories (634-40) led to the capitulation of all major Byzantine-controlled cities in Syria-Palestine. Many Christians reacted to the Muslim conquest by re-appropriating biblical motifs to reassess their status in world history and to explain why, for example, God sent the Arabs to punish them.[7] But there were also attempts to describe these conquerors accurately and explain their motivations. A mid-7th-century East Syrian history, known as the *Chronicle of Khuzistan*, recounts the Arab conquests of Sasanian Persian cities and includes an appendix that describes Muslim worship in Mecca, indicating the author's attempt to understand why this nascent faith was engaged in conquest.[8] Some Christians tried to describe the doctrines and political concerns of their Muslim conquerors in order to explain the possibility of a fruitful relationship with them. Ishoʿyahb III of Adiabene, the Patriarch of the Church of the East, is known for two letters he wrote that argue for the compatibility of Christian doctrines with the views of their new Muslim rulers. Letter 48 (before 637) suggests that the East Syrian Christology of the two natures in Christ was closer to that of Muslims than the one-nature Christology of the Syrian Orthodox. Letter 14 (after 649) also praises God for giving Muslims political power over the formerly Persian domain, even noting that some Arabs praise the Christian faith.[9] The *History of Sebeos* suggests that Armenians would be part of a greater collection of leaders who would help establish the Islamic Empire, regardless of their confessional differences.[10]

A number of early encounters took place under the Umayyads (661-750), in markets, during trade negotiations and in simple exchanges that involved legal matters in daily life. In fact, issues such as interreligious marriage, multi-religious families, and Christian and Muslim legal rulings about contact between groups reveal that such meetings took place on a

[6] See for example B. Roggema, *The legend of Sergius Baḥīrā*, Leiden, 2009; B. Roggema, '*The legend of Sergius Baḥīrā*', in *CMR* 1, 600-3.

[7] H. Suermann, 'The use of biblical quotations in Christian apocalyptic writings of the Umayyad period', in D. Thomas (ed.), *The Bible in Arab Christianity*, Leiden, 2007, 69-90; H. Suermann, 'The Apocalypse of Pseudo-Ephrem', in *CMR* 1, 160-2.

[8] C.F. Robinson, 'The conquest of Khuzistan. A historiographical reassessment', *BSOAS* 67 (2004) 14-40; H. Teule, '*The Chronicle of Khuzistan*', in *CMR* 1, 130-2.

[9] O. Ioan, 'Arabien und die Araber im kirchenleitenden Handeln des Katholikos Patriarchen Ischoʿjahb III. (649-659)', in M. Tamcke and A. Heinz (eds), *Die Suryoye und ihre Umwelt*, Münster, 2005, 43-58; H.G.B. Teule, 'Ishoʿyahb III of Adiabene', in *CMR* 1, 133-6.

[10] T. Greenwood, 'The history of Sebeos', in *CMR* 1, 139-44.

regular basis.[11] Evidence can be found in a number of works. Thus, the acts of the synod called in 676 by the Patriarch of the Church of the East, Mar Ghiwarghis I, to outline proper canonical relations, declared that Christians were forbidden to bring legal cases to Muslim courts rather than Christian courts, or to marry Muslims.[12] Likewise, Athanasius of Balad (d. 687) grudgingly noted that daily interactions were common in marriage, eating food together and celebrating festivals,[13] while Jacob of Edessa (d. 708) wrote letters about official relationships between church and state leaders as well as daily issues such as apostasy, violence against Christian sites, providing blessings for Muslims, and teaching Muslims.[14]

Social meetings were sometimes a channel for explaining the intricacies of daily relations. The *Chronicle of Zuqnīn* (775) describes the Islamic tax system and its collection process in great detail, including poll taxes exacted from Christians and their economic impact on the region.[15] Slightly later, the monk Leontius of Damascus (d. early 9th century) also described some of the practices of Muslims when they collected taxes from Christians,[16] while Theophanes the Confessor (d. 818) in his *Chronographia* ('Chronography') details the daily life of Christians under Islamic rule, noting that Muslim naval forces were composed mostly of Christian Greeks and Copts, and describing the transition of the language of the Umayyad administration from Greek into Arabic.[17] The letters of David of Damascus (d. after 887), the city's Melkite bishop, show how relations between the two communities affected everyday business, communal issues, Christian ecclesiastical decisions, and travel within Syria.[18]

Theological inquiries into the doctrines of the religious other led to the composition of several important treatises and letter exchanges. The

---

11 L. Weitz, *Between Christ and caliph. Law, marriage, and Christian community in early Islam*, Philadelphia PA, 2018; M. Penn, *Envisioning Islam. Syriac Christians and the early Muslim world*, Philadelphia PA, 2015.

12 H.G.B. Teule, 'Ghiwarghis I', in *CMR* 1, 151-3.

13 R. Hoyland, *Seeing Islam as others saw it. A survey and evaluation of Christian, Jewish and Zoroastrian writings on early Islam*, Princeton NJ, 2007, 147-9; H.G.B. Teule, 'Athanasius of Balad', in *CMR* 1, 157-9.

14 R. Hoyland, 'Jacob of Edessa on Islam', in G.J. Reinink and A.C. Klugkist (eds), *After Bardaisan. Studies on continuity and change in Syriac Christianity*, Louvain, 1999, 149-60; H.G. Teule, 'Jacob of Edessa', in *CMR* 1, 226-33.

15 A. Harrak, *The Chronicle of Zuqnin*, Toronto, 1999 (part IV); A. Harrak, 'Joshua the stylite of Zuqnin', in *CMR* 1, 322-6.

16 J.C. Lamoreaux, 'Leontius of Damascus', in *CMR* 1, 406-10.

17 C. Mango and R. Scott, *The Chronicle of Theophanes Confessor. Byzantine and Near-Eastern history AD 284-813*, Oxford, 1997; M. Vaiou, 'Theophanes the Confessor', in *CMR* 1, 426-36.

18 J.C. Lamoreaux, 'David of Damascus', in *CMR* 2, 79-82.

Umayyad policy that opened conversion to Islam for non-Arabs impelled Christians to consider Islam's claims, including for those who wanted to convert, those who wanted to refute Islamic doctrines, and those who wanted to explain Christian doctrines using an Islamic vocabulary. Thus, the Christian Arabic-speaking author of the 8th-century work *Fī tathlīth Allāh al-wāḥid* ('On the Triune nature of God') employed qur'anic-style vocabulary in his opening invocation:

> Praise be to God before whom nothing was, and who was before everything, after whom there is nothing, and He is the heir of all things, and to Him all things return, who by His knowledge kept the knowledge of all things, and nothing but His work is sufficient for this in whose knowledge is the end of all things, and he counts everything by His knowledge.[19]

However, many such theological works were tied to apologetic and/or polemical interests, and therefore any accurate depictions of the other group contained in them were usually included for the purpose of refutation, indicating that encounter could be tied to proximity and intellectual curiosity as much as to hostility or the desire to distinguish – sometimes even distance – one community from the other. For instance, the scathingly critical Arabic letter of the Christian ʿAbd al-Masīḥ al-Kindī accurately quotes passages from the Qur'an and from later Islamic traditions on its origins, correctly cites from the biographies of Muḥammad, and reflects an accurate understanding of how Muslims utilised oral traditions and historical writings.[20]

The medieval *majlis* was a place of relatively open debate and discussion. In the context of this freedom, it was assumed that opponents would reliably portray the religious perspective of the other side. Many disputes failed in this regard (e.g. the *Debate of Theodore Abū Qurra* cites numerous passages from the Qur'an accurately but only as a tool for reinterpreting and critiquing Islam), but some faithfully recorded the doctrines of the other religious group without polemic.[21] In 781, the East

---

[19] M.D. Gibson, *An Arabic version of the Acts of the Apostles and the seven Catholic Epistles from an eighth or ninth century ms. in the Convent of St. Katherine on Mount Sinai, with a treatise On the Triune nature of God with translation, from the same codex*, London, 1899 (repr. Piscataway NJ, 2003), p. 2; M. Swanson, '*Fī tathlīth Allāh al-wāḥid*', in *CMR* 1, 330-3.

[20] M. Beaumont (ed.), *Arab Christians and the Qur'an from the origins of Islam to the medieval period*, Leiden, 2018; J.S. Bridger, *Christian exegesis of the Qur'ān*, Eugene OR, 2015; C. Wilde, *Approaches to the Qur'an in early Christian Arabic texts (750-1258 CE)*, Palo Alto CA, 2014.

[21] W. Nasry, *The caliph and the bishop*, Beirut, 2008; D. Bertaina, '*The debate of Theodore Abū Qurra*', in *CMR* 1, 556-64.

Syrian patriarch Timothy I (d. 823) and the Caliph al-Mahdī discussed how Christians and Muslims understood the status of Jesus Christ differently, their understanding of God's nature, the continuity of Islam with earlier biblical tradition, and the interpretation of certain passages in the Bible and the Qur'an.[22] Timothy's letter, which was later published and circulated across the Middle East, reflects knowledge of Muslim doctrines and key passages in the Qur'an concerning Christians.

Several Muslim writings also showed detailed knowledge of Christianity, raising the question of the sources used. The free-thinking Muslim theologian Abū ʿĪsā Muḥammad ibn Hārūn al-Warrāq (d. after c. 860) was the author of the most thorough refutation of the doctrines of the three Christian denominations that has survived from the early medieval period. His *Kitāb al-radd ʿalā l-thalāth firaq min al-Naṣārā* ('Refutation of the three Christian sects')[23] sets out his arguments against the doctrines of the Trinity and Incarnation as they were presented by the Melkites, Nestorians and Jacobites with a detailed and very accurate, if schematised, description of the doctrines, in which he displays impressive knowledge and understanding of his opponents' different positions.[24] He clearly had a very well-informed source (presumably Christian, though he gives no information at all about what or who this was), indicating that he was in touch with a conduit of information that served his purposes well.

Similarly, the Baghdad Muʿtazilī theologian Abū l-ʿAbbās ʿAbd Allāh ibn Muḥammad, known as al-Nāshiʾ al-Akbar (d. 906), in his assessment of Christianity, which forms part of his *Fīl-maqālāt* ('On religious teachings'), gives summaries of more than 20 Christological positions, suggesting an extremely well-informed source, but one that has not been identified.[25] Both Abū ʿĪsā and al-Nāshiʾ moved in circles where information about the teachings of Christianity was available, pointing to shared forms of thinking and common terminology between Muslims and Christians. The fact that information regarding their oral and documentary sources is completely unknown raises the possibility that much more

[22] S.K. Samir and W. Nasry, *The patriarch and the caliph. An eighth-century dialogue between Timothy I and al-Mahdī*, Provo UT, 2018; M. Heimgartner, 'Timothy I: Letter 59', in *CMR* 1, 522-6.

[23] D. Thomas (ed. and trans.), *Anti-Christian polemic in early Islam. Abū ʿĪsā al-Warrāq's 'Against the Trinity'*, Cambridge, 1992; D. Thomas, *Early Muslim polemic against Christianity. Abū ʿĪsā al-Warrāq's 'Against the Incarnation'*, Cambridge, 2002.

[24] Thomas, *Anti-Christian polemic*, pp. 66-77.

[25] D. Thomas (ed. and trans.), *Christian doctrines in Islamic theology*, Leiden, 2008, pp. 38-59.

interaction and discussion about the intricacies of belief took place than the surviving evidence immediately suggests.

Muslims were also interested in the Bible and how to integrate elements from it into the Islamic tradition as part of the continuing attempt to prove that Muḥammad had been foretold in earlier scriptures, as the Qur'an states (Q 61:6; 7:157). Among the earliest examples, the convert from Christianity ʿAlī ibn Rabban al-Ṭabarī (d. c. 860) and Ibn Qutayba (d. 889) included in their works lists of verses from both the Old and New Testaments which they believed referred to Muḥammad.[26] Other Muslims were interested in Jesus as a figure who could help them understand their own Islamic practices, and so biblical or ascetic stories in which he featured were adapted to fit new contexts.[27] Likewise, the fact that a number of Hadith narratives utilised New Testament citations to prove the truth of Islam, mostly produced in the 8th and 9th centuries during these encounters, indicate a willingness among Muslims to find and engage with Christian sources for Islamic purposes. For instance, one Hadith paraphrases Jesus' words in Matthew 5:4 as: 'Blessed is he who controls his tongue and opens his home, and weeps over his sins.'[28]

The field of history was a major area of collaboration among religious intellectuals who were willing to share their knowledge with one another. The Muslim historian al-Yaʿqūbī (d. after 905) composed a universal history from the creation to the middle of the 9th century. For his accounts of early centuries, he makes free use of such Christian sources as the Syriac *Cave of treasures*, while for his account of Jesus he quotes from the Gospels to supplement his Qur'an-based narrative. It is not at all unlikely that he discovered these sources through discussions with Christians and inquiries he made into their sources.[29] His accurate use of Christian narratives and technical terms indicates his readiness to portray the past through the lens of a Christian worldview perspective.

---

26 D. Bertaina, 'Early Muslim attitudes towards the Bible', in D. Thomas (ed.), *Routledge handbook on Christian-Muslim Relations*, London, 2018, 98-106; D. Thomas, 'Abū ʿĪsā l-Warrāq', in *CMR* 1, 695-701; D. Thomas, 'Ibn Qutayba', in *CMR* 1, 816-18.

27 T. Khalidi, *The Muslim Jesus. Sayings and stories in Islamic literature*, Cambridge MA, 2001.

28 D. Cook, 'New Testament citations in the ḥadīth literature and the question of early Gospel translations into Arabic', in E. Grypeou, M.N. Swanson and D. Thomas (eds), *The encounter of Eastern Christianity with early Islam*, Leiden, 2006, 185-223, p. 207.

29 S. Griffith, 'The Gospel, the Qur'ān, and the presentation of Jesus in al-Yaʿqūbī's *Ta'rīkh*', in J. Reeves (ed.), *Bible and Qur'ān. Essays in scriptural intertextuality*, Atlanta GA, 2003, 133-60; D. Thomas, 'Al-Yaʿqūbī', in *CMR* 2, 75-8.

The Byzantine Christian Maḥbūb ibn Qusṭanṭīn al-Manbijī (Bishop Agapios of Manbij) composed an Arabic world history around 942 that covered everything from the creation down to the 10th century. His work was read within several Christian communities, as well as by Muslim readers. In it he analyses early Islamic history, uses the Islamic calendar, and employs Islamic sources that indicate his familiarity with Muslim repositories of learning. Muslim readers of al-Manbijī's history included al-Masʿūdī (d. 956), who commended the work and was personally interested in Christianity. The Muslim geographer Ibn al-Shaddād (d. 1285) also read his history.[30] Al-Manbijī's contemporary, the Melkite Patriarch Saʿīd ibn Baṭrīq of Alexandria (Eutychius of Alexandria, d. 940), also composed a historical book, known as the *Annales*, which relied upon Islamic sources for its accounts of the conquest of Egypt and other local events.[31] Finally, Metropolitan Elias of Nisibis (d. 1046) made ample use of Islamic scriptures, traditions, and historical writings in the dialogue sessions he held with the Muslim vizier Abū l-Qāsim al-Ḥusayn ibn ʿAlī al-Maghribī (d. 1027), as well as in his historical works.[32]

Muslims also sought to understand Christian historical claims regarding Jesus Christ and his crucifixion in novel ways.[33] In his *Aʿlām al-nubuwwa* ('Signs of prophethood'), Abū Ḥātim al-Rāzī (d. 934) defended Ismāʿīlī Islam as well as other religious groups against sceptics. This led him to agree with the claim that Jesus died on the cross, and he quotes passages from the New Testament.[34] The group of authors known as the Ikhwān al-Ṣafāʾ (Brethren of Purity), who flourished during the 10th century, used their philosophy of a single truth to treat Christian scriptures, views of Jesus, and practices in an accurate and sympathetic manner. They considered the Gospels as part of God's revelation and faithfully

---

[30] J. den Heijer, 'Coptic historiography in the Fāṭimid, Ayyūbid and early Mamlūk periods', *Medieval Encounters* 2 (1996) 67-98; M. Swanson, 'Maḥbūb ibn Qusṭanṭīn al-Manbijī', in *CMR* 2, 241-5.

[31] M. Breydy, *Das Annalenwerk des Eutychios von Alexandrien. Ausgewählte Geschichten und Legenden kompiliert von Saʿīd ibn Baṭrīq um 935 AD*, 2 vols (*CSCO* 471-2), Louvain, 1985; U. Simonsohn, 'Saʿīd ibn Baṭrīq', in *CMR* 2, 224-33.

[32] A. Borrut, 'La circulation de l'information historique entre les sources arabo-musulmanes et syriaques. Élie de Nisibe et ses sources', in M. Debié (ed.), *L'historiographie syriaque*, Paris, 2009, 137-59; D. Bertaina, 'An Arabic Christian perspective on monotheism in the Qur'an. Elias of Nisibis' *Kitab al-majalis*', in D. Bertaina, S.T. Keating, M.N. Swanson and A. Treiger (eds.), *Heirs of the Apostles. Studies on Arabic Christianity in honor of Sidney H. Griffith*, Leiden, 2019, 3-21; J.P. Monferrer Sala, 'Elias of Nisibis', in *CMR* 2, 727-41.

[33] See D. Thomas, 'Muslim regard for Christians and Christianity', in *CMR* 2, 15-27.

[34] S. Nomoto and D. Thomas, 'Abū Ḥātim al-Rāzī', in *CMR* 2, 200-9.

quoted from them in several of the letters they wrote. Here, Jesus is portrayed as a healer who gathered disciples, died in his human nature on the cross, and was raised from the dead. Christian practices, especially relating to the asceticism practised by monks, are highly respected in these texts and probably reflect their authors' efforts to acquaint themselves with Christianity.[35] Likewise, the Neoplatonist Ismāʿīlī thinker Abū Yaʿqūb al-Sijistānī (d. after 971) quoted from the Bible (Matthew 25:35-46) and suggested that the cross should be an object of veneration in his *Kitāb al-yanābīʿ* ('Wellsprings').[36] Among Christians who utilised Islamic sources, the Syrian biblical commentator Moses bar Kephā appropriated portions of a Muʿtazilī work on divine unity in order to describe the characteristics of God in the introduction to his commentary on the *Hexaemeron*, continuing a tradition of employing Muslim doctrines about God that is attested as early as the 9th century.[37] These examples demonstrate that some Muslims and Christians were familiar with each other's interpretations, and made efforts to incorporate the other's ideas into their own presentations of religious doctrine.

Islamic encounters with Christian monastic life were recounted multiple times in poetry and literature. A master of pre-Islamic Arab history, Ibn al-Kalbī (d. 819 or 821), made the effort to document the names of the churches and monasteries in the region of al-Ḥīra, the traditional home of the Arab Lakhmid Christians of the Church of the East.[38] Pre-Islamic Arab Christian poets were also well regarded in literary circles. The poet and historian Abū l-Faraj al-Iṣbahānī (d. 973-4) is known for collecting some of these poems and assembling music from Christian sources as well. Al-Iṣbahānī also composed a book on monasteries, the *Kitāb al-diyārāt* ('Book of monasteries'), which fondly recollects monastic landmarks among countryside locations associated with drinking and romance.[39] His work, though lost, is cited in passages that portray Christian monks and their holy sites as places of hospitality, where visitors enjoyed conversation, poetry recitals and attractive buildings and grounds. Ibn

35 Y. Marquet, 'Les Iḫwān al-Ṣafāʾ et le Christianisme', *Islamochristiana* 8 (1982) 129-58; O. Ali-de-Unzaga, 'Ikhwān al-Ṣafāʾ', in *CMR* 2, 306-11.

36 D. Thomas, 'Abu Ya'qub al-Sijistani', in *CMR* 2, 381-5.

37 S. Griffith, 'Free will in Christian kalām. Moshe Bar Kepha against the teachings of the Muslims', *Le Museon* 100 (1987) 143-59; H.G.B. Teule, 'Moses bar Kephā', in *CMR* 2, 98-101.

38 His work is now lost; D. Thomas, 'Ibn al-Kalbī', in *CMR* 1, 510-14.

39 H. Kilpatrick, 'Monasteries through Muslim eyes. The diyārāt books', in D. Thomas (ed.), *Christians at the heart of Islamic rule*, Leiden, 2003, 19-37; H. Kilpatrick, 'Abū l-Faraj al-Iṣbahānī', in *CMR* 2, 386-9.

Abī l-Dunyā (d. 894/5) collected sayings from several sources concerning Muslims who were able to gain spiritual wisdom from monks. The 24 sayings in his *Kitāb al-ruhbān* ('Book of monks') retell stories of monks instructing Muslims on how to achieve detachment from the world: 'A certain monk said: "O Mālik ibn Dīnār! If you are able to construct a wall of iron between yourself and people, then you must do it!"' In another narrative, a monk is able to pacify a lion that approached him; this was a common trope in Christian monastic literature. In two separate stories, a monk advises a caliph on the spiritual life. Others evoke the Muslim pietistic tradition: 'Renounce the world and divest yourself of its people. Become like the bees that consume only that which is good and leave behind only that which is good. Whenever they come upon something, they do not spoil it.'[40] The Muslim author al-Shābushtī (d. 999 or 1008) also composed a book on monasteries for the Fāṭimid Caliph al-ʿAzīz, which was a compilation of descriptions, poetry and anecdotes about monasteries, and historical reports that praised the holy sites, their services and festivals.[41] These writings reveal relaxed mixing of Christians and Muslims at monasteries, as well as the common pursuit of knowledge and wisdom among monks and ascetically-pious Muslims.

Translation and language studies were further paths to involvement between Muslims and Christians. Ḥunayn ibn Isḥāq was a celebrated translator tasked by his Muslim patrons to transmit knowledge from Greek into Arabic in the fields of medicine, philosophy, astronomy, theology, mathematics and linguistics.[42] His son Isḥāq ibn Ḥunayn also collaborated with him on translating texts from Syriac into Arabic, including the works of Euclid and Ptolemy, for Muslim sponsors.[43] The Melkite deacon and theologian ʿAbd Allāh ibn al-Faḍl al-Anṭākī (d. after 1052) was part of the translation movement in 10th-century Antioch that rendered numerous Greek patristic writings into Arabic. His education reveals that training in Arabic grammar and poetry could be a shared religious endeavour, as is indicated by his studies under the former Muslim-turned-sceptic Abū l-ʿAlā l-Maʿarrī, with whom he studied Arabic lexicography by reading the *Iṣlāḥ al-manṭiq* (Correction of Logic) by

40 D. Thomas, 'Ibn Abī l-Dunyā', in *CMR* 1, 829-31; S. Mourad, 'Christian monks in Islamic literature. A preliminary report on some Arabic *Apophthegmata Patrum*', *Bulletin of the Royal Institute for Inter-Faith Studies* 6 (2004) 81-98. See the quotes in MS Rampur, Uttar Pradesh, Raza Library - 565 *al-Muntaqā min Kitāb al-ruhbān*, fols. 190b-192a.

41 H. Kilpatrick, 'Al-Shābushtī', in *CMR* 2, 565-9.

42 J.P. Monferrer Sala, 'Ḥunayn ibn Isḥāq', in *CMR* 1, 768-74.

43 M.N. Swanson, 'Isḥāq ibn Ḥunayn', in *CMR* 2, 121-24.

the Persian Shīʿī Ibn al-Sikkīt.[44] The fact was that several Christians and Muslims among the elite were conversant with the works of both religions. Sometimes class membership was more important than religious identity.

Philosophy was a remarkable bridge of inquiry among Christians and Muslims. In the 9th and 10th centuries in particular, religious communities employed Aristotelian and Neoplatonic principles to explain their doctrines concerning God's unity and attributes, knowledge of God and other matters such as the status of human will. Interactive engagement between Christians and Muslims contributed to the doctrines of both on matters such as divine inspiration, free will and human action.[45] In these accounts, the authors had to reproduce faithfully the doctrines of the other with whom they agreed or disagreed. The Muslim philosopher Abū Yūsuf al-Kindī (d. 870) was known for interacting with Christians who shared his interests,[46] while in the Baghdad school of philosophy there were a number of fruitful relationships between Christians and Muslims, such as the Christian philosopher Abū Bishr Mattā (d. 940) and the Muslim philosophical master Abū Naṣr al-Fārābī (d. 950), as well as their Christian student Yaḥyā ibn ʿAdī (d. 974). Ibn ʿAdī's treatise on the moral life was inspired by his study of several Islamic sources.[47] Later, Muslim pupils studied under his guidance, including Abū Sulaymān al-Sijistānī (d. c. 985), who composed an explanation of God's unity using philosophical terminology utilised by Christians to explain the Trinity.[48] In the same way, the Muslim theologian Abū l-Ḥusayn al-Baṣrī (d. 1044) studied Aristotle under the Christian priest and physician Ibn al-Ṭayyib (d. 1043).[49] In short, philosophical studies were a fruitful area for instruction and collaboration, as well as exploring the other's systematic thought.

Politics were occasionally a site of interaction between the faiths, as Christians tried to navigate Islamic political structures and Muslims sought to govern non-Muslims in an orderly and stable fashion. Between

---

44 S. Noble and A. Treiger, 'Christian Arabic theology in Byzantine Antioch', *Le Muséon* 124 (2011) 371-417; A. Treiger, "Abdallāh ibn al-Faḍl al-Anṭākī', in *CMR* 3, 89-113, pp. 92-103.

45 See the examples in A. Treiger, 'Mutual influences and borrowings', in D. Thomas (ed.), *Routledge handbook on Christian-Muslim relations*, London, 2018, 194-206.

46 D. Thomas, 'al-Kindi', in *CMR* 1, 746-50.

47 Yaḥyā ibn ʿAdī, *The reformation of morals*, trans. S.H. Griffith, Provo UT, 2002; E. Platti, 'Yaḥyā ibn ʿAdī', in *CMR* 2, 390-438.

48 G. Troupeau, 'Un traité sur les principes des êtres attribué à Abū Sulaymān al-Siǧistānī, *Pensamiento* 25 (1969) 259-70; D. Thomas, 'Abū Sulaymān al-Sijistānī', in *CMR* 2, 480-4.

49 D. Thomas, 'Abu l-Husayn al-Basri', in *CMR* 2, 698-702.

the 10th and 13th centuries, the Middle East was a battleground between the Byzantines, Latins, Armenians, Syrians, Turks, Kurds, and Arabs. The Byzantine resurgence under the Emperor Nicephorus Phocas (d. 969) resulted in the re-conquest of Antioch and western Syria in 969, and there was further expansion under his successor John I Tzimisces (d. 976). Faithful depictions of Christian-Muslim relations during this period were accurate insofar as they sometimes related the violence of certain moments. For instance, Ibrāhīm ibn Yūḥannā al-Anṭākī (d. c. 1025) recorded the *Martyrdom of Christopher*, the Patriarch of Antioch (d. 967), which describes the bishop's administration under the Muslim ruler at the time, Sayf al-Dawla (d. 967). Al-Anṭākī's work accurately describes the tax concessions given to Christians and the political relations around the time of the Byzantine reconquest.[50] In a similar fashion, the Melkite historian Yaḥyā ibn Saʿīd al-Anṭākī (d. after 1033) fled the Fāṭimid Caliph al-Ḥākim's (d. 1021) persecutions for Byzantine Antioch, where he composed a history of Egypt and Syria during his lifetime. His history provided an accurate and detailed look at the reign of al-Ḥākim, as well as the political and social relations between religious groups in Egypt in the 11th century. His narrative was read by Muslim historians as well.[51]

Festivals and holy sites were key places of inquiry and encounter well into the medieval era. Christians and Muslims sometimes participated in each other's religious feasts. This was initially so popular that the Jacobite Bishop Athanasius of Balad (d. 687) discouraged his faithful from participating in Muslim festal observances, or eating meat there.[52] Other records indicate that Muslims participated in Christian liturgical and paraliturgical ceremonies such as Christmas, the Birth of St John the Baptist,[53] New Year's Eve and the Circumcision of Christ on 1 January.[54] The subject of the holy site of Mecca became a contact point when the Melkite physician and translator Qusṭā ibn Lūqā composed a work *On the regimen for the pilgrimage*, advising a Muslim about the Greek

---

50 J. Nasrallah, 'Deux auteurs melchites inconnus du Xe siècle', *Oriens Christianus* 63 (1979), 75-86; J. Lamoreaux, 'Ibrāhīm ibn Yūḥannā al-Anṭākī', in *CMR* 2, 611-16.

51 I. Kratchkovsky (ed.), F. Micheau and G. Troupeau (trans), *Histoire de Yaḥyā ibn Saʿīd d'Antioche*, Turnhout, 1997; M. Swanson, 'Yaḥyā ibn Saʿīd al-Anṭākī', in *CMR* 2, 657-61.

52 F. Nau, 'Littérature canonique syriaque inédite', *Revue de l'Orient Chrétien* 14 (1909) 113-30; H. Teule, 'Athanasius of Balad', in *CMR* 1, 157-9.

53 M. Fierro, 'Ibn Waḍḍāḥ', *CMR* 1, 837-8. Ibn Waḍḍāḥ was writing in Córdoba, though evidence of such practices (and consequently critiques) in the Middle East are available.

54 See the chapter in this volume by J.P. Monferrer Sala, Chapter 13. 'Conduits of interaction. The Andalusi experience', 307-29.

medical tradition to help him on his journey.[55] The Melkite Ṣāliḥ ibn Saʿīd al-Masīḥī (d. c. 1050) recollected two events in his life that highlight a degree of interactive encounter between Christians and Muslims. His first narrative is of a festival for Mār Mārī (St Cyrus). A Muslim threw a scorpion into the church in the middle of the liturgy, and when the scorpion failed to sting anyone, he approached it and was stung himself. He was given some holy water to drink and was miraculously healed so that 'everyone present at the festival, both Christians and outsiders [Muslims], glorified God'. Ṣāliḥ's second narrative recounts the positive treatment Christians experienced under the tribal leader Mufarrij ibn Daghfal ibn al-Jarrāḥ. Ṣāliḥ describes Mufarrij's respect for the local bishop Ayyūb, even attending his services and offering up prayers. He was also said to have called Christians 'the salt of the earth' (Matthew 5:13). Mufarrij supported the rebuilding of the Church of the Holy Sepulchre in Jerusalem after its destruction on the orders of the Caliph al-Ḥākim. His reports reveal how daily contacts between Christians and Muslims shaped positive views of the other.[56]

Theological inquiries by Muslims in Central Asia and other regions in the medieval era at times showed impartial interest in Christian faith and practices, although this was more often tinged with polemic.[57] For instance, one of the most popular Muslim genres in which the teachings of Christianity were set out was heresiography, which sought to explain the essential doctrines of non-Muslim groups and their differences for the purpose of refutation. The Muslim author al-Īrānshahrī, who was active in the later 9th century, made an objective analysis of various religious doctrines and their scriptures, including those of Jews, Christians and Hindus,[58] while the great theologian Abū l-Ḥasan al-Ashʿarī (d. 935) is recorded as having made a survey of Christian confessions.[59] Maybe the best-known heresiographer was Abū al-Fatḥ al-Shahrastānī (d. 1153), whose account of the Christian doctrines of the Trinity and Incarnation, the history of the Church, and the confessional differences between the Melkites, Jacobites and Church of the East is steadfastly descriptive, without any discernible bias or polemical misinterpretation.[60]

55 M.N. Swanson, 'Qusṭa ibn Lūqā', in *CMR* 2, 147-53.
56 A. Treiger, 'Ṣāliḥ ibn Saʿīd al-Masīḥī', in *CMR* 5, 644-50.
57 See examples in D. Thomas, *Christian doctrines in Islamic theology*, Leiden, 2008.
58 This text, which is now lost, is referred to by al-Bīrūnī; D. Thomas, 'Al-Īrānshahrī', in *CMR* 1, 889-91.
59 D. Thomas, 'al-Ashʿarī', in *CMR* 2, 210-16.
60 D. Thomas, 'al-Shahrastānī', in *CMR* 3, 549-54.

Several Muslim authors made what appear to be serious analyses of ecclesiastical organisation. Among the most remarkable figures of the medieval period was the Muslim polymath Abū Rayḥān Muḥammad al-Bīrūnī (d. 1048), who made detailed and astute observations about Christian customs and other practices, including a summary of the Melkite and East Syrian liturgical calendars.[61] He was also familiar with and defended the teachings of the Christian philosopher John Philoponus on the creation of the world. Likewise, a certain Abū l-Maʿālī (early 12th century) wrote, in Persian, an analysis of various creeds, and his account of Christian churches, doctrines, and leaders provides a further example of descriptions of Christians that do not enter into polemics.[62]

Works from the crusader period shed light on the addition of Frankish Latin Christians to the Melkite, Armenian, Syrian Orthodox Christian groups interacting with Sunnī and Shīʿa Muslim groups, showing the result as a complex mix of suspicion and curiosity.[63] The Franks gave Muslims (and Jews) protected legal status and freedom of worship, not unlike what earlier Muslims had done for Christians and others in according them protection under the conditions of the *dhimma*. The Muslim historian ʿUsāma ibn Munqidh's (d. 1188) autobiographical *Kitāb al-iʿtibār* ('Book of instructions') is one of the best sources for Muslim-Christian relations in crusader Syria-Palestine. It accurately describes daily relations between sides, and the various misunderstandings that arose from differences in culture and language.[64] His contemporary Ibn ʿAsākir (d. 1176) composed a history of Damascus during the crusader period that also discusses Christian beliefs and practices.[65] In a notably positive account, the Muslim historian Ibn al-Azraq (d. 1176/7) commends the Georgian King Dmitri, who was a Christian, for his benevolent treatment of his Muslim subjects.[66]

The crusades also led Westerners to compose more accurate descriptions of Islam for European readers. For instance, descriptions of Muḥammad's life and several key doctrines of Muslims were transmitted from the much earlier works of Anastasius of Sinai (d. c. 700), and

---

61 G. Strohmaier, 'al-Bīrūnī', in *CMR* 3, 73-80.

62 A. Mallett, 'Abū l-Maʿālī', in *CMR* 3, 214-16.

63 See P. Cobb, *The race for paradise. An Islamic history of the crusades*, Oxford, 2016.

64 P. Cobb, *Usama ibn Munqidh, warrior poet of the age of the crusades*, Oxford, 2005; A. Mallett, 'Usāma ibn Munqidh', in *CMR* 3, 764-8.

65 S.A. Mourad, 'A twelfth-century Muslim biography of Jesus', *ICMR* 7 (1996) 39-45; S. Mourad, 'Ibn ʿAsākir', in *CMR* 3, 683-9.

66 C. Hillenbrand, *A Muslim principality in crusader times*, Leiden, 1990; A. Mallett, 'Ibn al-Azraq', in *CMR* 3, 690-4.

further developed by Hugh of Fleury; they were later adapted in a historical work by William of Malmesbury (d. 1143 or after) to explain why Muslims venerated Muḥammad.[67] Walter the Chancellor (d. after 1122) composed a history entitled *Bella Antiochena* ('The Antiochene wars') dealing with Latin-Turkish battles in northern Syria and other religious issues. Burchard of Strasbourg (d. after 1194) in his *Itinerarium* recorded his journey to the Middle East, portraying Christian-Muslim interactions as largely marked by civility and mutual respect, extending to Muslim veneration of Mary at Christian holy sites such as Matariyya in Egypt and Saydnaya in Syria.[68] The Jerusalem-born William of Tyre (d. c. 1185) in his now-lost work, which was possibly entitled *Gesta orientalium principum* ('The deeds of the rulers of the East'), was said to have composed a history of the Islamic world using Christian Arabic (and presumably Muslim) sources. His better known *Chronicon* ('Chronicle') depicts a number of diplomatic relations and social occasions between Christians and Muslims.[69] In his *Maktbōnut zabnē* ('Chronography'), the Syrian Orthodox historian Michael the Syrian (d. 1199) also gives positive accounts of day-to-day relations between various ethnic and religious groups.[70] However, records on both sides suggest they were not always well-informed of each other's history, traditions and theologies. Muslim and Christian historical chronicles showed both admiration and condescension toward the other.[71]

The Mongol conquest of Baghdad and the Middle East destabilised new channels of religious interaction. After the Egyptian Mamlūk Sultan Baybars (r. 1260-77) defeated the Mongols in 1260, the Mamlūks sacked Antioch in 1268 and expelled its Christian population. They signed a treaty with the Mongols in 1323, after which they continued to control the region until 1517, when the Ottoman Turks took it. This period was a time of rough tolerance, with a mix of occasional destruction and persecution on both sides.

---

67 E. Mégier and M. de Ruiter, 'Hugh of Fleury', *CMR* 3, 341-50; J. Tolan, 'William of Malmesbury', in *CMR* 3, 483-7.

68 J. Tolan, 'Burchard of Strasbourg', in *CMR* 3, 679-82.

69 A. Mallett, 'William of Tyre', in *CMR* 3, 769-77.

70 J. van Ginkel, 'Michael the Syrian and his sources. Reflections on the methodology of Michael the Great as a historiographer and its implications for modern historians', *Journal of the Canadian Society for Syriac Studies* 6 (2006) 53-60; H.G.B. Teule, 'Michael the Syrian', in *CMR* 3, 736-41.

71 See more examples in A. Mallett, *Popular Muslim reactions to the Franks in the Levant, 1097-1291*, London, 2016.

From the following centuries, very few examples of serious inquiry are preserved. Theological debate for the purpose of refutation became instead the primary mode of engagement, particularly as the Christian minority became less significant, and most polemical arguments were in any case becoming quite repetitive. Perhaps the best exception to this trend was Gregory Barhebraeus (d. 1286), a West Syrian polymath and the most prolific writer of the medieval Syrian Orthodox Church. His works such as *Mnōrat qudshē* ('Lamp of the sanctuary') and *Ktōbō d-maktbōnut zabnē* ('Chronography') show intimate knowledge of Muslim authors, including the scientific works of Fakhr al-Dīn al-Rāzī (d. 1210), the philosophy of Ibn Sīnā (Avicenna, d. 1037) and Nāṣir al-Dīn al-Ṭūsī (d. 1274), and the theological writings of al-Ghazālī (d. 1111). Barhebraeus also made use of the works of Muslim historians such as Ibn al-Athīr (d. 1233) and ʿAlā' al-Dīn Jovaynī (d. 1283).[72] He provides a stellar example of knowledge as the highest pursuit, regardless of its origins.

However, Christian-Muslim interactions in this period were challenged by mutual distrust and internal divisions on both sides. Latin and Eastern Christians were at odds with each other over differences in politics, language, worship and theology. Muslims disagreed over territory, and Muslim Arabs, Kurds and Turks were separated by ethnic divisions. There were also rising tensions between Sunnī Muslims, Druze and ʿAlawīs (a Shīʿa sect, sometimes called Nusayrīs). The results were greater intolerance of native Christians. They faced stricter rules regarding such matters as clothing and freedom of movement. Among Muslims, there was also a revival of books, poems and rhetoric about jihad. Polemical writing became more popular, especially after the Mongol conquest of Baghdad in 1258, for which Muslims accused Christians of being collaborators or unsupportive of Muslim leaders.

To combat this trend, some authors composed works that implicitly accepted the authenticity of the Qur'an to prove Christian truths, and argued that Muslims and Christians should not be at odds with each other theologically, but could exist together. The Melkite Bishop Paul of Antioch (d. c. 1215) composed a *Risāla ilā baʿḍ aṣdiqā'ihi alladhīna bi-Ṣaydā min al-Muslimīn* ('Letter to a Muslim friend in Sidon') in which he suggested that the Qur'an supports the notion that Christianity is the true religion. Later, this letter was edited to make it more irenic in

---

[72] H. Takahashi, *Barhebraeus. A bio-bibliography*, Piscataway NJ, 2013; H. Teule, 'Gregory Barhebraeus and his time. The Syriac Renaissance', *Journal of the Canadian Society for Syriac Studies* 3 (2003) 21-43; H.G.B. Teule, 'Barhebraeus', in *CMR* 4, 588-609.

tone and distributed to leading Muslim scholars in Damascus under the title *Risāla min ahl jazīrat Qubruṣ* ('Letter from the people of Cyprus').[73] The Ḥanbalī jurist Ibn Taymiyya of Damascus (d. 1328) rejected its conclusions and composed a reply, *Al-jawāb al-ṣaḥīḥ li-man baddala dīn al-Masīḥ* ('The correct reply to those who have corrupted the religion of Christ'), which criticises point-by-point the theology and religious practices of Christians.[74]

The reliability of the Christian scriptures also became a controversial topic in Mamlūk Egypt. In a commentary on the Gospels that shows unusually detailed knowledge, Najm al-Dīn al-Ṭūfī (d. 1316) argues that Christian doctrines did not align with their Old Testament sources in scripture.[75] On the other hand, Abū l-Ḥasan Ibrāhīm al-Biqāʿī (d. 1480), who spent most of his life as a Qur'an commentator in Cairo, used the Bible to illustrate and interpret the meaning of qur'anic verses, and wrote a defence of this method, in which he argued that the Bible could be cited as an authority.[76] In a similar fashion, the famous Muslim historian Ibn Khaldūn (d. 1406) made insightful analyses of the rise of Christianity, the main Christian communities and the crusades.[77]

The Ottomans under Sultan Selim I (r. 1512-20) annexed Mamlūk Syria in 1517, bringing the Levant back under the same rule as Constantinople and Asia Minor for the first time since the 10th century. Under Ottoman rule, Christians were classified according to their religious community (*millet*), and religious leaders were also regarded as political representatives of their communities. The Ottoman aim in this was strong government, though the result was discouragement of social and intellectual exchanges between communities, with the exception of political and economic alliances among the elite.

In the early modern period, the advent of European global trade and diplomacy meant that inquiries were focused less on demonstrating

---

73 R. Ebied and D. Thomas (eds), *Muslim-Christian polemic during the crusades. The letter from the people of Cyprus and Ibn Abī Ṭālib al-Dimashqī's response*, Leiden, 2005; D. Thomas, 'The letter from the people of Cyprus', in *CMR* 4, 769-72.

74 T.F. Michel, *A Muslim theologian's response to Christianity. Ibn Taymiyya's* Al-jawab al-sahih, Delmar NY, 1984; J. Hoover, 'Ibn Taymiyya', in *CMR* 4, 824-78.

75 Al-Ṭūfī, *Muslim exegesis of the Bible in medieval Cairo. A critical edition and annotated translation with an introduction*, ed. and trans. L. Demiri, Leiden, 2013; L. Demiri, 'Al-Ṭūfī', in *CMR* 4, 724-31.

76 W.A. Saleh, *In defense of the Bible. A critical edition and an introduction to al-Biqāʿī's Bible treatise*, Leiden, 2008; D. Thomas, 'al-Biqāʿī', in *CMR* 5, 537-43.

77 M. Whittingham, 'The value of *taḥrīf maʿnawī* (corrupt interpretation) as a category for analysing Muslim views of the Bible. Evidence from *Al-radd al-jamīl* and Ibn Khaldūn', *ICMR* 22 (2011) 209-22; M. Whittingham, 'Ibn Khaldūn', in *CMR* 5, 300-8.

theological truth than on describing the religious practices of the other faith and analysing them in a perceived 'rational' manner. Most inquiries were unrelated to religious identity, and had more to do with travel and personal experience. Bertrandon de la Broquière (d. 1459) was a European Catholic who recounted his journey from Jerusalem to Istanbul in the company of Turkish pilgrims returning from Mecca. His colourful story recalls his drinking bouts with the caravan, his choice of clothes, details of Islamic religious practices, and how certain Turkish *beys* were baptised according to the Greek Orthodox rite.[78] The Greek envoy Laonicus Chalcocondyles (d. after 1464) composed *Apodeixeis historiōn* ('Demonstrations of histories') about the rise of the Ottomans.[79] His observations about the Muslim veneration of Mary and Jesus, and the similarities of other Muslim devotional practices to practices in Christianity showed how divergent religious beliefs could not maintain clear boundaries when they were put into practice in everyday social contexts.

One genre that embraced the rationalist attitude towards inquiry was the travelogue. Ludovico de Varthema (d. 1517 or 1525) of Bologna was the first European to recount the pilgrimage to Mecca and Medina to a Western audience, in Italian in 1510.[80] His observations about Arabia, the Mamlūks in Damascus and Muslim social practices greatly popularised the travelogue genre for audiences interested in Middle Eastern narratives. Luigi Bassano (d. after 1552) spent close to a decade in Istanbul as an envoy and recounted the religious practices of the Turks, including the call to prayer, public displays of religion and a description of Hagia Sophia.[81] The diplomat Pierre Belon (d. 1564/5) was the first French author to recount life in Egypt, the Holy Land and the Turkish capital, without religious commentary.[82] Unlike these official accounts, Giovanni Antonio Menavino, who was taken by pirates off Corsica and served Sultan Bayezid II (d. 1512), and then his son Selim I (d. 1520), until he was able to escape in 1513, was in a position to witness intimate details of the day to day activities of the Ottoman rulers. He recorded them in many books on the laws, religion and social life of the Turkish court.[83] These 16th-century observations saw Islam through the lens of its daily practice in the community.

---

[78] J. Tolan, 'Bertrandon de la Broquière', in *CMR* 5, 443-6.
[79] J. Preiser-Kapeller, 'Laonicus Chalcocondyles', in *CMR* 5, 481-9.
[80] A. Fuess, 'Ludovico de Varthema', in *CMR* 6, 405-9.
[81] P. Madsen, 'Luigi Bassano', in *CMR* 6, 501-5.
[82] A. Merle, 'Pierre Belon', in *CMR* 6, 703-11.
[83] P. Schwarz Lausten, 'Giovanni Antonio Menavino', in *CMR* 6, 512-22.

Conclusion

Christians and Muslims established a common informational network in the medieval period via their conduits of communication and various interactive engagements. Some historical examples include shared images (e.g. biblical figures), shared concepts (e.g. philosophical definitions), and/or shared perceptions and experiences (e.g. history and festivals). While these conduits were driven by competition, intellectual and experiential activities were shaped by collaborations in scriptural, legal, doctrinal and a host of other pursuits. The hunt for knowledge was sometimes characterised by accommodating others' views and inquiring into the origin and principles of their claims. While their aim was often to engage in apologetics or polemics, Christians and Muslims sometimes imitated, esteemed and adapted alternative models of thought via inquiries into the other religious tradition in order to express their own religious claims. In exceptional cases, the knowledge base of the other religion became a conduit for mutual affinities between the religious communities.

Chapter 4
Christians, Muslims and the True Religion

Mark N. Swanson

This chapter examines how Christians have perceived Islam; in particular, it looks at the *categories* Christians have used in order to find for Islam a comprehensible place within a Christian imagination. The essay will first present a survey of such categories, derived mainly from the Bible and the experience of the early Church. It will then turn, as a kind of case study, to one particular category that became prominent in Christian Arabic writing about Islam: the notion of Islam as a *dīn* among the *adyān*, or as we would say today, a religion among the religions. This notion set off a search for the criteria by which one could discern the true religion, a search that took a number of surprising twists and turns and that remains instructive to the present day. Through this case study we may see how a particular set of ideas developed over time – and how we may trace this development through the pages of a resource such as *Christian-Muslim relations: a bibliographical history*. In other words, there are stories buried in the pages of the *CMR* volumes of this history: the stories of the ebb and flow, the rise and fall, of particular forms of inter-religious discourse – as well as intimations of the human stories that produced that discourse.

Categories available to suffering Christians

For the earliest decades of what we call 'Christian-Muslim relations' (and about which we can provide a 'bibliographical history'), it is important to remember that the system of beliefs and practices that we call 'Islam' was in a process of development and gradual consolidation.[1] The Christians who had dealings with the Arab followers of the Prophet Muḥammad often acquired little more than incidental knowledge about their beliefs

---

[1] For one recent historical reconstruction, see F.M. Donner, *Muhammad and the believers. At the origins of Islam*, Cambridge MA, 2012.

(to the extent to which these were defined and owned).[2] However, Christians whose worlds had been upended by the rapid Arab conquests of the mid-7th century did not require detailed insight into developing Islamic beliefs in order to turn to the Bible and search for ideas that might help explain their plight and make it bearable. One could argue that such ideas – since they were portrayals and assessments not so much of Islam as of the conquering Arabs – fall outside the scope of this chapter. However, there are two biblical resources that are appealed to so frequently throughout the history of Christian-Muslim encounter that they deserve a brief mention here.

Instruments of God's wrath

In the book of the prophet Isaiah, God addresses 'Assyria, the rod of my anger—the club in their hands is my fury' (Isaiah 10:5, NRSV).[3] This text provides language for a common idea: that God can use the nations as instruments of God's wrath, including against God's own people as a punishment for their apostasy. From such wrath, the only remedy is repentance (e.g. Jeremiah 36:7). Thus, in 7th-century Christian literature, we frequently find references to the invading Arabs as the instrument of God's wrath against a sinful or doctrinally deviant people (with frequent emphasis on sexual sins, or on the doctrinal deviance of one's theological opponents).[4] And, as in the 7th century with regard to the Arabs, so also in the 16th with regard to the Turks: Martin Luther thought of 'the expansion of the Ottomans into central Europe as God's chastising punishment upon a theologically and morally corrupt Christendom'.[5] Any war against them could only succeed if accompanied by 'proper spiritual preparation' and 'the appropriate repentance'.[6]

---

[2] On the earliest perceptions of Islam by Christians (and others), see R.G. Hoyland, *Seeing Islam as others saw it. A survey and evaluation of Christian, Jewish and Zoroastrian writings on early Islam*, Princeton NJ, 1997; to which we may now add (for Syriac-speaking Christians), M.P. Penn, *When Christians first met Muslims. A sourcebook of the earliest Syriac writings on Islam*, Oakland CA, 2015.

[3] In this chapter, all English renderings of biblical passages are from the text (or the notes) of the New Revised Standard Version Bible (NRSV), Division of Christian Education of the National Council of the Churches of Christ in the United States of America, 1989.

[4] See, for example, the section 'Seventh-century searches for scapegoats', in W.E. Kaegi, *Byzantium and the early Islamic conquests*, Cambridge, 1992, pp. 213-18.

[5] A.S. Francisco, 'Martin Luther', in *CMR* 7, 225-34, p. 226.

[6] Francisco, 'Martin Luther', p. 231.

Actors in an apocalyptic drama

Another biblical resource that could provide meaning in the midst of difficult realities was apocalyptic, and *CMR* is a testimony to the importance of this literary genre. Muslims could readily be portrayed as actors in an apocalyptic drama. Christian texts that refer to Muslim invaders or rulers liberally exploit apocalyptic passages from the Bible: the figure of Muḥammad may be associated with the Beast of Revelation 13,[7] or one of the heads of the seven-headed Dragon of Revelation 12,[8] or the little horn of the fourth beast in Daniel 7.[9] Invading Muslim armies could be associated with Gog and Magog (Ezekiel 38-9; Revelation 20:7-10).[10] Christian writers' apocalyptic scenarios did not, however, limit themselves to an exegesis (or eisegesis) of canonical biblical material, but drew on and added to a rich tradition of Jewish and Christian apocalyptic that had by no means come to an end with Daniel or the Book of Revelation.[11]

Apocalyptic texts provided both encouragement and entertainment to their readers and hearers.[12] They assured them that the tribulations

[7] As in the 8th-century Coptic *Apocalypse of Pseudo-Athanasius*; B. Witte, 'The apocalypse of Pseudo-Athanasius', in *CMR* 1, 274-80.

[8] As in Joachim of Fiore's *Liber figurarum* or *Expositio in Apocalypsism*; B. McGinn, 'Joachim of Fiore', in *CMR* 4, 83-91.

[9] There is a long history of interpreting Muslim polities in the light of Daniel 7, going back to the *Doctrina Iacobi nuper baptizati* (J. Pahlitzsch, 'Doctrina Iacobi nuper baptizati', in *CMR* 1, 117-19), the 7th-century *History of Sebeos* (T. Greenwood, 'The History of Sebeos', in *CMR* 1, 139-44, here p. 142); the 8th-century *Apocalypse of Pseudo-Athanasius* (Witte, 'Apocalypse of Pseudo-Athanasius', p. 275); and the 9th-century *Indiculus luminosus* of Paul Alvarus (K.B. Wolf, 'Paul Alvarus', in *CMR* 1, 647-8). At the time of the Reformation, an interpretation of Daniel 7 that identified the 'little horn' (v. 8) with the Turk was eagerly taken up by a number of Lutherans. See J. Hund, 'Justus Jonas', in *CMR* 7, 161-7; Francisco, 'Martin Luther', pp. 228-9 (Luther's *Heerpredigt wider den Türcken*); J. Balserak, 'Philipp Melanchthon', in *CMR* 7, 246-52, pp. 248-50.

[10] The Arabs are interpreted in terms of Gog and Magog already in the 7th-century Syriac apocalyptic literature: H. Suermann, '*The Apocalypse of Pseudo-Ephrem*', in *CMR* 1, 160-2; L. Greisiger, '*The Apocalypse of Pseudo-Methodius* (*Syriac*)', in *CMR* 1, 163-71; L. Greisiger, '*The Edessene Apocalypse*', in *CMR* 1, 172-5. Centuries later, the Ottoman Turks can be similarly interpreted: K.S. Brokaw, 'John Bale', in *CMR* 6, 689-98; J. Balserak, 'John Calvin', in *CMR* 6, 732-45 (pp. 735, 740 speaking about Martin Luther).

[11] On this Jewish and Christian apocalyptic, see, for example, J.J. Collins (ed.), *The Oxford handbook of apocalyptic literature*, New York, 2014. For a recent survey of the material touched upon here, see E. Grypeou, '"A people will emerge from the desert": apocalyptic perceptions of the early Muslim conquests in contemporary Eastern Christian literature', in H. Amirav, E. Grypeou, and G. Stroumsa (eds), *Apocalypticism and eschatology in late antiquity: encounters in the Abrahamic religions, 6th-8th centuries*, Leuven, 2017, pp. 291-309.

[12] That apocalyptic texts may in part be seen as *entertainment* was made clear to me by Jos van Lent, author of a number of generous articles on Coptic and Copto-Arabic apocalyptic texts in *CMR* 1-5.

of the present time and the trials of the faithful all fell within the plan of God – and were temporary. The ultimate vindication of the believers was certain. Apocalyptic texts provided these assurances in allusive and richly imaginative passages that frequently included puzzles of identification that readers could solve with enjoyment and a sense of satisfaction. Take, for example, the *Arabic Sibylline prophecy*'s mention of the '"man of the South" [...] the "number of whose name" is 40-8-40-4' – which is readily understood to be Muḥammad, where the Arabic letters of his name have been read as numerals.[13] Such texts provided amusement as well as reassurance and exhortation.

Furthermore, apocalyptic texts could readily be recycled and updated, as we can see in the 'last emperor' tradition that reaches back to the 7th-century Syriac *Apocalypse of Pseudo-Methodius* but which was transmitted in most of the languages of the Christian world;[14] or in the several recensions of the aforementioned *Arabic Sibylline prophecy*.[15]

It is worth stressing that Christian writers might depict Muslim armies or Muslim rulers as instruments of God's wrath, or as actors in an apocalyptic drama, without any examination of or portrayal of their beliefs. Elements of these beliefs might sometimes be mentioned in passing. For example, the *Apocalypse of Shenoute* (c. 695) refers to the Arabs as those who deny Christ's crucifixion – which provides us with an important early witness to a standard Islamic belief.[16] However, in the context of the apocalypse it serves more to establish the Otherness of the apocalyptic actors than to provide any insight into the nature of their beliefs.

13 M.N. Swanson, '*The Arabic Sibylline prophecy*', in *CMR* 1, 492-7, p. 494.

14 Greisiger, '*The Apocalypse of Pseudo-Methodius* (*Syriac*)', in *CMR* 1, 163-71; P. Ubierna, '*The Apocalypse of Pseudo-Methodius* (*Greek*)', in *CMR* 1, 245-8; and J.P. Monferrer Sala, '*The Apocalypse of Pseudo-Methodius* (*Latin*)', in *CMR* 1, 249-52. Monferrer Sala speaks of the text's 'immense influence on apocalyptic literature throughout the Middle Ages' (p. 250). An important early study of this influence was P.J. Alexander, *The Byzantine apocalyptic tradition*, Berkeley CA, 1985.

15 Swanson, '*The Arabic Sibylline prophecy*'; J. van Lent, 'The Copto-Arabic Sibylline prophecy', in *CMR* 3, 270-3. The recensions of the *Prophecy* date from the 8th to the 11th century, and contain many allusions to identifiable figures (in addition to the Prophet Muḥammad): the 9th-century recension refers to the 'Abbasid Caliph Hārūn al-Rashīd and his sons al-Amīn and al-Ma'mūn, while the 11th-century recension refers to the Fāṭimid caliph al-Mustanṣir and the emir Badr al-Jamālī.

16 J. van Lent, '*The Apocalypse of Shenute*', in *CMR* 1, 182-5, p. 183.

Categories available to Christians pondering Islamic beliefs

For Christian writers who wanted to make sense of (and pass judgment on) the beliefs of the conquering Arabs and their successors, the Bible and the early Christian tradition provided some useful categories, specifically: idolatry, Judaism (or something like it), and heresy. Let us take these in turn.

Idolatry

Idolatry is an important category in the Bible's representations of non-Yahwistic religion. The Old Testament polemic against idolatry perhaps reaches its climax in the satire of Isaiah 44:9-20, with the story of a man who grows a tree, uses half of it to warm himself and cook food, and the other half to make an idol, which he worships. The polemic is picked up in the New Testament, especially by St Paul, who denies 'that an idol is anything' (1 Corinthians 10:19) and can only see demonic disorder in the public religion of the Roman Empire (vs. 20).

The charge that Islamic belief is somehow idolatrous might seem to be a strange one, given the absolutely monotheistic and anti-idolatrous character of (what we now know of) the message of the Qur'an. Still, this charge was a staple of Christian writing about Islam, particularly among authors in Greek and Latin (and European vernaculars) – and especially in contexts of war. For the Byzantines, already in the 8th century John of Damascus was recalling the idolatrous pagan past of the Ishmaelites and charging them (even post-Muḥammad) with worshipping the Black Stone of the Kaʿba.[17] A century later, Nicetas of Byzantium played an important role in misinterpreting God's name *al-Ṣamad* in Q 112 as *holosphyros*, something impersonal and material, which then allowed him to present Islamic worship as idolatrous.[18] This (mis-)perception is mirrored in the *Ritual of abjuration* that was long used in the Byzantine

---

17 R.F. Glei, 'John of Damascus', in *CMR* 1, 295-301, p. 298. For this entire section (including echoes of the charges of idolatry even when the Muslims' monotheism is acknowledged), see B. Roggema, 'Muslims as crypto-idolaters. A theme in the Christian portrayal of Islam in the Near East', in D. Thomas (ed.), *Christians at the heart of Islamic rule. Church life and scholarship in 'Abbasid Iraq*, Leiden, 2003, pp. 1-18.

18 A. Rigo, 'Nicetas of Byzantium', in *CMR* 1, 751-6; and see D.H. Sahas, '"Holosphyros"? A Byzantine perception of "The God of Muḥammad"', in Y.Y. Haddad and W.Z. Haddad (eds), *Christian-Muslim encounters*, Gainesville FL, 1995, pp. 109-25.

Church for Muslims who converted to Christianity; in its Article 22, the convert anathematizes 'the God of Muḥammad'.[19]

As for the western European world, portrayals of Saracens as idolaters proliferated, especially in the context of the early crusades (as in the *Gesta Francorum et aliorum Hierosolimitanorum* and the later historians who made liberal use of it)[20] or of the Reconquista (as in the *Chronicle of Pseudo-Turpin*).[21] The *Gesta Tancredi* reports the discovery of an idol of Muḥammad in the Temple in Jerusalem (the Dome of the Rock).[22] The *Chanson de Roland* presents the Muslims as pagans who worship a trinity of idols, Mahumet, Apollin and Tervagant.[23] Throughout the 12th century (and beyond, especially in popular vernacular literature), extraordinary tales about Muḥammad and the rise of Islam flourished as Western Christian authors, in the memorable phrase of R.W. Southern, 'luxuriated in the ignorance of triumphant imagination'.[24] Even an honest chronicler like Guibert of Nogent passed on stories about Muḥammad that he knew full well to be false,[25] in the assurance that 'it is safe to speak evil of one whose malignity exceeds whatever ill can be spoken'.[26] In such a literature, the name Muḥammad itself was transformed into an idol and mosques became 'mahumeries' full of idols – such as those, according to the *Chanson de Roland*, that the Franks destroyed at Saragossa, before the forced baptism of its populace.[27]

Judaism. 'The new Jews'

If idolatry is one category for religious difference that can be found in the pages of the Bible, another comes from 1st-century Christians' experience of processes of differentiation between the hybrid *ekklēsia* gathered around Jesus the Messiah on the one hand, and 'Israel according to the

---

19 A. Rigo, '*Ritual of abjuration*', in *CMR* 1, 821-4. See also N. Zorzi, '*Tomos*', in *CMR* 3, 759-63, for the controversy over this at the time of the Emperor Manuel I Comnenus (in 1180).

20 M. Bull, '*Gesta Francorum*', in *CMR* 3, 249-56, p. 252; followed by B. Packard, 'Raymond of Aguilers', in *CMR* 3, 297-300; M. Bull, 'Robert the Monk', in *CMR* 3, 312-17; and so on. For this entire section, see J.V. Tolan, *Saracens. Islam in the medieval European imagination*, New York, 2002, ch. 5, 'Saracens as pagans'.

21 M. Cheynet, '*Chronicle of Pseudo-Turpin*', in *CMR* 3, 455-77.

22 B. Packard, 'Ralph of Caen', in *CMR* 3, 375-8.

23 S. Kinoshita, '*La Chanson de Roland*', in *CMR* 3, 648-52, p. 648.

24 R.W. Southern, *Western views of Islam in the Middle Ages*, Cambridge MA, 1962, p. 28.

25 J. Tolan, 'Guibert of Nogent', in *CMR* 3, 329-34, p. 331.

26 Quoted in Southern, *Western views*, p. 31.

27 Kinoshita, '*Chanson de Roland*', p. 649.

flesh' (1 Corinthians 10:18) on the other. These processes would eventually result in distinct communities of Christians and Jews – and Judaism would become, for Christians, a category of religious otherness, despite shared scriptures and history.

Many early Christian texts that deal with Islam appear, in various ways, to be attempting to locate the somewhat mysterious Arab Muslims in relationship to this known Other, the Jews. The Arabs were widely known to be the children of Ishmael[28] and the children of Hagar,[29] and were thus located as a branch on a family tree not distant from that of the children of Israel, a proximity that might help account for the Muslim Arabs' monotheism.[30] John of Damascus famously suggested that the word regularly used for these people, *Saracens*, derived from *Sara kenē*, 'Sarah is empty' or barren, thus rooting the 'Saracens' linguistically in the text of Genesis 16.[31]

Christian writers gradually learned some basic tenets of Islamic teaching – many of which were close to Jewish beliefs: one God; prophets; books, including the *Tawrāt* sent down to Moses and the Psalms sent down to David. By the 8th century, the East Syrian writers Theodore bar Kōnī and the Catholicos Timothy I could refer to the Muslims as 'the new Jews',[32] and engage them accordingly as monotheists. This same sense of the closeness of Muslims to Judaism, while not always explicitly expressed, may help account for a notion found in much early Syriac and Arabic apologetic literature: that Muslims would be responsive to arguments based on the Old Testament, especially the books of Moses. Such is the case in the Syriac *Disputation of John and the Emir* (which claims to be from c. 640), where the teaching of Moses is stressed;[33] or in the chapter on the Cross in the 8th-century Arabic apology *Fī tathlīth Allāh al-wāhid* ('On the triune nature of God'), where Deuteronomy 28:66 (LXX, 'you shall see your life hanging before your eyes') and Numbers 21:6-9 (the bronze serpent) figure prominently.[34]

---

28 This is taken for granted in one of the earliest Christian texts to refer to the Muslim Arabs, *The History of Sebeos* from c. 655; Greenwood, 'History of Sebeos', p. 141.

29 As in another 7th-century work, the *Edessene Apocalypse*; Greisiger, '*Edessene Apocalypse*', p. 173.

30 For example, in the *Ktābā d-rēsh mellē* of John bar Penkāyē; Greisiger, '*Edessene Apocalypse*', p. 177.

31 Glei, 'John of Damascus', p. 298.

32 M. Heimgartner and B. Roggema, 'Timothy I', in *CMR* 1, 515-31, p. 520.

33 B. Roggema, '*The disputation of John and the Emir*', in *CMR* 1, 782-5, p. 783.

34 M.N. Swanson, '*Fī tathlīth Allāh al-wāhid*', in *CMR* 1, 330-3.

The notion that Muslims would be responsive to scriptural arguments, especially from the Old Testament, led to the translation and redeployment of a literary genre with a long history in Christian-Jewish debate: *testimonia* catalogues, that is, lists of Old Testament verses that had been interpreted as foretelling or foreshadowing events in the life of Christ or specifically Christian teachings and practices.[35] Such lists are to be found everywhere in early Arabic Christian apologies, beginning with the 8th-century *Fī tathlīth Allāh al-wāhid*, the longest part of which is a list of 34 Old Testament witnesses to the life of Christ, baptism and the Cross.[36] Sometimes such lists follow and underscore arguments that are crafted on some other basis, e.g. *kalām*-type arguments;[37] we see this regularly in the work of the great early 9th-century Christian *mutakallim* Theodore Abū Qurra.[38] And sometimes *testimonia* catalogues were stand-alone texts, even if part of a wider apologetic ensemble. Examples include the 9th-century apologetic *corpora* of Ḥabīb Abū Rā'iṭa (where a *testimonia* catalogue is one treatise among others);[39] the anonymous author of *Al-jāmiʿ wujūh al-īmān* (where, of its 25 chapters, chapter 13 is a *testimonia* catalogue);[40] and Peter of Bayt Ra's (whose *Kitāb al-burhān* consists of four parts, a major theological treatise followed by three different *testimonia* catalogues).[41]

---

35 An excellent study of the *testimonia* is M.C. Albl, *'And scripture cannot be broken'. The form and function of the early Christian testimonia collections*, Leiden, 1999.

36 Swanson, '*Fī tathlīth Allāh al-wāhid*'; see also M.N. Swanson, 'Beyond prooftexting (2). The use of the Bible in some early Arabic Christian apologies', in D. Thomas (ed), *The Bible in Arab Christianity*, Leiden, 2007, pp. 91-112.

37 Although it could also be argued that the *kalām*-style arguments are in effect entryways to a world shaped by biblical arcs of prophecy and fulfilment; see Swanson, 'Beyond prooftexting (2)', pp. 111-12.

38 J.C. Lamoreaux, 'Theodore Abū Qurra', in *CMR* 1, 439-91, e.g. Theodore's 'Questions on the Son of God' (pp. 458-60) where the third section in particular 'is accompanied by a lengthy collection of biblical testimonies affirming that God has a Son' (p. 459). Similar examples can be found throughout Theodore's works; as Lamoreaux puts it for Theodore's apology for the Trinity, '[h]is arguments are based on both scripture and reason' (p. 453).

39 S.T. Keating, 'Abū Rā'iṭa l-Takritī', in *CMR* 1, 567-81, noting especially the *Shahādāt min qawl al-Tawrāt wa-l-anbiyā' wa-l-qiddīsīn* ('Witnesses from the words of the Torah, the prophets and the saints'), pp. 576-7.

40 M.N. Swanson, '*Al-jāmiʿ wujūh al-īmān*', in *CMR* 1, 791-8.

41 M.N. Swanson, 'Peter of Bayt Ra's', in *CMR* 1, 902-6.

Heresy

Another category available to Christians for the classification of the religious Other was that of heresy. Already in the 370s, the Church father Epiphanius of Salamis had composed a list and refutation of some 80 heresies in his *Panarion*.[42] When much later (early-mid 8th century) John of Damascus composed a similar catalogue of heresies as the second of his three-volume *Pēgē gnōseōs* ('Fount of knowledge'), its concluding Chapter 100 dealt with the 'heresy of the Ishmaelites'.[43] And jumping ahead another four centuries, we find Peter the Venerable, abbot of Cluny, debating in his *Summa totius haeresis Saracenorum* (of 1143-4) whether Muslims were best considered heretics or pagans.[44]

The classification of Islam as a heresy has been useful to Christian theologians and controversialists throughout the centuries: it has allowed for the existence of elements held in common between the two belief systems as well as divergences. Writers could take these elements either as a baseline from which to stress the divergences, or as common ground upon which to build bridges of understanding. We thus find the idea of heresy put to work in the service both of Christian polemics and of more irenic approaches.

For example, the influential legend of Sergius Baḥīrā, which took shape in Syriac in the 9th century and spread throughout the Christian world, makes the claim that Christian teachings lie at the core of the Qur'an, which had its genesis as an attempt to preach Christianity to the Arabs. In the Long Arabic recension of the text, even the *basmala* is claimed to be an assertion of the Holy Trinity![45] However, for the Christian Baḥīrā tradition, the presence of these Christian teachings does nothing to prompt readers to take the religion of Islam seriously; rather, Islam is dismissed as an attempt at Christian missionary enculturation gone very badly awry.

In contrast to this, the idea that the Qur'an contained Christian truth *could* lead to attitudes other than scornful dismissal. Nicholas of Cusa in his *Cribratio Alchorani* ('Sifting the Qur'an') of 1461 sought to identify elements of truth in the Qur'an. His innovative (and irenic) approach

---

42 See *The Panarion of Epiphanius of Salamis*, trans. F. Williams, 2 vols, Leiden, 2009-13^2.

43 Glei, 'John of Damascus'.

44 D. Iogna-Prat and J. Tolan, 'Peter of Cluny', in *CMR* 3, 604-10, pp. 606-7.

45 B. Roggema, '*The legend of Sergius Baḥīrā*', in *CMR* 1, 600-3; and her *The legend of Sergius Baḥīrā. Eastern Christian apologetics and apocalyptic in response to Islam*, Leiden, 2009, where the text about the *basmala* is at pp. 458-9.

was that wherever the Qur'an appeared to deviate from Christian teaching, Nicholas sought to find a *pia interpretatio* or generous interpretation that recognised Muḥammad's monotheism, good intentions and need to make compromises in order to preach to his people effectively.[46]

Islam as one of the religions (*dīn min al-adyān*)

A striking feature of the early Christian apologetic literature that arose in Arabic in the second half of the 8th century and began to flourish in the 9th is the matter-of-fact acknowledgement of what today we might call 'religious plurality' in the world. Islam is recognised along with Christianity, Judaism, Zoroastrianism, Manichaeism (and others) as a *dīn* (conventionally translated 'religion') that comprises a certain 'way' of believing and behaving (*madhhab*, *sharīʿa*), defined by a scripture (*kitāb*), to which people have been called by particular founders who claim to have been sent by God. The question for Christian apologists, then, was this: in this world of many religions (*adyān*), how does one discern which religion (*dīn*) is the true one, the one that is pleasing to God?[47]

The question as just formulated contains but does not explicate a presupposition: that at least within the horizons of the Christian apologists' world, only one religion at a time can be pleasing to God. This is apparent in the strict supersessionism that we encounter in several early Christian Arabic texts with respect to Judaism. One very early Melkite (Chalcedonian Orthodox) Arabic apology, *Fī tathlīth Allāh al-wāḥid*, claims to have been written 746 years after the 'establishment' of Christianity,[48] while the Melkite apologetic collection *Al-jāmiʿ wujūh al-īmān* claims to have been written 825 years after Judaism had been 'abolished'.[49] There has been some scholarly discussion about how one should calculate a date from these statements, in particular whether one should work from the date of the Incarnation or from that of the crucifixion of Christ.[50] In

46 J. Tolan, 'Nicholas of Cusa', in *CMR* 5, 421-8, p. 425.

47 On this line of apology, see also M. Takawi and G.S. Reynolds, Chapter 6. 'Muslim perceptions of Jesus', 123-51 below. The seminal study of what I am going to call the True Religion Apology is S.H. Griffith, 'Comparative religion in the apologetics of the first Christian Arabic theologians', *Proceedings of the PMR [Patristic, Mediaeval and Renaissance] conference* 4 (1979) 63-87.

48 Swanson, '*Fī tathlīth Allāh al-wāhid*', p. 331.

49 Swanson, '*Al-jāmiʿ wujūh al-īmān*', pp. 791-2.

50 For a recent discussion that presents another supersessionist text and finds evidence for regarding the Incarnation itself as marking the 'abolition' of Judaism / 'establishment' of Christianity divide, see A. Treiger, 'New works of Theodore Abū Qurra

either case, it seems clear that the 'abolition' of Judaism and the 'establishment' of Christianity are conceived of as a single hinge in biblical history, a particular point in time at which God's good pleasure is transferred from one *dīn* to another.

Discerning the true religion. Some basic resources

'If God is only pleased with one *dīn* among the *adyān* available, how can one discern which *dīn* that is?' For answers, medieval Christian apologists needed resources for creating an argument – and these had long been at hand.

Very early in the history of Christian-Muslim encounters, Christian leaders pointed to miracles, especially those performed by monks and holy men, as evidence of Christianity's truth.[51] As noted above, Christian apologists had ready-made catalogues of Old Testament *testimonia* with which to make the argument that the true religion was the one confirmed by prophecy. Such a scriptural argument could then be extended with the claim that the Qur'an as well, properly read, bears witness to Christian truth.[52]

The place of miracles in the case for the truth of Christianity remained important for centuries (as we shall see below). With the passage of time, however, arguments from scripture appear to move from a leading to a supporting role. Christian apologists learned that Muslims did not simply accept the Christian Bible as an authority; that Muslims could also search the Bible and seek out prophecies of Muḥammad and the rise of Islam;[53] and that arguments from the Qur'an were risky, exposing the

---

preserved under the name of Thaddeus of Edessa', *Journal of Eastern Christian Studies* 68 (2016) 1-51.

[51] As in Letter 14C of Isho'yahb of Adiabene (H.G.B. Teule, 'Isho'yahb III of Adiabene', in *CMR* 1, 133-6; and see Penn, *When Christians first met Muslims*, 29-36, here p. 35); or the *Narrationes* of Anastasius of Sinai (A. Binggeli, 'Anastasius of Sinai', in *CMR* 1, 193-202, p. 198). Note that the miracle-workers are usually men, although of course there is a long history of saintly ascetic women as well.

[52] As in *Fī tathlīth Allāh al-wāḥid*; Swanson, '*Fī tathlīth Allāh al-wāḥid*', p. 331. An early Christian Arabic example of exploitative prooftexting of the Qur'an is Papyrus Schott-Reinhart no. 438; M.N. Swanson, 'A Christian Arabic Disputation (PSR 438)', in *CMR* 1, 386-87. On Christian engagement with the Qur'an, see U. Cecini, Chapter 10. 'Latin Christianity engaging with the Qur'an', and G. Nickel, Chapter 11. '"Our Friendly Strife": Eastern Christianity engaging the Qur'an' 227-54 and 255-79 below.

[53] As seen in the *Disputation* of the Catholicos Timothy I with the Caliph al-Mahdī; M. Heimgartner, 'Letter 59', in *CMR* 1, 522-6, p. 523, where the prophet like Moses (Deuteronomy 18:18), the rider on the camel (Isaiah 21:6-9), and the Paraclete of St John's Gospel, are understood by the Muslim interlocutor as prophecies of Muḥammad. This project of finding Muḥammad foretold in the Bible is taken to an extreme in *Kitāb al-dīn*

Christian interpreter to delicate questions about its authority. We can see this shift in the role of scriptural arguments in the earliest Christian Arabic literature. In the 8th-century *Fī tathlīth Allāh al-wāḥid*, an argument for the truth of the doctrine of the Trinity begins with the Bible (Isaiah 6:3, Genesis 1:1-3) before moving to simple rational arguments.[54] By the 9th century, however, Christian apologists (such as Theodore Abū Qurra, Ḥabīb Abū Rā'iṭa and ʿAmmār al-Baṣrī),[55] do not lead with arguments *min al-naql* ('from transmitted texts') but rather with arguments *min al-ʿaql* ('from reason'). Rational arguments – often constructed in ways that mirrored those of the early Islamic *kalām* – would then provide the framework into which other apologetic elements (scriptural arguments or the argument from miracles) might be inserted.

The rise of the True Religion Apology

It is especially to the three 9th-century Christian apologists just mentioned that we owe the development of what I shall call the 'True Religion Apology': an argument that one can, on the basis of reason, discern that Christianity is the true and God-pleasing *dīn* among the various possibilities on offer.

Let us begin with the first identifiable (by name) Christian theologian who composed treatises in Arabic, Theodore Abū Qurra. His *Maymar fī wujūd al-Khāliq wa-l-dīn al-qawīm* ('Treatise on the existence of the Creator and the true religion') is, as John Lamoreaux has pointed out, in fact a collection of three treatises.[56] Here I want to call attention to the second, which Lamoreaux in his volume of translated texts has called *Theologus autodidactus*, where the 'self-taught theologian' of the text is its first-person narrator who claims to be on a quest for truth, exercising a rationality unformed and undistorted by any particular faith

---

wa-l-dawla by 'Alī al-Ṭabarī; D. Thomas, '*Kitāb al-dīn wa-l-dawla*', in *CMR* 1, 672-4. See also the edition and English trans. in R. Ebied and D. Thomas, *The polemical works of ʿAlī al-Ṭabarī*, Leiden, 2016, 170-473, pp. 326-435.

54 Swanson, '*Fī tathlīth Allāh al-wāḥid*', p. 331. The 'simple rational arguments' here are analogies from nature: phenomena that are simultaneously one and threefold (such as a tree, known in roots, branches and fruit; or water, manifest in spring, river and lake; and so on).

55 See, respectively, Lamoreaux, 'Theodore Abū Qurra'; Keating, 'Abū Rā'iṭa l-Takriti'; and I.M. Beaumont, ''Ammār al-Baṣrī', in *CMR* 1, 604-10.

56 Lamoreaux, 'Theodore Abū Qurra', pp. 448-50. The combined *maymar* was edited by I. Dick, *Maymar fī wujūd al-Khāliq wa-dīn al-qawīm*, Jounieh: al-Maktaba al-Būlusiyya, 1982.

tradition.[57] The fundamental idea of this text is that the true religion may be discerned as the one that has doctrines about God, morality and the afterlife that conform to what reason teaches. Rational arguments lead the text's narrator to assert 'the inner-communal nature of God, the imperative of love in this life, and the incorporeal sublimity of reward in the next life'.[58] Unsurprisingly, it is the doctrines of Christianity, and Christianity alone, that measure up to these 'rational' deductions.[59]

This 'positive', all-at-once approach to discerning the true religion requires some rather brazen moves that belie the text's claim to religious neutrality.[60] It does not appear to have caught on with other apologists of Theodore's era, although they and later apologists were, of course, happy to take individual doctrines one by one and make arguments for their rationality (rather than trying to make one sweeping, comprehensive argument for the truth of Christianity as a whole). However, the main line of the True Religion Apology took a different path, a 'negative' one: it focuses on the reasons for which people might choose a religion other than the true one. Ironically enough, one of the earliest examples of this negative approach is the third part of the *Maymar fī wujūd al-Khāliq wa-l-dīn al-qawīm*, which Lamoreaux has called 'That Christianity is from God'.[61] This small treatise is closely paralleled by another one from the Abū Qurran corpus, called 'On the confirmation of the Gospel'.[62]

For this pair of treatises, the role of human reason is much more modest than what is claimed in *Theologus autodidactus*. Here, what reason can do is to discern and analyse the reasons for which a religion, any religion, was accepted by people and spread.[63] Most religions are accepted

---

57 J.C. Lamoreaux, *Theodore Abū Qurrah*, Provo UT, 2005, pp. 1-25.

58 As summarised in M.N. Swanson, 'Apology or its evasion? Some ninth-century Arabic Christian texts on discerning the true religion', in M. Root and J.J. Buckley (eds), *Christian theology and Islam*, Eugene OR, 2013, 45-63, p. 48.

59 Theodore's apology is described in detail in S.H. Griffith, 'Faith and reason in Christian *kalam*. Theodore Abū Qurrah on discerning the true religion', in S.K. Samir and J.S. Nielsen (eds), *Christian Arabic apologetics during the Abbasid period (750-1258)*, Leiden, 1994, pp. 1-43.

60 Theodore's 'assertion of precisely three attributes of "begetting", "procession" and "headship" [in his argument for God's triunity] has all the subtlety of a Hail Mary pass'; M.N. Swanson, 'The Trinity in Christian-Muslim conversation', *Dialog. A Journal of Theology* 44 (2005) 256-63, p. 259.

61 Lamoreaux, *Theodore Abū Qurrah*, 41-7.

62 Lamoreaux, 'Theodore Abū Qurra', pp. 456-7. Edition: Qusṭanṭīn al-Bāshā [Bacha], *Mayāmir Thāwudūrus Abī Qurra usquf Ḥarrān*, Beirut: Maṭbaʿat al-Fawāʾid, 1904, pp. 71-5; English trans., Lamoreaux, *Theodore Abū Qurrah*, pp. 49-53.

63 For this and the next two paragraphs, see Swanson, 'Apology or its evasion?', pp. 49-50, summarising 'That Christianity is from God', in Dick, *Maymar*, pp. 259-70, and 'On the confirmation of the Gospel', in al-Bāshā, *Mayāmir*, pp. 71-5.

for human (that is, psychologically, sociologically, economically or politically comprehensible) reasons, such as: constraint by the sword; the hope of gain (whether of wealth, power or status); ethnic or tribal solidarity; licence to indulge the appetites; or the approval (*al-istiḥsān*) of familiar or easy doctrines (which Theodore also called 'the satisfaction of the mercantile mind').[64] Theodore's point is this: the true religion must be the one that did not spread for any of these humanly comprehensible reasons, that is, because of human power. Thus we have a criterion by which a religion may possibly be dismissed from consideration as the true one.

Theodore does not bother to run all the various religions of the world through the filter he has constructed, but rather leaves it to the reader to work out the ways in which religions other than Christianity – Islam in particular – may have spread as a result of humanly comprehensible factors, such as coercion, hope of gain, tribal solidarity, licence or satisfying teachings. What he does do, as the second step in his argument, is make an argument that the Christianity of the apostolic era did not spread for any of these reasons. The apostles coerced no one; offered nothing in the way of wealth, power or status; overcame boundaries of ethnicity and tribe; called their followers to lives of ascetic virtue; and came with teachings that, rather than being familiar and easy, were new and strange.

The third step in the argument begins with an observation: in spite of the absence of humanly understandable reasons for the earliest spread of the Christian religion, it did in fact spread, with the result that the majority of people in the known world in Abū Qurra's day was Christian! If this did not take place through human power, then it must have come about through divine power – as made manifest in miracles. Here, finally, is the place of evidentiary miracles in the argument. Theodore is thinking especially of the miracles worked by the Apostles; he tells the story of St Thomas, whose preaching in India was without fruit until he raised a dead man 'in the name of Jesus Christ, who was crucified in Jerusalem'.[65]

This form of the True Religion Apology reconfigured the elements of miracle, scripture and reason that were available to Christian apologists.

---

64 *Qunūʿ al-ʿaql al-sūqī*, in 'On the Confirmation of the Gospel', in al-Bāshā, *Mayāmir*, p. 73.

65 'That Christianity is from God', in Dick, *Maymar*, p. 269 (no. 48), with a parallel passage in 'On the confirmation of the Gospel', in al-Bāshā, *Mayāmir*, p. 74.

Here reason does not peer into the nature of God, morality and the afterlife (as in Theodore's *Theologus autodidactus*), but rather brings its disjunctive and analytical capacities to observable phenomena in human history. Scripture does not provide evidence in the form of prophecies fulfilled in evangelical history, but rather functions as a historical source for the mission of the Apostles and early Christian teachings and practice. Miracles are invoked at the end of the argument, in order to support and add an exclamation mark to a conclusion that has already been reached: that Christianity must have spread because of other-than-human reasons, that is, because of divine power.

This form of the True Religion Apology became a staple of Christian Arabic apologetics for centuries. Different apologists developed slightly different lists of the humanly-comprehensible reasons for accepting a religion. So, for example, Ḥabīb Abū Rā'iṭa offered six reasons for the spread of a religion that have nothing to do with 'the religion of God'. They are: desire with respect to the things of this world; craving for the (corporeal) delights of the world to come; coercing fear; licence with respect to desired but forbidden things; approval, *al-istiḥsān*; and collusion and ethnic or tribal solidarity for the purpose of group advancement. Ḥabīb then contrasts these with the seventh (and only proper) reason for accepting a religion: the evidentiary miracles by which God establishes the truth of God's religion.[66]

Ḥabīb's East Syrian contemporary ʿAmmār al-Baṣrī has similar lists of 'worldly' motives for accepting a religion, which may be compiled into something like this: collusion; the sword; bribes and flattery; ethnic/tribal solidarity; *al-istiḥsān*, reasoned approval; licence with respect to the laws; and the illusions and specious proofs of sorcery.[67] These various lists of humanly-understandable (or 'worldly') reasons for accepting a religion have a common core (coercion, gain, tribal/ethnic solidarity, 'approval' of teachings, licence), to which individual apologists might find something else to add. Ḥabīb adds the promise of corporeal delights in the world to come, while ʿAmmār is concerned about trickery of various

---

66 As summarised in Swanson, 'Apology or its evasion?', pp. 53-4 (with slight emendations), from Ḥabīb's 'On the proof of the Christian religion', in S.T. Keating (ed.), *Defending the 'people of truth' in the early Islamic period. The Christian apologies of Abū Rā'iṭah*, Leiden, 2006, 82-95.

67 As summarised in Swanson, 'Apology or its evasion?', p. 55, from ʿAmmār's *Kitāb al-Burhān* ('The book of the proof'), ed. M. Hayek, *ʿAmmār al-Baṣrī. Apologie et controverses*, Beirut: Dar el-Machreq, 1977, pp. 32-41.

sorts, whether collusion between the founders of a religion, or of sorcery resulting in counterfeit miracles.

Later apologists would often pare down these more expansive lists. In the fourth 'session' of his *Kitāb al-majālis* (from about the year 1026),[68] Elias of Nisibis reduces the worldly reasons for accepting a religion to an elegantly rhymed pair: *al-raghba* (desire) and *al-rahba* (terror).[69] But then he proceeds with the standard analysis: Christianity did not spread for these reasons. But it did spread, accepted by philosophers and rulers, by 'Byzantines, Franks, Bulgars, Copts, Nubians, Armenians, Syrians, Persians, Turks and Chinese'. In the absence of *al-raghba* and *al-rahba*, it can only have been divine miracle that attracted all these people to the Christian faith.[70]

The place of reason

A notable feature of this True Religion Apology as developed by Theodore Abū Qurra, Ḥabīb Abū Rāʾiṭa and ʿAmmār al-Baṣrī is their unanimous judgement that one of the humanly-understandable or worldly reasons for accepting a religion is *al-istiḥsān*, 'approval', in particular of a religion's teachings. There are subtle differences in the ways these apologists understand this word. Theodore focuses on the approval that 'the mercantile mind' (*al-ʿaql al-sūqī*) gives to teachings that are easy and familiar. Ḥabīb gives the term an aesthetic twist, thinking of teachings that gain for their bearers' approval as persons of refinement and taste (*al-istiḥsān li-tanmīqihi wa-zakhrafatihi*, 'approval because of elegance and adornment'). ʿAmmār stresses the capacity of human reason, and by *al-istiḥsān* means the approval of doctrines that human reason can devise and that it deems plausible.[71] In each case, however, the human approval of religious teachings (whether because of their familiarity and simplicity, their elegance or their rational plausibility) is taken as a humanly-understandable or worldly reason for the acceptance of a religion. And then all of the Christian apologists considered here argue that such *istiḥsān* could not be a factor in the earliest spread of Christianity. Theodore more or less recites the Creed, with its narration of

---

68 See J.P. Monferrer Sala, 'Elias of Nisibis', in *CMR* 2, 727-41, pp. 730-2. For the edition of the fourth *majlis*, see L. Cheikho, 'Majālis Īliyyā muṭrān Naṣībīn', *Al-Mashriq* 20 (1922) 267-70.

69 Cheikho, 'Majālis', p. 268.

70 Cheikho, 'Majālis', pp. 268-9.

71 Summarised in Swanson, 'Apology or its evasion?', pp. 51-3 (for Theodore), p. 54 (for Ḥabīb), and pp. 55-7 (for ʿAmmār).

the suffering and death of the Incarnate one – and points out that such teaching, rather than being familiar and easy, is new and strange. Ḥabīb focuses on the crucifixion of the one claimed to be God – a teaching about which there is nothing of elegance or refinement. ʿAmmār gives a summary of Christian doctrine culminating in the doctrine of the Trinity – a teaching about God that does not occur to the human intellect (unlike, for example, dualisms or sheer monotheisms) and that it does not deem plausible.[72]

What is striking about this way of arguing is the way it takes Theodore's approach in *Theologus autodidactus* and turns it on its head. Theodore had tried out the 'positive' argument that human reason is capable of discerning truth about the nature of God, morality and the afterlife; indeed, that religiously unformed human reason is able to find its way to positing the existence of a triply inter-communal and self-giving God. The 'negative' form of the True Religion Apology, however, goes the other way: Christian teachings are not accessible to and 'approved' by human reason. Quite the contrary, as Theodore (in this mode of argumentation) points out: people's rational minds (*ʿuqūl*) find Christianity's teachings about the suffering and death of the incarnate Son of God to be repulsive.[73] Nor can one say that this is true only of the minds of the common people; after summarising Christian beliefs, Theodore can say: 'No one is convinced by this or accepts it, not the wise, nor the ignorant, nor the one in between.'[74]

The ironic result of all this is that the incapacity of reason to anticipate or grasp Christian teachings is folded into a (presumably reasonable) argument for Christianity's truth. As already noted, this form of True Religion Apology gained considerable popularity among Christians. It allowed for a very forthright statement of Christian teachings – the Triune God, the suffering and crucifixion of the Incarnate Son/Word for the redemption of the world – in all their paradoxical splendour (or palpable nonsense, depending on one's point of view).[75] Just so, the texts may well

---

72 See n. 71, above.

73 [...] *tastashniʿuhu ʿuqūl al-nās*; 'On the confirmation of the Gospel', in al-Bāshā, *Mayāmir*, p. 75. Interestingly, Gerasimos, abbot of the monastery of St Symeon, made use of *both* Theodore's positive and negative arguments in Parts 1 and 2 of his apology *Al-kāfī fī maʿnā l-shāfī*; A. Bakhou and J. Lamoreaux, 'Gerasimos', in *CMR* 4, 666-71.

74 Swanson, 'Apology or its evasion?', p. 53, translation from 'On the confirmation of the Gospel', in al-Bāshā, *Mayāmir*, p. 74.

75 For the argument that such claims are nonsensical, see, for example, the 'Refutation of the Christians' of ʿAlī al-Ṭabarī (D. Thomas, '*Al-Radd ʿalā l-Naṣārā*', in *CMR* 1, 671-2), now available in Ebied and Thomas, *Polemical works*, pp. 61-169.

have served as a kind of emergency catechesis for Christians who needed strengthening in their faith, in the first ʿAbbasid centuries when conversion of Christians to Islam was a real and accelerating phenomenon.

Over the course of time, however, it would be difficult for Christians to give their full endorsement to an argument that seemed to call into question reason's capacity to discern divine realities. The eager adoption (from the 9th century on) of neoplatonically-tinged Aristotelianism by Arabic-speaking elites from all religious communities infused new energy into arguments *min al-ʿaql* for the truth of the doctrines of the Trinity or the Incarnation;[76] the contributions of Yaḥyā ibn ʿAdī (d. 974) would be of great importance for generations of arabophone theologians.[77] Examples of the True Religion Apology might continue to follow older (negative) models, but with positive elements mixed in.

An early example would be that of Ḥunayn ibn Isḥāq's *Jawāb* ('Response') to Ibn al-Munajjim's *Burhān* ('Proof').[78] Ḥunayn's list of reasons for accepting *falsehood* is mostly a standard one: coercion, deliverance from need or trial, gain in social position or power, the combination of a deceptive founder and an ignorant public, and ties of kinship. In addition, Ḥunayn makes a point of saying that, of all the religious doctrines on offer, those of the Christians are 'the most difficult, the farthest from convincing [people]'.[79] But then Ḥunayn continues with not just one reason for accepting the truth (evidentiary miracles), but three more: that the outer bears witness to the inner; a compelling *burhān*; and that the end corresponds to the beginning.[80] Ḥunayn simply states these three positive criteria without explanation, a lacuna that an otherwise

76 This can be seen already in the 9th century in the use of Aristotle's *Topics* in arguing for and against the triunity of God by, respectively, Ḥabīb Abū Rā'iṭa (Keating, 'Abū Rā'iṭa l-Takriti', 572-4) and Abū Yūsuf Yaʿqūb al-Kindī (D. Thomas, 'Al-Kindī', in *CMR* 1, 746-50, p. 747).

77 E. Platti, 'Yaḥyā ibn ʿAdī', in *CMR* 2, 390-438. Yaḥyā would have an enormous influence on later thinkers, as his understanding of God (the divine Intellect) as *ʿaql, ʿāqil* and *maʿqūl* provided a sophisticated and brilliant response to the 'Why *three*?' question concerning God. See also I.M. Beaumont, Chapter 5. 'Debating the concept of God', 99-121.

78 B. Roggema, "Alī ibn Yaḥyā ibn al-Munajjim', in *CMR* 1, 762-7, and '*Kayfiyyat idrāk ḥaqīqat al-diyāna*', in *CMR* 1, 775-9. Edition of the *Jawāb*, in S.K. Samir and P. Nwyia (eds), *Une correspondence islamo-chrétienne entre Ibn al-Munağğim, Ḥunayn ibn Isḥāq et Qusṭa ibn Lūqā*, Turnhout, 1981, pp. 686-701.

79 *Jawāb* (ed. Samir and Nwyia), p. 698 (nos 78-80).

80 *Jawāb* (ed. Samir and Nwyia), p. 692 (nos 36-42); B. Roggema, 'Kayfiyyat idrāk ḥaqīqat al-diyāna', p. 775; and see M.N. Swanson, 'A curious and delicate correspondence. The *Burhān* of Ibn al-Munajjim and the *Jawāb* of Ḥunayn ibn Isḥāq', *ICMR* 22 (2011) 173-83, p. 178.

unknown Copt named Yūḥannā ibn Mīnā attempted to fill in. For Yūḥannā, consistency in the careers of the founder and earliest followers, that is, an almost aesthetic sense of integration and wholeness, is a criterion of a religion's truth, alongside evidentiary miracles and (as Yūḥannā interprets Ḥunayn's 'compelling *burhān*') the prophecies of scripture.[81] Forms of the argument from consistency – in particular, Christian disciples' actual embodiment of Christian teachings – would have some staying power, even as other elements of the True Religion Apology would erode over time.[82] It is to that erosion that we now turn.

The decline of the True Religion Apology

What miracles?

The True Religion Apology is founded on the conviction that the true religion is established and the true messenger authenticated by evidentiary signs and miracles (*āyāt, āʿlām; ʿajāʾib, aʿājīb*). This was one of the oldest and most widespread notions in the Christian apologetic arsenal in the encounter with Islam; after all, the Qur'an appeared to deny such wonders to Muḥammad, as a number of Christian apologists were eager to point out.[83] The charge appears to have elicited a response, so that an Islamic version of a True Religion Apology such as ʿAlī ibn Rabban al-Ṭabarī's *Kitāb al-dīn wa-l-dawla* includes a chapter on Muḥammad's miracles;[84] these would become a standard part of the Prophet's biography.[85] Christian pressure at this point undoubtedly contributed to the development of the doctrine of *iʿjāz al-Qurʾān*, the status of the Qur'an itself as Islam's decisive evidentiary miracle.[86]

---

81 M.N. Swanson, 'Yuḥannā ibn Mīnā', in *CMR* 3, 720-3.

82 Already Theodore Abū Qurra points to the transformed behaviour of the early Christians as something that points to Christianity's truth; 'That Christianity is from God', in Dick, *Maymar*, pp. 265-68 (nos 29-41). And see the discussion of the late-14th-century Copt al-Makīn Jirjis ibn al-ʿAmīd, below.

83 See, for example, ʿAmmār al-Baṣrī in *Kitāb al-burhān*, ed. Hayek, p. 31, where Q 17:59 and Q 6:105 are cited.

84 D. Thomas, "Alī al-Ṭabarī', in *CMR* 1, 669-74; and see the text in Ebied and Thomas, *Polemical works*, pp. 249-59 ('The book of religion and empire', ch. 3).

85 See, for example, A. Schimmel, *And Muhammad is his Messenger. The veneration of the Prophet in Islamic piety*, Chapel Hill NC, 1985, pp. 67-80.

86 The fundamental idea appears early, as in *Kitāb al-ḥujja fī tathbīt al-nubuwwa* by al-Jāḥiẓ (D. Thomas, 'Al-Jāḥiẓ', in *CMR* 1, 706-12), but receives its classical formulation in the 10th-century *Iʿjāz al-Qurʾān* by al-Bāqillānī (D. Thomas, 'Al-Bāqillānī', in *CMR* 2, 446-50).

We find some interesting variation in the way that different Christian apologists talked about the character of the evidentiary miracles. For Theodore Abū Qurra, the exemplary miracle was the raising of the dead 'in the name of Jesus Christ who was crucified in Jerusalem',[87] thus placing the primary scandal of Christian teaching – the lordship of one who was crucified – front and centre. ʿAmmār al-Baṣrī was concerned to distinguish true miracles from the counterfeits of sorcery: true miracles were dependable responses to real requests for genuine healing from actual diseases.[88] Būlus al-Būshī examined a number of Christ's miracles to show how they rhymed with God's works of creation – thus emphasising their divinely-given character.[89]

One serious point of discussion in these True Religion texts is whether one can look to miracles in the present as evidences of a religion's truth. Already in the 9th century, ʿAmmār al-Baṣrī not only asserted that evidentiary miracles had come to an end after the apostolic age, but made an argument for this end's necessity: otherwise, miraculous deeds would have become a kind of bludgeon coercing people into faith.[90] For ʿAmmār, the presence of evidentiary miracles in the early spread of Christianity is something to be deduced more from the lack of any other plausible explanation for Christianity's acceptance and spread than from observation of similar phenomena.[91]

ʿAmmār's scepticism concerning present-day miracles, however, does not appear to have been widely shared by Christians who were defending their faith within the *Dār al-Islām*. Among these Christians, the marvellous deeds of holy men and women were eagerly related and collected, leading both to a historiography with marked hagiographical elements (as in the composite *History of the patriarchs of Alexandria*)[92]) and the hagiographical genre of a saint's *Life* immediately followed by a collection

[87] 'That Christianity is from God', in Dick, *Maymar*, p. 269 (no. 48), with a parallel passage in 'On the Confirmation of the Gospel', in al-Bāshā, *Mayāmir*, p. 74.

[88] *Kitāb al-burhān*, ed. Hayek, pp. 39-41.

[89] S.K. Samir (ed.), *Maqāla fī l-tathlīth wa-l-tajassud wa-ṣiḥḥat al-masīḥiyya li-Būlus al-Būshī*, Dayr al-Malāk Mīkhāʾīl: al-Turāth al-ʿArabī l-Masīḥī, 1983, pp. 254-5. On Būlus al-Bushī, see M.N. Swanson, 'Būlus al-Bushī', in *CMR* 4, 280-7.

[90] Other authors, e.g. Gerasimos (Bakhou and Lamoreaux, 'Gerasimos'), speak of the time of need for miracles having passed.

[91] *Kitāb al-burhān*, ed. Hayek, pp. 26-7.

[92] For example, the source for the *History of the patriarchs* written by Michael of Damrū (M.N. Swanson, 'Michael of Damrū', in *CMR* 3, 84-8), is our earliest source for the well-known story of the Muqaṭṭam miracle: at a delicate moment for the Coptic community, there was found within it the faith to move mountains, in a dazzling public display before the Fāṭimid caliph.

of miracles.[93] Debate texts of varying degrees of historicity – from the Arabic disputation of Ibrāhīm al-Ṭabarānī[94] to the story of St Francis before the Ayyubid Sultan al-Malik al-Kāmil[95] – can end with (at least a proposal of) a trial by poison or fire. The miracle gives testimony to the truth of the teaching.

In between ʿAmmār's scepticism and an uncritical enthusiasm for miracles, we find the rather modest position of the *Letter* of Makkīkhā, preserved in the 14th-century collection *Asfār al-asrār* by Ṣalībā ibn Yūḥannā.[96] For Makkīkhā ibn Sulayman al-Qankānī, Catholicos of the Church of the East (1092-1109), the traces (*āthār*) of the great evidentiary miracles of Christianity's earliest period do continue to the present day, 'so that the little that is present may be an indication of the much that is lost'.[97] He points to the miracle of the holy fire in the Church of the Resurrection in Jerusalem,[98] as well as to marvels in monasteries, from healing formulae to perfectly preserved corpses. Such miracles should be 'sufficient and convincing for the one who seeks the truth'.[99]

Whose spread?

The fundamental observable fact upon which the True Religion Apology was built was that the Christian religion had somehow spread throughout the known world, to be embraced by people of very different social

---

93 An early example in Arabic is *The life of Timothy of Kākhushtā* (J.C. Lamoreaux, 'The life of Timothy of Kākhushtā', in *CMR* 1, 919-22). The genre became popular among the Copts in the 14th and 15th centuries, with the *Life* and *Miracles* of Barṣawmā al-ʿUryān, Marqus al-Anṭūnī, and Anbā Ruways (M.N. Swanson, 'The life and miracles of Barṣawmā al-ʿUryān', in *CMR* 5, 114-18; 'The life and miracles of Marqus al-Anṭūnī', in *CMR* 5, 203-6; 'The life and miracles of Anbā Ruways', in *CMR* 5, 287-90).

94 M.N. Swanson, *'The disputation of the monk Ibrāhīm al Ṭabarānī'*, in *CMR* 1, 876-81, and *CMR* 5, p. 730; similarly, M.N. Swanson, 'The disputation of Jirjī the monk', in *CMR* 4, 166-72.

95 First reported by Jacques de Vitry (J. Tolan, 'Jacques de Vitry', in *CMR* 4, 295-306), and later much elaborated.

96 For Ṣalībā, see M.N. Swanson, 'Ṣalībā ibn Yuḥannā', in *CMR* 4, 900-5; for Makkīkhā, see H.G.B. Teule, 'Makkīkhā ibn Sulaymān al-Qankāni', in *CMR* 3, 323-38, with a description of the *Letter* at pp. 324-6.

97 G. Gianazza, 'Lettre de Makkīḫā († 1109), sur la vérité de la religion chrétienne', *Parole de l'Orient* 25 (2000) 493-555, pp. 520-1 (no. 43).

98 Perhaps precisely because this annual miracle was seen as confirmation of the truth of Christianity it drew the debunking energies of Muslims, sometimes in an actively destructive way (e.g. T. Pratsch, 'Nicetus Clericus', in *CMR* 2, 263-5; A. Treiger, 'Destruction of the Cathedral of Our Lady Mart Maryam in Damascus', in *CMR* 5, 698-704, p. 703). In contrast, the Muslim polymath al-Bīrūnī described the miracle without polemic; G. Strohmaier, 'Al-Bīrūnī', in *CMR* 3, 73-80, p. 75.

99 Gianazza, 'Lettre de Makkīḫā', 520-7; the quotation is at p. 523 (no. 48).

standings, intellectual abilities, ethnicities and languages. Theodore Abū Qurra quantified this spread: according to him, at least five-sixths of the people of the world had embraced Christianity.[100] This, then, was the extraordinary fact that needed accounting for, especially when normal worldly (i.e., military, economic, sociological and psychological) explanations for the spread of an ideology had failed.

Over time, however, this cornerstone of the True Religion Apology began to erode. Muslims too could and did take the rapid spread of Islam into an argument for its truth, as we find already in an 8th-century(?) composition that claims to be a *Letter of ʿUmar II to Leo III*.[101] And within the expanding *Dār al-Islām*, demographic changes were taking place that made the traditional argument more difficult to defend. In the (perhaps) 13th-century apology of Abbot Gerasimos of the Monastery of St Symeon, the Christian apologist's assertion that the worship of Christ had spread to the ends of the earth draws an objection: 'The matter is not like this! For we see in our current time that more than half of the world does not know Christ, or they know Him but are not worshipping Him.'[102] In response, Gerasimos doggedly asserts that Christians still outnumber non-Christians in the world, but he is forced to acknowledge that some Christians have abandoned their faith.[103]

The popularity of the True Religion Apology among Christians is evident in its widespread use even when experience pointed to the decline rather than an increase in the number of Christians. It may come as a surprise when from 14th-century Egypt – during a period of difficulty and demographic decline among the Copts – the liturgical expert Yūḥannā ibn Sabbāʿ[104] could blithely trot out the True Religion Apology and claim: 'As the years followed in succession, they [the Christians] increased and grew and ruled cities and regions and became greater in number and power than all the previous kings of the earth in previous ages [...]'[105]

100 'On the confirmation of the Gospel', in al-Bāshā, *Mayāmir*, p. 74.

101 B. Roggema, '*Pseudo-ʿUmar II's letter to Leo III*', in *CMR* 1, 381-5.

102 A. Bakhou, *Defending Christian faith. The fifth part of the Christian apology of Gerasimus*, Warsaw, 2014, pp. 45-6; Bakhou's translation.

103 Bakhou, *Defending Christian faith*, pp. 46-7. Bakhou has a helpful discussion of how Fakhr al-Dīn al-Rāzī and Ibn Taymiyya used the spread of Islam as evidence for its truth; Bakhou, *Defending Christian faith*, pp. 42-5 (and see: M. Iskenderoglu, 'Fakhr al-Dīn al-Rāzī', in *CMR* 4, 61-5, and J. Hoover, 'Ibn Taymiyya', in *CMR* 4, 824-78).

104 M.N. Swanson, 'Ibn Sabbāʿ', in *CMR* 4, 918-23.

105 *Jûḥannâ ibn Abî Zakarîâ ibn Sibâʿ, Pretiosa margarita de scientiis ecclesiasticis*, ed. V. Mistrīḥ, Cairo, 1966, p. 63.

Historically speaking, that may have been true; but there was a more recent example of such spread in number and power. This fact was acknowledged by a Copt writing towards the end of the same 14th century, named al-Makīn Jirjis ibn al-ʿAmīd.[106] In a chapter on discerning the true religion in his compilation *Al-ḥāwī*, he wrote:

> Another *sharīʿa* has appeared since the '*sharīʿa* of perfection' [i.e., Christianity], and has grown, and many from the nations have entered into it. It is present in many regions of the earth; its sword is victorious, its tower is lofty, and many people have believed in it.[107]

Jirjis goes on to argue that no argument from worldly success has any legitimacy. Looking over human history, a variety of (now discarded) religious systems have held wide sway in times past; taking the earth as a whole, different religious systems have held sway in different places, at one and the same time.[108]

> Therefore, the inference [of the truth of a religion] from the aspect of its continuing existence, victory and the exaltedness of its word in a particular place and a particular time amounts to nothing: the argument based on it is flimsy and its bases failing and empty.[109]

While Jirjis undoubtedly here was responding to Muslims' claims that Islam's success was evidence for its truth, his argument also undercut the Christians' True Religion Apology – at least the version of it that had been popular for so long.

For Jirjis, what remained of the True Religion Apology? In a sense, he returned to our starting point: the sort of 'positive' apology represented by Theodore Abū Qurra's *Theologus autodidactus*, and its confidence that reason can discern right teaching. For Jirjis, this right teaching is the Way (*sharīʿa*) of grace (*al-faḍl*), which is revealed in the Gospel; this is the 'pinnacle of goodness' (*nihāyat al-jūd*)[110] from which any other *sharīʿa* is a falling away. Jirjis even believes that the lives of Christians can provide evidence for this: 'The conditions of those who put it into effect and

---

106 A. Sidarus and M.N. Swanson, 'Al-Makīn Jirjis ibn al-ʿAmīd', in *CMR* 5, 254-61. This *CMR* entry laid the groundwork for the study mentioned in the next note.

107 Translation by M.N. Swanson, 'Discerning the true religion in late fourteenth-century Egypt', in G. Gabra and H.N. Takla (eds), *Christianity and monasticism in Middle Egypt: al-Minya and Asyut*, Cairo, 2015, 133-44, p. 139. The text of *Al-ḥāwī* was published by a monk of Dayr al-Muḥarraq, *Al-mawsūʿa l-lāhūtiyya al-shahīra bi-l-ḥāwī l-Ibn al-Makīn*, 4 vols, Cairo, 1999-2001.

108 Swanson, 'Discerning the true religion', pp. 139-41.

109 Swanson, 'Discerning the true religion', p. 141.

110 Swanson, 'Discerning the true religion', pp. 138-9.

cling to its principles and ramifications bear witness to the veracity of the claim.'[111] That is to say, Christians who live their lives in accordance with the precepts of the Messianic *sharīʿa* – in particular, by observing the commandment to love all people, including one's enemies – provide evidence for the truth of that *sharīʿa*. This evidence, however, is rather shaky. Jirjis himself records the immediate objection: 'One does *not* find this commandment [being observed] in any of the Christians!'[112] In the end, the Christian apologist is left commending the excellence of Christ's teaching and life – whether or not Christ's followers actually live up to that standard.

Conclusion

Michael Philip Penn has usefully written about the processes by which Syriac authors came to portray their Arab conquerors not in the first place in ethnic terms but rather in accordance with their 'beliefs and practices' – a process by which 'Muslims essentially "got religion".'[113] In this essay, we have encountered a number of categories that Christians have used to make a place for Islam in a scripturally-formed Christian imagination, but have moved rather quickly to the situation where Muslims had 'gotten religion' – or, in Arabic, where Islam had become a *dīn* among the *adyān*. In this situation, the Christian apologist had to deal with a world where the Christian religion was one option out of several, and where the Christian religion and the Islamic religion were in competition, whether for good (a possibility intimated by the Qur'an, 5:48) or for ill.

Other chapters in this volume will highlight various aspects of this competition. The bulk of the present chapter has followed one particular line of argument through the centuries, namely the True Religion Apology that strove to prove Christianity's truth through the wonder of its worldwide spread despite the lack of humanly comprehensible reasons for that spread – which therefore meant that it spread because of divine power (as manifest in evidentiary miracles). Here is an example of a kind of apologetic discourse that spread like wildfire (among arabophone Christian apologists in the 9th century), but then very gradually

111 Swanson, 'Discerning the true religion', p. 139.
112 Swanson, 'Discerning the true religion', p. 139.
113 M.P. Penn, *Envisioning Islam. Syriac Christians and the early Muslim world*, Philadelphia PA, 2015, p. 59.

lost plausibility and popularity until it was nearly abandoned (by the end of the 14th). While the truths of faith may stand forever, particular apologetic strategies flourish and fade.

The volumes (*CMR* 1-7, and beyond) of *Christian-Muslim relations, a bibliographical history* project (*CMRBH*) may help us in mapping the vicissitudes of such strategies. And as we do this mapping, perhaps we can make an effort at empathetic imagination, trying to understand what was at stake in these various apologetic moves. Behind the rise and fall of particular forms of discourse, we may faintly discern the enthusiasm of triumphant imagination (say, of the apologist who exults in a knock-down argument); or the boldness, or desperation, of an attempt to preserve community identity (e.g. with an apology that makes the paradoxical strangeness of Christian doctrine into an argument for its *truth*); or a slow coming-to-terms with difficult realities (e.g. with the reminder that Christian teaching is beautiful, even when evidentiary miracles are not 'on tap' and demographic realities are discouraging). It is good to remember that, behind the apologetic ideas, there are people who are doing their best to live, and to preserve and shore up their communities.

Chapter 5
Debating the concept of God

I. Mark Beaumont

When Muslims brought their belief in the radical oneness of God to their conquered Christian populations in the Middle East, Christians looked to the Qur'an to support their belief in the Trinity. They argued that texts such as Q 4:171, which states that God has Word and Spirit, supported the Christian concept of the Trinity of Father, Son and Holy Spirit. Muslims replied that Jesus was created by God's word, and they turned to the Christian Gospels to show that Jesus did not claim to be equal to God, or to be the second person of the Trinity. They noticed that Jesus taught that his relationship to God as a son to a father could be experienced by his followers. Christians tried to convince Muslims that statements made by Jesus in the fourth Gospel indicated his equality with God.

Muslims were focused on defining the unity of God. How could the many attributes of God be understood within God's unity? Christians argued that God's attributes of fatherhood, sonship and spirit were essential to his being, thus proving his three-in-one nature. But Muslims failed to see how isolating three attributes from among the many that were regarded as essential to God could be justified. They accused Christians of denying the absolute unity of God. Later, medieval Western Christians understood that Muslims rejected the rationality of the Trinity; so they mostly argued that the Trinity was an aspect of revealed, rather than natural, knowledge. However, they lacked awareness of Middle Eastern Christian writings about the Trinity that might have enabled them to develop a more thorough dialogue with Muslims.

Christian appeal to the Qur'an to defend the Trinity

When Christians who had become subjects of Muslim rule in the Middle East began to pay attention to the message of the Qur'an, they discovered that, alongside the repeated declaration of the oneness of God, there were hints of diversity in the presentation of the names of God that could indicate the Trinity of Father, Son and Holy Spirit in Q 4:171: 'Christ

Jesus, son of Mary, was the messenger of God, and His word which He cast on Mary, and a spirit from Him.' The earliest extant example of the use of this verse to argue that the Qur'an refers to the Son and the Holy Spirit comes in an early 8th-century debate written in Syriac between a monk of the Bēt Ḥālē monastery and an Arab dignitary who visited him to discuss the differences in their beliefs. In his defence of the Trinity, the monk argues that 'the Qur'ān's concept of Christ as "the Word of God and his spirit" can be traced back to Muḥammad's knowledge of the Gospel of Luke' (Luke 1:35).[1] Barbara Roggema points out that, if the disputation comes from the early 8th century, it is the oldest Christian writing to show knowledge of the Qur'an.[2]

In the fourth decade of the 8th century, John of Damascus (d. c. 750) wrote a three-volume work in Greek entitled *Pēgē gnōseōs* ('The fount of knowledge') after his withdrawal from serving the Muslim caliph in Damascus. The second volume, *De haeresibus* ('Heresies'), critiques one hundred heresies, concluding with 'The heresy of the Ishmaelites', in which John attempts to defend the Trinity against Muslim attack by referring to Q 4:171 as support for a Trinitarian faith. He reports that Muslims accuse Christians of associating Christ with God in an unacceptable way because Christians say that 'Christ is the Son of God and God'.[3] John suggests that Christians should quote the Muslim belief that 'Christ is Word and Spirit of God', and say, 'If the Word is in God it is obvious that he is God as well.'[4] But if Muslims deny that the Word and Spirit are in God, they can be accused of cutting off these attributes of God from Him: 'Thus, trying to avoid making associates to God you have mutilated him.'[5] John is making the assumption here that the hypostases of the Word and the Holy Spirit are actually meant in Q 4:171, which is ironic given that John has disparaged the message of Islam as being filled with absurdities. According to Reinhold Glei, 'The significance of *De haeresibus* can hardly be overestimated. It formed the image of Islam in the Greek world and exerted wider influence among Christian readers, at least until the mid-14th century.'[6]

---

1 B. Roggema, *'The disputation between a monk of Bēt Ḥālē and an Arab notable'*, in *CMR* 1, 268-73.

2 Roggema, '*The disputation*'.

3 John of Damascus, 'The heresy of the Ishmaelites', trans. D.J. Sahas, in *John of Damascus on Islam*, Leiden, 1972, 132-41, p. 137.

4 John of Damascus, 'Heresy of the Ishmaelites', p. 137.

5 John of Damascus, 'Heresy of the Ishmaelites', p. 137.

6 R.F. Glei, *'Peri haireseōn'*, in *CMR* 1, 297-301.

The author of an anonymous apology for Christianity written in Arabic around the middle of the 8th century appeals to Q 4:171 as support for the Trinity. This apology comes from the same Chalcedonian community as John, but demonstrates that the language of the Muslim rulers was now being used by some Christian theologians to attempt to persuade Muslims that Christians were in basic agreement with Islamic monotheism.[7] His use of Q 4:171 is designed not only to strengthen fellow Christians in their faith but also to challenge Muslims quite directly to attend to their own scripture in order to discover that God is essentially Triune: 'You find in the Qur'ān that God and His Word and His Spirit is One God and One Lord. You have said that you believe in God and His Word and His Spirit, so do not reproach us, you people, for believing in God and His Word and His Spirit.'[8] The difference between this work and that of John is the absence of John's ridiculing much of the teaching of Islam as absurd. This writer never mocks his Muslim reader, but appeals to one who 'knows the truth and opens his breast to believe in God and His Scriptures'.[9] The tone of this apology is respectful, even when the writer challenges his Muslim reader to desist from quoting qur'anic texts that attack the Trinity. Muslims should not reproach Christians because, as a matter of fact, the latter do not believe in three gods. Muslims should rather listen carefully to Christians when they explain their belief in God and His Word and His Spirit.[10]

Q 4:171 is central to the argument of the monk Abraham in his debate with the Muslim emir in Jerusalem, which Krisztina Szilágyi argues may have taken place in the early 9th century, but was written up later by an anonymous author.[11] When Abraham is accused of slandering God, who will exercise judgement, he responds by saying that his Muslim accuser

---

[7] The Arabic text (Sinai 154) is edited and translated into English by M.D. Gibson as '*A treatise on the Triune nature of God*'. See M.D. Gibson (ed. and trans.), *An Arabic version of the Acts of the Apostles and the seven Catholic Epistles from an eighth or ninth century MS. in the Convent of St. Katherine on Mount Sinai, with a treatise on the triune nature of God, and translation from the same codex*, Cambridge, 1899. See M.N. Swanson, '*Fī tathlīth Allāh al-wāhid*', in *CMR* 1, 330-3, p. 332.

[8] Gibson, *A treatise on the triune nature of God*, pp. 77-8.

[9] Gibson, *A treatise on the triune nature of God*, p. 75.

[10] For a more detailed study of the way this author appeals to qur'anic language to defend the Trinity, see I.M. Beaumont, 'Speaking of the Triune God. Christian defence of the Trinity in the early Islamic period', *Transformation* 29 (2012) 111-27. See also M.N. Swanson, 'Beyond prooftexting. Approaches to the Qur'ān in some early Arabic Christian apologies', *The Muslim World* 88 (1998) 113-48.

[11] K. Szilágyi, 'The disputation of the monk Abraham of Tiberias', in S. Noble and A. Treiger (eds), *The Orthodox Church in the Arab world 700-1700, An anthology of sources*, De Kalb IL, 2014, 90-111, p. 92.

must testify that 'Christ is the Word of God and His Spirit'. The Muslim replies: 'You speak the truth, monk. It is as you said about Christ.'[12] Despite the fact that Q 4:171 does not call Christ 'the' word but 'a' word from God, the Muslim is portrayed as acquiescing in the Christian assumption that Christ is uniquely the Word of God in the sense of John 1:1: 'The Word was God.' The popularity of this disputation can be measured by the large number of manuscripts held by the various Christian denominations of the Middle East.[13]

The appeal by Christians to Q 4:171 as evidence for the Trinity may not have had the intended results in debate with Muslims. In his *Tathbīt dalā'il al-nubuwwa* ('Confirmation of the proofs of prophethood'), the rational theologian ʿAbd al-Jabbār (d. 1025) records that some Christians quote Q 4:171 to Muslims and say, 'This is what we say, that he is from the substance of his Father. We do not intend by our statement "from Him" that [Christ] is part of Him but rather that he is of the same genus and like him.'[14] He goes on to advise his Muslim reader to reply to such Christians that their view of Christ is based not on the actual teaching of Jesus but on the developed doctrine of the church expressed in the Creed, 'Jesus Christ is true God from true God, from the substance of his Father'.[15] These Christians have 'ended up with arrogance and impudence', because they are not concerned to distinguish the facts of Jesus from the interpretation they have been taught.[16] Gabriel Reynolds points out the lasting significance of ʿAbd al-Jabbār's argument that 'appears again in the circle of Ibn Taymiyya and his disciples, who evidently valued the *Tathbīt*'.[17]

Another example of a Muslim rebuttal of this Christian interpretation of Q 4:171 comes in a refutation of the divinity of Jesus attributed to Abū Ḥāmid al-Ghazālī (d. 1111), but probably written by an Egyptian admirer of the great scholar sometime in the 12th century. Right at the end of his demonstration that Jesus never intended to teach that he was divine or equal with God in the Gospels, the writer argues against Christians who

12 Szilágyi, 'Disputation of the monk Abraham of Tiberias', pp. 102-3.
13 Szilágyi, 'Disputation of the monk Abraham of Tiberias', p. 92.
14 ʿAbd al-Jabbār, *Critique of Christian origins*, ed. and trans. G.S. Reynolds and S.K. Samir, Provo UT, 2010, pp. 38-9.
15 ʿAbd al-Jabbār, *Critique of Christian origins*, pp. 39-40.
16 ʿAbd al-Jabbār, *Critique of Christian origins*, p. 40.
17 G.S. Reynolds, '*Tathbīt dalā'il al-nubuwwa*', in *CMR* 2, 604-8.

hold that 'the word' of God in Q 4:171 is 'exactly what they have defined for their hypostases'.[18] On the contrary, he points out that:

> Everyone is created by the word of God, the One who says to every creature 'Be and it exists' [...] He made this clear by saying 'cast into Mary', which means that although a child is created from the sperm cast into its mother, this child [Jesus] was only created by the casting of the word into his mother, that is to say the command about the creation. So then the word 'cast' is metaphorical.[19]

In other words, Christians should not attempt to read Q 4:171 as referring to the hypostasis of the Word.

The longevity of this Christian appeal to Q 4:171 to support the Trinity can be seen in a letter sent by a Christian scholar in Cyprus to Ibn Taymiyya (d. 1328) in 1316, and to Ibn Abī Ṭālib al-Dimashqī (d. 1350) in 1321, both of whom were moved to write replies. The Christian believes that Q 4:171 'approves of God appearing through a veil, and Christ in his humanity is God's veil, through whom God spoke to creation'.[20] However, al-Dimashqī replies,

> You said to yourselves: The Muslims name the Word of God and a Spirit from him, and some of our prophets name him Word, while speech is the attribute of one who is speaking, and the attribute is the adjunct of the one whose attribute it is. The Word came to dwell in Mary and united with her human nature. It became incarnate and was fully man and godly divine, perfect human and perfect divinity, and he did the work of his Father [...] Are you not troubling and bothering your souls beyond their ability in turning one who is below divinity into a divinity, making him into a Creator when he was created?[21]

Clearly, the Christian use of Q 4:171 to indicate the divine status of Jesus fails to move the Muslim scholar to respond with any exegesis of the text. Al-Dimashqī has already said to Christians that their belief that God could be divided into three attributes, Father, Son and Spirit, yet be one God, is impossible: 'You said that the three are one, not realising the

---

[18] M. Beaumont and M. El Kaisy-Friemuth (eds and trans.), *Al-radd al-jamīl. A fitting refutation of the divinity of Jesus, attributed to Abū Ḥamid al-Ghazālī*, Leiden, 2016, p. 181.

[19] Beaumont and El Kaisy-Friemuth, *Al-radd al-jamīl*, p. 185.

[20] 'The letter from the people of Cyprus', in *Muslim-Christian polemic during the Crusades*, ed. R. Ebied and D. Thomas, Leiden, 2005, 53-148, p. 99.

[21] 'Al-Dimashqī's response to the Letter from the people of Cyprus', in Ebied and Thomas (eds and trans), *Muslim-Christian polemic during the Crusades*, Leiden, 2005, 149-498, p. 319.

whole world's marvelling at you and laughing at the ignorance of people who had no idea what divinity is.'[22]

Ibn Taymiyya does not respond directly to the Christian interpretation of Q 4:171, but he argues that Christ is a creation of God's word.

> Even if Christ were himself the knowledge of God and His speech, it would not be permissible that he be the worshipped divinity. So how can it be possible when he himself is not the knowledge and speech of God, but rather is created by God's speech when He said to him 'Be!' and he was?[23]

This long history of Christian appeal to Q 4:171 to support the Trinity demonstrates a certain tenacity among Middle Eastern Christians in believing that appeal to a qur'anic text would convince Muslims that the oneness of God held to be central to the message of the Qur'an could in fact encompass a threefold revelation of Father, Son and Holy Spirit. However, Muslims responded by challenging Christians on the essential nature of the Trinity by arguing that Jesus never claimed to be divine.

Muslim appeal to the Gospels to deny the Trinity

While Christians were looking for the Trinity in the Qur'an during the 8th century, some Muslims responded by noticing that the Gospels of the Christians did not speak the same language as the creed that the Christians followed. The earliest extant example is a letter written in 796 for Caliph Hārūn al-Rashīd (r. 786-809) addressed to the Byzantine Emperor Constantine VI (r. 790-7) by Abū l-Rabīʿ ibn al-Layth, who 'claims that Christians have fallen victim to wrong interpretations of their scripture [...] Jesus calls God "our father" in the presence of the disciples, indicating that his own relation to God is comparable to theirs'.[24] This use of the Gospels to play down the divine status Christians claimed for Jesus was repeated in the earliest known refutation of Christianity by a Muslim, written by the Zaydī imam al-Qāsim ibn Ibrāhīm (d. 860), possibly after debating with Christians in Egypt during a stay between 815 and 826.[25]

---

[22] Ebied and Thomas, 'Al-Dimashqī's response', p. 317.

[23] Ibn Taymiyya, 'The correct answer to those who have changed the religion of Christ, *Al-jawāb al-ṣaḥīḥ li-man baddala dīn al-Masīḥ*', in T.F. Michel (trans.), *A Muslim theologian's response to Christianity. Ibn Taymiyya's* al-Jawab al-sahih, New York, 1984, 1-369, p. 269.

[24] B. Roggema, 'The Letter of Abū l-Rabīʿ Muḥammad ibn al-Layth which he wrote for al-Rashīd to the Byzantine Emperor Constantine', in *CMR* 1, 349-53.

[25] W. Madelung, 'Al-Qāsim ibn Ibrāhīm', in *CMR* 1, 540-3.

Al-Qāsim ibn Ibrāhīm quotes from the Qur'an verses that criticise those who associate with God other persons worthy of worship, especially Q 112:1-4: 'Say, He is God the One, God the Eternal, who does not beget and is not begotten, and there is none like Him.' Then he challenges Christians to pay heed to them: 'Whoever talks about God having a son, all those who associate anyone with God, among Jews, Christians, and any other people, should listen to God's clear arguments against them concerning this.'[26]

Al-Qāsim urges Christians to read their Gospels correctly rather than interpret them from the vantage point of more developed beliefs about there being one God in the form of Father, Son and Holy Spirit. On the contrary, the Gospels show that: 'The testimony of Christ to his disciples was that they were all sons of the Father. If God was the Father of all of them then it demonstrates that the interpretation of fatherhood and sonship is not what you Christians say in your teaching.'[27] Christians should consider the word of the angels to Mary: 'You will give birth to a son.' They did not say: 'You will give birth to the Son of God.'[28] Al-Qāsim reports the Sermon on the Mount from Matthew 5-7 but, when he quotes the Lord's Prayer, he changes 'Our Father' to 'Our Lord'.[29] His rather ambivalent attitude to quotation reflects an unease with the data in the Gospels. For example, he notes that Christians 'claim that God said in their Gospels about the Messiah, son of Mary, "This is my beloved son I have chosen" [sic], and Simon Peter said, "You are truly the Son of God."'[30] However, he goes on to suggest that this sonship is akin to people who adopt a child that is not physically generated from them, yet they love him as their son. 'This distinction is well known among them [the Christians] both in recent and ancient times. The wise among them recognise this.'[31] Al-Qāsim can then call on Christians to interpret fatherhood and sonship 'according to the way the Gospels present them'.[32]

Similar arguments can be found in the *Radd ʿalā l-Naṣārā* ('Refutation of the Christians') written in the mid-9th century by ʿAlī ibn Rabban al-Ṭabarī (d. c. 860), who says he was a Christian for the first 70 years of

26 Al-Qāsim ibn Ibrāhīm, 'Refutation of the Christians', ed. I. di Matteo, 'Confutazione contro i Cristiani dello zaydita al-Qāsim b. Ibrāhīm', *Rivista degli Studi Orientali* 9 (1921-2) 301-64, p. 310.

27 Al-Qāsim ibn Ibrāhīm, 'Refutation', p. 321.

28 Al-Qāsim ibn Ibrāhīm, 'Refutation', p. 322.

29 Al-Qāsim ibn Ibrāhīm, 'Refutation', p. 328.

30 Al-Qāsim ibn Ibrāhīm, 'Refutation', p. 322.

31 Al-Qāsim ibn Ibrāhīm, 'Refutation', p. 323.

32 Al-Qāsim ibn Ibrāhīm, 'Refutation', p. 324.

his life before he became a Muslim. He argues that Christians have forsaken the metaphorical sense of Jesus' language by attributing a literal meaning to the term 'father'. When Jesus called God his 'father', he was thinking of the relationship people have with the elders of their family.[33] However, the Christian creed says that Jesus is equal to the Father in a way that Jesus never claimed.

> Why is the Father called Father and the Son, Son? For if the term 'fatherhood' is required for the Father because of his eternity, then the Son too would merit this very term because he is eternal like him [...] For what superiority and power does the Father have over him, to command him and prohibit him, for the Father to be the sender and the Son the one sent, and the Father the one followed and obeyed and the Son the one following and obeying?[34]

Christians should return to the real meaning of Jesus' teaching in the Gospels, as al-Ṭabarī himself has done.

The rationalist theologian from Baghdad, al-Nāshi' al-Akbar (d. 904), blames Greek philosophical thinking for the change in Christian interpretation of the language of Jesus, who thought of his relationship to God in figurative terms.

> As for those who take refuge in the literal meaning of the Gospel, they hold only to the teachings narrated in the Gospel from Christ, who said: 'Consecrate people in the name of the Father and the Son and the Holy Spirit.' Here, there is no indication that they are eternal or temporal or that they are one substance or otherwise, nor in the Gospel is there any utterance which suggests substance or hypostases. Such utterances are philosophical, Greek; they passed down to the people, and they employed them in their discussions.[35]

If only Christians had not been misled by philosophy they would have been faithful to Jesus' own understanding of his relationship to God as a subordinate servant. Jesus included his disciples as sons of God and did not think of himself as the eternal Son uniquely equal to the Father. Indeed, 'Jesus is recorded in the Gospel as saying, "I am going to my Father and your Father, to my Lord and your Lord", associating himself

---

33 ʿAlī ibn Rabban al-Ṭabarī, *Refutation of the Christians*, in R. Ebied and D. Thomas (ed. and trans.), *The polemical works of ʿAlī al-Ṭabarī*, Leiden, 2016, 84-163, pp. 154-5.

34 ʿAlī ibn Rabban al-Ṭabarī, *Refutation*, pp. 158-61.

35 Al-Nāshi' al-Akbar, 'Refutation of the Christians', in D. Thomas (ed. and trans.), *Christian doctrines in Islamic theology*, Leiden, 2008, 35-77, p. 59.

jointly with them in both instances'.[36] Therefore, Christians must interpret Christ's reference to Father, Son and Holy Spirit in Matthew 28:19 in line with his assertion (John 20:17) that he was going to his Father and the Father of his followers.

Martin Accad has pointed out that this verse, John 20:17, is 'the most extensively used Gospel verse in the whole Islamic exegetical discourse of the second/eighth to the eighth/fourteenth centuries'.[37] He shows that, by the time Ibn Qayyim al-Jawziyya (d. 1350) cited the verse, he was repeating a standard Muslim view that Jesus regarded himself merely as a servant of God and that, by inviting his disciples also to call God 'Father', he was indicating that his sonship was not unique to him but could be shared by those who had faith in God. If Christians insist on isolating the sonship of Jesus as a mark of Jesus' divine status, they must reckon with John 20:17. 'In this case make yourselves all gods, for in another place he [Jesus] called him [God] "his Father and their Father", as in what he said: "I go to my Father and your Father".'[38]

The Christian response to this use of Gospel texts to deny the Trinity by playing down the divine status of Jesus was to assert the difference between the sonship of Jesus and that of his followers. Ḥabīb ibn Khidma Abū Rā'iṭa (d. c. 830), a West Syrian theologian from Takrit, addresses Muslim quotations from the Gospels in his *Letter on the Incarnation* (*fī l-tajassud*). He notices that John's Gospel includes sayings by Jesus that Muslims have used to argue that Jesus did not claim to be God, especially John 14:28: 'The Father is greater than I', and John 20:17: 'I am returning to my Father and your Father, to my God and your God.' Then he goes on to list other sayings of Jesus from John's Gospel that unmistakably uphold Jesus' claim to divinity.

He whom you describe as saying: 'I am going up to my Father and your Father, to my God and your God' [...] is he who said: 'The one who sees me sees my Father' [John 14:9], 'I am in my Father, and my Father is in me' [John 10:38], and 'I and my Father are one' [John 10:30] [...] and that

[36] Al-Nāshi' al-Akbar, 'Refutation', pp. 59-61.

[37] M. Accad, 'The ultimate proof-text. The interpretation of John 20:17 in Muslim-Christian dialogue (second/eighth-eighth/fourteenth centuries)', in D. Thomas (ed.), *Christians at the heart of Islamic rule*, Leiden, 2003, 199-214, p. 200.

[38] Ibn Qayyim al-Jawziyya, *Guidance concerning the incoherence of the answers of the Jews and Christians,* Hidāyat al-ḥayārā fī ajwibat al-Yahūd wa-l-Naṣārā, ed. A.Ḥ. al-Saqā, Cairo, 1980, p. 280, quoted in Accad, 'The ultimate proof-text', p. 208.

he always was, before Abraham existed [John 8:58], and other sublime statements that point to his divinity.[39]

Būlus al-Rāhib, a 12th-century Melkite bishop of Sidon, in his *Risāla fī l-firaq al-mutaʿārifa min al-Naṣārā* ('Letter concerning common differences of the Christians') interprets Jesus' statement in John 20:17 to mean that Jesus differentiates himself from his followers because of his divine status. He is the eternal Son of God but they can become sons of God by adoption. Accad indicates that Būlus uses a traditional Christian understanding of two kinds of sonship inherited from the Syriac tradition that had been established long before the advent of Islam, when he speaks 'of the "natural" sonship of Christ versus the disciples' sonship "by grace"'.[40]

Muslim appeal to the Christian Gospels to prove that Jesus did not claim to be equal to God, but rather taught that he was a subordinate servant of God and that his relationship to God as a son to a father could be experienced by his followers, became a standard argument against the theologising of the Christians. The Trinity was merely a later development that detracted from the message that Jesus himself brought. Christian reaction to this approach depended on stressing the uniqueness of Jesus' sonship, and holding that statements made by Jesus in the fourth Gospel truly indicated his equality with God. But Muslim thinkers were concentrating on the way to define the unity of God, and Christians who dialogued with Muslims had to join their discussion of the attributes of God in order to argue that God's attributes of fatherhood, sonship and spirit were essential to his being.

Islamic *kalām* and Eastern Christian theology on the attributes of God

By the end of the 8th century, Muslim thought about God had become concerned with defining epithets applied to God in the Qur'an, such as Almighty, All-seeing, and Wise. Discussion among practitioners of *kalām* centred on how these attributes related to the unity of God, and debate with Christians centred concomitantly on how confession of a Trinity could possibly accord with the absolute oneness of God. Christian

[39] Abū Rā'iṭa, 'Letter on the Incarnation', in S.T. Keating (ed. and trans.), *Defending the 'People of truth' in the early Islamic period. The Christian apologies of Abū Rā'iṭah*, Leiden, 2006, 268-71.

[40] Būlus al-Rāhib, 'Risāla fī l-firaq al-mutaʿārifa min al-Naṣārā', in L. Cheikho (ed.), *Vingt traités philosophiques et apologetiques d'auteurs arabes chrétiens* (*IX-XIII siècles*), Beirut, 1920, 19-38, p. 33, quoted in Accad, 'Ultimate proof-text', p. 212.

theologians responded by distinguishing between essential and non-essential attributes, and argued that God's Word and Spirit, as essential attributes, did not undermine the unity of God when revealed as the Son and the Spirit.

Three theologians from the three main denominations in the Middle East, the Chalcedonian Theodore Abū Qurra (d. after 816), the West Syrian Ḥabīb ibn Khidma Abū Rā'iṭa (d. c. 830) and the East Syrian 'Ammār al-Baṣrī (d. c. 850), all writing in Arabic, led the attempt to explain the Trinity to Muslim *mutakallimūn*. Abū Qurra and 'Ammār al-Baṣrī received written responses from leading Muslim thinkers: 'Īsā ibn Sabīh al-Murdār (d. 840) wrote a refutation entitled *Against Abū Qurra the Christian* and, according to the *Fihrist* of Ibn al-Nadīm Abū l-Hudhayl al-'Allāf (d. c. 840), wrote a 'Refutation of 'Ammār the Christian in his reply to the Christians'.[41] Unfortunately, neither of these Muslim refutations is extant, but the fact that they were known to Ibn al-Nadīm in the late 10th century suggests that Christian apologists were making an impact on their intended readership.

Abū Qurra begins his defence of the Trinity by stating that 'the one who negates Christian teaching' objects to the Trinity because their 'reason is confused by the Christian claims that the Father, the Son and the Holy Spirit are three hypostases (*aqānīm*) in one God (*ilāh wāḥid*), and that each of the hypostases is perfect God in himself'.[42] For the negators, reason dictates that either none of the hypostases is a god or each one of them is a god. He makes an analogy between the human names Peter, Paul and John and the hypostases (*aqānīm*), arguing that, just as these names refer to persons (*wujūh*) who share the one human nature (*ṭabī'a*), so the three hypostases share the one divine nature. Here, Abū Qurra employs the term *wajh* (pl. *wujūh*) to translate the Greek term *prosōpon*, which was a synonym for *hypostasis* in Greek theology.[43] According to Abū Qurra, there are 'three Persons (*wujūh*), one God [...] because the term "person" (*wajh*) is attributed to the Father, the Son and the Holy Spirit'.[44] But he recognises that the analogy with three men must not lead to the supposition that the Father, Son and Holy Spirit are separated

41 See B. Dodge (trans.), *The Fihrist of al-Nadīm, a tenth century survey of Muslim culture*, New York, 1970, pp. 388, 394.

42 Abū Qurra, 'Treatise on the Trinity', in C. Bacha (ed.), *Les oeuvres arabes de Theodore Aboucara*, Beirut, 1904, 23-47, p. 27. See also the English translation of the treatise in J.C. Lamoreaux, *Theodore Abu Qurrah*, Provo UT, 2005, pp. 175-93.

43 See R. Haddad, *La Trinité divine chez les théologiens arabes 750-1050*, Paris, 1985, p. 172.

44 Abū Qurra, 'Treatise on the Trinity', p. 34.

or differentiated, since they would then be three divine beings rather than one divine being.[45]

He refers to the divine nature in various ways. The three Persons (*wujūh*) share the same non-physical nature (*laṭāfa*).[46] Therefore, all of them share the same essence (*dhāt*).[47] The three Persons share the same oneness of divinity (*wāḥidiyyat al-lāhūt*),[48] and the same nature (*ṭabīʿa*).[49] Najib Awad has argued that Abū Qurra uses the term *wajh* 'to explain to Muslims the uniqueness of the Person of the Father (as well as that of the Son and the Spirit) that makes him alone Father (as it makes the Son alone "Son" and the "Spirit" alone "Holy Spirit") in the Trinity, without this *wajh* conveying the sense of a separate nature or an additional deity'.[50]

Abū Rāʾiṭa's *Letter on the Trinity* (*fi l-thālūth*) offers guidance in answering Muslim questions about Christian beliefs from someone who had experience of debate with Muslim intellectuals.[51] Abū Rāʾiṭa says he will try to answer the objection of 'the People of the south' that, since God is one, we Christians are wrong to teach the threeness (*tathlīth*) of God along with his oneness (*tawḥid*).[52] He proposes that 'the People of truth' agree with 'the People of the south' that God is one, but they should ask them what kind of oneness they mean. Do they mean one as genus (*jins*), one as species (*nawʿ*) or one as number (*ʿadad*)?[53] Sandra Keating has noted that these are distinctions drawn from Aristotle that Abū Rāʾiṭa clearly thinks will be decisive for his argument with Muslim opponents, who were reading Aristotle in Arabic translations made by Christian translators, and suggests that, among Christian apologists, 'He is one of the first to build his argument using principles of logic and elements drawn from Greek thought.'[54]

If 'genus' is meant, then God encompasses various species, which is not possible for the Creator of all species. If 'number' is meant, then God is subject to division since the number one is a species of number which

45 Abū Qurra, 'Treatise on the Trinity', p. 35.
46 Abū Qurra, 'Treatise on the Trinity', p. 38.
47 Abū Qurra, 'Treatise on the Trinity', p. 39.
48 Abū Qurra, 'Treatise on the Trinity', p. 37.
49 Abū Qurra, 'Treatise on the Trinity', pp. 39, 44.
50 N.G. Awad, *Orthodoxy in Arabic terms. A study of Theodore Abu Qurrah's theology in its Islamic context*, Berlin, 2015, p. 234.
51 Abū Rāʾiṭa, 'The first letter on the Holy Trinity', in Keating, *Defending the 'People of truth'*, 164-215, pp. 166-7.
52 Abū Rāʾiṭa, 'First letter on the Holy Trinity', pp. 168-9.
53 Abū Rāʾiṭa, 'First letter on the Holy Trinity', pp. 170-3.
54 Keating, *Defending the 'People of truth'*, p. 157.

is included in the perfection of number, and this contradicts the belief that God is perfect without being divided into parts. If 'species' is meant, then God is comprised of different beings and this is unacceptable.[55] According to Abū Rā'iṭa, the Christian should bring clarity to the debate by stating that 'We describe Him as "one" perfect in essence (*jawhar*) and not in number, because He is in number "three" in the hypostases (*aqānīm*)'. This is a perfect description of God because, first, it upholds His complete difference from His creation in his essence so that nothing can be compared with Him; and, second, it upholds His encompassing all of the species of number, even and odd, in His hypostases.[56]

Keating points out a second reliance on Aristotle in Abū Rā'iṭa's discussion of the attributes of God such as 'living', 'knowing', 'hearing' and 'seeing', which Muslims presume that Christians believe in as well.[57] He asks the Muslim, 'Are they single, absolute names or predicative names?' Single or absolute names are not predicated of anything such as 'earth' or 'fire', whereas predicated names are related to something else such as 'knower' and 'knowledge', because the knower knows through knowledge, a differentiation that derives from Aristotle. If a Muslim understands 'living' and 'knowing' as acquired by God as predicates of action, then he must describe God as Creator only after He created. But if he thinks of them as belonging to God eternally, then he must describe God as eternally creating. Sidney Griffith demonstrates that these were the very issues debated among the *mutakallimūn*, who distinguished between 'attributes of the essence' (*ṣifāt al-dhāt*) and 'attributes of action' (*ṣifāt al-fi'l*).[58] Abū Rā'iṭa goes on to argue that life and knowledge must be eternal in God because there cannot be a time when God does not have life and knowledge.[59] If the Muslim asks why there are only three hypostases and not ten or twelve, then the answer should be that 'God possesses knowledge and spirit, and the knowledge of God and His spirit are permanent and perpetual, not ceasing. For it is not permitted in a description of God for Him in His eternity to be without knowledge and spirit'.[60]

---

55 Abū Rā'iṭa, 'First letter on the Holy Trinity', pp. 172-3.

56 Abū Rā'iṭa, 'First letter on the Holy Trinity', pp. 174-5.

57 Abū Rā'iṭa, 'First letter on the Holy Trinity', pp. 176-7.

58 See S.H. Griffith, 'Ḥabīb ibn Ḫidmah Abū Rā'iṭah, a Christian *mutakallim* of the first Abbasid century', *Oriens Christianus* 64 (1980) 161-201, p. 182.

59 Abū Rā'iṭa, 'First letter on the Holy Trinity', pp. 182-5.

60 Abū Rā'iṭa, 'First letter on the Holy Trinity', pp. 196-7.

ʿAmmār al-Baṣrī wrote two defences of the Trinity, a longer one as part of *Kitāb al-masāʾil wa-l-ajwiba* ('The book of questions and answers'), and a shorter one as a section in his *Kitāb al-burhān* ('Book of the proof'). Since Abū l-Hudhayl wrote a (now lost) work entitled *Kitāb ʿalā ʿAmmār al-Naṣrānī fī l-radd ʿalā l-Naṣārā* ('Refutation of ʿAmmār the Christian in reply to the Christians'), it is probable, as Sidney Griffith argues, that ʿAmmār was attempting to answer this leading Muʿtazilī thinker.[61] The longer presentation is a series of answers to nine questions posed by a Muslim about the Trinity, and these may well be the kind of questions raised by Abū l-Hudhayl in his refutation of ʿAmmār.

The first question is 'Since the Creator is one, how can one be three and three one?'[62] The answer is that there is one eternal substance (*jawhar*) in three essential properties (*khawāṣṣ jawhariyyāt*) that are not differentiated or separated. The Creator lives and speaks, so 'life' and 'speech' can be attributed to Him: 'The principal substance (*jawhar al-ʿayn*) has the attributions of His life and His speech; His speech is the source of His wisdom and His life is the source of His spirit.'[63] A second question concerns the outcome of these attributions to the Creator: they appear to establish His existence first, then his life second, and His wisdom third, and so He is counted as three, divided and partitioned. ʿAmmār replies that God is not a body so He cannot be divided or partitioned.[64] If the opponents suggest that God's attributes such as 'hearing', 'seeing' and 'almighty' mean that Christians cannot limit God to threeness, then they need to distinguish between God's names (*asmāʾ*) and His attributes (*ṣifāt*). The names refer to actions of God, whereas the attributes refer to properties essential to Him. Only 'life' and 'speech' are essential properties in God.[65]

ʿAmmār has chosen to begin on ground familiar to Muslim theologians, who, at the time, he wrote were attempting to determine whether the names of God referred to actions of God. Abū l-Hudhayl is reported to have denied that the names referred to actions of God. While it is

---

[61] See S.H. Griffith, 'The concept of *al-uqnūm* in ʿAmmār al-Baṣrī's Apology for the doctrine of the Trinity', in K. Samir (ed.), *Actes du premier congrès international d'études arabes chrétiennes*, Rome, 1982, 169-91, pp. 180-1; and S.H. Griffith, "Ammār al-Baṣrī's *Kitāb al-burhān*. Christian Kalām in the first Abbasid century', *Le Museon* 96 (1983) 145-181, pp. 169-72.

[62] ʿAmmār al-Baṣrī, *Kitāb al-masāʾil wa-l-ajwiba*, in M. Hayek (ed.), *ʿAmmār al-Baṣrī. Apologie et controverses*, Beirut, 1977, 92-265, p. 148.

[63] al-Baṣrī, *Kitāb al-masāʾil wa-l-ajwiba*, p. 149.

[64] al-Baṣrī, *Kitāb al-masāʾil wa-l-ajwiba*, p. 154.

[65] al-Baṣrī, *Kitāb al-masāʾil wa-l-ajwiba*, pp. 156-7.

acceptable for created human beings to be described as performing an act of knowing by virtue of which they can be said to be knowing, it is necessary to interpret the statement 'God is knowing' as 'there is an act of knowing that is God' and 'there is an object that he knows'.[66] Abū al-Hudhayl was concerned to defend God's unity (*tawḥīd*) by denying that there is an entity called 'knowledge' that can be identified in God. In his argument, ʿAmmār is tackling this reticence head on by isolating life and speech as inherent qualities in God as distinct from actions, which are not.

The fourth of these nine questions is, 'Why do you call these three properties three individuals (*ashkhāṣ*), even though you lead the hearers of your teaching to believe that you reject three gods?' The answer is that ʿAmmār does not call them individuals (*ashkhāṣ*), since that term applies only to beings with physical bodies. Rather, he calls them by the Syriac term *aqānīm*. In order to explain the meaning of this term, he appeals to the categories of Aristotle, 'substance' (*jawhar*), 'power' (*quwa*) and 'accident' (*ʿaraḍ*), and then he adds 'hypostasis' (*qunūm*) to them. Of these, 'substance' and 'hypostasis' are alike in that they exist without depending on anything else, whereas 'power' and 'accident' depend on something other than themselves for their existence.[67] In her analysis of the Trinitarian defences of Abū Qurra, Abū Rāʾiṭa and ʿAmmār al-Baṣrī, Sara Husseini has shown that ʿAmmār 'displays the deepest engagement with Islamic thought of the three authors'. He is the only one to 'really question a Muʿtazilī conception of the nature of God'.[68]

A Muslim response to arguments such as these can be found in the very detailed *Radd ʿalā l-tathlīth* ('Refutation of the Trinity') by the little-known scholar Abū ʿĪsā al-Warrāq (d. after c. 860). He reports that Christians agree over the definition of the Trinity as 'one substance (*jawhar*), three hypostases (*aqānīm*)', and that the three hypostases are Father, Son and Spirit.[69] They have different terms for the hypostases, such as 'properties' (*khawāṣṣ*), 'individuals' (*ashkhāṣ*), and 'attributes' (*ṣifāt*), yet, 'despite their differences over explanation and terminology they keep

---

66 See R.M. Frank, *Beings and their attributes. The teaching of the Basrian school of the Muʿtazila in the classical period*, Albany NY, 1978, p. 12.

67 Frank, *Beings and their attributes*, pp. 161-3.

68 S.L. Husseini, *Early Christian-Muslim debate on the unity of God. Three Christian scholars and their engagement with Islamic thought*, Leiden, 2014, p. 200.

69 Abū ʿĪsā l-Warrāq, 'Refutation of the Trinity. The first part of the Refutation of the three Christian sects', in D. Thomas (ed. and trans.), *Anti-Christian polemic in early Islam*, Cambridge, 1992, 66-181, pp. 66-7.

more or less the same meaning, as they themselves admit'.[70] He goes on to subject the language of the Trinity to a sustained assault based on the presupposition that God must be one, and that the definition of oneness necessarily excludes threeness.

He develops an argument which mirrors that of John of Damascus and his successors, that God's Word and Spirit are eternally of God, by showing the Christians that, if the three hypostases are equivalent to the substance, then the threeness of the hypostases must attach to the one substance. 'Every number attaching to the properties will attach to the substantiality (*jawhariyya*).'[71] Christians end up having to admit three substantialities rather than one and thus the Trinity is negated. The same applies to the concept of divinity. If Christians claim that Father, Son and Holy Spirit are divine, they are asserting that there are three divinities that must share the one divine substance, and the result is that there must be two definitions of divinity, one for the substance and the other for the hypostases.[72] This principle also applies to the characteristics of the three hypostases. If Fatherhood is essential to the Father and not the Son, then the Son lacks an essential quality and so is less than God in his substance. If fatherhood and sonship are eternal qualities, they must be attributed to both, so that the Son must be Father alongside the Father.[73]

Abū ʿĪsā does not usually refer to individual Christian writers but prefers to speak about the teaching of the three main Christian communities of his time, but he says that 'one Trinitarian theologian (*mutakallim*) has presented arguments in support of the substance (*jawhar*) and the hypostases (*aqānīm*), that the one he worships lives eternally by "life" and speaks eternally by "speech", and that life and speech are two properties (*khāṣṣatān*) which confer perfection on His substance'.[74] This choice of life and speech as the essential properties of God reflects ʿAmmār al-Baṣrī's way of writing among the theologians examined above, and it may be that he is the unnamed Christian *mutakallim* here. Abū ʿĪsā counters this by examining the substance (*jawhar*) in this presentation. In essence, he argues that if the substance is specified by 'life', then the definition of any substance in the created world must also be specified by 'life' and even stones would have to be specified as 'living', which is absurd. But if the substance is specified by 'life' by virtue of a cause (*ʿilla*)

70 al-Warrāq, 'Refutation of the Trinity', pp. 68-9.
71 al-Warrāq, 'Refutation of the Trinity', pp. 78-9.
72 al-Warrāq, 'Refutation of the Trinity', pp. 112-13.
73 al-Warrāq, 'Refutation of the Trinity', pp. 126-9.
74 al-Warrāq, 'Refutation of the Trinity', pp. 130-1.

which is other than the substance, then an eternal cause other than the substance and the hypostases has been established, and this falsifies the argument.

He finds the appeal to the generation of a word from the intellect, light from the sun, and heat from a fire as analogies for the generation of the Son from the Father to be useless to support the Christian case for the Trinity. No matter whether Christians intend to compare the generation of the Son by the Father directly or only approximately with these other types of generation, the Christians cannot escape from ascribing to the eternal Father the same status as a created being or object.[75] Like other Muslim rationalist thinkers, Abū ʿĪsā rejected analogies from the created and temporal world for the uncreated and eternal God, since there is nothing like Him (Q 112:4). The problem with Christians is precisely that they think it appropriate to compare God with what resembles Him, with the result that 'they are openly introducing anthropomorphism (*tashbīh*), and they do not remove anthropomorphism from their teaching'.[76] David Thomas comments that the *Radd* 'is the longest and most detailed Muslim attack devoted to the two major Christian doctrines that has survived, and the longest extant pre-14th century anti-Christian polemic', and he notes: 'Descriptive accounts and arguments from it influenced anti-Christian polemic for more than a century after its appearance.'[77]

A later example of rejection of the Trinity comes from the judge and Ashʿarī theologian Abū Bakr al-Bāqillāni (d. 1014), who repeats many of the arguments of Abū ʿĪsā al-Warrāq. He denies the distinction between attributes essential to God such as life and knowledge, and other attributes that Christians claim are not essential to Him. 'We say that the eternal One is existent, living, knowing and powerful, and one who is powerful must obviously have power. So it necessarily follows that the hypostases are four.'[78] The same point can be made about any of the attributes of God, such as 'willing, everlasting, hearing, seeing, articulating. And the everlasting, seeing, articulating, willing One cannot thus be without the existence of everlastingness, will, hearing, sight and speech.'[79]

---

75 al-Warrāq, 'Refutation of the Trinity', pp. 166-71.

76 al-Warrāq, 'Refutation of the Trinity', pp. 168-9.

77 D. Thomas, '*Al-radd ʿalā l-thalāth firaq min al-Naṣārā* (longer version)', in *CMR* 1, 698-9.

78 Al-Bāqillānī, 'Refutation of the Christians from the Book of the introduction', in D. Thomas, (ed. and trans.), *Christian doctrines in Islamic theology*, Leiden, 2008, pp. 152-3.

79 Al-Bāqillānī, 'Refutation', pp. 154-5.

Such incredulity at Christian limitation of certain attributes as essential to God became a typical argument in subsequent Muslim rejections of the Trinity.

The West Syrian Christian Yaḥyā ibn ʿAdī (d. 974) had a profound impact upon later Christian understanding of the Trinity. As well as being an outstanding philosopher who engaged in debate with Muslims on the basis of Aristotelian premises, he wrote a point by point refutation of Abū ʿĪsā l-Warrāq's refutation of the Trinity (and of the same writer's refutation of the Incarnation). Emilio Platti summarises his defence of the Trinity within the unity of God as follows:

> The constituent attributes (*ṣifāt*) of the First Cause are evident from the effects (*āthār*) of his activity, while the substance itself remains hidden. What is to be attributed in this way to the Creator are bounty (*jūd*), wisdom (*ḥikma*), and power (*qudra*); and these three attributes are necessary (*yuḍṭarru ilayhā*), but also sufficient (*yustaghnā bihā*).[80]

However, while he retained this articulation of the essential attributes as bounty, wisdom and power, Ibn ʿAdī also developed a new view of the Trinity in his work against al-Warrāq. The relationships within the Trinity are now *al-ʿaql* (intellect), *al-ʿāqil* (the intelligent one) and *al-maʿqūl* (intellection), which Platti points out 'is likely to be more suitable to his way of thinking'.[81]

This more psychological analogy for the Trinity became popular among Christian theologians. Julian Faultless notes that the Nestorian Ibn al-Ṭayyib (d. c. 1043), in his treatise on the Trinity, modifies it to *ʿilm* (knowledge), *ʿālim* (knowing) and *maʿlūm* (known).[82] He defends these attributes as essential rather than contingent, and even though he does not mention Islam he evidently seeks to defend the unity of God 'from the common Muslim accusation that Christians were tritheists'.[83] A later West Syrian theologian actually used Yaḥyā ibn ʿAdī's *ʿaql, ʿāqil* and *maʿqūl* in the title of his treatise on the Trinity. Muḥyī l-Dīn al-ʿAjamī l-Iṣfahānī (fl. 12th century) wrote for what Herman Teule believes would

[80] E. Platti, 'Treatise on the Unity (of God)', in *CMR* 2, 123-4.

[81] E. Platti, 'Demonstration of the error of Muḥammad ibn Hārūn known as Abū ʿĪsā l-Warrāq in what he mentioned in his book "Refutation of the three Christian denominations"', in *CMR* 2, 413-15.

[82] J. Faultless, '*Maqāla fī l-tathlīth*, Treatise on the Trinity', in *CMR* 2, 690-1.

[83] Faultless, 'Treatise on the Trinity', p. 691.

have been a Muslim reader[84] *Kalām fī l-ʿaql wa-l-ʿāqil wa-l-maʿqūl* ('Discussion on intellect, the intelligent one, and intellection').

Ibn ʿAdī's conceptualisation of the Trinity was adopted by Egyptian Coptic theologians as well. The Egyptian Muslim author of *Al-radd al-jamīl li-ilāhiyyat ʿĪsā bi-ṣarīḥ al-Injīl* ('The fitting refutation of the divinity of Jesus'), written probably in the 12th century and often ascribed to al-Ghazālī (d. 1111), refers to Christians holding the view that the Father is pure intellect (*ʿaql*), the Son is the intelligent one (*ʿāqil*), and the Holy Spirit is the status of intellection (*maʿqūl*).[85] Intriguingly, he uses this definition of the Trinity to argue that the word of God in the Gospel of John 1:1 does not refer to Jesus of Nazareth but rather to God Himself. When the writer of the Gospel of John said, 'In the beginning was the Word',

> He meant, in the beginning was the knowledgeable one, and when he said, 'And the word was with God', his meaning was, the knowledgeable one is eternally an attribute of God [...] When he said, 'And God was the word', his meaning was, this word that indicates the knowledgeable one, this knowledgeable one is God [...] to counter the supposition of those who claim that the knowledgeable one, who is indicated by 'the word', is other than God [...] The beginning of this chapter shows no indication at all of the divinity of Jesus, on him be peace.[86]

Thus, the psychological analogy for the Trinity is turned against the normal interpretation of the opening section of the fourth Gospel. The Word is not equated with Jesus, despite the long Christian tradition of believing that John did indeed make this identification.

Another analogy for the Trinity made by Yaḥyā ibn ʿAdī was taken up by Ibn Taymiyya in the 14th century, when he quoted Yaḥyā ibn ʿAdī's comparison of the essential attributes of the Trinity with the essential properties of the human being Zayd, who is at one and the same time a doctor, an accountant and a writer.[87] Platti comments that this analogy is 'used over and over again in Yaḥyā's refutation of Abū ʿĪsā'.[88] Ibn Taymiyya rejects the psychological paradigm in describing God, arguing that it is absurd to view God as an amalgam of three kinds of activity:

---

84 H.G.B. Teule, '*Kalām fī l-ʿaql wa-l-ʿāqil wa-l-maʿqūl*, Discourse on the intellect, the intelligent one, and the intellection', in *CMR* 3, 757-8.

85 Beaumont and El Kaisy-Friemuth, *Al-radd al-jamīl*, pp. 158-9.

86 Beaumont and El Kaisy-Friemuth, *Al-radd al-jamīl*, pp. 160-1.

87 Ibn Taymiyya, *Al-jawāb al-ṣaḥīḥ* in Michel, *A Muslim theologian's response*, p. 271.

88 Platti, 'Demonstration of the error of Muḥammad ibn Hārūn', pp. 413-14.

> There is no defense for your saying, as do Yahya ibn ʿAdi and others like him, that this is the same as saying 'Zayd the doctor, the accountant, the writer' [...] Zayd here is one substance having three attributes of medicine, accounting, and writing. These are not three substances here, but each attribute offers a definition which the other does not.[89]

Christian appeals to the difference between essential and contingent attributes of God were regarded by Muslims as rather arbitrary. Muslims argued that the separation of word and spirit as essential to God over against other attributes was not acceptable. They suspected that Christians only made this case because they had already decided that God was to be defined as Father, Son and Holy Spirit. From the Muslim point of view, none of the attributes of God could be understood to be preferred over others. There was no logical case for the Trinity, but rather all the logic lay with the absolute unity of God. When Western Christians came to write about the Trinity in the light of Islamic convictions about God, they understood that Muslims rejected the rationality of the Trinity.

Western Christian theologians and the One God of Islam

Medieval Christians in the West began to take the Islamic view of God seriously from the 13th century onwards, after the Dominican and Franciscan orders started missionary work among Muslim communities. For example, Thomas Aquinas (d. 1274), the outstanding Dominican theologian, was asked to write a treatise to help with such mission by the Dominican leader Ramon de Penyafort (d. c.1275) who had established training schools in Arabic for missionaries around 1245 in Tunis and in Murcia in Spain. In his four-volume *Summa contra gentiles*, written between 1259 and 1264, he recognises that Muslims cannot be approached using scripture, but that reason also has limitations.

> The Mohammedans and the pagans, do not agree with us in accepting the authority of any scripture, by which they may be convinced of their error. Thus, against the Jews we are able to argue by means of the Old Testament, while against heretics we are able to argue by means of the New Testament. But the Mohammedans and the pagans accept neither the one nor the other. We must, therefore, have recourse to natural reason, to which all

[89] Ibn Taymiyya, *Al-jawāb al-ṣaḥīḥ* in Michel, *A Muslim theologian's response*, p. 271.

> men are forced to give their assent. However, it is true, in divine matters natural reason has its failings.[90]

The limitations of reason relate to discussing the Trinity, which is based on Revelation. 'Since natural reason ascends to a knowledge of God through creatures and, conversely, the knowledge of faith descends from God to us by a divine revelation [...] We must treat of the things about God Himself which surpass reason and are proposed for belief: such is the confession of the Trinity.'[91] In the final analysis, Thomas can only repeat Augustine's conceptualisation of the Trinity and seems unable to deal with Muslim objections: 'There is in the divine nature God unbegotten, who is the source of the whole divine proceeding, namely the Father; there is God begotten by way of a word conceived in the intellect, namely the Son; there is God by way of love proceeding, namely the Holy Spirit.'[92] Aquinas had read Muslim philosophers (though his knowledge of Islam was superficial; John Tolan writes, 'There is no evidence that he had ever seen a Latin translation of the Qur'an or that he had read any major Latin polemical text against Islam'),[93] but he had no awareness of the Eastern Christian theological tradition that had sought to hold that belief in the Trinity was rational.

Ramon Llull (d. 1316) had been attracted to the Franciscans, but ended as an independent missionary to Muslims in North Africa from his home in Majorca, where he set up a training school for missionaries to learn Arabic and Islamic thought. He is unique among missionaries of the period in his attempt to persuade Muslims of the rationality of the Trinity, as is evident from his *Llibre del gentil i dels tres savis* ('The book of the gentile and the three wise men'), written between 1274 and 1276. Its influence is shown 'not only by the number of manuscripts in which it is preserved, but also by the fact that we possess medieval translations of the work from the original Catalan into Latin, French, and Spanish'.[94] Llull structures it as a dialogue between the 'gentile', a man with no faith, and a Jew, a Christian and a Muslim.

---

90 Thomas Aquinas, *Summa contra gentiles*, 1:2, trans. A.C. Pegis, Notre Dame IN, 1975, p. 62.

91 Thomas Aquinas, *Summa contra gentiles*, 4:1, trans. C.J. O'Neil, Notre Dame IN, 1975, p. 39.

92 Aquinas, *Summa Contra Gentiles*, 4:1, p. 146.

93 John of Damascus, 'The heresy of the Ishmaelites', trans. D.J. Sahas, in *John of Damascus on Islam*, Leiden, 1972, 132-41, p. 137.

94 Ramon Llull, *The book of the gentile and the three wise men*, in A. Bonner (ed.), *Selected works of Ramon Llull (1232-1316)*, Princeton NJ, 1985, vol. 1, p. 100.

> In the first book we prove that God exists. In the second book the Jew tries to prove that his belief is better than those of the Christian and the Saracen. In the third book the Christian tries to prove that his belief is worthier than those of the Jew and the Saracen. In the fourth book the Saracen tries to prove that his belief is worthier than those of the Jew and the Christian.[95]

When the Christian presents his teachings, he uses the following argument to prove the Trinity.

> If in God there exists one begetting Good which is infinite goodness, greatness, eternity, power, wisdom, love, perfection, and which begets a Good infinite in goodness, greatness, power, wisdom, love, perfection, and if from this begetting Good and this begotten Good there issues forth a Good infinite in goodness, greatness, power, wisdom, love, perfection, then the flower is greater in God than it would be if the above-mentioned things did not exist in God [...] Therefore, the Trinity, by what we have said above, is demonstrable.[96]

This conception of the flowering of goodness through a good God begetting goodness which becomes begotten in his creation is Llull's attempt to demonstrate the logic of the Incarnation and infilling of the Spirit in humans as essential to the definition of God. However, he shows how a Muslim might respond to this when he puts into the mouth of the Muslim the following argument about the perfection of God's goodness.

> Rather, in every way He is one, without there existing in Him any Trinity or plurality. For if there did, then He would have to be compound, and His goodness, greatness, eternity, power, wisdom, love, would have to be contrary to perfection; and since this is impossible, it is therefore evident that God does not exist in Trinity.[97]

Llull does not allow the Christian to respond to this demolition of his case, but perhaps he hopes that the listening gentile will be persuaded by the power of the Christian presentation about the flowering of goodness in humanity.

Some Western Christians were impressed by the monotheism of Islam. Nicholas of Cusa (d. 1464), who wrote *Cribratio Alchorani* (Sifting the Qur'an) in 1461 at the request of Pope Pius II (r. 1458-64), held an innovative view of Muḥammad and the Qur'an.

---

95 Llull, *Book of the gentile*, p. 111.
96 Llull, *Book of the gentile*, p. 194.
97 Llull, *Book of the gentile*, pp. 259-60.

> Where the Qur'an differs from the Bible, it was the result of Muḥammad's ignorance of Christ, not of his hostility. Thus, the Qur'an's rejection of the Trinity is best understood as a refusal of polytheism and idolatry [...] Where other polemicists had seen Muḥammad to be malign and mendacious, Nicholas sees a laudable (if at times misplaced) attempt to lead infidels to true faith.[98]

Conclusion

After the arrival of Islam in the Middle East, Christians looked to the Qur'an to support their belief in the Trinity. They continued for centuries to argue that Q 4:171 supported the Trinity by declaring that God had revealed himself as having Word and Spirit. Muslims responded by pointing out that Jesus was created by God's word. They appealed to the Christian Gospels to prove that Jesus did not claim to be equal to God, or to be the second Person of the Trinity, and they noticed that Jesus taught that his relationship to God as a son to a father could be experienced by his followers. Christians tried to convince Muslims that statements made by Jesus in the fourth Gospel pointed to his equality with God.

Christians who dialogued with Muslim thinkers, who debated among themselves the status of the many divine attributes within the unity of God, argued that God's attributes of fatherhood, sonship and spirit were unlike the other attributes in alone being essential to his essence. However, their appeal to the difference between essential and contingent attributes was not acceptable to Muslims, who did not think that speech and life could be essential to God while attributes of power and justice were not. The Christian case for the Trinity failed the test of the absolute unity of God.

When late medieval Western Christians came to write about the Trinity in the light of Islamic convictions about God, they generally understood this Muslim rejection of the rationality of the Trinity. As a result, they tended to present the Trinity as a datum of revelation that could not be defended by rational argument. They were largely unaware of Middle Eastern Christian writing about Islam, which might have enabled them to develop a deeper dialogue with Muslim convictions about the unity of God.

---

98 J. Tolan, 'Cribratio Alchorani', in *CMR* 5, 425-7.

Chapter 6
Muslim perceptions of Jesus

Mourad Takawi and Gabriel Said Reynolds

Several verses of the Qur'an have God declare that He makes no distinction between the various prophets (Q 2:136, 285; 3:84). According to later Islamic teaching, the prophets are equal with regard to their message, 'paternal brothers' proclaiming one religion.[1] If any distinction is given to a particular prophet, it is to Muḥammad himself, the one who has been chosen (*al-muṣṭafā*). This is seen, for example, in the traditions associated with the ascension of Muḥammad, according to which he attains to a level of heaven beyond that of other prophets, even Abraham. Nevertheless, the Qur'an itself and later Islamic texts also recognise the distinctiveness of Jesus.

The Qur'an distinguishes Jesus among other prophets by attributing to him a conception and birth through the Spirit of God (21:91; 66:12), assigning to him titles such as Word (3:45; 4:171; cf. 3:39) and Spirit (4:171) of God, and Christ (11 times), by his miracles (some of which are said to have been achieved by the 'permission' of God), and by the mysterious end of his life and ascension into heaven (4:157-8). Moreover, Islamic tradition develops the figure of Jesus in distinct ways. Many of the later traditions associated with him are clearly exegetical in nature: they are meant to explain qur'anic allusions to his words and deeds. However, the Jesus of Islamic tradition is also closely associated with asceticism and wisdom sayings, elements that do not appear in the Qur'an. The Jesus of Islamic tradition, particularly in his apocalyptic role, is also shaped by sectarian rivalry with Christianity.

---

[1] Hammām ibn Munabbih, *Ṣaḥīfat Hammām ibn Munabbih 'an Abī Hurayra raḍī Allāh 'anhu*, ed. R.F. 'Abd al-Muṭṭalib, Cairo, 1985, p. 43, no. 134; al-Bukhārī, *K. Aḥādīth al-anbiyā'*, Damascus, 2002, 'Bāb qawl Allāh wa-dhkur fī l-kitāb Maryam idh intabadhat min ahlihā', p. 853, nos 3442 and 3443; Muslim ibn al-Ḥajjāj. *Ṣaḥīḥ Muslim*, ed. A.Ṣ. al-Karmī, Riyadh, 1998, Kitāb al-faḍā'il, 'Bāb fāḍā'il 'Isā', pp. 962-3, no. 2365. Cf. al-Ṣan'ānī, *Al-Muṣannaf*, ed. Ḥ. al-R. al-A'ẓamī, Beirut, 1983, vol. 11, 'Bāb nuzūl 'Isā b. Maryam', pp. 401-2, no. 20845.

Jesus in the Qur'an

The Qur'an refers to Jesus as 'Son of Mary', a title that affirms at once the Virgin Birth and the humanity of Christ, 23 times; *al-Masīḥ* 11 times; *rasūl* (messenger) four times (3:49; 4:157, 171; 5:75), and *nabī* (prophet) once (19:30). The Qur'an also speaks of Jesus as *min al-muqarrabīn* ('among those close to God'; 3:45), *wajīh* (high-ranking, 3:45), *mubārak* (blessed, 19:31), and *'abd allāh* ('servant of God'; 19:30 – perhaps also *qawl al-ḥaqq*, 'statement of truth', 19:34).

Although the Qur'an refers to Jesus as *al-Masīḥ*, which is cognate with Hebrew *Mashiaḥ* (cf. Greek *Christos*), the Jesus of the Qur'an is not messianic in the sense of the mighty king of Isaiah 9 or the suffering servant of Isaiah 53. As Georges Anawati notes, the historical perspective of the New Testament regarding the title 'Messiah' is not found in the Qur'an.[2] Nevertheless, the Qur'an demonstrates remarkable interest in the virgin birth of Jesus. It describes the annunciation to Mary of his birth on two different occasions. In Sūra 3 (v. 45), the Qur'an has angels (in the plural) declare to Mary, 'Surely God gives you good news of a word from Him: his name is the Messiah, Jesus, son of Mary, eminent in this world, and the hereafter, and one of those brought near.' The description of Jesus as a 'word' (*kalima*) from God (see also 3:39 and 4:171; Q 19:34, according to the reading of Ibn Mas'ūd, refers to Jesus as a 'statement [*qawl*] of truth'), is evocative of the *logos* theology of Christians. However, the Qur'an explicitly denies the divinity of Christ (cf. 5:116; 9:30).

The Qur'an also speaks of Jesus' creation from the Spirit of God. Q 21:91 has God breathe His spirit into Mary (66:12 has a variant – God breathes into 'him' or 'it', meaning, possibly, Mary's vagina [*farj*]) to create Jesus (Adam too is created by God's spirit: 15:29; 32:9; 38:72). This may account for the description of Jesus as a spirit 'from God' in 4:171. This description has led to debates among Muslim commentators (the Austrian convert Muhammad Asad translates the key phrase 'and a soul created by Him').[3] It does not reflect the Christology of early Christians, for whom 'spirit' was not a typical title of Jesus. The Qur'an also associates the 'holy spirit' (or literally, the 'spirit of holiness', *rūḥ al-qudus*) with Jesus. Three of the four appearances of 'holy spirit' in the Qur'an appear

2 G. Anawati, art. "Isā', in *EI2*.
3 M. Asad, *The message of the Quran*, London, 2003, p. 156.

in the phrase 'We supported [Jesus] with the holy spirit' (2:87, 253; 5:110; the fourth appearance is in 16:102).

While these titles seem to indicate a particular regard for the status of Jesus, and distinguish him from other prophets, the Qur'an nevertheless emphatically denies the Christian doctrine of his divinity. In 5:75 (a verse that also seems to reflect a concern with the divinisation of Mary), the Qur'an declares: 'The Messiah, son of Mary was only a messenger. Messengers have passed away before him. His mother was a truthful woman. They both ate food.' A few verses earlier, the Qur'an seems to declare that Christian teaching on Christ's divinity is a form of associationism (*shirk*), an unforgivable sin (see 4:48, 116) whose punishment is hellfire:

> Certainly they have disbelieved who say, 'Surely God – He is the Messiah, son of Mary', when the Messiah said, 'Sons of Israel! Serve God, my Lord and your Lord. Surely he who associates (anything) with God, God has forbidden him (from) the Garden, and his refuge is the Fire.' (5:72)

The Qur'an's objection to the Christian doctrine of the divinity of Christ is repeated in the following verse (5:73), which denies that God is the 'third of three'.

Although the presentation of Christian teaching in these two verses is unusual (Christians would declare 'Christ is God' but not 'God is Christ' and they do not speak of God as "third of three"), the sentiment agrees with the Qur'an's conviction that Christ is a human who never would claim to be a god, and never taught his followers to think of him as one. Later in that same sura, the Qur'an reports a conversation apparently meant to transpire in heaven after the ascension of Christ:

> (Remember) when God said, 'Jesus, son of Mary! Did you say to the people, "Take me and my mother as two gods instead of God (alone)?"' He said, "Glory to You! It is not for me to say what I have no right (to say). If I had said it, You would have known it. You know what is within me, but I do not know what is within You. Surely You – You are the Knower of the unseen." (5:116)

This verse (which again shows a concern with the divinisation of Mary) presents Jesus as a model servant of God (cf. 19:30, where the first words of the infant Christ are: 'I am the servant of God'). Like all of the prophets (see 5:109), Christ insists that God alone has knowledge of the unseen (*ghayb*). In several other verses (3:51; 5:72, 117; 19:36 [unless this is Muḥammad speaking]; 43:64), the Qur'an has Jesus declare to his followers, 'God is my Lord and your Lord', and reminds them that God alone is to be worshipped. These declarations help one understand the Qur'an's report in 5:14 that Christians have 'forgotten part of what they were reminded of' (said also of the Jews in 5:13). From this perspective, the Qur'an is a 'reminder' (*dhikr*) to the Christians about the human/servant nature of Christ.

The Qur'an also imagines Jesus to have faced a scenario similar to that of its own Prophet. Q 61:14 has the Prophet call on his followers to join themselves to him in a struggle against enemies, as the disciples once joined themselves to Jesus in a similar struggle. The Qur'an declares, 'One contingent of the Sons of Israel believed, and (another) contingent disbelieved. So We supported those who believed against their enemy, and they were the ones who prevailed' (61:14b). This scenario does not reflect the relationship between Jesus and the disciples in the Gospels. Jesus in the Gospels calls on his disciples to be itinerant preachers; Jesus in Sura 61 seems to call on them to fight. This verse thus reflects the context of Muḥammad in Medina as he engaged in armed conflict with his enemies (the Jews and the pagans of Mecca) for their refusal to believe in him.

As for the apocalyptic role that the later Islamic tradition attributes to Jesus, the Qur'an contains only hints. The Qur'an seems to have Jesus in mind when, in 43:61, it declares 'surely he [or, according to another interpretation, 'it'] is indeed knowledge of the Hour'. Q 4:159 speaks of Jesus' ascension to heaven and describes him as a 'witness' against his enemies on the Day of Resurrection.

Outside of the Virgin Birth and certain miracles of Jesus, the Qur'an has little in common with the New Testament. None of Jesus' parables, none of the Johannine discourses, none of the anecdotes of Jesus' adult ministry, appear in the Qur'an. The idea has occasionally been suggested that Jesus in the Qur'an preserves the teaching of the early Jewish Christian movement.[4] In fact, and even though the Qur'an has Jesus 'confirm' Moses's scripture (3:50; 61:6), the Jesus of the Qur'an does not appear as a memory of a primitive, pre-Nicene 'Semitic' perspective. Indeed, much of the Jewishness of Jesus in the Gospels is lost in the Qur'an (which, for example, has no comment on his teaching on the Sabbath or his relationship to the Jerusalem Temple). Instead, and as Kenneth Cragg has

[4] See, e.g. C. Geffré, 'La portée théologique du dialogue islamo-chrétien', *Islamochristiana* 18 (1992) 1-23; and more recently M. Akyol, *The Islamic Jesus. How the king of the Jews became a prophet of the Muslims*, New York, 2017.

argued, the Jesus of the Qur'an is a character shaped by the mould of Muḥammad himself.[5] Like Muḥammad, he is concerned with those who associate things with God (*shirk*; Q 5:72) and intent on rallying his followers (*ḥawāriyyūn*) around him as 'helpers' (*anṣār*) in a struggle against their enemies (61:14).

The Islamic Jesus is distinguished by the name ʿĪsā given to him in the Qur'an. Arabic Christian tradition knows Jesus (on the basis of the Hebrew or Syriac form of the name) as Yasūʿ, though in the Qur'an the letter *ʿayn* appears at the front of the name. It is possible that this form owes something to a desire to have Jesus' name rhyme with that of Moses (Mūsā). For our purposes, however, it is symbolically important that the Qur'an gives to Jesus a new name. Noting the problem of Jesus' name in the Qur'an, Cragg concludes: 'Two names, if remotely cognate, for one persona: one persona divergently revered and received'.[6]

Jesus in Islamic tradition before 1600

The Qur'an is the primary point of departure for later Muslim perceptions of Jesus, but the corpus of narratives and traditions that Tarif Khalidi calls the 'Muslim Gospel' goes far beyond elaborations of qur'anic material. Khalidi comments that this corpus comprises 'the largest body of texts relating to Jesus in any non-Christian literature [...] scattered in works of ethics and popular devotion, works of *adab* (belles-lettres), works of Sufism or Muslim mysticism, anthologies of wisdom, and histories of prophets and saints'.[7] In the following, we shall start with an overview of the various genres that preserve the Islamic Jesus – inscriptions, *akhbār*, and polemical writings – followed by a detailed discussion of the major themes of the Muslim Jesus, in particular his miracles, wisdom and asceticism, and end of life and return, with reference to relevant CMR entries as and where appropriate.

---

5 K. Cragg, *Jesus and the Muslim*, Oxford, 1999, p. 31.
6 Cragg, *Jesus and the Muslim*, p. 38.
7 T. Khalidi, *The Muslim Jesus*, Cambridge MA, 2001, p. 3.

Overview of genres

Inscriptions

The earliest Muslim writings on Jesus are found in inscriptions, which include graffiti inscriptions on rocks as well as monumental inscriptions (i.e. on Islamic monuments). In the early inscriptions from the Negev, which date to the first two centuries of the Islamic era, the name Jesus appears some dozen times, typically listed among other prophets, mostly in the locution 'the Lord of Jesus', associated with another prophet such as Moses.[8] One graffito, dated to the year 170 AH (786/7 CE), has the author, a certain Saʿīd, testify: 'Muḥammad and ʿIsā and ʿUzayr [see 9:30] and all the created ones are subordinate worshippers (*ʿibād marbūbīn*), and he testifies unto Allah, and Allah suffices as a witness, that he is One (*aḥad*), indivisible (*ṣamad*), neither begetting nor begotten (*lā wālid wa-lā walad*) [see 112:3]'.[9] Saʿīd's testimony seems to be more a personal profession of faith than polemical, notwithstanding his use of qur'anic references that often feature in anti-Christian contexts (9:30 and 112).

The famous mosaic inscriptions from the Dome of the Rock present one of the earliest anti-Christian polemical writings, dated to the last quarter of the first Islamic century.[10] The majestic octagonal structure erected by the Umayyad Caliph ʿAbd al-Malik ibn Marwān (r. 685-705) sits atop the Temple Mount, overlooking the blueish dome of the Holy Sepulchre, and effectively replacing it as the sacred centre of the city. The outer inscriptions emphasise the oneness of God (*allāh al-aḥad, allāh al-ṣamad*), who neither begets nor is begotten (*lam yalid wa-lam yūlad*; cf. Q 112), who has no divine partners (*lā sharīk lahu*), and who has not taken a son (*lam yattakhidh waladān*; see 17:111). While the mosaic inscriptions do not reproduce the qur'anic references verbatim, they evidently employ qur'anic language and motifs in their polemic.

---

8 Of the 12 mentions of Jesus in the Negev inscriptions, the expressions '*rabb ʿĪsā wa-Mūsā*' and '*rabb Mūsā wa-ʿ Īsā*' appear seven times. Interestingly, one graffito has Aaron inscribed in lieu of Moses: '*rabb Hārūn wa- ʿĪsā*'. Another graffito has the author asking forgiveness for Mary, the Mother of Jesus: '*ighfir li-umm ʿĪsā, Maryam*'; Y. Nevo, Z. Cohen, and D. Heftman, *Ancient Arabic inscriptions from the Negev*, Midreshet Ben-Gurion, 1993, vol. 1, p. 24.

9 Nevo, Cohen and Heftman, *Ancient Arabic inscriptions*, vol. 1, p. 54.

10 The inscriptions give the clear date of 72 (691-2), which probably refers to the foundation of the Dome. See M. Milwright, *The Dome of the Rock and its Umayyad mosaic inscriptions*, Edinburgh, 2016, p. 214.

In the same vein, the inscriptions on the inner part of the octagonal arcade specifically address and reject Christian views of Jesus and recast the qur'anic judgement:

> O People of the Book, do not exaggerate (*lā taghlū*) in your religion / nor say anything but the truth about God, the Messiah. Jesus son of Mary is only God's messenger and word that he committed to Mary, and a spirit proceeding from him, so believe in God and his messengers and do not say 'three' / Refrain! It is better for you. For God is only one god. Glory to him that he should have a son [...] The Messiah will not disdain to be / a servant of God, nor do the angels in proximity to him [...] God bless your messenger and servant Jesus / son of Mary and peace on him the day he was born, the day he dies, and the day he is raised alive. That is Jesus son of Mary in word of truth, about which you are doubting. It is not fitting that God should take a son. Glory be to him.[11]

Weaving in closely paraphrased qur'anic verses – 4:171-2; 19:15; and 19:34 – the mosaic inscriptions present a thoroughly qur'anic Jesus in the religiously contested and crowded space of Umayyad Jerusalem.

Akhbār: historiographical reports

The Islamic tradition presents a rich panoply of recollections of Jesus, contained in discrete historiographical reports called *akhbār*. Each *khabar* (a report or tradition) is transmitted through a chain of transmitters (*isnād*), tracing the report to an authoritative figure with the purpose of giving authority to its content (*matn*). Threaded together, these various *akhbār* constitute the building blocks for Muslim historical and narrative literature in which we meet a Jesus who is more than a counterpoint to the Jesus of Christianity. For example, the early Muslim chronicler Sayf ibn 'Umar (fl. 8th century) presents Jesus as a prophet to the Jews whose followers were led astray by the convert Paul.[12] The history of al-Ya'qūbi (d. 897), however, depicts Jesus in a way that is largely faithful to the New Testament. Similar is the account of Jesus in the history of al-Mas'ūdī (d. 956), who writes in the following century.[13] In

[11] Milwright, *Dome of the Rock*, p. 72.

[12] Sayf ibn 'Umar, *Kitāb al-ridda wa-al-futūḥ wa-kitāb al-jamal wa-maṣīr 'Ā'isha wa-'Alī*, no. 133, ed. Q. al-Samarrai, Leiden, 1995, pp. 132-5. See also S. Anthony, 'The composition of S. b. 'Umar's "Account of King Paul and his corruption of ancient Christianity"', *Der Islam* 85 (2010) 164-202. More generally, see D. Thomas, 'Sayf ibn 'Umar', in *CMR* 1, 437-8.

[13] D. Thomas, 'al-Mas'ūdī', in *CMR* 2, 298-305.

the histories of al-Yaʿqūbī and al-Masʿūdī, as in the history of Abū Jaʿfar al-Ṭabarī (d. 923), the story of the life of Jesus is told as one element of a universal history. In a certain group of works known as *qiṣaṣ al-anbiyāʾ* ('Stories of the prophets'), such as that attributed to al-Kisāʾī or authored by al-Thaʿlabī (d. 1035) and Ibn Kathīr (d. 1373),[14] the life of Jesus is told as one 'story' in a sequence of stories exclusively dedicated to the prophets, from Adam to Muḥammad. A more detailed thematic discussion of the contents of the various *akhbār* will follow.

Polemical exchanges and writings

With the flowering of Muslim anti-Christian polemical writings in the early ʿAbbasid era, known as the Refutation of Christians (*al-radd ʿalā l-Naṣārā*), qur'anic depictions of Jesus were presented and defended in a rationalist garb and supported with biblical proof-texts. While many works have been lost, including those authored by the rationalist theologians and controversialists Ḍirār ibn ʿAmr (d. early 9th century)[15] and Abū l-Hudhayl al-ʿAllāf (d. between 840 and 850),[16] the surviving refutations such as those by the Zaydī al-Qāsim ibn Ibrāhīm (d. 860),[17] ʿAlī l-Ṭabarī (d. c. 860),[18] the Muʿtazilī Abū ʿĪsā Muḥammad al-Warrāq (d. c. 864),[19] the Muʿtazilī Abū ʿUthmān al-Jāḥiẓ (d. 869),[20] and the Ashʿarī jurist Abū Bakr al-Bāqillānī (d. 1013),[21] among many others, exhibit a variety of approaches employed by Muslim polemicists at the time in addressing the differences between Christian and Muslim doctrines, ultimately arguing for the superiority of the latter. While as a rule the refutations do not directly cite the Qur'an to advance their apologetic goals, and prioritise instead rational argumentation in tandem with biblical prooftexts, the qur'anic account of Jesus informs and shapes the apologetic agenda. As ʿAlī l-Ṭabarī notes at the beginning of his Refutation: 'My intention is not to refute Christ (peace be upon him) or the people of his truth, but those Christian sects that oppose Christ and the Gospels and corrupt the

---

14 On the attribution of *Qiṣaṣ al-anbiyāʾ* to al-Kisāʾī, see T. Nagel, art. 'al-Kisāʾī', in *EI2*.

15 See D. Thomas, 'Ḍirār b. ʿAmr', in *CMR* 1, 371-4.

16 See D. Thomas, 'Abū l-Hudhayl al-ʿAllāf', in *CMR* 1, 544-9.

17 See W. Madelung, 'al-Qāsim ibn Ibrāhīm', in *CMR* 1, 540-3. For a detailed study on Qāsim's *Radd*, see R. Schaffner, 'The Bible through a Qurʾānic Filter: Scripture Falsification (*Taḥrīf*) in 8th and 9th-Century Muslim Disputational Literature', Columbus OH, 2016 (PhD Diss. The Ohio State University).

18 See D. Thomas, "ʿAlī l-Ṭabarī', in *CMR* 1, 669-74.

19 See D. Thomas, 'Abū ʿIsā l-Warrāq', in *CMR* 1, 695-701.

20 See D. Thomas, 'al-Jāḥiẓ', in *CMR* 1, 706-12.

21 See D. Thomas, 'al-Bāqillānī', in *CMR* 2, 446-50.

words'.[22] A Muslim who peruses his book, al-Ṭabarī promises his readers, will only increase in faith, and a Christian will have to either abandon his faith or remain in it and doubt it for the rest of his life.

The letter of Abū l-Rabīʿ Muḥammad ibn al-Layth (d. c. 819), which he wrote to the Byzantine Emperor Constantine VI on behalf of the ʿAbbasid Caliph Hārūn al-Rashīd (r. 789-809) presents an early epistolary example of refutation literature.[23] Composed sometime between 790 and 797, during the short reign of Constantine VI, the threatening letter demands that the emperor continue to pay tribute, lest martial hostilities ensue. Ibn al-Layth incorporates major themes of Christian-Muslim controversy in his letter, providing a rather detailed defence of the prophethood of Muḥammad combined with a refutation of Christian beliefs. Addressing the emperor and his theologians, Ibn al-Layth asks, 'On what basis do you attribute divinity to Jesus?'[24] Ibn al-Layth conjures up a list of scriptural examples meant to undermine Christian claims (e.g. scriptural comparisons of the sonship of Jesus to the sonship of Israel, Jesus' raising the dead to Ezekiel's raising the dead, Jesus' miracles to the wonders performed by Moses). It is worth noting that Ibn al-Layth justifies his use of scripture by noting that God's books are preserved (*maḥfūẓa*), and his proofs protected (*maḥrūsa*), and that Jews and Christians have gone astray by falsifying the meaning of its words (*taḥrif tāʾwīl al-kalām*), and the altering of the interpretation of books (*taṣrīf tafsīr al-kutub*).[25]

The correspondence of ʿUmar II (r. 717-20) and Leo III (r. 717-41), most likely a fiction purportedly between the pious Umayyad caliph and the Byzantine emperor, presents another early epistolary witness. According to the Greek chronicler Theophanes (d. c. 818), ʿUmar 'composed a theological letter for Leo the emperor, thinking to persuade him to become a Muslim'.[26] Agapius of Menbij (d. 950) gives a longer statement on ʿUmar's letter and mentions a reply from Leo.[27] The fuller letter attributed to ʿUmar has been reconstituted on the basis of a 9th- or

---

22 R. Ebied and D. Thomas (ed. and trans.), *The polemical works of ʿAlī al-Ṭabarī*, Leiden, 2016, p. 65.

23 See B. Roggema, 'Ibn al-Layth', in *CMR* 1, 347-53.

24 A.F. al-Rifāʿī, *ʿAṣr al-Maʾmūn*, Cairo, 1927, vol. 2, p. 226.

25 Al-Rifāʿī, *ʿAṣr al-Māʾmūn*, vol. 2, p. 226.

26 See R. Hoyland, 'The correspondence of Leo III (717-41) and ʿUmar II (717-20)', *Aram* 6 (1994) 165-77. The quotation is Hoyland's translation of Theophanes, *Chronographia*, Leipzig, 1883-85, p. 399.

27 On the Leo-ʿUmar correspondence, see B. Roggema, '*Pseudo-Leo III's first letter to ʿUmar II*', in *CMR* 1, 375-6; M.N. Swanson, '*The Arabic letter of Leo III to ʿUmar II*', in *CMR* 1, 377-80; and B. Roggema, '*Pseudo-ʿUmar II's letter to Leo III*', in *CMR* 1, 381-5.

10th-century Arabic manuscript and a 16th-century Aljamiado manuscript in which ʿUmar (or pseudo-ʿUmar) asks who ruled the world when Christ was in his mother's womb and describes biblical verses that present the human nature of Jesus.[28]

The Muʿtazilī scholar ʿAbd al-Jabbār (d. 1025) discusses at some length the character of Jesus in his work on the 'signs' of the prophethood of Muḥammad, *Tathbīt dalāʾil al-nubuwwa*. In a section of that work known as the 'Critique of Christian origins', ʿAbd al-Jabbār challenges the claims of Christians to be the community that preserves authentic accounts of Jesus.[29] To that end, he reports numerous traditions that vary from the New Testament accounts. For example, whereas the Gospel of John (19:26-7) has the crucified Jesus speak to his mother and the beloved disciple, ʿAbd al-Jabbār has a different person on the Cross (i.e. the one who was substituted for Jesus in accordance to his understanding of Q 4:157), and Jesus and Mary standing by: 'The crucified one looked at [Mary] and said, while he was on the cross, "This is your son." He said to Christ, "This is your mother."'[30] Otherwise, in order to argue that Christians have deviated from the teaching and practice of Christ, ʿAbd al-Jabbār reports that he lived and worshipped as other Israelites did, holding fast to the law of Moses and Israelite religious customs. He writes, 'Christ read his prayers as the prophets and the Israelites did both before him and in his era when they read from the word of God.'[31] And 'Christ was circumcised and required circumcision'; 'He never took Sunday as the holiday ever, nor did he ever build a church. He did not annul the Sabbath, even for one hour.'[32]

The late medieval period witnessed the scholarly pinnacle of anti-Jewish and anti-Christian Muslim polemics, and numerous Muslim scholars responded to Christian apologetics with long and exquisitely detailed polemical treatises. In one such, *Fī l-radd ʿalā l-milla l-kāfira*, called by Carl Brockelmann 'the greatest apologetic achievement in Islam', the author and Mālikī scholar Shihāb al-Dīn al-Qarāfī (d. 1285) presents a systematic defence of the Islamic faith following a question and answer format.[33] While he disputes the authenticity of the canonical Gospels – and even

28 Roggema, '*Pseudo-ʿUmar II's letter*', p. 382.

29 See G.S. Reynolds, 'ʿAbd al-Jabbār's *Tathbīt dalāʾil al-nubuwwa*', in *CMR* 2, 604-9. For the text, see ʿAbd al-Jabbār, *Critique of Christian origins*, ed. and trans. G.S. Reynolds and S.K. Samir, Provo UT, 2010.

30 ʿAbd al-Jabbār, *Critique of Christian origins*, p. 79.

31 ʿAbd al-Jabbār, *Critique of Christian origins*, p. 87.

32 ʿAbd al-Jabbār, *Critique of Christian origins*, p. 87.

33 M. El Kaisy-Friemuth, 'Al-Qarāfī', in *CMR* 4, 582-7, p. 585.

presents what he takes to be contradiction (*al-tanāquḍ wa-l-taʿāruḍ*), intentional misinformation (*takādhub*), and conflict (*muṣādama*) in the four Gospels – he appeals to the Gospels' authority in his presentation of the Muslim Jesus' arguing for the departure of the Christian dogma from its biblical foundation.[34] Al-Qarāfī thus argues that Jesus' Incarnation from the Holy Spirit is not found in the Gospel (*bāṭil bi-naṣṣ al-injīl*), citing the descent of the Spirit of God as a dove on the baptised Jesus as his proof-text.[35] Al-Qarāfī elsewhere takes up the old anti-Christian Muslim polemical theme of Jesus' allowing Mary's suffering and death, and argues that the Christian portrayal of Jesus' silence in the face of his mother Mary's accusers, committing her to a life of prayer and fasting that ended in her death and the corruption of her body, is too scandalous 'to have been ascribed to the most contemptuous of sons' (*lam yunsab ilā aqbaḥ walad min al-awlād*).[36]

While al-Qarāfī engages with the Christian apologetic tract, *Letter to a Muslim friend*, authored by the Melkite bishop Paul of Antioch whom he cites anonymously, the Ḥanbalī jurist Ibn Taymiyya (d. 1328) writes his *Al-Jawāb al-ṣaḥīḥ li-man baddala dīn al-Masīḥ* as a more detailed refutation of the Christian *Letter from the People of Cyprus*, which is a revised version of Paul's letter.[37] As has been noted, the main aim of Ibn Taymiyya's *Jawāb* is to set out Christianity as an example of what Muslims ought to avoid, and therefore presents the Muslim Jesus in sharp contradistinction to Christian beliefs.[38] To this end, Ibn Taymiyya effectively refutes Christian attempts to employ the Qur'an in their apologetic argumentation, and questions the biblical foundations of the Christian Jesus, likening the Gospels not to the Qur'an, but to the *sīra* literature (which he comments 'may on the overall be true [*wa-in kāna ghālibuhā*

34 Al-Qarāfī, *Al-Ajwiba l-fākhira ʿan al-asʾila l-fājira fī l-radd ʿalā l-milla l-kāfira*, ed. M.M. al-Shahāwī, Beirut, 2005, p. 46. Al-Qarāfī notes that there are five Gospels: the four well-known (*mashhūra*) Gospels in addition to the fifth infancy gospel (pp. 43-5), and then enumerates some 15 contradictions between the four canonical accounts (pp. 46-52). See also D.S. Cucarella, *Muslim-Christian polemics across the Mediterranean. The splendid replies of Shihāb al-Dīn al-Qarāfī (d. 684/1285)*, Leiden, 2015.

35 Al-Qarāfī, *Al-Ajwiba*, p. 133. Al-Qarāfī's proof-text is from Matthew 3 (given as Matthew 2 in his tract).

36 Al-Qarāfī, *Al-Ajwiba*, p. 150.

37 J. Hoover, 'Ibn Taymiyya', in *CMR* 4, 824-78. See D. Thomas, 'Paul of Antioch', in *CMR* 4, 78-82.

38 Hoover, 'Ibn Taymiyya', p. 835.

ṣaḥīḥan] […] though it may be prone to errors [*fa-innahu qad yaqa'u fī ba'ḍi alfāẓihā ghalaṭ*]').[39]

Ibn Taymiyya's disciple, the prolific Ḥanbalī scholar Ibn Qayyim al-Jawziyya (d. 1350), following in his master's footsteps, composed an anti-Christian polemical opus, *Hidāyat al-ḥayārā fī ajwibat al-Yahūd wa-l-Naṣārā*, seen as perhaps the last massive scholarly Muslim polemic.[40] As one scholar notes, 'Thereafter only very simple popular writings seem to have been written in Arabic by Muslim authors, who reiterate earlier polemical arguments.'[41] Compared with Ibn Taymiyya, Ibn Qayyim is more sceptical of the reliability of the Gospels' overall presentation of Jesus, arguing that, contrary to Christian views, the Gospel (*al-injīl*) in various places seems to deny Jesus' miracles.[42] Moreover, he mocks the divergent Christian views of Jesus, jestingly remarking: 'if ten of them [Christians] gathered to discuss religion, eleven sects would form.'[43] Ibn Qayyim also maintains that the Jews also differ in their views of Jesus, and that they only mockingly ascribed divinity to him.[44] Given these divergent accounts and their unreliability, he argues that the true knowledge of Jesus is anchored in Muḥammad's revelation.[45]

The prominence of the anti-Christian polemical tradition in the medieval Islamic world is undeniable, yet it is important to emphasise that Jesus was not only an occasion for religious dispute. He was also a figure of substantial interest to Muslim historians and storytellers for his own sake.

---

39 See Ibn Taymiyya, *al-Jawāb al-ṣaḥīḥ li-man baddaladīn al-Masīh*, ed. 'A. b. Ḥ. b. Nāṣīr, 'A. al-'A. b. I. al-'Askar and Ḥ. b. M. al-Ḥamdān, Riyadh, 1999, vol. 3, pp. 22-3.

40 J. Hoover, 'Ibn Qayyim al-Jawziyya', in *CMR* 4, 989-1002.

41 H.L.-Y. Hava, *Intertwined worlds. Medieval Islam and Bible criticism*, Princeton NJ, 1992, p. 139. On more recent polemical views of Jesus, see D. Pinault, 'Images of Christ in Arabic literature', *Die Welt des Islams* 27 (1987) 103-25.

42 Ibn Qayyim al-Jawziyya, *Hidāyat al-ḥayārā fī ajwibat al-Yahūd wa-l-Naṣārā*, ed. M.A. al-Ḥājj, Damascus, 1996, p. 533.

43 Ibn Qayyim, *Hidāyat al-ḥayārā*, p. 533.

44 Ibn Qayyim, *Hidāyat al-ḥayārā*, pp. 530-3.

45 Ibn Qayyim, *Hidāyat al-ḥayārā*, p. 538.

Thematic study

In one of the earliest extant Hadith collections from the first half of the 8th century, the Successor and traditionist Hammām ibn al-Munabbih (d. early 8th century) provides a tradition that aptly recapitulates Jesus' place in Islamic prophetology.[46]

> The Messenger of God said: 'I am the closest (*awlā*) of humankind to Jesus son of Mary in this world (*ūlā*) and the hereafter (*ākhira*).' They asked, 'How, O messenger of God?' He responded: 'The prophets are brothers from different mothers but their religion is one, and there is no prophet between us.'[47]

While all the prophets are descendants of Adam, the prophet Jesus has a special place as the prophet who immediately precedes Muḥammad, the 'seal of the prophets' (Q 33:40). Another tradition cited in al-Bukhārī's Hadith collection reiterates the important place that Jesus assumes in Islamic prophetology and adds his name to the Muslim proclamation of faith (*shahāda*):

> The Prophet said: 'Whoever proclaims that there is no god but God alone with no partner, and that Muḥammad is his servant and messenger, and that Jesus is his servant and messenger and word that he cast unto Mary and a spirit from him, and that paradise is true and that hell fire is true, God will grant him entry to paradise from one of its eight doors as he wishes.'[48]

In addition to belief in God, his messenger, and the afterlife, this prophetic tradition reiterates the qur'anic characterisation (4:171) of Jesus as God's spirit (*rūḥ*) and word (*kalima*) that He cast into Mary.[49] This special attention to Jesus is further manifested in the host of narratives and

---

46 See more generally, D. Cook, 'Christians and Christianity in ḥadīth works before 900', in *CMR* 1, 73-82.

47 See n. 1 above.

48 Al-Bukhārī, *Aḥādīth al-anbīyā'*, 'Bāb qawlih yā ahl al-kitāb lā taghlū fī dīnikim[…]' no. 3435, p. 851.

49 See the commentary by al-ʿAsqalānī (d. 1449) on this Hadith, *Fatḥ al-bārī bi-sharḥ Ṣaḥīḥ al-imām Abī ʿAbd Allāh Muḥammad b. Ismāʿīl al-Bukhārī*, ed. M.F. ʿAbd al-Bāqī and M. al-D. al-Khaṭīb, Beirut, 1959, vol. 6, pp. 474-6. The *Sīra* of Ibn Hishām (d. 828 or 833) retains a tradition attributed to Muḥammad ibn Isḥāq (d. 768) in which the Christian Ethiopian king, the Negus, affirms his newfound Islamic faith by adding faith in Jesus to the *shahāda*: 'He testifies that there is no god but God, and that Muḥammad is his servant and messenger, and he testifies that Jesus son of Mary is his servant and messenger and spirit, and his word that he cast into Mary'; Ibn Hishām, *Al-Sīra l-nabawiyya*, ed. ʿU.ʿA. al-S. Tadmurī, Beirut, 1990, vol. 1, p. 366.

sayings in Islamic tradition covering a wide array of themes and aspects of his prophetic career, ranging from his physical description and miracles to his role as an ascetic exemplar and an apocalyptic figure.

Description

A number of Hadiths provide the physical description of Jesus, whom the Prophet Muḥammad encounters during the Night Journey. A tradition narrated by Abū Hurayra and recorded in both al-Bukhārī's and Muslim's collections has the Prophet provide descriptions of Moses, Jesus and Abraham during his Night Journey. Jesus, Abū Hurayra relates, 'was of moderate height (*rab'a*) and ruddy as if he had just come out of the bathroom (*dīmās*).'[50] Other traditions provide variant physical descriptions. Ibn 'Abbās reportedly transmits a tradition confirming Jesus' red complexion and adds that he has curly hair (*ja'd*) and a broad chest.[51] Elsewhere, Ibn 'Abbās transmits a Hadith describing Jesus as of moderate height (*marbū' al-khalq*) of a red-white complexion and lank hair (*sabṭ al-rā's*).[52]

Mālik ibn Anas in his *Muwaṭṭa'* reports a Prophetic tradition transmitted on the authority of Ibn 'Umar providing a variant description of Jesus from a vision Muḥammad had in a dream:

> I saw a man of a fine brown complexion (*ādam*) with long abundant hair recently styled and still dripping water leaning on two men and circumambulating the House. I asked 'Who is this?' I was told, 'He is the Christ (*masīḥ*) son of Mary.' Then I saw a man with frizzy curly hair, blind in the right eye, which looked like a bulging grape. I asked, 'Who is this?' I was told, 'This is the lying-Christ (*al-masīḥ al-dajjāl*).'[53]

---

[50] Al-Bukhārī, *Aḥādīth al-anbīyā'*, 'Bāb qawl Allāh wa-dhkur fī l-kitāb Maryam idh intabadhat min ahlihā', pp. 852-3, nos 3437, 3442, 3443; Muslim, *Ṣaḥīḥ Muslim, K. al-Īmān*, 'Bāb al-isrā' bi-rasūl Allāh', p. 94, no. 168.

[51] Al-Bukhārī, *Aḥādīth al-anbīyā'*, 'Bāb qawl Allāh wa-dhkur fī l-kitāb Maryam idh intabadhat min ahlihā', p. 853, no. 3438.

[52] Al-Bukhārī, *Aḥādīth al-anbīyā', K. Bad' al-khalq*, 'Bāb idhā qāl aḥadukum āmīn', p. 800, no. 3239; Muslim, *Īmān*, 'Bāb al-isrā' bi-rasūl Allāh', pp. 93-4, no. 165.

[53] Malik ibn Anas, *Al-Muwaṭṭa', K. Ṣifat al-nabī*, 'Bāb mā jā' fī ṣifat 'Īsā ibn Maryam wa-l-Dajjāl', ed. M.F.'A. al-Bāqī, Beirut, 1985, vol. 2, p. 920; Ibn 'Abd al-Barr, *Al-Tamhīd li-mā fī l-Muwaṭṭā' min al-ma'ānī wa-l-asānīd*, ed. M.b.A. al-'Alawī and M.'A. al-K. al-Bakrī, Rabat, 1967, vol. 14, p. 187; al-Bukhārī, *Aḥādīth al-anbīyā', K. al-Libās*, 'Bāb al-Ja'd', p. 1488, no. 5902. Cf. al-Bukhārī, *Aḥādīth al-anbīyā* ', 'Bāb qawl Allāh wa-dhkur fī l-kitāb Maryam idh intabadhat min ahlihā', p. 853, no. 3441; Muslim, *Īmān*, 'Bāb dhikr al-Masīḥ ibn Maryam wa-l-Masīḥ al-Dajjāl', p. 95, no. 169.

Commenting on this tradition, the Andalusian Mālikī scholar Ibn ʿAbd al-Barr (d. 1071) in his *Tamhīd* gives different possible etymologies for the title *masīḥ* given in this tradition to both Jesus, called *al-masīḥ al-siddīq*, and to the lying-Christ, *al-masīḥ al-dajjāl*. On the one hand, Jesus was called *masīḥ* either due to his roaming the earth (*siyāḥatihi fī l-arḍ*),[54] for having flat feet (*mamsūḥ al-rijl*),[55] because he was born anointed (*mamsūḥān bi-l-dihn*), or because he wipes (*yamsaḥ*) those who are sick to heal them. The Dajjāl, on the other hand, also bears this same title possibly for roaming the earth, or because he is blind in one eye (*mamsūḥ al-ʿayn al-wāḥida*), or possibly due to his flat feet.[56] In both cases, the title *masīḥ* is not understood in its biblical sense but is imagined to denote a physical characteristic.[57]

Miracles

In his *Al-Milal wa-al-niḥal*, the famed heresiographer and historian of religions al-Shahrastānī (d. 1153) prefaces his discussion on Christianity and the three major Christian sects with a description of Jesus that corresponds to the major contours of Christian belief:

> Christ Jesus son of Mary, messenger of God and his word (peace be upon him). He is the truly sent (*mabʿūth ḥaqqān*) after Moses (peace be upon him), the one proclaimed (*mubashshar*) in the Torah, and he demonstrated clear signs, lustrous evidence, and dazzling proofs such as resurrecting the dead, curing the blind and the leper. His very existence and nature is a complete sign of his sincerity. For he was brought about with no originating sperm, and he eloquently spoke with no prior education. While all the prophets attained their revelation at the age of 40, God had inspired him to speak (*awḥā ilayh inṭāqan*) in the cradle and inspired him to preach

---

54 On this, Ibn Kathīr further explains that Jesus roamed (*masaḥa*) the earth as he escaped from the discords (*fitan*) of his times, especially the Jewish denial and allegations against him and his mother. *Al-Bidāya wa-l-nihāya*, Beirut, 1990, vol. 2, p. 96.

55 Ibn ʿAbd al-Barr explains that *mamsūḥ al-rijl* means that his foot is without an arch, with no *akhmaṣ*, the part of the foot that does not touch the ground. Ibn ʿAbd al-Barr, *Tamhīd*, vol. 14, p. 188. Ibn al-Athīr (d. 1232) in his *Al-Nihāya fī gharīb al-ḥadīth* gives a different explanation for the expression, which he renders *masīḥ al-qadamayn*, meaning soft and smooth feet (*malsāwān layyinatān*) with no coarseness or cracks (*laysa fīhimā takassur wa-lā shuqāq*). Ibn al-Athīr, *Al-Nihāya fī gharīb al-ḥadīth wa-l-athar*, ed. Ṭ.A. al-Zāwī and M.M. al-Ṭanāḥī, Cairo, 1963, vol. 4, p. 327.

56 Ibn ʿAbd al-Barr, *Tamhīd*, vol. 14, p. 187.

57 While Ibn al-Athīr cites similar traditions in his entry under the letters *msḥ*, he reports one tradition that has the term *masīḥ* as an Arabised form of the Hebrew *mashīaḥ*; *Nihāya*, vol. 4, p. 327.

> (*awḥā ilayh iblāgh*) at the age of 30. His call lasted for three years, three months and three days.[58]

Recapitulating the major descriptive elements of Jesus in the Qur'an and Islamic tradition, al-Shahrastānī's pithy representation enunciates the centrality of Jesus' signs: Jesus' very existence and nature, he notes, are themselves clear signs of his special prophetic office.

Following the qur'anic presentation, Islamic accounts of Jesus' prophetic career start with a Marian prelude. Introducing his account of Jesus, Ibn Kathīr discusses Mary's prophetic lineage and miraculous birth, following Q 3:33-6. After years of failure to conceive a child, Ḥannah bint Fāqūdhā, the wife of ʿImrān from the House of David, conceived Mary in her old age, promising her to serve in the Jerusalem temple (*bayt al-maqdis*). Like her son Jesus, Mary was also protected from the touch of Satan at birth. Ibn Kathīr relates two Prophetic traditions narrated by the Companion and transmitter of Hadith Abū Hurayra to this effect: 'No baby is born except that it is touched by Satan at the time of its birth, and it comes out screaming from the touch of Satan, except Mary and her son Jesus'.[59] Addressing his Companions, the Prophet elucidates:

> 'Every human when he is given birth, Satan kicks him on his two sides, except Mary and her son. Do you not see how the baby cries when he comes out?' The Companions said: 'Yes, O Messenger of Allāh.' He said: 'That happens when Satan kicks him on his two sides.'[60]

Ibn ʿAbd al-Barr in his *Tamhīd* weaves this tradition into a larger account narrated by Anas ibn Mālik on the events unfolding in the wake of Jesus' miraculous birth. When Jesus was born, every idol that was worshipped beside God fell on its face. Lamenting, the demons brought their concern before Satan, who verified that the prophet Jesus was born in Jerusalem (*bayt al-maqdis*),[61] protected by angels. Failing to touch the newborn, Satan vouched, 'By the God of Jesus, I will use him to misguide the

---

[58] Al-Shahrastānī, *Al-Milal wa-l-niḥal*, ed. A.F. Muḥammad, Beirut, 1992, vol. 2, pp. 244-5. More generally on his presentation of Christianity, see D. Thomas, 'al-Shahrastānī', in *CMR* 3, 549-54.

[59] Ibn Kathīr, *Qiṣaṣ al-anbīyā'*, ed. I. Ramaḍān, Beirut, 1996, p. 503; Ismāʿīl ibn 'Umar ibn Kathīr, *Stories of the prophets*, trans. R.A. Azami, Riyadh, 2003, p. 540.

[60] Ibn Kathīr, *Qiṣaṣ*, p. 503.

[61] Al-Thaʿlabī suggests that Jesus was born en route to Egypt (Joseph wanted to kill Mary but Gabriel persuaded him not to). Al-Thaʿlabī, *Qiṣaṣ al-anbiyā' al-musammā ʿarā'is al-majālis*, ed. ʿA. al-L. al-Raḥmān, Beirut, 2004, p. 337.

people a misguidance the like of which I have never applied to anyone coming before or after him'.[62]

Jesus' miraculous birth reverberated in the natural order, with rain falling and the earth becoming more fertile (*amṭarat al-samāʾ wa-akhṣabat al-arḍ*).[63] Jesus did not cry at his birth, but instead spoke in the cradle (Q 3:46; 19:30).[64] Al-Bukhārī and Muslim relate a prophetic tradition narrated by Abū Hurayra listing Jesus along with two others from Banū Isrāʾīl who spoke in the cradle.[65] Other traditions have Jesus speaking and praising God while still in the womb. A tradition transmitted by Mujāhid has Mary saying that she would hear the unborn Jesus praising God, and that they would engage in conversation with each other whenever they were alone.[66] Jesus also spoke again at an early age, the chronicler Ibn ʿAsākir (d. 1176) relates on the authority of Abū Hurayra, eloquently praising God with words 'ears have not hitherto heard' (*fa-takallama fa-ḥamida Allāha ayḍān bi-taḥmīdin lam tasmaʿ al-ādhānu bi-mithlihi*).[67]

Muslim writers present a colourful account of the young Jesus' miraculous career prior to his prophetic mission. At nine months old, according to one tradition attributed to the fifth Shīʿī Imām Muḥammad al-Bāqir, Jesus eloquently unravelled to his tutor the spiritual mysteries of the Arabic alphabet.[68] During the family's flight to Egypt, al-Kisāʾī relates, the young Jesus calmed a fearsome lion they encountered in the middle of the road.[69] Another tradition, cited by al-Kisāʾī as also taking place en route to Egypt, has the young Jesus aid the wife of a king in her difficult

---

[62] Ibn ʿAbd al-Barr, *Tamhīd*, vol. 14, pp. 194-5. Cf. variations of this narrative in Ibn ʿAsākir, *Tārīkh madīnat Dimashq*, ed. M. al-ʿAmrawī, Beirut, 1995, vol. 47, pp. 356-9; al-Thaʿlabī, *Qiṣaṣ*, p. 338.

[63] Ibn ʿAbd al-Barr contrasts the prosperity (*rakhāʾ*) associated with the birth of Jesus with the adversity (*balāʾ*) accompanying the birth of other prophets; *Tamhīd*, vol. 14, p. 196.

[64] Al-Shahrastānī, as we have seen above, distinguishes between Jesus' miraculous speech (*inṭāq*) in the cradle and his prophetic preaching (*iblāgh*).

[65] Al-Bukhārī, *Aḥādīth al-anbīyāʾ*, 'Bāb qawl Allāh wa-dhkur fī l-kitāb Maryam idh intabadhat min ahlihā', p. 852, no. 3436. Aḥmad ibn Ḥanbal relates a tradition narrated by Ibn ʿAbbās that includes Jesus in a list of four who spoke at this young age; *Musnad*, ed. A.M. Shākir, Cairo, 1995, vol. 3, pp. 253-4, no. 2822.

[66] Ibn ʿAsākir, *Tārīkh*, vol. 47, pp. 351-2; al-Thaʿlabī, *Qiṣaṣ*, p. 339. This may be a reflection of Q 19:24 with its reference to a voice calling out to Mary from 'below' (sometimes explained as a report that Jesus spoke to her while still in her womb); see further S.A. Mourad, 'Ibn ʿAsākir', in *CMR* 3, 683-9.

[67] Ibn ʿAsākir, *Tārīkh*, vol. 47, p. 362.

[68] Al-Thaʿlabī, *Qiṣaṣ*, p. 340.

[69] Al-Kisāʾī, *Qiṣaṣ al-anbīyāʾ*, ed. I. Eisenberg, Leiden, 1922, pp. 304-5.

delivery, and even predict the physical characteristics of her soon-to-be-born son.[70] The young Jesus continued to perform miracles while residing in Egypt. According to al-Thaʿlabī, the first miracle he performed there has the 12-year old boy helping the charitable landowner (*dihqān*) on whose property the family resided to reclaim money that was stolen from him.[71] Moreover, Muslim writers also present rich accounts of Jesus' miracles performed after his mission (*mabʿath*) and during his prophetic career. For instance, expanding on the qur'anic banquet (*māʾida*) passage (Q 5:112-15), Ibn Kathīr provides a detailed exegetical account of the circumstances leading up to the sending down of the *māʾida*, as well as the items of food included.[72]

While Muslim writings on Jesus' miracles are mostly rooted in the Qur'an, other non-qur'anic biblical details are sometimes woven into the presentation in creative ways that are not necessarily in line with Christian usage. Thus, in his retelling of the episode of Jesus' walking on water – a Gospel account not mentioned in the Qur'an – al-Thaʿlabī replaces Peter with an unnamed companion who is short (*qaṣīr*).[73] In discussing Jesus' miraculous raising of the dead, al-Thaʿlabī recapitulates the Johannine account of Lazarus, and relates the account of the raising of the daughter of a tax collector, perhaps alluding to the synoptic Gospels' account of the raising of the daughter of Jairus. He also integrates non-qur'anic and non-biblical material, such as Jesus' resurrecting Shem son of Noah and Ezra (ʿUzayr) (cf. Q 9:30).[74]

Even as certain traditions emphasised the miracles that accompanied Jesus, or that he himself performed, Muslim scholars were also eager to downplay the importance of his miracles. The principal strategy of medieval scholars was to note that Jesus was not the only prophet to perform miracles. In his response to a letter sent to him by Christians from Cyprus, Ibn Abī Ṭālib al-Dimashqī (d. 1327) writes the following: 'In case you should say that he performed miracles, I say to you that other prophets performed greater miracles than he did, but they have never been taken as gods nor made partners with him in the way that you take Christ as God and make him a partner'.[75]

---

[70] Al-Kisāʾī, *Qiṣaṣ*, p. 305.

[71] Al-Thaʿlabī, *Qiṣaṣ*, p. 341.

[72] Ibn Kathīr, *Qiṣaṣ*, pp. 546-8 (*Stories*, pp. 567-8).

[73] Al-Thaʿlabī, *Qiṣaṣ*, p. 347.

[74] Al-Thaʿlabī, *Qiṣaṣ*, pp. 345-7. On the resurrection of Shem, son of Noah, see tradition no. 23 in Khalidi, *Muslim Jesus* (with references there), pp. 66-7.

[75] Al-Dimashqī, *Muslim-Christian polemic during the Crusades*, ed. and trans. R.Y. Ebied and D. Thomas, Leiden, 2005, p. 385.

Al-Dimashqī goes on to claim that the birth of Adam was more miraculous than that of Christ (since Adam had neither a father nor a mother), that Elisha, Elijah and Ezekiel raised the dead as Christ did (Ezekiel raising many more than Christ, an allusion to Ezekiel 37 and the 'valley of dry bones') and Moses turned a staff into a serpent, which al-Dimashqī calls 'more wonderful than raising the dead' (since it involves the transformation of an inanimate object).[76] Al-Dimashqī concludes that his Christian adversaries are compelled either to acknowledge that Christ is merely a prophet, or 'to worship these prophets and associate them as you associate him' [with God].[77]

On the other hand, from the view of the Islamic tradition, there seems to be a link between Jesus' eventful prophetic career and prolific miracles, and his divine status in Christianity – which may have served a polemical function, especially given the Christian emphasis on miracles in their polemic and apologetical tracts at the time. This is aptly represented in a tradition related by Ibn ʿAsākir. Approaching Jesus at the Temple, the account goes, Satan addressed him:

> 'Are you Jesus son of Mary [...] Are you the one who came into being without a father, indeed you are of great status (*ʿaẓīm al-khaṭar*)?' Jesus replied, 'All might belongs to Him who made me.' Satan said: 'You are Jesus son of Mary who have attained divine might (*ʿiẓam rubūbiyyatik*) to cure the blind and the leper and the sick.' Jesus said: 'All power is to the One by whose permission I cured them, and if He wills He would make me sick.' Satan said: 'You are Jesus son of Mary, you raise the dead, you are indeed mighty.' Jesus said: 'All might belongs to the One with whose permission I resurrect them, and it is inevitable that He will make me die.' Satan said: 'You are Jesus, whose might enabled you to walk on water.' Jesus said: 'All might belongs to the One with whose permission I walked [on water], and if He so wills he would drown me.' Satan said: 'You are Jesus, son of Mary, who are so glorious that you can attain the heavens (*taʿlū l-samāwāt*) and manage all affairs (*tudabbir fīhā al-amr*). Indeed, I know of no equal or likeness to God other than you.'[78]

Terrified by Satan's words, Jesus collapses and casts the demon away. Regrouping, Satan recharges:

> Did I not say to you that you are a mighty god, and that no one is like God apart from you? But you do not know yourself. Order the demons to

[76] Al-Dimashqī, *Muslim-Christian polemic*, p. 387.
[77] Al-Dimashqī, *Muslim-Christian polemic*, p. 387.
[78] Ibn ʿAsākir, *Tārīkh*, vol. 47, pp. 358-9.

> worship you for they have not acknowledged any human before you, for if people saw that the demons worship you, they will worship you and you will become the god on earth and the God whom you describe in heaven.[79]

The exchange between Satan and Jesus, which evidently riffs on the Synoptic Gospels' account on the temptation of Christ, could be seen as an Islamic rebuke of the Christian belief in Jesus's divinity.[80] Indeed, the exchange prioritises the miracles attested in the canonical Christian accounts – walking on water, healing the sick, and resurrecting the dead – and does not include the qur'anic miracles of Jesus such as speaking in the cradle and creating a bird from clay. This passage also places the doctrine of Christians in the mouth of the devil and has the devil tempt Jesus with the possibility of becoming a god, as Christians consider him to be. Jesus, however, resists this temptation (cf. Q 4:172), thereby rebuking both Satan and Christians.

Wisdom and asceticism

Scholars have long noted the role of Jesus in medieval Islamic traditions as a wisdom figure and an ascetic. These traditions have Jesus warn his followers of the danger that this world (*al-dunyā*) presents to their spiritual progress. For example, Abū Ḥāmid al-Ghazālī (d. 1111) reports in his *Iḥyāʾ ʿulūm al-dīn* that Jesus declared: 'Do not take this world as a lord for it will take you as slaves. Store up treasures with the one who will not lose it. For the owner of the treasure of this world will fear it will decay (cf. Luke 12:33). The owner of treasure of God does not fear that it will decay'.[81]

In a following saying, Jesus is made to warn his followers about rulers and women:

> He also said, 'I have spread out this world for you and you have seated yourselves upon its back. Kings and women will not dispute with you over it. As for the kings, do not dispute with them over this world, for they will not oppose you if you leave them with their world. As for women guard yourselves from them with fasting and prayer.'[82]

---

[79] Ibn ʿAsākir, *Tārīkh*, vol. 47, p. 359.

[80] Cf. Matthew 4:1-11; Mark 1:12-13; and Luke 4:1-13. Ibn ʿAsākir's narrative concludes with God's sending three angels, Jibrīl, Mikāʾīl and Isrāfīl to assist Jesus, which is reminiscent of the conclusion in Matthew 4:11 and Mark 1:13, where the devil departs and angels minister to Jesus.

[81] Al-Ghazālī, *Iḥyāʾ ʿulūm al-dīn*, ed. A. al-Khālidī, Beirut, 1998, vol. 3, p. 263.

[82] Al-Ghazālī, *Iḥyāʾ ʿulūm al-dīn*, vol. 3, p. 263.

This dimension of the Muslim Jesus is distinctive inasmuch as it has no firm qur'anic basis. The Qur'an never hints at Jesus' ascetic lifestyle and neither does not make Jesus into a wisdom figure. Nevertheless, and as Tarif Khalidi has described in his work *The Muslim Jesus* (following the earlier studies of Miguel Asín Palacios), an enormous body of sayings of this type is found in medieval Islamic literature.[83] It is possible that the growth of the idea of Jesus as an ascetic sage is connected to the standard Islamic conviction that Jesus was celibate, or to the qur'anic description of Jesus as a 'spirit from God' (Q 4:171); in these Islamic traditions, Jesus is often referred to as 'God's spirit' (*Rūḥ Allāh*). It is also possible that this distinctive perspective on Jesus was shaped by the encounter of early Sufis with Christian monks who sought to live out their religious life in imitation of the asceticism of Christ. In his classic study of early Islamic mysticism, Tor Andrae describes Islamic reports of encounters with monks, and comments: 'The sense of spiritual affinity with Christianity, or rather with that form of Christianity which was regarded as original and orthodox, is also expressed in the dominant position Jesus occupies in the pronouncements and ideas of the ascetics.'[84]

As Georges Anawati has noted, the appearance of Jesus in collections such as the *Iḥyā' 'ulūm al-dīn* of al-Ghazālī and other works, including the *Nawādir* of al-Ḥakīm al-Tirmidhī (d. c. 905), *Qūt al-qulūb* of al-Makkī (d. 996), *Ḥilyat al-awliyā'* of Abū Nu'aym (d. 1038), the *Rawḍ al-rayāḥīn* of al-Yāfi'ī (d. 1367) offers a distinctive presentation of Jesus, emphasising: 'Poverty [...] detachment from the life of this world, denunciation of false wisdom and of the specious sureties of this world, dialogues, pilgrim stories, the resurrection of the dead who bear witness against the vanity of the world against which Jesus constantly warned his Companions, his Apostles, the Children of Israel and his listeners in general'.[85]

Anawati continues: 'His description is based on that of the Christian ascetics and monks wearing a woollen habit, detachment, a life of solitude, the power of the initiate to perform cures.'[86] Indeed, the very woollen garments worn by ascetics, and from which the name *ṣūfī* is usually believed to have originated, are also associated with Jesus.[87] According to

---

83 See M. Asín Palacios, 'Logia et agrapha Domini Jesu', in F. Nau et al. (eds), *Patrologia orientalis*, Paris, 1919, vol. 13, fasc. 3, 335-431; 1926, vol. 19, fasc. 4, 531-624.

84 T. Andrae, *In the garden of myrtles. Studies in early Islamic mysticism*, trans. A. Schimmel, Albany NY, 1987, p. 15. On Ṣūfī encounters with Christian monks, see also Y. Ṣādir, *Ruhbān 'arab fī ba'ḍ siyar al-mutaṣawwifīn al-muslimīn*, Beirut, 2009.

85 Anawati, "Īsā'.

86 Anawati, "Īsā'.

87 L. Massington et al., art. 'Taṣawwuf', in *EI2*.

a tradition transmitted by the *muḥaddith* Ibn Abī Shayba (d. 849), when the disciples (*ḥawāriyyūn*) asked Jesus about what he wore, he responded: 'wool (*ṣūf*)'.[88] In a similar vein, the ascetic traditionist Hannād al-Sarī (d. 857), whose telling sobriquet is the 'monk (*rāhib*) of Kūfa', reports: 'The day Jesus was raised to heaven, he left behind nothing but a woollen garment (*midraʿa*), a slingshot, and two sandals.'[89] Another variant tradition, transmitted on the authority of the Shīʿī exegete al-ʿAyyāshī (fl. late 9th century), has Jesus ascend to heaven donning the woollen garment that his mother Mary had made for him.[90]

It is no coincidence, therefore, that ascetic themes permeate the various sayings attributed to Jesus that are preserved under the rubric of ascetic sayings (*kitāb al-zuhd*) in the Hadith collections of al-Sarī l-Shaybānī (d. 783-4), ʿAbd Allāh ibn al-Mubārak (d. 797), and Aḥmad ibn Ḥanbal (d. 855), among others. At the heart of the various themes presented in these sayings is worldly renunciation. A representative report transmitted by Ibn Ḥanbal has Jesus teach:

> 'Love of the world is the root of all sin. Worldly wealth is a great sickness.' They asked, 'What is that sickness?' He said, 'Its owner cannot avoid pride and self-esteem.' They asked, 'Suppose he avoids this?' Jesus replied, 'The cultivation of wealth distracts man from the remembrance of God.'[91]

Jesus' teachings also convey fear of the Hour. 'Whenever the Hour was mentioned in the presence of Jesus', Ibn al-Mubārak reports, 'he would cry out and say, "It is not fitting that the son of Mary should remain silent when the Hour is mentioned in his presence."'[92] Disdainful of this world and fearful of the impending divine judgement, Jesus is presented as an embodiment and exemplification of key ascetic characteristics and practices, while maintaining the frailty of his humanity.

Scholars have long noted that various sayings from the Gospels permeate the Islamic tradition, whether given to Jesus or to Muslim scholars

---

[88] Ibn Abī Shayba, *Al-Muṣannaf*, ed. A.M. Muḥammad, Cairo, 2007, vol. 10, *K. al-zuhd*, 'Bāb mā dhkur fī zuhd al-anbīyāʾ wa-kalāmihim ʿalayhīm al-salām', p. 8, no. 35233.

[89] Hannād al-Sarī, *K. al-Zuhd*, ed. ʿA. al-R. al-Faryawāʾī, Kuwait, 1985, 'Bāb man yastaḥibb al-mawt wa-qillat al-māl wa-l-wild', p. 311, no. 553. Khalidi suggests that the description of what Jesus left behind may echo Mark. 6:7-9, *Muslim Jesus*, p. 94, no. 77 (trans. and notes).

[90] Al-ʿAyyāshī, *Tafsīr al-ʿAyyāshī*, ed. H.al-R. al-Maḥallātī, Beirut, 1991, vol. 1, p. 199.

[91] Ibn Ḥanbal, *K. al-Zuhd*, ed. M.ʿA. al-Salām Shāhīn, Beirut, 1983, p. 117; Khalidi, *Muslim Jesus*, p. 87, no. 62 (trans. and notes).

[92] Ibn al-Mubārak, *K. al-Zuhd wa-yalīh K. al-Raqāʾiq*, ed. Ḥ. al-R. al-Aʿẓamī, Beirut, 2004, p. 104, no. 229; Khalidi, *Muslim Jesus*, p. 54, no. 6 (trans. and notes). Cf. Ibn Ḥanbal, *Zuhd*, p. 75.

and ascetics.[93] One of the early traditions transmitted by Ibn Ḥanbal presents a verbatim translation of a Gospel saying: 'Jesus said, "Place your treasures in heaven, for the heart of man is where his treasure is."'[94] Other traditions reiterate parts of Jesus' teaching while remaining faithful to the spirit of the Gospels. A report related by Ibn al-Mubārak thus fuses different parts of Jesus' teachings in Matthew 6 into one tradition:

> Jesus said, 'If it is a day of fasting for one of you, let him anoint his head and beard and wipe his lips so that people will not know that he is fasting. If he gives with the right hand, let him hide this from his left hand. If he prays, let him pull down the door curtain, for God apportions praise as He apportions livelihood.'[95]

Khalidi observes that, while the concluding statement ('for God apportions') is part of a process of Islamicising sayings, it does not detract from the meaning of the Gospel account. Elsewhere, such glosses may further Islamicise a saying while preserving an identifiable Gospel reference. Thus, a tradition transmitted by Ibn Abī Shayba preserves a near verbatim quotation of Luke 11:27-8, substituting the 'word of God' in the Gospel account with the Qur'an, effectively Islamicising the saying: '"Blessed (*ṭūbā*) is the womb that carried you, and the breast that nourished you." Jesus responds, "Blessed (*ṭūbā*) is he who reads the Qur'an and follows what is in it".'[96]

Islamicising glosses may also be more substantial. A tradition transmitted by Ibn Ḥanbal connected to the Synoptic Gospels' account of the temptation of Jesus in the desert, concludes with Jesus' rebuking Satan as follows: 'God ordered me not to put myself to the test, for I do not know whether He will save me or not.'[97] Another report by Ibn Ḥanbal reshapes the account of the woman caught in adultery (John 8:1-11):

---

93 On this see I. Goldziher, 'Influences chrétiennes dans la littérature religieuse de l'Islam', *Revue de l'Histoire des Religions* 18 (1888) 180-99; M. Asín Palacios, 'Influencias evangélicas en la literatura religiosa del Islam', in T.W. Arnold and R.A. Nicholson (eds), *A volume of Oriental studies presented to Professor Edward G. Browne*[...] *on his 60th birthday*, Cambridge, 1922, 8-27; in addition to Palacios, 'Logia et agrapha Domini Jesu', see also the references in Khalidi, *Muslim Jesus*, pp. 221-2, n. 2.

94 Ibn Ḥanbal, *Zuhd*, p. 74; Khalidi, *Muslim Jesus*, pp. 71-2, no. 33 (trans. and notes). Khalidi notes that this may be an example of an early Muslim access to an Arabic Gospel translation or to a lectionary. Cf. Matthew 6:20-1; Luke 12:33-4.

95 Ibn al-Mubārak, *Zuhd*, p. 84, no. 150; Khalidi, *Muslim Jesus*, p. 53, no. 4 (trans. and notes).

96 Ibn Abī Shayba, *Muṣannaf*, *K. al-Zuhd*, 'Bāb mā dhukira fī zuhd al-anbīyā' wa-kalāmihim 'alayhīm al-salām', vol. 12, p. 8, no. 35235; cf. Ibn Ḥanbal, *Zuhd*, p. 75.

97 Ibn Ḥanbal, *Zuhd*, p. 74; Khalidi, *Muslim Jesus*, p. 72, no. 34 (trans. and notes).

> A man who had committed adultery was brought to Jesus, who ordered them to stone him. Jesus said, 'But no one should stone him who has committed what he has committed.' They let the stones fall from their hands, all except John son of Zachariah.[98]

The departures from the Johannine account notwithstanding (indeed, it reverses the teaching, as it implies that John the Baptist was able to carry out the stoning), this tradition preserves clearly identifiable traces of the Gospel narrative. While in this instance the overarching narrative invokes the Gospel account, other traditions employ evident biblical idioms to establish their unequivocal connection to the biblical text. This is exemplified in a report transmitted on the authority of the traditionist and *tābiʿ* Wahb ibn Munabbih, in which he draws attention to Jesus' Gospel idiom: 'Jesus said to his disciples, "In truth I say to you" – and he often used to say "In truth I say to you" – "those among you who sorrow most in misfortune are the most attached to this world."'[99]

Concomitant with Jesus' portrayal as an ascetic exemplar, as this and many other traditions evince, is his presentation as a mystic and a wisdom figure. This is perhaps captured in a pithy aphorism transmitted by Ibn al-Mubārak: 'Jesus said to the disciples, "Just as kings left wisdom to you, so you should leave the world to them."'[100] As Anawati summarises, 'Jesus became for the Muslim mystic writers "the model of the pilgrims", "the imām of the wanderers", "the example of the mystics".'[101]

Certain Muslim figures have also described mystical encounters with Jesus who, according to the standard doctrine, did not die but ascended body and soul to heaven. The Andalusian mystic Ibn ʿArabī (d. 1240) describes a vision of Jesus that he received when he was a young man. He recounts how Jesus urged him to a life of asceticism (*zuhd*) and self-denial (*tajrīd*), and interceded for him. Ibn ʿArabī calls Jesus his first 'master' (*shaykhunā l-awwal*),[102] and also dedicates a chapter to Jesus in his *Fuṣūṣ al-ḥikam*, with a special focus on the role of the Spirit (*rūḥ*) in his creation.[103]

---

98 Ibn Ḥanbal, *Zuhd*, p. 97; Khalidi, *Muslim Jesus*, pp. 82-3, no. 54 (trans. and notes).

99 Ibn Ḥanbal, *Zuhd*, p. 78; Khalidi, *Muslim Jesus*, p. 80, no. 51 (trans. and notes).

100 Ibn al-Mubārak, *Zuhd*, pp. 117-18, no. 284; Khalidi, *Muslim Jesus*, pp. 55-6, no. 8 (trans. and notes).

101 Anawati, "Īsā'.

102 Ibn ʿArabī, *Al-Futuḥāt al-makkiyya*, ed. ʿU. Yahya, Cairo, 1972-92, vol. 3, p. 341, quoted in C. Addas, *Quest for the red sulphur*, trans. P. Kingsley, Cambridge, 1993, p. 39. See S. Hirtenstein, 'Ibn ʿArabī', in *CMR* 4, 145-9.

103 See Ibn ʿArabī, *The ringstones of wisdom*, trans. C.K. Dagli, Chicago IL, 2004, pp. 157-76.

End of life and return

The standard Islamic understanding of the Qur'an's one reference to the Crucifixion (Q 4:157), shaped by the passive verb *shubbiha* (which may mean 'someone was made to appear' or 'it was made to appear') has another figure transformed into the likeness of Jesus and killed in his place.[104] Various scenarios (some of which have a disciple of Jesus killed, and others an enemy of Jesus, or Judas) are found in Islamic tradition that develop this theme. For example, one narrative related by Abū Jaʿfar al-Ṭabarī recounts that, towards the end of his life, Jesus was with his disciples (*ḥawāriyyūn*) on the day the Jews were looking to kill him, when all the disciples were miraculously transformed into his image. The Israelites, arriving at the spot where they were gathered, threatened: 'Show us which one is Jesus or we will kill all of you.' At this Jesus asked, 'Which one of you will win paradise for his soul today?' One faithful disciple who assented remained in the image of Christ, went out to the Jews, was taken and crucified, while God took Jesus into heaven through an opening in the roof of the house.[105]

The notion that Jesus did not die but was raised body and soul to heaven opened the door to speculation that he has been preserved for some future task on earth. Moreover, the Qur'an seems to hint at or allude to a role that Jesus will play in the Islamic end times scenario. Q 4:159, a verse that follows allusions to the crucifixion (4:157) and the ascension (4:158) of Jesus, relates: '(There is) not one of the People of the Book who will not believe in him before his death, and on the Day of Resurrection he will be a witness against them.' This verse could be read (and indeed was read) to imply that, before the death of Jesus, Jews and Christians will believe in him (as a Muslim prophet). The logical consequence of this reading is that Jesus has not yet died, that he ascended body and soul to heaven and will return to earth in the last days. Confirmation for this interpretation was found in 43:61: 'Surely it [or *he*] is indeed knowledge of the Hour.' This verse is preceded by a discussion in which Jesus apparently meant to reprimand Jews, and which was consequently seen to affirm an apocalyptic role for Jesus. The idea that Jesus would return in the end times was also thought helpful in explaining the remark of the angels in 3:46 that Jesus would be 'high-ranking' both 'in the cradle'

---

104 On this, see T. Lawson, *The crucifixion and the Qur'an. A study in the history of Muslim thought*, Oxford, 2009.

105 Al-Ṭabarī, *Jāmiʿ al-bayān fī taʾwīl al-Qurʾān*, ed. M.A. Bayḍūn, Beirut, 1988, vol. 6, pp. 12-13, on Q 4:157. This tradition is on the authority of Wahb ibn Munabbih.

and 'in maturity' (*kahlan*). It was widely understood that Jesus was taken to heaven when he was still young (*shābb*), and so his return in the end times would indeed allow him to reach a mature age.

From this relatively modest qur'anic basis, detailed traditions of Jesus' role in the last times emerged in the early Islamic centuries. A full consideration of Islamic traditions on Jesus' role in the eschaton would also involve a study of the development of the doctrine of a figure – not mentioned in the Qur'an – known as the *Mahdī*. Here we might mention only that, at an early stage, the title of Mahdī seems to have been associated with certain political figures, including the Umayyad Caliph 'Umar II (r. 717-20). However, in the end times traditions that spread in the early 'Abbasid period, the Mahdī is portrayed as a righteous leader who will appear, lead the Muslims in battle against the unbelievers, and establish a reign of justice. Most traditions have the Mahdī accomplish these feats together with Jesus, who is given the special role of confronting al-Dajjāl, or al-Masīḥ al-Dajjāl ('the lying Christ'). A long Hadith reported in *Sunan Ibn Mājah* describes the appearance of al-Dajjāl in detail and continues:

> Allah will send 'Isā ibn Maryam, who will come down on the white tower at the east of Damascus, wearing two *mahrūds*, resting the palms of his hands on the wings of two angels. When he lowers his head, droplets will fall from it and when he raises it drops like pearls will come down from it. It is not possible for the unbelievers to smell the fragrance of his breath without dying. His breath will stretch as far as his eyes can see. He will set forth until he reaches [al-Dajjāl] at the gate of Ludd (near Jaffa) and then kill him.[106]

The principal role of Jesus in the end-times scenarios in most Hadiths, including that quoted just above, is to confront and kill al-Dajjāl. The idea that Jesus – who during his lifetime exemplified an ascetic and mystical ethic – would be violent upon his return may reflect Christian apocalyptic expectations shaped in turn by the Book of Revelation, with its violent imagery. It may also be a way of shaping the image of Christ in a way that makes him more like the figure of Muḥammad, who confronted and killed his enemies. To this end, it is notable that certain apocalyptic traditions have Jesus take on a distinctly anti-Christian role. A widespread Hadith has Jesus break crosses, kill pigs (animals eaten by Christians) and refuse to accept the *jizya* (meaning that Christians, or Jews, might only choose Islam or death): 'The Hour will not begin until

---

106 Ibn Mājah, *Sunan Ibn Mājah*, *K. al-Fitan*, 'Bāb fitnat al-Dajjāl', ed. M.M.H. Naṣṣār, Beirut, 2012, vol. 4, p. 443, no. 4071.

'Isā ibn Maryam comes down as a just judge and an equitable ruler. He will break crosses, kill pigs and abolish the *jizya*, and money will become so abundant that no one will accept it.'[107]

Finally, we should note the view found in a Hadith transmitted by al-Ḥasan al-Baṣrī (d. 728) that Jesus himself will be the Mahdī: 'The situation will only become more trying and worldly affairs will only become more difficult, and people will only become more stingy, and the Hour will only come upon the worst of people, and the only Mahdī is 'Isā ibn Maryam.'[108] On this view, Jesus is not only the apocalyptic hero who overcomes and kills the enemies of Islam, but also the just judge who will rule over the final peaceful period of human history in anticipation of the Day of Resurrection.

Conclusion: After the ascension of Jesus

Preserved in various communities and genres across the large swathes of *dār al-Islām* over the centuries, the richly diverse accounts of Jesus in the Islamic tradition are nonetheless anchored in the Qur'an. Indeed, the qur'anic account at once draws the broad contours that the diverse portrayals of Jesus fill and effectively acts as their underlying unifying principle. In a similar vein, Muslim scholars developed varying accounts of the historical developments of the early Church after the ascension of Jesus, tracing the lives of the disciples up to the formation of the three major ecclesiastical groups: the Melkite Chalcedonians, West Syrian Miaphysites and the Church of the East.[109]

The early Muslim historiographer, Sayf ibn 'Umar, traces the development of Christianity to Paul, whom he takes to be a king and gives him the teknonym 'the Father of Saul'. After his conversion to Christianity, Ibn 'Umar relates, Paul enclosed himself in a hermitage/temple (*bayt*) which he ordered to be built and furnished with ashes, only to come out of it each time with a different opinion (*ra'y*) that his followers (*ahl al-bayt*) would soon espouse, such as directing prayers to the east, abandoning food laws and the teaching to turn the other cheek and to abandon warfare (*jihād*). Coming out of his hermitage for a fourth time,

[107] Ibn Mājah, *Sunan*, *K. al-Fitan*, 'Bāb fitnat al-Dajjāl', vol. 4, pp. 448-9, no. 4078. Cf. 'Abd al-Razzāq (d. 827), *Al-Muṣannaf*, vol. 11, pp. 400-1, nos 20843, 20844, and 20855.

[108] Ibn Mājah, *Sunan*, *K. al-Fitan*, 'Bāb shiddat al-zamān', vol. 4, p. 420, no. 4039.

[109] On the qur'anic presentation of the disciples, see G.S. Reynolds, 'The Quran and the Apostles of Jesus', *BSOAS* 76 (2013) 209-27.

Paul instructs all his followers to depart, except for four with the telling eponyms: Yaʿqūb (Jacob), Nasṭūr (Nestorius), Malkūn and al-Muʾmin (the Believer), with all except the Believer accepting Paul's newly introduced teaching: 'God appeared to us and then concealed himself from us' (*anna Allāh taʿālā tajallā lanā thumma iḥtajaba*). In this way, Ibn ʿUmar traces the development of the three major ecclesiastical groups – the West Syrians, known as Jacobites; the Church of the East, known as Nestorians; and the Chalcedonians, known as Melkites – to these three disciples. The Believer, effectively presented as a proto-Muslim, refused Paul's *raʾy*, so the account goes, and remained steadfast in keeping Jesus' original teachings.[110]

Other chroniclers present Islamic historical accounts for the development of Christianity that constructively engage Christian sources. The great scholar Ibn Khaldūn (d. 1406) presents an example of a Muslim historiographical account of Christian origins that is informed by Christian sources (notably al-Makīn Jirjis Ibn al-ʿAmīd [d. ca. 1280]) while remaining faithful to Islamic orthodoxy.[111] Ibn Khaldūn suggests that Jesus' followers were faithful to his teachings for some three centuries:

> Three hundred and twenty-eight years elapsed from the birth of Christ to the discovery of the cross. These Christians appointed their patriarchs and bishops, upholding the religion of Christ (*dīn al-Masīḥ*) according to what the disciples (*ḥawāriyyūn*) had laid down with regard to laws, beliefs and rules (*qawānīn wa-ʿaqāʾid wa-aḥkām*). Disagreements then arose in their beliefs (*ʿaqāʾid*) and all that they upheld in their faith in God and His attributes (*ṣifātih*) – far from what God, Christ and the disciples upheld, that is, their belief in the Trinity (*tathlīth*). But they were encumbered by the apparent meaning of Christ's words in the Gospel, whose original meaning (*tāʾwīl*) they failed to capture, and whose meanings they failed to understand.[112]

While both Sayf and Ibn Khaldūn distinguish Jesus from what they believed to be later distortions of the Christian faith, Ibn Khaldūn traces the 'turning point' in which Christians are thought to have abandoned

---

110 Sayf ibn ʿUmar, *Kitāb al-Ridda*, no. 133, pp. 132-5. Interestingly, Ibn al-Qayyim (*Hidāyat al-ḥayārā*, p. 548) traces the 'corruption' of the Christian faith not to the Apostle Paul, but to the third century bishop of Antioch Paul of Samosata.

111 See M. Whittingham, 'Ibn Khaldūn', in *CMR* 5, 300-8.

112 Ibn Khaldūn, *Tārīkh Ibn Khaldūn al-musammā dīwān al-mubtadaʾ wa-l-khabar fī tārīkh al-ʿarab wa-l-barbar wa-man ʿāṣarahum min dhawī al-shaʾn al-akbar*, ed. K. Shiḥāda and S. Zakkār, Beirut, 2001, vol. 2, pp. 175-6. Ibn Khaldūn introduces Jesus and Christianity in vol. 1, pp. 289-92, and then presents a more detailed account in vol. 2, pp. 167-80.

the (Islamic) teachings of Jesus and about Jesus, not to the apostle Paul, but to the rise of imperial Christianity. Despite this polemical perspective, Muslims scholars through the centuries continued to be enamoured by the figure of Christ. Far from limiting themselves to the Qur'an, they sought out a deeper understanding of his life and teaching in the New Testament and Christian tradition.

Chapter 7
Christian perceptions of Muḥammad

Clinton Bennett

Introduction: Setting the scene

Christian writings about Muḥammad during the first thousand years of Christian-Muslim encounter were almost all negative and hostile, presenting an attitude of virtually unrelieved antipathy. Tropes and legends developed that continued to shape Christian ideas about Muḥammad well into the early modern period, some of them still lurking in Christian writings even today. Major foci were Muḥammad's moral conduct, how he spread Islam, how he allegedly compiled the Qur'an, and what supposedly happened to his body after death. In this period, a small number of Christians did express affinity with Islam by writing more sympathetically about Muḥammad or, at the very least, by debating whether he met the criteria for prophetic legitimacy (as they devised these). Some expressed aversion towards Muḥammad but identified more positively with Islamic culture. Others tried to appeal to Muslims by way of affirming common ground, thus inviting Muslims to 'come on over', or by allowing for some measure of coexistence. A minority attempted to accommodate Muḥammad within a Christian theological view that recognised some legitimacy regarding his status as a prophet. When Christians wrote about Muḥammad, they did not always expect Muslims to read their works, though this was less true within the Islamic world when Arabic rather than Greek (or later Latin) was used. Those living among or in proximity to Muslims often wrote to reassure their own constituency that, despite Islam's political ascendancy, it was illegitimate and could not survive.

Apocalyptic views frequently shaped what Christians wrote about Muḥammad. Christians who lived at a distance and had no contact with Muslims, simply set out to demonise and dehumanise a potential enemy. Whether living under Muslim or Christian rule, few who wrote on Muḥammad appear to have had much interest in consulting Muslim sources until the end of this period. Many allowed their imaginations free reign. Legends and fictional tropes – such as pigs killing Muḥammad and eating his corpse, or his body being suspended in an iron coffin by magnets – proved remarkably durable. Antipathy produced a picture of Muḥammad that had no resemblance to the way Muslims saw him (though, of course, it is unlikely that any Christian who attempts an appreciation of him could replicate a Muslim view and remain Christian).

Works selected for discussion in this chapter either contributed tropes to the developing antipathetic tradition, significantly perpetuated them, or at least provided Christians with tools or ideas that could allow a reimagining of Christian-Muslim relations. They are mainly introduced chronologically, with later examples that contain similar tropes described together with them. The spelling of the name 'Muḥammad' is used throughout, although non-Arabic works used a range of renditions, including Mahun, Mahound, Mahomet, Mahumet, Mammet and Machomet.

Accounts of Christian encounters with Muḥammad in Muslim sources

Descriptions of encounters between Muḥammad and Christians in Muslim sources provide an important background to later Christian writings on the Prophet.[1] First, Muḥammad's early encounter with Baḥīrā, who is portrayed as a solitary monk, during a trade mission to Syria features prominently in Christian writings. Baḥīrā appears to have recognised Muḥammad as someone whose coming had been predicted in scripture, 'finding traces of his description' there.[2] The account given by Ibn Isḥāq (d. 767), the first major biographer of Muḥammad, of Christian visitors from Najrān engaging in dispute with him over the Trinity and the status of Jesus, and of how they were permitted to pray in the Prophet's mosque, informed subsequent Christian-Muslim relations in significant ways, but is ambiguous with respect to what they thought about him.[3] Ibn Isḥāq claims that their own chief advisor declared that the delegates knew 'right well that Muḥammad is a prophet sent by God', even though they chose not to submit to his religious authority but entered a political pact with him that allowed them to maintain their religious practices.

---

[1] See J. Hämeen-Anttila, 'Christians and Christianity in the Qur'ān', in *CMR* 1, 21-30.

[2] A. Guillaume, *The life of Muhammad. A translation of Isḥāq's Sīrat rasūl Allāh*, Oxford, 1955, p. 80.

[3] Guillaume, *Life of Muhammad*, pp. 270-7.

Ibn Isḥāq also records the Byzantine Emperor Heraclius (r. 610-41) telling a delegation sent by Muḥammad that he knew their master was a prophet who was mentioned 'in our scriptures', but that he would not acknowledge him for fear of his life under the bishop, whose authority was greater than his.[4] This resonates with Gregory Barhebraeus's later account of Heraclius's reaction to Muḥammad, which is discussed below.

Accounts such as these serve Muslim purposes by declaring that Christians who met Muḥammad and knew about him recognised his legitimacy on the basis of scriptural prophecies. Following his death in 632, and until John of Damascus wrote *Peri haeresiōn* ('On heresies', known by its Latin title *De haeresibus*) in the mid-8th century, the rapid expansion of the Islamic state probably preoccupied Christians more than theological reflection on Muslim claims for Muḥammad.

Christian perceptions of Muḥammad in 8th- and 9th-century works from Greater Syria and Iraq

John of Damascus

Before becoming a monk, the Melkite theologian John of Damascus served in senior administrative capacities under two caliphs. He thus probably had conversational Arabic, although his extant writings are in Greek. His are some of the earliest recorded Christian perceptions of Muḥammad.[5] In the light of R.F. Glei's comment that the 'significance of ch. 100 of *De haeresibus* cannot be overestimated', it calls for detailed discussion.[6] Although *De haeresibus* is often taken to refer to Muḥammad himself, it is largely a description of his religion. Also known as Saracens, John says, the Ishmaelites had worshipped idols down to time of Heraclius, when the 'false prophet' Muḥammad 'appeared in their midst'. Having 'chanced upon' the Old and New Testaments, and having conversed with an Arian monk (who is not named by John), he pretended piety, 'devised his own heresy', and claimed that 'a certain book' had been 'sent down to him from heaven'. In this book, he gave the Saracens 'ridiculous compositions', including what he called the chapter of the 'She-camel', which drank a 'whole river' and 'passed through two

4 Guillaume, *Life of Muhammad*, p. 656.
5 F.H. Chase (trans.), *Saint John of Damascus. Writings* [The Fathers of the Church 37], Washington DC, 1958, p. 153.
6 R.F. Glei, 'John of Damascus', in *CMR* 1, 295-301, p. 299.

mountains'.[7] This is mistaken, because there is no such chapter or story in the Qur'an (although there is the recurring story of a she-goat that was cruelly hobbled to prevent her grazing on common pasture). However, other qur'anic references name chapters correctly – 'The heifer', 'Women', 'The table spread' – and accurately summarise much of what the Qur'an says about Jesus: he was a 'word' and a 'spirit' from God (Q 4:171), was not crucified (Q 4:157), and was emphatically not God's son or God himself.[8] John is also aware of the Muslim charge that Jews and Christians have corrupted their scriptures, exaggerated Jesus' status, and obscured the truth that Muḥammad fulfils scriptural promises.[9]

John ridicules Muḥammad's claim to have received revelation because no one witnessed this event.[10] His laws that allow a man four wives and 'if possible' a thousand concubines, and the summary divorce of wives, are among other 'stupid things' attributed to him, while his fabrication of a revelation to justify his conduct with the wife of his former slave and adopted son, is reprehensible.[11] (John must have heard about the Zayd-Zaynab affair because it cannot be reconstructed from the Qur'an itself. It became a favourite of polemical Christian writers, who devoted many pages to condemning it as an example of Muḥammad's debauchery.) Despite all this, John acknowledges that Muḥammad condemned idolatry, believed in one God who was Creator of all things, and acknowledged that Jesus was 'begotten without seed' of Mary. Problematic for him was Muḥammad's rejection of the Trinity and of Jesus' crucifixion, and the charge that Christians commit *shirk* (associating Jesus with God as God's partner). His response asserts that Muslims are inconsistent because they accept Jesus as a 'word' and 'spirit' from God (as Q 4:171 openly states) yet separate these from the Being from which they 'naturally have their existence', and he accuses them of idolatry in worshipping the Black Stone, which they rub, kiss and embrace, and which he identifies as a representation of Venus.[12]

Three negative tropes can be identified in John's chapter. First, that at least one heterodox Christian helped Muḥammad concoct Islam, which can therefore be considered a type of Christian heresy. This figure, together with other imagined Christian and Jewish sources of

[7] Chase, *Writings*, p. 158.
[8] Chase, *Writings*, p. 154.
[9] Chase, *Writings*, pp. 155-6.
[10] Chase, *Writings*, p. 155.
[11] Chase, *Writings*, p. 157.
[12] Chase, *Writings*, p. 156.

Muḥammad's information, features in later works, where he is sometimes named Sergius; some of these works are discussed below.[13] Usually identified as a heretic (later routinely as a Nestorian rather than an Arian), this monk (or sometimes monks) receives credit for instructing Muḥammad and helping launch his career as a heretic, or for leading him into error, which some suggest he might otherwise have avoided. Perhaps aware that, to a degree, this could exonerate Muḥammad, one variation transforms the monk into an Orthodox teacher. Second, that Muḥammad used his alleged revelations to justify his immoral behaviour, with the imputation that he was lustful and sexually promiscuous. Third, that, although he condemned idolatry, Muḥammad permitted a pagan practice, a charge that over time developed into the belief that Muslims worshipped idols of Muḥammad. Writing from his abbey in distant England, in later centuries William of Malmesbury (d. 1143) informed readers that Saracens did not worship Muḥammad but 'God the Creator and believe that Muḥammad is his prophet'; he then described the Turks placing an image of him (*simulacro Mahomet*) in the Dome of the Rock in Jerusalem, apparently without seeing any incongruity between his statements.[14] In the *Chanson de Roland* (late 12th century) Muslims worship a Trinity of Mahumet, Apollin and Termagant in places of worship called mahumeries.[15] The *Chansons d 'Antioche*, part of the Old French Crusade cycle (end of the 12th and early 13th centuries) has an idol of Muḥammad floating in the air suspended by magnets and 'later carried on an elephant [...] with a devil inside uttering prophecies'.[16] Several terms found in English works, such as 'mawmet' and 'mummery', meaning respectively a 'doll' and 'absurd ceremony', appear to have their origin in versions of the spelling of Muḥammad. The Christian Arab known as ʿAbd al-Masīḥ al-Kindī (see below) picked up and supported the specific charge that the annual pilgrimage was pagan, 'borrowed from heathens', though he pointed to Indian rather than Hellenic influences.[17]

---

13 See B. Roggema, *The legend of Sergius Baḥīrā. Eastern Christian apologetics and apocalyptic in response to Islam*, Leiden, 2009, for the developments of this myth in various forms.

14 J. Tolan, 'William of Malmesbury, in *CMR* 3, 483-7, pp. 485-6.

15 S. Kinoshite, *'La Chanson de Roland'*, in *CMR* 3, 648-52.

16 C. Sweetenham, *'Chanson d'Antioche'*, in *CMR* 3, 422-6, p. 424. See also A. Shalem et al., *Constructing the image of Muhammad in Europe*, Berlin, 2013, p. 29.

17 W. Muir, *The Apology of al Kindy. Written at the court of al Mâmûn (circa A.H. 215, A.D. 830), in defence of Christianity against Islam: with an essay on its age and authorship*, London, 1882, p. 38.

Intended to reassure Christians that they might be subject to Muslim political rule, although their religion was superior and Islam an absurd forgery, John's chapter easily qualifies as antipathetic. Yet, some affinity with Islam can be identified in what he says. Muḥammad's teaching on Jesus provided a foundation for John to argue or reason with Muslims on the rationality of the Christian belief in a Triune God. In *Dialogue between a Saracen and a Christian*, a work that has been attributed to him but was probably written by someone influenced by him, the allusion in Q 4:171 to God's 'spirit' and 'word' is utilised in debate with Muslims on the Trinity and Incarnation, with stock answers given to questions that Muslims ask.[18] This suggests willingness to engage with Muslims on questions of belief, not merely to write about Islam from a distance. Even if minimally, John recognised some common ground with them. His view of Islam as a heresy suggests that efforts should be made to bring them into the orthodox fold by confessing their errors, repenting and affirming the Nicene Creed. John 'builds his case' for Christianity 'on foundations acceptable to Muslims'.[19]

Theodore Abū Qurra (d. c. 823)[20]

Theodore's literary corpus includes a version of the *Dialogue between a Saracen and a Christian*, which, if it is not by John, Theodore could have written or edited.[21] A Melkite bishop in northern Mesopotamia, he may well have taken part in a number of debates with Muslims. He wrote in Arabic as well as in Greek and was understandably much more circumspect in his Arabic works, though he does not always identify his interlocutors as Muslims,[22] and may not have intended 'any of his Arab works to focus on Islam'. However, in this period when Christians named Jews in their writings as their targets they were usually targeting Muslims,[23] and his expression 'those who lay claim to faith' probably refers to Muslims.

---

[18] I.M. Beaumont, *Christology in dialogue with Muslims. A critical analysis of Christian presentations of Christ for Muslims from the ninth and twentieth centuries*, Eugene OR, 2011, p. 16.

[19] Beaumont, *Christology*, p. 17.

[20] See P. Schadler, 'The dialogue between a Saracen and a Christian', in *CMR* 1, 367-70, and J.C. Lamoreaux, 'Theodore Abū Qurra', in *CMR* 1, 439-91.

[21] Schadler, 'Dialogue between a Saracen and a Christian', p. 368.

[22] P. Schadler, *John of Damascus and Islam. Christian heresiology and the intellectual background to earliest Christian-Muslim relations*, Leiden, 2018, p. 189.

[23] Schadler, *John of Damascus and Islam*, p. 190.

In Theodore's Greek works, Muḥammad is a demon-possessed, truth-distorting 'insane false prophet',[24] guilty of 'moral turpitude'.[25] Throughout his writings, he accuses Muḥammad of succeeding only by inducing people to follow him with the offer of sexual indulgence, wealth and power. He offered booty, and laws that catered to the same base human desires that had caused Adam's fall. Like John of Damascus, Theodore refers to an unnamed Arian (but does not describe him as a monk) who is the sole source of Muḥammad's knowledge of Christianity. Other authors added additional encounters and extended the relationship between Muḥammad and the monk from a brief meeting in his youth to a longer, more mature and formative one.

Theodore cites the Qur'an accurately and does not hesitate to employ terms used in Muslim theological discourse about the relationship between God and God's uncreated and eternal attributes, including the Word and how it can also be present within a book. There are continuing debates about the nature of Christian-Muslim exchanges in this period, and to whether Christians did or did not influence developments in Islamic theology.[26] Whether there was influence or not, it seems likely that by utilising the terms he did Theodore was aware that Muslims would find them familiar and might draw conclusions based on this language.

Like John, Theodore lived among Muslims and interacted with them, yet his writings are distinctly more antipathetic and polemical. He may have had some cultural affinity with Muslims, but they would not have found his works very appealing; he probably did not intend to confront Muslims but to provide Christians with material 'to refute Muslim arguments'.[27]

Again, we have the trope that Muḥammad learned about religion from a heterodox Christian. Added to this, there are others in later works, about his being possessed by a demon, being insane and constructing a self-serving religion that led people into error. The Qur'an itself reflects similar criticisms of Muḥammad by his Meccan opponents (see Q 68:2), to which can be added his own fear that he had become a *kāhin* (soothsayer, who he believed were demon possessed or fraudsters).[28]

24 Schadler, *John of Damascus and Islam*, p. 200.
25 Lamoreaux, 'Theodore Abū Qurra', p. 441.
26 Schadler, 'Dialogue between a Saracen and a Christian', p. 368.
27 Schadler, 'Dialogue between a Saracen and a Christian', p. 368.
28 Guillaume, *Life of Muhammad*, p. 106.

Q 16:103 also reports the accusation that a young Christian slave taught Muḥammad all that he knew.[29]

Theophanes the Confessor (d. c. 818)[30]

Theophanes the Confessor is best known for his *Chronographia*, a chronicle of world events of which a Latin translation was made between 873 and 875. In this work, when he recounts the expansion of the caliphate, Theophanes describes Muslims torturing and killing prisoners, destroying churches, forcibly converting their subjects, taxing them heavily and deporting them.[31] He credits their victory over the Byzantine Empire as the result of the Emperor Heraclius deviating from Christian orthodoxy, suggesting that Islam was used by God to punish Christians – a trope that attracted support from other writers.[32] For Theophanes, Arabs are 'God's enemies', 'deniers of Christ', 'cowards', 'stupid', 'boorish' and 'impure'.[33]

Theophanes pioneered the new and enduring trope that Muḥammad's delusional visions about receiving divine revelation were the result of epileptic seizures.[34] Like the accusation of insanity, this removes any possibility that Muḥammad's religious claims could be legitimate. In his brief biography of Muḥammad, as well as diagnosing epilepsy, Theophanes describes how, as a 'poor orphan', he attached himself to a rich widow in order to advance himself by taking control of her camels and property. When he went to Palestine, he met Christians and Jews and 'hunted for certain writings among them'. His wife was alarmed when she saw him in one of his fits, and she regretted that she had married a man who was not only poor but also epileptic. Muḥammad soothed her by explaining that the cause of his faints was visions of the Angel Gabriel. When his wife told this to her friend, an exiled false monk, he identified the angel as the one whom God sent to prophets. So, from that point, she believed in Muḥammad and told other women. Abū Bakr was the first man to believe, and was appointed by Muḥammad to succeed him. After practising his heresy secretly for ten years, Muḥammad was able to conquer the town of Yathrib by force. He told his followers that paradise was a place of carnal delight (a popular Christian trope) where they would

[29] Guillaume, *Life of Muhammad*, p. 180.
[30] See M. Vaiou, 'Theophanes the Confessor', in *CMR* 1, 426-36.
[31] Vaiou, 'Theophanes', p. 428.
[32] Vaiou, 'Theophanes', p. 429.
[33] Vaiou, 'Theophanes', p. 428.
[34] H. Turtledove (ed. and trans.), *The Chronicle of Theophanes. Anni mundi 6095-6305 (A.D. 602-813)*, Philadelphia PA, 1982, p. 35.

enjoy intercourse with women and drink wine, while any who killed an enemy or who were killed by them would enter heaven. He said many other 'foolish things', yet he also taught his followers to 'have sympathy for one another and help those treated unjustly'.[35]

While the *Chronographia* is an important historical work, in part corroborated by 'Arab sources',[36] it did nothing to improve Christian-Muslim understanding. The myth that epileptic seizures were the cause of Muḥammad's 'revelations' virtually became a fixed explanation of Muḥammad and his visions. The popular *Travels of John Mandeville* (mid-14th century)[37] did much to spread it in Europe; the 1582 London version has a woodcut of Muḥammad being treated for this illness.[38] Much later, physician and Orientalist Aloys Sprenger (1813-93) depicted Muḥammad as 'a complete maniac' at times, because for him epilepsy undermined any possibility of religious sincerity or of receiving genuine revelations from God.[39] Other than correctly naming Abū Bakr, Khadīja, Gabriel and the city to which Muḥammad migrated (by invitation not invasion) in 622, nothing in this account corresponds with Muslim belief. Writing in Greek, Theophanes was evidently reassuring Christians that their political overlords were only temporary and acting as instruments of divine punishment while purveying a debased and ridiculous religion.

Christian-Muslim debates: two examples

The next two works represent types of debate between Arabic-speaking Christians and Muslims in the ʿAbbasid period. *The apology of Timothy the Patriarch* is the report of a two-day dialogue between the Nestorian Catholicos Timothy I and the Caliph al-Mahdī that took place in about 782,[40] while *The apology of al-Kindī* (or *Risāla*), written under a pseudonym, purports to be a literary exchange between a Christian and his Muslim friend (it is usually dated to the 830s).[41] Timothy wrote his account in Syriac (there is also an Arabic version), and al-Kindī in Arabic. As head of the Church of the East in his time, Timothy was also

---

35 Turtledove, *Chronicle*, p. 35.

36 Vaiou, 'Theophanes', p. 431.

37 I.M. Higgins, 'John Mandeville', in *CMR* 5, 147-64.

38 'Machomet treated for the "falling evil"', in *Travels of John Mandeville* (Sig. Kv2). See M. Dimmock, *Mythologies of the Prophet Muhammad in early modern English culture*, Cambridge, 2013, p. 49.

39 A. Sprenger, *The life of Mohammad from original sources,* Allahabad, 1851, p. 114.

40 M. Heimgartner and B. Roggema, 'Timothy I', in *CMR* 1, 515-31.

41 L. Bottini, 'Al-Kindī, ʿAbd al-Masīḥ ibn Isḥāq (pseudonym)', in *CMR* 1, 587-94.

leader of the Christian *dhimma* within the Islamic world, and as such had regular audiences with the caliph. In return for paying the *jizya* (tax payable by non-Muslims), his community in theory received the state's protection, was allowed some measure of internal civil autonomy and freedom to practise its own faith, and was usually exempt from attempts at conversion by Muslims. Nestorians and other non-Chalcedonians, and also some Orthodox Christians who were at odds with the Patriarch of Constantinople, may have preferred Muslim rule because this was more conducive than Byzantine domination had been. The Nestorians (like some others) made themselves indispensable in the caliphal administration, so much so that Theophanes the Confessor reports two occasions when non-Muslims were removed from their posts 'out of envy', only to be quickly restored because the 'ignorant Arabs' could not maintain their own accounts and records.[42]

Much less is known about al-Kindī and his Muslim friend al-Hāshimī. They were probably fictitious characters invented by a Christian who used the pretext of an invitation by al-Hāshimī to al-Kindī to convert to Islam and al-Kindī's explanation of why he would not accept to produce a scathing critique of the foundations of Islam. Written under a pseudonym, it understandably differs markedly in both tone and content from Timothy's eirenic replies to al-Mahdī given in a public debate.

Rendel Harris thought that Timothy agreed to the debate at al-Mahdī's invitation only reluctantly, believing that this type of exchange was an exercise in futility.[43] The exchanges contain several references to Muḥammad, mainly concerned with whether he was predicted in scripture, received true revelation or worked miracles, as he would have if he had been a genuine prophet. Timothy rejects all claims in favour of Muḥammad, but he never ridicules or insults him or imputes lack of sincerity to him. The most significant exchange concerning Muḥammad is on the second day, when the caliph asks Timothy, 'What do you say about Muḥammad?' To this he responds:

> Muḥammad is worthy of all praise by all reasonable people, O my Sovereign. He walked in the path of the prophets, and trod in the track of the lovers of God. All the prophets taught the doctrine of one God, and since

42 Turtledove, *Chronicle*, pp. 73, 120.
43 R. Harris, 'Introduction', *Woodbrooke Studies* 2 (1928) 1-10, p. 5.

> Muḥammad taught the doctrine of the unity of God he walked, therefore, in the path of the prophets.[44]

Timothy goes on to observe that Muḥammad drove his people away from bad works towards good, separated them from idolatry and polytheism, and taught them about God, his word and his spirit, all of this following in the path of the prophets. Muḥammad ardently loved God more than his own soul, he praised those who worshipped God, he opposed idolatry and warned of the perils of hell. In a word, what Abraham did in opposing idolatry, Muḥammad also did. For this, God honoured Muḥammad and made him victorious over 'two powerful kingdoms',[45] Persia and Byzantium.

It can be seen that, on the one hand, Timothy does not explicitly call Muḥammad a prophet, though on the other, saying that he walked in the path of the prophets means that Muḥammad practised what they had preached. This leaves open the possibility that Muḥammad and those who imitated him enjoyed a genuine relationship with God. Some centuries after this, Thomas Aquinas (d. 1224) developed the notion that explicit faith in Jesus' Incarnation, suffering and resurrection is not essential for salvation. Provided that non-Christians (and those within the Church who do not fully understand Christian doctrine) have 'some kind' of belief 'in the mystery of Christ's incarnation, implicit faith which God will eventually bring to explicit faith in the Trinity', this will suffice.[46] If Christians choose to see Muḥammad's acceptance of Jesus as a word and spirit from God (see Q 4:171) as implying implicit belief in the Incarnation of Christ (at which John of Damascus hinted), he could qualify as an unbaptised Christian, which might be what Timothy had in mind. However, when Aquinas mentions Muḥammad, he points out that, unlike Christ, he worked no miracles. He saw him as a carnal man whose followers were 'beastlike' and 'irrational',[47] unable to perceive that God could have a son without needing a wife.[48] Muḥammad forced people to follow him, he had ten wives, he perverted the Bible and fabricated

---

44 A. Mingana, 'Timothy's Apology', *Woodbrooke Studies* 2 (1928) 11-162, p. 61. The Syriac text runs from p. 91.

45 Mingana, 'Timothy's Apology', p. 62.

46 F.V. Bauerschmidt, *Holy teaching. Introducing the Summa theologiae of St. Thomas Aquinas*, Grand Rapids MI, 2005, p. 137.

47 J. Tolan, '*Liber de veritate catholicae fidei contra errores infidelium qui dicitur Summa contra gentiles*', *CMR* 4, 523-7, p. 524.

48 J. Tolan, '*De rationibus fidei contra Saracenos, Graecos et Armenos ad cantorem Antiochenum*', in *CMR* 4, 527-9, p. 528.

his own scripture, and he thus failed the tests of authentic prophethood. On every point, Muḥammad serves Aquinas as a 'black foil to the light of Christ'.[49]

In contrast to Timothy, al-Kindī's view of Muḥammad is closer to what Christians had written up to his time. He dismisses any claim that Muḥammad had worked miracles or was predicted in scripture, and sees nothing commendable or praiseworthy in him; he describes Muḥammad as a womaniser or a demoniac, which Timothy does not. For al-Kindī, who declares that he has received a guarantee of immunity to speak his mind,[50] Muḥammad's mission was neither inspired by the divine nor motivated by the human, but was of Satan,[51] and all he offered was worldly inducements. His 'chief object was to take beautiful women to wife, to attack surrounding tribes, slay and plunder'.[52]

Al-Kindī makes much of the way Muḥammad allegedly had enemies assassinated, and 'besieged and forced' the Jewish tribe Banū Qaynuqāʿ to surrender.[53] Aware of Muslim accounts of Muḥammad's miracles, al-Kindī describes several of these and dismisses them as fabrications, citing for support what he takes to be the Qur'an's disclaimer that Muḥammad did not perform any miracles.[54] In an allusion to the involvement of the monk Baḥīrā in the composition of the Qur'an, he declares that a Nestorian monk called Sergius and two Jewish rabbis interpolated biblical stories into the text, which is anyway full of contradictions. Muḥammad also fabricated Q 33:36-7 to justify his forcing his adopted son Zayd to divorce his wife Zaynab so that he himself could marry her.[55] Those who followed him were invited to rape, pillage, make war and take people captive, while Jesus' followers will enter paradise.[56] Thus, Muḥammad fails on every count when compared with Jesus.

Both these works became popular guides for Christians debating with Muslims. Timothy's, which may represent the first serious attempt by a Christian author to move towards an accommodation with Islam, did not

---

49 P. Valkenberg, 'Can we talk theologically? Thomas Aquinas and Nicholas of Cusa on the possibility of a theological understanding of Islam', in A.K. Min (ed.), *Rethinking the medieval legacy for contemporary theology*, South Bend IN, 2014, 131-66, p. 136.

50 W. Muir *Apology of al Kindy*, p. 49.

51 Muir, *Apology*, p. 20. Muir also entertained the possibility that Muḥammad's inspiration was Satanic, see W. Muir, *Life of Mahomet*, London, 1858, vol. 2, p. 90.

52 Muir, *Apology*, p. 9.

53 Muir, *Apology*, pp. 6-7. Muir was to highlight this in his *Life of Mahomet*.

54 Muir, *Apology*, p. 12. See Q 17:59 (Muir has 17:60).

55 Muir, *Apology*, p. 9.

56 Muir, *Apology*, pp. 57-8.

achieve as wide an exposure beyond the Islamic world because, although it was quickly translated into Arabic, it was not translated into Latin or a European vernacular until Alphonse Mingana's English translation in 1928 (one Arabic version substitutes Theodore Abū Qurra as author).[57] Al-Kindī's reply was among the works of apology and polemic that Peter of Cluny (1094-1156) commissioned to be translated into Latin during his visit to the Iberian Peninsula in 1142-3, resulting in Peter of Toledo's *Epistula Saraceni*.[58] In turn, an epitome of this was included in the publication by Theodor Bibliander of Robert of Ketton's Latin translation of the Qur'an in 1543.[59] Many Christians regarded it as the guide *par excellence* to refuting the false, even satanic, religion and its founder's spurious claims. Attributing Muḥammad's inspiration to Satan finds expression elsewhere, when William of Tyre describes him as a 'destroyer not a prophet' and Satan's first-born.[60] Peter of Cluny, despite calling for a new, peaceful appeal to Muslims, nevertheless dubbed Muḥammad's religion diabolical, and one through which more people had been led into error than by any other heresy.[61] In the 19th century, William Muir in his *Life of Mahomet*, which, though antipathetic to its subject, was based on early Islamic sources, strongly hints that he subscribed to this accusation.[62] All the works discussed so far were written by Christians living among Muslims under Muslim rule, and who all, to some degree, enjoyed cordial or even friendly relations with Muslims and had some knowledge about Muḥammad and the Qur'an.

However, with the exception of Timothy, they combined this with calumny and suspicion, so that references to incidents in the life of Muḥammad that many Muslims accepted as fact would frequently be presented in ways that discredited Muḥammad morally. Al-Kindī's inability to see anything admirable in Muḥammad suggests that he had no interest in trying to see him from a Muslim viewpoint, though he probably had the best access to Islamic sources of all these writers. Timothy's attempt to avoid openly insulting Muḥammad, and his effort to recognise something praiseworthy in him, could suggest that neither acquaintance with Muslims nor direct access to Islamic sources could

57 M. Heimgartner, 'Timothy', p. 524.

58 F. González Muñoz, '*Epistula Saraceni* [*et*] *rescriptum Christiani*', in *CMR* 3, 479-82.

59 See B. Gordon, '*Machumetis Saracenorum principis, eiusque successorum vitae, ac doctrina, ipseque Alcoran*', in *CMR* 6, 680-5.

60 A. Mallett, 'William of Tyre', in *CMR* 3, 771-7.

61 D. Iogna-Prat and J. Tolan, 'Peter of Cluny', in *CMR* 3, 604-10.

62 Muir, *Life of Mahomet*, vol. 2, p. 91.

influence opinions about Muḥammad over *a priori* assumptions, agendas and theological dispositions. The starting position discernible in John and Timothy that Muslims in some measure participated in the 'light that gives light to everyone' (John 1:9) – even though the fullness of that light is revealed in Christianity – may be more important than other factors in shifting Christians towards a less hostile perception.

Early Latin works from Spain in the 8th and 9th centuries

The Muslim invasion of Iberia in 711 led to the first major encounter in Europe between Christians and Muslims. The *Chronicle of 741* was probably the first Latin work to mention Muḥammad,[63] and the *Chronicle of 754* was the second.[64] Both cover Islam's rise and expansion up to the writers' own times in the 8th century. Neither gives much biographical detail, although both describe Muḥammad as the leader of an anti-Byzantine rebellion. The earlier work identifies Muḥammad as of noble birth, a wise or prudent man about whom many stories were told, after whose death his followers revered him as a prophet.[65] The second work adds the date of Muhammad's death as 666, when Abū Bakr of his own tribe was chosen to succeed him as leader of the Arabs.[66] The Arabs won victories more 'through trickery' than through Muḥammad's leadership. Kenneth Wolf, who has translated the *Chronicle of 754*, comments that the author hardly refers to any distinctive rites or teachings in the Arabs' religion, which has led to speculation that the work could not have been written by a Muslim. Others remark that it is highly unlikely that a Muslim would refer to Islam's rise as a rebellion, the term used here, added to which the authors (both works are presumed to have been written by Christians) seemed to think that Mecca was in Mesopotamia. Ethnic rather than religious terms are used throughout, and except for hinting that the Arabs' victories were due to their craftiness and use of bribes, these two chronicles do not seem to show hostility, unlike other works where Arabs are dismissed as ugly, cowardly, barely human and followers of a diabolical sect.[67]

---

63 C. Ailett, '*The Chronicle of 741*', in *CMR* 1, 284-9.

64 K.B. Wolf, '*The Chronicle of 754*', in *CMR* 1, 302-4.

65 A.R. Christys, *Christians in al-Andalus*, Abingdon, 2002, p. 43.

66 K.B. Wolf, *Conquerors and chroniclers of early medieval Spain*, Liverpool, 1990, vol. 9, p. 115; see also his '*Chronicle of 754*', pp. 302-4.

67 Wolf, *Conquerors and chroniclers*, pp. 29, 36; see also Sweetenham, *Chanson d'Antioche*, p. 116.

Most relevant for Christian-Muslim relations, apart from the two works' religiously neutral tone, is the date 666 given for Muḥammad's death. Initially in Iberia, but later well beyond, this fed into ideas that associated Muḥammad with the beast of the Book of Revelation and the Book of Daniel in various ways. In his bull calling for the fifth crusade (1213), Pope Innocent III (r. 1198-1216) predicted the imminent end of the Saracens, because almost 600 of the allotted 666 years had passed since the death of 'a certain son of perdition, Muḥammad the pseudo-prophet'.[68] Others found ways to read the number 666 into Muḥammad's name.[69]

In the immediate Iberian context, it was from this association that the martyrs of Córdoba, who were executed over a number of years in the mid-9th century for publicly insulting Muḥammad, took their cue. Eulogius of Córdoba, who recounted and defended their actions, and was himself executed in 857, left more evidence that Iberian Christians quickly came to link Muḥammad with notions and fables about the Antichrist who would appear at the Endtime by copying and using the *Istoria de Mahomet* (c. 850).[70] The opening sentence of this work refers to Muḥammad as a 'heresiarch', and goes on to describe him as an orphan who was 'put under the charge of a certain widow', and attended 'assemblies of Christians' while travelling on business. A 'shrewd son of darkness', he learned some sermons off by heart and surpassed his fellow 'irrational Arabs in all things'. Inflamed by lust, he 'was joined to his patroness by some barbaric law'. The 'spirit of error' began to appear to him in the form of a vulture with a golden mouth, which he said was Gabriel who ordered him to present himself to the people as a prophet.[71] Preaching to 'irrational animals', he told people to worship a 'corporeal God' and to abandon idolatry. He composed 'false psalms' from the 'mouths of irrational animals', and sayings about a hoopoe and a frog as well as songs about Joseph, Zachariah 'and even the mother of the Lord, Mary'. He fabricated a divine message to justify taking his neighbour's wife (Zayd is named as the neighbour, though he is identified in most versions of this story as Muḥammad's adopted son) as his own. Soon after that, 'the death of his body and soul approached simultaneously'.

---

68 J. Tolan, *Saracens. Islam in the medieval European imagination*, New York, 2002, p. 194.

69 See M.N. Swanson, 'Būlus al-Būshī', in *CMR* 4, 280-7, p. 281.

70 K.B. Wolf (trans.), 'Eulogius, A Christian account of the life of Muhammad', in O.R. Constable (ed.), *Medieval Iberia. Readings from Christian, Muslim, and Jewish sources*, Philadelphia PA, 1997, pp. 48-50.

71 Wolf, 'Eulogius, Christian account', p. 48.

His followers guarded his corpse, expecting him to rise again after three days as he had predicted, but his body began to stink and dogs 'devoured his flank' (p. 49). Muḥammad committed other sins which were not recorded, and condemned both his own soul and those of many others to hell.[72]

The debased death trope

Although they lived in close proximity to Muslims, the writer of the *Istoria de Mahomet* and Eulogius, who copied it, evidently had no interest in learning about Islam or Muḥammad from Muslims. Their source was almost certainly the 'meagre' information available in Latin texts possibly derived from John of Damascus (which is supported by the use of the term 'heresiarch' for Muḥammad and the inclusion of the Zayd-Zaynab incident).[73] Two tropes developed from the details they give. The first was a profusion of myths about how Muḥammad pretended to receive revelation through birds, often doves, that were supposed to be the Holy Spirit, and the second was the debased or horrible death he suffered, involving a stinking corpse and attacks by dogs (later more usually pigs), that in some accounts actually killed him.

Some accounts link Muḥammad's horrible death with epilepsy, so that it was during a seizure that swine attacked him. Originally, this trope was borrowed from legends about the demise of the Antichrist, which establishes another link between early Iberian responses to Muḥammad and expectations that the End was near. There are also some parallels between the development of this trope and Jewish mockery of Jesus' death that are found, for example, in the *Toledot Yeshu*[74] (possibly from the 2nd century), in which Jesus is a magician who enticed Jews away from their religion, seduced women and died a shameful death. The early biographer of Muḥammad, Ibn Isḥāq, records that even after his death Muḥammad smelled 'sweet', suggesting a hint of reaction to Christian accusations.[75]

---

72 Wolf, 'Eulogius, Christian account', p. 50.

73 R.W. Southern, *Western views of Islam in the Middle Ages*, Cambridge MA, 1962, p. 25.

74 Possibly 2nd century; see R.E. Van Voorst, *Jesus outside the New Testament. An introduction to the ancient evidence*, Grand Rapids MI, 2000, p. 127; and the translation by M. Meerson, P. Schäfer and Y. Deutsch, *Toledot Yeshu. The life story of Jesus*, Tübingen, 2014.

75 Guillaume, *Life of Muhammad*, p. 688.

Among works in which pigs eat Muḥammad's corpse or actually kill him are Embrico of Mainz's rhymed Latin text, *Vita Mahometi*, from the early 12th century,[76] which describes how Muḥammad, who was a magician, ties his book of law to the horns of a bull, which then comes up to him with it, passing this off as a miracle. After God smites him dead for his sins, pigs start to devour him, and his followers arrange for his tomb to be suspended in mid-air by magnets. In the *Vita Machometi*, also from the early 12th century, by the little-known author Adelphus,[77] Muḥammad also trains a cow to appear before the people with his law book tied to its horns. Initially tutored by Nestorius, a heretic and false monk, Muḥammad later kills Nestorius out of jealousy because of his fame. Furthermore, after accusing a companion of drunkenness, he prohibits alcohol (see below for a variant of this legend). Muḥammad is then attacked and killed by pigs during a hunting expedition. In *Iniquus Mahometus*, from the late 13th century,[78] Muḥammad is also depicted as a magician and a womaniser (although here he also has sexual relations with boys and girls, which extends the sexual debauchery trope). He makes use of a bull and a trained dove to convince people that he receives revelation. He is killed by relatives of a Jewish woman whom he tried to seduce. She cuts up his corpse and feeds it to pigs leaving only his left leg, which his followers rescue and reverently bury.

Guibert of Nogent's *Dei gesta per Francos* (1109) has Muḥammad pass off epileptic seizures as the 'effects of a divine presence'. He is tutored by a 'heretical hermit', and he makes use of the horns of a cow to convince people that he is a prophet, purveying a law that permitted 'sexual license and debauchery'.[79] In the end, pigs attack and devour him while he is suffering an epileptic seizure, and only his heels are left for the Saracens to venerate. Gautier de Compiegne's *Otia de Machomete* (1155) also has Muḥammad passing off epileptic seizures, which alarm his rich, older wife, Khadīja, as divine visitations, and using trickery to convince people that he is a prophet, including the use of the horns of a bull,[80] and intimidating a hermit to support his claims. He gives permission for men to take ten wives, and after his death his iron coffin is suspended by magnets in mid-air at Mecca. Here, the trickster-scoundrel trope is seen in fully developed form.

---

76 V. Valcarcel, '*Vita Mahometi*', in *CMR* 4, 208-11.
77 J. Tolan, '*Vita Machometi*', in *CMR* 3, 572-3.
78 J. Tolan, '*Iniquus Mahometus*', in *CMR* 4, 654-6.
79 J. Tolan, 'Guibert of Nogent', in *CMR* 3, 329-43.
80 J. Tolan, 'Gautier de Compiègne', in *CMR* 3, 601-3.

Many of these tropes continued into the early modern period. For example, almost all, including the tame dove and an ass (instead of a bull), as well as the 'use of the sword', appear in Henry Smith's *God's arrow against atheists* written in 1593,[81] while an illustration in a 15th-century manuscript of Giovanni Boccaccio's *Le cas de nobles*, now in the Bibliothèque nationale de France, depicts Muḥammad preaching with a dove on his right shoulder and a bull bringing his book tied to its horns.[82]

Attempts at appeal

The Cluniac initiative

Many, if not all, of these texts were written in support of the crusades, so they depict Muslims as enemies to be defeated by force of arms. A few Christians questioned this violent approach and called for a move away from hostility towards peaceful efforts at proclamation and persuasion. Peter of Cluny (d. 1156) was one who pioneered this new approach, writing to Muslims that he would not attack them as others did by 'arms, but by words, not by force, but by reason, not in hatred but in love'.[83] He wanted to win Muslims over to Christianity, although his approach fell somewhat short of an appeal. He saw Islam as diabolic, and Muḥammad as the devil's instrument in mixing 'good and evil', the 'sublime and the ridiculous' into a 'monstrous cult'. It was during a visit to Cluniac daughter monasteries in Iberia in 1142-3 that he decided to help equip Christians for the verbal rather than violent confrontation with Islam by commissioning twelve translations, including the Qur'an and al-Kindī's *Apology*. The translation of the Qur'an, *Lex sive doctrina Mahumeti*, by Robert of Ketton, was actually a paraphrase incorporating commentaries that drew on Islamic sources. It has been judged that Ketton made real efforts to 'understand what he was translating' and, while he attacked Muḥammad and the Qur'an viciously, he did justice to the poetic quality of the original by rendering it into high Latin prose.[84] His paraphrase shows 'sensitivity to Qur'anic language and its layered meaning'.[85] Despite

---

81 H. Smith, *God's Arrow against atheists*, London, 1617, 50. See C. Bennett, 'Henry Smith', in *CMR* 6, 826-32.

82 Shalem, *Constructing the image*, pp. 23-4; Ms. Fr. 226, fol. 243r.

83 J. Kritzeck, *Peter the Venerable and Islam*, Princeton NJ, 1964, p. 161.

84 O. de la Cruz Palma and C. Ferrero Hernandez, 'Robert of Ketton', in *CMR* 3, 508-19, p. 510.

85 B. Lawrence, *The Qur'an. A biography*, New York, 2007, p. 105.

being 'hostile to Islam' he 'was willing to trust Muslim scholars in trying to understand what Muslims found believable in the "false prophecy of Muhammad"'.[86] As a result, and until the appearance of other translations in later centuries, this effort made Muḥammad's book available in some form to Europeans for the first time.

William of Tripoli

Francis of Assisi (d. 1230) signalled an alternative to confrontation. In the first draft of the rule of life he made for his followers (the *Regula non bullata*), he wrote that there were two ways to go out among the Saracens. 'One way is to make disputes or contentions', and the other is to 'announce the word of God to them' when the friars see 'it as pleasing to God'.[87] In a similar manner, the Dominican friar William of Tripoli,[88] who is mentioned in papal documents in 1264, became convinced that, while they were in error 'learned and wise Muslims are very near the Christian faith' and could easily be won for Christ.[89] When he writes about the Qur'an he was surprisingly positive. Although he tended to make use of favourite passages that Christians had long 'seized upon [...] for apologetic purposes', when he comments on what the Qur'an says about Jesus and Mary he describes this as so pious and devout 'that the uneducated might believe that these words are truer than those of the text of the holy Gospel'.[90] This may be the earliest praise of the Qur'an by a Christian writer, and it contrasts sharply with the way in which al-Kindī had made fun of its alleged contradictions and absurdity, rejecting any claim to literary excellence.[91]

Despite this, when William wrote about Muḥammad he noted nothing praiseworthy even though Christians routinely credited Muḥammad with compiling or composing the Qur'an. Here, William offered a somewhat different view of Muḥammad's role in an unusual version of the Baḥīrā legend. He transformed the monk into an Orthodox Christian who taught Muḥammad the true faith. His relatives and friends 'formed

---

86 Lawrence, *The Qur'an*, p. 107.

87 P. Robinson (ed.), *The writings of Saint Francis of Assisi*, Philadelphia PA, 1905, pp. 48-9.

88 See T.E. Burman, 'William of Tripoli', in *CMR* 4, 515-20.

89 Burman, 'William of Tripoli', p. 519. See p. 517 for the issue of attribution of the two works associated with William.

90 Burman, 'William of Tripoli', p. 517.

91 Muir, *Apology of al Kindy*, pp. 30-1.

an army and proclaimed him messenger of God',[92] and they did not like the way in which Muḥammad continued to consult the monk for advice because they wanted a different type of religion. So, one night when Muḥammad was sleeping, they used his sword to kill the monk, telling him afterwards that it was he who had done this while he was drunk. This led him to prohibit the consumption of alcohol. Without the monk, Muḥammad 'lost all moral control and began raiding and plundering the surrounding territories'. This version of the legend found its way into the *Travels of John Mandeville*, which is probably from the 1350s, illustrations in printed editions of which show the killing of the hermit.[93]

In similar vein, Bartholomew of Edessa (d. c. 1300)[94] attributes anything that is true in Islam to Baḥīrā and its lies to changes made to the Qur'an after Muḥammad's death by 'Uthmān, the third caliph.[95] But Bartholomew certainly did not intend his version of the Baḥīrā legend to exonerate Muḥammad: he called him a 'murderer', 'brigand' and 'voluptuary', who was 'defiled to the core'.[96] He may also have popularised the tendency to satirise and ridicule the story of Muḥammad's Night Journey and Ascent, which became another incident that Christians singled out from the Prophet's biography. Later, Aloys Sprenger also attributed the founding of Islam to Muḥammad's followers, especially Abū Bakr, and blamed Muḥammad himself for defiling the faith with his 'immorality' and 'perverseness'.[97]

Ramon Llull

The second way of approaching Muslims that Francis of Assisi had set out in the first version of his Rule appealed to Ramon Llull[98] (d. 1315), a tertiary Franciscan, who argued that the Christian duty was to win Muslim souls through rational discourse. He believed that Muslims could be convinced that Christian doctrines were true through reason and through the art of discovering the truth (*Ars inveniendi veritas*). Realising

---

[92] M. Di Cesare, *The pseudo-historical image of the Prophet Muḥammad in medieval Latin literature. A repertory*, Berlin, 2011, p. 349.

[93] Dimmock, *Mythologies*, pp. 50-1.

[94] J. Niehoff-Panagiotidis, 'Bartholomew of Edessa', in *CMR* 3, 715-19.

[95] B. Roggema, 'A Christian reading of the Qur'an. The legend of Sergius-Baḥīrā and its use of Qur'an and Sīra', in D. Thomas (ed.), *Syrian Christians under Islam. The first thousand years*, Leiden, 2001, 57-74, pp. 70-1.

[96] N. Khan, *Perceptions of Islam in the Christendoms. A historical survey*, Oslo, 2005, p. 209.

[97] Sprenger, *Life of Mohammad*, p. 175.

[98] H. Hames, 'Ramon Llull', in *CMR* 4, 705-17.

that Christians needed better knowledge of Islamic sources (like Peter of Cluny before him), he called for professorial chairs of Arabic to be set up at various universities. Considered by many to be the first Christian missionary to Muslims, Llull tried out his new approach in three visits to Tunisia. He ended up in jail in Tunis, was expelled from the country (commuted from the death penalty) and, on his final attempt, was stoned by a crowd. He died while sailing home.

In *Doctrina pueril* (1274-6), which he wrote for his son, he states that Muḥammad had seven wives and 'a host of mistresses', and that when he conquered Mecca he ordered the execution of everyone who did not embrace Islam.[99] He 'lived a life of excess' with his wives, his promise of a carnal paradise luring people to his false religion. Even some Muslims themselves did not believe he was a prophet.

Llull could see nothing admirable in Muḥammad. In fact, while the first article of the Islamic declaration of faith at least affirmed belief in one God (but one that lacked love, and it was only half-true because it denied the Trinity), the problem with Islam lay in its second article, belief in Muḥammad as messenger of God. He could not resist insulting Muḥammad when he preached and, on one occasion when he was thrown into jail and asked to embrace Islam, his reply was, 'Do you have for me four wives and all sorts of worldly pleasure if I accept the law of Mohammed?'[100] Others had lost their lives for similar behaviour, including the five friars sent by Francis to Morocco in 1219.[101]

Gregory Barhebraeus

Barhebraeus (d. 1286)[102] was a Syrian Orthodox *maphrian* (one rank below the patriarch) in Iraq and Azerbaijan from 1264. His responsibilities included 'relations with the highest Islamic authorities of Baghdad'. He composed an important corpus of writing of which his world chronicle, *Ktōbō d-maktbōnut zabnē*, achieved wide circulation. His preferred residence was Marāgha, where he had access to 'a famous observatory [...] an extensive library' and 'contact with Islamic scholars'.[103] One of his aims was to 'emulate [...] the greatest Islamic scholars and literary

99 Hames, 'Ramon Llull', p. 706.
100 S.M. Zwemer, *Raymond Lull. First missionary to the Moslems*, New York, 1902, p. 109.
101 S. Lay, *The Reconquest kings of Portugal. Political and cultural reorientation on the medieval frontier*, Basingstoke, 2009, p. 427.
102 H.G.B. Teule, 'Barhebraeus', in *CMR* 4, 588-609.
103 Teule, 'Barhebraeus', p. 589.

specialists'.[104] His admiration for Muslim scholars and his writings show that he felt at least a cultural affinity with Muslims. He wrote poems that contain 'styles and themes' characteristic of Arabic poetry, while his *Laughable stories* represent 'the most telling proof' of his 'acculturation to the Muslim-Arabic literary world'.[105]

Gregory's best-known work was neither an apology for Christianity nor a polemic against Islam, but one of serious historical scholarship, which offers a 'balanced account of secular history' from Christian and Islamic sources.[106] He describes many peace treaties between Christians and Muslims, but also instances when he thought Christians were unjustly treated. He may have admired the Muslim theologian Abū Ḥāmid al-Ghazālī (d. 1111), whose work he consulted, because he thought that, unlike him, Muslims were too concerned with outer matters to the detriment of inner, spiritual concerns.[107] In his chapter on the Arab kings, he devotes a paragraph to a brief life of Muḥammad,[108] which in its general tone is not stridently anti-Islamic. It provides some information that is lacking in the other works considered in this chapter, such as the names of the Prophet's father and uncle, although he mistakenly identifies Muḥammad's city as Yathrib. Referring to Muḥammad's marriage with Khadīja, although he describes her as wealthy, he does not impute any sinister motive to Muḥammad in marrying her.

In Palestine, Muḥammad met Jews who told him that God had given them the land because they rejected idols, which led him to desire 'this land earnestly', and he persuaded his countrymen 'about this matter when he was forty years of age'. Rumour among the leaders of Mecca that he was introducing a foreign religion led him to flee to Yathrib (which seems inconsistent with the above identification that this was already his home). He taught the people to worship one God, to abandon useless gods, to perform ablutions, because Arabs were a 'dirty people', and to fast until daybreak once a year, and he sent raiding parties into Palestine that returned with 'riches and goods'. After leading some raids, he no longer used persuasion but the sword. Those who joined him were permitted to 'much copulation with women', both wives and concubines,

---

104 Teule, 'Barhebraeus', p. 592.

105 Teule, 'Barhebraeus', p. 592.

106 Teule, 'Barhebraeus', p. 602.

107 D.M. Freidenreich, 'Muslims in Eastern Canon Law, 1000-15000', in *CMR* 4, 45-59, p. 49.

108 E.A.W. Budge, *The Chronography of Gregory Abû 'l Faraj, the son of Aaron, the Hebrew physician commonly known as Bar Hebraeus. Being the first part of his political history of the world*, London, 1932, vol. 1, pp. 90-2.

and could divorce their wives at will. He told his followers that after the Resurrection, they would enter a paradise with rivers of milk and honey, fruit-laden trees, golden couches and beautiful women. After ten years and two months he had conquered much of Rome (Rhomaye, meaning the Eastern Roman Empire) and the land of the Persians.

While this account reflects many standard Christian criticisms, it does not include the accusation that Muḥammad was a false prophet or refer to a Christian monk, though Gabriel is not mentioned either. The next paragraph praises the intellectual and cultural flowering of the early ʿAbbasid period:

> There arose among them [the Muslims] philosophers, mathematicians and physicians who surpassed the Ancients by their precise understanding [...] to the extent that we from whom they acquired wisdom through translators who were all Syrians find ourselves now in the necessity of asking for wisdom from them.[109]

Barhebraeus's admiration for Islamic literary and scientific achievement was such that he did not hesitate to express it. Later, Christians would dismiss the role of Muslim scholars as only borrowers who merely preserved Greek and Persian knowledge without adding anything new, prevented by their faith from any type of innovative thought or scientific discovery. However, an even better clue to his view of Islam may be found in the opening paragraph of his section on the Prophet, where he cites the Emperor Heraclius saying of the Arabs:

> Yea, indeed, they are remote from the darkness, inasmuch as they have rejected the worship of idols, and they worship one God. But they lack the perfectly clear light because of their remoteness from the light and because of their imperfect knowledge of our Christian faith and Orthodox confession.[110]

This sounds very much like an affirmation that Muslims are close to Christian faith and would not have to move very far to attain the fullness of the truth, which presumably would also apply to Muḥammad. This leaves open the possibility that Muslims are close enough to the truth to qualify as possessors of an implicit faith sufficient for salvation, which would shift Barhebraeus towards some degree of accommodation with Islam. Through the translation made by Edward Pococke (d. 1691),[111]

---

109 Budge, *Chronography of Gregory Abû 'l Faraj*, vol. 1, p. 92.
110 Budge, *Chronography of Gregory Abû 'l Faraj*, vol. 1, p. 90.
111 N. Matar, 'Edward Pococke', in *CMR* 8, 445-58.

Barhebraeus's history became widely read in Europe, where for many readers his brief sketch of Muḥammad's life was actually the oldest and least polemical to which they had access, and almost the only text 'not based on European sources and legends'.[112]

Attempts at an accommodation

Paul of Antioch

The last works discussed in this chapter moved towards accommodation with Islam perhaps more intentionally than Barhebraeus's *Ktōbō d-maktbōnut zabnē*. Paul of Antioch (fl. early 13th century),[113] a Melkite bishop of Sidon, wrote a *Letter to a Muslim friend* around the year 1200. This brief text (24 pages) was later revised and expanded (known as *The letter from the people of Cyprus*),[114] and sent to the Muslim scholar Ibn Taymiyya in 1316 and to another scholar, Ibn Abī Ṭālib al-Dimashqī, in 1321. This is 'less a new edition of the earlier letter than a new composition',[115] although it more or less offers the same argument. Paul saw the Melkites as 'privileged interlocutors of the Muslim community'.[116] Both works portray Islam as a valid faith for Arabs, and Muḥammad as a legitimate prophet for the people to whom he had been sent. These were the 'ignorant Arabs', and did not include Christians because they had already received messengers who had spoken to them in their own languages.

Paul's unambiguous recognition of Muḥammad as a prophet goes further than Timothy's view that Muḥammad had 'walked in the path of the prophets'. However, as David Thomas remarks, this 'gesture towards reconciliation with Islam' turns its prophet 'into a local preacher who may be authentic' but whose mission was limited to the Arabs to whom he preached an initial monotheism that still fell short of 'the full Trinitarian form'.[117] This infuriated Ibn Taymiyya,[118] whose response emphatically

---

112 Matar, 'Pococke', p. 451.

113 D. Thomas, 'Paul of Antioch', in *CMR* 4, 78-82; see also the English trans. by N. Abdelsadek at: https://www.researchgate.net/publication/268216125_Paul%27s_Letter_to_the_Muslims_English_Translation_from_Arabic_and_French_source_documents.

114 D. Thomas, '*The letter from the People of Cyprus*', in *CMR* 4, 769-71.

115 Thomas, '*Letter*', p. 770.

116 D.R. Sarrió Cucarella, *Muslim-Christian polemics across the Mediterranean. The splendid replies of Shihāb al-Dīn al-Qarāfī (d. 684/1285)*, Leiden, 2015, p. 139.

117 See Thomas, 'Paul of Antioch', p. 81.

118 J. Hoover, 'Ibn Taymiyya', in *CMR* 4, 824-72.

called for belief in Muḥammad as the universal prophet necessary for salvation. When Christians claimed that the Qur'an (e.g. 5: 82) affirms their salvation, this referred to Christians from before Muḥammad's time not to those who lived after his death, who must accept his prophethood to have any hope of salvation.[119] Yet a limited affirmation of Muḥammad's prophetic mission might be as close as Christians can go without denying their own faith. On the other hand, some Muslims adopt a similar approach to Christianity. It is adequate for salvation but less desirable than the fullness of truth that Islam brings. Thus, 'a person [...] who declares that he or she is not a Muslim and lives accordingly still has the possibility that he or she might be Muslim in her or his inner being', just as someone who conforms to Muslim belief and practice 'might not be Muslim in fact'.[120]

Juan de Segovia and Nicholas of Cusa

The final two writers to be examined, Juan de Segovia (d. 1448)[121] and Nicholas of Cusa (d. 1464),[122] continued the trajectory evidenced in Francis of Assisi, Peter of Cluny and Ramon Llull. Both rejected the way of violence against Muslims, and were instead interested in evangelising them, and both believed that Christians needed to know more about Islam, and engaged in extensive personal study of it. Especially concerned that few Christians had read the Qur'an, Juan embarked on a remarkable collaboration with the Iberian Muslim scholar Yça Gidelli to produce a trilingual translation. This is lost, and only the *Prefacio* survives, standing out as the sole example known by this time of such a partnership between a Muslim and a Christian who wanted to learn from a Muslim first-hand about Muslim beliefs. When he wrote about Muḥammad, Juan made it clear that he did not regard him as genuine and thought that 'Christians should insist that Muslims prove' to them 'that Muḥammad was God's prophet'.[123] On the other hand, he also knew that 'Muhammad did not consider himself the founder of a new religion' but a reformer of the religion of Abraham, which Juan thought opened up possibilities for Christians to demonstrate that Muslim notions about Christianity were

---

119 T.F. Michel. *A Muslim theologian's response to Christianity*, Delmar NY, 1984, p. 247.
120 A. Aslan, *Religious pluralism in Christian and Islamic philosophy. The thought of John Hick and Seyyed Hossein Nasr*, London, 1994, p. 195.
121 A.M. Wolf, 'Juan de Segovia', in *CMR* 5, 429-42; A.M. Wolf, *Juan de Segovia and Western perspectives on Islam in the fifteenth century*, Minneapolis MN, 2003.
122 J. Tolan, 'Nicholas of Cusa', in *CMR* 5, 421-8.
123 Wolf, 'Juan de Segovia', p. 438.

'mistaken, and that Christians were not [...] unbelievers'.[124] He thought that, after the fall of Constantinople in 1453, Christians should abandon fighting the Turks except with God's word. However, instead of sending preachers to them, Muslim representatives should be invited to a conference.

Nicholas had little favourable to say about Muḥammad. In his eyes, he was a 'pseudo-prophet', a 'deceiver' and an 'instrument of the devil' whose book glorified himself not God.[125] Yet, despite the Qur'an's depiction of a carnal paradise, its encouragement of promiscuity and laws that God could never have revealed, he saw examples of God's glory shining through. When he proposed an End of Time congress of religions, he cited what he thought were Muḥammad's words from the Qur'an: 'The law or faith of all is one, but the rites of the different prophets were undoubtedly different.'[126] A gathering of wise men would discuss religious differences, before agreeing one single expression of religious truth that would unify all in a single faith.

Conclusion

What carried over into the next 500 years from this first millennium of Christian writings on Muḥammad was mainly myth, legend and calumny, with little resemblance to Muslim accounts of his life. Nothing close to a Muslim view can be seen in any of the works discussed above, with their portraits of a war-mongering, womanising trickster, a Satan-serving, demon-possessed pseudo-prophet whose corpse was attacked by pigs (or who was killed by pigs). These myths surfaced in places far from the Islamic world, though they flourished just as vigorously among Christians who lived under Islamic rule. In general, little was known about the details of Muḥammad's life, and even the chronology was vague to many. Apart from favourite incidents used for polemical purposes, such as Muḥammad's meeting with Baḥīrā, his marriage to Khadīja, the Zayd-Zaynab affair and later the Night Journey and Ascent, details are absent. No effort was made to understand how Muslims saw the alleged moral blemishes in Muḥammad's character, and why they were not persuaded of his perfidy when Christians alluded to them. Even after travel accounts reached Europe informing readers that Muḥammad was buried

124 Wolf, 'Juan de Segovia', p. 433.
125 Valkenberg, 'Can we talk', pp. 151-2.
126 Tolan, 'Nicholas of Cusa', p. 423.

in Medina and not Mecca, Christian writers still referred to his coffin being suspended by magnets at Mecca. It is, however, difficult to state categorically that any writer discussed here, with the possible exception of al-Kindī, had access to early Muslim lives of Muḥammad. Except for Robert of Ketton and Juan de Segovia, it is difficult to identify any who showed interest in learning directly from Muslims, even though several of these writers were culturally at home in the Islamic world.

What almost everyone missed, even those who wanted to appeal to Muslim hearts and minds, was the place Muḥammad occupied devotionally and spiritually in Muslim life. Traducing the Prophet and his book as a device to convince Muslims of Jesus' superiority would hardly encourage Muslims to listen to anything else Christians had to say. More often than not, an ability to see some truth or light in Islam and even in the Qur'an did not translate into seeing anything praiseworthy in Muḥammad, apart maybe from the Patriarch Timothy. Timothy's and Paul of Antioch's approaches appear to have deliberately avoided insulting Muḥammad, which distinguishes their works from the rest of those discussed.

Chapter 8
Defending the faith. Lines of apology

Sandra Toenies Keating

Introduction

With the expansion of Arab rule around the Mediterranean basin from the 7th century, indigenous Christians experienced increasing challenges on many levels of their daily lives. There is little evidence of Christian awareness early on that the revelation announced by the Arabian prophet Muḥammad, preserved in writing in the Qur'an, laid out a theological framework for the relationship between his community of believers and themselves. It was only after Muḥammad's death and decades of interaction between well-established Christian communities and their new rulers that the implications of the Qur'an and the new religion based upon it revealed clear points of contention and responses to them.

Scholars have established that the first encounters with the unexpected strength of Arab invaders from the desert were met with mixed reactions. Initially, the conquest itself was seen by many as divine judgement on the Christian community, but not as a serious threat to Christian faith. For some, especially Jews and those Christians who rejected the conclusions of the Council of Chalcedon (451), the promise of an alternative to Melkite Byzantine rule was attractive.[1] For others, the conquest signalled the expected end times, setting in motion the final conflict with the armies of the Antichrist.[2] Still others apparently regarded the incursions as only particularly intense episodes of the regularly occurring raids by desert peoples, which would pass as they always did. For

[1] These groups were accused of cooperating with the invaders, which is probably true since Christians of the (Nestorian) Church of the East hoped for more neutral treatment by rulers who did not take a particular side in the Chalcedonian debates. An especially useful compilation of these sources is found in R.G. Hoyland, *Seeing Islam as others saw it. A survey and evaluation of Christian, Jewish and Zoroastrian writings on early Islam*, Princeton NJ, 1997.

[2] Apocalyptic and eschatological themes are ubiquitous in the literature of the first century of Arab rule. See, e.g. H. Suermann, '*The Apocalypse of Pseudo-Ephrem*', in *CMR* 1, 160-2; L. Greisiger, '*The Apocalypse of Pseudo-Methodius* (*Syriac*)', in *CMR* 1, 163-71; L. Greisiger, '*The Edessene Apocalypse*', in *CMR* 1, 172-5.

all of these reasons, the first century of Arabian conquests did not spark extensive theological responses to the vision laid out in the Qur'an. It was only after the establishment of the ʿAbbasid caliphate in 750 that the implications of the religious beliefs of the new rulers began to have serious effects on the Christian communities. Consequently, the end of the 8th century signals the beginning of the flowering of intellectual engagement between Muslims and Christians, as well as the start of significant religious apologetical writing. It took several decades for arguments and strategies to be honed, but by the end of the 9th century the lines of argumentation were well established.[3] Among the changes that prompted an increase in apologetic literature was the fact that the ʿAbbasids were more interested than their Umayyad predecessors in gaining converts to Islam, and Christians reported an intensification of efforts to bring about submission to the religion of their rulers. In response, Christian intellectuals mobilised to arm their communities with the tools necessary to defend the faith when challenged.

Although numerous references to famous debates, often between a high-ranking Muslim and a Christian cleric, have been recorded, it is likely that the most common exchanges occurred among friends and acquaintances, in the market place, and perhaps in families that included religiously mixed marriages. These concrete experiences produced typical questions that were later compiled and given substantial responses that could be used to prepare Christians who found themselves in a similar context. Very early on, a fixed set of topics that covered Christian doctrine fairly systematically were developed, so that by the end of the 9th century a standard apologetic canon can be identified. It included defences of the integrity of the Christian scriptures, the Holy Trinity, the Incarnation, and Christian practices (such as baptism, veneration of icons and the direction of prayer). These were often supplemented by lists of biblical proof-texts to substantiate the teachings, which might be convincing to a Muslim listener. An additional, though less common, type of writings focused on exposing Muḥammad and his scripture as false, and the followers of the new religion as misguided. In the centuries that followed, these questions and responses were refined and adjusted to fit particular situations, but the central corpus of material remained stable well into the modern period.

---

[3] For an excellent survey of the early context for the development of Christian responses to Islam, see S.H. Griffith, *The Church in the shadow of the mosque*, Princeton NJ, 2008.

It is useful to define some of the terms of these inter-communal exchanges from the outset. In general, we can identify a variety of strategies employed by the authors of extant texts to counter the challenge of Islam. In many cases, the aim of the author was to explain or clarify Christian teachings, often in response to an explicit invitation to convert to Islam. These apologetic writings may focus entirely on the defence of Christian faith without making an explicit reference to Islam or Muslim beliefs. Frequently, even if the text was addressed to a Muslim, the intended readership was those Christians facing pressure to convert. Such apologetic literature was preserved and passed on within Christian ecclesial communities for their own edification and encouragement, and may not even have been written in a language readily accessible to the average Muslim. A popular format for this literature was 'question and answer', written to offer guidance to those who might be confronted on the street or in the court with an invitation to accept Islam. The emphasis in these texts was on giving clear, convincing, but non-confrontational, responses to those questioning Christian faith – Muslim and Christian alike.

A different objective can be identified in writings that were more polemical and intended to expose fallacies in the opponent's religious beliefs. Although the impetus for these texts may have been similar to apologies for Christianity, especially in the case of perceived threats to Christian faith, the tone and strategy were markedly different. These authors were clearly intent on identifying what they took to be weak or indefensible aspects of Islamic beliefs in order to undermine and eliminate them as viable. Often the texts were explicitly directed against the Qur'an, Islam, Muslims, and especially Muḥammad, and were frequently aggressive in tone, sometimes openly disparaging and hostile towards the other community. Where dismantling Islam was the objective, the audiences might be both Muslims and Christians, with the aim of converting Muslims away from Islam while giving assurance to Christians that their beliefs were not foolish. These texts were generally composed in Arabic, although they may have been translated into another language at a later date.[4]

---

4 The purported literary exchange between 'Abd Allāh ibn Ismā'īl al-Hāshimī and 'Abd al-Masīḥ ibn Isḥāq al-Kindī is an excellent example of this type of polemic. For centuries, it was the best-known Christian response to Islam in both the Eastern and Western churches, but the exact route of its dissemination remains unclear. It was heavily redacted and translated into Latin in the 12th century and included in the *Collectio*

Scholars have disagreed on whether the stated purpose and context of many of these writings can be trusted. A common rhetorical strategy found in this literature is the formulation of a coherent exposition of the truth of Christian faith and the falsity of Islam through questions allegedly posed by a Muslim and answers given by a devout Christian. The material may be structured as written correspondence (e.g. *The apology of al-Kindī*),[5] an account of a conversation between a Muslim and a Christian (e.g. Timothy I's Letter 59 (*Disputation with the Caliph al-Mahdī*)),[6] or discussion between representatives of one or more Christian denominations (and sometimes a Jew) in the presence of a Muslim official (e.g. *A Christological discussion*).[7] It is, however, unlikely that any extant texts are actual transcripts of conversations, although some of the literary exchanges have been identified as reconstructions of such discussions. For example, the '*Correspondence between 'Umar II and Leo III*',[8] preserved in the Armenian History of Ghewond,[9] has been determined by scholars as most likely a reconstruction of original questions and comments from 'Umar II, followed by highly developed Christian answers, probably composed first in Greek. It was then translated into Armenian, perhaps as early as the late 8th century, to be employed in defence of Christianity.

Like the '*Correspondence between 'Umar II and Leo III*', most early apologetic works were written in Greek, Syriac, Coptic, Armenian or Georgian, languages not readily accessible to Muslims, suggesting that they were not primarily intended for that community. A notable exception is one of the earliest known Arabic apologies for Christian faith, constructed by an unknown author in the mid-8th century, which has been given the modern title *On the triune nature of God*. It includes a broad apology for Christian faith and was specifically directed towards Muslims.[10] By the end of the 8th century, however, many more original works were being written in Arabic and at the conclusion of the 9th century the language of the ruling class was widely employed in apologetic writings. The shift to Arabic doubtless occurred for two major reasons. First, unlike the Umayyad caliphate, which maintained its bureaucracies

---

toletana, making it a principal source for knowledge of Islam in medieval Europe; L. Bottini, '*The Apology of al-Kindī*', in *CMR* 1, 585-94.

5 Bottini, '*Apology of al-Kindī*'.

6 M. Heimgartner, 'Letter 59 (Disputation with the Caliph al-Mahdī)', in *CMR* 1, 522-6.

7 S.T. Keating, '*A Christological discussion*', in *CMR* 1, 553-5.

8 T. Greenwood, '*The Letter of Leo III* in Ghewond', in *CMR* 1, 203-8.

9 T. Greenwood, 'Ghewond', in *CMR* 1, 866-71.

10 M.N. Swanson, '*Fī tathlīth Allāh al-wāḥid*', in *CMR* 1, 330-3.

in the languages of the local populace, the ʿAbbasid caliphs insisted on conducting official business in Arabic, which required most people to be conversant in the language and made it the *lingua franca* of areas under Arab rule. In addition, the translation movement of the late 8th and early 9th centuries established Arabic as a language of intellectuals, giving Muslims and Christians alike ready access to the Classical heritage.[11] Second, Christians defending their faith needed responses crafted to answer the challenges of the Qur'an in the language of the Qur'an. Without an established Christian lexicon, it was difficult to explain the subtleties of the Incarnation or the unity of God to Muslims in a foreign language whose parameters were controlled by the Qur'an. By the beginning of the 9th century, theologians such as Theodore Abū Qurra[12] and Abū Rā'ita l-Takrītī[13] were devoting considerable effort to constructing clear and effective means of communicating Christian doctrine in Arabic, eventually claiming a space for Arabic-speaking Christians within the growing Muslim sphere of influence.

General apologetics

Within this evolving context, with a few notable exceptions, the general concern of early Christian theologians was defence of the faith, not dismantling Islam, and apologetic works dominate the extant literature. The reasons for the decision to focus on apologetics are hinted at by many of the early writers. The first is the obvious imprudence of criticising one's powerful rulers on a subject as sensitive as religious beliefs. For example, Abū Rā'iṭa l-Takrītī noted at the beginning of his first *risāla, 'On the Holy Trinity'*, that one must make a wise judgment based on one's own situation as to how deeply to enter into debates about religious matters. One can and should, however, respond to questions about Christian doctrine to the best of one's ability, and so it is necessary to be prepared.[14]

---

11 An excellent study of the translation movement can be found in D. Gutas, *Greek thought, Arabic culture*, London, 1998.

12 J.C. Lamoreaux, 'Theodore Abū Qurra', in *CMR* 1, 439-91.

13 S.T. Keating, 'Abū Rā'iṭa l-Takrītī', in *CMR* 1, 567-81.

14 Abū Rā'iṭa specifically mentions consideration of one's own knowledge and abilities to speak about the subjects, as well as the consequences for one's dependents, presumably if engagement with the interlocutor could lead to imprisonment or execution. See S.T. Keating, *Defending the 'People of Truth' in the early Islamic period*, Leiden, 2006, pp. 82-5.

Scholars and clergy needed complex, carefully constructed responses to navigate delicate exchanges with those in power.

A second reason can be found in Q 2:111, where the direct challenge is given to Christians and Jews to provide a proof (*burhān*) of the truth of their teachings. Although the term *burhān* in philosophical thought comes to mean a particular method of arriving at true statements through argumentation, in the earliest Christian responses to Muslims it is defined as the clear evidence of an irrefutable truth – the truth Muḥammad's followers claimed was manifested in the Qur'an.[15] Many texts were given titles that included the terms *burhān*, *ithbāt* (demonstration) or *dalīl* (proof), indicating that their purpose was to provide a response to this challenge.[16] Christian apologists developed structured arguments that began with the ostensible agreement between Muslims and Christians on the unity of God, moved to the necessity of the Trinity and the Incarnation, and then situated Christian practice within these beliefs. The goal was to provide a coherent (and rational) account of Christian faith, with the subtle implication that the Qur'an was not the *burhān* Muslims claimed. Some Christian apologists did take the next step of challenging the coherence and truth of Islam, but this was not typical.[17]

The need for catechesis of the faithful was a third significant reason why Christian theologians emphasised apology rather than polemic. As the theological challenges of Islam were more carefully articulated by Muslim *mutakallimūn*, the necessity of providing clear explanations of

---

15 L. Gardet, art. 'Al-Burhān', in *EI2*, and M.N. Swanson, art. 'Proof' in *EQ*.

16 See, for example, M. Beaumont, 'Ammār al-Basrī', in *CMR* 1, 607-10 (*Kitāb al-burhān*); B. Roggema, 'Yūḥannā ibn al-Ṣalt', in *CMR* 1, 849-51 (*Kitāb al-burhān* and *Kitāb dalīl al-ḥā'ir*), and Keating, 'Abū Rā'iṭa l-Takrītī', pp. 571-2 (*Risala fī ithbāt dīn al-naṣrāniyya wa-ithbāt al-Thālūth al-muqaddas*).

17 Two notable and very influential examples of anti-Islamic polemic are found in the writings of John of Damascus (d. 750) and 'Abd al-Masīḥ ibn Isḥāq al-Kindī's *Apology*. John, a Melkite Christian closely associated with the court of the Caliph 'Abd al-Malik and known for his influential theological treatises, presents an unflattering summary of Islam in the last chapter of *De haeresibus*. This text was widely known in both the Greek and Latin churches, and greatly influenced Christian perceptions of Islam; see, e.g. P. Schadler, *John of Damascus and Islam*, Leiden, 2018, and D. Janosik, *John of Damascus*, Eugene OR, 2016. Al-Kindī includes a very critical account of the origins and collection of the Qur'an, as well as numerous derogatory statements about Muḥammad and his claim to prophethood; see: E. Platti, 'Abd al-Masīḥ al-Kindī on the Qur'an', 66-82, and S.T. Keating, 'Manipulation of the Qur'an in the epistolary exchange between al-Hāshimī and al-Kindī', 5-65, in M. Beaumont (ed.), *Arab Christians and the Qur'an from the origins of Islam to the medieval period*, Leiden, 2018. Both al-Hāshimī and al-Kindī became authoritative sources for Christian writers in subsequent centuries and their arguments appeared in various forms in Eastern and Western literature.

Christian doctrine became critical. References to questions and doubt that might lead to conversion away from Christianity became ubiquitous in the prefaces of apologies, suggesting this was of great pastoral concern for those living under Islamic rule. Now the Qur'an's demand to provide a *burhān* afforded an opportunity to formulate new expressions of doctrine that had been settled for most Christians at ecumenical councils in the previous centuries. Bishops, priests and theologians began to produce literature to address the crisis, working to communicate traditional doctrine in a new idiom more effectively. This task required both the translation of terms and ideas into the language of Arabic, as well as the development of creative strategies and expressions that responded to the peculiar claims of Islam.

The continual expansion of apologetic strategies to address Muslim challenges is evident in the first few centuries of engagement between the two communities. For example, in their initial encounters, Christians seem to have regarded Muḥammad and his followers as belonging to a deviant form of Christianity or Judaism. Such sects were ubiquitous as local communities were affected by their acceptance or rejection of synods and ecumenical councils, or by charismatic leaders proclaiming innovative doctrines. Christians recognised important beliefs that they held in common with Muslims, such as the unity and absolute oneness of God, but realised that some teachings of the Qur'an were in direct conflict with Christian faith. Consequently, in the earliest apologies one finds significant efforts to explain and clarify biblical passages, as well as to bolster Christian doctrines with biblical evidence. For example, in the *Disputation between a monk of Bēt Ḥalē and an Arab notable*, the author presented a series of Muslim questions with responses from the monk that included extensive exegesis of biblical passages.[18] Christian apologists responding to Islam in this early period followed the lead of their spiritual ancestors who answered the Jews, emphasising proper biblical exegesis as the key to understanding the Trinity, the Incarnation, and many practices such as veneration of icons, prayer facing east and monasticism. Among the best-known articulations of this approach is John of Damascus's inclusion of Islam in the final chapter of his catalogue of known heresies.[19] John seems to have followed previous writers

---

18 B. Roggema, *'The disputation between a monk of Bēt Ḥālē and an Arab notable'*, in *CMR* 1, 268-73.

19 R.F. Glei, *'Peri haireseōn'*, in *CMR* 1, 297-301. Schadler argues that John's inclusion of Islam as a heresy should be understood not only as a theological concept, but also as a legal and historical category consistent with contemporary understandings of

in this assessment, notably Anastasius of Sinai (d. c. 700), who also referred to Islam in his refutation of heresies.[20] The expectation appears to have been that, if the true meaning of the biblical text could be clearly explicated, those aspects of Islam that contradict Christian faith could be refuted.[21]

This strategy failed. The seeds of the response that delegitimises biblical authority are found already in the Qur'an and, within a century, the doctrine of *taḥrīf*, which asserts that the Bible has been tampered with, became a significant factor in Muslim-Christian engagement. Further, one of the most important tools of theology, that of analogy, fell under a shadow with the qur'anic command that nothing can be regarded as 'like' God (e.g. Q 42:11, 112:4), leaving Christian apologists without an easy way to illustrate complex church teaching. More will be said about the latter below. With two of the most important apologetic devices rendered ineffective, Christian writers began to seek new approaches to defending the faith.

Claims for the superiority of Islam and the preservation of the faith

In recent years, scholars have raised serious questions about the initial motivations of Muḥammad and his followers concerning the inauguration of a new religious movement, in particular, how they regarded themselves in relation to the more established Christian and Jewish communities they encountered. Whatever the impetus, the earliest evidence suggests that Muḥammad understood that it was his role as God's Messenger to deliver a warning to those who had strayed from the revelation given to the prophets who preceded him. Embedded in his message was

---

heresiography. He concludes that the description does not reflect any particular animus to Islam on John's part, but may indicate he did not have direct access to the Qur'an; Schadler, *John of Damascus and Islam*, esp. pp. 210-17.

20 A. Binggeli, '*Hodegos*', in *CMR* 1, 196-7.

21 It is significant that Christians recognised the Muslim claim of continuity with the Jewish and Christian traditions. Muslims themselves appear to have asserted this belief in multiple ways, including using churches for worship, visiting Christian pilgrimage sites and venerating Mary. These practices would have been noticeable to the average person, and contributed to the fear of Church authorities that Christians might be enticed by the advantages of following the religion of their rulers. Based on this evidence, some scholars in recent years have speculated that Muḥammad's interest was not in establishing a new religion, but rather in creating an ecumenical community to overcome the divisions between Christians and Jews. Most notable of these is F. Donner, *Muhammad and the believers*, Boston MA, 2010.

the view that the revelation sent down to him both confirmed and corrected the scriptures of Jews and Christians. Consequently, Muḥammad should be regarded as a prophet like those who preceded him (Q 4:163-5), while errors that had crept into the religion preached by these previous messengers should be eradicated (Q 4:171; 5:116-17). He came to be seen by his followers as the 'Seal of the prophets' (*khātam al-nabiyyīn*) (Q 33:40), whose message superseded all that had gone before. But Muḥammad's message was not accepted by everyone and he faced significant resistance throughout his prophetic career. He continually responded to this opposition, as well as criticised beliefs and practices he encountered and formulated principles that became the foundation of relations between Muslims and Christians. In many cases, his responses articulated strong condemnations, and polemical language is a significant feature of the Qur'an and Hadith.[22] This censure was especially concerned with anything that compromised *tawḥīd*, the belief in the absolute oneness and unity of God, which Christian teachings about the Trinity and the Incarnation seemed to undermine. Although a full-blown teaching on abrogation of suspect biblical texts did not appear immediately, the charge of *taḥrīf* had its roots in the Qur'an, and was developed and elaborated by Muslim thinkers in subsequent centuries in exchanges with Christian apologists and polemicists. The specific admonitions in the Qur'an against problematic doctrines alleged that their source lay in the mishandling of scripture; where the revelation to Muḥammad differed from the religion of the *Ahl al-kitāb*, the People of the Book,[23] his message was understood to supersede it.

The Qur'an makes reference to various types of alteration, ranging from misinterpretation to actual substitution of text, whether knowingly or inadvertently (e.g. Q 2:59, 75; 4:46; 6:13; 7:162). These verses were later supplemented by Hadith and commentary to give a more complete picture of the superiority of the Qur'an and Islam over the 'books' that were currently in the hands of other monotheists. Over the centuries, Muslim writers engaged Christians and Jews with varying degrees of scepticism, depending on their positions on *taḥrīf* and how responsible they thought their opponents were for their own error.[24] Among the earliest to address the issue explicitly and systematically, Ibn al-Layth (d. 819)

---

22 K. Zebiri, art. 'Polemic and polemical language' in *EQ*.
23 M. Sharon, art. 'People of the Book' in *EQ*.
24 H. Lazarus-Yafeh, art. 'Taḥrīf' in *EI2*, and F. Buhl, art. 'Taḥrīf' in *EI1*. See also S.H. Griffith, art. 'Gospel', in *EQ*, and G.D. Newby, art. 'Forgery' in *EQ*.

was aware of various forms of alteration and specifically mentioned the false doctrines of the Trinity and the Incarnation,[25] while al-Qāsim ibn Ibrāhīm (d. 860) concluded that the problem lay with the interpretation of the scriptures, not with the actual texts.[26]

Even without a systematic Islamic formulation of the principle, however, the charge of *taḥrīf* was well enough known for Christians (and Jews) to feel the need to counter it in their apologetic writings. Fairly well developed responses to the assertion that the biblical text had been tampered with are found in the *Correspondence between 'Umar II and Leo III*,[27] which points to the existence of a common reliable redactor of the Jewish scriptures in the person of Ezra as a defence of its integrity. But the trustworthiness of those who later transmitted the text soon fell under suspicion, raising serious questions of how the authenticity of any revealed text could be ascertained. The study of *tawātur*, developed by Muslim scholars to authenticate the chain of transmission of each Hadith, proposed systematic methods for determining textual reliability.[28] The expectations of *tawātur* ultimately forced Christians to explain the existence of translations and multiple textual traditions, as well as the acceptance of four Gospels and the inclusion of texts such as the Pauline letters in the biblical corpus.

The challenges of *taḥrīf* and demand for verifiable *tawātur* often lay just below the surface in Christian apologetics in the first centuries of Islam, though only a few writers confronted it head on. One of these was the author of the so-called *Apology of al-Kindī* (early 9th century).[29] In this lengthy response to a purported invitation to submit to Islam, al-Kindī presented a defence of Christ as a perfect moral teacher with a coherent and rational message, whose followers accepted his teachings because they were authentic and accompanied by divine miracles. Section three of the *Apology* then turns to a scathing critique of the origins of Islam, including an examination of the codification of the Qur'an and inconsistencies that indicated that Muḥammad's followers had tampered with the text for their own personal gain. Al-Kindī turned the charges of *taḥrīf* and lack of *tawātur* against his Muslim interlocutor, forcing him to

---

25 B. Roggema, 'Ibn al-Layth', in *CMR* 1, 347-53.

26 W. Madelung, '*Kitāb al-radd 'alā l-Naṣārā*', in *CMR* 1, 542-3.

27 Greenwood, '*The Letter of Leo III* in Ghewond', pp. 203-8. See also B. Roggema, '*Pseudo-'Umar II's letter to Leo III*', in *CMR* 1, 381-5.

28 G.H.A. Juynboll, art. 'Tawātur' in *EI2*.

29 Bottini, '*Apology of al-Kindī*'.

explain, for example, the differences between the *muṣḥaf* (written text of the Qur'an) of the Shīʿa and that of Ahl al-Sunna.[30]

Other Christian writers addressed the issues more subtly, mentioning the particular concern in passing or including a defence of the integrity of the Bible in answers to related questions. Of special interest here is the *risāla, 'On the Holy Trinity'*, by Abū Rā'iṭa l-Takrītī (d. c. 830), who concluded his lengthy exposition of the rationality of the doctrine of the Trinity with arguments against those who claimed the scripture had been altered.[31] His second *risāla, 'On the Incarnation'*, is a continuation of the treatise on the Trinity, and includes numerous biblical proof-texts carefully chosen to demonstrate the coherence and integrity of the Bible.[32] A third text associated with Abū Rā'iṭa includes a list of proof-texts that could be used in responding to Muslim questions about Christian doctrine, and exhibits great care to avoid evidence that could lead to the charge of *taḥrīf*.[33]

The concern for *taḥrīf* grew significantly in the 11th-14th centuries, with numerous extensive works produced by Muslims against Christians, including those by al-Jaʿfarī (d. 1270),[34] al-Ṭūfī (d. 1316),[35] and many others. Among the most significant is the work of Ibn Taymiyya (d. 1328), especially his response to an anonymously edited version[36] of the Christian *Letter to a Muslim friend* written by Paul of Antioch.[37] Ibn Taymiyya's extensive treatise is the longest medieval refutation of Christianity, and represents a verified literary exchange between Muslims and Christians. It also includes one of the most developed expositions of Muslims' concerns about the Bible ever written.[38] This increasingly systematic refutation of biblical texts that contradicted the Qur'an prompted further responses from Christians, such as those of Ishoʿyahb bar Malkon

---

30 J. Burton, art. 'Muṣḥaf' in *EI2*.

31 S.T. Keating, *'Al-risāla l-ūlā fī l-Thālūth al-muqaddas'*, in *CMR* 1, 572-4.

32 S.T. Keating, *'Al-risāla l-thāniya li-Abī Rā'iṭa l-Takrītī fī l-tajassud'*, in *CMR* 1, 574-5.

33 S.T. Keating, *'Shahādāt min qawl al-Tawrāt wa-l-anbiyā' wa-l-qiddīsīn'*, in *CMR* 1, 576-7.

34 L. Demiri, *'Kitāb al-radd 'alā l-Naṣārā'*, in *CMR* 4, 485, and L. Demiri, *'Takhjīl man ḥarrafa l-Tawrāh wa-l-Injīl'*, in *CMR* 4, 481-3.

35 L. Demiri, *'Al-intiṣārāt al-Islāmiyya fī kashf shubah al-Naṣrāniyya'*, in *CMR* 4, 729-31.

36 D. Thomas, *'Risāla ilā baʿḍ aṣdiqā'ihi alladhīna bi-Ṣaydā min al-Muslimīn'*, in *CMR* 4, 79-82.

37 D. Thomas, *'The letter from the people of Cyprus'*, in *CMR* 4, 769-72. Many of Ibn Taymiyya's arguments have been revived in the modern period, and continue to play a significant role in theological debates between the two communities.

38 J. Hoover, *'Al-jawāb al-ṣaḥīḥ li-man baddala dīn al-Masīḥ'*, in *CMR* 4, 834-44.

(d. 1246)[39] and al-Makīn Jirjis ibn al-ʿAmīd (d. c. 1398),[40] defending the biblical scripture and its integrity.

As noted above, there is evidence towards the end of the 8th century that Christian apologists were beginning a concerted search for alternatives to biblical proof-texts in their response to Islam. While proof-texts remain an important aspect of apologetics, they were now included more for the benefit of Christians looking for substantiation of their own faith than as convincing arguments for Muslims. The most influential new approach relied on philosophical categories to establish common ground between Islamic and Christian teachings. Of course, philosophical principles had played a significant role for the Church Fathers in the explication of Christian doctrine and had been used in intellectual debates with pagans and heretics. By the end of the 8th century, with the beginning of widespread translation of classical Greek texts into Arabic, Muslim intellectuals now had access to these resources.[41] Increasingly, *ʿilm al-kalām*,[42] which can be loosely translated as 'theology', began to engage pagan sources and work within ancient, predominantly Aristotelian, categories. Many Christian apologists recognised this opening as an opportunity to find common ground apart from scripture. Their assumption was that they and their opponents shared the goal of understanding the nature of the One God, and that establishing a common method of inquiry would lead to the truth.

Among the many examples of this shift in methodology, is the letter of the East Syrian (Nestorian) Patriarch Timothy I, dated around 782, which engages an interlocutor well-versed in Aristotelian philosophy. This letter uses both philosophical categories and scriptural (biblical and qur'anic) proof-texts to argue for the existence of three divine hypostases in one God.[43] The association of the persons of the Trinity with divine attributes became a standard defence in Christian apologetics that will be examined more carefully below. One of the best-known Christians of the ʿAbbasid period to develop these philosophical arguments is Yaḥyā ibn ʿAdī (d. 974), an extremely prolific writer, a philosopher and theologian, and a translator of Aristotle and other ancient commentators.[44] He

39 H.G.B. Teule, *'Barāhīn ʿalā ṣiḥḥat al-Injīl'*, in *CMR* 4, 335-6.

40 A. Sidarus and M.N. Swanson, *'Al-ḥāwī l-mustafād min badīhat al-ijtihād'*, in *CMR* 5, 256-61.

41 C. D'Ancona, art. 'Greek into Arabic', in *EI*3, and D. Gutas and K. van Bladel, art. 'Bayt al-Ḥikma', in *EI*3.

42 L. Gardet, art. 'Kalām', in *EI*2, and L. Gardet, art. "Ilm al-Kalām' in *EI*2.

43 B. Roggema, 'To Sergius, Letter 40', in *CMR* 1, 519-22.

44 E. Platti, 'Yaḥyā ibn ʿAdī', in *CMR* 2, 390-415.

took up the challenge to defend the rationality of Christianity, producing at least 18 works defending the faith against Islam. His writings also demonstrate a true engagement with Muslim thinkers, addressing questions concerning *tawḥīd*, human action and 'acquisition' (*kasb* or *iktisāb*), the nature of the possible (*ṭabīʿat al-mumkin*), and divine foreknowledge. Among his most influential works, is one that uses logical demonstration to disprove the Muslim theologian Abū ʿĪsā al-Warrāq's (d. c. 864) refutation of the incarnation, and of the Trinity in his *Refutation of the three Christian sects*.[45]

By the 11th century, the arguments employing philosophical methodology in defence of Christian doctrine and practice had been carefully honed through continual engagement with Muslim opponents. In this period, an extremely prolific Christian writer in Arabic was Ibn al-Ṭayyib (d. c. 1043), a philosopher and biblical commentator, who also produced numerous texts explicating doctrine through the lens of Aristotle.[46] Among his most significant theological writings are his lengthy *Treatise on the foundations of the religion*,[47] and substantial treatises on the Trinity and the Incarnation.[48] In the medieval period, European scholars gained access to this method through translations of texts into Latin, which led to a separate body of apologetic literature.

Proofs of prophethood and the true religion

Perhaps the first issue that arose between Muḥammad and his followers and the Christians they encountered was the authenticity of his prophethood. Muḥammad's initial mission was to those Arabian polytheists who had not yet accepted the authority of the One God as professed by Christians and Jews, and the first verses of his revelation accentuated the need for his message to them. As his prophetic career progressed, however, his expectation that the Christian and Jewish communities would accept him as one of their own was greatly disappointed. Not only did they not accept him as a messenger from God, but allegations that he had received his teachings from disreputable Jewish or Christian figures

---

45 E. Platti, '*Tabyīn ghalaṭ Muḥammad ibn Hārūn al-maʿrūf bi-Abī ʿĪsā l-Warrāq*', in *CMR* 2, 413-14. See also D. Thomas, 'Abū ʿĪsā l-Warrāq', in *CMR* 1, 695-701.

46 J. Faultless, 'Ibn al-Ṭayyib', in *CMR* 2, 667-97.

47 J. Faultless, '*Maqāla fī l-uṣūl al-dīniyya*', in *CMR* 2, 683-4.

48 J. Faultless, '*Maqāla fī l-tathlīth*', in *CMR* 2, 690-1; J. Faultless, '*Maqāla fī l-tathlīth wa-l-tawḥīd*', in *CMR* 2, 692-3, and J. Faultless, '*Maqāla mukhtaṣara fī l-aqānīm wa-l-jawhar, wa-anna l-fiʿl li-l-jawhar*', in *CMR* 2, 694.

began to surface. This prompted an on-going debate on Muḥammad's status and the source of his revelations.[49]

The Qur'an makes numerous allusions to those who rejected Muḥammad's claim to prophethood, and Christians and Jews appear to have argued that he had received his messages from sources other than God (e.g. Q 25:4-9). At the centre of the controversy is the tradition that a Christian monk named Baḥīrā identified Muḥammad as one who was expected to come after Jesus.[50] Accounts of the encounter between Muḥammad and Baḥīrā are contained in *al-sīra l-nabawiyya*, the traditional biography of the prophet.[51] According to Muḥammad's followers, Baḥīrā's recognition was confirmation of his prophethood and the veracity of his revelations. Christians, on the other hand, argued that the monk was a charlatan and a heretic whose testimony meant nothing. The trustworthiness of Baḥīrā as a witness to the authenticity of Muḥammad's prophethood raised multiple questions later taken up in Christian apologetics. Foremost among them was the charge of *taḥrīf* discussed above. According to Muslim tradition, Baḥīrā claimed that 'another' prophet was predicted in the Gospel, yet efforts to locate this prediction were unsuccessful. Some, such as Ibn Hishām (d. 833), quoting Ibn Isḥāq (d. 767), suggested that Q 61:6, which foretells one who will be named 'Aḥmad', can be identified with the Paraclete in John 14:16, 15:23-7. The absence of support in the New Testament for the Muslim claim fuelled suspicions that the Christian scriptures had been tampered with or were being misinterpreted.[52]

Christians rejected the notion that Muḥammad was a prophet promised by Jesus, arguing instead that true prophets must be accompanied by miracles and good works, which are compelling evidence for all people. Theodore Abū Qurra (d. c. 830) claimed that a true religion would be associated with authentic miracles, and even that no true religion would be without them. The earliest disciples of Christ could not offer wealth,

---

[49] For a succinct summary of the life and significance of Muḥammad, see F. Buhl et al., art. 'Muḥammad' in *EI2*.

[50] A. Abel, art. 'Baḥīrā', in *EI2*, and B. Roggema, '*The legend of Sergius Baḥīrā*', in *CMR* 1, 600-3. For an extensive study of the extant literature, see B. Roggema, *The legend of Sergius Baḥīrā*, Leiden, 2009, also the brief, though important treatise outlining the corruption of the Qur'an and Baḥīrā's role in the deceit: B. Roggema, '*'Eltā d-Quran*', in *CMR* 1, 595-6.

[51] G.L. Della Vida, art. 'Sīra' in *EI1*; W. Raven, art. 'Sīra' in *EI2*. S.A. Mourad, 'Christians and Christianity in the *Sīra* of Muḥammad', in *CMR* 1, 57-71.

[52] S.T. Keating, 'The Paraclete and the integrity of scripture', in C.L. Tieszen (ed.), *Theological issues in Christian-Muslim dialogue*, Eugene OR, 2018, 15-25; J. Schacht, art. 'Aḥmad' in *EI2*.

power, lax morality or increased status to those to whom they preached; rather, to follow Christ was to expect suffering and poverty. According to Abū Qurra, converts accepted Christianity because they believed its truth.[53] In response to a Muslim request for a proof of the truth of Christianity, Abū Rā'iṭa l-Takrītī composed a brief logical demonstration of the universality of the faith, arguing that its intellectual sophistication could reach the intelligent, while its miracles appealed to the ignorant. Abū Rā'iṭa left his reader to draw the conclusion that Islam had neither, and so could not be universal.[54]

Muḥammad, however, did not claim to have performed any miracles. The Qur'an says that no one can perform miracles unless they be signs granted by God to authenticate his true prophets. These *āyāt* (signs or tokens; sing. *āya*) are divine acts that cannot be contradicted. They came to be identified specifically as verses (also called *āyāt*) sent to God's messengers. Although the *sīra* and Hadith contain traditions attributing miracles to Muḥammad, his primary and only universally accepted *āya* was his reception of the Qur'an.[55] Eventually, the rejection of Muḥammad's prophethood by Christians and Jews because of his lack of miracles prompted a spate of Muslim writings often given the general title of 'Proof of Muḥammad's prophethood', many of which are now lost. These works both collected and systematised traditions of miracles associated with Muḥammad and constructed a more complete picture of the authenticity of his call based on divine confirmation. Among these are the 8th-century treatise by Ibn al-Layth mentioned above,[56] *Kitāb al-ḥujja fī tathbīt al-nubuwwa* by al-Jāḥiẓ (d. 869),[57] al-Hādī ilā l-Ḥaqq's (d. 911) *Tathbīt nubuwwat Muḥammad*,[58] the *Kitāb ithbāt nubuwwat al-nabī* by al-Mu'ayyad bi-llāh (d. 1020),[59] and the *Munāzara fī l-radd ʿalā l-Naṣārā* by Fakhr al-Dīn al-Rāzī (d. 1209),[60] to name only a very few.

The task of determining whether Muḥammad was a true prophet remained a point of contention between Muslims and Christians, and

---

53 J.C. Lamoreaux, 'Theodore Abū Qurra', in *CMR* 1, 439-91.

54 S.T. Keating, *'Min qawl Abī Rā'iṭa l-Takrītī al-Suryānī usquf Nasībīn mustadillan bihi ʿalā ṣiḥḥat al-Naṣrāniyya l-maqbūla min al-dāʿīn al-mubashshirīn bihā bi-l-Injīl al-muqaddas'*, in *CMR* 1, 578-80.

55 A. Jeffery, art. 'Āya' in *EI2*; A.J. Wensinck, art. 'Muʿdjiza' in *EI2*.

56 B. Roggema, *'Risālat Abī l-Rabīʿ Muḥammad ibn al-Layth allatī katabahā li-l-Rashīd ilā Qusṭanṭīn malik al-Rūm'*, in *CMR* 1, 349-53.

57 D. Thomas, *'Kitāb al-ḥujja fī tathbīt al-nubuwwa'*, in *CMR* 1, 707-8.

58 G.S. Reynolds, *'Tathbīt nubuwwat Muḥammad'*, in *CMR* 2, 127-9.

59 D. Thomas, *'Kitāb ithbāt nubuwwat al-nabī'*, in *CMR* 2, 235-6.

60 M. Iskenderoglu, *'Munāzara fī l-radd ʿalā l-Naṣārā'*, in *CMR* 4, 63-5.

inspired scholars in both communities to produce writings that delineated criteria for identifying the 'true religion', along with grounds for authentic conversion when one discerned that religion's authenticity. This literature is extensive and came in many different formats, some of which have been noted already. In some cases, texts had as their primary focus the identifying characteristics of the authentic religion from God and signs of genuine conversion, and in many instances, extensive defences of particular doctrines and practices were collated in longer treatises of the genre 'On the true religion'. One finds examples compiled by both Muslim and Christian scholars, and many common themes run through the texts; in some cases, the authors were responding to a particular argument or representative of the other religion, but in most the impetus appears to be the desire to make a general contribution to an ongoing debate concerning the truth of Christianity or Islam.[61]

Extant texts indicate that the genre became popular with Christians beginning in the late 8th century, probably in connection with the rise of the ʿAbbasid caliphate, which began to encourage conversion to Islam. Three of the best-known Christian apologists of this period, Theodore Abū Qurra,[62] Abū Rāʾiṭa,[63] and ʿAmmār al-Baṣrī (d. c. 840),[64] wrote such treatises to encourage their communities in this time of transition. Their arguments became the standard responses in the following centuries, apparently even crossing denominational lines, as Christians fought to preserve their religious identity under their Muslim rulers. The genre experienced a revival in the medieval period, this time with significant contributions from Muslim intellectuals. From the Ashʿarī school, al-Juwāynī (d. 1085) constructed an extensive systematic theology that included a refutation of the central Christian doctrines and provided the reader with the principles of the 'true religion'.[65] Somewhat later, al-Shahrastānī (d. 1153) assembled a very extensive outline of all religions and sects, and criteria for determining pure monotheism. Although it is primarily descriptive, this work was influential in its conclusion that Christianity is a distortion of the true religion revealed to Muḥammad.[66] A century later, al-Jaʿfarī (d. 1270) elaborated further on these arguments

61 See in this volume, chs 4, 6, and 7 for further examples and discussion.

62 J.C. Lamoreaux, *'Maymar fī wujūd al-Khāliq wa-l-dīn al-qawīm'*, in *CMR* 1, 448-50; J.C. Lamoreaux, *'Maymar yuḥaqqiqu anna dīn Allāh'*, in *CMR* 1, 467-8.

63 S.T. Keating, *'Risāla li-Abī Rāʾiṭa l-Takrītī fī ithbāt dīn al-Naṣrāniyya wa-ithbāt al-Thālūth al-muqaddas'*, in *CMR* 1, 571-2.

64 I.M. Beaumont, *'Kitāb al-burhān ʿalā siyāqat al-tadbīr al-ilāhī'*, in *CMR* 1, 607-10.

65 D. Thomas, *'Kitāb al-Shāmil fī uṣūl al-dīn'*, in *CMR* 3, 124-6.

66 D. Thomas, *'Kitāb al-milal wa-l-niḥal'*, in *CMR* 3, 550-2.

in his last polemical work, using arguments from scripture and from reason to compare the prophethood of Jesus and of Muḥammad.[67]

Christians responded to these, drawing on previous authors while at the same time addressing local concerns. The Copt Yuḥannā ibn Mīnā (11th century?), about whom very little is known, authored a short treatise concerning false conversion that was added to the well-known work of Ḥunayn ibn Isḥāq on discerning the true religion, which suggests this was a special concern for the Coptic Christian community.[68] Somewhat later, Makkīkhā ibn Sulaymān al-Qankānī (11th century), writing during a period of difficult relations between Muslims and Christians in Baghdad, included in his treatise on the truth of the 'religion of the Messiah' accounts of miracles associated with Christians steadfast in their faith, as well as encouragement to those who might face martyrdom.[69] One of the most extensive extant Coptic works of this genre, from Būlus al-Būshī (d. c. 1250), follows the traditional question-answer format, explaining the doctrines of the Trinity and the Incarnation, and then turning to an examination of the characteristics of true prophets and criteria for the true religion. He argued that only a religion known through prophecy and substantiated by miracles and rational arguments could be from God, with the implication that Muḥammad's message fell short.[70]

The question of the authenticity of Muḥammad's prophethood raised a host of issues that continued to be addressed by Muslims and Christians in the centuries following his death, including the necessity of miracles as proof of the true religion and the accuracy of the biblical text. These problems led to a relative impasse between scholars of the two communities; each continued to examine the questions, and applied traditional arguments taking into account the current context of the author, but few new insights made their way into the debate after the medieval period.

Christology and soteriology

The question of the status of Jesus lies at the very heart of Christian debates with Muslims. Already in the Qur'an, Christian claims about the divine nature of Jesus Christ were being challenged and, as was noted

67 L. Demiri, '*Kitāb al-radd ʿalā l-Naṣārā*', in *CMR* 4, 485.
68 M.N. Swanson, 'Untitled appendix to Ḥunayn ibn Isḥāq, *Kayfiyyat idrāk ḥaqīqat al-diyāna*', in *CMR* 3, 721-3.
69 H.G.B. Teule, '*Kitāb fī ḥaqīqat al-dīn al-Masīḥī*', in *CMR* 3, 324-6.
70 M.N. Swanson, '*Al-maqāla al-ūlā min qawl al-qiddīs Būlus al-Būshī*', in *CMR* 4, 283-6.

above, contributed to the Muslim concern that the Bible was no longer reliable. The Christian assertion that the first-century Jew, Jesus, son of Mary, was the expected Messiah, who was crucified, died and raised from the dead, seemed to compromise God's absolute divinity. The Qur'an instead emphasises the humanity of Jesus, asserting that he himself made no claims to divinity, and was only a messenger like those before him (Q 5:115-16, 72, 75; 19:30-1). Further, according to the qur'anic account, Jesus was a prophet who only 'appeared' (*shubbiha*) to have been crucified, and was raised up to God from his earthly life (Q 4:158-9). Some of the earliest preserved debates between Muslims and Christians took up questions about the historicity, and even the necessity, of the crucifixion. Indeed, for Christians, the Incarnation and Resurrection are the foundations of orthodox faith – without the Resurrection, Christian 'faith is in vain' (1 Corinthians 15:17), making it *the* doctrine *sine qua non*.

An added difficulty to defending the biblical account of Jesus, though, was the divisions that had arisen between Christians as a consequence of the various ecumenical councils, especially the Council of Chalcedon (451) at which the Church made a formal creedal statement concerning the relationship between the human and divine natures of Christ. The controversy that precipitated the Council was complex, involving concerns about the usefulness of Greek (especially Aristotelian) philosophy for understanding biblical concepts, political infighting, and general disagreement on the interpretation of key passages of scripture. At the time of Muḥammad, three major (and many smaller) denominations flourished around the Mediterranean basin: the Melkite (Chalcedonian/Byzantine) Church, the Jacobite (Syrian Orthodox/Miaphysite) Church, and the Nestorian (Church of the East) community. To these one could add the Egyptian Coptic and Armenian Miaphysite churches, who also produced unique apologetic traditions. The Christological controversies of the 4th and 5th centuries and continuing rancour among the factions prevented Christians from presenting a unified front to address the challenge of a new religion, a situation of which Muslims were well-aware. The Qur'an alludes to these controversies in Q 3:55, where God declares he will settle that over which Christians dispute on the Day of Resurrection. In the centuries following Muḥammad's death, Christians from each denomination were occasionally called before Muslim officials to give an account of the teachings of their community and explain their differences. There is little evidence that Muslims found these arguments convincing, although the staged discussions seem to have prompted Christians to prepare arguments in order to present a coherent and understandable case for their positions.

Some explanations and arguments did cross the denominational divide, but extant texts reveal that many apologists were as concerned with defending the Christological position of their own church against other Christians as against Muslims. Consequently, the apologetic tradition included at least three separate streams associated with the various churches. As noted above, some of the earliest theological engagement between Muslims and Christians addressed questions of the status of Jesus as a prophet, as, for example, the 8th-century *Disputation between a monk of Bēt Ḥalē and an Arab notable.* Similarities between this text and others authors such as John of Damascus and Theodore Abū Qurra have led scholars to believe it belongs to the Melkite tradition; other anonymous texts also indicate that increasingly developed Arabic presentations of Christological doctrine were circulating. By the end of the 8th century, each denomination had come to be associated with its own particularly articulate and creative writer whose works formed the foundation for later apologists: the Melkite bishop Theodore Abū Qurra, the Syrian Orthodox (Jacobite) Abū Rā'iṭa, and the Patriarch of the Church of the East (Nestorian) Mar Timothy I (d. 823).

The earliest of these three, Abū Qurra, was an extremely prolific writer whose texts are preserved in both Arabic and Greek. Among the topics he addressed directly were the truth of the crucifixion and whether Christ was crucified willingly,[71] and the manner of his death. According to Abū Qurra, the Orthodox teaching was that God became incarnate and died in his human, not divine nature, in contrast to the Nestorians, who claimed Jesus was only human, and the Monophysites, who argued that his divine nature died. Following the Chalcedonian position, Abū Qurra stated that the core of the dispute was the necessity for God to become human, and for humanity to be redeemed through the human nature of the Incarnate One. Without the Cross and Christ's suffering humanity, there could be no salvation.[72]

One of his most ardent opponents was Abū Rā'iṭa, who mentioned Abū Qurra by name in his writings. Abū Rā'iṭa addressed issues of properly

---

71 J.C. Lamoreaux, *'Su'ila Abū Qurra Anbā Thādhurus usquf Ḥarrān 'an al-Masīḥ bi-hawāhi ṣuliba am bi-ghayr hawāhi'*, in *CMR* 1, 468-9.

72 J.C. Lamoreaux, *'Maymar fī mawt al-Masīḥ'*, in *CMR* 1, 454-6. See also M.N. Swanson, 'The cross of Christ in the earliest Arabic Melkite apologies', in S.K. Samir and J. Nielsen (eds), *Christian Arabic apologetics during the Abbasid period (750-1258)*, Leiden, 1994, 115-45.

understanding the Incarnation and soteriology in nearly all his extant texts. His most complete explication, however, is his *risāla* on the Incarnation, which was written as the second of three treatises responding to Muslim questions about Christian doctrine. Like Abū Qurra and others, he presented a defence of the crucifixion and its necessity, as well as Jesus Christ's willingness to accept such an ignominious death. As a Syrian Orthodox (Jacobite) theologian, Abū Rā'iṭa was very cautious about compromising the unity of the *person* of Christ, and spent considerable time examining such issues as Christ's foreknowledge and whether his divinity remained unified with his body in death.[73]

The third author, Mar Timothy I, is known from his many letters, his treatises, and an account of a disputation with the Caliph al-Mahdī. While the disputation is not specifically concerned with the Incarnation, it engages questions of Jesus' humanity, and especially how one can speak of Jesus as 'good' (since only God is 'good'), and that he was truly crucified.[74] Although Mar Timothy represented the East Syrian (Nestorian) Church, his arguments were adapted by other denominations and later appeared in various forms. In subsequent centuries, the debate continued as Christians sought to refine arguments that had already been fashioned to respond to Muslim intellectuals.

As noted above, the increased use and translation of Greek philosophy introduced opportunities to clarify in Arabic doctrines expressed (or rejected) at the ecumenical councils. Another popular literary form developed by Christians for internal use was the *florilegium*, which collected passages suitable as proof-texts in situations that called for apology. Many Christian writers produced these as separate documents or included them in longer treatises. For example, Abū Rā'iṭa is associated with a list of 'witnesses' from the Torah to be used in defence of Christian doctrine.[75] Two centuries later, Sāwīrus ibn al-Muqaffa' (d. 987) produced an important *florilegium* of quotations from the Fathers, primarily dealing with Christology.[76] These texts attested to the ongoing need for Christians to search the Bible and tradition for evidence of the validity of their faith.

Many of those who participated in the medieval intensification of Muslim-Christian engagement also contributed significant defences of

73 Keating, '*Al-risāla l-thāniya li-Abī Rā'iṭa l-Takrītī fī l-tajassud*', pp. 574-5.
74 M. Heimgartner, 'Letter 59 (Disputation with the Caliph al-Mahdī)', in *CMR* 1, 522-6.
75 Keating, '*Shahādāt min qawl al-Tawrāt wa-l-anbiyā' wa-l-qiddīsīn*', pp. 576-7.
76 M.N. Swanson, '*Al-durr al-thamīn*', in *CMR* 2, 508-9.

Christological and soteriological doctrines. Notable among these is ʿAbd Allāh ibn al-Faḍl al-Anṭākī (d. c. 1052), who included within a longer defence of the Holy Trinity an explanation of how one can speak of Christ's death as not touching his divinity, and responses to other questions concerning the two natures, why Christ was crucified and how he suffered.[77] Yaḥyā ibn Jarīr's (d. 1103/4) extensive theological compendium contains several chapters devoted to Christ's crucifixion, passion and humanity.[78] Later, al-Makīn Jirjis ibn al-ʿAmīd (d. 1398) constructed a massive exposition of Christian beliefs, including a Christological treatise and an explanation of the Fall, the effects of sin, free will and salvation.[79] Muslims also carried forward arguments that had been articulated before in order to address new situations. An important contribution in this regard comes from al-Khaṭīb al-Iskandarī (d. mid-13th century), who formulated an extensive response to Francis of Assisi's attempt to convert al-Malik al-Kāmil (d. 1238), the Muslim ruler of Egypt, Palestine and Syria. This understudied work contains an outline of the Christian positions he intended to address, including misguided beliefs about Jesus Christ (crucifixion, conciliar doctrines, Old Testament prophecy and prefiguration of Christ), followed by his refutation of these. It is, in many ways, a summary of the Muslim response to the Christian doctrine of Christ's Incarnation.[80]

Finally, a significant point of contention between Muslims and Christians related to questions of Christology was the issue of iconoclasm. This complex problem touched deep concerns on both sides about the relationship between God and creation, and the possibility of the Incarnation. John of Damascus was one who was well aware of the implications of the Qur'an's rejection of the existence of anything that could be 'like' God (Q 42:11; 112:1-4). Although his three treatises *On the divine images* are not usually considered to be directed specifically at Islamic teaching, he is squarely situated in the midst of the iconoclastic controversy, writing against those who 'attack the Holy Icons'. He argued that Christ was the true and perfect image of God, which could be represented in appropriate holy images.[81]

---

77 A. Treiger, *'Kalām fī l-Thālūth al-muqaddas'*, in *CMR* 3, 98-100.

78 H.G.B. Teule and M.N. Swanson, *'Kitāb al-murshid'*, in *CMR* 3, 282-6.

79 Sidarus and Swanson, *'Al-ḥāwī l-mustafād min badīhat al-ijtihād'*.

80 D. Thomas, *'Adillat al-waḥdāniyya fī l-radd ʿalā l-milla l-Naṣrāniyya'*, in *CMR* 4, 265-6.

81 A. Louth, *St John Damascene*, Oxford, 2009, pp. 193-22; A. Louth (trans.), *Three treatises on the divine images*, Crestwood NY, 2003.

John's ideas were taken up by his spiritual son Abū Qurra in several of his writings, but especially in the short treatise on the necessity of venerating icons.[82] Usṭāth al-Rāhib (d. end of 9th century) included in his Christological treatise the question of the veneration of icons and their meaning for the Christian faithful.[83] Later in the 13th century, Ishoʿyahb bar Malkon reiterated previous arguments in favour of venerating icons, adding that such intermediaries were in fact a 'remembrance' (*dhikr*), as one finds in many Muslim practices, and were even necessary to avoid the impudence of approaching God directly.[84]

Muslims did not find these arguments convincing, and continued to produce extensive refutations of Christian teachings concerning the Incarnation, crucifixion, miracles and prophecies about Jesus, veneration of icons and other expressions of devotion to Christ. Christian converts to Islam certainly contributed to the increasing articulation of anti-Christian rhetoric, and some, such as Naṣr ibn Yaḥyā (d. 1163/93), produced extensive systematic critiques of their former religion[85] as a justification for their conversions, adding to the corpus of apologetic literature and keeping the topics alive in scholarly exchanges.

Divine unity and the doctrine of the Trinity

Another central disagreement between Muslims and Christians concerned the nature of the unity of God. Whereas from its inception the Christian community had affirmed a threefold relationship within the single Godhead,[86] the Qur'an insists on rejection of any form of plurality associated with God (Q 112:1-4; 59:22-4; 2:255). Underlying the Qur'an's injunction is the concern that Trinitarian doctrine might lead to polytheism; indeed, it is sometimes unclear in the Qur'an whether Christians are

---

82 J.C. Lamoreaux, *'Maymar qālahu Anbā Thāwudhūrūs usquf Ḥarrān al-muqaddas wa-huwa Abū Qurra yuthbitu fīhi anna l-sujūd li-ṣūrat al-Masīḥ ilāhinā lladhī tajassada min Rūḥ al-Qudus wa-min Maryam al-adhrā' al-muṭahhara wa-ṣuwar qiddīsīhi wājib 'alā kull Naṣrānī'*, in *CMR* 1, 463-6.

83 E. Salah and M.N. Swanson, *'Kitāb Usṭāth (al-rāhib)'*, in *CMR* 1, 908-10.

84 H.G.B. Teule, *'Al-radd ʿalā l-Yahūd wa l-Muslimīn alladhīna yattahimūna l-Naṣārā bi-ʿibādat al-aṣnām li-sujūdihim li-l-ṣalīb wa-ikrāmihim ṣuwar al-Masīḥ wa-l-Sayyida wa-l-qiddīsīn'*, in *CMR* 4, 333-5.

85 L. Demiri, *'Al-naṣīḥa l-imāniyya fī faḍīḥat al-milla l-Naṣrāniyya'*, in *CMR* 3, 751-4.

86 Christians generally trace the basis for doctrine of the Trinity to Jesus' command to 'Go, therefore, and make disciples of all nations, baptising them in the name of the Father, and of the Son, and of the holy Spirit' (Matthew 28:19). Over the centuries, exegesis of this injunction led to the complex dogma of the threefold unity of God that is identified as the foundation of Christian faith; see W.J. Hill, *The three-personed God*, Washington DC, 1982.

included with polytheists in condemnations of idolatry as *shirk* – associating anything with God – which is the worst form of unbelief (*kufr*).[87] The teaching of the Trinity is especially problematic for Islam because of the Incarnation – how could the One Transcendent God become incarnated in an historical human being? The worship of a person seems the very definition of idolatry, even if he is a member of the Holy Trinity! The Qur'an denounces this as an 'excess', commanding Christians to desist from it (Q 4:171; 5:72-3).

The challenge posed by Islam to the doctrine of the Trinity was in many ways a combination of those presented by pagans and Jews in the first centuries of Christianity, and initially the Christian apologists followed the well-trodden lead of the early Church Fathers in their responses. Biblical images and analogies were translated into Arabic, and arguments were constructed to demonstrate that Christian faith was not polytheistic. Nonetheless, two important obstacles to these strategies quickly emerged: the charge that the biblical text had been manipulated (*taḥrīf*), and Muslim suspicions of analogy (*qiyās*). Because both have their roots in the Qur'an, it became increasing difficult for Christian writers to rely on them in apologetic responses. Consequently, within a century of the death of Muḥammad, Christian apologists began to shift their strategy towards emphasising the common faith of both Christians and Muslims in one God, and then demonstrating that Christian doctrines about the Holy Trinity and the Incarnation were not only falsely considered to be irrational, but were in fact the necessary logical conclusions of important theological and philosophical questions.

This issue of *taḥrīf* has been discussed above, and it is sufficient to note that, by the early 9th century, Christian apologists were developing new strategies of defence, independent of biblical proof-texts. The most significant of these employed Greek philosophical texts to explain and clarify the mysterious doctrine of the Trinity. A constant Muslim charge against Christians was that this doctrine was irrational, since it was impossible that something could be absolutely one and unified, and also simultaneously multiple. Abū Rā'iṭa was the first apologist whose name is known who developed the notion that the Persons of the Trinity can be understood in a way similar to the Muslim concept of the 'beautiful names' of God (*al-asmā' al-ḥusnā*).[88] He argued that those 'names', or attributes (*ṣifāt*), of God that were recognised as necessary – life,

---

87 D. Gimaret, art. 'Shirk' in *EI2*; D. Thomas, art. 'Tathlīth' in *EI2*; C. Adang, art. 'Belief and unbelief', in *EQ*.

88 G. Böwering, art. 'God and his attributes', in *EQ*.

knowledge, and wisdom[89] – were attributes or properties (*khawāṣṣ*) without which God had never existed and which Christians identified as the Divine Persons.[90] His arguments relied heavily on a sophisticated understanding of analogy accepted by most Christians.

This approach enjoyed long-lived popularity as others, such as ʿAbd al-Masīḥ al-Kindī, developed and refined it. Al-Kindī's *Apology*, which quotes extensively from Abū Rāʾiṭa's writings, especially the first *risāla*, *'On the Holy Trinity'*, became widely known in Europe in the medieval period through translation into Latin.[91] Israel of Kashkar (d. late 9th century), of the East Syrian (Nestorian) church, adopted the description in his surviving work on 'the Unity of the Creator and the Trinity of his properties'.[92] A century after Abū Rāʾiṭa, the great translator and theologian Yaḥyā ibn ʿAdī (d. 974) continued in this vein, producing several treatises that attempted fully to exploit Aristotelian philosophy as a means to explain the Trinity in logical terms.[93] Ibn ʿAdī's work reflects the pinnacle of this method and became the model that most Christian apologists subsequently adopted.

Muslims, however, were suspicious of the comparisons Christian apologists made between the created world and God, lest it lead to idolatry, and had cautiously developed carefully delineated rules for the use of analogy (*qiyās*) in legal spheres.[94] Concerns about analogy were closely related to those about the Incarnation and veneration of icons – if nothing is like God (Q 42:11), how can analogy lead to knowledge of God? For Christians, however, scripture had definitively established that one could arrive at authentic, though limited, knowledge of God through observation of the created world (Genesis 1:27; John 12:45, 14:8). Many analogies had become standard in patristic explanations of the Trinity, and these were carried over into Christian Arabic apologetics and theology. Abū Qurra, Abū Rāʾiṭa, ʿAbd al-Masīḥ al-Kindī and most others employed the common comparisons of the sun and its disc, light and heat, and the human being (or soul) and its life, knowledge/speech and power. Muslims for their part continued to voice scepticism about the legitimacy of using analogy when discussing the Divine Being. Al-Nāshiʾ al-Akbar

---

89 These are three of the most commonly used terms, although there was significant variation as the doctrine was developed by Christian intellectuals.

90 Keating, *'Al-risāla l-ūlā fī l-Thālūth al-muqaddas'*.

91 Bottini, *'Apology of al-Kindī'*.

92 B. Holmberg, *'Risāla fī tathbīt waḥdāniyyat al-bāriʾ wa-tathlīth khawāṣṣihi'*, in *CMR* 1, 759-61.

93 E.g. E. Platti, *'Maqāla mawsūma bi-l-ʿaql wa-l-ʿāqil wa-l-maʿqūl'*, in *CMR* 2, 419-21.

94 M. Bernand and G. Troupeau, art. 'Ḳiyās', in *EI*2.

(d. 906) wrote a text refuting the Christian doctrines of the Trinity and the Incarnation, focusing particularly on Christians who made arguments based in scripture, and used reason to draw analogies with characteristics of physical matter.[95] In his own refutation of Christian teachings, Abū l-Qāsim al-Anṣārī (d. 1118) dismissed the idea that there could be comparison or analogy between physical substances and the Divine Being. Rather, he argued that the divine attributes (*ṣifāt*) that could be attributed to God were known through revelation, not through the material world.[96]

This debate persisted well into the Middle Ages, as Christians continued to insist that the use of analogy was both sanctioned and necessary for a proper of understanding of God. Some, such as ʿAbd Allāh ibn al-Faḍl al-Anṭākī (d. c. 1052), argued that analogy was a tool that was absolutely central to Christian theology and essential for grasping the concept of the Trinity.[97] As both religious communities based their acceptance and concerns about analogy in scripture, the stalemate was not overcome, and the topic recurred intermittently into the modern period.

Conclusion

The development of apologetic literature reflects the long and often painful relationship between Muslims and Christians as they worked to articulate common beliefs and differences. As each community was confronted with new situations, questions of religious identity and the meaning and significance of beliefs and practices often surfaced, prompting renewed interest in old themes. The topics, and many, if not most, of the arguments remained the same in the first millennium after the rise of Islam: the authenticity of Muḥammad and his message, the integrity of the Bible, the possibility of the Incarnation and the truth of the doctrine of the Holy Trinity. Questions and responses were refined and made more complex, but in the end the differences were not settled. Nor did the communities expect that they would be. Muslim and Christian apologists were well aware that the decision to submit to either religion was ultimately a matter of faith, and a dispute that could only be settled by God.

---

95 D. Thomas, *'Kitāb al-awsaṭ fī l-maqālāt'*, in *CMR* 2, 86-8.

96 D. Thomas, *'Al-ghunya fī l-kalām'*, in *CMR* 5, 666-7.

97 A. Treiger, *'Kalām fī l-thālūth al-muqaddas'*, in *CMR* 3, 98-100.

Chapter 9
Muslims engaging the Bible

Ayşe İçöz

Introduction

From the very beginning of the Islamic era, the attitude of Muslims towards the Hebrew Bible and the New Testament was determined by the Qur'an. The following verse epitomises the way in which the Qur'an regards the Bible:

> And we have revealed to you [O Muḥammad], the book in truth, confirming that which preceded it of the Scripture and as a criterion over it. So, judge between them by what Allāh has revealed and do not follow their inclinations away from what has come to you of the truth. To each of you We have prescribed a law and a method. Had Allāh willed, He would have made you one nation [united in religion], but [He intended] to test you in what He has given you; so race to [all that is] good. To Allāh is your return all together, and He will [then] inform you concerning that over which you used to differ. (Q 5:48)

As verses such as this show, the Qur'an understands itself as continuing the earlier divine message that was revealed in the Bible,[1] and in addition as preserving what is true in it, which implies that, although the original form of the Bible has been changed and corrupted, it still contains some truth.[2] As may be expected, in the early Islamic era the issue of the corruption of the Bible (*taḥrīf*) constituted one of the major topics in Muslim refutations of Christianity, though at the same time many Muslim polemicists used verses from the Bible to support their arguments against Christians (and also Jews). Similarly, some Muslim authors valued it as a reliable source for their historical books or Qur'an commentaries. The Bible was employed by Muslims in many ways.

---

1 Q 4:47; Q 5:46.

2 Q 2:42, 59, 75, 79; Q 3:71, 78; Q 4:46; Q 5:13, 41; Q 6:91; Q 7:162.

Early Muslim use of the Bible: ʿAlī al-Ṭabarī

The *Kitāb al-dīn wa-l-dawla* (c. 860) by the 9th-century convert to Islam, Abū l-Ḥasan ʿAlī ibn Sahl Rabbān al-Ṭabarī, is one of the earliest examples of the *ithbāt al-nubuwwa* (confirmation of prophethood) genre, which sought to prove the divine mission of the Prophet Muḥammad.[3] As a former Christian from a scholarly family, ʿAlī al-Ṭabarī possessed an understandably good command of the Bible, which he very likely read in Syriac.[4]

ʿAlī al-Ṭabarī organises his work into ten chapters. In the first nine, he relies heavily on traditional Islamic materials, and then in the last chapter, by far the longest, he turns to proofs from the Bible.[5] He quotes verses from throughout the Old Testament and the Gospels, and follows each with an interpretation that identifies a reference in it to the Prophet or Islam. For example, in the opening section, which deals with the prophecies of Moses, he quotes Deuteronomy 33:2–3:

> The lord came from Mount Sinai and appeared to us from Seir, and became manifest from Mount Paran. With him on his right hand were myriads of the holy ones. To these he granted power and made them to be loved by the people, and he invoked blessing on all his saints.[6]

This interpretation, ʿAlī al-Ṭabarī contends, is supported by Genesis 21:20–1, where Ishmael is referred to as learning archery in the desert of Paran, which includes Mecca and its surroundings. Thus, in this verse Paran refers to Mecca, and 'The lord' refers to the Prophet Muḥammad.[7] Later in the same chapter, ʿAlī al-Ṭabarī recounts Jesus' testimonies regarding the Prophet. He quotes John 14:26: 'The Paraclete, the Spirit of truth, whom the Father will send in my name, will teach you all things.' His point is that, since, after Jesus and his disciples, the only one who taught anything in addition to Jesus' message was the Prophet Muḥammad, here 'Paraclete' refers to him and 'all things' refers to the Qur'an.[8]

It is clear that ʿAlī al-Ṭabarī was fully aware of the supportive function of certain Bible verses, as long as they were interpreted appropriately. So,

---

3 See D. Thomas, "Ali l-Ṭabarī', in *CMR* 1, 669-74; also R. Ebied and D. Thomas (ed. and trans.), *The polemical works of ʿAlī al-Ṭabarī*, Leiden, 2016, here especially pp. 1-24.

4 A. Mingana (trans.), ʿAlī al-Ṭabarī, *The book of religion and empire*, London, 1922, p. xviii.

5 Ebied and Thomas, *The polemical works*, pp. 340-473.

6 Ebied and Thomas, *The polemical works*, p. 343.

7 Ebied and Thomas, *The polemical works*, p. 343.

8 Ebied and Thomas, *The polemical works*, p. 425.

by and large he accepted the biblical text, though at one point near the beginning of his work he does complain that 'the bearers of the book [...] concealed his name and distorted the outline of him that was found in the books of the prophets'.[9] This may refer to misinterpretation or corruption of the text; if the latter, ʿAlī al-Ṭabarī seems to have harboured reservations about the reliability of the text of the Bible.

ʿAlī al-Ṭabarī's contemporary Ibn Qutayba (d. 889)[10] composed his *Dalāʾil al-nubuwwa* ('Proofs of prophethood') to prove in a similar manner that the coming of the Prophet Muḥammad was foretold in the Bible.[11] Ibn Qutayba employs many of the same Gospel verses as ʿAlī, and also similar arguments. In the two places where he addresses the issue, he appears, like ʿAlī, to think of biblical corruption as misinterpretation rather than as alteration of the text.[12]

Differing Muslim perspectives on the Bible

Although many early Muslims accepted that the Bible, as possessed by contemporary Christians, was a corrupted version of the original revelations, they nevertheless valued it as a source of information. The historians Abū l-ʿAbbās Aḥmad al-Yaʿqūbī (d. c. 905) and Abū Jaʿfar Muḥammad ibn Jarīr al-Ṭabarī (d. 923) are good examples from the 10th century of scholars who used biblical material to construct and recount the history of prophets who preceded the Prophet Muḥammad. The influence of the biblical narratives can be seen on both the structure and content of their histories.

Al-Yaʿqūbī's *Tārīkh* ('History'), one of the first Muslim historical works, deals with world history from the time of Adam, relying on the biblical books of Kings, Chronicles and Psalms for much of pre-Islamic history.[13] The biblical narrative is fundamental to the organisation and chronology of the work. Al-Yaʿqūbī likes to blend together the biblical and Islamic versions of a story, as can be seen in the first section of his

---

9 Ebied and Thomas, *The polemical works*, p. 203.

10 See D. Thomas, 'Ibn Qutayba', in *CMR* 1, 816-18.

11 For a translation of biblical passages in this work, which is lost but selectively quoted in Ibn al-Jawzī's *Kitāb al-wafā fī faḍāʾil al-Muṣṭafā*, see C. Adang, *Muslim writers on Judaism and the Hebrew Bible. From Ibn Rabban to Ibn Hazm*, Leiden, 1996, pp. 267-77. For an edition of the first eight sections, based on a single manuscript held in Dār al-Kutub al-Ẓāhiriyya in Damascus, see S. Schmidtke, 'The Muslim reception of biblical materials. Ibn Qutayba and his *Aʿlām al-nubuwwa*', *ICMR* 22 (2011) 249-74, pp. 254-60.

12 Adang, *Muslim writers*, p. 225.

13 See D. Thomas, 'Al-Yaʿqūbī', in *CMR* 2, 75-8.

Tārīkh, which tells about Adam and Eve. The initial part follows both the biblical and Islamic accounts,[14] though it becomes explicitly Islamic when it recounts Adam's first pilgrimage in Mecca. After he has been expelled from Paradise and has settled in the earth, God sends down to him the black stone (*al- ḥajar al-aswad*) and asks him to go to Mecca and build the Kaʿba. When he has done this, he walks around it and offers a sacrifice, thus performing the first Muslim *ḥajj* by God's command.[15] In this way, al-Yaʿqūbī skilfully and smoothly amalgamates the biblical and Islamic materials.

The influential Persian historian, Abū Jaʿfar al-Ṭabarī also employed biblical material in his voluminous *Tārīkh al-rusul wa-l-mulūk* ('History of messengers and rulers').[16] This work starts with an account of the creation of the universe and of Adam. It is based on the Bible, but as in al-Yaʿqūbī's work, the influence of the Islamic tradition is unmistakable. For example, al-Ṭabarī devotes a lengthy section to the importance of Friday in Adam's life.[17]

Franz Rosenthal observes that although there is a certain amount of biblical material in the text, it relies heavily on traditional Islamic sources.[18] The following quotation is one of the rare examples of an almost literal translation of Genesis 4:9-16:

> The people of the Torah suppose that when Cain killed his brother Abel, God said to him: Where is your brother Abel? Cain replied: I do not know. I was not his keeper. Whereupon God said to him: The voice of the blood of your brother calls out to Me from the earth. Now you are cursed from the earth which opened its mouth to accept the blood of your brother from your hand. If you work the earth, it will not again give you its produce, and eventually you will be an errant fugitive on earth. Cain said: My sin is too great for You to forgive. Today, you have driven me from the face of the earth (and I shall keep concealed) from before You and be an errant fugitive on earth. Everybody who meets me will kill me. God said: This is not so. He who kills someone shall not be requited sevenfold, but he who kills Cain will be requited seven(fold). God put a sign upon Cain so that

---

[14] His main source here is the Arabic translation of the Syriac *Book of the cave of treasures*; see Adang, *Muslim writers*, p. 117.

[15] Al-Yaʿqūbī, *Tārīkh al-Yaʿqūbī*, Beirut, 1960, vol. 1, p. 6.

[16] See D. Thomas, 'Al-Ṭabarī', in *CMR* 2, 184-7.

[17] Al-Ṭabarī, *The history of al-Ṭabarī*, trans. F. Rosenthal, vol. 1, Albany NY, 1989, pp. 282-90.

[18] F. Rosenthal, 'The influence of the biblical tradition on Muslim historiography', in B. Lewis and M. Holt (eds), *Historical writings of the peoples of Asia*, vol. 4. *Historians of the Middle East*, London, 1962, 35-45, p. 42.

> those who found him would not kill him, and Cain left from before God (and settled) east of the Garden of Eden.[19]

Although he benefits from the Bible in his history, al-Ṭabarī does not ignore the issue of *taḥrīf*. He addresses it in his Qur'an commentary entitled *Jāmiʿ al-bayān ʿan taʾwīl āy al-Qurʾān* ('Collection of statements on interpretation of the verses of Qur'an'), which contains compilations of interpretations from earlier exegetes. He says that the history of corruption of the Torah dates back to the time of Moses, though it did not stop there, because the Jewish community of Medina at the time of the Prophet Muḥammad was also guilty of it.[20] This argument revolves around the rejection of Muḥammad's divine mission by the Jews of Medina. In opposing him and misrepresenting the descriptions of him in their scripture, they were doing the same as their ancestors had done when they distorted the divine message that was revealed to Moses. But, as Camilla Adang points out, the corruption that al-Ṭabarī refers to here was not textual alteration but misinterpretation.[21] In fact, for obvious reasons, all the authors who argued that the coming of the Prophet was foretold in the Bible understood *taḥrīf* as Jewish and Christian misreading or misrepresentation of the divine message, rather than wholesale corruption of the text itself.

This same approach of accepting the integrity of the text of the Bible can be seen in *Kitāb al-ʿibar* ('The book of examples') by the renowned 15th-century historian and historiographer ʿAbd al-Raḥmān ibn Muḥammad ibn Khaldūn (d. 1406).[22] The work is divided into three main parts, the first of which contains the famous *Muqaddima*. The second part deals with pre-Islamic history, focusing on various peoples, before moving on to the history of early Christians, Persians and Romans, and lastly recounting the history of Islamic civilisation from its origins to the author's own time. The third part deals with the history of North Africa and Ibn Khaldūn's autobiography.

Ibn Khaldūn relies extensively on the Bible for the section on the history of the Israelites, which is structured into six main sections that focus on various phases of the Israelites' history. The first section recounts the story of Moses and is mostly constructed according to the Book of Exodus.

---

19 Al-Ṭabarī, *History*, p. 312. According to Rosenthal, this is based on one of the early translations of the Aramaic/Syriac Bible rather than on the Hebrew; see Al-Ṭabarī, *History*, p. 312, n. 877.

20 Adang, *Muslim writers*, p. 228.

21 Adang, *Muslim writers*, pp. 227-31.

22 See M. Whittingham, 'Ibn Khaldūn', in *CMR* 5, 300-8.

At the beginning, Ibn Khaldūn emphasises the Abrahamic origins of this people, reminding the reader that they come from the prophet Jacob, the son of Isaac, who is named 'Israel' in the Bible.[23] The second and the third sections focus on events from the time of Joshua to the death of Solomon, including the conquest of Canaan and the building of the First Temple. The remaining three sections cover the period from Rehoboam to the coming of Jesus and include the division of the Kingdom of Israel from Judah, and the Second Temple period.[24] It is striking to see that Ibn Khaldūn often quotes from two Christian historians, namely Ibn al-ʿAmīd (d. after 1280) and Paulus Orosius (5th century). Further, throughout the text, he often refers to the historian Abū Jaʿfar al-Ṭabarī for details of events. His approach clearly shows that, like his earlier counterparts, he looked on the Bible as a reliable historical source.

The 10th century witnessed one of the most vibrant periods in the history of Islamic literature, and various approaches to the Bible can be seen in the writings of the Muslim intellectuals of the period. The well-known esoteric fraternity called the Ikhwān al-Ṣafāʾ had a good command of the Gospels and used them in their *Rasāʾil Ikhwān al-Ṣafāʾ wa-khillān al-wafāʾ* ('The epistles of the Brethren of Purity and friends of loyalty'), which were composed around the middle of the 10th century.[25] The authors, who followed the Ismāʿīlī tradition, not only employed the Gospels but also advised their brethren to read them. This suggests they had easy access to Arabic versions of Christian scripture, while the variations in the translations of some Gospel verses in different parts of their composite work implies that they had a number of different Arabic translations of the New Testament at their disposal.[26]

Borrowings from Christian scripture can be seen in many parts of the *Rasāʾil*. For example, the life of Jesus is constructed according to the Gospel records. There are references to the boy Jesus in the Jerusalem temple telling his parents that this is where he is meant to be. The Ikhwān liken this to the beginnings of the prophet Moses's career, and to the Prophet Muḥammad's divine mission, as they both initially informed their close relatives and friends about their experiences.[27] The stories of Jesus' final

---

[23] Ibn Khaldūn, *Tārīkh, Kitāb al-ʿibar wa-dīwān al-mubtadaʾ wa-l-khabar*, vol. 2, Beirut, 1992, p. 92.

[24] Ibn Khaldūn, *Tārīkh, Kitāb al-ʿibar*, vol. 2, pp. 92-139.

[25] See O. Ali-de-Unzaga, 'Ikhwān al-Ṣafāʾ", in *CMR* 2, 306-11.

[26] I. Netton, *Muslim Neoplatonists. An introduction to the thought of the Brethren of Purity*, Edinburgh, 1991, p. 54.

[27] Netton, *Muslim Neoplatonists*, p. 55.

days and crucifixion, including the Last Supper and his appearances after the resurrection, generally parallel the Gospel narratives, as the following passage demonstrates:

> So His humanity (*nāsūtuhu*) was crucified and His hands were nailed to the two planks of wood of the cross. He remained crucified from the forenoon to the afternoon. He asked for water and was given vinegar to drink, and He was pierced by the lance. Then He was buried in the vicinity of the cross and forty men were set to guard the tomb. All this took place in the presence of His friends and disciples and when they saw what had happened, they were convinced and knew that He had not ordered them to do anything which He Himself had not done. Then they gathered after three days in the place in which He had promised them that He would appear to them and they saw that sign which was between Him and them. The news spread among the Jews that Christ had not been killed so the tomb was opened and His human body (*al-nāsūt*) was not found [there].[28]

Distinguishing Jesus' divine (*lāhūt*) and human (*nāsūt*) natures, the Ikhwān state that it was his human nature that was killed on the cross. Although they seem here to prefer the Christian version of the narrative, which clearly contradicts the qur'anic account, Ian Netton points out that, elsewhere in the *Rasā'il*, the Christian beliefs in the Incarnation and the crucifixion are openly criticised. These conflicting views can be ascribed to the composite nature of a work with multiple authors, but one thing is clear: the Ikhwān were very well acquainted with most parts of the New Testament, as well as with elements of Christian doctrine, and had no problem in drawing from them.[29]

Another Ismāʿīlī author from the 10th century who freely employed Bible verses in his writings is Abū Yaʿqūb al-Sijistānī (d. after 971). This Persian author composed his *Kitāb al-yanābīʿ* ('The book of wellsprings') in 40 short chapters, each of which deals with an issue arising from Neoplatonic theosophy.[30] Although he uses Bible verses to support his ideas, he is careful to provide his own interpretation of them in order to make them fit into the Islamic context. This approach can be seen clearly in the following quotation echoing the Gospel of Matthew:

> Verily the Lord will gather the pious and the wicked in one place. Then he will say to the pious, 'How good is what you did and brought about in regard to me. I was hungry and so you brought me food. I was thirsty and

---

28 Translation in Netton, *Muslim Neoplatonists*, pp. 59-60.
29 Netton, *Muslim Neoplatonists*, p. 61.
30 See D. Thomas, 'Abū Yaʿqūb al-Sijistānī', in *CMR* 2, 381-5.

> you provided me drink. I was naked and you clothed me. I was in prison and you freed me.' They shall respond to Him, saying, 'Our Lord! When were You hungry and thirsty and naked and imprisoned so that we fed You, provided You drink, clothed You, and freed You?' Then God will say to them, 'You are right [to ask], but all that you have done for yourselves, that you have done for me.' Thereupon God will say to the wicked, 'How evil is what you have done in regard to me. I was hungry but you did not feed me [...] (to the end of this).' They shall say to Him, 'Our Lord, when were You like this?' He will reply, 'Yes, you are right but all of that which you did not do for yourselves, it was as if you did not do that for me.'[31]

This quotation does not agree fully with the standard version of the biblical verse, because there it is Jesus who speaks, whereas here it is God.[32] Thus, although he uses the biblical passage to support his point, al-Sijistānī converts it into a form compatible with Islamic teachings.

While such Muslim authors as these regarded the Bible as a reliable source and alluded to Christian misinterpretations of the text, the 11th-century Cordoban scholar Abū Muḥammad ʿAlī Ibn Ḥazm (d. 1064)[33] argued that the Bible had undergone complete and deliberate textual corruption.[34] To establish his point, he provides examples of contradictory accounts of the same incident, and immoral behaviour ascribed to the earlier prophets. One of the very first issues he refers to is found in Genesis 1:27. He states that there appears on the first page of the Torah a statement attributed to God, namely, 'I created humankind in my own likeness and resemblance.' In Ibn Ḥazm's view, the problem with this statement is the word 'resemblance' (*shubh*), because it clearly leaves no room for further interpretation and equates the Creator with humankind.[35] Unworthy or immoral behaviour attributed to some of the Israelite prophets is another topic that Ibn Ḥazm addresses in detail. He is particularly critical about their marriages with the close relatives:

---

[31] P. Walker (ed.), *The wellsprings of wisdom. A study of Abū Yaʿqūb al-Sijistānī's* Kitāb al-yanābīʿ, Salt Lake City UT, 1994, p. 105.

[32] Walker, *Wellsprings of wisdom*, p. 185.

[33] See J.P. Monferrer Sala and D. Thomas, 'Ibn Ḥazm', in *CMR* 3, 137-45.

[34] This appears in his *Kitāb iẓhār tabdīl al-Yahūd wa-l-Naṣārā li-l-Tawrāt wa-l-Injīl wa-bayān tanāquḍ mā bi-aydīhim min dhālika min mā lā yaḥtamil al-taʾwīl* ('An exposure of the Jews and Christians' alteration to the Torah and Gospel, and a demonstration of the contradiction in what they possess of this that will not permit metaphorical interpretation'), which is included in his *Kitāb al-faṣl fī l-milal wa-l-aḥwāʾ wa-l-nihal* ('The book of judgement on the religions and sects'), Cairo, 1899.

[35] Ibn Ḥazm, *Kitāb al-faṣl*, vol. 1, pp. 117-18.

> By God, I have not seen a nation ascribe to their prophets [such conducts] as those infidels do. Once they claimed that Abraham, peace be upon him, married his sister who gave birth to Isaac, peace be upon him.[36] Later, they say Jacob married a woman, but he was brought another woman who was not his wife who gave birth to children from whom Moses, Aaron, David, Solomon and other prophets are descended.[37] They also claim that Reuben, the son of Jacob, fornicated with his step-mother, who was at the time married to his father, the prophet, and mother of his two brothers.[38]

He addresses in chronological order the lives of the prophets narrated in the Torah, continuing with examples from the lives of Judah, Joshua son of Nun, Amram the son of Levi's son Kohath, and David. Although it is claimed that he took some of his examples from the work of the Jewish sceptic Ḥīwī al-Balkhī, it is clear from the text that Ibn Ḥazm had a good command of the Torah, as his quotations closely follow the biblical text.[39] Despite this, he challenges the authenticity of the Torah, addressing problems concerning the transmission of the text. He argues that the original Torah went through certain changes and the name of God was removed from the text, and that it was finally burned by Jehoiakim.[40] Following the collapse of the kingdoms of Israel and Judah, the Temple in which the Torah had always been kept was destroyed, and when they were taken into exile for 70 years the Israelites did not have any written record of the Torah or a prophet among them.[41] Following their return to Jerusalem the Jews had to produce a new scripture. This was made by Ezra,[42] who introduced changes while he was dictating or writing the text from memory. The result is that none of the Jewish scriptures is original, and therefore they cannot be considered as reliable sources of truth.[43]

---

36 Genesis 12:13, 19; 20:2, 12.

37 Genesis 29:23.

38 Genesis 35:22; Ibn Ḥazm, *Kitāb al-faṣl*, p. 147.

39 Adang, *Muslim writers*, pp. 240-1.

40 Ibn Ḥazm, *Kitāb al-faṣl*, p. 193. Adang suggests that he sometimes goes beyond the biblical material and uses the Talmud, as here. As he sees it, the one who corrupted the Bible and removed the name of God was Jehoahaz, though in the Talmud these are the kings Manasseh and Ahaziah; see Adang, *Muslim writers*, p. 244.

41 Ibn Ḥazm, *Kitāb al-faṣl*, pp. 196-7.

42 Although Ibn Ḥazm mentions various names regarding the author of the new Torah, in most cases he identifies Ezra, and he is not depicted very favourably. See further: Adang, *Muslim writers*, pp. 245-6.

43 Ibn Ḥazm, *Kitāb al-faṣl*, p. 202. For a detailed analysis of the issue of *taḥrīf* in Ibn Ḥazm's writings, see Adang, *Muslim writers*, pp. 237-48.

Ibn Ḥazm regards the Bible as internally contradictory and historically unreliable. Compared with earlier understandings of *taḥrīf*, Ibn Ḥazm's is the most explicit and direct criticism of the authenticity of the scripture, because he suggests deliberate and complete textual corruption. Thomas Michel refers to the division in attitudes among Muslim authors on the issue of *taḥrīf* into the two main categories of *taḥrīf al-lafẓ* (corruption of the word), which refers to the alteration of the actual revealed text, and *taḥrīf al- maʿnā* (corruption of the meaning), the misinterpretation of the largely intact text. As has been mentioned, the latter approach can be observed in the writings of the earlier authors ʿAlī al-Ṭabarī, Ibn Qutayba and Abū Jaʿfar al-Ṭabarī. Ibn Ḥazm's approach stands as an example of the first category, as he states that the Bible was re-written centuries after its revelation and has no credibility. Although his position is not followed by many subsequent authors, it marks the 11th-century turning point in Islamic literature on the issue of *taḥrīf*.[44]

Novel Muslim approaches to the Bible

A completely different approach to the Bible appears in the writings of Ibn Ḥazm's compatriot, the Andalusian mystic Ibn al-Barrajān (d. 1141), who was known as 'the al-Ghazālī of Andalus'. According to his biographer Ibn al-Zubayr (d. 1308), he was proficient in the fields of theology, Arabic language and literature. He was also known for his Sufi tendencies, which later led him to be seen as a political threat by the Almoravid emir at the time, who had him imprisoned. He died in prison two months after his trial.[45]

Three of Ibn al-Barrajān's works contain quotations from the Bible, namely *Sharḥ al-asmāʾ al-ḥusnā* ('Commentary on the beautiful names of God'), and two Qur'an commentaries, *Tanbīh al-afhām ilā tadabbur al-kitāb al-ḥakīm wa-taʿarruf al-āyāt wa-l-nabaʾ al-ʿaẓīm* ('Alerting intellects to contemplation on the wise book and recognition of signs and the tremendous news') and *Iḍāḥ al-ḥikma bi-aḥkām al-ʿibra* ('Explaining wisdom according to the principles of examples'). The latter was planned as a supplement to the *Tanbīh* and contains a transcription of

---

[44] T.F. Michel, *A Muslim theologian's response to Christianity. Ibn Taymiyya's* Al-jawāb al-ṣaḥīḥ, Delmar NY, 1984, pp. 89–90.

[45] See J.P. Monferrer Sala, 'Ibn Barrajān', in *CMR* 3, 488-9. For detailed information about his biography, see Y. Casewit, *The mystics of al-Andalus. Ibn Barrajan and Islamic thought in the twelfth century*, Cambridge, 2017, pp. 91-125.

Ibn Barrajān's lectures given during the final years of his life.[46] He states that the Torah has a special status among other revealed scriptures as it contains the epitome of God's knowledge.[47] Thus, when he interprets Q 11:7, which explains the creation,[48] he liberally employs passages from Genesis. He also quotes verses about the creation of Adam and Eve, the depiction of Paradise, the tree of life, the tree of knowledge of good and evil, and the stories of Abraham and the people of Lot.[49] From the New Testament, he quotes verses from the Gospel of Matthew.[50]

Ibn Barrajān's position is almost the opposite of Ibn Ḥazm's. These two examples, originating from the same region and around the same time, show how vibrant and diverse were the attitudes of Muslim authors towards the Bible.[51]

Jalāl al-Dīn Rūmī on *taḥrīf*

The 13th-century mystic Mawlānā Jalāl al-Dīn Rūmī (d. 1273) addressed the issue of *taḥrīf* in his own particular manner.[52] The well-known Sufi poet was born in Balkh in present-day Afghanistan and spent most of his life in Anatolia, which led to his being known as Rūmī (Anatolian). In his *Mathnawī* he tells the story of a certain Jewish vizier who intended to mislead the Christian community and create confusion among them. The vizier asks the king to punish him publicly by cutting off his ears, hands and nose, and then driving him out of his presence so that he could reach the Christian community. This happens, and when he meets Christians he claims that he is secretly a Christian and that the king wants to take his life. Thus, he gains their trust[53] and it does not take long for the vizier to become a most revered leading member of the Christian community

46 See Y. Casewit, 'A Muslim scholar of the Bible. Prooftexts from Genesis and Matthew in the Qur'an commentary of Ibn Barrajān of Seville (d. 536/1141)', *Journal of Qur'anic Studies* 18 (2016) 1-48.

47 Casewit, 'Muslim scholar', pp. 6-7.

48 And it is He who created the heavens and the earth in six days – and His Throne had been upon water – that He might test you as to which of you is best indeed. But if you say, 'Indeed, you are resurrected after death', those who disbelieve will surely say, 'This is not but obvious magic'.

49 He quotes Genesis 2:8-14, 16-19; 3:1-7, 24.

50 Casewit, 'Muslim scholar', pp. 28-33.

51 For a comparison of Ibn al-Barrajān and Ibn Ḥazm's approaches, see Casewit, *Mystics of al-Andalus*, pp. 262-5.

52 See L. Lewisohn, 'Mawlānā Jalāl al-Dīn Rūmī', in *CMR* 4, 491-508.

53 Mawlānā Jalāl al-Dīn Rūmī, *The Mathnawī of Jalālu'ddīn Rūmī*, ed. and trans. R.A. Nicholson, London, 1926, vol. 2, pp. 21-2.

whose commands will be followed without question, even by the twelve emirs who were then guiding the Christians.[54]

The vizier then prepares a scroll in the name of each emir. These contain numerous contradictions. For example, one of them teaches that strict asceticism is the ideal way of piety while another rejects the laws of observance and abstinence as the necessary components of piety.[55] After creating different scrolls for each emir, the vizier tells the Christians that Jesus has commanded him to retreat into seclusion. Before he leaves, he secretly appoints each of the emirs as his successor. Thus, when he finally kills himself in seclusion, he leaves the Christian community with numerous different scrolls and emirs who all claim to be appointed as the next leader of the Christian community.[56] This, for Rūmī, reflects the chaotic state of Christian scripture and church order.

Rūmī also refers to the Muslim argument that the coming of the Prophet Muḥammad was foretold in the Gospels:

> The name of Mustafa was in the Gospel – (Mustafa) the chief of the prophets, the sea of purity.
>
> There was mention of his (external) characteristics and appearance; there was mention of his warring, fasting and eating.
>
> A party among the Christians, for the sake of the divine reward, whenever (in reading the Gospel) they came to that name and discourse,
>
> Would bestow kisses on that noble name and stoop their faces towards that beauteous description.
>
> In this tribulation of which we have told, that party were secure from tribulation and dread,
>
> Secure from the mischief of the amirs and the vizier, seeking refuge in the protection of the name Aḥmad [Muḥammad].
>
> Their offspring also multiplied: the Light of Ahmad aided and befriended them.
>
> And the other party among the Christians (who) were holding the Name of Aḥmad in contempt,
>
> They became contemptible and despised through dissensions caused by the evil-counselling and evil-plotting vizier;
>
> Moreover, their religion and their law became corrupted in consequence of the scrolls which set forth all perversely.[57]

---

54 Rūmī, *The Mathnawī*, p. 27.
55 Rūmī, *The Mathnawī*, p. 29.
56 Rūmī, *The Mathnawī*, pp. 32-41.
57 Rūmī, *The Mathnawī*, pp. 41-2.

As can be seen, Rūmī does not seek historical or textual proofs to support his arguments. The credibility of the stories is never his main concern. Rather, he addresses issues surrounding the Bible in his own style and makes it clear that both the faith and the scripture of Christians are corrupted.

A Muslim commentary on the Gospels: Sulaymān al-Ṭūfī

The Hanbalī jurist, poet and theologian Najm al-Dīn Sulaymān al-Ṭūfī (d. 1316) was extremely unusual among Muslims in that he composed a commentary on the Gospels.[58] Born in the village of Ṭūfā near Baghdad, he travelled to Baghdad, Damascus and Cairo, and joined the circles of the renowned theologian Ibn Taymiyya (d. 1328) and the Hanbalī chief judge Sa'd al-Dīn Mas'ūd al-Ḥārithī l-Baghdādī (d. 1312). But he was accused of writing poems ridiculing the Companions of the Prophet Muḥammad and was exiled to Damascus, though he could not enter the city because he had written sarcastic poems about its residents. He spent some time in Damietta and in Qūs in Egypt, and died in Hebron in 1316 while on pilgrimage.[59]

Al-Ṭūfī was a very prolific, multifaceted author who penned more than 50 works in the fields of Islamic jurisprudence, interpretation of the Qur'an, dogmatic theology, poetry and interreligious polemics.[60] He dressed and lived modestly and, although he does not seem to have been a member of any Sufi order, a number of Sufi ideas, along with Sufi terminology, can be detected in his writings. He also thought that the study of rational theology (*kalām*) was obligatory for the whole community (*farḍ al-kifāya*), because rational thinking should be employed to establish Islamic doctrinal principles derived from the Qur'an and tradition. This is an unusual profile for a Hanbalī author, as the followers of this school are known not to favour speculative theology or esoteric Sufism.[61]

Sometime around 1308, al-Ṭūfī wrote a commentary on the Bible to show the shortcomings of Christianity, *Al-taʿlīq ʿalā l-anājīl al-arbaʿa wa-l-taʿlīq ʿalā l-Tawrāh wa-ʿalā ghayrihā min kutub al-anbiyā'* ('Critical commentary on the four Gospels, the Torah and other books of the

58 See L. Demiri, 'Al-Ṭūfī', in *CMR* 4, 724-31.

59 For a fuller biography of al-Ṭūfī, see L. Demiri, *Muslim exegesis of the Bible in medieval Cairo. Najm al-Dīn al-Ṭūfī's (d. 716/1316) commentary on the Christian scriptures*, Leiden, 2013, pp. 3-7.

60 Demiri, *Muslim exegesis*, p. 4.

61 Demiri, *Muslim exegesis*, p. 20.

prophets').[62] It starts with a prologue in which he outlines the origins and doctrines of Christianity and states that the Gospels currently held by Christians are not the same as the message originally revealed to the prophet Jesus. They contain only a small portion of Jesus' teachings, and they should be considered biographies (*siyar*) of Jesus compiled by his disciples.[63]

The commentary starts with a critique of the four Gospels, and this is followed by a short defence of the prophethood of Muḥammad. In this, al-Ṭūfī rejects the claims of some Christians and Jews that the Prophet came with a sword and was a 'destructive king' rather than a prophet. He argues that the sovereignty of all destructive kings disappeared after their death, but the legacy of the Prophet Muḥammad has continued for more than seven centuries, proof that he was truly a prophet.[64] After this, he deals with the Old Testament books of Isaiah, Hosea, Jonah, Habakkuk, Malachi, Jeremiah, Ezekiel, Daniel and Genesis.

A striking feature of the work is that al-Ṭūfī uses the Qur'an as the 'proof-text' for the Bible, because the Gospels are not the same as what was revealed to Jesus.[65] Further, he has no hesitation in giving metaphorical interpretations of verses when they contradict Islamic teachings. This can be clearly observed in his interpretation of Matthew 4:6-11, where the devil challenges Jesus' divine sonship.

> Among other things, (there is the following account) in the remainder of this chapter: When Satan said to Christ: 'If you are the Son of God, then throw yourself down from this temple', he replied to him: 'It is written, you shall not make trial of the Lord your God'. Again Satan spoke to him: 'If you fall down prostrating yourself to me, I shall give you the kingdoms of the world'. Then Jesus said to him: 'Get behind me, Devil! It is written, To the Lord your God you shall prostrate yourself, and Him only shall you worship'. At that moment Satan left him. This is a declaration by Christ that God is his god, and that Christ worships God and is a servant of his Lord. By this and similar passages it becomes obvious to any intelligent person that what is meant by the expressions of 'sonship', wherever applied, is the very 'servanthood' that has been determined in the present situation, because of the following fact: had Christ been God, it would have been inconceivable of him to be his own god and to worship himself, and had he been His Son, he would have said instead, 'You shall not make trial

62 Demiri, *Muslim exegesis*, pp. 50-1.
63 Demiri, *Muslim exegesis*, pp. 100-1.
64 Demiri, *Muslim exegesis*, pp. 354-7.
65 Demiri, *Muslim exegesis*, p. 55.

> of your Father, and to the Lord, your Father, you shall prostrate yourself.' Thus, what he declared by using expressions indicating 'divinity' proves what we have mentioned.[66]

Al-Ṭūfī's Bible commentary is an example of the lively exchanges that took place between Christians and Muslims following a turbulent period during which the Middle East and North Africa were threatened by the crusades and Mongol invasions. The *Taʿlīq* also witnesses to al-Ṭūfī's close engagement with earlier Muslim polemical works.[67]

Qur'anic scholarly use of the Bible: al-Biqāʿī

The Qur'an commentary of the 15th-century scholar Abū l-Ḥasan Ibrāhīm ibn 'Umar al-Biqāʿī (d. 1480) is one of the very rare examples of biblical quotations being extensively employed to support Islamic teachings. Born in Lebanon, al-Biqāʿī travelled to Damascus, Jerusalem, Alexandria and finally Cairo, where in 1431 he joined the circle of Ibn Ḥajar al-ʿAsqalānī (d. 1449) to learn the qur'anic sciences. He then worked for most of his life as the Qur'an commentator in the Ẓāhir mosque.[68] His Qur'an commentary, *Naẓm al-durar fī tanāsub al-āyāt wa-l-suwar* ('The string of pearls, on the harmonious relationship of verses and chapters'), contains a substantial number of citations from the Hebrew Bible and the Gospels, which are used to explain the backgrounds of biblical narratives in the Qur'an.[69] The Gospel quotations appear as combined versions of the same narratives as they are found in the various Gospels, with Matthew as the narrative frame. Al-Biqāʿī himself is very much aware that he is doing this, and explains it at the beginning of his work.[70]

---

66 Demiri, *Muslim exegesis*, pp. 143-5.

67 See Demiri, *Muslim exegesis*, pp. 29-37.

68 See D. Thomas, 'Al-Biqāʿī', in *CMR* 5, 537-43, and more fully W.A. Saleh, *In defense of the Bible. A critical edition and an introduction to al-Biqāʿī's Bible treatise*, Leiden, 2008, pp. 7-20.

69 Walid Saleh observes that these Bible quotations are unique in Islamic tradition. See W. Saleh, 'Sublime in its style, exquisite in its tenderness. The Hebrew Bible quotations in al-Biqāʿī's Quran commentary', in Y. Tzvi Langermann and J. Stern (eds), *Adaptations and innovations. Studies on the interaction between Jewish and Islamic thought and literature from the Early Middle ages to late Twentieth century*, Paris, 2007, 335-80.

70 Saleh, *In defense of the Bible*, pp. 23-4. For a list of Gospel citations in *Naẓm*, see the appendix in W.A. Saleh and K.C. Waled, 'An Islamic Diatessaron. Al-Biqāʿī's harmony of the four Gospels', in S. Binay and S. Leder (eds), *Translating the Bible into Arabic. Historical, text-critical and literary aspects*, Beirut, 2012, 89-115.

His interpretation of Q 4:157-8, the denial that the Jews crucified Jesus, provides a good example of his use of Bible verses in his commentary. He explains that some of the Jews claimed that they had killed Jesus, some said 'He did not die', others believed that 'It [the figure on the cross] was looking like him'. Their uncertainty left them suspicious about the whole issue, though in reality they killed someone who resembled Jesus.[71] Al-Biqāʿī then details Jesus' last days, starting from his departure from the Temple after his debate with the Jews, reconstructing the sequence of the events according the Gospel accounts. His approach can be clearly seen in the following passage:

> Luke said: Certainly, I will give you mouth [speech] and wisdom that none of your opponents will be able to answer. The brother will betray his brother to death and the father his son; and children will rise up against their parents. Matthew said: Then, they will leave you to persecution and kill you, all the nations will hate you. At that time, many will doubt [about the faith] and betray and hate each other. A lot of false prophets will appear and deceive many of them. The love of the masses will grow cold; the ones who remain patient till the end will be saved. And, this Gospel of the kingdom will be preached everywhere as a testimony to all nations. Mark said: When you see the abomination that causes destruction which was mentioned by the prophet Daniel standing in the holy place, let the reader understand, then let those who remain in Judea escape to the Galilee. Let no one on the top [of the house] step down to the house to take something. Pity on the women who are pregnant or nursing on those days.[72]

As can be seen, al-Biqāʿī quotes the Gospel verses one after another with hardly any commentary, though when he comes to the crucifixion of Jesus he feels obliged to make a remark that this is how it was explained in the New Testament and not his own opinion, saying: 'After that, all of their Gospels agree that they crucified him between two thieves.'[73] This little remark makes a lot of sense when the Muslim version of the crucifixion story and the socio-political circumstances of the day are recalled. Seven years after al-Biqāʿī started writing his Qur'an exegesis, a dispute broke out over the acceptability of using biblical quotations to explain the Qur'an.[74] It led the author to compose a defence of his actions, entitled

[71] Al-Biqāʿī, *Naẓm al-durar f ī tan āsub al- āyāt wa al-suwar*, Hyderabad, 1978, vol. 5, p. 465.
[72] Al-Biqāʿī, *Naẓm*, pp. 469-70.
[73] Al-Biqāʿī, *Naẓm*, p. 493.
[74] See Saleh, *In defense of the Bible*, pp. 25-33.

Al-aqwāl al-qawīma fī ḥukm al-naql min al-kutub al-qadīma ('Just words on the permissibility of quoting from the ancient books'). Here, al-Biqāʿī explains why his Qur'an commentary is superior to any similar works in the field, and he supports his method of employing the Bible by referring to precedents from the Prophet Muḥammad himself, as well as to those of chief judges of his own time.

Ottoman narratives: the conversion of priests

Stories of Christian priests converting to Islam were very popular in Ottoman circles from the 15th century onwards. In the Ottoman world, priests and monks were representative of Christendom as the advisors of kings and emperors, and the fiercest adversaries of Islam, and as senior members of the Christian community, because they were the teachers of the religion. Thus, stories of their conversion were one of the main components of polemics between Muslims and Christians.[75] A 16th-century work entitled *Bir râhib ile bir pîr-i Müslim arasında İsa (a.s.) hakkında mükâleme* ('A dialogue between a monk and a Muslim elder about Jesus, peace be upon him') illustrates the main aspects of this type of literature.[76] It narrates a conversation between a Muslim elder called 'the shaykh' and a monk who has converted to Islam and is referred to as *râhib-i Müslim* ('Muslim monk'). The latter appears to have some reservations, so the shaykh, who is probably a Sufi, shows him the flaws in Christian beliefs and assures him that he has made the right choice.

The conversation starts with a discussion of the Paraclete (a common theme in Muslim defences of the Prophet). The shaykh refers to John 16:7, and says that the appearance of the *Faraklit* in this verse can only be an allusion to the Prophet Muḥammad.[77] The monk agrees and the shaykh goes on to explain inconsistencies in Christian beliefs in the divinity of Jesus and the Incarnation. He explains that a divine being cannot have the same characteristics as a human being:

> A divine being should be necessarily existent (*vājib al-vujūd*). Thus, he should not be physical, concrete or an accident (*ʿaraḍ*). [However] Jesus, peace be upon him, was a human being who was brought into existence.

75 T. Kristić, *Contested conversions to Islam. Narratives of religious change in the early modern Ottoman Empire*, Stanford CA, 2011, pp. 68-9.

76 See M. Kahveci, 'A dialogue between a monk and a Muslim elder about Jesus (peace be upon him)', in *CMR* 7, 740–2.

77 MS Konya, Koyunoğlu Museum Library – 10812, fol. 1r-v.

> After that, according to your claims, he disappeared when the Jews killed him. According to the Christian faith, the Jews killed Jesus. It is mentioned at the end of the Gospel of Matthew that the Messiah called to God before he was executed: 'O my Lord, O my Lord. You have abandoned me!' These are the last words of Jesus.[78]

Here the shaykh asks the Muslim monk to confirm that this is found at the end of the Gospel of Matthew. When the former Christian agrees, he continues:

> He is such a person who eats and drinks, was born of a woman, grew to be a child, adolescent and adult. He slept and woke up. According to the words of the Christians, he was pursued by the Jewish community. He escaped and hid. He whimpered and cried out, but they did not care. They took him to the cross, he remained alive there for a while. Then, they crucified him and slit open his flesh. How can a community who confesses all these issues still claim his divinity! If he really was God, why could he not save himself from the Jews? Why did he not confound the Jewish community who persecuted him? O Muslim monk, this claim is invalid. Jesus, peace be upon him, was just a prophet who had his own legacy (*sharīʿa*) and he was the harbinger of my ancestor [the Prophet Muḥammad]. The Jews did not crucify or kill him. If the claims of the Jews and Christians were true, the universe would have been left with no God. Also, how is it that, God forbid, a god cannot save himself from a community such as the Jews?[79]

There is another reference to the Gospels when the shaykh explains the flaws in Christian views on the divinity of Jesus. He says:

> Another proof of the errors in the words of the Christians is that Jesus, peace be upon him, was repeatedly referred to[80] as a pious man. In the third chapter of the Gospel of Luke, the fifteenth chapter of the Gospel of John, the twentieth chapter of the Gospel of the apostle Matthew, the eleventh chapter of the apostle Mark and all the other apostles' Gospels, it is explained that Jesus, peace be upon him, did not cease being obedient to God and worshipping Him. Not for a moment would he cease from prayer and entreaty.[81]

---

[78] MS Konya, fols 2v-3r.

[79] MS Konya, fols 3v-4r.

[80] Interestingly, *tevâtür*, the verb used here, is normally used with regard to Hadiths that have been multiply transmitted and must therefore be authentic.

[81] MS Konya, fol. 7r.

For the shaykh, this is another proof that Jesus cannot be God, because all the apostles agree that Jesus was a pious man. If he worships another being, he must certainly be a creature, not the Creator, for it is not possible to be God and a worshipper at the same time. To sum up, the shaykh never challenges the textual authenticity of the Gospels, but rather tries to prove his points by referring to them. This is probably because his interlocutor is a new convert from Christianity who has until recently accepted the validity of the Bible. Finally, the monk is convinced and he and the audience who have been listening join the shaykh's Sufi order.[82]

Conclusion

The version of the Bible that was in the possession of Christians was generally seen by Muslims as a corruption of the divine message that had been revealed to Jesus. While some Muslim authors held the view that it was textually intact, this was challenged by many who wrote against Christianity. In the earliest years, some Muslims such as ʿAlī al-Ṭabarī and Ibn Qutayba used it to support the Muslim belief that the Prophet Muḥammad's mission was foretold in the Bible. These authors understood *taḥrīf* as misinterpretation of the text rather than complete textual alteration.

The attitude of the 11th-century Andalusian Ibn Ḥazm, who challenged the integrity of the text itself and also the process of its transmission, resulted in one of the strictest interpretations of *taḥrīf* in Islamic tradition. He claimed that, as the scripture had been completely altered, it no longer had any validity. Although subsequent authors did not take such an extreme approach, the issue of the corruption of the Bible continued to be one of the major subjects in Muslim writings against Christianity.

Despite these widespread views about the authenticity of the Bible, it served as a source for some Muslim exegetes to interpret verses of the Qur'an. Ibn Barrajān from al-Andalus, and al-Biqāʿī from Egypt are two authors who actually employed biblical verses in their Qur'an commentaries to support and explain the meaning of qur'anic passages.

When the picture is taken as a whole, the majority of Muslims authors in the period 600-1600 regarded the Bible as unreliable because its text had been corrupted; this is how they interpreted the allusions in the Qur'an to *taḥrīf*. Others, however, granted it a measure of veracity, as

82 MS Konya, fol. 10.

long as it was interpreted correctly, and thus profited from its contents. It is important to note, however, that all Muslims who knew and used the Bible read it with the help of the Qur'an, and saw it as concurring or diverging from the teachings in their own scripture.

Chapter 10
Latin Christianity engaging with the Qur'an

Ulisse Cecini

Introduction

The history of Latin Christianity engaging with the Qur'an is the history of a process. The Qur'an entered gradually into the argumentation of Christian authors who dealt with Islam, moving from mere mentions to become more and more the centre of attention and an object of discussion. From the first appearance of Latin works on Islam in the 9th century down to the year 1600, varying degrees of knowledge of the Qur'an can be detected, generally increasing with time, and various presentation strategies, from utter demonisation of it to analytical presentation of its contents and translations. This trajectory can be seen in a wide range of works: anti-Islamic polemical tracts, texts supposedly aimed at promoting peace between Christianity and Islam, and texts whose target is not Islam but rather Christian opponents; in the 16th century, for example, both Catholics and Lutherans used the Qur'an in order to accuse the doctrines of their Christian opponents of being even more deviant than the Qur'an.

We shall see that, while the history of the use of the Qur'an is mainly one of recurring topics, there are sometimes moments of originality and breaking with the past. On the one hand, a general discourse is built-up century after century, fed by interweaving motifs and specific *loci classici* in the Qur'an. Later works transmit and develop arguments in earlier works, and along the way there are milestones in the form of works and authors that become continuing points of reference. On the other, there are also moments when there is a break with what has gone before, occurring when there is a change in direction that arises from a new body of work or line of interpretation, or initiated by an innovative perspective from a single author that creates an alternative strand of thinking. Some works proved influential and became sources of reference over periods of centuries, while others had no impact when they first appeared but sprang up later to provide a reference for a new perspective. This essay will try to illustrate these dynamics, tracing the path and its milestones, the turning points, and the various currents that flowed and intersected. In such a survey, a measure of simplification cannot be avoided, and not every author can be mentioned or treated in the detail he deserves.

The Qur'an on the margin: First appearances of the Qur'an in works from the Latin West (9th-11th centuries)

The first item of interest and object of argumentation for Latin Christian authors was not the Qur'an as such, but the Prophet Muḥammad. In both historiography and polemics, he is the centre of attention. The first Latin historiographical sources that dealt with Muḥammad, namely the *Chronicle of 741*[1] and the *Chronicle of 754*,[2] do not mention the Qur'an at all. Rather they point out the political relevance of the figure of Muḥammad as a 'prince' and military leader who united and guided the 'Saracens' in wresting 'the provinces of Syria, Arabia and Mesopotamia' from the Byzantine Empire.[3] Although the *Chronicle of 741* states that he was regarded as an 'apostle and prophet of God',[4] no connection is made between him and the Qur'an.

---

1 C. Aillet, '*The Chronicle of 741*', in *CMR* 1, 284-9.

2 K.B. Wolf, '*The Chronicle of 754*', in *CMR* 1, 302-4.

3 See the anonymously authored *Chronicle of 741*, para 13, in J. Gil (ed.), *Corpus scriptorum muzarabicorum*, vol. 1, Madrid, 1973, p. 9. The *Chronicle* refers to Muḥammad's ability to foresee the future, and this may have its source in the Qur'an. Indeed, for Muslims one of the proofs of the inimitability (Arabic, *iʿjāz*) of the Qur'an is the fact that it contains the foretelling of future events (see R.C. Martin, art. 'Inimitability', in *EQ*). Inimitability is in turn a proof of Muḥammad's prophethood. This 'hidden' reference to the Qur'an in the *Chronicle* shows that, even if it not mentioned or discussed in the text, the Qur'an was certainly known through oral or written sources, and material was drawn from it. Generally speaking, a statement made by Christians about Islam or the Qur'an most likely came from an Islamic source, even if it was misunderstood or decontextualised, misrepresented or exaggerated by Christians for polemical purposes.

4 *Chronicle of 741*, para 17 (Gil, *Corpus scriptorum*, vol. 1, p. 9): *Quem hactenus tanto honore et reverentia colunt, ut Dei apostolum et prophetam eum in omnibus sacramentis suis esse scriptisque adfirment.* The terms *apostolus* and *propheta* show a hint of qur'anic knowledge, most probably being renditions of the Arabic *rasūl* ('apostle', or better 'messenger') and *nabī* ('prophet'), designations of Muḥammad in the Qur'an (e.g. Q 3:144, 'And Muḥammad is not but a messenger, as the messengers who have existed before him'; Q 33:1, 'O Prophet, fear God and do not follow the infidels and the hypocrites'). The designation *rasūl* also appears in the Islamic profession of Faith, which is probably meant or included in what in this text is called *sacramenta*.

Istoria de Mahomet

The first explicit reference to the Qur'an comes in the first known biography of Muḥammad in the Latin West, the so-called *Istoria de Mahomet*[5] included by Eulogius of Cordova (d. 859) in his *Liber apologeticus martyrum*.[6] The *Istoria* conforms to the Latin West's first strategy for disputing with Islam, which discredits Muḥammad as a *bona fide* prophet and depicts him as a liar, deceiver and pseudo-prophet, immoral in conduct and character, and a precursor of the Antichrist, if not indeed the Antichrist himself. The Qur'an appears quite marginally, and only to support criticisms of Muḥammad. He is described as a *tenebrae filius* ('son of darkness') and his prophetic mission is inspired by an *erroris spiritus* (spirit of error, deception) that appears to him in the form of a golden-mouthed vulture claiming to be the archangel Gabriel ordering Muḥammad to be a prophet for his people.[7] The Qur'an is presented as a work composed by Muḥammad himself:[8] the 'pseudo-prophet' who 'composed psalms' dedicated to dull animals (*insensibilia animalia*), such as the spider, the hoopoe, the frog and the red calf, or heifer. The last is found in the Hebrew scriptures,[9] and all of these appear in passages of the Qur'an:[10] Q 29:41-3 for the spider,[11] Q 27:20-2 for the hoopoe,[12] Q 2:67-74 for the

---

5 J. Tolan, '*Istoria de Mahomet*', in *CMR* 1, 721-2.

6 Eulogius of Cordova, *Liber apologeticus martyrum*, para 16, in Gil, *Corpus scriptorum*, vol. 2, pp. 483-6; see also J. Tolan, 'Eulogius of Cordova', in *CMR* 1, 679-83, p. 683.

7 Gil, *Corpus scriptorum*, vol. 2, p. 484, lines 15-17.

8 Gil, *Corpus scriptorum*, vol. 2, pp. 484-5, lines 29-34.

9 See, e.g. Numbers 19.

10 These have been identified by, among others, D. Millet-Gérard, *Chrétiens mozarabes et culture islamique dans l'Espagne des VIIIe-IX^{e}siècles*, Paris, 1984, pp. 105-8, and F. González Muñoz, 'El conocimiento del Corán entre los mozárabes del siglo IX', in M. Domínguez García et al. (eds), *Sub luce florentis calami. Homenaje a Manuel C. Díaz y Diaz*, Santiago de Compostela, 2002, 390-409, p. 395.

11 Q 29:41-3: 'The likeness of those who have taken to them protectors, apart from God, is as the likeness of the spider that takes to itself a house; and surely the frailest of houses is the house of the spider, did they but know. God knows whatever thing they call upon apart from Him; He is the All-mighty, the Allwise. And those similitudes – We strike them for the people, but none understands them save those who know' (trans. A.J. Arberry, *The Koran interpreted. A translation*, London, 1955, vol. 2, p. 101).

12 Q 27:20-2: 'And he reviewed the birds; then he said, "How is it with me, that I do not see the hoopoe? Or is he among the absent? Assuredly I will chastise him with a terrible chastisement, or I will slaughter him, or he bring me a clear authority." But he tarried not long, and said, "I have comprehended that which thou hast not comprehended, and I have come from Sheba to thee with a sure tiding"' (Arberry, *Koran*, vol. 2, p. 78).

heifer,[13] and Q 7:133 for the frogs.[14] What the author of the *Istoria* intends by mentioning these animals found in the Qur'an is not simply to say that the holy book of the Muslims talks about things that may be considered vile. He rather links them to traditional Latin knowledge about them in order to associate their typical bad qualities with Muḥammad, thus using the Latin Western tradition known to his audience to apply a negative interpretation of the Qur'an and Muḥammad. Frogs, according to the etymology of their name offered by Isidore of Seville,[15] are supposed to utter loud, nonsensical chattering; such is the sound coming from the prophet's mouth imagined to be. In the same way, the hoopoe, associated in the classical Western tradition with a bad smell (*foetor*),[16] refers to his supposed foul breath. With reference to the description of a spider catching flies, found in St Jerome's commentary on Isaiah 59:4-5,[17] Jerome speaks of the enemies of God's law who meditate all night against it and whisper old wives' tales, which are like a spider's web, catching flies, mosquitos and other little bugs.[18] In the intention of the author of the *Istoria*, Muḥammad's teachings and the words contained in the Qur'an capture simple minds so that they follow Muḥammad, rather like a spider's web catching flies. The actual metaphor used in the qur'anic verse (those who build their faith in others than God build on something as frail as a spider's web),[19] is completely discarded in favour of a more negative interpretation, drawing on a Western tradition not connected at all with the qur'anic context. Thus, the reader of the *Istoria* is led into a misinterpretation of the Qur'an based on association with earlier Western conceptions.

Another perspective on the contents of the Qur'an is that, in order to make his text more appealing (*ad condimentum sui erroris*), Muḥammad

---

13 Q 2:67-9: 'And when Moses said to his people, "God commands you to sacrifice a cow." […] They said, "Pray to thy Lord for us, that He make clear to us what her colour may be." He said, "He says she shall be a golden cow, bright her colour, gladdening the beholders"' (Arberry, *Koran*, vol. 1, pp. 36-7).

14 Q 7:133: 'So We let loose upon them the flood and the locusts, the lice and the frogs, the blood, distinct signs; but they waxed proud and were a sinful people' (Arberry, *Koran*, vol. 1, p. 186).

15 W.M. Lindsay (ed.), *Isidori Hispalensis Etymologiarum sive originum libri*, Oxford, 1966, book 12, chap. 6, para. 58.

16 Lindsay, *Isidori Hispalensis Etymologiarum*, book 12, chap. 7, para. 66.

17 See González Muñoz, 'El conocimiento del Corán', p. 395.

18 Jerome, *Hieronymi Commentariorum in Esaiam libri XII-XVIII*, ed. M. Adriaen, Turnhout, 1963, p. 680.

19 For this image, compare with Job 8:13-15; see, González Muñoz, 'El conocimiento del Corán', p. 395.

inserted other 'psalms' about biblical figures.[20] Besides the reference to Moses and the red heifer, the author mentions Joseph (Q 12), Zachariah (Q 3:37-41; 19:2-11) and the Virgin Mary (Q 3:33-7, 42-8; 19:16-40). The presence of biblical figures in the Qur'an is therefore nothing but a trick to give the text the appearance of a holy book, using the 'condiment' (*condimentum*) of another known and acknowledged holy book, i.e. biblical patriarchs, prophets and saints. Earlier in the *Istoria*, the author has already mentioned that Muḥammad used to attend Christian events and to learn by heart what was said in order to be considered the wisest among his own people who were not cultivated in such matters.[21] Once again, we have the concept of the Qur'an as a cunningly composed text, even inspired by a demon, that contains Jewish-Christian elements in order to make it more seductive. The motif of Jewish and Christian influences in Islam and in the Qur'an is one that recurs in Christian polemics with various ramifications, as we shall see below. It is a motif already present in Greek, Arabic and Syriac anti-Islamic polemics.

Influences on the West from the East

Many motifs appearing in the West come from the Eastern polemical tradition. A very good example is that of John of Damascus (c. 675-c. 749),[22] a Melkite monk of the monastery of Mār Saba and former member of the financial administration of the Umayyad Caliphs ʿAbd al-Malik (r. 685-705) and maybe al-Walīd I (r. 705-15). In the *Peri haireseōn* ('On heresies'), the second part of his *Pēgē gnōseōs* ('Fount of knowledge'), John lists and describes all the heresies known to him. Chapter 100 is on 'the heresy of the Ismaelites', namely Islam, acknowledging the tradition that regards the Arabs as having their origin in Ismael, son of Abraham. After describing the former paganism of the Arabs, John introduces the figure of their 'pseudo-prophet' who on his travels came across both the Hebrew and Christian scriptures (i.e. Old and New Testaments), and was acquainted with an Arian monk. As a result, he went on to create his own heresy and write his own book, which he claimed had come down from heaven.[23] Another motif, which is present both in John of Damascus and

---

20 Gil, *Corpus scriptorum*, vol. 2, p. 485, lines 34-6.

21 Gil, *Corpus scriptorum*, vol. 2, p. 484, lines 11-13.

22 R.F. Glei, 'John of Damascus', in *CMR*, 1, 295-301.

23 Iohannes Damaskenos, *De haeresibus*, ch. 100, lines 12-14, ed. R. Glei, in R. Glei and A.T. Khoury (eds), *Johannes Damaskenos und Theodor Abū Qurra. Schriften zum Islam*. Würzburg, 1995, p. 74.

in the *Istoria de Mahomet*, is the episode of Zayd, in which Muḥammad marries Zaynab, the former wife of his adoptive son Zayd, with the permission of God. Q 33:37, states:

> When thou saidst to him whom God had blessed and thou hadst favoured, 'Keep thy wife to thyself, and fear God', and thou wast concealing within thyself what God should reveal, fearing other men; and God has better right for thee to fear Him. So when Zaid had accomplished what he would of her, then We gave her in marriage to thee, so that there should not be any fault in the believers, touching the wives of their adopted sons, when they have accomplished what they would of them; and God's commandment must be performed.[24]

This verse is paraphrased in the *Istoria de Mahomet*.[25] The point that underlies this argument, present in both John of Damascus and the *Istoria*, is that Muḥammad created qur'anic revelations *ad hoc* to justify his own lust. This episode, and the related qur'anic quotation, became one of the recurring tropes in anti-Islamic polemics. It is also found in another very influential work of Christian-Muslim polemic, the so-called letter (or apology) of al-Kindī, originally written in Arabic in the first half of the 9th century and translated into Latin in the 12th century.[26] The episode is also found in a variant of the *Istoria de Mahomet*, contained in a letter of John of Seville to Albarus of Cordova, known as *Adnotatio Mammetis Arabum principis*. It calls Muḥammad a heretic and a precursor of the Antichrist.[27] About the episode of Zayd and Q 33:37, it says: 'And the followers of such a nasty prophet say that he was shining with so many miracles, that, drawn by his burning lust, he took away the wife from another one and joined himself with her in matrimony'.[28]

Eulogius and Albarus of Cordova

Eulogius and Albarus of Cordova, the authors who transmitted these biographies of Muḥammad, are also the authors of apologetic works in support of the so-called martyrs of Cordova – about 50 people who, in 850-60, during the reigns of ʿAbd al-Raḥmān II (822-52) and Muḥammad

---

[24] Arberry, *Koran*, vol. 2, p. 125.
[25] Gil, *Corpus scriptorum*, vol. 2, p. 485, lines 36-43.
[26] L. Bottini, '*The Apology of al-Kindī*', in *CMR* 1, 585-94. See further, below.
[27] This is also a motif present in John of Damascus: at the very beginning of the paragraph about Islam he describes the 'superstition of the Ismaelites' as the precursor of the Antichrist; see Glei and Khoury, *Johannes Damaskenos*, p. 74, lines 3-4.
[28] Gil, *Corpus scriptorum*, vol. 1, pp. 200-1, lines 5-8.

I (852-86), were executed for publicly insulting the Prophet Muḥammad. In his *Memoriale sanctorum* and *Liber apologeticus martyrum*, Eulogius records the events of every execution, while Albarus, in his *Indiculus luminosus*, attacks Muḥammad and tries to show how he can be linked with biblical passages that refer to the Antichrist. The Qur'an, regarded as composed by Muḥammad who is connected in some way to the devil himself, is used to support attacks on him. Moreover, Muḥammad is regarded as having used the Qur'an to justify his lust (the episode of Zayd is also mentioned by one of the martyrs, Perfectus).[29] In Albarus, we find another argument, which will recur as a polemical trope, namely the argument against the Islamic paradise as a place of sensual pleasure (e.g. Q 2:25; 4:57), used to show the lustful nature of Muḥammad, and because of which he cannot be a genuine prophet.[30]

These Latin Christian texts present a pattern of rejection of and attack on the Qur'an, although this was by no means the only attitude towards the Qur'an in 9th-century Cordova. The very fact that Eulogius and Albarus had to write apologetic works to defend the behaviour of the Christians who voluntarily sought martyrdom shows that the majority of the Christian community of Cordova were critical of them. From the arguments Eulogius and Albarus employ, we can infer that the Christians of Cordova did not consider those who died as real martyrs, for martyrdom is not something to be sought and forced; they were rather considered as provocateurs. The confrontation and the rejection of Islam and the Qur'an promoted by the 'martyrs' was counterbalanced among the wider Christian population by a more tolerant attitude in which can be found patterns of some sort of acceptance and assimilation. For example, Christians in Cordova, although criticised by Albarus, referred to Jesus by the qur'anic terms 'Word of God' or 'Spirit of God', avoiding 'Son of God'.[31] While they accepted his divine Sonship, they sought compromise by using qur'anic language,[32] which they found quite acceptable.

---

29 Gil, *Corpus scriptorum*, vol. 2, p. 398, lines 24-8.

30 Albarus, 'Indiculus Luminosus', para. 24, in Gil, *Corpus scriptorum*, vol. 1, pp. 297-8.

31 Albarus, 'Indiculus Luminosus', para. 9, in Gil, *Corpus scriptorum*, vol. 1, p. 281.

32 Cf. Q 4:171: 'People of the Book, go not beyond the bounds in your religion, and say not as to God but the truth. The Messiah, Jesus son of Mary, was only the Messenger of God, and His Word that He committed to Mary, and a Spirit from Him' (Arberry, *Koran*, vol. 1, p. 125).

Other texts

Other texts, such as the *Historia ecclesiastica* or *Chronographia tripertita* by Anastasius Bibliothecarius (d. c. 878),[33] enjoyed considerable circulation. It was the source of Landolfus Sagax's *Historia Romana* in the last quarter of the 10th century.[34] It was used by Peter the Venerable in the 12th century and, furthermore, it was responsible for the transmission of Eastern knowledge about Muḥammad in the West. It is a translation of three Byzantine historiographical works, namely the *Chronicon* of George the Synkellos (d. 810), the *Chronographikon syntomon* by Nicephorus of Constantinople (d. 828) and the *Chronographia* by Theophanes the Confessor (d. 817). While it contains a detailed biography of Muḥammad taken from Theophanes, it does not mention the Qur'an, apart from a reference to the qur'anic teaching about paradise.[35]

The commentary on the Gospel of Matthew by Pascasius Radbertus (d. c. 860) mentions the bare fact that the Saracens have a new law built on the Old and the New Testaments.[36] It is worth noting that Radbertus connects the Saracens with the ancient heretical movement of the Nicolaites. Traditionally, the Nicolaites were associated with loose sexual conduct and this could explain their supposed connection to Muḥammad, who was also criticised by polemicists for his perceived sexual appetite.[37] This connection with the Nicolaites created a whole branch of the Muḥammad legend, culminating in the identification of Muḥammad with the Christian cleric Nicholas, the supposed founder of this movement. It was the flourishing of legends of this kind, far removed from Islam itself and its prophet, that provided impulses and a focus for Qur'an translations during the 12th and 13th centuries. These aimed to give access to the Islamic sources and to discredit the legends that were circulating.[38] An example of such legends is that of the 'Passio Pelagii'

---

33 B. Neil, 'Anasthasius Bibliothecarius', in *CMR* 1, 786-90.

34 J. Tolan, 'Landolfus Sangax', in *CMR* 2, 524-5.

35 See 'Anastasius the Librarian, History of the Church', in M. Di Cesare, *The pseudo-historical image of the prophet Muhammad in medieval Latin literature. A repertory*, Berlin, 2012, 52-4, p. 53.

36 See 'Pascasius Radbertus, Commentary on the Gospel of Matthew', in Di Cesare, *The pseudo-historical image of the prophet Muhammad*, 49-51, p. 50, lines 39-40.

37 Ireneus of Lyon (130-202) is a case in point. See J.P. Migne (ed.), *Contra haereses*, vol. 1, 26, at p. 7, col. 687.

38 For an overview of the development of the Nicholas legend in the West, see F. González Muñoz, 'Liber Nycholay. La leyenda de Mahoma y el cardenal Nicolás', *Al-Qanṭara* 25 (2004) 5-43, pp. 20-7. See also, F. González Muñoz, '*Liber Nycholay*', in *CMR* 4, 650-3.

by Hrothsvita of Gandersheim,[39] written around 955, in which Muslims are described as pagans and idolaters, worshipping gods made of gold.

Other significant works about Islam from the 10th century, such as Raguel's 'Passio Pelagii' (before 967)[40] and the life of John of Gorze, by John of St Arnoul (978-84),[41] while still critical, are not as aggressive as other sources. The former only describes the Muslims as dissolute degenerates, while the latter, which refers to an embassy to Cordova carried out by John of Gorze in 953, so giving information about life in Cordova and etiquette at the emir's court, does not indulge in attacks on the doctrines of Islam or the Qur'an. By contrast, Adémar of Chabannes (989-1034),[42] goes back to the pattern of hostility. He returns to the motifs of the Antichrist, linking Islam with the devil and moral perversion. He also connects Islam with Christian heresies and tries to draw correspondences between individual aspects of Islam and specific Christian heresies, anticipating in this Peter the Venerable. However, Adémar shows no interest in the text of the Qur'an, in contrast to the 12th-century abbot of Cluny, Peter the Venerable. This indicates the difference between the period traced so far and the turning point that follows.

During the period from the 9th to the 11th century, apart from some exceptions represented by legends, Christian circles had relatively good knowledge of the Qur'an. Latin Christianity knew its *content*, though the Qur'an as *text* was not the centre of attention. Starting with use of the qur'anic content, polemical motifs and arguments were in process of formation and transmission and the qur'anic text 'hidden' behind them can be discerned, although it was not normally discussed in itself. Argumentation leans frequently on interpretations distorted by Christian cultural tradition, while biblical authorities, the Church Fathers and other ancient Latin sources supported anti-Islamic interpretations and even the interpretation of the Qur'an. Another general theme of this period is the demonisation of Islam, and connection of the Qur'an with an evil spirit, the devil and hell. Nonetheless, it seems that, in everyday life, there was a lessening of the earlier confrontational attitude towards Islam, which can be inferred from the apologetic works of Eulogius and Alvarus that denounce the tolerant and rather assimilating attitude of

39 L.A. McMillin, 'Hrotsvit of Gandersheim', in *CMR* 2, 293-7.
40 P. Henriet, 'Raguel', in *CMR* 2, 377-80.
41 M. Frassetto, 'John of St Arnoul', in *CMR* 2, 475-9.
42 M. Frassetto, 'Ademar of Chabannes', in *CMR* 2, 648-56.

Christians towards Muslims, and is also represented by the historical works of the 10th and 11th centuries.

The Qur'an at the centre: Qur'an translations and treatises on the Qur'an (12th-14th centuries)

With the 12th century, there is a shift in the engagement of the Latin West with Islam as the Qur'an as text gradually becomes the centre of attention. Furthermore, in the 12th century, reason and rationality gain importance as directing principles of argumentation. These enhanced efforts to distinguish historical reality from legend and to develop discourse on Islam from reliable sources. Texts were required to pass through the filter of reason, rather than being built on the imagined connection of Islam with the devil and supernatural evil.

Petrus Alfonsi

The first key figure at this turning point is Petrus Alfonsi (d. after 1116).[43] Petrus was a Jewish convert to Christianity (formerly named Moses Sefardi) from al-Andalus who was baptised in Huesca on the feast day of Ss Peter and Paul (29 June) in 1106, under the patronage of King Alphonsus of Aragon (r. 1104-34), from whom Petrus, named after Peter, gained his surname Alfonsi. In 1108-10, Petrus Alfonsi wrote the *Dialogi contra Iudaeos*, in which he discusses his conversion with his Jewish alter ego, Moses, explaining why his choice was dictated by reason. In the fifth chapter of the work, Moses becomes convinced that 'the faith of the Jews' is 'shallow, incoherent, irrational and displeasing to God', which Petrus has proved with 'most evident rational arguments'.[44] However Moses asks Petrus why, if rationality was his criterion, did he not convert to Islam given that he was well acquainted and grew up with it? He knew their books and he understood their language. Moreover, continues Moses, Islam seemed more straightforward and practical than either of the other two religions. Its 'law' is relaxed about the pleasures of this life, and its commandments show how God loves Muslims, and promises

---

[43] J. Tolan, 'Petrus Alfonsi', in *CMR* 3, 356-62.

[44] Pedro Alfonso de Huesca, *Diálogo contra los Judíos*, ed. K.P. Mieth, Huesca, 1996, p. 91: *Hactenus Iudaicae gentis fides quam inanis et inconstans in omnibus esset, eorumque obsequium quam irrationabile existeret deo atque ingratum, vel cur ab eiusdem fide recesseris, et evidentissimis edidisti probastique rationibus et michi, in quanto permanserim hactenus errore, monstrasti.*

the rewards of ineffable pleasures in the hereafter. More important, if one examines the essence of this religion, one will see how it is founded on the stable basis of reason.

This is the occasion for Petrus to speak not only of Judaism, but also of Islam. He is in the privileged position of having grown up with Islam around him, and of being conversant with its books and its language. These, in fact, will be the objects of the discussion: the texts as they are. The Prophet himself is not to be discussed, but rather the *Lex*, a word that designates not only Islam, but in a narrower sense the book of its law, the Qur'an. The criterion and focus of the discussion is Islam's 'rationality', and the starting point is a positive one. Islam is presented as the most reasonable and practical religion, the closest to human understanding, the most grateful to God, until it can be proved wrong. Moses presents the obligations required of Muslims: the five daily prayers (a number which seems acceptable and not too heavy); the ablutions before prayer (cf. Q 4:43, a reasonable process of purification); the profession of faith (which is monotheistic); the reasonableness of the fast during the month of Ramaḍān (cf. Q 2:185, only during the day and only if one is not sick or travelling); the pilgrimage to Mecca, in which pilgrims have to stone the devil 'as the law [i.e. the Qur'an] orders'[45] (cf. Q 2:196-202; Q 81:25); the 'house of God' (*domus Dei*) in Mecca (i.e., the Kaʿba), which is said to have been built by Adam when he was expelled from paradise, and to have been a place of prayer since then (cf. Q 2:125), having also been used as a sacrificial altar by Abraham, who improved its structure and left it as an inheritance to Ismael (cf. Q 2:127). The enemies of the faith as well as their prophets –Moses continues the explanation– should be fought, robbed and killed in every possible way, until they convert to Islam, or pay a tax (cf. Q 9:29). Every kind of meat is permitted to them, except pork and the blood and meat of any animal that has died naturally rather than being slaughtered (cf. Q 2:173). All that has not been blessed in the name of God is to be rejected. Regulations concerning the number of wives permitted and the divorce process are also described (cf. Q 2:226), as are abstention from wine (cf. Q 2:219), and for believers a carnal paradise in the hereafter and the tortures in hell that await unbelievers (cf. Q 2:80-1).

Almost every element in the description of Islam is supported by a qur'anic passage, as also are arguments of refutation, and the discrediting

---

45 Pedro Alfonso, *Diálogo*, p. 92.

of the Prophet as a cunning, self-proclaimed pseudo-prophet.[46] Petrus's source is the 9th-century Arabic *Risālat al-Kindī* ('Letter [or Apology] of al-Kindī'), an important source for Latin texts engaging with the Qur'an, especially after the middle of the 12th century when it was translated into Latin by Peter of Toledo (d. after 1142) for the abbot of Cluny, Peter the Venerable.[47] Of course, this was after the time of Petrus Alfonsi – which underscores his pioneering efforts in working with original sources.

Petrus mentions what he regarded as the Christian heresies that underlie Islam, especially that of the Jacobites, who maintained that Jesus is not God and was not crucified (Q 4:157). He also speaks of Jewish influences on Islam, represented by the Companion of the Prophet 'Abdias' (*scil.* 'Abdallāh ibn Salām) and 'Cahbalhabar' (*scil.* Kaʿb al-Aḥbār), and other Christian heretical influences, represented by the Jacobite cleric Sergius. He also uses another motif that will be frequent in anti-Islamic polemics (found, e.g., in Peter the Venerable and Riccoldo da Monte di Croce), namely the violent nature of Islam in that it seeks conversion by the sword.[48] In relation to the fact that Muḥammad did not perform any miracles, Petrus warns against believing any stories that tell of miracles performed by Muḥammad and he does this using the Qur'an, underlining that nothing is said there about any miracles by Muḥammad. Furthermore, Petrus continues, the Prophet himself commanded followers not to believe what he did not explicitly write in *his* Qur'an (notice here the motif that the Qur'an was written by Muḥammad, and did not come from God).[49] In discrediting the Prophet, such textual support gains importance.

Peter the Venerable and Robert of Ketton

If in Petrus Alfonsi we find the beginning of a new trend, albeit as a parenthesis within an anti-Judaic work, we find in Peter the Venerable (1092/4-1156) a figure who makes a great systematic effort to enhance the work of Petrus Alfonsi.[50] While he was visiting Cluniac abbeys in the Iberian Peninsula, Peter charged two translators, Robert of Ketton[51]

---

[46] The quotations from the Qur'an in the *Dialogus* are listed and analysed in detail in G. Monnot, 'Les citations coraniques dans le "Dialogus" de Pierre Alfonse', in *Islam et chrétiens du Midi, XIIe-XIVe s.*, Toulouse, 1983, 261-77, pp. 272-3.

[47] See F. González Muñoz, 'Peter of Toledo', in *CMR* 3, 478-82.

[48] Pedro Alfonso, *Diálogo*, p. 95.

[49] Pedro Alfonso, *Diálogo*, p. 96.

[50] D. Iogna-Prat and J. Tolan, 'Peter of Cluny', in *CMR* 3, 604-10.

[51] O. de la Cruz Palma and C. Ferrero Hernández, 'Robert of Ketton', in *CMR* 3, 508-19.

and Hermann of Carinthia,[52] together with Peter of Toledo and Peter of Poitiers,[53] with translating a corpus of Arabic texts about the Prophet and Islam.[54] This yielded the first Latin translation of the entire Qur'an, carried out by Robert of Ketton in 1143. The purpose was to offer reliable material for the refutation of Islam that would dismiss any legend in circulation, such as the legend of Nicholas.[55] The rational way of refuting Islam through a written tract that would disclose Islamic errors using its own sources and texts, especially the Qur'an, was also seen as an alternative to violence at a time when the idea of crusade was flourishing.[56]

Robert of Ketton's translation is a milestone in the history of Christianity engaging with the Qur'an.[57] Copied in several manuscripts, it was the primary source for a number of authors, such as Riccoldo da Monte di Croce, Juan de Segovia and Nicholas of Cusa, up to the 17th century at least. It was the basis for the first translations of the Qur'an into European vernacular languages and it was the first Latin Qur'an to be printed (in 1543 in Basel, by Theodor Bibliander). Qur'anic verses are merged into long, elaborate sentences, which reflect the style of the high prose of the time. However, if one compares the Latin translation with the Arabic original, the rendition is substantially correct. From the very beginning, Robert's translation was surrounded in the manuscripts with glosses, in a layout that resembles glossed Bibles or juridical works. This exemplifies the understanding of the work in Latin circles as both a sacred and a juridical text (the two meanings of the word *lex*, through which the Qur'an was often defined: *Lex Sarracenorum*).

The translation does not contain polemics. On the contrary, one can see the effort on Robert's part to render the text in objectively and clearly. This can also be seen in his way of translating a single Arabic word with two in Latin, to make the translation as clear and complete as possible. The translation also reveals the use of Islamic exegetical literature to

52 O. de la Cruz Palma and C. Ferrero Hernández, 'Hermann of Carinthia', in *CMR* 3, 497-507.

53 González Muñoz, 'Peter of Toledo'.

54 See de la Cruz Palma and Ferrero Hernández, 'Robert of Ketton', pp. 510-15.

55 Cf. Peter the Venerable, 'Summa totius haeresis Saracenorum', chap. 3 in R. Glei, (ed.), *Petrus Venerabilis. Schriften zum Islam*, Altenberge, 1985, p. 4. Note: the wording gives clear reference to Ireneus of Lyon.

56 Cf. Peter the Venerable, 'Contra sectam Saracenorum', book I, chap. 24, lines 6-8, in Glei, *Petrus Venerabilis*, 62.

57 An excellent overview about medieval and early-modern Latin Qur'an translations can be found in T.E. Burman, *Reading the Qur'ān in Latin Christendom, 1140-1560*, Philadelphia PA, 2007. On Robert of Ketton and Mark of Toledo's translations, see also U. Cecini, *Alcoranus Latinus*, Berlin, 2012.

reflect the Islamic understanding of the text. On the other hand, polemic is evident in the glosses. These were not written by Robert, and their original core most likely comes from the pen of Peter of Poitiers. In these glosses, polemical topics are underlined and singled out in very aggressive language: Christological errors, biblical misunderstandings, internal incongruences in the text, moral corruption, and so on.

As noted above, the translation was intended to be used to write a refutation of Islam. Not finding anyone disposed to do this, Peter the Venerable himself wrote two works on the subject: the shorter *Summa totius haeresis Sarracenorum* and the *Contra sectam Sarracenorum*. The former is a brief summary of the contents of Islam, whose refutation is once again based on the Prophet's biography: the sources are Anastasius Bibliothecarius, the *Apology of al-Kindī* and Petrus Alfonsi. The latter, planned as a longer treatise of refutation against Islam, was probably left unfinished. In it, Muslims, to whom the book is addressed, are intended to find a rational deconstruction of Islamic arguments. In the introduction one finds an analytical dissection of Islam in different doctrines, each of which is associated to an early Christian heresy. Again, the denial of the prophetic status of Muḥammad has pre-eminence, though even if quotations from Ketton's translation are included, the polemical potentiality of the Qur'an translations was not fully exploited by Peter, who focussed mainly on the figure of the Prophet.

Further translation work

In 1210, around 60 years after the first Qur'an translation, a second was made. The Archbishop of Toledo, Rodrigo Jiménez de Rada,[58] commissioned Canon Mark of Toledo[59] to produce a new translation.[60] The result was remarkable for two reasons: the style of the translation and its (presumed) purpose. The style is diametrically different from that of Robert of Ketton. In Robert's translation the sentences are reformulated and the verses are merged to create the appearance of a refined Latin text, while Mark's translation follows the Arabic almost word for word as far as that is possible without doing violence to the Latin syntax. If the translation is compared with the Arabic original, exact correspondences concerning word order can usually be observed, and some idiomatic

---

[58] M. Maser, 'Rodrigo Jiménez de Rada', in *CMR* 4, 343-55.

[59] T.E. Burman, 'Mark of Toledo', in *CMR* 4, 150-6.

[60] Nàdia Petrus Pons (ed.), *Alchoranus Latinus quem transtulit Marcus canonicus Toletanus*, Madrid, 2016.

phrases are translated literally. This may have had something to do with the (alleged) purpose of the translation, because, while it was meant to be a pacific means of combatting the Saracens, the aim of converting at least few of them is explicitly mentioned. Its closeness to the original makes it suitable for use as an aid to preachers reading the Qur'an in Arabic.

Used within Dominican circles, and notably by Riccoldo da Monte di Croce,[61] the translation itself, which can be regarded as philological, attentive to the original text and to Islamic exegesis of it, gives no evidence of polemic. However, the prologue contains a biography of Muḥammad that features some motifs traceable to traditional polemic before the 11th century. Latin interpretation was used to discredit the Prophet. For example, the meaning of 'Mecca', where Muḥammad was born, is explained as coming from the Latin verb *moechari*, meaning 'to commit adultery', thus suggesting it was a polytheistic city, unfaithful to the one God. Traditional motifs are explained according to the new sensibility of the time, as, for example, that there was no supernatural revelation *per se* through Muḥammad. Rather, he simply gave the appearance of manifesting a supernatural event by faking epileptic fits, the symptoms of which Mark describes with medical accuracy. Such polemical motifs are confined to the preface in which stories that are patently legends are dismissed.

From translation to polemic

In this period, translation of texts from Arabic seems to have been thought more important than writing polemical works. Apart from his polemical prologue, Mark himself did not write any work of refutation, and neither did Jiménez de Rada, who commissioned his translation. Nevertheless, polemic can be carried out through translation, as happened in the case of the translation of the *Risālat al-Kindī* and the translation that was also undertaken in this period and attributed, probably falsely, to Mark of an Arabic work known in Latin as *Contrarietas alfolica* (meaning the contradictions of the *fuqahā'*, experts in Islamic jurisprudence) or *Liber denudationis* (original between about 1050 and 1132).[62] The work of an Islamic

[61] T.E. Burman, 'How an Italian friar read his Arabic Qur'an', *Dante Studies* 125 (2007) 93-109.
[62] T.E. Burman, '*Liber denudationis*', in *CMR* 3, 414-17.

convert,[63] with the Qur'an at its very centre, this had the aim of exposing all the errors of Islam by using its own sources,[64] and showing how the Qur'an contradicts itself.[65] It perfectly reflects the trend of the time, and was to have great influence as a source for authors such as Ramon Llull, Ramon Martí and Riccoldo da Monte di Croce.

A new argument, introduced by the *Contrarietas*, derives from the complex redaction history of the Qur'an. After Muḥammad's death, says the *Contrarietas* in the sixth chapter, different people transmitted the Qur'an, and 'each of them fixed the [text of the] Qur'an in a different way than the others, and they fought one another, not accepting until their death the authenticity of [what was transmitted by] others'.[66] Also, the contents of the suras changed over time: 'The chapter of Repudiation [Q 66], which before consisted of two hundred and thirty verses and today only twelve, used to surpass [in length] the chapter of the Cow [Q 2]. Also, they say that the chapter of the Cow contained a thousand verses and today only two hundred eighty-five.[67] All this is clearly intended to refute the argument of the inimitability of the Qur'an and its divine origin. Its style is also criticised: 'In this book, really, there are many things so obscure, so abruptly interrupted, that they do not make any sense and rather cover foolishness and lies.'[68]

In the seventh chapter, we find again the argument that the Qur'an contains *ad hoc* revelations to justify Muḥammad's own lust, in support of which Q 66:1-2 and Q 5:89 are cited. The beginning of the latter verse *Lā yu'ākhidhukum Allāh bi-l-laghw fī aymānikum* ('God will not punish you for unintentional words in your oaths') is translated quite strongly in regard to the word *laghw* (foolish talk, nonsense, ineffectual language), which appears as *fraudatio* (fraud).[69] Thus, even though it is not the

---

63 *Liber denudationis*, ed. T.E. Burman, in T. Burman, *Religious polemic and the intellectual history of the Mozarabs, c. 1050-1200*, Leiden, 1994, 240-385, p. 240.

64 *Liber denudationis*, 1.2, in Burman, *Religious polemic*, p. 242.

65 *Liber denudationis*, 2.3, in Burman, *Religious polemic*, p. 246.

66 *Liber denudationis*, 6.2, in Burman, *Religious polemic*, pp. 275-6. Burman remarks on this argument: 'The textual history of the Qur'an outlined in this paragraph is rather distorted at points for polemical effect, but it is recognizably based on the traditional history of the text as found, for example, in al-Ṭabarī, "Khuṭbat al-kitāb", 1, pp. 25ff.'; see *Religious polemic*, p. 277, n. 2.

67 *Liber denudationis*, 6.3, in Burman, *Religious polemic*, p. 276, with the reading 'octoginta quinque' based on MS Paris, BnF – Ms. Lat. 3394, fol. 244v.

68 *Liber denudationis*, 6.4, in Burman, *Religious polemic*, p. 278.

69 *Liber denudationis*, 7.3, in Burman, *Religious polemic*, p. 282: *Non imputabit vobis Deus fraudationem iuramenti vestri*. Burman notes that Ramon Martí later quotes this verse in the same context (p. 283, n. 5).

norm, a translation may sometimes, for polemical purposes, exaggerate the meaning of a word. Here, what is meant is an unintentional mistake in an oath, but the translation makes it a deliberate fraud, which supports the argument that someone could bypass oaths at will, or lie while swearing an oath, to satisfy lust. Further, it is argued that most of the Qur'an comes from the Old and New Testaments,[70] and that, when God speaks in the Qur'an, it is Muḥammad who, in effect, gives voice to the divine. Further, Q 17:88, on the inimitability of the Qur'an,[71] is refuted with the argument that what men and spirits allegedly cannot replicate, as the verse claims, is in fact self-contradictory and written in deficient or bad (*foedus*) language.[72] Indeed, the whole of chapter 9 of the *Contrarietas* is devoted to inner contradictions in the Qur'an.

Chapter 10 compares Jesus with Muḥammad to show how the former is presented in the Qur'an as greater than the latter. The traditional disqualification of Muḥammad's character is achieved by quoting verses from the Qur'an that testify, for example, to his humble condition (Q 93:6), or his past as an idolater (Q 93:7, 48:2). By contrast, Jesus is presented as the Word of God (Q 4:171). Also, two Muslim objections are presented and refuted with both biblical and qur'anic quotations: how the infinite God could be enclosed in the Virgin's womb, and how he could be crucified. So, here in the *Contrarietas*, Muslim opinions are made known, taken into account and, in what may be intended as the preliminary to an attitude of dialogue, discussed, even if ultimately refuted.

The path traced by Petrus Alfonsi, Peter the Venerable, and the *Contrarietas* was soon followed by Ramon Martí, Riccoldo da Monte di Croce and Ramon Llull. These authors have in common knowledge of Arabic and the experience of living in Arab countries. Ramon Martí (c.1120-c.1284)[73] began studying Arabic in 1250, and was in Tunis in 1269. Besides Arabic, he knew Hebrew and Aramaic, and he was a key figure in Christian-Jewish relations, having written a monumental work on the Talmud and Midrashim, the *Pugio fidei*, with quotations in the original language and his own Latin translations. Interestingly, this work quotes the Qur'an in support of Christian belief and against Judaism.[74] In his

---

70 *Liber denudationis*, 7.13, in Burman, *Religious polemic*, p. 294. Note: the Latin *computator* should be translated as 'plagiarist'; see p. 295, n.3.

71 'Say: "If men and jinn banded together to produce the like of this Koran, they would never produce it like, not though they backed one another"' (Arberry, *Koran*, vol. 1, p. 312).

72 *Liber denudationis*, 8.1 and 8.2, in Burman, *Religious polemic*, p. 296.

73 T.E. Burman, 'Ramon Martí', in *CMR* 4, 381-90.

74 See R. Szpiech, 'Citas árabes en caracteres hebreos en el *pugio fidei* del dominico Ramón Martí: Entre la autenticidad y la autoridad', *Al-Qanṭara* 22 (2011) 71-107, pp. 84-9.

Explanatio simboli apostolorum, Martí intersperses his explanation of the Apostles' Creed with refutation of Islamic beliefs, basing his arguments on biblical and qur'anic verses and, again, quoting the Qur'an to support Christian beliefs.[75] While the *Explanatio* is a fusion of a catechetical work for Christians with a refutation of Islam, *De seta Machometi*, also known as *Quadruplex reprobatio*, focusses on Islam, discrediting the figure of Muḥammad as prophet.

The title of this four-fold refutation relates to the four characteristics that a true prophet must have, which, as the author aims to show, do not belong to Muḥammad. The text displays comprehensive knowledge of Arabic sources: we find a vast number of quotations not only from the Qur'an, but also from the Hadiths (as was also the case in the *Contrarietas*, one of the sources of *De seta*). The author is clearly also familiar with philosophical works by Ibn Sīnā and al-Ghazālī. A recent work by Pieter van Koningsveld[76] identifies the 13th-century Christian Arabic work *Al-sayf al-murhaf fī-l-radd ʿalā-l-Muṣḥaf* ('The whetted sword in refutation of the Qur'an'),[77] as the main source of Martí's *De seta*. This would imply that the primary sources quoted by Martí were accessed indirectly. Nevertheless, he would have drawn them from an Arabic text, which can be considered a more primary source than a Latin translation of an original Arabic work.

Directly drawn from *De seta* is the *Tractatus seu disputatio contra Saracenos et Alchoranum*,[78] attributed – even if not unanimously – to Riccoldo da Monte di Croce (c. 1240-1320).[79] Like Martí, Riccoldo was a scholar learned in Arabic, as well as Syriac, Hebrew and Greek. He spent 13 years in the eastern Mediterranean (1288-1301) between Acre, Turkish territories and Baghdad, a period he describes in the *Liber peregrinationis*, or *Itinerarius*. The last part has a section specifically devoted to the Qur'an (Cap. 24: *De lege Sarracenorum*) about which he says that the *lex Sarracenorum* is *larga* (broad / easy), *confusa* (confused), *occulta*

---

75 One of his sources is surely the *Contrarietas*. For example, against the Islamic belief that Jews and Christians corrupted their scriptures, he quotes Q 10:94, which affirms that the 'book' that was read before the Qur'an itself attests to the Qur'an. If the Bible was corrupted before the Qur'an came into existence, it could not confirm it. See J.M. March, (ed.), 'En Ramón Martí y la seva "Explanatio Simboli Apostolorum"', *Anuari de l'Institut d'Estudis Catalans* (1908 [1909]) 443-96, p. 454. The same argument is found in the third chapter of the *Contrarietas* (and it was also used by Riccoldo in *Itinerarium* 34, p. 27).

76 P.S. van Koningsveld, *An Arabic source of Ramon Martí*, Leiden, 2018.

77 L. Demiri, '*Al-sayf al-murhaf fī-l-radd ʿalā-l-Muṣḥaf*', in *CMR* 4, 662-5

78 Ricoldus de Monte Crucis, *Tractatus seu disputatio contra Saracenos et Alchoranum*, ed. D. Pachurka, Wiesbaden, 2016.

79 T.E. Burman, 'Riccoldo da Monte di Croce', in *CMR* 4, 678-91.

(mysterious / difficult to interpret), *mendacissima* (most mendacious), *irrationabilis* (irrational) and *violenta* (violent), explaining each adjective by using qur'anic quotations in support. Nonetheless, in the previous part of the work he describes the good qualities of Muslims he encountered in the Islamic world: their devotion, generosity and hospitality. Although their religion is erroneous, many Christians could yet learn from their exemplary behaviour.

Riccoldo's human response to Islam is also shown in his five *Epistolae de prosperitate Sarracenorum*, written in the face of the political success achieved by Muslims in Palestine (notably, the conquest of Acre, the last city held by the Latin Crusaders, in 1291). In these letters, he calls on God to defend Christians and to make clear that He is on their side or, if not, to make known that Islam is the true religion, so that Christians may change and 'venerate Muḥammad'.[80] Nevertheless, he intersperses the letters, especially the third, with refutations of qur'anic passages and Christian apologetic. In the end he trusts in the Bible, although doubt on which side God stands remains latent. Even a fervent polemicist like Riccoldo was tormented by doubt, a sentiment that may have affected more than one author discussed here and which should never be forgotten when reading the apparently steely determination and clearness of Latin Christianity engaging with the Qur'an.

Riccoldo's great treatise on the Qur'an is the *Contra legem Sarracenorum*. Thomas Burman defines it as 'a thorough-going attack on the Qur'an and Islam, with little direct attempt at Christian apologetic'.[81] It can be considered a *summa* of the preceding tradition of arguments of refutation against the Qur'an. It develops the arguments presented in the *Itinerarius* and adds more, going through them analytically in its 17 chapters, which are largely based on the *Contrarietas Alfolica*, from which Riccoldo draws most of his arguments. For its qur'anic quotations it uses the Qur'an translation by Mark of Toledo, correcting it where needed with Riccoldo's own translations. Being so systematic and exhaustive, it was used as a basis by later scholars, such as Nicholas of Cusa. It was translated into Greek and retranslated into Latin and printed in the 16th century and represents the culminating point of the period we are dealing with here, reuniting Arabic knowledge, using Arabic sources in the original and in translation for its arguments and refutations, and drawing

80 See Epistle 1:11-12; 31, ed. E. Panella, 2010; http://www.e-theca.net/emiliopanella/riccoldo/epi.htm; Burman, 'Riccoldo da Monte di Croce', p. 681.

81 Burman, 'Riccoldo da Monte di Croce', p. 688.

together the whole of the earlier tradition. It shows the most 'scholarly' side of Riccoldo, which coexisted with the more 'human' side, ever ready to see the positive aspect of the alleged opponent.

William of Tripoli and Ramon Llull

The scholarly and human side is also found in William of Tripoli (d. after 1273)[82] and Ramon Llull (c. 1232-c. 1315).[83] William was the author of two works, the *Notitia de Machometo* and *De statu Sarracenorum*, the most remarkable thing about which is the fact that, while they include *loci classici* of Christian apologetics, they also see and underline an Islamic devotion to Jesus and Mary that originates from the qur'anic passages about them. Thus, they contemplate the real possibility of the conversion of Muslims to Christianity.

While this attitude towards Jesus and Mary in the Qur'an is the point in common between Christians and Muslims in William of Tripoli, in Ramon Llull rationality is the common ground. From among the enormous number of works he wrote, the *Liber de gentili et tribus sapientibus*,[84] a Latin translation almost contemporary with the Catalan original from 1274, is perhaps the most significant. In it, Llull rejects controversy based upon the authority of any scripture, and instead seeks a way in which shared rational elements can be found among the three participants.

In the work, three wise men, a Jew, a Christian and a Muslim, each outline their own faith before a pagan who is looking to see which contains truth. Each presents his faith without interruption and only the pagan may ask questions. In the fourth book, it is the turn of the *Lex Sarracenorum*, and it is the Saracen who presents his faith; *he* is the one to talk and not, as was the case in earlier works, the Christian author commenting on the Qur'an and judging it. There is, with the two *obiectiones Sarracenorum*, an anticipation of this in the *Contrarietas* but even then it was the (converted) Christian author who reported the objections. Here, the born Christian (not a convert), Ramon Llull, lets the Saracen talk and only the pagan, as a third, objective party, makes objections. It is true, as Harvey Hames says,[85] that one should not exaggerate Llull's tolerance towards members of other faiths, for the ultimate objective of all

82 T.E. Burman, 'Humbert of Romans', in *CMR* 4, 509-14.

83 H. Hames, 'Ramon Llull', in *CMR* 4, 703-17.

84 Ramon Llull, *Liber de gentili et tribus sapientibus*, ed. Ó. de la Cruz Palma, Turnhout, 2015, pp. 125-481.

85 Hames, 'Ramon Llull', p. 710.

his works is the conversion of infidels. Nonetheless, Llull is ready to talk with his opponent on a level, hear him and take his arguments seriously.

At the end of the book, the three wise men do not let the pagan say which religion he has chosen, as they wish to continue debating. Thanks to this open ending, the reader is not provided with a solution. However, through the pagan's objections to the Saracen, 'the dialogue clearly indicates that it is Christianity'[86] that he chooses. Nonetheless, the reader is given the opportunity to think further and decide for himself. In any case, the presentation of the three religions opens the way for comparison and for a search of common ground. Such perspectives may be regarded as minor in light of the great number of treatises against Islam and the Qur'an, though such openness, running alongside lines of refutation, flourishes again in the 15th century in figures such as Nicholas of Cusa.

A reflection on the preceding tradition, new translations and new perspectives (1400-1600)

By the 15th century, Latin Christianity had built a large repository of resources on the Qur'an: translations, treatises, dialogues and epistles. From this time onwards, such material is found in both large treatises and in dialogical form (e.g. in the work of Dionysius the Carthusian,[87] 1402/3-71 and Alonso de Espina,[88] 1412-61/4) and in works that evaluate and elaborate further on earlier material. In addition, there now comes into play the challenge presented by the conquest of Constantinople by the Turks in 1453. New intellectual tools and new perspectives emerge, for it appears that all the preceding efforts could not stop the advancement of Islam to the detriment of Christianity: a situation that recalls Riccoldo's epistles at the time of the fall of Acre (1291). One method of analysis of the pre-existing material employed in the 15th and 16th centuries was the indexation and summarisation of the Qur'an. Juan de Segovia (c. 1390-1458), in his *Errores legis Mahometi*,[89] lists excerpts from Robert of Ketton's translation of the Qur'an according to topics of polemics:

86 Hames, 'Ramon Llull', p. 710.

87 About Dionysius the Carthusian and his works, *Contra perfidiam Mahometi* and *Dialogus disputationis inter Christianum et Sarracenum*, see A. Mallett, 'Dionysius the Carthusian', in *CMR* 5, 522-5.

88 About Alonso de Espina and his *Fortalitium fidei*, see A. Echevarría, 'Alonso de Espina', in *CMR* 5, 451-5.

89 A. Bündgens et al. (eds), 'Die *Errores legis Mahumeti* des Johannes von Segovia', *Neulateinisches Jahrbuch* 15 (2013) 27-60.

De paradisi felicitate (against the carnal pleasures in the Islamic Paradise); various errors about creation (of the world, of man, of angels and demons); *de Iudaeis*; *contra divina mandata*, etc.

Ketton's translation is also behind the monumental work *De gladio divini spiritus in corda mittendo Sarracenorum*,[90] begun in 1453, in which Juan de Segovia rejects war as a way of converting Muslims; conversion should happen only through peaceful and intellectual means.[91] In this work, Juan de Segovia remembers his personal discussions with a Granadan emissary, who showed him the possible effectiveness of rational argumentation. He explains further that Muslims may sometimes have misconceptions about Christianity through the portrayal of it given in the Qur'an – which also contains correct teachings. One of the purposes of the *De gladio* is to highlight these misconceptions in the Qur'an in order to persuade Muslims of the veracity of the Christian religion. A thorough study of Ketton's translation, compared with the Arabic original, permitted Juan de Segovia to evaluate it and see its flaws. He describes them in the prologue to a new translation, which he decided to produce in cooperation with the Segovian *faqīh* Yça Gidelli.[92] Robert of Ketton, skilled in rhetoric and poetry,[93] rendered the Arabic Qur'an into eloquent Latin.[94] However, some deficiencies occurred, in word order, for example, and some words were mistranslated, and even changed in meaning. Explanations were also added to the text, which are absent from the Qur'an, and which give guidance and instruction as a teacher would to students.[95] Nonetheless, 'almost all the contents of the Qur'an are to be found in the translation',[96] but they are difficult to locate because of the re-elaboration of the text, so the translation does not exactly replicate the original text. Thus, a new, etymologically correct translation was needed that would follow the word order of the original text, and so Yça Gidelli translated the text into Spanish, taking care to keep close to the Arabic, and Juan translated the Spanish into Latin. The

---

[90] Johannes von Segovia, *De gladio divini spiritus in corda mittendo Sarracenorum*, ed. U. Roth, 2 vols, Wiesbaden, 2012.

[91] Johannes von Segovia, *De gladio divini spiritus*, praefatio (p. 6). See also Juan de Segovia, *Praefatio in translationem noviter editam ex Arabico in Latinum vulgareque Hyspanum libri Alchorani*, in J. Martínez Gázquez (ed.), 'El prólogo de Juan de Segobia al Corán (*Qur'ān*) trilingüe (1456)', *Mittellateinisches Jahrbuch* 38 (2003) 389-410, p. 400, line 200.

[92] G. Wiegers, 'Içe de Gebir', in *CMR* 5, 462-8.

[93] See Juan de Segovia, *Praefatio*, p. 405, line 406.

[94] Segovia, *Praefatio*, p. 405, line 408.

[95] Segovia, *Praefatio*, p. 405, lines 417-21.

[96] Segovia, *Praefatio*, p. 405, lines 424-5.

layout of the translation should have included all three versions, alongside each other: Arabic, Spanish and Latin.[97]

The 15th and 16th centuries saw new Latin Qur'an translations, by Flavius Mithridates, also known as Guillelmus Raymundus de Moncada, who translated Q 21 and 22 for Federigo da Montefeltro,[98] and by Iohannes Gabriel Terrolensis (1518) for Cardinal Egidio da Viterbo.[99] These translations have as their underlying impulse the humanistic principle of return to the sources, also shown by the fact that they display the original text along with the translation. They are not of good quality throughout and the one by Flavius Mithridates contains evident mistakes.[100] Also, they contain no overt polemic, even though the commentaries that are part of Iohannes Terrolensis's translation include issues regarding Christianity and topics frequently debated. They also display an ethnographic interest. One prominent source of such commentaries is the *Confusión de la secta mahometana* by the Muslim convert Juan Andrés.[101] This focussed not only on the topics debated, but also on practical reciprocal knowledge between Christians and Muslims. None of these translations overshadowed Ketton's translation. It continued to be copied and was the first to be printed, in 1543. This translation, together with Riccoldo's *Contra legem Sarracenorum*, was also behind the works of Nicholas of Cusa (1401-64),[102] friend and correspondent of Juan de Segovia and author of two fundamental works: *De pace fidei* and *Cribratio Alcorani*. In the former appears the principle of *una religio in rituum varietate*: all religions are founded on a common base and their differences only reflect different ways of presenting it. Also, in the *Cribratio Alcorani*, despite its drawing on a traditional repertoire of anti-Muslim polemic, such as

97 The translation has not survived in its entirety. However, apart from fragmentary quotations, at times paraphrased, in the same prologue and in letters, a fragment of it (Q 5:110-15) has been found in the margin of a manuscript of *De gladio* and published (see U. Roth and R. Glei, 'Die Spuren der lateinischen Koranübersetzung des Juan de Segovia. Alte Probleme und ein neuer Fund', *Neulateinisches Jahrbuch* 11 (2009) 109-54, which also includes the other fragments, already published, and U. Roth and R. Glei, 'Eine weitere Spur der lateinische Koranübersetzung des Juan von Segovia', *Neulateinisches Jahrbuch* 13 (2011) 221-8). Juan revised his work, which used Ketton's translation, in the light of his new translation, correcting the previously incorrect translations.

98 Edition of Sura 21 by H. Bobzin, 'Guglielmo Raimondo Moncada e la sua traduzione della sura 21 ('dei profeti')', in M. Perani (ed.), *Guglielmo Raimondo Moncada*alias *Flavio Mitridate. Un ebreo converso siciliano*, Palermo, 2008, 173-83.

99 K.K. Starczewska (ed.), *Latin translation of the Qur'ān (1518/1621)*, Wiesbaden, 2018.

100 On this and other early modern Latin translations of the Qur'an, see T.E. Burman, 'European Qur'an translations, 1500-1700', in *CMR* 6, 25-38.

101 Z. Zuwiyya, 'Juan Andrés', in *CMR* 6, 79-84.

102 J. Tolan, 'Nicholas of Cusa', in *CMR* 5, 421-8.

Riccoldo's *Contra legem*, there is a conciliating effort. As in Juan de Segovia's *De gladio*, although the errors of the Qur'an are underlined, there is also a desire to find in the Qur'an confirmation of Christian truth. Moreover, through the *pia interpretatio*, possible errors can be linked to Muḥammad's misunderstandings of Christian teachings, or to decisions he took in good will and not out of hostility. In the words of John Tolan: 'Where other polemicists had perceived Muḥammad's malignancy and mendacity, Nicholas sees a laudable (if at times misplaced) attempt to lead infidels to true faith.'[103]

In the 15th century, the fall of Constantinople represented a challenge both to the self-awareness of Christianity as the true religion, which was supposedly meant to triumph over Islam, and to the vision of unity and peace that was pursued by many intellectuals. The 16th century saw Christianity itself suffering division and experiencing a challenge to its own unity as a consequence of the rise of Protestantism. At the same time, the idea of universal sovereignty was increasingly prevalent on the political level: the various rulers of Mediterranean areas, such as the Ottoman Sultan Süleyman, the Shīʿī prophet and Shah Ismail, the Holy Roman Emperor Charles V, and the kings of France, all struggled for absolute dominion. The same was true on the religious and cultural level: Nicholas of Cusa's efforts to find unity between the different religions, and the vision of a universal religious discourse in the search of an ancient theology common to all humankind as portrayed by Egidio da Viterbo, for example, were continued and enhanced by scholarly engagement with the Qur'an, including by Guillaume Postel (1510-81)[104] and Johann Albrecht von Widmanstetter (1506-57).[105] Moreover, their efforts were not only, and not primarily, directed towards Islam but rather towards their Protestant counterparts, such as Martin Luther (1483-1546)[106] and Theodor Bibliander (1505-64),[107] who, in turn, each took part in the debate around the Qur'an. The Qur'an, therefore, while still playing its role in the relationship between Christianity and Islam (now represented by the Ottoman Turks), was also involved in the confrontation between Catholics and Protestants.

In this dialectic, a major role was played by the advent of the printed book. The polemical battle was now conducted not only by the

103 Tolan, 'Nicholas of Cusa', p. 425.
104 C. Isom-Verhaaren, 'Guillaume Postel', in *CMR* 6, 712-25.
105 U. Cecini, 'Johann Albrecht Widmanstetter', in *CMR* 7, 235-45.
106 A.S. Francisco, 'Martin Luther', in *CMR* 7, 225-34.
107 B. Gordon, 'Theodor Bibliander', in *CMR* 6, 675-85.

composition of new works, but also by older manuscript works being printed for the first time. The key year for Christianity engaging with the Qur'an in this new age of communication and dissemination was surely 1543. In this year, three works were printed. First, a work edited by the Protestant Theodor Bibliander, supported in his effort by Martin Luther, and published in Basel as *Machumetis Saracenorum principis eiusque successorum vitae, ac doctrina, ipseque Alcoran*. This contained the Qur'an as translated by Robert of Ketton, along with the other texts about Islam translated by Peter the Venerable, as well as some traditional texts about the Qur'an, such as Riccoldo's *Contra legem* and Nicholas of Cusa's *Cribratio Alcorani*, and, finally, contemporary texts about the Turks, who in this period were the most important representatives of the Muslims. Second, the Catholic humanist Johann Albrecht von Widmanstetter published in Nuremberg a book called *Mahometis Abdallae filii theologia dialogo explicata* [...] *Alcorani epitome*, containing an annotated abridgement of Ketton's Qur'an, and third, the Catholic scholar Guillaume Postel published in Paris *Alcorani seu legis Mahometi et Evangelistarum concordiae liber, in quo de calamitatibus orbi Christiano imminentibus tractatur*.

Bibliander's effort to publish Ketton's Qur'an translation in Basel was not unopposed. The city council confiscated the first printed copy and had the publisher Oporinus arrested. The Protestant humanists were divided between opponents and supporters of the publication. Opponents were against what they saw as the circulation of a book in which all the worst heresies of history were reunited, very much according the traditional narrative since the 11th century. On the other side, a number of humanists and theologians supported the publication for various reasons. The most prominent was Martin Luther, who wrote a letter-preface to the edition, which was very influential for the eventual publication of the Qur'an. While he shared resistance to the Qur'an as a heretical book, he promoted its publication for the very reason that it was a heretical book, because nothing could be said about, let alone against, something that was not known, and through knowledge of it not only could the Qur'an be better refuted and possibly some Muslims converted, but Christians would also be better warned.[108]

This inner Christian warning applied not only to Islam, but also to deviant Christian doctrines, principally Catholicism. Luther defined the

108 See H. Bobzin, *Der Koran im Zeitalter der Reformation*, Beirut, 2008, p. 156.

pope and the Turks as two aspects of the Antichrist[109] and the fight against Islam and Catholicism was for him along the same path. Widmanstetter and Postel's publications in the same year can be seen, among other things, as a symmetrical reaction to this attitude. The German and French scholars aimed in fact to underline the similarity between Islam and Protestantism and while Widmanstetter did this in his prologues and his annotations to the Qur'an, Postel openly dedicated his book to this purpose from the title itself, *Alcorani seu legis Mahometi et Evangelistarum concordiae liber*, which would be included and enhanced in his *magnum opus*, *De orbis terrae concordia* (1544).

Moreover, both men, while having followed different paths and possessing quite different personalities, tried to promote a universalistic view that reconciled classical philosophy, the Kabbalah and Islam, interpreting the Qur'an in the context of the search for a primordial theology. One could see this as an enhancement of the way traced by Nicholas of Cusa, with the difference that they also placed great emphasis on linguistic competence – in this following Egidio da Viterbo – being also authors of grammatical books and treatises on languages.

Conclusion

In the period 850-1600, even though the approach of Latin Christianity to the Qur'an can generally be characterised as negative and expressed in the form of refutation, there was clearly modulation in the intensity of rejection and some positive elements did emerge from time to time. First of all, there was a marked distinction between the attitude shown in intellectual refutation and in armed conflict, as the latter was increasingly discarded as a viable solution to differences (of course, also in light of Muslim military successes). Second, there were efforts to look for common elements between Christianity and Islam, which more often than not was approached as a Christian heresy, less frequently as a distinct religion, and occasionally as a pagan, idolatrous cult.

While the Qur'an was not regarded as an inspired book but the creation of Muḥammad, it was nevertheless treated with respect: although the first translation attacks the Qur'an in its glosses on the text and its polemical prologue, it presents the actual text in a layout similar to that

[109] Luthers Tischreden, no. 330: *Martin Luthers Werke, Weimarer Gesamtausgabe*, vol. 1, Weimar, 1912, p. 135.

of the Bible or the most important legal collections, and employs rhetorically elevated language. At first, the Qur'an was often overlooked in the first treatments of Islam, which mostly centred on the figure of the Prophet. It gradually came into focus, concerning first its nature and origin (revealed or not, demonic, human or divine), later its contents, and eventually its underlying message, which was supposedly common to every religion.

A discourse of refutation made up of recurring topics was gradually constructed and from time to time retransmitted and enhanced. Typical points of criticism included the following: material taken from the Old and New Testaments but inaccurately presented in the Qur'an, the carnal paradise, permitted licentiousness, and the support of violence to spread the religion. Formal aspects were also objects of accusation: it was a confused, obscure and self-contradictory book. Nonetheless, alongside this discourse can also be found figures who did not indulge in polemics, but instead, while they still aimed at conversion to Christianity, stressed that there were in the text traces of universal religious sentiment and of the best of human nature to promote a peaceful dialogue. In addition, more often than not, Latin discourse on the Qur'an was only superficially directed against Muslims. In reality, it often had a Christian target audience. It was used to recall fellow Christians to a presumed lost, or misunderstood, Christian orthodoxy; to move Christians to repentance, or to interpret their own scriptures correctly; and also to encourage them to behave as devoutly and generously as Muslims did.

The Qur'an was also used as a negative model compared with which Christian deviations were even worse. It was investigated to look for unity in difference, for what was common in all humankind, whether this was rationality or an analogous way of perceiving the supernatural that was only expressed differently. It was also used as an aid to learning Arabic and coming to know the customs of people with whom Christians had to live in the same kingdom, or with whom they wanted to make an alliance to pursue their own interest in ruling over the world. Finally, it was studied by Christian intellectuals to find answers about themselves, looking for traces of a common language of humanity interspersed in its lines. Ultimately, despite all the polemics, violence, attacks and misunderstandings, the history of Christianity engaging with the Qur'an is, indeed, the history of humanity investigating itself in its relationships with the divine and with the other, in the relentless effort to understand who they were and what it meant to live as human beings in a complex and variegated world.

Chapter 11
'Our Friendly Strife'. Eastern Christianity engaging the Qur'an

Gordon Nickel

Introduction

The engagement of Eastern Christianity with the Qur'an in the earliest centuries of Islam is distinguished from that of its Latin counterpart by virtue of developing within an empire that was dedicated to the propagation and defence of a new religion. Assuming that the available documents give us a representative picture of that engagement, these particular circumstances drew out of Eastern Christians new ways of thinking about and expressing their own faith, as well as responding to the claims of a conquering Arab power. They could hardly have anticipated the cataclysmic circumstances that would require new thoughts and expressions.

In the year 691, the Umayyad Caliph 'Abd al-Malik (r. 685-705) constructed a beautiful building on the Temple Mount in Jerusalem, thereby announcing to the region, with a flourish, that a new ruling regime and a new religion had come to stay. Along the top of both sides of the outermost galleries within this octagonal building, known as the Dome of the Rock, the caliph had inscribed in mosaic a 240-metre line of Kufic Arabic script. The contents of the text are remarkable for the high proportion that addresses Christian beliefs.

Jerusalem was 'the Christian city par excellence' when the second caliph, 'Umar ibn al-Khaṭṭāb (r. 634-44), and his troops had first arrived in 638.[1] Its Church of the Holy Sepulchre was considered one of the wonders of the world at the time. Just over 50 years later, the Dome of the Rock, constructed in the style of an Eastern church and placed on the most prominent platform in the city, was competing for attention with the older Christian buildings. Inside, the inscriptions along its spacious colonnades directly addressed 'the people of the book' with the words,

---

[1] O. Grabar, *The shape of the holy. Early Islamic Jerusalem*, Princeton NJ, 1996, p. 63.

'Do not go beyond the limits in your religion and do not say about Allāh but the truth.' Some 175 out of a total of 370 words in the inscription concern the identity of Jesus, here called 'Īsā. Interspersed with words about 'Īsā are claims for a new name, 'the messenger of Allāh'.[2]

The walled city of Jerusalem in the late 7th century, and for many centuries since, can be seen as an intriguing picture of Eastern Christian engagement with the Qur'an. The text and challenges of the Qur'an came to Christians from outside of their familiar world, from an alien conquering power. Christians were not generally the ones who brought theological challenges to their new rulers, but rather were themselves challenged by their rulers to respond to new religious claims.

Eastern Christians continued their lives among the Muslims who brought the challenges. This led to face-to-face encounters and authentic interfaith conversation. At the same time, the playing field was not level. The conversation was between conqueror and conquered, and the restrictions imposed on Christian expression could change according to the whims of whichever caliph was ruling. Eastern Christians did not have the freedom of Latin Christians to say and write whatever they thought about the Qur'an.

Christians who wanted to respond effectively to the Muslim challenges would need to do so in what for many was a new language – although there were substantial numbers of native Arabic speakers in parts of the pre-Islamic Christian East. Like the inscriptions in the Dome of the Rock, Muslim challenges that came in Arabic needed to be deciphered and understood before Christians could compose a response. At their best, Eastern Christians not only learned to comprehend and engage with the contents of the Qur'an, but those whose first language was Arabic were able to turn the spotlight towards the literary style of the Qur'an and the claims that Muslims made for it. They needed to learn to fashion their responses in the terms of the Muslim societies in which they lived and take into account the constraints these imposed. These are some of the circumstances that distinguish Eastern Christian engagement with the Qur'an from the treatment of the Qur'an in Latin Christianity. Knowing the context for Eastern engagement should help us to appreciate it more fully and not to judge it inappropriately according the to the standards of other times and places.

---

2 Grabar, *Shape of the holy*, pp. 59-61.

Relevant documents

Examples of Eastern Christian engagement with the Qur'an come from a variety of documents, from the earliest centuries of Islam. Their authors express themselves in Greek, Syriac, Coptic, Armenian and Arabic, and there are striking differences in how directly they write or speak as well as in the extent of their knowledge about the Qur'an.

This essay will frequently mention the *Risāla* of al-Kindī[3] because it shows the most extensive range and depth of engagement with the Qur'an of all existing records from early Eastern Christianity. It was written sometime in the mid-9th century by an anonymous Christian purporting to report an exchange of letters between the Muslim ʿAbd Allāh ibn Isḥāq al-Hāshimī, who sets out the superior advantages of Islam and calls his correspondent to convert, and a much longer response from the Christian ʿAbd al-Masīḥ al-Kindī, who explains why he finds Islam inferior to his own faith. In addition to its engagement with many qur'anic passages that are also treated by other Christian authors, this Christian letter is unique in its prescient investigation of the claims that the Qur'an makes for itself, and it also presents an extensive section on the development of the Qur'an in history, a passage that prompted Sidney Griffith to write in 1983, 'Unfortunately, thus far little scholarly attention has been paid to this valuable ninth century discussion of such an important issue.'[4] Actually, this discussion has been noted with interest by scholars of qur'anic studies and the origins of Islam for more than a hundred years. Fortunately, in recent years that discussion has received more attention from scholars of Christian-Muslim relations.

The title of this essay, 'our friendly strife', indeed comes from al-Kindī's *Risāla*. The author offers this surprising expression at the end of the long and lively response to the Muslim interlocutor's summons to him to 'wage war in the way of Allāh'.[5] Al-Kindī's vigorous advocacy in the opposite direction, the way of 'the Messiah, the Saviour of the world', is

---

3 L. Bottini, '*The Apology of al-Kindī*', in *CMR* 1, 585-94.

4 S.H. Griffith, 'The Prophet Muḥammad, his scripture and his message according to Christian apologies in Arabic and Syriac from the first Abbasid century', in G. Monnot (ed.), *La vie du Prophète Mahomet. Colloque de Strasbourg* (*octobre 1980*), Paris, 1983, 99-146, p. 144.

5 A. Tien (trans.), 'The Apology of al-Kindi', in N.A. Newman (ed.), *The early Christian-Muslim dialogue. A collection of documents from the first three Islamic centuries* (*632-900 AD*), Hatfield PA, 1993, 365-545, p. 391 (summons from al-Hāshimī), pp. 478-86 (response from al-Kindī); W. Muir, *The Apology of al Kindi, written at the court of al Mâmûn* (*A.H. 215, A.D. 830*), *in defence of Christianity against Islam*, London, 1882 (partial trans.), pp. 40-8.

straightforward and unapologetic, and yet he is able to ask his opponent to let reason – 'impartial and incorruptible reason' – be their umpire in the debate.[6] The concept of peaceful debate may appear counter-intuitive in circles where debate itself is anathema. For Christians living in the midst of Muslim-majority societies, however, the concept may not seem so strange.

Variety of approaches and strategies

Among the approaches to the Qur'an by Eastern Christians were several that made use of the Qur'an itself, sometimes extensively, but that arguably did not engage with the Qur'an in regard to its challenging perspectives on Christian beliefs. One approach was to say that the text of the Qur'an came originally from a Christian monk named Baḥīrā who taught Muḥammad. One Arabic version of this story, probably from the 9th century, quotes around 40 verses from the Qur'an.[7] The unknown author of this version makes extensive use of apparently 'pro-Christian' verses (such as Q 10:94 and 5:82), comments on a small number of anti-Christian verses, then interprets 'neutral' verses in such a way that they seem to come from a Christian source. Verses that are undeniably anti-Christian are explained as later corruptions of the original text composed by Muḥammad. The goal of the story is to argue that the Qur'an confirms Christian beliefs, and therefore to plead that Muslims should not attack Christians for their beliefs.[8]

A second approach was to argue that, while for the most part the Qur'an affirms Christian beliefs, it is simply not relevant to Christians because it is for the Arabs alone. The strategy of Paul of Antioch's *Risāla ilā baʿḍ aṣdiqāʾihi alladhīna bi-Ṣaydā min al-Muslimīn* ('Letter to a Muslim friend in Sidon'), written in Arabic by the Melkite Bishop Paul of Sidon sometime around the year 1200, includes the comparatively rare Christian acceptance that Muḥammad was sent, and the Qur'an was revealed, by God,[9] but that the Qur'an was given in Arabic specifically for the pagan Arabs, and that it can only be fully understood when read

[6] Tien, 'Apology of al-Kindi', p. 486.
[7] B. Roggema, 'A Christian reading of the Qur'an. The Legend of Sergius-Baḥīrā and its use of Qur'an and Sīra', in D. Thomas (ed.), *Syrian Christians under Islam. The first thousand years*, Leiden, 2001, 57-74, p. 58. See also, B. Roggema, '*The Legend of Sergius Baḥīrā*', in *CMR* 1, 600-3.
[8] Roggema, 'Christian reading of the Qur'an', p. 70.
[9] See D. Thomas, 'Paul of Antioch', in *CMR* 4, 78-82.

in line with the Bible. His subtle interpretations of verses about Jesus create the impression that, 'if read judiciously and with Christian intentions, the Qur'an can be seen to support Christian doctrines'.[10] Paul of Antioch's approach was substantially picked up a century later in the early 14th century in the anonymous *Risāla min ahl jazīrat Qubruṣ* ('The letter from the people of Cyprus').[11]

Differing from the approaches in these two letters written at the time of the crusades, but like them declining to criticise the Qur'an openly, is the document known as *Fī tathlīth Allāh al-waḥīd* ('On the triune nature of God'), from the 8th century.[12] This has been praised for its use of qur'anic language to explain the identity of Jesus in a Muslim context,[13] though its references to the contents of the Qur'an are light and suggestive in a peculiar way. For example, after a detailed proclamation of the deity of Jesus, the author writes, 'You will find all this about the Messiah in your book.'[14] This claim seems to show either an unaccountably sanguine approach to the qur'anic teaching on 'Īsā, or an assumption that Muslims do not know the Qur'an well.

The qur'anic materials most often engaged by Eastern Christians were the verses in the Qur'an about Jesus, where he is named 'Īsā. Some responses show knowledge of the wording of the verses themselves, while others may deal with the arguments of the verses as heard in interfaith conversation. In some cases, Christians sought to take advantage of actual teachings in the Qur'an in order to present their faith, while in others Christians needed to answer strong claims that their Muslim opponents anchored confidently in the Qur'an. In addition to defending

---

10 D. Thomas, 'Paul of Antioch's *Letter to a Muslim Friend* and *The Letter from Cyprus*', in D. Thomas (ed), *Syrian Christians under Islam. The first thousand years*, Leiden, 2001, 203-21, p. 211.

11 R.Y. Ebied and D. Thomas (ed. and trans.), *Muslim-Christian polemic during the crusades. The letter from the people of Cyprus and Ibn Abī Ṭālib al-Dimashqī's response*, Leiden, 2005. See also D. Thomas, '*The letter from the people of Cyprus*', in *CMR* 4, 769-72.

12 M.D. Gibson (ed. and trans.), *An Arabic version of the Acts of the Apostles and the seven Catholic Epistles from an eighth or ninth century MS. in the Convent of St. Katherine on Mount Sinai, with a treatise on the triune nature of God, and translation from the same codex*, Cambridge, 1899. See also S.K. Samir, 'The earliest Arab apology for Christianity', in S.K. Samir and J.S. Nielsen (eds), *Christian Arabic apologetics during the Abbasid period (750-1258)*, Leiden, 1994, 57-114; M.N. Swanson, '*Fī tathlīth Allāh al-wāḥid*', in *CMR* 1, 330-3.

13 M.N. Swanson, 'Beyond prooftexting. Approaches to the Qur'ān in some early Arabic Christian apologies', *The Muslim World* 88 (1998) 297-319; S. Griffith, 'The Qur'an in Christian Arabic literature. A cursory overview', in I.M. Beaumont (ed.), *Arab Christians and the Qur'an from the origins of Islam to the medieval period*, Leiden, 2018, 1-19, pp. 5-8.

14 Gibson, *An Arabic version of the Acts of the Apostles*, p. 12.

their own faith in the face of qur'anic denials, Christians were sometimes summoned to respond to qur'anic claims for the Qur'an, its messenger and Islam.

The death of Jesus

According to the earliest available documents, Christians quickly became familiar with the Muslim denial of the death of Jesus. Writing in the mid-8th century, John of Damascus, who functioned as an official under the Umayyad caliphs before withdrawing to the monastic life, notes this denial in chapter 100 of his *Peri haeresiōn* ('On heresies') in words that summarise Q 4:157-8: '[...] the Christ was not crucified, nor did he die; for God took him into heaven unto Himself [...]'.[15] John does not respond to the denial, except to write that 'all the prophets' foretold the death and resurrection of Jesus.[16]

Some writers sought to respond to the Qur'an's assertion that the Jews lied when they claimed to have killed the Messiah by saying that the assertion was partly true. The 9th-century Jacobite Abū Rā'iṭa, for example, argues that the Jews lied when they claimed to have killed the divine nature of the Messiah, although they did indeed kill his human nature.[17] The 9th-century Nestorian ʿAmmār al-Baṣrī takes a different approach, engaging the Muslim accusation that belief in the crucifixion of the Messiah imputes weakness to God or humiliation to the Messiah. John the Baptist was beheaded, asks ʿAmmār rhetorically, so why then should Muslims be offended that Jesus also met a humiliating end?[18]

In his well-known dialogue with the ʿAbbasid Caliph al-Mahdī (r. 775-85), the Nestorian Patriarch Timothy I confesses the redemptive significance of the death of Jesus and especially the demonstration of the love of God in 'the death in the flesh' of his beloved Son.[19] In response, the

---

15 D.J. Sahas, *John of Damascus on Islam. The 'heresy of the Ishmaelites'*, Leiden, 1972, p. 132. See also R.F. Glei, 'John of Damascus', in *CMR* 1, 295-301.

16 Sahas, *John of Damascus*, p. 136.

17 I.M. Beaumont, 'Early Christian interpretation of the Qur'an', *Transformation* 22 (2005) 195-203, p. 201. See also S.T. Keating, 'Abū Rā'iṭa l-Takrītī', in *CMR* 1, 567-81; S.T. Keating, 'On the Incarnation', in *CMR* 1, 574-5.

18 I.M. Beaumont, ''Ammār al-Baṣrī. Ninth century Christian theology and qur'anic presuppositions', in I.M. Beaumont (ed.), *Arab Christians and the Qur'an from the origins of Islam to the medieval period*, Leiden, 2018, 83-105, pp. 99-101. See also M. Beaumont, ''Ammār al-Baṣrī', in *CMR* 1, 604-10.

19 A. Mingana (trans.), 'The apology of Timothy the Patriarch before the Caliph Mahdi', *Bulletin of the John Rylands Library* 12 (1929) 137-226, p. 176. See also

caliph denies Jesus' death by quoting Q 4:157, to which Timothy argues that, on the contrary, the Qur'an bears witness to Jesus' death, making his point by quoting Q 19:33, where Jesus says, 'Peace be upon me the day I was born, and the day I die, and the day I am raised up alive.' Timothy notes that the sequence of verbs here follows the order of the Gospel accounts, and Jesus cannot be 'raised up alive' unless he first dies.

Timothy also quotes Q 3:55, 'When God said, "Jesus I will cause you to die (*mutawaffīka*) and will raise you to me."' Again, the sequence of verbs follows the Gospel order, but here Timothy faces a challenge in the Arabic text. The verb *tawaffā* is most naturally translated as 'cause to die', and in most occurrences in the Qur'an that are not related to Jesus it is habitually translated this way. With the two occurrences of the verb that are connected with Jesus (Q 3:55; 5:117), however, both Muslim commentators and translators were (and still are) accustomed to render it in ways not related to death (e.g. 'take', Yusuf Ali; 'gather', Pickthall).

Timothy also makes the case for the death of Christ from several other angles. It was appropriate, he says, because without it people would have no sign to assure them of eternal life. Furthermore, both the death and resurrection of Jesus were witnessed publicly, so that all people could enjoy the expectation of everlasting life and the world to come. He adds that the Muslim claim that Allāh deceived the witnesses of the crucifixion by making another person look like ʿĪsā (a frequent interpretation of Q 3:54; see 4:157) is 'entirely unfitting' for God.[20] This argument, which was developed further by later Christian apologists, may have produced echoes in Muslim writings such as the Qur'an commentary of Fakhr al-Dīn al-Rāzī (1149-1210), where he says that the idea of throwing the witnesses of the crucifixion into confusion and ignorance 'is not worthy of the wisdom of God'.[21]

M. Heimgartner, 'Timothy I', in *CMR* 1, 515-19, and also pp. 522-6 on Letter 59, which contains the Syriac text of Timothy's account of the debate.

20 M.N. Swanson, 'Folly to the *ḥunafāʾ*. The crucifixion in early Christian-Muslim controversy', in E. Grypeou, M. Swanson and D. Thomas (eds), *The encounter of Eastern Christianity with early Islam*, Leiden, 2006, 237-56, pp. 248-55.

21 G. Nickel, '"Self-evident truths of reason". Challenges to clear thinking in the *Tafsīr al-kabīr* of Fakhr al-Dīn al-Rāzī', *ICMR* 22 (2011) 161-72, pp. 166-7.

The deity of Jesus

The Arabic message above the galleries within the Dome of the Rock does not touch on the death of Jesus but chooses instead the deity of Jesus as its central theme. The longest units of text in the inscription target the Christian confession that Jesus is the Son of God, and along with that belief in the Trinity.[22] In the Qur'an as well, it is the deity of Jesus that draws the strongest denials and arguably the harshest tone.[23] Correspondingly, a large part of the apologetic responses and debates from Eastern Christian pens strive to make a case for the Trinity and for the deity of Jesus.

The most common text from the Qur'an to spark Eastern Christian reaction to the qur'anic denials was Q 4:171,[24] the words of which also appear on the inner face of the Dome's colonnades. In order to appreciate the Christian reaction in full, it is important to note that the challenge came to Eastern Christians, probably for the first time, in the form of a command to a subject population under Arab military occupation. Q 4:171 is actually a collection of affirmations and denials, and Eastern Christian writings sought both to answer the denials and take advantage of the apparent affirmations. It commands Christians not to say about Allāh anything 'except the truth'. The concern is explicitly theological, and the epistemology is traditional. The verse then immediately brings forward 'the Messiah, 'Īsā son of Mary': he was only a messenger of Allāh. 'Do not say "three"', the verse continues. Far be it from Allāh 'that he should have a son'.

In the extensive explanations that Eastern Christians composed to try to make a case before Muslims for the Trinity and the divine sonship of Jesus,[25] they made use of the first part of this verse, which they found supported their claim. Here, 'Īsā is also called '[Allāh's] word which he cast into Mary, and a spirit from him'. Eastern Christians learned to use this apparent reference to the three Persons of the triune Godhead,

22 Grabar, *Shape of the holy*, pp. 59-61.

23 G. Nickel, 'Jesus', in A. Rippin and J. Mojaddedi (eds), *The Wiley Blackwell companion to the Qur'ān*, Oxford, 2017, 288-302, pp. 291-4.

24 Beaumont, 'Early Christian interpretation', pp. 199-200.

25 E.g. Mingana, 'Apology of Timothy', pp. 153-63, 199-215; Tien, 'Apology of al-Kindi', pp. 412-25; A. Jeffery, 'Ghevond's text of the correspondence between 'Umar II and Leo III', *Harvard Theological Review* 37 (1944) 269-332, pp. 300-19.

Allāh, his Word, and his Spirit, from as early as John of Damascus and *Fī tathlīth Allāh al-wāḥid* in the mid-8th century.[26]

Of the few direct quotations from the Qur'an that appear in *Fī tathlīth Allāh al-wāḥid*, one verse is used to support the anonymous author's affirmation of the deity of Jesus as it is demonstrated in his miracles. He argues: 'The Messiah created (*khalaqa*), and no one creates but God. You will find in the Qur'an [the words of Jesus], "I shall create (*akhluqu*) for you the form of a bird from clay. Then I will breathe into it and it will become a bird by the permission of Allāh"' (Q 3:49, cf. 5:110). The author's point is that, elsewhere in the Qur'an, there are 171 occurrences of forms of the verb *khalaqa* in the active voice. The subject of 162 of these is Allāh, and in the remaining verses the verb is used mockingly in relation to false claims made for pagan deities or humans.[27] Perhaps sensing the implications of this (or possibly in response to Eastern Christians), Muslim commentators found ways to interpret *khalaqa* here with other words (and the practice continues today in most Muslim translations of the Qur'an into English, e.g. 'fashion', Pickthall, 'determine', Shakir).

In his brief chapter in *Peri haeresiōn* devoted to the group he calls the Ishmaelites, John of Damascus remarks on their accusation that Christians are 'associators', because when Christians say the Messiah is the Son of God and God, they introduce an associate alongside the one God.[28] It would have been very important for Christians living within the Islamic Empire to reject this term, which in John's Greek must represent the Arabic *mushrikūn* (derived from the verb *ashraka*, 'to make a partner', 'to associate'), because the Qur'an contains very threatening verses about the treatment of *mushrikūn* (e.g. Q 4:48; 9:5, 36, 113).[29] Interestingly, the outer face of the inscriptions within the Dome includes the words 'Praise to Allāh who has not taken a son, nor has he any associate (*sharīk*) in the kingdom'; and above the north door of the Dome appear the words, 'Muḥammad is the servant of Allāh and his apostle, whom he sent with the guidance and the religion of truth so that he may cause it to prevail over religion – all of it – even though the associators (*mushrikūn*) dislike (it)'.[30]

---

26 Sahas, *John of Damascus*, p. 137; Gibson, *An Arabic version of the Acts of the Apostles*, pp. 2-36.

27 Nickel, 'Jesus', p. 296.

28 Sahas, *John of Damascus*, pp. 134-7.

29 Roggema, 'Christian reading of the Qur'an', p. 59. See also G. Hawting, art. 'Idolatry and idolaters', in *EQ*.

30 Grabar, *Shape of the holy*, pp. 59, 61.

In response, John notes that Muslims agree that Christ is word and spirit of God (following this with Q 4:171), and goes on to argue that 'the word and the spirit are inseparable from the one in whom they are by nature'. That is, as attributes, they must be intrinsic constituents of the being that possesses them. Where Muslims falsely call Christians 'associators', John argues, in reply 'we call you mutilators of God'.[31] For John is implying that, in their concern to preserve the unity of God, Muslims implicitly deny the reality of any of God's attributes, including 'word of God' on the basis they might be understood to exist independently of the essence or being of God. The word of God (Christ) is thus not a separate entity to be associated, or not, with Allah; it is a necessary attribute or element of the divine being.

Accusations against the Bible

Writings from Eastern Christian authors also deal extensively with Muslim accusations against the Bible. The qur'anic materials that may support such accusations are sometimes assumed to be the series of verses that use the verbs *baddala* and *ḥarrafa*, or perhaps the 'woe' pronounced upon 'those who write the book with their hands (Q 2:79). However, the writings of Eastern Christians do not seem to mention any of the 'tampering' verses that are often cited in Muslim polemic,[32] whether Christian writers knew these verses or not. Rather, the qur'anic material with which Eastern Christians most needed to engage were the claims in the Qur'an that the '*ummī* prophet (Q 7:157) or *aḥmad* (a possible synonym for the name Muḥammad, Q 61:6) is referred to in the Torah and the Gospel.[33] In the dialogue between Patriarch Timothy and al-Mahdī, the caliph asks Timothy, 'How is it that [...] you do not accept Muḥammad from the testimony of the Messiah and the Gospel?'[34] No matter how reasonably, and patiently, Timothy presents his answer, the caliph keeps coming back to the same question. Timothy replies firmly, 'So far as Muḥammad is concerned I have not received a single testimony either from Jesus the Messiah or from the Gospel which would refer to his name or to his

[31] Sahas, *John of Damascus*, p. 137.
[32] See G. Nickel, *Narratives of tampering in the earliest commentaries on the Qur'ān*, Leiden, 2011, pp. 26-9.
[33] G. Nickel, '"They find him written with them". The impact of Q 7:157 on Muslim interaction with Arab Christianity', in I.M. Beaumont (ed.), *Arab Christians and the Qur'an from the origins of Islam to the medieval period*, Leiden, 2018, 106-30.
[34] Mingana, 'Apology of Timothy', p. 168.

works.'[35] Finally the caliph insists, 'There were many testimonies but the books have been corrupted, and you have removed them.'[36] If Timothy's dialogue is representative of a general trend, then Muslim accusations against the Bible may be seen as a function of an apologetic requirement to claim attestation for Muḥammad in the earlier scriptures.[37]

Eastern Christians made great efforts to answer Muslim accusations of falsification of the Bible, partly because, as a *dhimmī* population within the Islamic empire, they had no other authority than the Word of God. Writers demonstrated remarkable ingenuity in defending the Bible against this attack,[38] and sometimes it was Jewish scholars, fellow *dhimmī*s with Eastern Christians, who supplied the strongest answers.[39] In constructing their answers Christians sometimes appealed to verses in the Qur'an that show a positive and respectful view of the Bible.[40]

Christian and Jewish engagement with Muslim accusations against the Bible seems to have caught the attention of some Muslims, if al-Rāzī's exegesis of Q 3:78, 4:46, 5:13, and 6:91 is any indication. Al-Rāzī concedes the points of faithful transmission and dissemination of the Torah, concluding that 'it is impossible to introduce additions or omissions' to such a holy text that has been faithfully preserved in its original form. On this point, al-Rāzī seemed to allow to the Torah the same claim to the guarantee of preservation through time that he makes for the Qur'an.[41] In general, however, and despite the best efforts of Eastern Christians, the accusation of biblical falsification continued to be extremely popular in Muslim polemic, probably because the accusation made it so easy to rebuff any arguments based on the Bible.[42] There seems to be an almost-audible groan of frustration on the part of al-Kindī in his *Risāla* when he says to his Muslim correspondent: 'You escape the inference on the

---

35 Mingana, 'Apology of Timothy', p. 169.

36 Mingana, 'Apology of Timothy', p. 171.

37 Nickel, '"They find him written with them"', pp. 128-9.

38 G. Nickel, *The gentle answer to the Muslim accusation of biblical falsification*, Calgary, 2015, pp. 117-20. See also I.M. Beaumont, "Ammār al-Baṣrī on the alleged corruption of the gospels', in D. Thomas (ed.), *The Bible in Arab Christianity*, Leiden, 2007, 241-55; S.Toenies Keating, 'Refuting the charge of *taḥrīf*. Abū Rā'iṭah (d. c. 835 CE) and his first *risāla* on the Holy Trinity', in S. Günther (ed.), *Ideas, images, and methods of portrayal. Insight into classical Arabic literature and Islam*, Leiden 2005, 41-57. On this text, see S. T. Keating, 'On the Trinity', in *CMR* 1, 572-4.

39 Nickel, *Gentle answer*, pp. 120-4.

40 For example, Q 10:94, in Tien, 'Apology of al-Kindi', pp. 498-9.

41 Nickel, '"Self-evident truths of reason"', pp. 164-5; Nickel, *Gentle answer*, pp. 52-3.

42 W.M. Watt, *Muslim-Christian encounters. Perceptions and misperceptions*, London, 1991, p. 30.

plea that the text has been corrupted, so that you can apply your favourite argument and shelter behind it. I do not know that I have found an argument more difficult to dislodge, more desperate to disarm than this which you advance as to the corruption of the sacred text.'[43]

The Qur'an supported by miracle?

Another area of Eastern Christian engagement with the Qur'an surrounded the question of whether Muḥammad performed miracles. Eastern Christians must have become familiar with the idea that, according to the Qur'an, he did not, because a number of writers quoted verses such as Q 6:109, 17:59, and 17:90 to back their questions.[44] These verses are part of a longer series in which the audience asks for 'signs' (*āyāt*) but none are given (also Q 13:7, 27; 20:133; 29:50; 43:40). 'They say, "We shall not believe you [Muḥammad] until you cause a spring to gush forth for us from the earth[...]"', runs one such scene (Q 17:90). Within the early Islamic empire, both Jews and Christians began to ask the conquerors whether the new teaching was backed up by divine signs.[45] They argued that, just as the authority of the Torah is supported by the miracles of Moses, and the Gospel by the miracles of Jesus, so the Qur'an requires the attestation of miracles by its messenger.[46]

The morality of the Qur'an

Eastern Christian writers raised matters of morality in the Qur'an about which they had either read or heard. For example, John of Damascus mentions the Qur'an's teaching on divorce, referring to Q 4 (*al-Nisāʾ*, 'Women'; he calls it *Hē graphē tēs gynaikós*, 'The discourse of the woman'),

---

43 Tien, 'Apology of al-Kindi', p. 498.

44 Griffith, 'Prophet Muhammad, his scripture and his message', p. 145; Roggema, 'Christian reading of the Qur'an', p. 66; Beaumont, 'Early Christian interpretation', pp. 197-8 ('Ammār al-Baṣrī).

45 S. Stroumsa, 'The signs of prophecy. The emergence and early development of a theme in Arabic theological literature', *Harvard Theological Review* 78 (1985) 101-14, pp. 105, 109. A Jewish writer who asked this question was the 13th century Jewish philosopher, Ibn Kammūna. See M. Perlmann (trans.), *Ibn Kammūna's examination of the three faiths. A thirteenth-century essay in the comparative study of religion*, Berkeley CA, 1971, pp. 92-3.

46 E.g. Sahas, *John of Damascus*, pp. 156-9, Mingana, 'Apology of Timothy', pp. 172-3; Tien, 'Apology of al-Kindi', p. 439.

which contains much of it.[47] Al-Kindī's *Risāla* quotes Q 24:11 and comments on 'the affair of 'Ā'isha' – the rumour of a scandal in Muslim tradition according to which Muḥammad's young wife 'Ā'isha was once left behind alone by a Muslim raiding force and reappeared in the camp with a young man.[48] The anonymous *Disputation of the monk Ibrāhīm al-Ṭabarānī*, thought to have been written in the later 9th century, probes the question of the imputed sinlessness of Muḥammad. A representative Muslim claims that Muḥammad was without sin, though his interlocutor, a monk, denies this, referring for support to Q 48:2, '[…] so that Allāh may forgive you what is past of your sin and what is to come' ,[49] one of a number of verses that address this issue (also Q 40:55 and 47:19; cf. 3:147; 4:106; 110:3). The Muslim's claim may indicate the development of the Islamic dogma of prophetic sinlessness or immunity known as *'iṣma*.[50]

John of Damascus also refers to the story of Zayd, Muḥammad's adopted son, and his wife Zaynab, in which Zayd divorces Zaynab so that Muḥammad can marry her, in Muslim tradition related to Q 33:36-40. Other writings that mention this story include al-Kindī's *Risāla* and the correspondence between the Byzantine Emperor Leo III (r. 717-41) and the Umayyad Caliph 'Umar II (r. 717-20).[51] John of Damascus shows no awareness of any qur'anic anchor but tells the story along the same general lines as Muslim historians such as Abū Ja'far al-Ṭabarī,[52] though al-Kindī is able to quote most of Q 33:37-8.[53] Zayd's name does indeed appear in Q 33:37, one of very few contemporary names to appear in the Qur'an, but al-Kindī inserts the name Zaynab where the canonical text has simply, '[…] when Zayd had gotten what he needed from her […]'.

Considering these verses, al-Kindī says, 'I have too much respect for the paper on which I write to mention' the story, but says he does so because Q 33:37 claims that Allāh arranged the Prophet's union with the woman ('[…] we married her to you […]'). In his letter, Leo comments, 'Of all these abominations the worst is that of accusing God of being

---

47 Sahas, *John of Damascus*, pp. 137-8.

48 Tien, 'Apology of al-Kindi', p. 433. Cf. A. Guillaume (trans.), *The life of Muhammad. A translation of Isḥāq's* Sīrat rasūl Allāh, Karachi, 1955, pp. 493-7.

49 Beaumont, 'Early Christian interpretation', p. 198. See M.N. Swanson, *'The disputation of the monk Ibrāhīm al-Ṭabarānī'*, in *CMR* 1, 876-81.

50 See T. Andrae, *Die Person Muhammeds in Lehre und Glaube seiner Gemeinde*, Stockholm, 1917, pp. 139-45.

51 T. Greenwood, '*The Letter of Leo III* in Ghewond', in *CMR* 1, 203-8. See also, B. Roggema, *'Pseudo-Leo III's first letter to 'Umar II'*, in *CMR* 1, 375-6; M.N. Swanson, 'The *Arabic Letter of Leo III to 'Umar II'*, in *CMR* 1, 377-80.

52 Al-Ṭabarī, *Ta'rīkh al-rusul wa-l-mulūk*, Cairo, 1967, vol. 2, pp. 562-4.

53 Tien, 'Apology of al-Kindi', pp. 432-3.

the originator of all these filthy acts [...] Is there indeed a worse blasphemy than that of alleging that God is the cause of all this evil?'[54] Such Christian engagements with the qur'anic text should not automatically be characterised in the most pejorative terms. This is a Muslim story that was widely retold in early Muslim commentaries on the Qur'an.[55] The Christian writers said that their main concern was theological. If their concern was rather Muḥammad, however, his behaviour as reported by Muslim tradition is not irrelevant to the evaluation of his claim to prophethood. The story was also of considerable interest within the early Muslim community, writes David Powers, where it raised discomfiture over 'the manner in which God's decree appears to have been designed to satisfy the sexual desires of the Prophet'.[56]

The Qur'an as prophetic *bona fides*

Eastern Christian engagement with moral issues in the Qur'an tends inexorably towards interaction with claims for Muḥammad. Emilio Platti makes the interesting suggestion that al-Kindī wrote about the Qur'an as a way of addressing what for him was the larger question of Muḥammad's prophetic status.[57] This seems to fit well with the insight of John Wansbrough that a dominant concern of Islam in its formative period was the notion of authority, 'acceptance or rejection on the basis of a scriptural dispensation in the possession of a prophet. In dispute are the authenticity of the former and the qualifications of the latter.'[58] Wansbrough finds Muslim dogmas about the Qur'an as the word of God as they developed in the third and fourth centuries of Islam to be 'secondary to acceptance of scripture as prophetical bona fides'.[59] In this

---

[54] Jeffery, 'Ghevond's text', p. 324.

[55] G. Nickel, 'Muqātil on Zayd and Zaynab. "The *sunna* of Allāh concerning those who passed away before" (Q 33:38)', in M. Daneshgar and W.A. Saleh (eds), *Islamic studies today. Essays in honor of Andrew Rippin*, Leiden, 2017, 43-61, pp. 46-51; 'Abdallāh Maḥmūd Shiḥāta (ed.), *Tafsīr Muqātil ibn Sulaymān*, Beirut, 2002, vol. 3, pp. 490-9; *Tafsīr al-Ṭabarī musamma Jāmiʿ al-bayān fī taʾwīl al-qurʾān*, Beirut, 2005, vol. 10, pp. 301-5.

[56] D.S. Powers, *Muḥammad is not the father of any of your men. The making of the last prophet*, Philadelphia PA, 2009, p. 48.

[57] E. Platti, ''Abd al-Masīḥ al-Kindī on the Qur'an', in I.M. Beaumont (ed.), *Arab Christians and the Qurʾan from the origins of Islam to the medieval period*, Leiden, 2018, 66-82, pp. 67-8.

[58] J. Wansbrough, *The sectarian milieu. Content and composition of Islamic salvation history*, Oxford, 1978, p. 56.

[59] Wansbrough, *Sectarian milieu*, p. 58.

scenario, the Qur'an serves as proof, or disproof, of Muḥammad's qualifications for prophethood.

The Dome inscriptions bear witness to a development in Muslim veneration for Muḥammad from a very early point in the emergence of Islam. After stating that Allāh does not beget and was not begotten (Q 112:3), the outer face declares that Allāh and his angels pray for the Prophet, and exhorts the believers to pray for the Prophet and greet him.[60] The same wording appears in Q 33:56. Again on the inner face of the Dome, immediately preceding two long passages on the identity of Jesus, reads 'Muḥammad is the servant of Allāh and his Apostle. Allāh and his angels pray for the prophet. You who believe, pray for him and greet him.'[61] That Allāh would 'pray for', rather than being the object of being 'prayed to', may appear odd, but it is the essential meaning of *Ṣallā Allāhu 'alayhi*' and implies a superlative spiritual status imputed to Muḥammad. Questions raised by this include how Eastern Christians engaged this Qur'anic theological claim, and whether this claim made it difficult to even raise the subject of Muḥammad's identity. If the Dome's proclamation about Muḥammad is representative of how challenges from conqueror to conquered may have run in other parts of the Islamic empire, this would presumably have made it very difficult for Eastern Christians to criticise Muḥammad directly.

Platti gives an example of al-Kindī's method of evaluating the status of Muḥammad by discussing 'law'.[62] He says that there are three kinds of law used in making judgements:[63] divine law, the law of nature or justice, and the law of Satan, identifying the last as 'the law of violence' and 'the law your master brought'. The *Risāla* describes the divine law as having been revealed by the Messiah. Al-Kindī quotes the affirmative Q 5:46, 'And in their footsteps we followed up with Jesus, son of Mary, confirming what was with him of the Torah, and as guidance and admonition to the ones who guard themselves.' He immediately joins this to Jesus' command to love one's enemies in Matthew 5:44-5. In describing the law of nature, 'based on reason', al-Kindī quotes Exodus 21:23-4, but further on quotes its apparent echo in Q 5:45, 'the life for the life, and the eye for the eye, and the nose for the nose [...] and the tooth for the tooth'. The second part of this verse is 'but whoever remits it as a freewill offering,

60 Grabar, *Shape of the holy*, p. 59.
61 Grabar, *Shape of the holy*, p. 60.
62 Platti, ''Abd al-Masīḥ al-Kindī', pp. 66-8.
63 Tien, 'Apology of al-Kindi', pp. 449-52.

it will be an atonement for him'. Al-Kindī suggests that since the first part of Q 5:45 is the law of nature brought by Moses, and the last part of the verse is the divine law brought by Jesus, there is nothing left for 'your master' to bring but the law of Satan, 'I mean the law of violence, opposed alike to the law of God and contrary to those of nature'.[64]

Elsewhere in the *Risāla*, al-Kindī discusses the teachings in the Qur'an on peace and war more extensively than any other Eastern Christian writer. Though the work is often characterised as hostile towards Islam, the author does not present the long list of commands to fight and kill that are found in the Qur'an as part of his attack, but instead responds to a summons from his Muslim correspondent to 'smite men with the edge of the sword'[65] by quoting verses from the Qur'an that command or recommend good treatment of non-Muslims (Q 3:104; 2:272; 10:99-100a, 108-9; 11:118-19a).[66] He is trying to show that these verses contradict the violent summons of his correspondent and, he writes, the conduct of Muḥammad. In this remarkable passage, he pleads for better treatment of Eastern Christians, 'the saints of God, a people who had no defence except in His name, who kept His laws and humbled their hearts before Him, believing in the Messiah and truly reverencing Him, men who had been led into the truth so that their faces shone'.[67] He continues to quote from the Qur'an, starting with the famous Q 2:256 ('no compulsion in religion') and ending with Q 29:46 ('Do not dispute with the People of the Book except with what is better') (also Q 3:20; 2:253b; 109:6).[68]

Platti suggests that here the author is making his Christian character ask his Muslim interlocutor to drive the theory of abrogation in the opposite direction from Muslim dogma: that they let peaceful verses like 'no compulsion in religion' abrogate the violent verses.[69] He knows the Qur'an well enough to be familiar with the commands to fight and kill (he quotes from Q 9:29, the *jizya* verse). He says he has heard Jews say that the Qur'an is self-contradictory, but declines to say this himself. He is straightforward in his disapproval of the violence of Muḥammad as described in Muslim tradition, and he freely recommends the conduct and teachings of Jesus about responding to conflict. However, he chooses to highlight the peaceful verses in the Qur'an.

---

64 Tien, 'Apology of al-Kindi', pp. 449-52.
65 Tien, 'Apology of al-Kindi', pp. 391, 478.
66 Tien, 'Apology of al-Kindi', p. 478.
67 Tien, 'Apology of al-Kindi', p. 479.
68 Tien, 'Apology of al-Kindi', p. 479.
69 Platti, ''Abd al-Masīḥ al-Kindī', p. 69.

The Christian character's response here to his Muslim correspondent's summons to 'wage war in the way of Allāh'[70] indicates a possible distinguishing feature of Eastern Christian engagement with the Qur'an. All told, he evaluates the 'law' that he finds in Qur'an and *sunna*, challenges his opponent to favour peaceful verses over violent, and provides a striking contrast in the life and teachings of Jesus.[71] This is significant because the part of the Eastern Church that had lived under Sasanian dominance prior to Islam had had no experience of combining the Christian faith with political power and force.

Intriguingly, Western scholars by and large do not seem to have given due acknowledgement to this important material in the *Risāla*. Samir Khalil Samir, however, points out the theme of non-violence in *Fī tathlīth Allāh al-wāḥid*,[72] which 'is almost entirely lacking' in the first translation of the document made by Margaret Gibson.[73] The work here portrays the Apostles of Christ as weak and poor and having no authority. 'They did not fight anybody, and they did not force the people [...]', Samir translates, suggesting that the text makes 'a discrete allusion as to how, right from their birth, Christianity and Islam spread: Christianity in a non-violent manner, while Islam in a violent way'. Samir also finds in the second part of the document 'a clear defence of non-violence in religious matters', adding that this theme would become very important in later Arab Christian apologetics.[74] To what extent, one wonders, in a document which quotes the Qur'an sparingly but uses qur'anic language to explain Christian meanings, could this theme be a reaction to qur'anic teachings about fighting?

Responding to Islamic claims for the Qur'an

The 'qualifications' of Muḥammad also depended on the status of the Qur'an. While they accuse the Bible of falsification or corruption, Muslims who feature in dialogues written by Christians are portrayed as confident in their claims for the Qur'an. While the questions raised in the Qur'an about Muḥammad performing miracles do not evoke examples

---

70 Tien, 'Apology of al-Kindi', p. 391.

71 Tien, 'Apology of al-Kindī', pp. 481, 503-14.

72 Samir, 'Earliest Arab apology, pp. 102-4.

73 Samir, 'Earliest Arab apology', p. 101. See Gibson, *An Arabic version of the Acts of the Apostles*, p. 15.

74 Samir, 'Earliest Arab apology', pp. 102-4.

of miracles from him, with time Muslims began to claim that the Qur'an itself is a miracle.

Eastern Christian ways of evaluating the Qur'an include John of Damascus's comment that its contents are merely 'worthy of laughter',[75] and comprise nothing more than 'idle tales'.[76] Likewise, when the Patriarch Timothy is asked by al-Mahdī, 'Do you not believe that our book was given by God?', he replies indirectly that when God wished to abrogate the Mosaic law He confirmed by the signs and miracles of the Messiah and his Apostles that the words of the Gospel were from Him, 'but your book has not been confirmed by a single sign or miracle. Since signs and miracles are proofs of the will of God, the conclusion drawn from their absence in your book is well known to your majesty.'[77]

The Muslim claim of the Qur'an's inimitability (*iʿjāz*) seems to have received its formal articulation in the third and fourth centuries of the Islamic era, when it was connected with a series of 'challenge' (*taḥaddī*) verses in the Qur'an. Al-Kindī's *Risāla* actually quotes two of these verses, which may be represented by Q 2:23, 'If you are in doubt about what we have sent down on our servant, then bring a *sūra* like it, and call your witnesses, other than Allāh, if you are truthful' (also Q 17:88; cf. 10:38; 11:13; 28:49; 52:34).[78] What follows is a remarkable response to this challenge.[79]

As Andrew Rippin observes about this, the Muslim claim about the Qur'an's inimitability is a dogmatic argument that operates 'within the presuppositions of Islam alone'.[80] The advantage of the author of the *Risāla* was that he (assuming he speaks personally through the character of al-Kindī) had an excellent mother-tongue knowledge of Arabic[81] and was also 'versed in textual criticism'.[82] He thus addresses the overall form of the Qur'an, showing what seems to be an intimate familiarity with the text and confidently appealing to the same knowledge in his Muslim correspondent.[83] On the basis of this, he asserts that the Qur'an 'is loosely

75 Sahas, *John of Damascus*, pp. 133, 141.

76 Sahas, *John of Damascus*, pp. 137, 141.

77 Mingana, 'Apology of Timothy', p. 173.

78 Tien, 'Apology of al-Kindi', pp. 452-3.

79 Tien, 'Apology of al-Kindi', pp. 452-70. Muir, *Apology of al-Kindi*, pp. 22-33.

80 A. Rippin, *Muslims. Their religious beliefs and practices*, London, 2001[2], p. 34.

81 Tien, 'Apology of al-Kindi', pp. 463, 489. See also Clare Wilde's comparison of al-Kindī's ability with that of Theodore Abū Qurrā and other Christian Arabic writers, 'Is there room for corruption in the "books" of God?', in D. Thomas (ed.), *The Bible in Arab Christianity*, Leiden, 2007, 225-40, pp. 235-6.

82 Tien, 'Apology of al-Kindi', p. 460.

83 Tien, 'Apology of al-Kindi', pp. 458-9.

put together often without any meaning, and that again and again it contradicts itself'.[84]

The *Risāla* also deals with the Muslim claim that the vocabulary of the Qur'an is especially rich. The Christian notes that every nation considers its own language rich and beautiful, and then he questions the presence of the many foreign words in the Qur'an. If Arabic is such a special language, he asks, why does the Qur'an 'borrow' words from other languages when Arabic equivalents are available and used in other Arabic writings?[85] He quotes Q 12:2, 'We have sent it down as an Arabic Qur'an' (one in a series of verses that draw attention to the Arabic nature of the recitation; also Q 20:113; 39:28; 41:3; 43:3), evidently to query this special claim for Arabic. He also compares the qur'anic style unfavourably with the great pre-Islamic Arab poets, saying the Qur'an 'is broken in its style, hybrid in its diction and, while high-sounding, often destitute of meaning'.[86] Examining this argument, Rippin observes, 'The literary state of the Qur'ān is used against the Muslims by al-Kindī as proof of its non-divine origin.'[87]

'What ignorance could be more dense than his who appeals to such a book as evidence and proof that its author was a prophet sent by God?'[88] Al-Kindī's question to his correspondent may well be seen as rude and insensitive by today's standards of interfaith dialogue. But for the author and the church he represented the stakes were high. Those who ruled over them were claiming that the Qur'an was a miracle of language, and on that basis asserting the divine origin of the book, the prophethood of Muḥammad, and the truth of Islam. From a distance of centuries, the inimitability argument 'is difficult, if not impossible, to evaluate, due to the lack of contemporaneous profane literature by which the rhetorical accomplishment of the Qur'ān can actually be assessed'.[89] Who today is as close to the claim as was this Christian author? Sandra Keating suggests that the strength of the arguments of al-Kindī and perhaps other Eastern Christians may be reflected in Muslim laws that banned Christians from owning a Qur'an or teaching it to their children. 'Limited

84 Tien, 'Apology of al-Kindi', p. 459.

85 Tien, 'Apology of al-Kindi', pp. 460-1; S.T. Keating, 'Manipulation of the Qur'an in the epistolary exchange between al-Hāshimī and al-Kindī', in I.M. Beaumont (ed.), *Arab Christians and the Qur'an from the origins of Islam to the medieval period*, Leiden, 2018, 50-65, p. 62.

86 Tien, 'Apology of al-Kindi', p. 461.

87 Rippin, *Muslims*, p. 33.

88 Tien, 'Apology of al-Kindi', p. 460.

89 Rippin, *Muslims*, p. 34.

access to the text assured that non-believers could not use it to undermine settled teachings.'[90]

On the development of the Qur'an

Another apparently unique contribution to Eastern Christian engagement with the Qur'an is the section of the *Risāla* on the origin and history of the Qur'an.[91] Griffith describes this passage as 'one of the earliest testimonies to the process of the Qur'ān's canonization'.[92] The *Risāla* claims to its Muslim correspondent, 'We have said nothing more than your own writings allow. We have confirmed nothing on our authority which is not confirmed by the traditions of your own scholars, men of weight among you.'[93] If dispassionate academic scholars can describe the traditional Muslim collection and canonisation stories as 'a mass of confusions, contradictions and inconsistencies',[94] and as transparently polemical,[95] why should an Arab Christian not discuss the traditions as he has heard them from Muslims in the earliest centuries of Islam?

The discussion in the *Risāla* features the same cast of characters that one meets in the Muslim traditions: Abū Bakr, ʿAlī, Ibn Masʿūd, Ubayy ibn Kaʿb, ʿUthmān, Zayd ibn Thābit, Ibn ʿAbbās, ʿUmar. The author refers to the enmities between the first caliphs and queries the impact of their conflicts on the formation of the Qur'an.[96] He also refers to a number of characters who seem to appear less frequently in some modern non-Muslim summaries of the collection stories, among them Ḥajjāj ibn Yūsuf (d. 714), governor of Iraq under the Umayyad Caliph ʿAbd al-Malik. The *Risāla* describes Ḥajjāj as gathering up all copies of the Qur'an that he could find, revising the text and deleting material, sending copies of the revised text to six cities in the Arab empire, then destroying all the

---

90 Keating, 'Manipulation of the Qur'an', p. 63.

91 Tien, 'Apology of al-Kindi', pp. 452-70; Muir, *Apology of al-Kindi*, pp. 22-9.

92 Griffith, 'Prophet Muhammad, his scripture and his message', p. 144.

93 Tien, 'Apology of al-Kindi', p. 459; Muir, *Apology of al-Kindi*, p. 29.

94 J. Burton, *The collection of the Qur'an*, Cambridge, 1977, p. 140.

95 Wansbrough, *Sectarian milieu*, p. 57. See also J. Wansbrough, *Quranic studies. Sources and methods of scriptural interpretation*, Oxford, 1977, p. 50.

96 For comments by academic scholars who have recently pursued this and similar questions, see, for example, G. Böwering, art. 'Chronology and the Qur'ān', in *EQ*; F.E. Peters, *The voice, the word, the books. The sacred scriptures of the Jews, Christians and Muslims*, Princeton NJ, 2007, p. 148; L.I. Conrad, 'Qur'ānic studies. A historian's perspective', in M. Kropp (ed.), *Results of contemporary research on the Qur'an. The question of a historico-critical text*, Würzburg, 2007, 9-15, p. 12; C.F. Robinson, *'Abd al-Malik*, Oxford, 2005, p. 103.

earlier copies.[97] The *Risāla* is not alone in narrating this episode. Two other Eastern Christian works that make reference to the role of Ḥajjāj ibn Yūsuf in the collection of the Qur'an are the *Dispute of the monk Ibrāhīm al-Ṭabarānī*[98] and the correspondence between Leo III and 'Umar ibn 'Abd al-'Azīz.[99] Scholars who have continued to discuss the Ḥajjāj episode in recent decades include François Déroche,[100] Alfred-Louis de Prémare[101] and Omar Hamdan.[102] Al-Kindī's discussion of the history of the development of the Qur'an has been respectfully noted by scholars of the emergence of Islam and especially of qur'anic studies for more than a hundred years: Paul Casanova, Alphonse Mingana, Arthur Jeffery, John Wansbrough, Harald Motzki, Chase Robinson, Stephen Shoemaker, Nicolai Sinai.[103] Such scholars seem willing to consider evidence from any early sources, however characterised by others.

The *Risāla* suggests that inconsistencies arose in the Qur'an between material that came from different sources. It discusses variant readings between manuscripts, disagreements about the inclusion of certain short suras and the length of longer suras, and traditions about missing verses.[104] Such matters were openly and widely discussed in Muslim works at least until the *Al-itqān fī 'ulūm al-Qur'ān* of al-Suyūṭī (d. 1505). The *Risāla* uses these discussions to turn the Muslim accusation of biblical falsification back upon the Qur'an.[105] In so doing, it makes the point that the text of the Qur'an is incomplete and unreliable. Al-Kindī's conclusion is that 'there is no ground to have faith in the text transmitted in his [Muḥammad's] days'.[106]

---

97 Tien, 'Apology of al-Kindi', p. 459; Muir, *Apology of al-Kindi*, p. 28.

98 K. Vollers, 'Das Religionsgespräch von Jerusalem (um 800 D); aus dem arabischen übersetzt', *Zeitschrift für Kirchengeschichte* 29 (1908) 29-71, 197-221, p. 48.

99 Jeffery, 'Ghevond's text', pp. 297-9, and p. 298 n. 48 for Arthur Jeffery's accompanying note on Ḥajjāj and several Muslim sources for this story.

100 F. Déroche, *Qur'ans of the Umayyads*, Leiden, 2014, p. 72.

101 A.-L. de Prémare, ''Abd al-Malik b. Marwān et le processus de constitution du Coran', in K.-H. Ohlig and G.-R. Puin (eds), *Die dunklen Anfänge*, Berlin, 2007, 178-210.

102 O. Hamdan, 'The second maṣāḥif project. A step towards the canonization of the qur'anic text', in A. Neuwirth, N. Sinai and M. Marx (eds), *The Qur'ān in context. Historical and literary investigations into the qur'ānic milieu*, Leiden, 2010, 794-835.

103 G. Nickel, 'Scholarly reception of Alphonse Mingana's "The transmission of the Ḳur'ān". A centenary perspective', in D. Pratt et al. (eds), *The character of Christian-Muslim encounter*, Leiden, 2015, 343-64, pp. 347, 349, 353, 358, 361. See also Wilde, 'Is there room for corruption?', p. 232.

104 Tien, 'Apology of al-Kindi', pp. 455-60; Muir, *Apology of al-Kindi*, pp. 25-8. Emilio Platti enumerates these helpfully in ''Abd al-Masīḥ al-Kindī', pp. 78-82.

105 Keating, 'Manipulation of the Qur'an', pp. 54, 64.

106 Platti, ''Abd al-Masīḥ al-Kindī', p. 81.

Characterisations of the legacy

Some of the scholarship on the literary legacy of Eastern Christianity has not only provided helpful description of the writings and their authors but has also characterised the writings in ways that would either recommend or discourage study of them.

When Griffith asked why scholars have paid so little attention to the vigorous engagement with the Qur'an in al-Kindī's *Risāla*, he suggested, 'Perhaps the polemical character of the text makes it suspect as an historical document.'[107] Actually, al-Kindī's discussion of the Qur'an has received the attention of key scholars of the history of the Qur'an's development for more than a hundred years, as shown above. But Griffith's suggested reason for neglect by others carries within it a challenge to scholars of Christian-Muslim relations. Arthur Jeffery also wrote in 1944 that al-Kindī's statements about the involvement of Ḥajjāj ibn Yūsuf in the collection of the Qur'an have 'been looked at askance as a piece of Christian polemic', but then went on to list a variety of early Muslim sources that tell the same story.[108] If this is true, why should scholars neglect 'one of the earliest testimonies to the process of the Qur'an's canonization'[109] because of a negative epithet?

Rippin has traced a comparable tendency in the academic study of the Qur'an and early Muslim writings, describing an 'irenic approach' in the discipline that aims towards 'the greater appreciation of Islamic religiousness and the fostering of a new attitude towards it'. He suggests this approach 'has led to the unfortunate result of a reluctance on the part of many scholars to follow all the way through with their insights and results'.[110] Rippin was concerned with what he saw as the mixing of intellectual history with sociology. To what extent has the legacy of Eastern Christian engagement with the Qur'an been characterised according to the changing philosophical currents in interfaith relations?

A famous example of disparate characterisations of Eastern Christian engagement is the framing of the answer of Timothy I to the Caliph al-Mahdī's question in the course of their debate: 'What do you say about

107 Griffith, 'Prophet Muhammad, his scripture and his message', p. 144.

108 Jeffery, 'Ghevond's text,' p. 298 n. 48.

109 Griffith, 'Prophet Muhammad, his scripture and his message', p. 144.

110 A. Rippin, 'Literary analysis of *Qur'ān, tafsīr,* and *sīra.* The methodologies of John Wansbrough', in R.C. Martin (ed.), *Approaches to Islam in religious studies*, Tucson AZ, 1985, 151-63, p. 159.

Muḥammad?'[111] David Kerr used Timothy's answer to make a case for accepting the Muslim claim that Muḥammad was a prophet of God. He acknowledged the ambiguity of Timothy's words but argued that they could still be used in 'the modern search for irenic dialogue between Christianity and Islam'.[112] By contrast, Samir concludes from a careful study of the passage in the Arabic recension of the debate and its context that Timothy refuses to answer the question of Muḥammad's prophethood positively.[113] 'Some Christian scholars have interpreted [Timothy's answer] as a recognition of the prophethood of Muḥammad [...] [T]he meaning which is sometimes derived today from Timothy's beautiful words *salaka fī sabīl al-anbiyā'* ['he – Muḥammad – walked in the way of the prophets'] has nothing to do with Timothy's own interpretation.'[114]

Appearances are not always what they seem. Characterisations of Eastern Christian works based on tone and style may lead to false evaluation. David Thomas writes insightfully about the approach of Paul of Antioch's 'Letter to a Muslim friend', which generally agrees with the content of the Qur'an and even offers the possibility that Muḥammad was sent by God. Though outwardly peaceful, friendly and reasonable, the work 'proves more provocative than any direct attack'.[115] 'Paul's *Letter* can only have outraged Muslims by the implicitly arrogant manner in which it shuts out any alternatives to the views it states', Thomas suggests.[116] The letter and its revised and extended version in the 'Letter from the people of Cyprus' drew 'some of the most substantial and intransigent refutations ever produced by Muslim authors',[117] including al-Qarāfī (d. 1285),[118] Ibn Taymiyya (d. 1328)[119] and Ibn Abī Ṭālib al-Dimashqī (d. 1327).[120] We know of no formal Muslim responses to al-Kindī's *Risāla*, but is it possible

111 Mingana, 'Apology of Timothy', p. 197.

112 D.A. Kerr, '"He walked in the path of the prophets". Toward Christian theological recognition of the prophethood of Muhammad', in Y.Y. Haddad and W.Z. Haddad (eds), *Christian-Muslim Encounters*, Gainesville FL, 1995, 426-46, p. 426.

113 S.K. Samir, 'The Prophet Muḥammad as seen by Timothy I and other Arab Christian authors', in D. Thomas (ed.), *Syrian Christians under Islam*, Leiden, 2001, 75-106, p. 96.

114 Samir, 'Prophet Muḥammad', pp. 96, 105.

115 Thomas, 'Paul of Antioch's *Letter*', p. 205.

116 Thomas, 'Paul of Antioch's *Letter*', p. 211.

117 D. Thomas, '*Risāla ilā baʿḍ aṣdiqā'ihi alladhīna bi-Ṣaydā min al-Muslimīn*', in *CMR* 4, 79-82.

118 M. El Kaisy-Friemuth, 'Al-Qarāfī', in *CMR* 4, 582-7.

119 J. Hoover, 'Ibn Taymiyya', in *CMR* 4, 824-78, and J. Hoover, 'The correct answer to those who have changed the religion of Christ', in *CMR* 4, 834-44.

120 D. Thomas, 'Ibn Abī Ṭālib al-Dimashqī', in *CMR* 4, 798-801.

that the author knew something about 'friendly strife' in interfaith conversation that does not seem apparent on the surface?

Regarding al-Kindī's *Risāla*, in recent years a number of scholars have been drawing attention to the value of the work. Platti notes that the author discussed Muslim traditions about the collection and canonisation of the Qur'an prior to the writing down of these traditions by Muslim authors in the great works of Hadith; therefore, he asserts, the author's early material 'should be included in any research on the collection of the Qur'an'.[121] Keating remarks on the extensive and accurate knowledge of the Qur'an demonstrated in the *Risāla*, 'rarely found in Christian writings from this period, even when it may be hinted at'.[122] Clare Wilde queries the significance of quotations from the Qur'an in early Christian Arab works such as this for the history of the development of the text of the Qur'an.[123] Wilde also gazes provocatively in the direction of Eastern Christianity: 'Rather than dismissing al-Kindī's text as unfit for insight into the *iʿjāz al-Qur'ān* debate due to its patronizing and polemical tone, Islamicists may want to examine the Arabness of his defense of Christianity more closely – especially in the light of other contemporary polemics within the Islamic world.'[124]

Like the erection of the Dome of the Rock upon the Temple Mount in sight of a Christian Jerusalem, the Qur'an with its affirmations, denials and insistent claims confronted the Christian communities of the Middle East with overwhelming force and presence. Beautiful in its standardisation of a new language, though a language foreign to most Christians, the Qur'an's greatest challenges came from the contents between the covers. Those challenges penetrated into the deepest convictions of the vanquished communities and drew out of those who dared many remarkable, and often courageous, expressions.

The legacy of Eastern Christianity's engagement with the Qur'an, as seen through surviving documents, is a treasure for the entire global Church, especially Christians who relate on a daily basis to Muslims in Muslim-majority societies. 'For the Arab Christian writers were honest with themselves and with their religion', writes Samir.[125] Christians in

121 Platti, "Abd al-Masīḥ al-Kindī', p. 82, cf. pp. 71-7.

122 Keating, 'Manipulation of the Qur'an', p. 56.

123 C. Wilde, 'Early Christian Arabic texts. Evidence for non-ʿUthmānic Qurʾān codices, or early approaches to the Qurʾān?', in G.S. Reynolds (ed.), *New perspectives on the Qurʾān. The Qurʾān in its historical context* 2, London, 2011, 358-71, pp. 362-3.

124 Wilde, 'Is there room for corruption?', p. 237.

125 Samir, 'Prophet Muḥammad', p. 106.

Muslim contexts will probably value the legacy differently from Western scholars who have made commitments to various current philosophies of religious difference. Most regions of Latin Christianity have never experienced the kinds of circumstances that produced the Eastern Christian writings. We therefore read these writings with sympathetic and grateful appreciation.

Chapter 12
The crusades to the eastern Mediterranean, 1095-1291

Nicholas Morton

The month of October 1242 was a rare moment for the Crusader Kingdom of Jerusalem; it was on the advance. For decades, it had played the weaker party to the Ayyubid Muslim territories lying to the east and south, and was capable of taking the offensive only with the assistance of massive crusader reinforcements from western Christendom. Recently, however, it had been able to flex its muscles and it was with this renewed strength that the Franks seized the town of Nablus. The Coptic author Yūḥannā ibn Wahb explains what happened next. The Frankish forces swiftly took control of the town, then assembled its inhabitants and divided Christians from Muslims, before killing or imprisoning all non-Christians.[1]

Twenty-one years later, in April 1263, the Mamluk Sultan Baybars staged one of his many incursions against the Kingdom of Jerusalem. All the Crusader states were by this time in brisk decline, brought about by the Mamluks' incessant incursions. On this occasion, as a deliberate act of hostility towards his Christian opponents, he ordered the destruction of the Church of the Annunciation in Nazareth, a site of fundamental importance to Christianity.[2] The recollection of such stories immediately evokes some of the darkest and best-known judgements made about the wars of the crusading period: the idea that cumulatively they represented a bitter and cruel contest between two diametrically opposed religions, each bent on the other's destruction. Even so, such tales need to be balanced with other reports.

In 1111, the Antiochene ruler Tancred decided that he could no longer maintain his siege on the Arab town of Shaizar. He then attempted to withdraw his forces, but immediately came under heavy attack. At that

---

[1] Yūḥannā ibn Wahb, *History of the patriarchs of the Egyptian Church*, ed. A. Khater and O.H.E. Burmester, vol. 4, pt 2, Cairo, 1974, pp. 268-9; see S. Moawad, 'Yūḥannā ibn Wahb', in *CMR* 4, 316-19, pp. 318-19.

[2] D. Pringle, *The churches of the Crusader Kingdom of Jerusalem. A corpus*, vol. 2, Cambridge, 1998, p. 121; Ibn al-Furāt, *Ayyubids, Mamlukes and Crusaders. Selections from the* Tārīkh al-duwal wa'l-mulūk, trans. U. Lyons and M.C. Lyons, Cambridge, 1971, vol. 2, p. 56.

moment, an unnamed warrior stepped out from the Christian ranks and single-handedly protected the Christian column, holding his enemies at bay so that the army could escape. Soon afterwards, this same warrior set off to Shaizar to converse with his erstwhile enemies and to compare notes about their martial skills. He arrived at Shaizar bearing a letter of introduction and clearly expected to receive his former foes' hospitality and welcome. The rulers of Shaizar were probably rather surprised by his arrival but, nonetheless, they had been impressed by his valour and it seems they received him warmly.[3]

In 1211, the German pilgrim Wilbrand of Oldenburg landed at the Crusader city of Acre and then began to make his way north on an embassage for his master, the Holy Roman Emperor Otto IV (r. 1209-15). En route, he visited the Templar stronghold of Tartus. Within the town was the famous Church of St Mary the Virgin, where Wilbrand not only noted the presence of Muslim worshippers, but even observed that the Virgin granted miracles to both Christians and Muslims.[4]

These four episodes have been plucked out from among the hundreds of reports arising from the history of the Crusader states on the Levantine mainland (1097-1291). As should already be clear, such tales are far from consistent in the way they report relations between Christians and Muslims, and thus reflect the diversity of contemporary interactions. This chapter offers a survey of the main features of Christian-Islamic relations in this period. It seeks to reveal the complexity of cross-cultural interactions whilst demonstrating how war, faith, trade and realpolitik could create some fascinating and – at times – bizarre relationships across ethnic and religious boundaries.

As a first step, it is necessary to begin with two important predicates, which will be discussed over the next few pages. The first is to recognise the sheer diversity of the ethnic and religious groups spread across the Middle East region. The second is to show that each of these communities had a complex range of objectives, alliances, enmities and interests that were defined by many factors – not simply their religious identity – creating an intricate web of relationships. Both these points became clear to the First Crusaders during their journey to Jerusalem, and they encountered a huge variety of societies en

[3] Usāma ibn Munqidh, *The book of contemplation. Islam and the crusades*, trans. P.M. Cobb, London, 2008, pp. 80-1; see A. Mallett, 'Usāma ibn Munqidh', in *CMR* 3, 764-8.

[4] Wilbrand of Oldenburg, 'Peregrinatio', in J.C. Laurent (ed.), *Peregrinatores medii aevi quatuor*, Leipzig, 1864, 169-70.

route. The first major empire they traversed was Byzantium. The Greeks had repeatedly appealed for Frankish aid in recent years, seeking assistance against the Seljuk Turks.[5] The Byzantines were fellow Christians (even if they were considered schismatics), and yet their agenda differed significantly from that of the incoming Franks, whom they tended to view deprecatingly as representatives of an inferior culture, or even as barbarians. Some crusaders, for their part, found the Byzantines patronising, effeminate and treacherous.[6] Both during and after the First Crusade, there were moments of cooperation between these two peoples, but their shared faith in no way guaranteed a common sense of purpose. At times, the disputes between Franks and Greeks could escalate to the point where they sought Turkish allies to assist them in their quarrelling; in 1110, for example, the Muslim historian Ibn al-Athīr reported that the Emperor Alexius I Comnenus (r. 1081-1118) sent an envoy to the Turkish sultan inciting him to fight against the Franks.[7]

Having crossed Byzantine territory, the First Crusaders then marched south into Anatolia, towards the great city of Antioch. Enroute they fought off the Turks, whose mounted archers exacted a heavy toll on the Franks' marching columns. During this time, the Anatolian Turks, like their cousins in the Seljuk Sultanate, were part-way through a process of cultural transition. Around the turn of the first millennium, various conglomerations of Turkic tribes had invaded and then conquered the Near Eastern Islamic world, ultimately seizing Baghdad in 1055. They then set up a sultanate led by the Seljuk family, assuming many of the traditions common to the Persian societies they now ruled. Where the Turks had originally been largely shamanistic in their spirituality, they steadily began to adopt an Islamic identity and faith. Some Turkish communities in western Anatolia likewise adopted some aspects of Byzantine Christian practices and beliefs.[8] In this way, the Turks' former steppe traditions and shamanistic beliefs were in the process of morphing and merging with those of the peoples they now ruled. For the most part, their long-term trajectory was one of steady Islamisation, but at the time of the First

5 See P. Frankopan, *The First Crusade. The call from the east*, London, 2012, pp. 57-100.

6 See for example: Odo of Deuil, *De profectione Ludovici in Orientem. The journey of Louis VII to the east*, ed. V.G. Berry, New York, 1948, pp. 10, 56, 88; Marino Sanudo Torsello, *The book of the secrets of the faithful of the cross. Liber secretorum fidelium crucis*, trans. P. Lock, Farnham, 2011, p. 301.

7 Ibn al-Athīr, *The chronicle of Ibn al-Athir for the crusading period from* al-Kamil fi'l-ta'rikh, part 1, trans. D.S. Richards, Aldershot, 2006, p. 155.

8 A.D. Beihammer, *Byzantium and the emergence of Muslim-Turkish Anatolia, ca. 1040-1130*, Abingdon, 2017, pp. 265-303.

Crusade many Turks retained the beliefs and practices of their forefathers. The crusade chronicle *Gesta Francorum* (c. 1099) reports the Turks burying their dead with weapons and grave goods – a steppe practice – while the later Antiochene author Walter the Chancellor (d. after 1122) likewise describes Turkish commanders scalping their opponents, practising astrology, and turning defeated foes' heads into drinking cups.[9] Robert the Monk (d. c. 1122) and Guibert of Nogent (d. c. 1125), among others, report them tying opponents to posts and shooting them with arrows, actions that stress the centrality of symbols connected to archery, held as sacred to nomadic Turkic peoples.[10] In this way, the Turks – the crusaders' primary opponent – were hardly the embodiment of Islamic culture; some would have been new converts, others would only have been lightly touched by this faith, whose former leaders they had overthrown.

As the crusaders crossed the Taurus and Amanus mountain ranges, moving towards Antioch and Syria, they entered a landscape populated in large part by a mixture of Arab Muslims (Sunnī and Shīʿa, as well as several minority groups) and Eastern Christians (Melkite, Jacobite and Armenian). Each of these peoples – whether Christian or Muslim – responded differently to their advance. For some Muslim Arabs, the chaos of the Frankish incursion represented an opportunity to rid themselves of their Turkish yoke and, both during the crusade and in later decades, several of the major Arab tribes started to offer resistance to their Turkish masters. These Arab tribes had formerly ruled Syria and the Jazira. They had little reason to love their Turkish overlords, who had seized the region only a couple of decades previously. The Banū Kilāb clan raided Aleppan territory during the crusade. Subsequently, two other leading Arab dynasties – the Banū ʿUqayl and later the Banū Mazyad – at various times worked with the Franks against the region's Turkish warlords.[11] At other times they fought against them. Many other leading Arab families, including the Banū Munqidh of Shaizar, as well

---

[9] R.M.T. Hill (ed.), *Gesta Francorum. The deeds of the Franks and other pilgrims to Jerusalem*, Oxford, 1962, p. 42; see M. Bull, '*Gesta Francorum*', in *CMR* 3, 249-56. Walter the Chancellor, *Bella Antiochena*, ed. H. Hagenmeyer, Innsbruck, 1896, pp. 66, 67, 91, 108-9; S.B. Edgington, 'Walter the Chancellor', in *CMR* 3, 379-82.

[10] D. Kempf and M. Bull (eds), *The Historia Iherosolimitana of Robert the Monk*, Woodbridge, 2013, p. 5; see M. Bull, 'Robert the Monk', in *CMR* 3, 312-17. Guibert de Nogent, *Dei Gesta per Francos*, ed. R. Huygens, Turnhout, 1996, p. 350; see J. Tolan, 'Guibert of Nogent', in *CMR* 3, 329-34.

[11] N. Morton and J. France, 'Arab Muslim reactions to Turkish authority in northern Syria, 1085-1128', in J. France (ed.), *Warfare, crusade and conquest in the Middle Ages*, Aldershot, 2014, 1-38.

as other leaders governing cities along the Levantine coast, assumed a position of neutrality, offering neither support nor sustained resistance to the advancing First crusaders.[12]

The region's Christian communities likewise adopted a variety of postures towards the crusaders. The Armenian author Matthew of Edessa effectively captured his people's reaction in his *Chronicle*. Initially, he depicted the Franks as long-anticipated saviours, liberating the Armenian people and, by so doing, fulfilling an important eschatological role in the advance of the end-times. Over time, however, this aspirational perspective wore thin as the cold reality of crusader conquest and rule settled in – reflected in the later chapters of the *Chronicle*[13] – yet many Armenians, both during the crusade and afterwards, worked closely with the Franks.[14]

As the crusaders made their final approach to Jerusalem, they came into ever-closer contact with the Egyptian Fatimids. This Shīʿī dynasty, ruling the diverse population of the Nile Delta, had been in negotiations with the Franks from an early stage in the crusade.[15] They, too, saw the Turks as a major threat, having defeated a Turkish invasion into the Delta as recently as 1077. In the intervening years, both the Turks and the Fatimids had fought over the Jerusalem region and, while the crusaders were besieging Antioch in 1098, the Fatimids seized the opportunity to take the holy city from the Turks. Both sides perceived the value of cooperative action against the Turks and were prepared to make substantial concessions to bring this about. The First Crusade chronicler, Raymond of Aguilers (d. after 1101), explains that the crusaders were willing to join forces with the Fatimids to reconquer their lost territories, provided that they themselves received Jerusalem in return. After long drawn-out negotiations, however, these talks collapsed and the crusaders moved immediately to besiege Jerusalem.[16]

Alongside these major political powers, the Franks encountered many other smaller groups, both during the crusade and afterwards. In

---

12 Raymond of Aguilers, *Le 'Liber' de Raymond d'Aguilers*, ed. J. Hill and L. Hill, Paris, 1969, pp. 103, 107, 111, 125; see B. Packard, 'Raymond of Aguilers', in *CMR* 3, 297-300.

13 T.L. Andrews, *Mattʿēos Uṙhayecʿi and his Chronicle. History as apocalypse in a crossroads of cultures*, Leiden, 2017; see T.L. Andrews, 'Matthew of Edessa', in *CMR* 3, 444-50.

14 For discussion on this theme, see C. MacEvitt, *The crusades and the Christian world of the East. Rough tolerance*, Philadelphia PA, 2008.

15 N. Morton, *Encountering Islam on the First Crusade*, Cambridge, 2016, pp. 141-7.

16 *Le 'Liber' de Raymond d'Aguilers*, pp. 109-10.

Anatolia they met the Paulicians, a heretical Christian group.[17] Likewise, following the First Crusade, the newly-founded territories of the Crusader states – Edessa, Antioch, Jerusalem and Tripoli – included many Jewish communities along with other peoples, such as the Assassins, the Druze and the Samaritans.[18] The Kingdom of Jerusalem also struck up a strong accord with many Bedouin tribes, whose loyalties were often mercurial but who nonetheless fought alongside the Franks during many of their campaigns. As should already be clear, reviewing this highly diverse ethnic and religious map, any simplistic notion of a monolithic 'Christianity' fighting a monolithic 'Islam' quickly falls apart.

In later years, political or economic expediency frequently found the Franks fighting side by side with non-Christian warriors, and in their early years the Crusader states were often allied with Arab tribes wishing to make common cause against the Turks. One Arab community travelled from as far afield as Basra in Iraq to the principality of Antioch seeking shelter from the Turks.[19] There were also moments, both during the crusade and afterwards, when Turkish renegades and fugitives sought refuge with Frankish leaders. For example, two separate Turkish governors of Azaz sought aid from the Franks in 1098 and also sometime in the years 1107-8.[20] For their part, some Frankish warriors took service under Muslim rulers, often as mercenaries. Instances of such recruitment can be found throughout the crusading period, but perhaps most conspicuously in 13th-century Seljuk Anatolia. The forces of Sultan Kaykhusraw II of Rūm (r. 1237-46) at the crucial battle of Kose Dagh against the Mongols in 1243 are said to have included 2,000 Frankish warriors led by two captains, the Cypriot John of Liminata and the Venetian Boniface of Molini.[21]

With the rise of the Crusader states in the early 12th century, the causes of conflict in the Middle East were as diverse as its many different

---

17 Z. Pogossian, 'The frontier existence of the Paulician heretics', in K. Szende and M. Sebők (eds), *Annual of medieval studies at CEU*, vol. 6, Budapest, 2000, 203-6.

18 For discussion on the Franks' relations with local Jewish populations, see J. Prawer, *The history of the Jews in the Latin Kingdom of Jerusalem*, Oxford, 1988.

19 Matthew of Edessa, *Armenia and the crusades, tenth to twelfth centuries. The Chronicle of Matthew of Edessa*, trans. A.E. Dostourian, New York, 1993, p. 202.

20 *Le 'Liber' de Raymond d'Aguilers*, pp. 88-9; Albert of Aachen, *Historia Ierosolimitana. History of the journey to Jerusalem*, ed. S. Edgington, Oxford, 2007, pp. 344-54; Kamāl al-Dīn, 'Extraits de la Chronique d'Alep', *Recueil des historiens des croisades. Historiens orientaux*, vol. 3, Paris, 1884, 571-690, p. 595.

21 Marino Sanudo Torsello, *Book of the secrets of the faithful of the cross*, p. 375. For an earlier deployment of substantial Frankish forces by the Seljuks, see Bar Hebraeus, *The Chronography of Gregory Abû'l Faraj, the son of Aaron, the Hebrew physician commonly known as Bar Hebraeus*, ed. E.W. Wallis Budge, vol. 1, Oxford, 1932, p. 406.

communities. One major determinant of fighting and diplomacy was the political turmoil within the Seljuk sultanate's core lands in Iraq. Located on the fringes of the repeated civil wars fought over the rule of the sultanate, the Turkish warlords in Syria were divided in their loyalties between the various political factions vying for supremacy. They were also determined to maintain their independence in the face of sporadic attempts by the current Seljuk sultan to bring them more directly under his authority. These Syrian warlords were resolute in their efforts to resist the sultan's demands for submission, and these reached a climax in 1115, when the Turkish warlords Ilghazi of Mardin and Tughtakin of Damascus sided with the Crusader states against a Turkish army sent from the sultanate, Tughtakin even pursuing and slaughtering the survivors from the sultan's force after its defeat at the Battle of Tell Danith.[22] Their motivation was to deny the sultan any territorial foothold in Syria that might ultimately enable him to bring them to heel. These events represent only one example of the many agendas shaping the political and military ecosystem of the Middle East. Demands for holy war – both Christian calls for crusading and subsequently Muslim calls for jihad – represented only one strand within a highly complex mesh of ethnic, political, commercial and dynastic concerns. The willingness manifested by all sides to join forces with warriors from other faiths underlines the fact that religious antagonism was very far from being the sole determinant of conflict (even if such alliances were occasionally denounced by pious observers from all sides).[23]

Viewing this confused world from the Latin Christian perspective, the Franks were prepared to ally themselves with any faction in the name of political expediency. At various points in the 12th century, they fought alongside Turks, Eastern Christians, the Muslim Fatimids, and Christian Byzantines. One example of such collaboration took place in the 1160s, when Fatimid Egypt descended into civil war. In this conflict, both the Franks and the Syrian Turks under Nūr al-Dīn saw an opportunity to profit from the Fatimids' internal conflict, and they each supported opposing sides. In this environment, from the perspective of the Frankish-backed faction, the Kingdom of Jerusalem was both their ally and their major hope for victory, one Egyptian writer even making the astonishing claim about the Franks that, 'You stood up in support of

22 Albert of Aachen, *Historia Ierosolimitana*, p. 856.

23 See, for example, O. Latiff, *The cutting edge of the poet's sword. Muslim poetic responses to the crusades*, Leiden, 2018, p. 166.

the Prophet and his family, so God the Most Merciful owes you a reward for that.'[24]

There is little to suggest that such alliances posed any significant ethical problem for either faction. After all, the First Crusaders' goal was to retake Jerusalem, and reviewing the tens of legal charters produced by the crusaders during their preparations to depart for the East reaching Jerusalem is namechecked in almost every case as their main objective, while notions of fighting 'Saracens' were only occasionally referenced.[25] To this end, they were prepared to enter into alliance with anyone who might facilitate that goal and, on the crusade itself, they often avoided unnecessary conflict where possible, purposely side-stepping Damascus when selecting their route to Jerusalem because it was a Turkish centre of power.[26]

In a similar vein, the First Crusaders knew very little about either the Turks or Islam when they set out on campaign. The Turks had only recently arrived on their knowledge horizon and the crusaders' charters (produced at the outset of their campaign) speak only vaguely about fighting 'pagans' or occasionally 'Saracens' – never 'Turks'.[27] During the crusade itself, these peoples necessarily came into closer contact, but while some aspects of the Turks' deeds filled them with anger, they also came to admire the Turks' war-craft and courage. The Crusader chronicle *Gesta Francorum* even endorsed the idea – voiced originally by the Turks, apparently – that their two peoples must be distantly related.[28]

The Franks' knowledge of Islam as a religion was equally feeble and, for the most part, remained feeble as the crusades progressed. The First Crusade chroniclers knew that the 'Saracen' religion included an important figure called 'Mohammed' but even then he was often described inaccurately as the 'Saracens' God'. Later in the 12th century, writers from the Crusader states such as William of Tyre (d. c. 1185) showed a marginally greater knowledge of Islam, but even he revealed only a very limited grasp of some of its basic ideas and precepts.[29] At a more popular

24 Latiff, *Cutting edge of the poet's sword*, p. 194.

25 Morton, *Encountering Islam*, p. 95.

26 Albert of Aachen, *Historia Ierosolimitana*, p. 395.

27 Morton, *Encountering Islam*, pp. 97-110.

28 For a discussion on the traditions surrounding this view, see Morton, *Encountering Islam*, pp. 99-101; M. Meserve, *Empires of Islam in Renaissance historical thought*, Cambridge MA, 2008.

29 N. Morton, 'William of Tyre's attitude towards Islam. Some historiographical reflections', in S.B. Edgington and H.J. Nicholson (eds), *Deeds done beyond the sea. Essays on*

level, the idea was frequently touted – in *chansons* (epic songs), such as the *Chanson de Roland* – that the 'Saracens' were idolaters worshipping multiple gods.[30] An especially strong indicator of this lack of knowledge, or even interest, about the Islamic religion can be seen in the chronicle of William of Malmesbury (d. 1143 or after). William felt it necessary to explain to his readers that there was *in fact* a difference between the 'Saracen' religion and the beliefs held by Baltic pagans.[31] True, during the 12th century there was a growing intellectual engagement with Islam, led by monastic heavyweights such as Peter the Venerable (d. 1186), but this seems to have taken place far more across the Iberian frontier than in the eastern Mediterranean.[32]

According to contemporary Western Christian theology, Islam was perceived as either a manifestation of paganism, or as a serious heresy.[33] For the crusaders and their chroniclers, this distinction was deemed largely irrelevant: either way the 'Saracen' religion (in so far as it was understood at all) was presented as a major theological error. For this reason, chroniclers were almost unanimous in their denunciation of it as an evil or even demonic ideology. This enmity towards the 'Saracen law [religion]' (the name 'Islam' was not commonly used in the French language until the late 17thcentury)[34] did not, however, extend to its believers. Muslims existed in a very different category from their religion, according to contemporary Christian thinking. Unlike their faith, they were fully accepted as manifestations of God's creation, intentionally made and loved by Him. According to this view, they may have been raised or led into theological error but they remained fully redeemable and eligible – at least theoretically – for inclusion into the Christian community should they choose to convert. As the 11th-century Norman

---

William of Tyre, Cyprus and the military orders presented to Peter Edbury, Farnham, 2014, 13-24. For further discussion on William of Tyre's attitude towards Islam, see R. Schwinges, *Kreuzzugsideologie und Toleranz. Studien zu Wilhelm von Tyrus*, Stuttgart, 1977; A. Mallett, 'William of Tyre', in *CMR* 3, 769-77.

30 J. Tolan, *Saracens. Islam in the medieval European imagination*, New York, 2002, pp. 105-34; see S. Kinoshita, *'La Chanson de Roland'*, in *CMR* 3, 648-52.

31 William of Malmesbury, *Gesta regum Anglorum*, trans. R.A.B. Mynors, R.M. Thomson and M. Winterbottom, Oxford, 1998, pp. 338-40; J. Tolan, 'William of Malmesbury', in *CMR* 3, 483-7.

32 Many works have been written on Peter the Venerable's view of Islam. For a recent example, see S.G. Bruce, *Cluny and the Muslims of La Garde-Freinet. Hagiography and the problem of Islam in medieval Europe*, Ithaca NY, 2015.

33 Tolan, *Saracens*, pp. 105-69.

34 J. Tolan, G. Veinstein and H. Laurens, *Europe and the Islamic world. A history*, Princeton NJ, 2013, p. 3.

chronicler Geoffrey Malaterra observed, Muslims might not practise Christianity but they remained nonetheless 'His [God's] creatures'.[35]

Perceived through this lens, the Franks deemed non-believers as being capable of virtuous behaviour, even to the point of being held up as role-models to fellow Christians. Many crusade chronicles express admiration for their Turkish, or Arab, or Kurdish allies and foes, with their praise extending well beyond a grudging recognition of their excellence in war-craft (Ṣalāḥ al-Dīn, Saladin, being the obvious example). Even so, given that they were adherents of a non-Christian faith, they were seen as more vulnerable to evil and demonic influence than their Christian opponents. This broad frame of reference recurs across many of the sources for the crusades.[36] Some chronicles are either softer or harder in tone, often reflecting the influence of a writer's lived experience or upbringing, but the basic lens of perception remained fairly consistent. Authors wishing to draw a harder line were often those who believed or implied that the Turks are unconvertable (thereby in their view leaving no alternative but their destruction). Writers viewing the crusade through a more apocalyptic stance seem likewise to have been more ready to reduce their opponents to the status of demons, but this is rare.

The Turks' perceptions of the Franks, especially in the early years of the 12th century, are exceptionally difficult to recreate. Very little of the material that survives records either their identity or world-view, and so it is necessary to rely upon the accounts of other peoples. The most obvious group of sources to consult on this point is the histories and poems written by Muslim (although non-Turkish) authors such as Ibn al-Qalānisī and Ibn al-Athīr, who knew the Turks well and had worked alongside them. The problem here is that such authors often depict the Turks according to idealised Islamic models. To take one example, the Damascene ruler Tughtegin is known to have carved his enemies heads into cups, to have indulged in massive drinking binges and to have maintained many distinctively steppe customs and rituals, but you would not learn this from the Damascene author Ibn al-Qalānisī, who depicts him as an exemplary Muslim leader.[37] In some cases, these chronicles were written many decades or centuries after the events, seemingly by authors

[35] G. Malaterra and E. Pontieri (eds), *De rebus gestis Rogerii Calabriae et Sicilae Comitis et Roberti Guiscardi Ducis fratris eius*, Bologna, 1927, p. 43.

[36] Morton, *Encountering Islam*, pp. 42-8. For context, see D. Iogna-Prat and J. Tolan, 'Peter of Cluny', in *CMR* 3, 604-10.

[37] See N. Morton, 'Walter the Chancellor on Ilghazi and Tughtakin. A prisoner's perspective', *Journal of Medieval History* 44 (2018) 170-86.

who wanted to supply their *contemporary* Turkish masters – who had fully assumed an Islamic identity – with the kind of history they would like to have.[38]

Often the best indicator of a Turkish ruler's character and priorities is his political and military conduct and the priorities implied by his behaviour and objectives. It is certainly notable that the Turkish rulers of Syria and the Jazira, such as Ilghazi, Balak and Jawuli, only occasionally fought the Crusader states during the early 12th century and devoted much of their attention to conflict with fellow Turks, Arabs or other enemies. Indeed, Balak – the man who became a bitter opponent of the principality of Antioch in the early 1120s – initially responded to the advent of the First Crusade by offering to join forces with the crusader commander Baldwin of Boulogne.[39]

In the early years of the 12th century, there is little to suggest that the Turks felt a faith-driven need to drive out the Franks, but this changed as the century progressed. Later rulers, such as Nūr al-Dīn, assumed a far more conspicuous Islamic mantle, deliberately cultivating an image for themselves of pious adherence to Sunnī Islam and intense devotion to the anti-Frankish jihad. Nūr al-Dīn founded tens of religious institutions and encouraged his followers and soldiers to make a deep and pious commitment to the faith. Exactly what motivated him to articulate a fuller and more explicit allegiance to Islam remains an open question. On the one hand, his newly assumed piety may simply reflect a profound sense of personal spiritual conviction. On the other, it is difficult to ignore the fact that this posture also played strongly to his political advantage. Assuming an overt and pious leadership role in the defence of Islam against the Franks would have the effect of entrenching the Turkish ruling classes' control over the broader Muslim populace who, for much of the early 12th century, were far from reconciled to Turkish rule (many Arab leaders adopting an overtly defiant stance when possible). It would also grant Nūr al-Dīn access to the rhetoric of jihad, a factor that would likewise help to legitimise his position while enhancing their ability to raise large and motivated armies.

Identifying the Kurdish ruler Ṣalāḥ al-Dīn's character represents similar challenges.[40] Contemporary Muslim chroniclers, such as Bahāʾ al-Dīn,

38 For an excellent discussion on related themes, see O. Safi, *The politics of knowledge in premodern Islam. Negotiating ideology and religious inquiry*, Chapel Hill NC, 2006.

39 Albert of Aachen, *Historia Ierosolimitana*, pp. 176-8.

40 Although it should be noted that he was a Kurdish ruler leading a predominantly Turkish empire, rather than a Turk himself.

assure their readers that Ṣalāḥ al-Dīn was a sincere and ideal Muslim ruler, but historians remain far from convinced.[41] There is a major debate surrounding him that essentially revolves around the question of whether we can believe the depictions offered by his propagandists and apologists. This is a complex issue. The fact that many Frankish authors – most notably William of Tyre – offer strikingly laudatory depictions of his virtues, which later became popularised in Western knightly culture, seems to bear out their claims.[42] On the other hand, many of Ṣalāḥ al-Dīn's actions and policies seem to imply a rather more worldly and power-hungry ambition. This is evidenced in his usurpation of his master's heirs following Nūr al-Dīn's death in 1174, his relentless campaigns against Muslim enemies during the period 1174-86, and his rather lacklustre attempts to make war on the Franks during the same period. This conflicting evidence underlines the problems faced by scholars attempting to look behind the idealised facade surrounding contemporary Muslim commanders created by suspiciously positive court writers or later scholars who had a didactic purpose.

Although the Turks' perceptions of the Franks remain, to some extent, veiled in mystery, the views offered by non-Turkish Muslim authors, whether pilgrims, historians or intellectuals, are rather clearer; certainly, they are far better evidenced. In such works, the Franks are almost ubiquitously presented as foes, but here too perceptions were complex. Many authors described their admiration for the Franks' courage and prowess in warfare, Ibn Shaddād once exclaiming, 'My God, what fighting men they are! How strong are they and how great their courage!'[43] Usāma ibn Munqidh also seems to have had a fair respect for the reasonably even-handed implementation of justice in Frankish territory (although under Frankish law Muslims were legally unequal).[44] Frankish women also received considerable attention in such works, being viewed with intense curiosity and fascination by many writers, coupled

---

41 For a summary of the debate on this topic, see C. Hillenbrand, *The crusades. Islamic perspectives*, Edinburgh, 2006, pp. 185-6; N. Christie, *Muslims and crusaders. Christianity's wars in the Middle East from 1095-1382, from the Islamic sources*, London, 2014, pp. 43-57 (esp. pp. 48-9).

42 William of Tyre, *Chronique*, ed. R.B.C. Huygens, H.E. Mayer and G. Rösch, Turnhout, 1986, pp. 925, 967.

43 D.S. Richards (trans.), *The rare and excellent history of Saladin. Or al-Nawādir al-Sulṭāniyya wa'l-Maḥāsin al-Yūsufiyya by Bahā' al-Dīn Ibn Shaddād*, Aldershot, 2002, p. 219.

44 For more detailed discussion, see B.Z. Kedar, 'The subjected Muslims of the Frankish Levant', in T. Madden (ed.), *The crusades. The essential readings*, Oxford, 2002, 233-64, pp. 256-7.

with disapproval for their many personal freedoms (a curiosity fully returned by the Franks whose *chansons* contain many vivid descriptions of Muslim noblewomen).[45] Some authors – although not all – were partial to deprecatory portrayals of the Franks, presenting them as uncouth and uncivilised. Usāma ibn Munqidh's chronicle is a case in point, frequently lampooning the Franks as stupid, gullible and without discretion. From a religious perspective, they were often labelled as polytheists, rather than fellow-monotheists, a point that stressed the religious divide separating them.[46]

Away from the field of battle or the negotiating table, encounters between Muslims and Christians occurred in a wide variety of contexts ranging from the marketplace and sacred spaces to chance encounters on the highway. The Crusader states encompassed many Muslim communities, which were swiftly incorporated into the machinery of Frankish rule following the First Crusade. One of the most famous and suggestive accounts describing Muslims living under Christian rule is that of the Iberian Muslim pilgrim Ibn Jubayr (d. 1217). He passed through the Crusader states in 1184 on his return journey to al-Andalus and was shocked to observe the many Muslim communities living peacefully under Frankish rule in the region of Tibnīn, Lebanon. He observed that they paid their taxes, but in other respects were left alone.[47]

The suggestion has been made that the Franks' pragmatic treatment of their Muslim populace – as described by Ibn Jubayr – represents a significant shift away from the language of holy war-driven hatred evinced by the First Crusaders. Extrapolating from this, one might argue that perhaps the realities of ruling a large and diverse populace (whose taxes and labour were essential for the new Frankish rulers) caused them to soften the hard rhetoric of holy war. This kind of argument has been made many times, but it should not be taken too far. Several writers, both Christian and Muslim, including Usāma ibn Munqidh and Ibn ʿAbd al-Ẓāhir, convey the idea that 'western' Franks newly-arrived from overseas were more hostile than 'eastern' Franks from the Crusader states, implying that eastern Franks had become more attuned to their

45 For further discussion, see, for example, Christie, *Muslims and crusaders*, pp. 82-4; Hillenbrand, *The crusades*, pp. 347-8.

46 See, for example, Latiff, *Cutting edge of the poet's sword*.

47 R. Broadhurst (trans.), *The travels of Ibn Jubayr. A mediaeval Spanish Muslim visits Makkah, Madinah, Egypt, cities of the Middle East and Sicily*, London, 1952, p. 316; A. Mallett, 'Ibn Jubayr', in *CMR* 4, 159-65.

Muslim neighbours and tolerant of them.[48] Nevertheless, the antipathy circulating among incoming crusaders should not be over-estimated; their primary concern was always Jerusalem itself and only secondarily the peoples who contested their control. It is equally important not to underestimate the ability of medieval Christianity to permit cooperation with non-Christians.

One striking feature of these Muslim communities within Frankish territory is that they hardly ever rebelled. There were a few minor uprisings in the north, but rebellions were very rare. Of course, one factor underpinning their quiescence would have been the overwhelming strength of Frankish authority and the implicit threat of reprisals should they offer resistance. This factor is certainly indicated by examples of reprisal attacks against the Franks, which occurred when Frankish power was in decline, implying that some local Muslims grasped eagerly at the chance to offer resistance. Following the Frankish defeat at Caroublier in August 1266, local Muslim peasants attacked the survivors, apparently seeking to seize their armour and clothes.[49] Even so, it is notable that, even at times of Frankish defeat, some former Muslim subordinates were prepared to defend their retreating Frankish overlords. In the same year, while the Mamluk Sultan Baybars was engaged in dismembering the Crusader states, he was appalled to learn that the Assassins, who had formerly been long-term tributaries of the military orders, had been offering to safeguard Frankish cattle and property from his attacks.[50]

There are also some examples of Muslim migration into (as well as out of) the Crusader states. At a slightly later stage in his journey, Ibn Jubayr discussed the fall of Tyre back in 1124. At the time, much of the Muslim population initially fled from Frankish territory, but then returned a little later.[51] Clearly, they anticipated that their return would be both in their interests and permitted by the Frankish authorities. Consequently, it should not be automatically assumed that fear and force were the dominant factors underpinning the acceptance shown by many Muslim communities for Frankish rule. Overall, the general principle seems to have

48 See Usāma ibn Munqidh, *The book of contemplation*, p. 147; A.A. al-Khowayter, 'A critical edition of an unknown source for the life of al-Malik al-Zahir Baibars: with introduction, translation, and notes', London, 1960 (PhD Diss. SOAS), vol. 2, p. 655.

49 L. Minervini (ed.), *Cronica del Templare di Tiro (1243-1314)*, Naples, 2000, p. 112. See also Kedar, 'Subjected Muslims', pp. 249-50.

50 Al-Khowayter, 'A critical edition', p. 589.

51 Broadhurst (trans.), *The travels of Ibn Jubayr*, p. 321.

been that, provided they paid their taxes and 'kept-their-heads-down', Muslim communities would generally be left alone.[52]

Certainly, for many decades in the 12th century, the Crusader states away from the frontier brought a degree of stability to the region that it had not known for a long time. Even so, that condition came sharply to an end on 4 July 1187, when the Kingdom of Jerusalem's field army was annihilated by Ṣalāh al-Dīn at the Battle of Haṭṭīn. The kingdom crumpled over the following months while the northern crusader states – left exposed by the kingdom's sudden collapse – were swiftly degraded. This dramatic event provoked the Third Crusade and the titanic duel between Salāḥ al-Dīn and Richard I of England.

Over the following half-century, the Crusader states staged a slow recovery, incrementally regaining many of their lost towns and cities. Multiple crusading armies were flung into the region, often following the logic that the permanent re-conquest of Jerusalem could only be attempted once Egypt – and its massive economic and agricultural resources – had been brought under control. None of these campaigns achieved a great deal. The German crusade of 1197-8 secured a few territorial advances. The Fourth Crusade veered off course and sacked the Byzantine capital Constantinople, and the few troops who did land at Acre achieved very little. The Fifth Crusade was a complete disaster, scarcely mitigated by the fact that the crusaders built up some of the Kingdom of Jerusalem's fortifications.

The subsequent expedition led by Emperor Frederick II of Germany in 1227-9 was rather more successful – if unconventional. Frederick made no attempt to fight the Ayyubids, but rather negotiated the return of Jerusalem and much of its hinterland. This bloodless achievement was a consequence of the longstanding enmity and infighting that riddled the Ayyubid dynasty. Since the death of Ṣalāḥ al-Dīn in 1193, the dynasty became locked in internecine conflict and their leaders were generally content to sign long-term treaties with the Kingdom of Jerusalem so that they could pursue their own disputes. The events of 1227-9 were no exception. When Frederick II arrived demanding territorial concessions, the Egyptian Ayyubid ruler al-Malik al-Kāmil I (r. 1218-38) chose to buy off the emperor so that the crusade would not interrupt his own struggle against his nephew, the Ayyubid ruler of Damascus, al-Malik al-Nāṣir II (r. 1227-9). His response serves as a valuable indicator of

52 For more detailed discussion on this theme, see Kedar, 'The subjected Muslims of the Frankish Levant', p. 254.

inter-faith relations. Clearly al-Malik al-Kāmil was prepared to prioritise his dynastic feuds over the need to retain a city as precious as Jerusalem. To this degree, realpolitik proved more decisive than the interests of his religion. Nevertheless, this point needs to be counter-balanced by the outrage provoked by this act among contemporary Muslims, who were horrified by the handover of the holy city. Such commentators had little interest in the Ayyubids' petty disputes and, on this occasion, as with every other concession or acquisition of territory by either Christian or Muslim commanders across this entire period, there were always plenty of protagonists on all sides paying close attention to how events might affect the broad advance or retreat of their religion's interests.[53]

The strategic situation began to change in the late 1230s-40s. Yet another crusade – known as the Barons' Crusade – arrived, only to suffer another massive battlefield defeat. Even so, it yielded some further concessions because the Ayyubids' internal quarrels were intensifying, and they were prepared to cede territory in return for Frankish support. By this stage, the Kingdom of Jerusalem was starting to re-assume its former position as a major Levantine power. Its army had recovered in size and quality and its strongholds were massively fortified through the consistent efforts of incoming crusaders and the military orders. This revival was badly dented, however, in October 1244, when an Ayyubid-Frankish coalition consisting of the of armies of Damascus, Jerusalem and Homs marched out to do battle with another Ayyubid coalition led by the sultan of Egypt, supported by a large force of warriors from the Empire of Khwarazm, far to the east, who had been displaced by the Mongols. Like so many battles in this period, this was very far from being an inter-faith duel, the battle lines having been determined primarily by the Ayyubids' internecine rivalries. Indeed, Muslim accounts describe the Ayyubid-Frankish army marching out under standards bearing the sign of the cross, with Christian priests moving among the squadrons blessing them in preparation for battle.[54]

In this same year, the already-convoluted world of the Middle East acquired a new level of complexity with the first major Mongol incursion into northern Syria. The Mongols had been a growing menace on the Ayyubids' eastern flank for some time, but now the threat was intensifying. The arrival of the Khwarazmians, along with tens of thousands

---

53 Al-Maqrīzī, *A history of the Ayyūbid sultans of Egypt*, trans. R.J.C. Broadhurst, Boston MA, 1980, p. 207.

54 Ibn al-Furāt, *Ayyubids, Mamlukes and crusaders*, vol. 1, p. 5.

of displaced Turkmen tribesmen, was itself a symptom of the Mongol advance as communities and tribes scrambled to get out of their way. The major blow landed in 1260, when a colossal army led by the Mongol commander Hulegu, founder of the Ilkhanate, advanced towards the Levant. His forces had conquered Baghdad two years previously, and this cleared the path for a major invasion into Syria.

The Mongol advance cleanly divided the region's Christian powers. Some, such as the Armenians, had already submitted to the Mongols. The Antiochenes likewise took the Mongol side and benefitted considerably from their overwhelming invasion, joining Hulegu's forces and regaining many former towns, including their vital port at Latakia. The Kingdom of Jerusalem was more cautious; a raid by one of their noblemen sparked a Mongol backlash, resulting in the destruction of the port of Sidon. The Ayyubids by this stage were in full decline. Back in 1250, there had been a revolt in Egypt among the sultan's slave soldiers, the Mamluks, who had taken power for themselves, thereby establishing the Mamluk Sultanate. By 1260, the Ayyubids' two other major centres of power, Damascus and Aleppo, were now in Mongol hands. The Mamluks' response to the Mongol advance was incredibly bold; they marched out to fight the Mongol army. By this stage, the majority of the Mongols had withdrawn from the Syria region and the remaining garrison of about 10,000 troops was defeated at the Battle of ʿAyn Jālūt. Crucially, before this battle the Mamluks contacted the Franks in Acre, asking for their assistance against the Mongols. The Franks refused this request, but nonetheless the mere fact that it was made reinforces the idea that the frontiers of war, during the 13th century especially, were rarely drawn along religious lines.

In the decades that followed, the major confrontation in the Middle East was between the Mamluks and the Ilkhans (Mongols). These two heavy-weight pugilists spent decades in conflict, relegating the Crusader states, the various Turkmen tribes and the Armenians to a secondary role in shaping the region's history. During the 1260s and 1270s, the Mamluks staged repeated campaigns against the Crusader states, destroying much of the Kingdom of Jerusalem and, in the north, conquering the city of Antioch in 1268. The Kingdom of Jerusalem finally collapsed in 1291 with the fall of Acre. The contemporary court writer Ibn ʿAbd al-Ẓāhir garlands these ventures with the language of jihad, and yet it is very clear that the Mamluks only reduced the Frankish states when troops could be spared from the Mongol frontier. Moreover, the Mamluks themselves depended heavily on Genoese shipping to maintain a steady supply of slaves from the Black Sea region, who could be trained as Mamluk slave warriors – the backbone of their army. This trade was facilitated in turn by the Byzantines, who permitted shipping to travel from the Black Sea through the Bosporus and into the Mediterranean (and who likewise had strong diplomatic ties with the Mamluks).[55]

Indeed, reviewing the period in its entirety, from 1095 to 1291, religion and holy war provide a very limited explanation for most of the region's wars, which were provoked in large part by a succession of factors. Perhaps the easiest way to visualise the causes of war is to imagine a Venn diagram consisting of five partially overlapping circles labelled respectively: religion and holy war; trade and commerce; ethnic and dynastic politics; political realpolitik; and migration and demographic change. In different decades, each of these circles overlapped one another to a lesser or greater degree and each circle either grew or shrank in significance as time went on, but none supplies a single over-arching explanation for the evolution of events. The 'religious' circle in such a diagram would have reached its greatest extent during periods of heightened crusading or jihad rhetoric (such as under Nūr al-Dīn and Ṣalāḥ al-Dīn, or during a major crusade), but the point needs to be made that these moments were only ever brief. For the most part, inter-faith rivalries supplied little more than background noise to the region's politics. This should not imply for a moment that any of the protagonist factions were in any way 'irreligious' or even that they held their beliefs lightly – indeed they watched every loss or gain of land for their faith with the closest attention; rather, the survival and pursuit of their interests, religious or otherwise, were only occasionally served through holy war.

Trade was a vital factor, playing its part in moulding events. The blunt commercial reality was that major trade routes ran through the Middle Eastern region, both local and international. The most important of these were the 'Silk' or 'Spice' routes from China and India, bringing high-value commodities across Eurasia and feeding markets as far afield as western Christendom and the Maghreb. Regional trade routes also played their part. Egypt, for example, was careful to maintain the flow of ship building and construction timber from Cilician Armenia and Asia Minor, given its lack of local sources. Egypt itself imported many commodities through the Frankish city of Acre, a fact that had to be considered carefully when making war, while the annual rise and fall of the Nile – and its effect in fertilising the Nile Delta – determined whether Egypt would

[55] The best survey of this period is R. Amitai-Preiss, *Mongols and Mamluks. The Mamluk Īlkhānid war, 1260-1281*, Cambridge, 1995.

be a mass importer or exporter of cereal crops. Likewise, the Frankish states were perennially reliant on materials and trade goods from Western Christendom, sending in return vast quantities of sugar raised on plantations located in the Crusader states' coastal regions. The Franks sourced other items from Muslim cities; Damascus in particular seems to have been crucial for supplying horn and glue, vital for the manufacture of crossbows.

In this context, Christian-Muslim relations needed to accommodate economic realities. The Italian cities of Genoa, Pisa and Venice were enthusiastic crusaders, and their troops played an important role conquering many of the ports along the Levantine littoral. Even so, these urban societies depended upon trade with Muslim powers, thereby creating potential conflicts of interest between commerce and crusade. One way to reconcile this problem was to separate the two zones of activity. Indeed, Ibn Jubayr reports that, during the intense warfare between Ṣalāḥ al-Dīn and the Crusader states in the 1180s, trade continued unabated.[56] Likewise, at the conclusion of the Third Crusade, one of the main stipulations of the Treaty of Jaffa was that trade should continue without the payment of tribute by the merchants of any party.[57] At various times throughout this period, the papacy attempted to erect a military and commercial blockade against Egypt, which relied upon Mediterranean commerce (especially in metals and timber), but this policy seldom had much effect. The actions of the Italian merchants were also guided by their own internal rivalries, which grew in intensity during the 13th century and often broke into violent conflict. Their navies frequently clashed in encounters spread across the Mediterranean, and at times these hostilities could trump both the demands of their common Christian faith and basic contemporary geo-political realities. From the late 1240s onwards, there was fighting between their various representatives in the Crusader states, and there are rumours in the 1260s of an agreement between the Genoese and the Mamluks to conduct a joint assault on the Frankish capital of Acre. This never occurred, but the suggestion that such a joint enterprise was even considered against the Kingdom of Jerusalem's capital city is deeply significant.[58]

---

56 Broadhurst (trans.), *The travels of Ibn Jubayr*, pp. 300, 301, 303.

57 M. Ailes and M. Barber (eds), *The history of the holy war. Ambroise's Estoire de la Guerre Sainte*, vol. 1, Woodbridge, 2003, p. 190, lines 11, 756-60.

58 Al-Khowayter, 'A critical edition', vol. 2, pp. 588-9. For discussion on this report and its sources, see P. Thorau, *The Lion of Egypt. Sultan Baybars I & the Near East in the thirteenth century*, trans. P.M. Holt, Harlow, 1992, p. 148.

Alongside the barter and bustle of the Near East's commercial centres, other forms of exchange also took place as ideas, concepts and technologies changed hands. Travelling masons and builders shared skills and construction techniques, leading to architectural works of art that reflect this cultural cross-pollination.[59] For example, the design and decorative elements of the Church of the Holy Sepulchre in Jerusalem represent a synthesis of Western and Eastern Christian (specifically Armenian) influences.[60] New encounters between different communities or logistical challenges could also provoke innovation, as leaders and artisans addressed themselves to unexpected problems or questions. These could range from the mundane to the warlike. Odo of Deuil, chaplain to King Louis VII (r. 1137-80) during the Second Crusade, advised future pilgrims in his chronicle to shun four-wheeled carts owing to the problems they caused on campaign.[61] On a more refined level, the artwork produced in the Middle East likewise reveals an exciting exchange of influences: Latin Eastern art drew heavily upon Armenian, Islamic and Byzantine ideas, while Turkish artisans adopted some distinctly European designs, such as the fleur-de-lys.[62]

On the battlefield, the region's various commanders watched one another closely, looking for a way to mitigate their own weaknesses whilst breaking down their enemy's strengths. For example, Nūr al-Dīn's commander Shīrkūh worked out how to negate the destructive impact of the Frankish heavy cavalry charge. He simply instructed his forces to divide their ranks moments before the Christian charge made contact, thereby evading the enemy horsemen, and subsequently to counterattack them as soon as their charge lost impetus. This was later used to devastating effect by Shīrkūh's nephew, Ṣalāḥ al-Dīn, in 1187 at the battle of Ḥaṭṭīn.[63]

---

[59] See, for example, R. McClary, 'Craftsmen in medieval Anatolia. Methods and mobility', in P. Blessing and R. Goshgarian (eds), *Architecture and landscape in medieval Anatolia, 1100-1500*, Edinburgh, 2017, 27-58.

[60] N. Kenaan-Kedar, 'Decorative architectural sculpture in crusader Jerusalem. The eastern, western and Armenian sources of a local visual culture', in A.J. Boas (ed.), *The crusader world*, Abingdon, 2016, 609-23.

[61] Odo of Deuil, *De profectione Ludovici in Orientem*, p. 52.

[62] J. Folda, *Crusader art in the Holy Land. From the Third Crusade to the fall of Acre, 1187-1291*, Cambridge, 2005; S.R. Canby et al. (eds), *Court and cosmos. The great age of the Seljuqs*, New York, 2016, pp. 69, 146.

[63] See, for example, R. Ellenblum, *Crusader castles and modern histories*, Cambridge, 2007.

Within this complex milieu, many relationships emerged across faith or ethnic boundaries. During the Third Crusade, Richard I became friends with Ṣalāḥ al-Dīn's brother al-ʿĀdil and they met on many occasions, sharing food from their respective cultures. Richard even knighted some of Ṣalāḥ al-Dīn's leading warriors.[64] Usāma ibn Munqidh likewise mentioned his friendship with a Frankish knight who was planning to return to Western Europe. During his sojourn in the East, they had become so comfortable in one another's company that the knight offered to take Usāma's son back to Christendom to be trained as a knight; an astonishing offer, even if Usāma understandably declined.[65]

The military dimension to the crusading period was perennially of the first importance to all sides, and the conduct of these wars varied considerably over time in intensity and brutality. As a rough rule, most sides broadly accepted that, if enemy cities surrendered to an attacker, their populace should be spared. Likewise, commanders generally considered it acceptable to sack cities – killing or enslaving the populace – if they refused to surrender and were subsequently taken by storm. Likewise, in skirmishes and pitched battles, it was ubiquitously the case that a victorious general, having routed and scattered his opponents, would seek to maximise his advantage by slaughtering, enslaving or imprisoning as many of his enemies as possible. To this extent, the practice of war was broadly similar across all societies, irrespective of faith-identity.

Viewed from a conqueror's perspective, it was rarely in the interests of any commander, whether Turkish-Muslim or Frankish-Christian, to massacre urban populations. They needed the population's labour if they were going to maintain permanent control and, conversely, harsh treatment might deter future cities from submitting to their rule. Consequently, massacres occurred only sporadically across this period. The Franks committed several during the First Crusade and in its immediate aftermath; examples include the conquest of al-Bāra in 1098, Maʿarrat al-Nuʿmān in 1098, Sarūj in 1101, Caesarea in 1101, Acre in 1104, and Beirut in 1110. A few occurred later, such as during the conquest of al-Balbein in Egypt in 1168.[66] For the most part – but not always – such brutal acts followed the pattern outlined above, namely, if cities refused to surrender and were then taken by storm, the crusaders tended to inflict a general sack. This grim practice was entirely normal for the medieval period.

---

64 *Rare and excellent history of Saladin*, pp. 193, 223.
65 Usāma ibn Munqidh, *Book of contemplation*, p. 144.
66 For further discussion, see Kedar, 'Subjected Muslims', pp. 241-3.

The conquest of Jerusalem in 1099, however, represents a notable and infamous exception. Here too the population held out until the city was conquered by force (and in this way was not dissimilar to other sieges), but the treatment of the citizens in the days following the conquest far exceeded the norms of medieval warfare. Crusader eyewitnesses recalling the massacre (possibly of about 3,000 people) describe the astonishingly bloody violence of these days and generally present the conquest as a spiritual cleansing, one which removed all vestiges of non-belief from the holy city. In this case, at least, the rhetoric of holy war provoked bloodletting on an astonishing scale.[67] The Turks also committed massacres against urban populations, early examples being Zangī's conquest of Edessa in 1144 and the raid on Nablus in 1184 by Ṣalāḥ al-Dīn's troops. Further massacres were committed in the late 13th century, during the Mamluks' relentless campaigns against the Crusader states, a clear example being the fall of Antioch in 1268.

Conquerors often garlanded such moments of conquest with acts of religious triumphalism. After Muslim victories, Christian buildings were often stripped of their crosses and Muslim authors frequently spoke of their wish to smash or expunge crosses (used as a symbol for the Frankish presence as a whole) from the region.[68] Likewise, churches were occasionally destroyed, defiled or turned into stables or Islamic religious institutions. The crusaders could be every bit as aggressive, destroying Islamic religious buildings or converting them into churches. In some cases, buildings changed hands multiple times. One Coptic author reports that a mosque in Acre had originally been converted into a church following the Frankish conquest in 1104. The Franks had then painted its walls with Christian images and scenes (as was their custom). When the city fell to Ṣalāḥ al-Dīn in 1187, the building was restored to its original function and Ṣalāḥ al-Dīn ordered Frankish prisoners to wipe off the paint before whitewashing the building with lime. Then, following the recapture of Acre in 1191, the building was converted into a church once again and the Franks made Muslim prisoners wash the whitewash off the walls and renew its paintings.[69] Both sides often spoke of such conquests as 'cleansing' acts, ridding a city of the polluting presence of the other's

---

67 B.Z. Kedar, 'The Jerusalem massacre of July 1099 in the western historiography of the crusades', *Crusades* 3 (2004) 15-75; Morton, *Encountering Islam*, pp. 174-83.

68 Latiff, *Cutting edge of the poet's sword.*

69 Maʿānī ibn Abī l-Makārim, *History of the patriarchs of the Egyptian Church*, ed. S. ibn al-Muqaffaʿ, vol. 3, pt 1, Cairo, 1968, p. 154.

religion.[70] It was at such moments that the underlying inter-faith antagonism between Christianity and Islam was at its most conspicuous, and yet it has to be remembered that, despite these symbolic acts of spiritual supremacy, both sides permitted the other faith to be practised in their territories.

Perhaps some of the most precariously situated communities in the Middle East were those living in the contested borderlands between Turkish and Frankish territory. In such liminal spaces, where the fortunes of war might swing violently and suddenly from one side to another, taking sides was a risky business. This kind of environment clearly encouraged many local communities to be cautious about aligning themselves too closely to any faction, a perspective that is revealed clearly by Maʿānī ibn Abī l-Makārim in his account of the early raids launched by the Fifth Crusade into the Jordan Valley in 1217.[71] Apparently, at one point a procession of local Eastern Christians set out to greet the arriving crusaders. The Franks then asked if there were any Muslims in their town – which there were – and the Christians answered that there were not (presumably fearful that if they said 'yes' the crusaders would kill their neighbours, thereby provoking reprisals from other Muslim settlements). Having received this answer, the Franks asked these local Christians to take care of four knights who had become too sick to participate in the campaign. Once the army had departed, the local Muslims then seized these knights and killed them, with their Christian protectors feeling unable to prevent them out of fear of the Ayyubid sultan. When the Franks found out that their trust had been betrayed and that their men had been executed, they sacked the town, killing the entire population. Treading a safe path through multiple hostile factions was a dangerous business.[72]

This theme of the crusaders' engagement with the local populace also connects to another important matter: conversion and religious change. This is perhaps the most complex issue of all. During this period, the region's religious identities were in rapid flux, and it is helpful to review a few of the most important macro-developments.

---

70 For examples of this in Islamic sources, see Latiff, *Cutting edge of the poet's sword*, p. 146.

71 J. Den Heijer *with* P. Pilette, '*History of the churches and monasteries of Egypt*', in *CMR* 4, 983-8.

72 Maʿānī ibn Abī l-Makārim, *History of the patriarchs*, vol. 3, pt 1, pp. 154-5.

1. The Seljuk Turks invaded and increasingly assumed a Persian/Sunnī Islamic identity. In many regions they became deeply influenced by Sufi thinking.
2. The Shīʿa Fatimids suffered overthrow at the hands of Shīrkūh and Ṣalāḥ al-Dīn, who were Sunnīs, and suffered the abolition of their Shīʿa caliphate.
3. The Mongols invaded and slowly converted to Islam.[73]
4. The Armenians engaged in long protracted talks over their union with Rome (and the Maronites united with Rome during this time).[74]
5. Former Byzantine territories were conquered by both Franks and Turks, and their inhabitants had to accommodate themselves to their new rulers' religious policies and identity.
6. The Assassins – Nizārīs – rose and expanded as a sect, winning converts in many regions, especially northern Syria, all the while being brutally persecuted by the Turks.

These were all major developments involving issues of religious change and conversion that affected communities at foundational levels. The basic compass of these societies' identities – and, by extension, their objectives and networks of natural friends and foes – was in flux.

It is beyond the scope of this essay to cover each of these processes, but two of the most indicative shifts directly impacting the character of the crusading movement were, first, the Turks' steadily deepening adherence to Sunnī Islam (covered above) and, second, Western Christendom's growing enthusiasm for evangelism to the Muslim world. This latter trend began to gather substantial momentum in the early decades of the 13th century. Before this, attempts at winning converts were sporadic at best. During the final phases of the First Crusade, there seems to have been some anticipation among participants that the sheer scale of their victories would be accepted as proof by the Turks that the Christian God was the true God, leading them to convert.[75] Nevertheless, no large-scale conversion took place. Some interest in evangelistic activity was shown in later years far to the west in Iberia, and it is in this context that Peter the Venerable (d. 1156) commissioned his translation of the Qur'an.[76] Even so, while this may have added a new dimension to Iberian inter-faith relations, it did not have much impact in the eastern Mediterranean.

---

[73] For discussion, see P. Jackson, *The Mongols and the Islamic world. From conquest to conversion*, New Haven CT, 2017, pp. 328-80.
[74] B. Hamilton, *The Latin Church in the Crusader states. The secular church*, London, 1980.
[75] Morton, *Encountering Islam*, pp. 154-82.
[76] Iogna-Prat and Tolan, 'Peter of Cluny'.

A major change occurred with the rise in the orders of friars (Franciscans and Dominicans), and their efforts to galvanise their institutions and the wider church to support crusading campaigns and evangelistic missions to the East.[77] An early indicator of this merging of mission and crusade was St Francis of Assisi's attempt to convert the Egyptian Sultan al-Malik al-Kāmil after the Fifth Crusade, although a strong interest in evangelistic activity is also discernible among other contemporary writers. These include Jacques de Vitry (d. 1240), whose works reflect his own enthusiasm for preaching.[78] There were also other authors who noted the presence of non-Latin preachers seeking converts to Christianity. For example, the Hospitaller master, Geoffrey of Donjon, in a letter to the order's English commander, mentioned a young Muslim convert who, by 1201, had led over two thousand Muslims to Christianity.[79]

From the early 13th century onwards, Dominican and Franciscan missionaries and envoys make frequent appearances in the sources. On some occasions, they were despatched on papal instructions to lead Mongol or Muslim leaders to Christ (with very little success); on others, they acted as crusade preachers, whipping up support for new campaigns.[80] Crusading strategists began to devise approaches by which crusading could support or interact with missionary activity,[81] while the Majorcan writer and missionary Ramon Llull (d. 1315-16) flirted with the idea of creating a new military order which would carry out both roles.[82] There is little to suggest that these missionaries won a landslide of new converts during this period; nonetheless, their appearance demonstrates a major shift in Christendom's engagement with the region.

Overall, the relationship between Christianity and Islam at the time of the crusades was highly complex and ever evolving. It differed in nuance and texture across the many different regions impacted by crusading to the eastern Mediterranean, from the Anatolian highlands in the north to the Nile Delta in the south. It included some moments of vicious

---

77 The major and unsurpassed study on this topic is B.Z. Kedar, *Crusade and mission. European approaches towards the Muslims*, Oxford, 1984.

78 J. Tolan, 'Jacques de Vitry', in *CMR* 4, 295-306.

79 M. Barber and K. Bate (trans.), *Letters from the East. Crusaders, pilgrims and settlers in the 12th-13th centuries*, Farnham, 2010, p. 96.

80 See P. Jackson, *The Mongols and the west, 1221-1410*, Harlow, 2005, 58-112; C.T. Maier, *Crusade propaganda and ideology. Model sermons for the preaching of the cross*, Cambridge, 2000.

81 Kedar, *Crusade and mission*, pp. 159-203.

82 Ramon Llull, *Blanquerna*, trans. E.A. Peters, ed. R. Irwin, London, 1987, pp. 327-31; H. Hames, 'Ramon Llull', in *CMR* 4, 703-17.

inter-faith killing, perpetrated at different moments by various factions, alongside far longer stretches of time when holy war was, at best, a secondary factor in shaping events. This political narrative likewise has to be intersected by the omnipresent demands of commerce, conversion and religious accommodation, alongside the need – common to many non-combatant communities – to plot a safe course through the cascading conflict. The resulting picture is one of diversity, encompassing moments of friendship, technological exchange, tolerance and inter-faith interest, alongside times of violence, hatred and aggressive polemic. The sum of these components is to render the crusading period a fascinating and confused moment in Middle Eastern history, but emphatically not one that can be captioned in any simple way as a 'clash of civilisations'.

Chapter 13
Conduits of interaction. The Andalusi experience

Juan Pedro Monferrer Sala

Introduction*

Works from al-Andalus in the period 700-1500 reveal a complex and varied picture of Christian-Muslim relations, which can be described as providing a socio-religious architecture of communities from the two faiths. These works make it possible to appreciate the complexity of the experience of Christians and Muslims, to consider how they saw the 'other' and to reflect on how they captured and adapted an image of the 'other'. Misunderstandings between the groups were certainly many, but so were the collaborations between them, collaborations that would lead to extensive intellectual interaction in later centuries. This chapter, begins with a context-setting discussion of land, people and faiths, then proceeds to the matters of Arabisation, Islamisation and acculturation. There follows a wide-ranging discussion of the perceptions that each held of the other that engage a complex and rich world of idea and image, and a concluding brief discussion of the impact, or lack thereof, of the sequence of expulsions – of Christians, then of Muslims, then of Moriscos. The conduit of interaction led to the formation, in effect, of a coexistence of knowledge, a coexistence that for a time enriched both communities and prompted an era of relative stability and peace.

Land, people and faiths

In the spring of 711, fighting men led by the Berber Ṭāriq ibn Ziyād (d. 722) under the orders of the *Ifrīqiya* governor Mūsā ibn Nuṣayr (d. 716?), entered Hispania (*Ishbāniya*) and a few weeks later defeated the army

* This study forms part of the Research Project FFI2014-53556-R: 'Study and edition of the Greek, Arabic and Latin biblical and Patristic MSS', funded by the Spanish Ministry of Economy and Competitiveness.

of the last Visigothic king, Ruderic (d. 711). The gates of the Iberian Peninsula were thus flung open to an army of several thousand mostly Berber men, who streamed virtually unopposed into the very heart of the Visigothic kingdom of Toledo. By the summer of 714, just over three years later, the whole of the Peninsula was in the hands of Arab contingents; by 716, they had also seized power in the Pyrenees and territories in what is now Portugal. A new socio-political and religious dispensation soon held sway in a land hitherto under Visigothic rule, which since 589 had gradually abandoned the Arianism of the Visigoths in favour of the Catholic faith of the Hispano-Roman population.[1]

The emergence of this new dispensation not only prompted a change from the feudal production model to the Asian model,[2] but also ushered in the dual process of Arabisation and Islamisation, in accordance with the policy pursued by the Umayyads of Damascus. The Islamic faith was not imposed on the peoples of the Peninsula, but rather, as followers of a revealed religion, they were classed as 'people of the Book' (*ahl al-kitāb*), and therefore allowed to retain their forms of worship though they were subject to the Islamic authorities in fiscal matters as *ahl al-dhimma*.[3] This situation favoured the conversion to Islam of those who had lost their possessions under the Visigoths, for, by converting, they assumed the status of Muslims and were able to avoid the taxes levied on *dhimmīs*.[4] These conversions created new social groupings within the Muslim population of al-Andalus, the so-called *musālima*, i.e. converts, or *muwalladūn*, a term denoting descendants – in various degrees – of converts. The rate of conversion to Islam remains a matter of debate, since the theory postulated by Richard Bulliet, though it was initially welcomed, has since been heavily criticised in terms both of the method used and of the percentages obtained.[5]

As was occurring in the Near East, the process of Arabisation in al-Andalus had a marked impact on various aspects of the socio-cultural and religious life of the Christian communities, who spoke a variant

[1] R. Izquierdo Benito, 'Toledo en época visigoda', in M. Cortés Arrese (ed.), *Toledo y Bizancio*, Cuenca, 2002, 43-74, p. 61.

[2] M. Acién Almansa, 'La herencia del protofeudalismo visigodo frente a la imposición del estado islámico', in L. Caballero Zoreda and P. Mateos Cruz (eds), *Visigodos y Omeyas. Un debate entre la Antigüedad Tardía y la Alta Edad Media*, Madrid, 2000, 429-41.

[3] M. Meouak, 'Ibn Ḥayyān', in *CMR* 3, 165-71, p. 167.

[4] M. Meouak, 'Ibn Bassām', in *CMR* 3, 318-22, p. 320.

[5] R. Bulliet, *Conversion to Islam in the medieval period. An essay in quantitative history*, Cambridge MA, 1979. Cf. the criticism of R. Schick, *The Christian communities of Palestine from Byzantine to Islamic rule. A historical and archaeological study*, Princeton NJ, 1995, pp. 139-41, and M. Penelas, 'Some remarks on conversion to Islam in al-Andalus', *Al-Qanṭara* 23 (2002) 193-200.

of Romance and whose prestige language was Latin. Arabisation led not only to the conversion of Christians, but also to the emergence of another social group that was to wield considerable influence in Andalusī Christian society, that of the so-called *Mozarabs*.[6] Its members included a number of excellent bilingual Latin-Arabic translators and intellectuals, who wrote in Arabic and at the same time had their works drafted in Latin. These Arabised Christians, who belonged to the urban elite and were in some cases clergy, have been viewed in opposition to the well-known group formed by Eulogius (d. 859), Albarus Cordubensis (d. c. 860-61) and their followers.[7] While Eulogius and Albarus represented loyalty to the Catholic faith and to Latin culture and tradition, the Arabised Christians have been regarded as traitors to that tradition, in that they abandoned Latin in favour of Arabic. This interpretative reductionism has even prompted the view that the only Christianity possible in al-Andalus was Catholicism, any other groups being dismissed as heretics of little or no importance.[8]

The impact of heresies on the Christian milieu in al-Andalus was by no means as negligible as was that of the non-Sunnī movements (Shīʿa, Muʿtazila, Khawārij, etc.) or of heretical groups in general (*zanādiqa*)[9] elsewhere in the Islamic world; heretical movements destabilised the Catholic Church in Baetica and particularly in Córdoba. For example, Samuel, the 9th-century bishop of Elvira and maternal uncle of Bishop Hostegesis of Malaga (d. c. 864), incited his followers to practise rites such as circumcision, as well as expounding views contrary to Catholic dogma, denying, for example, the resurrection of the flesh.[10] This, together with the complex fiscal situation in which Christians found themselves, prompted a certain amount of apostasy. Samuel himself, once deprived of his see, moved to Córdoba, denied Christ, shaved his head, converted to Islam and promptly started persecuting Christians. The situation of the Christian population in al-Andalus was very different from that

---

6 On this term, see R. Menéndez Pidal, *Orígenes del español. Estado lingüístico de la Península Ibérica hasta el siglo XI*, Madrid, 1980, p. 415, n. 1; D. Urvoy, 'Les aspects symboliques du vocable "mozarabe". Essai de réinterprétation', *Studia Islamica* 78 (1993) 117-53; R. Hitchcock, *Mozarabs in medieval and early modern Spain. Identities and influences*, London, 2008; and F. Corriente, 'Tres mitos contemporáneos frente a la realidad de Alandalús: romanticismo filoárabe, "cultura Mozárabe" y "cultura Sefardí"', in G.F. Parrilla and M.C. Feria García (eds), *Orientalismo, exotismo y traducción*, Cuenca, 2000, 39-47.

7 J. Tolan, 'Eulogius of Cordova', in *CMR* 1, 679-83; K.B. Wolf, 'Paul Alvarus', in *CMR* 1, 645-8.

8 J. Aguadé, 'Some remarks about sectarian movements in al-Andalus', *Studia Islamica* 64 (1986) 53-77, p. 73.

9 M.I. Fierro, *La heterodoxia en al-Andalus durante el periodo omeya*, Madrid, 1987.

10 E. Flórez, *España sagrada*, Madrid, 1754, vol. 12, p. 168.

traditionally described: Arabised Christians vs. non-Arabised Christians, but all within the Catholic fold.

Religious beliefs in the Peninsula derived essentially from a dual Visigothic and Hispano-Roman legacy. The conversion of the Visigothic kings to Catholicism had failed to eradicate the existing diversity among Christians, and this was exacerbated by the arrival of the Arabs. There were Christian soldiers in the occupying armies, and other Christians came to Hispania for a range of different purposes, among them the famous George, a monk from the Orthodox Monastery of Mār Sābā in the Judaean desert. He came in the mid-9th century to the Iberian Peninsula via North Africa with the aim (according to Eulogius) of raising money for his monastery (*ob stipendio monachorum*),[11] although his arrival may have been prompted by an agreement between the Catholic Church in Córdoba and Eastern monasteries such as Mār Sābā. Córdoba's Christians needed the assistance of monks who not only spoke Arabic but were also conversant with the Qur'an and Islamic tradition, for apologetic and polemical purposes. These requirements led to an agreement with Eastern monasteries, through a channel for dialogue with the *Oriens christianus* that had been set up earlier.[12] One possible proof of these contacts between Peninsular and Palestinian Christians may be the presence of a Latin Psalter at St Catherine's Monastery in Sinai.[13] The codex, probably of North African origin, may have entered St Catherine's from the Iberian Peninsula, where it arrived before the latter half of the 7th century, in other words, after the Arab conquest had taken place. But this was by no means the only Latin text that made its way to St Catherine's; a number of liturgical texts in the monastery also point to a relationship between Palestinian Melkites and Christians in al-Andalus.[14] One explicit datum

[11] *Evlogi Memoriale sanctorvm* II 10.23, in J. Gil (ed.), *Corpvs Scriptorvm Mvzarabicorvm*, Madrid, 1973, vol. 2, p. 425.

[12] H. Goussen, *Die christlich-arabische Literatur der Mozaraber*, Leipzig, 1909, pp. 10-11 (Spanish trans. by J.P. Monferrer Sala, *La literature árabe cristiana de los mozárabes*, Córdoba, 1999, pp. 20-1). See also C.E. Dubler, 'Sobre la Crónica arábigo-bizantina de 741 y la influencia bizantina en la Península Ibérica', *Al-Andalus* 11 (1946) 283-349; L.A. García Moreno, 'Elementos de tradición bizantina en dos *Vidas de Mahoma* mozárabes', in I. Pérez Martín and P. Bádenas de la Peña (eds), *Bizancio y la Península Ibérica. De la antigüedad tardía a la edad moderna*, Madrid, 2004, 250-60.

[13] E.A. Lowe, 'An unknown Latin Psalter on Mount Sinai', *Scriptorium* 9 (1955) 177-99; cf. G.D. Sixdenier, 'A propos de l'origine du Psautier latin du Sinaï: Une piste?', *Scriptorium* 41 (1987) 129.

[14] Cf. J. Gribomont, 'Le mystérieux calendrier latin du Sinai. Édition et commentaire', *Analecta Bollandiana* 75 (1957) 105-34; E.A. Lowe, 'Two new Latin liturgical fragments on Mount Sinai', *Revue Bénédictine* 74 (1964) 252-83; B. Fischer, 'Zur Liturgie der lateinischen

is provided by the author of the Latin-Arabic *Glossary of Leiden* (fl. 12th century),[15] who suggests that an Eastern version of the Pentateuch, of Syrian origin, was circulating in the Iberian Peninsula.[16] And the same can be said in the opposite direction, i.e. Latin translations of Eastern Christian works such as *Revelatio S. Methodii de temporibus nouissimis* ('Revelation of St Methodius on the most recent times'), a Latin translation from a slightly expanded Greek version of a Syriac original.[17]

This religious diversity accounts in great measure for certain aspects of Andalusī Christianity; without it, the circulation of some texts, translations and ideas cannot be readily explained. Islam is often adduced, for example, to account for the Adoptionist doctrine espoused by Elipandus of Toledo (717-808), though in theological terms his doctrinal views cannot possibly be explained by reference to Islam. Even so, scholars have systematically refused to link the ideas of Elipandus with the theology of the Church of the East (the misnamed Nestorians), whose presence in al-Andalus is by no means unlikely.

Prior to the arrival of the Arabs, the Catholic Church was facing dark times. The top-down shift from Arianism to Catholicism, intended to unite and homogenise the people in a kind of *gens gothorum*, did not penetrate to the grass roots. Although Catholicism won out, and succeeded in incorporating the whole of the Arian curia, it failed to extinguish entirely the lingering embers of earlier ethnic rifts between Visigoths and Hispano-Romans, or between the Arian and Catholic Churches over political and doctrinal issues, especially regarding the nature of the Trinity.[18]

This doctrine and the associated Trinitarian terminology, which set Arians against Catholics, among others, had been *disputandi causa* in the Latin West since the 5th century, and continued to be divisive; by the latter third of the 8th century, it was still a burning issue in the Iberian Peninsula. An interesting theological episode dating from this period was the debate between Beatus of Liébana and Elipandus of Toledo regarding

Handschriften vom Sinai', *Revue Bénédictine* 74 (1964) 284-97; E.A. Lowe, 'Two other unknown Latin liturgical fragments on Mount Sinai', *Scriptorium* 19 (1965) 3-29.

15 T.E. Burman, 'Glossarium latino-arabicum', in *CMR* 3, 742-4.

16 P.S. Van Koningsveld, *The Latin-Arabic glossary of the Leiden University Library. A contribution to the study of Mozarabic manuscripts and literature*, Leiden, 1977, pp. 65, 75-6, n. 245.

17 J.P. Monferrer Sala, '*The Apocalypse of Pseudo-Methodius* (*Latin*)', in *CMR* 1, 249-52. Cf. P. Ubierna, '*The Apocalypse of Pseudo-Methodius* (*Greek*)', in *CMR* 1, 245-8.

18 J. Orlandis, 'El cristianismo en la España visigoda', in J. Orlandis, *Estudios visigóticos*, Madrid, 1956, vol. 1, 7-9.

the Adoptionist controversy, which reached its fiercest expression from October 785.[19] But this dispute coincided with a new heresy, embodied by one Migetius, whose religious activities were certainly a danger to the Church in Córdoba in the late 8th century; so much so, in fact, that Elipandus himself took Migetius to task for preaching unorthodox views.[20]

Departures from orthodox theological teachings and rites were multiple: refusal to celebrate Easter in the manner prescribed by the Council of Nicea in 325; refusal to fast on Saturdays; mixed marriages, particularly with Arians but also with Jews and Muslims; the practice of divorce; and a dangerous diversity of beliefs regarding the dogma of predestination. This complex and at times uncontrolled situation led Wilcarius, the archbishop of Sens in Gaul, around 790 to suggest that an apostolic nuncio might be sent to the Peninsula in order to deal with the problems arising within the Spanish Catholic Church, which had been wholly destabilised by the emerging heresies. The person chosen for this mission was the recently-consecrated bishop Egila, who was sent by Pope Hadrian I in 777 to the Peninsula in the company of an assistant named Iohannes.[21] One of several enemies to be tackled was Migetius, but far from confronting him Egila actually associated with him, eventually enlisting in his ranks.[22]

Further heresies subsequently arose, some even enjoying the backing of certain religious authorities. There was the controversial schism within the church at Cabra in the 9th century, following its separation from the Catholic Church,[23] and the Cassianist heresy led by Cuniericus, which – though it had originated elsewhere – was very active in Córdoba and the province during that century. To this difficult doctrinal and ethnic situation for Peninsular Christians, the presence of a new religion, together with a new Andalusī socio-political structure, brought additional challenges. In the 9th and 10th centuries, ethnic considerations created new rifts in a society already divided by religious beliefs, and this led to numerous problems. The group of Córdoba Christians led by

---

19 F. Sáinz Robles, *Elipando y San Beato de Liébana, siglo VIII*, Madrid, 1934.

20 J.F. Rivera Recio, *El adopcionismo en España, siglo VIII: historia y doctrina*, Toledo, 1980, pp. 34-7, 45-6.

21 Cf. P. Jaffé, *Bibliotheca rerum germanicarum*, Paris, 1867, vol. 4, pp. 78-9.

22 Flórez, *España sagrada*, vol. 5, 527-36 (appendix X), cf. vol. 12, pp. 163-4; F.J. Simonet, *Historia de los mozárabes de España, deducida de los mejores y más auténticos testimonios de los escritores cristianos y árabes*, 4 vols Madrid, 1897-1903 (repr. 1983), vol. 2, pp. 262-5. Cf. C. Aillet, 'Pope Hadrian's epistles to Bishop Egila', in *CMR* 1, 338-42.

23 Cf. M. José Hagerty, *Los cuervos de San Vicente. Escatología mozárabe*, Madrid, 1978, 108-13.

Eulogius and Alvar was particularly active in religious matters, whilst in the social and ethnic sphere the Muladis (*muwalladūn*) were quite prepared to fight against the Arabs, making a major contribution to the destabilisation of the Caliphate of Córdoba.[24]

Arabisation, Islamisation and acculturation

The policy of Arabisation and Islamisation pursued by the Umayyad caliph of Damascus ʿAbd al-Malik (r. 685-705)[25] was also introduced in al-Andalus.[26] This political project, comprising the two separate but linked processes of Arabisation and Islamisation,[27] gave rise to a third integrating element – acculturation. The Latin Mozarabic texts on Arabisation as it affected certain Christian groups in al-Andalus have widely been interpreted as a negative reaction to the process. A good example is Paul Alvar of Cordoba's *Indiculus luminosus* (9th century):

> *Heu pro dolor, legem suam nesciunt Xpīani et linguam propriam non aduertunt Latini, ita ut omini Xp̄i collegio uix inueniatur unus in milleno hominum numero qui salutatorias fratri possit ratjonauiliter dirigere litteras, et repperitur absque numero multiplices turbas qui erudite Caldaicas uerborum explicet pompas, ita ut metrice eruditjori ab ipsis gentibus carmine et sublimiori pulcritudine finales clausulasunius littere coartatjone decorent, et iiuxta quod lingue ipsius requirit idioma, que omnes uocales ápices commata claudit et cola, rithmice, immo ut ipsis conpetit, metrice uniuersi alfabeti*

---

24 Ibn Ḥayyān, *Al-Muqtabis*, vol. 3, p. 51. Spanish trans. J. Guráieb, 'Al-Muqtabis de Ibn Ḥayyān', *Cuadernos de Historia de España* 20 (1953) 155-164, p. 156; *Una crónica anónima de ʿAbd al-Raḥmān III al-Nāṣir*, ed. E. Lévi-Provençal and E. García Gómez, Madrid, 1950, § 4 (pp. 36-7 Arabic, 100-1 Spanish trans.), § 52 (71-2 Arabic, 144 Spanish trans.). Cf. M. Fierro, *Abderramán III y el califato omeya de Córdoba*, Donostia-San Sebastián, 2011, p. 83.

25 G.C. Anawati, 'Factors and effects of Arabization and of Islamization in medieval Egypt and Syria', in S. Vryonis (ed.), *Islam and cultural change in the Middle Ages*, Wiesbaden, 1975, 17-41.

26 E. Manzano Moreno, *Conquistadores, emires y califas*, Barcelona, 2006, pp. 58-100, 113-20; A. Fernández Félix and M. Fierro, 'Cristianos y conversos al Islam en al-Andalus bajo los omeyas. Una aproximación al proceso de islamización a través de una fuente legal andalusí del s. III/IX', in Caballero Zoreda and Mateos Cruz (eds), *Visigodos y Omeyas*, 415-27; A. Fernández Félix, *Cuestiones legales del Islam temprano. La 'Utbiyya y el proceso de formación de la sociedad islámica andalusí*, Madrid, 2003, pp. 433-92, 549-63. Cf. J.P. Monferrer Sala, 'Al-ʿUtbī l-Qurṭubī', in *CMR* 1, 734-7; D. Serrano Ruano, 'Al-Khushanī', in *CMR* 2, 342-6.

27 Cf. M. Levy-Rubin, 'Arabization versus Islamization in the Palestinian Melkite community during the early Muslim period', in A. Kofsky and G.G. Stroumsa (eds), *Sharing the sacred. Religious contacts and conflicts in the Holy Land, first to fifteenth centuries CE*, Jerusalem, 1998, 149-62.

> *littere per uarias dictjones plurimas uariantes uno fine constringuntur uel simili apice.*[28]
>
> Oh pain! The Christians are ignorant of their own law and the Latins do not understand their own language, so much so that in the whole Christian community scarcely one in a thousand men can correctly address a letter to a brother in Latin, and yet there are countless multitudes who are able to explain the verbal bombastics of the Arabs, to the extent that, being more learned in metrics than these very peoples, and with more sublime beauty, they adorn their final clauses by shortening a letter, in keeping with the demands of expression in the Arabic, which closes all stressed vowels with a rhythmic or even metric accent, which is suited to all the letters of the alphabet, by means of diverse expressions, and many variations are reduced to one and the same ending.[29]

This fragment has been quoted extensively as an example of the existence of two Christian communities in the 9th century, a model that would eventually extend to the whole of al-Andalus: those who resisted Arabisation and were therefore unwilling to collaborate, opting to oppose the Andalusī state, and those who favoured Arabisation and were more than willing to collaborate with the Muslim authorities, although they continued to use their own language (*al-ʿajamiyya*) without this in any way undermining their standing.[30] But Alvar's text offers much more than this restrictive reading.[31] Certainly, he was complaining about the alarming ignorance of Latin among the Christians of the time,[32] but that was by no means his only – or even his principal – ground for complaint.

Alvar's distress was prompted not by the idea that Christians were familiar with the (classical) Arabic language, or by their skill at versifying, but rather by the idea that this might lead to acculturation, which might in turn favour the assimilation of Islamic ideas and practices that ran counter to Christian orthodoxy; and this is what was really happening among some Christian groups in al-Andalus.[33] This was the real

28 *Albari Indicvlvs lvminosvs* 35 (lines 53-62), in Gil (ed.), *Corpvs scriptorvm mvzarabicorvm*, vol. 2, 314-15.

29 F. Delgado León, *Álvaro de Córdoba y la polémica contra el islam. El Indiculus luminosus*, Córdoba, 1996, p. 185.

30 Ibn Ḥārith al-Jushanī, *Kitāb al-quḍāt bi-Qurṭuba. Historia de los Jueces de Córdoba por Aljoxani*, ed. and trans. J. Ribera, Madrid, 1914 (repr. Seville, 2005), ns. 1, 19.

31 Cf. R. Jiménez Pedrajas, *Historia de los mozárabes en Al Ándalus*, Córdoba, 2013, pp. 88-91, 296-9.

32 F. González Muñoz, *Latinidad mozárabe. Estudios sobre el latín de Álbaro de Córdoba*, Corunna, 1996, pp. 14-17.

33 M. de Epalza, 'Influences islamiques dans la théologie chrétienne médiévale. L'adoptionisme hispanique', *Islamochristiana* 18 (1992) 55-72; J. Tolan, 'Felix of Urgell', in *CMR* 1, 365-6.

cause of Alvar's pain, because the Christians of al-Andalus, and especially those belonging to the group led by Eulogius and Alvar,[34] sought above all to maintain their community identity at the heart of a complex milieu that continually favoured linguistic and cultural interaction between its varied elements.

The Christian community was by no means a community apart, placed in isolation by the ruling powers, although its members were officially defined by their legal status (*dhimma*), and their movements were thus bounded by certain limits imposed by the Islamic authorities.[35] The influence of Islamic law regarding *dhimmīs*, as is apparent in *Al-Qanūn al-muqaddas* ('The sacred canon'),[36] offered channels that facilitated social interaction and by extension the assimilation of Christians into Islam. As was the case with Muslim communities living under Christian rule in newly-reconquered areas, conversion to Islam occasionally provided Christians with a means of escaping the status of social and religious outcasts or worse, a life of slavery or manumission.[37] Within the limits of this legal control, Christians sought their own distinctive identity, drawing up the pre-emptive lines required to control acculturation, i.e. to avoid cultural contacts that might undermine that identity.[38]

But Alvar's text tells us something else: from the information provided, we can infer that he himself was conversant not only with the grammatical rules of classical Arabic, but also with the rules of Arabic prosody as indicated by Ḥafṣ ibn Albar al-Qūṭī (9th-10th centuries)[39] in the introductory *urjūza* to his translation of the Psalms;[40] this would appear to suggest that Alvar of Córdoba was an Arabised Christian.[41] Alvar cannot have been an isolated case in Andalusī urban religious circles; other

---

34 Cf. C.L. Tieszen, *Christian identity amid Islam in medieval Spain*, Leiden, 2013.

35 C. Aillet, *Les mozarabs. Christianisme, islamisation et arabisation en péninsule Ibérique* (*IX*e*-XII*e *siècle*), Madrid, 2010, pp. 33-9.

36 A. Echevarría, 'Vicentius', in *CMR* 3, 81-3.

37 E. Lapiedra, '*Ulūǧ, rūm, muzarabes* y mozárabes. Imágenes encontradas de los cristianos de al-Andalus', *Collectanea Christiana Orientalia* 3 (2006) 105-42, pp. 108-9.

38 A. Echevarría, 'Los marcos legales de la islamización. El procedimiento judicial entre los cristianos arabizados y mozárabes', *Studia Historica. Historia Medieval* 27 (2009) 37-52.

39 J.P. Monferrer Sala, 'Ibn Albar al-Qūṭī', in *CMR* 2, 281-4.

40 Ḥafṣ Ibn-Albar al-Qūṭī, *Le Psautier de Hafs le Goth*, ed. trans. and introduction M.-T. Urvoy, Toulouse, 1994, pp. 15-18. On this *urjūza*, see P.S. van Koningsveld, *The Arabic Psalter of Ḥafṣ ibn Albar al-Qûṭî. Prolegomena for a critical edition*, Leiden, 2016, pp. 71-4.

41 Cf. González Muñoz, *Latinidad mozárabe*, pp. 11-14; J.P. Monferrer Sala and U. Cecini, 'Once again on Arabic "alkaufeit" (Alb. Ind. 23,14). Between polemics and inculturation', *Mittellateinisches Jahrbuch* 49 (2014) 201-10.

educated clergymen must have found themselves in a similar situation. A good example is Abbott Samson (d. 890),[42] who was asked by Emir Muḥammad I (r. 852-86) to translate into Latin a letter to Charles the Bald, king of the Franks (r. 840-77):

> *Et ut mea oratio retrogradet paululum, dum epistole regis Hispanie ad regem Francorum essent sub era DCCCCIa dirigende appelatvs ex regione decreto ego ipse, quatenus, ut pridem facere consueueram, ex Caldeo sermone in Latinum eloquium ipsas epístolas deberem transferre, adfui et feci.*[43]
>
> Going back a little in my account, once when the king of Hispania had to write a letter to the king of the Franks, in the year 863, I was summoned by the king. As it had for some time been my practice, I was to translate the letter from Arabic into Latin; I attended the king, and did so.

As in the Near East,[44] not only did many Christians in al-Andalus understand and use Arabic,[45] but the members of some clans – among them the Banū l-Qasī and the Banū l-Ṭawī – occupied senior posts in the administration of the Umayyad state,[46] whilst others rose higher still, among them Rabīʿ ibn Tudulf, who held several key posts under Emir al-Ḥakam I (r. 796-822). The most important was that of *comes* (*qūmis*) or 'governor of the Christians', but he was also employed as collector of canonical taxes (*mushrif* = exactor) and farmer of non-canonical taxes (*ṣāḥib al-mukūs*); he was even appointed general of the mercenary force that had come from Galicia (*qāʾid ghilmān al-ʿajam*).[47]

The Arabisation of Christians was not regarded as a negative phenomenon by any sector of the Christian population. Quite the reverse: it reflected the sensibility, expressed in a wide variety of ways, triggered

---

42 J.A. Coope, 'Abbot Samson', in *CMR* 1, 691-4.

43 *Samsonis apologeticus* II Praef. 9,1-5, in Gil (ed.), *Corpvs scriptorvm mvzarabicorvm*, vol. 2, p. 554. Cf. *Apologético del Abad Sansón* ed. José Palacios Royán, 'introducción', G. del Cerro Calderón, Madrid, 1988, p. 76.

44 Cf. S.H. Griffith, 'The Manṣūr family and Saint John of Damascus. Christians and Muslims in Umayyad times'; and L. Yarbrough, 'Did 'Umar b. 'Abd al-'Azīz issue an edict concerning non-Muslim officials?', in A. Borrut and F.M. Donner (eds), *Christians and others in the Umayyad state*, Chicago IL, 2016, 29-51, and 173-216 respectively.

45 Cf. D. Millet-Gérard, *Chrétiens mozarabes et culture islamique dans l'Espagne des VIIIe-IXe siècles*, Paris, 1982, pp. 53-62.

46 Cf. M. Meouak, *Pouvoir souverain, administration centrale et élites politiques dans l'Espagne umayyade (IIe-IVe/VIIIe-Xe siècles)*, Helsinki, 1999, pp. 220-7.

47 Ibn Ḥayyān, *Crónica de los emires Alḥakam I y ʿAbdarraḥmān II entre los años 796 y 847* [*Almuqabis II-1*], trans. Maḥmūd ʿAlī Makkī and F. Corriente, Zaragoza, 2001, pp. 63, 170, 273. On this character, see also Á.C. López, 'El conde de los cristianos Rabīʿ ben Teodulfo. Exactor y jefe de la guardia palatina del emir al-Ḥakam I', *Al-Andalus-Magreb* 7 (1999) 169-84.

by a whole range of situations that had to be addressed. By adopting the Arabic language, Christians could be integrated into the new Andalusī society, enjoying any privileges to which their new legal status gave them access.[48] But they were not only absorbed into a new society; they also took part in its culture, which allowed them to create a valuable literary legacy in Arabic thanks to the skill of bilingual Latin-Arabic authors and translators,[49] and this gave rise to a kind of linguistic hybridity.

One example of that hybridity is Ḥafṣ ibn Albar al-Qūṭī's decision to use an Arabic meter (*ʿarūḍ*) when planning his verse translation of the Book of Psalms, noting that 'it is a pleasant metre for singing, which the Latins call iambic' (*wa-huwa ʿarūḍ fī l-ghinā' muʾanniq / ʿinda al-aʿājīm yusammā yanbaqu*).[50] This highlighting of the prosodic resemblance of the Arabic and Latin metres in order to account for his choice is highly revealing in the context of Arabisation, since Ḥafṣ is acknowledging that his choice was made on the basis of a Latin referent. But the comparison also enabled him draw a conceptual parallel between the two cultures, as a way of underpinning his claim that the Latin language and culture were superior to their Arabic counterparts, since the Latin governed the choice made in Arabic.

The *rajaz mashṭūr* metre, therefore, was chosen because it resembled the Latin metre.[51] This selection strategy was to some extent echoed by bilingual Latin-Arabic translators, whose versions were made from a Latin original that they sought to imitate as far as possible. The Arabic language, and by extension the Arabisation process, was for the Christians a means to various ends: amongst other things, it gave them access to the complex system of social promotion within the Andalusī state, allowed them to transmit their religious legacy to those for whom Arabic had replaced Latin as the cultural prestige language, and equipped them with an instrument with which to confound and attack their religious opponents.

This is not the only case of linguistic hybridity. The author of a 12th-century polemical text entitled *Tathlīth al-waḥdāniyya* ('Trebling the

48 Cf. H.E. Kassis, 'Some aspects of the legal position of Christians under Mālikī jurisprudence in al-Andalus', *Parole de l'Orient* 24 (1999) 113-28.

49 P.S. Van Koningsveld, 'Christian Arabic literature from medieval Spain. An attempt at periodization', in S.K. Samir and J. Nielsen (eds), *Christian Arabic apologetics during the Abbasid period (750-1258)*, Leiden, 1994, 203-24.

50 Cf. al-Qūṭī, *Le Psautier de Hafs le Goth*, 16, verse 47.

51 On this meter, see D. Norberg, *An introduction to the study of medieval Latin versification*, trans. G.C. Roti and J. de La Chapelle Skubly, ed. J. Ziolkowski, Washington DC, 2004, pp. 63-7.

Oneness')[52] – a converted Jew, probably from Toledo – refers to the Apostle John as *al-ḥawārī Yaḥyā*, although he goes on to clarify that his real name was *Juwānnish*, i.e. Latin *Iohannes*. He thus uses the qur'anic terms *ḥawārī* and *Yaḥyā* to refer to his Muslim interlocutor, but corrects the Arab name to the corresponding Latin form.

Verse translations like that made by Ḥafṣ ibn Albar al-Qūṭī show that, by the 9th century, the process of Arabisation had reached its zenith among Córdoba's Arabised clergy and aristocracy. The fruits of that trend included a new literary landmark, the publication, in the 10th century, of another translation, *Kitāb al-ʿālam* ('History of the world'), the Arabic title given to the Latin original *Historiæ adversus paganos* by the Spaniard Paulus Orosius (4th-5th centuries), also known as *Kitāb Harūshiyūsh* ('Book of Orosius').[53] The translation from the original Latin appears to have been made jointly by a Christian and a Muslim, probably Aṣbagh ibn Nabīl and Ḥafṣ ibn Albar al-Qūṭī, according to the hypotheses put foward by van Koningsveld and by Penelas.[54]

The translations of the Book of Psalms and the *Kitāb Harūshiyūsh*, as well as other texts translated in the same century, mark the culmination of the Arabisation process among the educated urban Christian classes, but at the same time they point to an intense process of linguistic acculturation, involving the use of Islamic terms and expressions;[55] the *Kitāb Harūshiyūsh* in addition uses expressions belonging to the qur'anic tradition.[56] This latter book, translated jointly by a Muslim and a Christian, marked a watershed in Arabic translation; Islamic nuances crept in through the terminology used. All this makes the *Kitāb Harūshiyūsh* a linguistically ecumenical text and, although other later translations shared similar features, none rivalled the degree of acculturation displayed in it.

---

[52] J.P. Monferrer Sala and P. Mantas-España, *De Toledo a Córdoba. Tathlīth al-waḥdāniyyah ('La Trinidad de la Unidad'), fragmentos teológicos de un judeoconverso arabizado*, Madrid, 2018, pp. 144, 183. Cf. T.E. Burman, 'Tathlīth al-waḥdāniyya', in *CMR* 4, 115-17.

[53] *Kitāb Hurūšiyūš* (*Traducción árabe de las Historiæ adversus paganos de Orosio*), ed. M.T. Penelas, Madrid, 2001.

[54] Cf. van Koningsveld, 'Christian Arabic literature from medieval Spain', p. 217; M.T. Penelas, 'A possible author of the Arabic translation of Orosius' *Historiae*', *Al-Masāq* 13 (2001) 113-35. See also *Kitāb Hurūšiyūš*, 27-33.

[55] H.E. Kassis, 'Arabicization and Islamization of the Christians of al-Andalus. Evidence of their scriptures', in R. Brann (ed.), *Languages of power in Islamic Spain*, Bethesda MD, 1997, 136-55; M.-T. Urvoy, 'Influence islamique sur le vocabulaire d'un Psautier arabe d'al-Andalus', *Al-Qanṭara* 15 (1994) 509-17.

[56] *Kitāb Hurūšiyūš*, pp. 38-40.

Changing political circumstances meant that the Arabised Christians who emigrated northwards took the opposite path, passing from Arabic to Latin. That shift is exemplified by the *Kitāb al-shurūḥ* (*Liber glossarium*),[57] which provides information on linguistic and intellectual trends among 12th-century Arabised Christians who left the south to settle in Toledo. Their new social and religious circumstances prompted a progressive immersion in Latin language and culture; one stage in that process is reflected in the *Kitāb al-shurūḥ*.[58] But the acculturation process taking place in al-Andalus was a two-way affair. While Arabised Christians underwent Arab acculturation, converts to Islam and their descendants were involved in a similar process but in the opposite direction, i.e. though now Muslims, they preserved the memory of their Visigothic past. A classic example is the 10th-century Córdoba historian Ibn al-Qūṭiyyah (lit. 'the son of the Gothic woman') who, in sustaining pride in his Visigothic background, at the same time highlighted the importance both of his Christian ancestors and of their culture, acknowledging in his account the key role played by Christians in the development of Andalusī society.[59]

Sensing the Other: a universe of perceptions

The universe of perceptions held by the Christians and Muslims of al-Andalus forms part of a long chronological process, in which the ideas expressed in their work – as a reflection of their outlook – constructed a discourse dictated largely by the personal views of the author concerned, the time and place in which he formulated his ideas and, above all, the purpose for which they were formulated.[60] In religious terms, the views expressed by Christians and Muslims with regard to each other reflected an attitude that was at not only negative but also actively hostile;[61] they sought to show that they and their faith were superior to their opponents.

---

57 Cf. *Glossarium latino-arabicum*, ed. C.F. Seybold, Berlin, 1900; Van Koningsveld, *Latin-Arabic glossary*, p. 55.

58 Burman, 'Glossarium latino-arabicum', pp. 742-4.

59 J.P. Monferrer Sala, 'Ibn al-Qūṭiyya', in *CMR* 2, 456-9. Cf. A. Christys, *Christians in al-Andalus, 711-1000*, Richmond, 2002, 158-83.

60 Cf. R. Barkai, *Cristianos y musulmanes en la España medieval* (*El enemigo en el espejo*), Madrid, 1991.

61 C.L. Tieszen, 'Christians under Muslim rule, 650-1200', in D. Thomas (ed.), *Routledge handbook on Christian-Muslim relations*, London, 2018, 75-9, pp. 77-8.

In the mid-10th century, the nun Hrotsvit provided a melodramatic account of the martyrdom of the young Pelagius.[62] The narrative was clearly intended as a piece of international propaganda seeking to praise the wisdom of King Otto I (r. 962-73) and highlight the ignorance of Caliph ʿAbd al-Raḥmān III (r. 912-61). The text, which is not based on any written source, presents Islam as an aggressive military power and Muslims as a pagan threat to Western Christendom.[63] It is not an alarmist account, although the author offers her own distorted description of Islam, with an obvious view to disparage it. This twisted vision of the faith of the Other persisted among Christians and Muslims throughout the Middle Ages; it is apparent, *inter alia*, in al-Dāwudi's *Kitāb al-amwāl* ('Book of property'), whose author, in his polemical references to Christian dogma on Christological issues, makes use of general basic theological concepts to refute Christian dogmas, although these dogmas do not in fact reflect the sense of Christian theology.[64]

With certain exceptions, this disparaging attitude was to become a routine feature of the medieval dialogue between Islam and Christianity. It is to be found in the preaching of clergymen such as Pedro Pascual (13th century), Bishop of Jaén, who was captured by Naṣrid troops and imprisoned in Granada, where he died in captivity around 1300. In one of the works attributed to him, *Sobre la seta Mahometana* ('On the Muḥammadan sect'),[65] he displays his familiarity with both Islam and Muslim society, though voicing an aggressively hostile attitude towards both: he attributes the divination practices used by Christians to the bad influence of Islam, tarnishes the name of the Prophet Muḥammad, and describes the Muslims (*Moros*) as fierce enemies of the people of God and as wild beasts (*bestias agri*).[66] His aim, yet again, is clear: to belittle Islam and to provide his Christian readers with arguments to brandish against the Muslims.

Yet in the latter third of the 10th century, John of Gorze (c. 900-74) in his *Vita*[67] offers a vivid account of friendly contacts and cooperation between Christians and Muslims when recounting his mission as

[62] Cf. L.A. McMillin, 'Hrotsvit of Gandersheim', in *CMR* 2, 293-7.

[63] Christys, *Christians in al-Andalus*, pp. 96-7; for the *Passion of Pelagius*, pp. 82-5, 88-91, 94-6, 98-100.

[64] J.P. Monferrer Sala, 'Al-Dāwudī', in *CMR* 2, 637-9.

[65] J. Tolan, 'Pedro Pascual', in *CMR* 4, 673-7.

[66] F. González Muñoz, *Pseudo Pedro Pascual. Sobre la se[c]ta mahometana*, Valencia, 2011, p. 124.

[67] M. Frassetto, 'John of St Arnoul', in *CMR* 2, 475-9. Cf. Jean de Saint-Arnoul, *La vie de Jean, abbé de Gorze*, ed. and trans. M. Parisse, Paris, 1999.

emissary of King Otto I to the Umayyad Caliph ʿAbd al-Raḥmān III in 953. It is true that the whole account underlines the friendly, cooperative attitude of the two monarchs, but there are political reasons for this: their fight against a common enemy, the pirates of the La Garde-Freinet. Even so, the *Vita* also highlights the persistent lack of real understanding between the two creeds, for all that many Córdoba Christians displayed a willingness to collaborate actively with the Islamic authorities.[68]

Contemporary chroniclers evinced a positive attitude to Christianity and simultaneously constructed – with a certain discursive logic – a negative view of Islam: Muḥammad was a repulsive figure, Islam a treacherous faith, and Muslims foolish, cheating infidels. A collective view of the enemy was thus constructed by interweaving all three components. Naturally, the issues covered by the chroniclers were selected with a negative purpose, and affected each of the components. The view propounded by chroniclers, polemicists and theologians was a negative one in which the person or individual (Muḥammad) formed part of a collective structure that encompassed his followers (Muslims) and his faith (Islam).

Although the author of *The chronicle of 741* offers a detailed positive image of the Umayyad conquests,[69] this was by no means the dominant tone amongst historiographers. *The chronicle of 754* describes the Muslim conquest of Hispania as disastrous,[70] whilst *The chronicle of Albelda* and *The chronicle of Alfonso III* contributed decisively to the transmission of the notion of a Gothic renaissance, praising the dynasty of Asturian and Leonese kings as descendants of the Gothic kingdom that fell to the perfidious Muslim enemy.[71] Both chronicles seek to present the Oviedo kings as Hispano-Christian monarchs engaged, as legitimate successors of the Gothic kings, in a battle against the Muslim enemy.[72] A number of texts of this kind give us an idea of the situation in the Peninsula after

68 Christys, *Christians in al-Andalus*, pp. 109-12.

69 Cf. Gil, *Corpvs scriptorvm mvzarabicorvm*, vol. 1, pp. 10-14. Cf. C. Aillet, '*The chronicle of 741*', in *CMR* 1, 284-9.

70 Cf. Gil, *Corpvs scriptorvm mvzarabicorvm*, vol. 1, pp. 31-54. Cf. K.B. Wolf, '*The chronicle of 754*', in *CMR* 1, 302-4.

71 T. Deswarte, '*The chronicle of Albelda and the prophetic chronicle*', in *CMR* 1, 810-15; T. Deswarte, '*The chronicle of Alfonso III*', in *CMR* 1, 882-8.

72 H. Sirantoine, 'Le discours monarchique des "Chroniques asturiennes", fin IXe siècle. Trois modes de légitimation pour les rois des Asturies', in J.M. Fernández Catón (ed.), *Monarquía y sociedad en el reino de León, de Alfonso III a Alfonso VII*, vol. 2, León, 2007, 793-819.

the 'disastrous' Arab invasion,[73] among them the *Historia Silense* ('The history of Silos'), a 12th-century chronicle that deplores the 'loss of Spain' and praises Alfonso VI (r. 1065-1109) for rescuing some territories from 'the sacrilegious hands of the Barbarians'.[74]

Muslim chroniclers offer a comparable view of Christians.[75] In his *Akhbār mulūk al-Andalus* ('Reports on the kings of al-Andalus'), Aḥmad al-Rāzī (d. 995), whilst he devotes considerable space to the history of Christianity in general and to the Christian faith in al-Andalus in particular, attributes the conquest of al-Andalus to the immorality of the Visigothic kings and the treacherous behaviour of their subjects.[76] This negative attitude to the Christian enemy is to be found in all the Islamic chronicles from the very beginning,[77] and even in a number of legal sources, among them *Al-aḥkām al-kubrā* ('The major legal judgements') by Ibn Sahl (d. 1093).[78] This document notes, in clearly authoritarian tones, that Christians are forbidden to walk on Muslim tombs[79] and to build new churches;[80] it also warns its readers against those Christians who, having converted to Islam, later return to the Christian faith,[81] and even conversions from Islam to Christianity, for instance in the 11th century.[82] Interestingly, while the Christian sources show an unexpected interest in Islam, the Islamic texts display little interest in Christianity.[83]

The chronicles of the Almohad period are particularly vitriolic in their condemnation of Christians as wicked and idolatrous, whereas Muslims are hailed as great, brave and heroic. This ideological underpinning, like the anti-Christian propaganda pervading the chronicles, is hardly surprising given that they were written during a *jihād*. The word, in fact was father to the deed: Almohad policy turned the complex situation

---

73 J. Horrent, 'L'invasion de l'Espagne par les musulmans selon l'*Historia Silense*, le *Chronicon Mundi* et l'*Historia de rebus Hispaniae*', in C. Alvar et al. (eds), *Studia in honorem prof. M. de Riquer*, Barcelona, 1986, vol. 2, 373-93.

74 P. Henriet, '*Historia Silense*', in *CMR* 3, 370-4.

75 Cf. A.M. Carballeira Debasa, 'Ibn Bashkuwāl', in *CMR* 3, 451-4, p. 453; M.D. Rodríguez-Gómez, 'Ibn Abī Zar', in *CMR* 4, 815-19, p. 817.

76 *Crónica del moro Rasis*, ed. D. Catalán and M. Soledad de Andrés, Madrid, 1975, pp. 278-9.

77 J.P. Monferrer Sala, 'Ibn Ḥabīb', in *CMR* 1, 825-8.

78 D. Serrano Ruano, 'Ibn Sahl', in *CMR* 3, 210-13. Cf. Ibn Sahl, *Dīwān al-aḥkām al-kubrā, al-nawāzil wa-l-i'lām*, ed. R.H. al-Nu'aymī, Riyadh, 1997, vol. 2, pp. 467, 672-4, 974-6, 1274, 1302-4.

79 Ibn Sahl, *Dīwān al-aḥkām al-kubrā*, vol. 2, p. 1171.

80 Ibn Sahl, *Dīwān al-aḥkām al-kubrā*, vol. 2, pp. 1173-4.

81 Ibn Sahl, *Dīwān al-aḥkām al-kubrā*, vol. 2, pp. 1261-3.

82 J.P. Monferrer Sala, 'Ibn Sa'īd al-Maghribī', in *CMR* 4, 361-4, p. 362.

83 Barkai, *Cristianos y musulmanes*, p. 285.

faced by Jews and Christians into an ever-greater tragedy, culminating in a degree issued by Caliph ʿAbd al-Muʾmin (r. 1133-63) ordering their obligatory conversion.[84]

One text that clearly reflects the regulations governing the daily life of Christians and Muslims in Seville during the 9th and 10th centuries is *Risāla fī l-qaḍāʾ wa-l-ḥisba* ('Epistle on the office of judge and of market inspector').[85] Its author, Ibn ʿAbdūn al-Ishbīlī (d. 12th century) used Islamic legislation as a basis for drawing up a set of rules aimed at destroying any relationship that might have grown up between Christians and Muslims in the city: Muslim women were forbidden to enter churches; Muslims were banned from attending Christian festivities, from shaking hands with Christians or Jews, and from selling them books of science; Christians and Jews were required to wear distinctive clothing.[86]

Andalusī Islamic sources include prophetic traditions and transmissions from the first generations of Muslims, with a view to stressing that Muslims were forbidden to attend Christian and Jewish festivities. Yet in al-Andalus, during the celebrations of *mīlād* (the nativity of Christ) and *ʿanṣara* (Pentecost?), Muslim children visited churches where they were given presents.[87] Other festivals, like *Yannayir* (New Year's Eve) and *Nayrūz* (Jesus' circumcision & also Coptic New Year), were also celebrated by both Christians and Muslims.[88] Regardless of the restrictions imposed by the *fuqahāʾ*, attendance at these Christian festivities testifies to a certain degree of real social interaction between the Muslim and Christian communities.

---

84 M. Fierro, 'A Muslim land without Jews or Christians. Almohad policies regarding the "protected people"', in M.M. Tischler and A. Fidora (eds), *Christlicher Norden – Muslimischer Süden. Ansprüche und Wirklichkeiten von Christen, Juden und Muslimen auf der Iberischen Halbinsel im Hoch- und Spätmittelalter*, Achendorff, 2011, 231-47.

85 C. de la Puente, 'Ibn ʿAbdūn al-Ishbīlī', in *CMR* 3, 397-400. Cf. *Thalātha rasāʾil andalusiyya fī ādāb al-ḥiṣba wa-l-muḥtasib*, ed. É. Lévi-Provençal, Cairo 1955, pp. 1-65. French trans. É. Levi-Provençal, *Seville musulmane au début du XII siècle. Le traité d'Ibn ʿAbdūn sur la vie urbaine et les corps de métiers*, Paris, 1947; Spanish trans. É. Lévi-Provençal and E. García Gómez, *Sevilla a comienzos del siglo XII. El tratado de Ibn ʿAbdūn*, Madrid, 1948.

86 J.P. Monferrer Sala, 'Christians and Muslims in the Iberian Peninsula, 1000-1600', in D. Thomas (ed.), *Routledge handbook on Christian-Muslim relations*, London, 2018, 149-57, pp. 150-2.

87 F. de la Granja, 'Fiestas cristianas en al-Andalus (materiales para su estudio). I: *Al-durr al-munaẓẓam* de al-ʿAzafī', *Al-Andalus* 34 (1969) 39-46. Cf. M. Fierro, 'Ibn Waḍḍāḥ', in *CMR* 1, 834-9, pp. 837-8.

88 Cf. *Le calendrier de Cordoue*, ed. C. Pellat, Leiden, 1961, pp. 26-7, 100-1, 182-3. See also A.-M. Eddé, F. Micheau and C. Picard, *Communautés chrétiennes en pays d'islam du début du VIIe siècle au milieu du XIe siècle*, Paris, 1997, pp. 18-19.

One genre that more than any other epitomised the antagonistic outlook of Christians and Muslims was polemics. Polemical works were more than simply texts designed to stimulate debate between the two communities. Their purpose went beyond expounding and defending certain ideas with a view to refuting opposing views. They were manuals on the faith of the other, aimed at providing a practical guide to the opponent's ideas and arguments. By this means, Christians and Muslims acquired direct, though not necessarily fully accurate, knowledge of the other faith, without mediators who might distort the polemicists' aims. Paradoxically, if anyone was intentionally engaged with the faith of his opponent, it was the polemicist.

The works of Christian polemicists such as Speraindeo and Alvar[89] display a clear Eastern Christian influence,[90] systematically presenting Islam as the arrival of the Antichrist in the person of Muḥammad, who is reviled as a lustful figure – a view extended to Muslims in general.[91] This and other commonplaces regarding the Prophet recurred throughout the Middle Ages among Peninsular Christian polemicists, and are to be found in works by the much later Ramón Llull (d. c.1315-16): *Doctrina pueril* ('Teachings for children'), *Llibre del gentil i dels tres savis* ('The book of the Gentile and the three wise men') and *De fine* ('The goal').[92]

Since the genre of polemics was intended as a means of teaching and providing knowledge, polemicists had to be highly trained. To achieve this, Christian authors unfamiliar with Arabic were provided with Latin translations. A classic case that was to exert considerable influence on later authors[93] was a 9th-century work presented as a correspondence between the Muslim ʿAbd Allāh ibn Ismāʿīl al-Hāshimī and the Christian ʿAbd al-Masīḥ ibn Isḥāq al-Kindī,[94] thought to have been written by

89 J.A. Coope, 'Speraindeo', in *CMR* 1, 633-5.

90 J.A. Coope, *The martyrs of Córdoba. Community and family conflict in an age of mass conversion*, Lincoln NB, 1995, pp. 46-7; León, *Álvaro de Córdoba*, pp. 63-73.

91 J. Flori, *L'islam et la fin des temps. L'interprétation prophétique des invasions musulmanes dans la chrétienté médiévale*, Paris, 2007, pp. 162-3.

92 H. Hames, 'Ramon Llull', in *CMR* 4, 703-17, pp. 706-15.

93 T.E. Burman, 'The influence of the *Apology of al-Kindī* and *Contrarietas alfolica* on Ramon Llull's late religious polemics, 1305-1313', *Mediaeval Studies* 53 (1991) 197-208; O. Lieberknecht, 'Zur Rezeption der arabischen Apologie des Pseudo-Kindi in der lateinischen Mohammedliteratur des Mittelalters', in A. Schönberger and K. Zimmermann (eds), *De orbis Hispani linguis litteris historia moribus*, Frankfurt am Main, 1994, vol. 1, 523-38.

94 L. Bottini, '*The Apology of al-Kindī*', in *CMR* 1, 585-94. Cf. G. Tartar, 'Dialogue islamo-chrétien sous le calife al-Ma'mun (813-834). Les épîtres d'al-Hâsimî et d'al-Kindî', Strasbourg, 1977 (PhD Diss. Université des Sciences Humaines de Strasbourg).

an anonymous Christian in Baghdad. It was translated in 1142 by Peter of Toledo (d. after 1142) in collaboration with Peter of Poitiers (d. 1205). The resulting Latin version, *Epistula Saraceni* [*et*] *rescriptum Christiani* ('The letter of a Saracen [and] the reply of a Christian'),[95] formed part of the corpus of works on Islam known as the *Collectio Toletana*, whose compilation was supervised by Peter of Cluny (d. 1156).[96]

Another work popular with Christian polemicists and apologists was the *Liber denudationis siue ostensionis aut patefaciens* ('The book of denuding or exposing'), a model piece of polemic crucial to our understanding of the way Christians viewed and refuted Islam. The author, now identified as Būluṣ ibn Rajā' (d. 10th-11th c.), of this 12th-century treatise – an abridged translation of what Ibn Rajā' originally composed – revisits all the commonplaces of Islamo-Christian polemics: it dismisses the Muslims as mad for following Muḥammad's law; it describes the Prophet himself as epileptic; it clears the biblical books of any charge of falsification (*taḥrīf*), it provides an account of the Prophet's marriage to Zaynab, and it rejects the miraculous nature of the Qur'an, highlighting, among other *topoi*, the contradictions within it.[97]

Yet another work that exerted considerable influence in the Iberian Peninsula during the Middle Ages was *Dialogi contra Iudaeos* ('Dialogues against the Jews'), written by Petrus Alfonsi (12th century),[98] which earned acclaim amongst those interested in Islam. Chapter 5, which shares certain features with *Risālat al-Kindī*, includes a fierce criticism of Islam: Muḥammad is presented as a false prophet, and attention is drawn to the pre-Islamic pagan origin of rites such as ablutions and pilgrimage.[99] Special emphasis is placed on Muḥammad's violent behaviour and on episodes in his sex life[100] that were widely remarked on and disseminated by Eastern Christian chronographers and polemicists.

---

[95] F. González Muñoz, 'Peter of Toledo', in *CMR* 3, 478-82. Cf. F. González Muñoz, *Exposición y refutación del Islam. La versión latina de las epístolas de al-Hāšimī y al-Kindī*, Corunna, 2005.

[96] On this character and his work, see D. Iogna-Prat and J. Tolan, 'Peter of Cluny', in *CMR* 3, 604-10.

[97] T.E. Burman, *Religious polemic and the intellectual history of the Mozarabs, c. 1050-1200*, Leiden, 1994, pp. 37-62, 108-120, 143-53, 196-7, 204-9, 215-39; T.E. Burman, '*Liber denudationis*', in *CMR* 3, 414-17.

[98] J. Tolan, 'Petrus Alfonsi', in *CMR* 3, 356-62.

[99] A. Ballestín, 'El Islam en los *Dialogi* de Pedro Alfonso', *Revista Española de Filosofía Medieval* 10 (2003) 59-66; B. Septimus, 'Petrus Alfonsi on the cult at Mecca', *Speculum* 56 (1981) 517-33.

[100] Cf. J. Tolan, '*Istoria de Mahomet*', in *CMR* 1, 721-2.

Christian authors throughout the 12th century showed a lively interest in producing polemical theological material such as the *Muṣḥaf al-ʿālam al-kāʾin* ('The book of the existing world'), consisting of a number of surviving fragments of al-Imām al-Qurṭubī's *Iʿlām,* which he attributes to one Aghushtīn.[101] Displaying clear Eastern influence, these focus on the doctrines of the Trinity and the Incarnation. The most significant of the works quoted in it is *Tathlīth al-waḥdāniyya* ('Trebling the Oneness').[102] The author reveals himself as highly conversant with both the Qur'an and the *sunna* and displays great mastery of the expository technique of the *mutakallimūn,* as well as notable familiarity with Christian theology in both the Eastern and the Latin traditions.[103]

Muslim polemicists were just as pointed in their refutations, illustrating with eloquent and forceful rhetoric the absolute truth of their faith. They were equipped to adduce a whole series of arguments, which were not always easy to refute. The most famous among these in al-Andalus was Ibn Ḥazm, who also displayed a remarkable familiarity with the Bible, which he used to criticise both the Jewish and Christian faiths. In his *Kitāb al-fiṣal fī l-milal wa-l-ahwāʾ wa-l-niḥal* ('Book of judgement regarding the confessions, inclinations and sects'),[104] he echoes the polemical stance developed in the East, but at the same time adds some original features to his discourse,[105] notably a vitriolic condemnation of Christian beliefs,[106] and above all a demonstration of what he sees as corruptions (*taḥrīf*) of the biblical text.[107] Significantly, in his description of the various Christian groups, including heretical groups, Ibn Ḥazm makes no reference to the Christians of al-Andalus.[108]

---

101 Burman, *Religious polemic,* pp. 80-4, 100, 117-18, 166-89, 202-4; T.E. Burman, 'Aghushtīn', in *CMR* 3, 745-7.

102 Monferrer Sala and Mantas-España, *De Toledo a Córdoba.*

103 Cf. Monferrer Sala and Mantas-España, *De Toledo a Córdoba*, pp. 17-108.

104 J.P. Monferrer Sala, *'Kitab al-fisal fi l-milal wa-l-ahwa wa-l-nihal'*, in *CMR* 3, 141-3. Cf. Ibn Ḥazm, *Al-fiṣal fī l-milal wa-l-ahwāʾ wa-l-niḥal,* ed. Muḥammad Ibrāhīm Naṣr and ʿAbd al-Raḥmān ʿUmayr, Beirut, 1996, vol. 2.

105 C. Adang, 'Islam as the inborn religion of mankind. The concept of *fiṭra* in the works of Ibn Ḥazm', *Al-Qanṭara* 21 (2000) 391-410.

106 G. Troupeau, 'Présentation et réfutation des croyances des chrétiens chez Ibn Hazm de Cordoue', in A.-M. Delcambre and R. Arnaldez (eds), *Enquêtes sur l'Islam. En homage à Antoine Moussali,* Paris, 2004, 193-210.

107 I. di Matteo, 'Le pretese contraddizioni della S. Scrittura secondo Ibn Ḥazm', *Bessarione* 39 (1923) 77-127.

108 B. Harakat, 'La communauté chrétienne et celle d'origine chrétienne en Espagne musulmane, vues par les sources arabes', in M. Hammam (ed.), *L'Occident musulman et l'Occident chrétienne au moyen âge,* Rabat, 1995, 197-205.

By the 9th century, Muslim theologians were able to draw on a whole series of *testimonia* to reinforce their anti-Christian arguments with regard to certain issues: the Trinity, the corruption of the Bible, the resurrection of the dead and the defence of Muḥammad as the true prophet.[109] This is evident in the *Jawāb ilā risālat rāhib Faransā ilā l-Muslimīn* ('Reply to the monk of France's letter to the Muslims') by Abū l-Walīd al-Bājī (d. 1081). To this routine polemical catalogue of arguments, al-Bājī adds his own aggressive profile of the Christians.[110]

A further tree in the vast forest of texts in the polemical genre (*radd*) is *Maqāmiʿ al-ṣulbān wa-marātiʿ* (*rawātiʿ*) *riyāḍ* (*rawḍat*) *ahl al-īmān* ('Mallets for crosses and provender in the meadows of the faithful'), composed by Aḥmad ibn ʿAbd al-Ṣamad al-Khazrajī (d. 1187) during his two years' captivity in Christian Toledo (1145/6-1147/8).[111] This includes the so-called *Risālat al-Qūṭī* ('Epistle of the Goth').[112] In his reply to this attack on Islam, al-Khazrajī refutes Christian beliefs concerning the divinity of Christ, his incarnation and crucifixion, and the Trinity. He defends the inimitability of the Qur'an (*iʿjāz al-Qurʾān*) and Muḥammad's mission as prophet, underlines the corruption of the Bible (*taḥrīf*), and attacks the Christian author's criticism of *jihād* and of polygamy amongst Muslims.[113]

The lively refutation of Christian doctrines and theological arguments persisted undiminished well into the 13th century, by which time Islamic power in the Peninsula was fast waning. Evidence is to be found in al-Imām al-Qurṭubī's *Iʿlām*,[114] which includes fragments of several Christian works[115] whose theological views are debated point by point; the refutation is accompanied by a lengthy defence of Muḥammad's prophethood and of the miracles attributed to him by Islamic tradition. The aim of his strategy was, as always, to demonstrate the truth of Islam as a revealed religion and the status of Muḥammad as the last prophet sent down (*khātam al-nabiyyīn*).

---

109 A.M. Turki, 'La lettre du "Moine de France" à al-Muqtadir billāh, roi de Saragosse, et la résponse d'al-Bāŷī, faqīh andalou', *Al-Andalus* 31 (1966) 73-153.

110 A. Zomeño, 'Al-Bājī', in *CMR* 3, 172-5.

111 J.P. Monferrer Sala, 'Al-Khazrajī', in *CMR* 3, 526-8.

112 J.P. Monferrer Sala, 'Al-Qūṭī', in *CMR* 3, 524-5. Cf. Diego R. Sarrió Cucarella, 'Corresponding across religious borders. The *Letter of al-Qūṭī*', *Islamochristiana* 43 (2017) 149-71.

113 Burman, *Religious polemic*, pp. 36, 63-4, 67, 70, 83, 253 n. 4, 321 n. 2, 347 n. 7.

114 J.P. Monferrer Sala, 'Al-Imām al-Qurṭubī', in *CMR* 4, 391-4. Cf. Al-Qurṭubī, *Kitāb al-iʿlām bi-mā fī dīn al-Naṣārā*.

115 J.P. Monferrer Sala, *Scripta theologica Arabica Christiana. Andalusi Christian Arabic fragments preserved in Ms. 83* (*al-Maktabah al-Malikiyyah, Rabat*), Diplomatic edition, critical apparatus and indexes, Porto, 2016.

Conclusion: The end of the road?

The expulsion of the Christians from al-Andalus in the mid-12th century and of the Muslims in 1492 (and indeed the exiling of the Moriscos in 1609-13) failed to bring an end to the complex and challenging socio-religious and intellectual situation shared through the centuries by Christians and Muslims in the Iberian Peninsula. However, their mutual interest in each other masked changing structural circumstances of considerable socio-historical interest.

Works by Muslims and Christians certainly presented the other as opponent and – albeit potential – enemy, and his religion as false. While the political image was of enormous value as propaganda in socio-political, and even in ethnic and historical, terms, both religious groupings focused largely on questions of faith. Their works, drawing on expositional and argumentation techniques to be found in Eastern works, both Christian and Muslim, unfailingly sought to demonstrate that theirs was the true faith. Christians vilified Muḥammad and his followers, mocked and scorned Islam, attacked its rites and dogmas, and refuted its theological arguments. Muslims, for their part, scorned and maligned Christianity, branded the Bible corrupt, and generally mocked Christian doctrines in general and Christological teachings in particular, accusing Christians of idolatry.[116]

These negative sentiments always underpinned the two sides' views of the other. Yet, though they sometimes took up violent positions, Christians and Muslims were able to give intellectual expression to their opinions and arguments, each constructing his own logical discourse aimed at capturing the interest and support of his readers and co-religionists. In this intellectual milieu, Christians and Muslims – though ideologically opposed – found a common space that enabled peaceful coexistence for some time;[117] and that coexistence in turn provided a channel of communication between them. It was not a harmonious coexistence in physical terms – something that occurred in al-Andalus only for occasional brief periods – but rather a real, everyday coexistence of competing prejudices and vested interests of all kinds: a 'coexistence of knowledge'.

But that in itself would not have been feasible if Christians – and non-Muslims in general – had not been involved in the process of Arabisation instituted by Muslim authorities. Linguistic integration, which entailed

116 Cf. Jiménez Pedrajas, *Historia de los mozárabes en Al Ándalus*, pp. 133-59.
117 Cf. M. Penelas, '*Dhikr Bilād al-Andalus*', in *CMR* 5, 593-5, p. 594.

acculturation, signified the acceptance by Christians of a new social and cultural situation in which they sought to retain their identity through certain attitudes, but above all through their intellectual activity in both Latin and Arabic. That 'coexistence of knowledge' had a twofold social and intellectual outcome: first, it enabled each of the groups to maintain its distinctive socio-religious and sometimes ethno-religious identity, and second, it led to the export of the intellectual and cultural dynamics of al-Andalus, inherited from the East, to the rest of Europe. This was a watershed moment in a centuries-long journey in which – for all their opposition – Jews, Christians and Muslims helped to create a new world order of knowledge, which would later be passed on to the people and lands of the north.

Chapter 14
Interactions in the early Ottoman period (1299-1518)

Tom Papademetriou

Introduction

To understand the nature of Christian-Muslim interactions in the early Ottoman era, it is important first to understand the background and historical development of the Ottomans in Asia Minor and, more importantly, their advancement into the Balkans. The Ottomans were not only shaped by their Turkmen cultural milieu, which dominated Asia Minor in the 13th century, but also by their rapid expansion in the Balkans. These experiences determined the way in which the Ottomans interacted with Christians they encountered. The ultimate success of the Ottomans was not based upon sheer military force, or the singular religious ideology of holy war, but rather upon a practical approach to conquest and governance that integrated the local populations into their emerging state. As a result, local populations were both victims and agents of the great transformation that took place.

In this chapter, we explore the interaction of Muslims and Christians in the early Ottoman period, that is, the two centuries or so from 1299 to 1518. We begin with brief contextualising discussions of Asia Minor in the 13th century and the origins of the Ottomans in Anatolia. We turn then to the role of Christian *Timariot*s, the competing motifs of *gaza* (holy war) and *istimalet* (accommodation through *dhimmī* regulations), the phenomenon of Christians boys taken into Ottoman service through the *Devshirme*, cultural transformations, and the 'holy man' motif. The case of Gregory Palamas, the topics of bishops and the emirs, Byzantine observers of Ottoman conquest and the 1453 conquest of Constantinople are also discussed, leading into a concluding section on the new emphasis on Islamic principles.

Asia Minor in the 13th century

Interactions between Byzantines and Ottomans were shaped by a series of events that weakened the Byzantine Empire and Seljuk Sultanate of Rum, the two significant 13th-century states in Asia Minor. The resulting power vacuum allowed for the Osman tribal group to emerge with dynamism and tremendous force. In 1204, the European crusader forces sacked the city of Constantinople in what is known as the Fourth Crusade. Byzantine imperial families fled to Nicaea, where they established an exiled government of the Empire of Nicaea. For the period between 1204 and 1261, Nicaea and the surrounding region in north-west Asia Minor remained in Byzantine control. In 1261, Michael VIII Palaeologus (r. 1261-82) retook Constantinople and established himself as the emperor in the historic capital. But the devastating sack of Constantinople in 1204 was so serious that the Byzantines never recovered. Realising their great weakness, the Palaeologan dynasty renewed its focus on the imperial capital, along with calls for rapprochement with the West, and appeals for assistance from that quarter. This Western focus arguably led to the Byzantines losing sight of the importance of their holdings in Asia Minor and the region of Nicaea.

It was at the end of the 13th century, in the region of Bithynia in the Sakarya River valley, that Ertoghrul, a Turkmen tribesman and father of the founder of the Ottoman dynasty, served as a border-lord. The Turkmen had entered Asia Minor as early as 1071, when the Seljuk leader Alp Arslen (r. 1063-72) defeated the Byzantine Emperor Romanus IV Diogenes (r. 1068-71) in the battle of Manzikert. The Seljuk Sultanate of Rum then set up its capital in Konya (Iconium) and remained in control of the greater part of Asia Minor until the late 13th century. Around the same time, nomadic Turkmen tribes migrated into Asia Minor from Central Asia and Khorasan as a result of pressure from Mongol invasions led by Jengiz Khan. It is likely that Ertoghrul first served the Seljuks and later became a vassal to the Ilkhanid Mongols when the Mongols defeated the Seljuks in 1255.

By the end of the 13th century, Seljuk power had been destroyed and Byzantine imperial power was all but erased from the landscape. What remained was a series of small but significant Turkmen tribes or emirates led by tribal leaders, emirs, and some Byzantine cities and fortresses still maintained by Byzantine military commanders who functioned as semi-independent warlords. It is out of these historical circumstances that the tribe of Osman originated. Certainly, there were other Turkmen nomadic groups that formed independent emirates throughout Anatolia, such as the emirates of Saruhan, Karaman, Germiyan, Menteshe, Aydın and Karasi, among others, and for the Byzantines, the tribe of Osman, the Osmanlis, was largely indistinguishable from the Turkmen who had been present since the 11th century.

Byzantine writers rarely spoke of the Turks in terms of a distinct ethnicity; rather they followed the traditional Byzantine designation of all Muslims as *Agarenoi* and *Ismaelitai*, descendants of Hagar and her son Ishmael. The Byzantine princess and historian Anna Comnena was among the first to mention the Turks by name, describing them as 'godless Turks' (*hoi atheōtatoi Tourkoi*).[1] Even so, she, as well as other Byzantine authors such as Michael Psellus, John Cinnamus, George Pachymeres and John Cantacuzenus, continued to use terms with ancient historical references, such as *Sarakenoi*, *Achaemenai*, *Parthoi* and *Persai*. Later Byzantine writers such as Nicephorus Gregoras began to take particular notice of the Ottomans, referring to them as *Persai* and *Tourkoi*, though terms such as *Sarakenoi*, *Agarenoi* and *Ismaelitai* were still prevalent. More rarely, authors such as John Cananus, who wrote in 1422 after the siege of Constantinople, used the term *Mousoulmanoi*.[2]

Origins of the Ottomans in Anatolia

The Ottomans' geographical location clearly offered them an immediate advantage with which to exploit Byzantine weaknesses. Poised in Bithynia, on the border of the Byzantine state, they enjoyed early advances and successes against Byzantine fortresses and cities. Their close proximity to Byzantine territory meant that Ertoghrul (d. c. 1260) and his son Osman (r. ?-1324) were acquainted with the geography and topography of the region. They probably had interaction and exchange with local Byzantine cities. Furthermore, as the historian George Arnakis has shown, the lack of security in Anatolia meant that farming, taxation, and ultimately also administration, were neglected and there was a general loss of morale among the Byzantine population. All this contributed to the weakening of Byzantine control and also caused a crisis in the cities. The decay of Bithynia was due to poor imperial policy and Byzantine

1 A. Comnena, *Alexias*, ed. D.R. Reinsch et al., 2 vols, Berlin, 2001, p. 114; English trans. E.R.A. Sewter, *The Alexiad of Anna Comnena*, Harmondsworth, 1969, p. 93. See discussion in K.-P. Todt, 'Islam and Muslims in Byzantine historiography of the 10th-15th centuries', in *CMR* 5, 35-46.

2 S. Kolditz, 'John Cananus', in *CMR* 5, 342-5, pp. 343-5.

civil wars. When they combined with Turkish inroads, the result was an economic crisis and a seeming state of anarchy. The consequent loss of morale made the Bithynians easy prey to Osmanli raiders.[3]

After initial successes by Osman and his son Orhan (r. 1324-62), the emirate expanded and gained its first foothold in Europe. Orhan captured Prousa (Bursa) in 1326, defeated the Byzantine emperor in Pelecanos in 1329 and Nicaea in 1331, and by 1337 had captured almost the entire province. By 1346, Orhan had agreed to marry the daughter of the Emperor John Cantacuzenus (r. 1347-54) in return for an alliance against the rebels who were threatening Cantacuzenus's rule. Thus, when they entered Europe for the first time in 1352, the Ottomans were serving as allies and mercenaries in support of the Byzantine emperor. By 1354, after a major earthquake destroyed the walls of Gallipoli, the city surrendered to the Ottomans. It then became a staging ground for Ottoman advances into the Balkans.[4]

In the following 50 years, the Ottomans grew from a small Turkish tribe to a major military force. Advances into the Balkans were swift, so much so that, by 1400, much of the Balkans had either been subdued or become vassals to the Ottoman sultan. After the brief but significant setback of the Timurid defeat of Bayezid I (r. 1389-1402) in 1402, and the subsequent civil war between his successors, the Ottomans recovered well enough to reconsolidate power and, under Fatih Sultan Mehmed II (r. 1444-6, 1451-81), they attained the major prize of Constantinople in May 1453.

In a 15th-century narrative by Theodore Spandounes, a member of the Byzantine imperial Cantacuzenus family, the origin of the Ottomans was discussed in reference to the presence of four Turkmen lords on the frontier of the Empire of Nicaea. Being in effect petty Turkmen chieftains, they felt vulnerable to attack by Michael VIII Palaeologus and therefore decided to establish a confederacy, voting for one of the four to be their leader. These four individuals are identified as *Köse* Mihal, *Gazi* Evrenos, Turachan and Osman. It is important to keep in mind that two of the four, *Köse* Mihal and *Gazi* Evrenos, were Christians who had

[3] G. Arnakis, *Oi protoi Othomanoi* [The first Ottomans], Athens, 1947.

[4] P. Charanis, 'On the date of the occupation of Gallipoli by the Turks', *Byzantinoslavica* 15 (1955) 113-16, p. 113.

converted to Islam, but they nevertheless functioned as equal partners under Osman's leadership.[5]

As Osman gained greater control over more towns, and utilised local Greek Christians in his fighting force, many converted to Islam, although mostly later on in their lives. Christian peasants paid tribute to the Ottomans and remained in their places to tend their fields while the local elite estate owners, with more formal ties to Byzantine rule, fled. Eventually, however, even the local elites understood the advantages of remaining, and so became Ottoman subjects. They were able to join the fighting force and thus transform their lands into even larger estates, so becoming part of the new feudal system. This situation encouraged the local population to join the Ottomans. The Ottomans absorbed many of the local social and legal institutions, as well as cultural mechanisms, and were able to exploit the friction between the local agriculturists and the ruling elites who had ties with Constantinople. Thus, pragmatism and utilitarianism were fundamental to the Ottomans' success in growing an empire. Local Christians not only provided them with tribute and resources but many joined forces with them, contributing their institutions and administrative skills. This was to continue as the Ottomans expanded their territory, especially in the Balkans.

Narrative sources confirm the mixing of the local Christian and Turkmen population during the early Ottoman era. According to a 15th-century Ottoman chronicler, Aşıkpaşazade, Osman captured the castles of Bilecik, Yar Hisar, Inegöl and Aya Nicola. When he took Yar Hisar, he gave the daughter of the Christian lord in marriage to his son Orhan. The chronicler remarks that Osman brought justice to the province through his conquests, and the local Christians, who had fled from their villages as a result of the anarchy and crisis, returned and settled down. Hearing how well the population was treated by Osman, other 'infidels' began to come to settle in his region.[6] For the Byzantine side, Nicephorus Gregoras, when he describes the population of Bithynia, identifies three groups: those of Osman, the Byzantines, and a third group of *mixobarbaroi*, the offspring of mixed Greek and Turkish marriages who were active among the Ottomans.[7]

5 T. Spandounes, *On the origin of the Ottoman emperors*, ed. and trans. D.M. Nicol, Cambridge, 1997, p. 15.

6 Aşıkpaşazade, *Vom hirtenzelt zur Hohen Pforte*, ed. R.F. Kreutel, Graz, 1959.

7 H.W. Lowry, *The nature of the early Ottoman state*, Albany NY, 2003, p. 94, n. 107; see D. Manolova, 'Nicephoras Gregoras', in *CMR* 5, 133-7, pp. 136-7.

Christian *timariots*

The process by which the Ottomans actually conquered territory, however, was heavily determined by their general lack of manpower in relation to the size of the conquered territory and subject populations. They formulated a clear method for conquering territory. First, they attempted to make the leaders of neighbouring states their vassals, who paid tribute and provided fighting forces. In effect, they reduced the local rulers to tributary subjects, who were thus able to preserve their autonomy and even political and religious identity. If these leaders refused, their territory would be subdued and annexed. After the success of such conquests, which could take years, a few soldiers would be assigned to key garrisons in the conquered territory. Another Ottoman strategy was to establish direct control by relying on the territory's former ruler. It was in this context that the institution of the *timar* (feudal fiefdom) became the chief fiscal and administrative mechanism. A *timar* was granted by the sultan for loyalty and meritorious service in battle, so giving an individual a vested interest in the territory. As a *timar* consisted of taxation of whole villages and regions, the Ottomans then sent out agents to register the land and the peasantry, and make assessments for the collection of taxes. There was no specific norm for taxation; it was largely dependent on the previous local practice with, often, a lessening of the tax burden – so appealing to the local populace. However, commensurate with their income, the *timariot*s also had to provide a fighting force.[8]

The *timar* system functioned to integrate talented manpower, whether Christian or Muslim, and it was a conservative reconciliation of local conditions and classes. Christian *timariot*s were used because the sultan wanted to preserve low-level authorities who were well recognised by the peasantry. During the early years of the Ottoman state, this policy preserved local laws and customs intact and allowed the Ottomans to incorporate both military and clerical groups into its administrative system.[9]

The great 20th-century Ottoman historian Halil Inalcik was the first to identify the Ottoman practice of incorporating Christians into their fighting force, and rewarding meritorious service with the feudal grant of the *timar*. By examining land registers (*tahrir defteri*) for the 15th-century

---

[8] H. Inalcik, 'Ottoman methods of conquest', *Studia Islamica* 2 (1954) 104-29.

[9] On the application of local codes, see J.C. Alexander, *Toward a history of post-Byzantine Greece. The Ottoman* kanunnames *for the Greek lands, circa 1500-circa 1600*, Athens, 1985.

Balkans with reference to the Arvanid region (today's Albania), Inalcik was able to show that Greek, Slavic and Albanian Christians served in the Ottoman ranks and received feudal rewards for fighting, without being required to convert to Islam.[10] Inalcik explains that, 'It is rather surprising to find that in some areas in the fifteenth century approximately half of the *timariots* were Christians. [...] These proportions were no doubt higher in these areas in the first years after the conquest.'[11]

One such example comes from a surprising Greek Christian source, a hagiographic collection of neomartyrs (*Synaxaristēs neomartyrōn*). This offers an account of an individual named George, who was probably martyred between 1437 and 1439.[12] The account describes him as a 30-year-old Orthodox Christian from Sofia, and a soldier in the Ottoman army. On a visit to Edirne to have his bow mended, he got into a quarrel with the bow-maker over the nature of Jesus Christ. In his anger, George defended Christ's divine nature but, in so doing, he blasphemed against Muḥammad. This led to his execution. In spite of the account being a text created to show the villainy of the Ottomans, it is significant that it identifies George as a soldier who served the Ottomans as a Christian, just like the multiple examples Inalcik identifies in the *tahrir defteri* of Arvanid. The case even caught the attention of the Grand Vizier, who sought a lesser punishment until the crowd clamoured for his death. While one could remain a Christian, the martyrdom account also indicates that there was enough social pressure to put Christians in jeopardy.[13] By the end of the 16th century, this tendency had all but vanished. Nevertheless, the presence of Christians in the earliest Ottoman organisation, with examples lasting well into the 16th century, raises the question of just how the Ottomans justified this, given that theirs was primarily a Muslim culture.

A first step in answering is to accept the principle that Osman led a 'predatory confederacy' that brought together people from various ethnic and religious backgrounds and focused their attention on the rewards of plunder.[14] This is in direct contrast to the traditional and outdated explanation of the Ottomans as being driven by the ideology of the *gaza*, or holy war, to which we now turn.

---

10 For the *tahrir* register, see H. Inalcik, *Suret-i Defter-i Sancak-i Arvanid*, Ankara, 1954.

11 Inalcik, 'Ottoman methods of conquest', pp. 113-14.

12 Synaxaristēs Neomartyrōn, *Ergon psychōphelestaton kai sōtēriōdestaton, periechon martyria 150 kai pleon Neophanōn Hagiōn Martyrōn tēs Orthodoxou tou Christou Ekklēsias mas tōn etōn 1400 eōs 1900 meta Christou*, Thessalonika, 1984, pp. 403-13.

13 K. Sokolov, 'Life of George the Younger', in *CMR* 5, 375-8, pp. 376-8.

14 Lowry, *Nature of the early Ottoman state*, pp. 56-7.

Gaza or *istimalet*?

First articulated by the Turkologist Paul Wittek in his lecture of 1938, the *gazi* thesis identifies the concept of holy war against the Christian Byzantine infidel neighbour as a prime cause of Ottoman success and, indeed, the *raison d'être* of the nascent empire.[15] Wittek's conceptions of the *gaza* were determined to a great extent by his Ottoman and contemporary German literary pursuits. A poem by Ahmedi and an inscription from Bursa formed the basis for considering the early Ottoman sultans as 'Sultan of the Ghazis'. Combined with the literary predilections for the super heroic figure, Wittek projected anachronistic ideas upon a period in which the Ottomans displayed very little in the way of religious fervour. The ideology, however, made it appear that the Ottomans were paving the way for Islam against a world full of infidels: the ideology of the *gazi* thesis thus placed Muslims and Christians in direct opposition to each other.[16] This presupposition became the predominantly accepted line of justification for Ottoman success.

Contrary to this thesis, however, Ottoman success depended on a policy of granting concessions to the local Byzantine population, the peasantry, townspeople, soldiery and clerics, which entailed going beyond the limits of Islamic law in order to incorporate the local population into the administrative system. Inalcik was the first to identify the term *istimalet*, 'the gaining of good will', as the Ottoman policy of accommodation offered to besieged inhabitants in order to encourage their surrender. In his 1991 article, Inalcik explains that *istimalet* facilitated conquest. Promises of generous concessions disposed the indigenous population favourably towards the Ottomans. Rather than imposing new laws as conquerors, the Ottomans maintained the laws, customs, statuses and privileges of the previous rulers, even when it meant exceeding the fairly tolerant legal stipulations of Islamic law towards non-Muslims who submitted. In this way, former Byzantine Christian nobles (*pronoia*-holders) became *timar* holders.[17]

As the historian Heath Lowry says, 'Osman sought to co-opt rather than to conquer his neighbours'.[18] He maintains that *istimalet* was the

---

15 P. Wittek, *The rise of the Ottoman Empire*, London, 1938.

16 For a comprehensive dismantling of Wittek's evidence, and an alternative explanation, see Lowry, *Nature of the early Ottoman state*.

17 H. Inalcik, 'The status of the Greek Orthodox Patriarchate under the Ottomans', *Turcica* 21-3 (1991) 407-36, p. 409; Lowry, *Nature of the early Ottoman state*, pp. 91-2.

18 Lowry, *Nature of the early Ottoman state*, pp. 64-5.

'carrot' in contrast to the 'stick' of conquest. It was by this policy that the Ottomans were able successfully to expand their rule over the Christian Balkan people. Individuals such as *Köse* Mihal and *Gazi* Evrenos, who perhaps were still Christians when they began their association with Osman, would not have wished to participate in a *gaza* system to spread Islam, but would be more inclined to pledge loyalty to Osman in order to share in the booty and spoils of conquest. Using these principles, *Gazi* Evrenos led the Ottoman forces into many battles in the Balkans, and eventually settled in the area of northern Greece in Yenice-i Vardar (modern-day Giannitsa).

Christians boys and the *devshirme*

While the *timar* system certainly favoured individuals who agreed to accept and join forces with the Ottomans, those people and towns that rejected the Ottoman offer of *istimalet* were subject to conquest and perhaps being taken as prisoners of war. Individuals who were captured became slaves (*kul*) to their captors. Those with financial means and connections sought to secure their ransom, while others would stay in servitude. According to the Ottoman practice of collecting *pençik*, a fifth of the captured population were turned over to be slaves of the sultan. This was a continuation of slave systems that had been practised by earlier dynasties in the Middle East. In 'Abbasid, Mamluk, and Seljuk times prisoners of war would be placed in palace schools in order to be trained for service as military or state officials. The procedure under the Ottomans included training in Turkish and perhaps Arabic or Persian as administrative scholarly languages; conversion to Islam, and the adoption of a new identity with a Muslim name and the epithet 'Abd Allāh', meaning slave of Allāh. Known as the *gulam* system, it was probably established in the reign of Murad I (1360-89), when there was a steady supply of prisoners from conquests.

The dating of the *devshirme* is generally thought to be confirmed by a sermon preached in 1395 by the Metropolitan of Thessaloniki, Isidore Glabas, who spoke of free children becoming slaves, 'forced to change over to alien customs' and taught to commit heinous acts on behalf of the barbarians.[19] However, it appears more likely that the *devshirme* system that provided the sultan with an independent force recruited from

---

19 M.St. Popovic, 'Isidore Glabas', in *CMR* 5, 220-5, pp. 222-5.

young Christian boys between eight and 18 years of age was established during the reign of Mehmed I, after the Interregnum (r. 1402-13). This was probably in response to a singular need for trustworthy soldiers who were not connected to or dependent on any of the Turkmen ruling elite families. The *devshirme* system produced the Janissaries, who would become the private army of the sultan. While for some Christian boys this meant being raised to the highest levels in the officialdom of the Ottoman Empire, where *devshirme* recruits rose to the ranks of vizier and grand vizier, it also meant that young boys were removed from their families.[20]

In a number of important cases, children from Byzantine and Serbian elite royal families were brought into the *devshirme* system and ended up being subsumed into the Ottoman ruling elite. These included the nephews of the last Emperor Constantine XII Palaologos (r. 1449-53), Mesih Pasha and Hass Murad Pasha, who had been taken into palace service by Mehmed II at the conquest. Mesih Pasha became the admiral of the Ottoman fleet and governor of the province of Gallipoli, and then finally Grand Vizier, and Hass Murad Pasha served as governor-general (*Beylerbey*) of Rumeli.[21] Another important figure was Mahmud Pasha (*Angelovic*), of Byzantine-Serbian nobility, who was captured and raised in the Ottoman palace in Edirne. In his case, he remained connected to his Christian mother and brother, Michael, who were often at his side in Istanbul.[22]

Cultural transformations and the holy man

The religious *milieu* of the Ottomans was also an important element in their success. As Ottoman religious practice was pragmatic and fluid, and offered a spirit of non-conformism with respect to traditional Islam, it was more palatable to both the Turkmen population and Christians. As the historian Speros Vryonis has demonstrated, the period from the 11th to the 15th century in Asia Minor was a time of great transformation from a Christian and Hellenic culture to a Muslim and Turkish one. However, the transformation was not due to any massive Turkmen migration or population pressure, or even religiously inspired raiding, but rather to a process of cultural conversion that continued well into the Ottoman era.

[20] N. Nazlar, 'Re-reading Glabas in terms of the question of the origin of the Devshirme', *International Journal of Turkish Studies* 22 (2016) 1-15.

[21] Lowry, *Nature of the early Ottoman state*, pp. 115-16.

[22] Lowry, *Nature of the early Ottoman state*, p. 124.

With the Byzantine state and church leadership in essence 'decapitated', regarded as agents of the enemy state, the Turkmen, including the Ottomans, replaced many of the social institutions of the churches, monasteries and poorhouses with their own dervish-inspired institutions. For many of the local Christian population, these came to replace their former religious institutions. Furthermore, the early Turkmen emirs, rather than maintaining strict, traditional Sunnī Islam, added a rather heterodox and even Turkmen shamanist substratum to their religion: they maintained their attachment to the shaman *baba*, or dervish holy man. These dervishes participated in religious practices in which men and women gathered in ritual services, believed in reincarnation and metempsychosis, and used alcohol and hashish for spiritual purposes. Their rituals were not constrained by traditional Sunnī practices, and so proved more palatable to local Christians, who could readily accept them without great resistance. To the local populations of Anatolia and the Balkans, where Byzantine society had suffered a crisis of leadership, the Sufi dervish or *baba* meant a continuation of the Christian holy man motif.[23]

One individual who rose to prominence as a holy man in Anatolia in the mid-13th century, attracting Muslims and non-Muslims alike, was Mawlānā Jalāl al-Dīn Rūmī (1207-73). His preaching reflected ecumenical inclusivism and anti-sectarian pluralism, and he had Christians among his followers. Trained originally as a scholar of the traditional sciences, he transitioned into a Sufi master, developing a form of whirling dance as integral to devotions. This practice, and his emphasis upon the person of Jesus as an important figure in Islam, captivated Christians.[24]

The Sufi holy man as dervish and *baba* continued and proliferated after Rūmī's death among the various frontier brotherhoods of Akhhis, Abdals and Hurufis. These dervishes participated in Ottoman conquests and also took on administrative roles in the emerging state. Sultan Orhan, the son of Osman, was even said to have had good relations with Geyikli Baba, a heterodox dervish who participated in the conquest of Bursa. After this conquest, in which many dervishes participated, Orhan sent Geyikli Baba wine. Additional figures such as Haji Bektash-i Veli became notable for their message of universal love, and the Bektashi brotherhood emerged to be a mystical, liberal and heterodox order. In the early Ottoman conquests, the Bektashi were the colonisers, educators and

---

[23] T. Papademetriou, 'The continuity of the holy man. Orthodox hesychasm and dervish mysticism in the late Byzantine and early Ottoman period', in D. Papademetriou and A.J. Sopko (eds), *The church and the library*, Boston MA, 2005, 32-74.

[24] L. Lewisohn, 'Mawlānā Jalāl al-Dīn Rūmī', in *CMR* 4, 491-508.

propagators of Islamic and Turkic culture. It is thus no surprise that Haji Bektash-i Veli was adopted as patron of the Janissary corps.[25]

While the more flexible, heterodox approach to religious beliefs maintained by the Ottomans may have made the passage to Islam more palatable to local Christian populations, Byzantine officials and religious leaders who resisted the Ottomans were still considered agents of the enemy. For even as Ottoman religious attitudes impacted the interactions they had with the local Christian populace, the Ottomans still considered Byzantines as adversaries, just as the Byzantines understood the Ottomans as Turkmen antagonists who posed an existential as well as religio-political threat. The Byzantines had a long record of experience of Turkmen emirates, including the Ottomans, taking over territory within Asia Minor.

The case of Gregory Palamas

One of the earliest and more significant interactions between the Ottomans and a high profile Greek Orthodox hierarch is recorded in a letter by Archbishop Gregory Palamas of Thessaloniki to his flock in July 1354.[26] Best-known for being the champion of the mystical tradition of silent meditation, or *hesychasm*, Palamas was captured by the Ottomans off the coast of Gallipoli in March 1354, and while waiting to be ransomed, he experienced life under Ottoman rule. Even while he was in captivity, the Ottomans gave him considerable freedom of movement, allowing him to walk about and engage with the local Greek Orthodox community.

Following his capture, Palamas and his fellow captives were initially mistreated, and the local Christian community was forced to care for them. At Biga (Pegai), a Christian leader named Mavrozoumis, a *heteriarch*, offered shelter, clothing and food. Mavrozoumis ensured that Palamas was well cared for, and that he could teach and conduct services in the church for local Christians and captives. It is after relating this first part of his captivity in his account that Palamas described the Ottomans as 'hated by God and cast out of his father's blessing – to live a prodigal life in swords and knives, indulging in slavery, murder, plundering, rape,

25 I. Melikoff, 'L'origine sociale des premiers Ottomans', in E. Zachariadou (ed.), *The Ottoman Emirate (1300-1389)*, Rethymnon, Crete, 1993, 135-44.

26 J. Pahlitzsch, 'Gregory Palamas', in *CMR* 5, 101-8, pp. 103-8.

licentiousness, adultery, and homosexuality', and he explained that he gained this impression 'now that I know their ways better'.[27]

After being taken to the cool mountainous region of Bursa (Prusa), where the emir spent the summer months, Palamas was visited by Ishmael, the grandson of Orhan. In a conversation that ranged from agreement about almsgiving and disagreement about the prophethood of Muḥammad, the crucifixion of Christ and the virgin conception of Jesus, Palamas remarked how Ishmael was not angrily disposed to him, even though the Muslim had a reputation for being enraged and unrelenting against Christians.

In his captivity, Palamas was cared for by a Christian physician named Taronites, who was also the physician of the Emir Orhan. Taronites sought to have Palamas moved to Nicaea explaining that he was a great teacher and theologian.[28] In response, Orhan proposed an extended dialogue with his own wise men, whom Palamas identifies as 'Chiones', probably a group of Jewish scholars who had converted to Islam. While their discussion of the differences between Islam and Christianity was formulaic, which has led some historians to question its veracity, Palamas offers compelling details that indicate it actually took place. For example, while the entire discussion is very respectful, after it was over one of the Chiones attacked Palamas and hit him in the eye, only to be rebuked and reprimanded by Orhan himself.

Palamas states that, when he was taken from town to town, the guards who accompanied him would ask questions to which he would respond. Often, they concurred with him and discussed matters in a very pleasant manner. In his final stop in Nicaea he was free to wander the town, and went to observe a Muslim funeral service performed by an imam. When it was over, Palamas and the imam began a lengthy discussion on the differences between Christianity and Islam. After this had gone on a while, many of the local Muslims were clearly getting irritated. The local Christians signalled Palamas to conclude, to which he replied, 'If we were in one accord, we would be of one and the same faith, too.'

As one of the first direct sources on the Ottomans, this account is significant and offers an opportunity to gain valuable insight into the relations between Christians and Muslims at this time. Easily identified is the aspect of violence against the Christians, whether it was the

[27] D. Sahas, 'Captivity and dialogue. Gregory Palamas (1296-1360) and the Muslims', *Greek Orthodox Theological Review* 25 (1981) 409-36, p. 415.

[28] M. Vucetic, 'Taronites', in *CMR* 5, 109-13.

captivity of Palamas and his companions, or the displaced local populations of Lapseki and Biga by the conquering Ottomans. Spurring on antipathy between the two groups, the reactions of the Ottomans and Palamas affirm their respective attitudes of social superiority and inferiority, as well as providing a taste of their mutual polemics. Yet even this gave way to what appear to be three sincere interactions and attempts to affirm common agreement and values, the first with Ishmael, the second with the Chiones, and the third with the imam. In none of these do the participants come to agreement as such, but they are clearly engaged in serious inquiry and discussion, with points of agreement and disagreement. In the context of these dialogues, extreme responses are restrained and they are discouraged when they do emerge.

Perhaps what is most interesting in this example, however, is the existence of individuals such as Mavrozoumis and Taronites, who were both significant Christians in a dominant Muslim Ottoman state. It may be that they were outliers and exceptional. However, their ability to intervene and perform important functions as Christians in an Ottoman setting may be more an indicator that, as long as the Christians accepted Ottoman rule, they could – and did – play significant roles in Ottoman society.

Bishops and the emirs

In the process of the Turkmen takeover of Asia Minor, many Byzantine officials and priests fled, with most retreating to Constantinople. They included bishops whose sees were located in the now-conquered territories. The patriarch of Constantinople was keenly aware of the state of the churches in Asia Minor, being informed by refugee clergy. Records of these interactions are found in the minutes of the Patriarchal Synod of Constantinople, preserved in the *Patriarchal acta*.[29]

For their part, the bishops who had fled understood that they represented an enemy state to the Turkmen emirs, and they had therefore left reluctantly. Theophanes of Nicaea wrote a pedagogical letter to his Christian flock in the 1360s concerning the state of the church in the region. He bemoans the fact that the metropolitans and bishops cannot officiate in Ottoman-controlled territory, and that priests still have difficulty tending

---

[29] F. Miklosich and J. Müller (eds), *Acta et diplomata medii aevi sacra et profana*, 6 vols, Vienna, 1860-90.

to pastoral needs and are hindered from administering and distributing the sacraments. He warns the local Christians not to be seduced by an 'immoral lifestyle' when they are living among the Muslims.[30] Yet, as this seemed to be happening at an alarming rate, a letter by the patriarch of Constantinople to the Christians of Nicaea urged any Christians who felt compelled to take on the exterior markings of Islamic faith to keep their Christian beliefs and continue in secret to practise them, and to follow God's commands in order to attain salvation.[31] In essence, they were urged to remain true to their faith as crypto-Christians.

The Patriarchal Synod of Constantinople had a keen sense of these challenges, and recorded multiple cases of bishops who had to be reassigned to other sees in non-occupied locations for 'reasons of sustenance' (*kata logon epidoseon*); in other words, to receive suitable financial compensation. Other bishops, however, continued steadfast in their sees after they had been overrun by Turkmen, at great risk to themselves. These bishops sought to ingratiate themselves with their new masters in order to serve a Christian populace that was unable to flee.

Ironically, we know of these individuals because the Patriarchal Synod viewed this situation with great concern. In numerous cases, bishops appealed to the local Turkmen emir and accepted his suzerainty. Often a financial gift, intended first as a type of bribe and identified later as an investiture gift (*pişkeş*), was given for him to be allowed to remain as bishop over the Greek Orthodox community in the territory. These interactions represented a new relationship with the Turkmen emirs in which the bishops openly acknowledged the authority of non-Christian rulers. But the Patriarchal Synod was greatly alarmed by these arrangements, and the *Patriarchal acta* record emphatic condemnations of individual bishops for being undisciplined and disobedient in this regard.

One of the chief complaints was that bishops who sought to collaborate with Turkmen emirs would disregard canonical administrative order. In some cases, under the direction of the emir, these bishops would take authority over a jurisdiction that was not their own. The condemnation of the metropolitan of Chalcedon in 1394 is such an example. When the Ottomans had taken over the region of Asia Minor across from the city of Constantinople, it included the Monastery of Akapnios together with its estate. It is not clear who initiated the arrangement, but the Ottoman Sultan Bayezid I (r. 1389-1402), who was firmly in control of the territory,

---

30 K.-P. Todt, 'Theophanes of Nicea', in *CMR* 5, 189-93, pp. 191-3.

31 Lowry, *Nature of the early Ottoman state*, p. 67.

granted the monastery and holdings to the metropolitan of Chalcedon. The monastery had been established as an ecclesiastical order dependent directly on the Patriarchate of Constantinople (*stavropegaic*), and not under the authority of the local bishop. As a result of the new arrangement, the Patriarchal Synod reacted with great condemnation, denouncing the transfer as an act of greed and the metropolitan for acting 'like an Ottoman'. They referred to St Gregory the Wonderworker's 'canonical epistle' from the 3rd century, which condemned the stealing of properties aided by foreign powers (referring to Goths invading the Pontos region). The Synod warned the metropolitan against becoming a 'publican' and a 'foreigner'.

A few years later, the Patriarch Matthew I (r. 1397-1410) was compelled to defend himself in a public letter against charges of collaborating with Sultan Bayezid. He emphatically denied secretly negotiating with the sultan during a siege of the city in 1401 to arrange for his personal security if Constantinople should ever be taken, saying it would be the same as a 'betrayal of Christ'. Interestingly, in the face of an Ottoman siege of the Byzantine capital, people considered it possible that even a patriarch could make a private negotiation for safety with the Ottomans.[32]

The Patriarchal Synod of Constantinople was perhaps justified in its alarmed response to the Turkmen emirates and the rise of the Ottomans. For it witnessed how local churches in Ottoman territory faced confiscations, and how their bishops were threatened and many fled because they were regarded as representing the enemy Byzantine state, which could no longer protect them. Those bishops who chose to remain in Turkmen-controlled territory took a more independent stance from that of the Patriarchate of Constantinople, establishing new terms for living under Muslim rule, initiated with financial payments or gifts.

As previously stated, in the Turkmen emirate era, metropolitans, archbishops and bishops made financial gifts to the Turkmen emirs, perhaps initially as bribes, in order to maintain their positions. This practice continued well into the Ottoman period and eventually became normalised in a practice known as the *iltizam* system, or tax farming system, grafted onto the church. While the church was important to the Christian population for spiritual and psychological reasons, it was also the owner of tremendous financial resources on account of the multiple

[32] T. Papademetriou, 'The Turkish conquests and decline of the church reconsidered', in D.G. Angelov (ed.), *Church and society in late Byzantium*, Kalamazoo MI, 2009, 183-200, pp. 194-5.

gifts and estates it had received from faithful Christians, and was also, in effect, a revenue-producing institution on account of its various fee collections (marriage, funeral, baptisms), saints'-day markets and rents from extensive landholdings. The Ottomans became aware of these financial opportunities but, because Islamic law did not allow for the direct taxation of religious institutions, it could not directly exploit them. Their solution was to make the church into a specialised revenue-producing concession, essentially a 'tax farm' (*iltizam*), that would be assigned to an individual bishop, who would become the 'tax farmer' (*mültezim*). Just as with other such arrangements, in ports and mines, the bishop was required to make a payment for the right to hold the concession, and a yearly payment thereafter, according to the assigned geographical jurisdiction.[33]

The collection of funds and yearly payments to the Ottoman treasury was based on the revenue production of the churches in the bishop's jurisdiction. However, it did not include the head (poll) tax on non-Muslims, the *cizye*. The administration of this tax was completely separate from ecclesiastical dues, and it was Ottoman officials originating from the military ranks (*sipahi*) who were assigned to collect it, and not members of the non-Muslim communities. The bishops were responsible only for collecting funds and submitting payments for the revenue generated by local parishes. In effect, the Ottoman state determined a way in which to exploit the Christian church financially.

This Ottoman practice of the ecclesiastical tax farm had direct and detrimental effects on the church and its leadership. For instance, individuals who sought to serve the church in positions of high office were immediately faced with a huge financial burden because, in order to serve, clergy were forced to make a payment to the Ottoman state, in return for which they received a *berât* of appointment. Only when they had this could they take their place in the church hierarchy, as in the case of a bishop being enthroned, and all the while they were conscious of their ongoing financial responsibilities towards the Ottoman state. Interestingly, the fact that the church became the locus of financial transactions actually attracted laypeople to become the financial sponsors of individual clerics who sought to attain higher ecclesiastical ranks, including that of the patriarch of Constantinople. This resulted in there being a great number of speculators who advanced various financial agendas in a

33 T. Papademetriou, *Render unto the sultan. Power, authority, and the Greek Orthodox Church in the early Ottoman centuries*, Oxford, 2015, pp. 139-75.

system that would become highly competitive. In time, competition was to become so severe that particular sees were often the objects of fierce bidding contests. Individual bishops, metropolitans and even patriarchs would hold office for only a short time, having made a down payment, but might be removed in short order in favour of another candidate. Entire fortunes were lost in this way, and it posed a huge financial strain on the church as it was ultimately responsible for the revenue stream. The Christian community also suffered the vagaries of this burdensome system, while the Ottoman treasury reaped the financial rewards. The church, as far at the state was concerned, provided a fiscal opportunity. The formation and use of this ecclesiastical *iltizam* system accompanied Ottoman expansion, for it was particularly well suited to putting the institution of the church at the service of the state; in other words, integrating the church into the Ottoman fiscal mechanism.

Monasteries under the Ottomans

As with local bishops, the fate of monasteries under Ottoman rule depended on the individual monastery's stance towards the Ottoman conquest of their region. In the heady times of Byzantine patronage, monasteries profited from generous benefactions. However, in times of uncertainty monasteries needed to secure their existence, and so vigorously protected any concessions and rights they were enjoying. In the early period of Ottoman rule, when the Ottomans took over large parts of the Balkans, they were faced with the challenge of monastic administrations. The initial Ottoman response was ambivalent, though the monks were not. They approached the Ottoman emirs to request that their monastic property should be recognised, as it had been in the past, with the goal of protecting, or even increasing, their rights. The monks of Mt Athos, in particular, were often successful in securing this protection of their rights and interests.

Among the first documents to be issued by the Ottoman state in respect of monastic institutions is a decree issued by Sultan Murad I (r. 1360-89) in late 1372 to the Monastery of St John Prodromos in Serres, in which he ordered that the monks, along with their villages, lands and mills, should be exempt from any taxation. In essence, the monastery had secured the right to exist without any harassment from the Ottoman state.[34]

[34] E. Zachariadou, 'Early Ottoman documents of the Prodromos Monastery', *Südost Forshungen* 28 (1969) 1-12, p. 3.

However, monasteries were complex entities in that they sometimes had much land and other properties, as well as dependencies, or *metochia*. These posed additional administrative problems for the Ottoman state, as each monastery sought to protect its own resources.

In 1568, the monasteries faced a major challenge as a direct result of the attempt by Sultan Selim II (r. 1566-74) to confiscate properties belonging to Mt Athos in order to satisfy an immediate need for cash. The sultan had ordered monastic properties to be treated like any other land holding, so if monasteries had not paid any yearly tithes according to the traditional land-holding regime (*tapu*), or had purchased their properties illegally with false documents, these properties would revert to the Ottoman imperial treasury. A *fetva* was even issued by the head Islamic jurist (*sheyh-ül-Islam*), Ebussuud Efendi (1490-1574), who justified the ruling according to *sharīʿa*. Once the property was in possession of the state, the monks would be able to purchase it. In response, monks made substantial payments to the Ottoman imperial treasury in order to redeem monasteries in the region of Thessalonike and Serres. However, they also aggressively negotiated to be recognised under the new status of pious foundation (*vakıf*), as with similar Islamic foundations. They even threatened to abandon all their monasteries and leave them fallow, and so worthless. As a result, Sultan Selim II recognised their status and Ebussuud issued a legal opinion acknowledging each monastery as a *vakıf*, and the monasteries were issued with *vakıf* foundation documents.[35]

Byzantine observers of the Ottoman conquest

To contemporary Byzantine observers, the Ottoman power were not simply a competing state and culture, but a direct existential threat. This was confirmed by the obvious fact that the Ottomans were successful in conquering territory and cities.[36] The Byzantine Emperor John VI Cantacuzenus (r. 1347-54) wrote both historical works and polemical *apologias*. In his *Historion biblia tessara* ('Four books of history'), he gives an extended account of his relations with Turkmen emirs, and with the Ottomans in particular. He describes how he became friends with Umur

35 J.C. Alexander, 'The Lord giveth and the Lord taketh away. Athos and the confiscation affair of 1568-9', in D. Komine-Dialete (ed.), *Athos in the 14th-16th centuries*, Athens, 1997, 149-200.

36 Todt, 'Islam and Muslims in Byzantine historiography'.

Pasha of Aydın, and then with Orhan, who had first been his enemy, laying siege to Constantinople in 1337, and then his ally, marrying John's daughter Theodora. John relies on the Turks in his civil war against John V Palaiologos (r. 1341-76), which is concluded by agreeing a joint regency, and later by Cantacuzenus's abdication in order to become a monk.[37] Preoccupied with religious ideas, Cantacuzenus wrote *Logoi tessares kata Moameth* ('Four orations against Muḥammad'), which contain highly informed arguments against Islamic religious principles. These include quotations from the Qur'an, while depending heavily on Demetrius Cydones's translation of the *Contra legem Sarracenorum* by the Florentine Dominican, Riccoldo da Monte di Croce. His grandson, Emperor Manuel II Palaeologus (r. 1391-1425), later refers to these very orations in composing his own work, *Dialogos meta tinos Persou* (Dialogue with a Persian) in 1392/3 in which Manuel and a *müderris* of Ankara debate the principles of Islam and Christianity. Ultimately, Cantacuzenus saw the Ottomans as an enemy force, although he regarded the losses of the Byzantines to the Ottomans as only a temporary setback.[38]

Demetrius Cydones was a Byzantine courtier who was sympathetic to Rome. He was a prolific writer and scholar who saw the Turks as *asebeis* ('ungodly') people who would bring the Christian faith to ruin. In a speech advising on the course of action in the struggle against Sultan Murad I, Cydones advised against the handing over of Gallipoli to the Ottomans, arguing that the result would be a definitive loss of religious freedom.[39] Furthermore, in a series of letters to the Emperor Manuel II Palaeologus, he talks of Christians despairing under Turkish rule, and the numbers succumbing to apostasy. He is alarmed that some Christians prefer to live under a restrictive Islamic legal code rather than have their liberty as Christians. When Manuel II was taken into the court of Murad I, Cydones wrote that he was concerned for the young man's soul, and prayed for him not to succumb to the pressure of Muslim blasphemies against God and apostatise. He was fearful that the emperor would suffer spiritually by his close association with the Muslims.[40]

The historian Doucas, who is best known for writing a well-informed account of the period 1347-1453, called Sultan Bayezid I 'a persecutor of Christians like no other around him', who contributed to 'intrigues and

[37] K.-P. Todt, 'John VI Cantacuzenus', in *CMR* 5, 165-78, pp. 168-73.

[38] Todt, 'John VI Cantacuzenus', pp. 173-8. See also: F. Tinnefeld, 'Manuel II Palaeologus', in *CMR* 5, 314-25, p. 222.

[39] Tinnefeld, 'Manuel II Palaeologus', pp. 318-19.

[40] F. Tinnefeld, 'Demetrius Cydones', in *CMR* 5, 239-49, pp. 248-9.

machinations against the rational flock of Christ'.[41] Ironically, Bayezid was criticised by fellow Muslims for turning against his co-religionists, the Muslim emirs in Anatolia. According to the early 15th-century Ottoman chronicler Ahmedi, Bayezid betrayed the *gaza* against the Christians and moved instead against his fellow emirs. It was this betrayal, Ahmedi argued, that brought Timur (Tamerlane) and his Mongol warriors as divine retribution against Bayezid in his defeat at the Battle of Ankara in 1402.[42] When Timur captured Bayezid there was in Constantinople a general sense of reprieve from the impending Ottoman threat. This continued when Bayezid's sons engaged in a civil war, known as the Ottoman Interregnum (1402-13).

The Byzantine emperors used Bayezid's defeat as an opportunity to regain the upper hand. However, by 1422, the Ottomans had once again returned to power, and under Murad II they set siege to Constantinople. The little-known John Cananus dedicates an entire work to this siege, *Diēgēsis peri tou en Kōnstantinoupolei gegontos polemou* ('Narration of the fighting that took place in Constantinople'), recounting how, with Emperor Manuel II too ill to lead the people, the populace rose up and destroyed the Ottoman siege engines. He portrays Sultan Murad as influenced by the divination and magic of the religious figure Mersaities, who is married to his daughter. Cananus explains the Christian triumph as a result of divine intervention. It was the apparition of the Virgin Mary on the walls of Constantinople that was responsible for the ultimate salvation of the city, just as in times past.[43]

In his account of the capture of Thessaloniki by Murad II in 1430, John Anagnostes describes the Turks as being not necessarily anti-Christian, but rather being motivated by the search for booty. Thus, their destruction of churches and relics, especially those of St Demetrius, were simply the acts of impious marauders looking for treasure. As an aside, Anagnostes mentions them being impressed by the power of the holy oil at the shrine of St Demetrius.[44]

The historian Laonicus Chalcocondyles, writing in 1463-4, seems to offer a different, and more balanced, perspective on the Ottomans. Rather than focusing on them as a scourge or a punishment for the Byzantines' unfaithfulness to God by signing a union with the West,

---

41 G. Prinzing, 'Doucas', in *CMR* 5, 469-77, pp. 470-7.

42 Lowry, *Nature of the early Ottoman state*, p. 25.

43 S. Kolditz, 'John Cananus', in *CMR* 5, 342-45, pp. 343-5.

44 E. Mitsiou, 'John Anagnostes', in *CMR* 5, 353-7.

Chalcocondyles presents the Ottomans in a more classical framework, in that their actions are not barbaric or brutish, but are governed by fate (*tychē*) and virtue (*aretē*). Such ideas perhaps emanated from his education under George Gemistos Plethon. His deep awareness of Muslim belief and practice is revealed in his descriptions of the Ottomans' daily prayers, fasting, pilgrimage, marriage and family law, their prohibitions against wine and pork, and various customs. What is even more impressive is his knowledge of Muslim rule in the empires of the Mongols and Timur, among the Mamluks of Egypt, and in the Iberian Peninsula (he includes the *Reconquista*). His detailed knowledge of Ottoman administrative practices makes him a valuable source for Ottoman history, including the period of the conquest of Constantinople.[45]

The conquest of Constantinople

In his account of the conquest of Constantinople in 1453, the Byzantine historian Doucas describes Fatih Sultan Mehmed II as the 'Antichrist, the spoiler of the flock of my Christ, the enemy of the Cross', entering the city and 'destroying and enslaving the inhabitants, trampling upon the blessed sacraments, demolishing the holy churches with their relics of the saints and martyrs'.[46] The religious rivalry between two main Christian factions in Constantinople threatened to split the population in the face of the impending threat of catastrophe. There was great antipathy between the two main parties of the Byzantines, namely the Unionists, who sought to join Rome through church union, as affirmed at the Council of Florence (1439), and those who were opposed, led by the monks Mark of Ephesus and Georgius Scholarius, who later became Patriarch Gennadius II Scholarius (r. 1454-56; 1463; 1464-65). It was Doucas who recorded the famous words of the Grand Duke Loucas Notaras: 'It would be better to see a turban of the Turks reigning in the centre of the City than a Latin imperial crown'.[47]

Doucas describes the dramatic defeat and slaughter of Byzantine fighters, including the Emperor Constantine XI (r. 1449-53), followed by the raiding of homes and monasteries, the enslavement of women

---

[45] J. Preiser-Kapeller, 'Laonicus Chalconydyles', in *CMR* 5, 481-9, pp. 483-9.

[46] Prinzing, 'Doucas', pp. 470-7.

[47] Prinzing, 'Doucas', pp. 470-7. See also Doucas, *Decline and fall of Byzantium to the Ottoman Turks by Doukas. An annotated translation of 'Historia Turco-Byzantina'*, ed. and trans. H.J. Magoulias, Detroit MI, 1975, p. 210.

and children, and the capture of Hagia Sophia (Aya Sofya). When Sultan Mehmed II entered the city, he went directly into the great church and 'marvelled at the sight'.[48] The Ottoman historian Tursun Beğ also describes how Mehmed caused the gates of the city to be opened, and how he went to Hagia Sophia, which was 'a sign from Paradise' with a dome that 'vies in rank with the nine spheres of heaven'; he climbed 'up to the convex outer surface, mounting as Jesus the spirit of God ascended the fourth sphere of heaven'.[49] Referred to by the Ottomans as the 'opening' of Constantinople to the domain of Islam (*İstanbul'un fethi*), the conquest became known by the Byzantines, and later by modern Greeks, as the 'fall' of Constantinople (*alōsē tēs Kōnstantinoupoleōs*). The Ottomans recalled the Hadith of the Prophet Muḥammad: 'Verily they will conquer *Konstantiniyye*. Truly their commander will be an excellent one. Truly that army will be an excellent one'. Yet, the relationship that Mehmed II had with the city of Constantinople was more complex than the accounts of conquest might seem to indicate.

The sultan had hoped the city would capitulate and be spared actual conquest, and would therefore not be sacked and looted. According to Islamic law, if the *ahl al-kitāb* (People of the Book) surrendered, they and their property would be spared. If they resisted they would be considered as polytheists (*mushrikūn*), and when they were defeated by force (*anwatan, qahran*) they would have no rights and so be reduced to slavery. In this instance, the ruler would be entitled to one-fifth of all movable property. Immovable property would become the property of the state, in essence the property of Mehmed himself. Knowing the consequences, he appealed three times to the Emperor Constantine to surrender. According to Doucas and the Ottoman chronicler Neshri, Constantine, together with Loucas Notaras, actually considered this appeal to surrender. However, it was rejected when the Italian soldiers defending Constantinople flatly refused to surrender to the Muslims. In the event, the city was conquered by force on 29 May 1453.[50]

Mehmed II had a clear vision for the city to be the capital of a world empire. Perhaps because of his rudimentary Greek education and training at the Ottoman court, as well as the influence of his stepmother, Mara Brankovic, a scion of the Byzantine imperial family, Mehmed and his

[48] Doucas, *Decline and fall*, p. 235.

[49] Tursun Beg, *The history of Mehmed the Conqueror*, Minneapolis MN, 1978.

[50] H. Inalcik, 'The policy of Mehmed II toward the Greek population of Istanbul and the Byzantine buildings of the city', *Dumbarton Oaks Papers* 23-4 (1969/1970) 229-49, p. 232.

successors considered themselves to be successors of the Roman emperors once they sat on the throne of the Caesars. This was affirmed by the Byzantine intellectual George of Trebizond, who wrote to Mehmed, 'No one doubts that you are emperor of the Romans. Whoever holds by right the centre of the empire is emperor, and the centre of the Roman Empire is Istanbul'. Mehmed claimed all the 'stones, and the land of the city', which included all the buildings, for himself, and allowed his soldiers to carry off their share of booty.[51]

However, in order to begin the process of building an imperial capital worthy of a world conqueror, Mehmed needed to repopulate the city. To do this, he sought to bring in builders, tradesmen and artisans, and he resettled his one-fifth share of prisoners along the shore of the Golden Horn, near the Phanar. From June 1453 to January 1454, he was relatively unsuccessful at attracting people back, and eventually he ordered some 4,000 to 5,000 Muslim, Christian and Jewish families, who had settled from the Balkans and Anatolia as part of the policy of forced migration (*sürgün*), to take part in the task of rebuilding. They were given tax exemptions, which became a vexed issue as non-Muslims were seen to be receiving special privileges in the context of the conquest.[52] He also decided to make a gesture so as to inspire confidence among the Christians, partly in the hope of enticing many to return. He chose Georgius Scholarius to be appointed patriarch of Constantinople, a position that had been vacant since before 1453. The new patriarch was given great honours by the sultan, and the two of them spent time together discussing issues of faith in a spirit of friendship. This moment was marked both in a contemporary account by Kritovoulos of Imvros, and later in 16th-century patriarchal chronicles.[53]

The appointment of the new patriarch has been marked by historians as a momentous occasion when the Ottoman *millet* system, the historical model in which non-Muslim religious leaders served as both civil and religious authorities, was established. According to the *millet* system, the non-Muslim religious leader became the ethnarch (*millet-bashı*) and was granted civil authority to govern all aspects of the entire Greek, Armenian or Jewish community of which he was head. Essentially, this set religious leaders to govern a state within the state. However, the *millet*

---

[51] Inalcik, 'Policy of Mehmed II', p. 233.

[52] Inalcik, 'Policy of Mehmed II', p. 247.

[53] Kritovoulos of Imvros, *History of Mehmed the Conqueror*, trans. C.T. Riggs, Princeton NJ, 1954; M. Crusius, *Turco-Graeciae, libri octo*, Basle, 1584.

system has recently been contested by historians of the early centuries as inadequate to describe Christian-Muslim relations as well as church-state relations under the Ottomans.[54] According to the Ottomans, the primary responsibilities of the patriarch granted by the Ottomans were not to govern the Greek Orthodox community as ethnarch, or even to collect and submit the non-Muslim dues, the *cizye*; these tasks were carried out by Ottoman administrators. Rather, the obligation of the church hierarchs to the Ottoman administration was to act as tax farmers (*mültezim*) for a cash income derived from the church's extensive holdings.

Patriarch Gennadius bemoaned the conditions within the city, and he resigned about eight months after his appointment. In his letter of resignation, he described how he had been saved by Mehmed, who had personally bought his freedom and brought him to Constantinople, where he gave him a monastery and restored a number of churches to the Christians. Gennadius looked on the re-establishment of the church in Constantinople and in the empire as a miracle of God, but as patriarch he had suffered great trials and hostility from members of the Greek community. He therefore tried to resign, but Mehmed prevented this.[55]

The relationship between the sultan and the patriarch is further punctuated by the request that Mehmed made of Gennadius to compose for him a treatise on the Christian faith. Gennadius wrote a longer and then a shorter version of the work, *Peri tēs monēs hodou pros tēn sōtērian tōn anthrōpōn* ('On the only way to salvation for humankind'). In this treatise, written first in Greek and then translated into Ottoman Turkish for Mehmed, he gives a summary of Christian beliefs. In 12 articles he treats the doctrine of God as creator, the doctrine of Christ, including his incarnation, death, resurrection and judgement of the world at his second coming, the doctrine of the immortality of the soul and life after death, and finally proofs for the Christian faith. Gennadius does not shy away from arguing why Christianity is the only faith to lead to eternal life, contending that the decline of Christian rule does not mean it is less true, as persecution and criticism do not have power over it.[56]

At about the same time as this, in 1455, a work in Arabic was also composed for Mehmed II by an unknown author to explicate why the Muslim faith was correct, and to disprove Christian beliefs. It reflects

---

[54] See 'Chapter 3: Millet system revisited', in Papademetriou, *Render unto the sultan*, 19-62.
[55] K.-P. Todt, 'Gennadius II Scholarius', in *CMR* 5, 503-18, pp. 506-8.
[56] Todt, 'Gennadius II Scholarius', pp. 510-12.

many popular ideas and attitudes towards the Christian religion, though it was written by someone with limited sophistication in his knowledge of both Christian and Muslim doctrines. Composed as a dialogue, a Christian asks a Muslim a number of questions related to the abrogation of Christianity by Islam, the prophethood of Muḥammad and the divinity of Christ, and also groups that oppose Muḥammad's prophethood. It shows that Ottoman Muslims knew little about the Christian faith, though they sought to understand it, to learn how it differed from Islam, and how they might respond to it.[57]

By 1460, Patriarch Gennadius had begun to reflect still further on the fate of Christians under Ottoman rule. In his lamentation on the fall of Constantinople, known as *Gennadiou thrēnos*, he worries that, while physical enslavement is bad, Christians falling away from their faith and corrupting their souls is worse. He observes that Christians no longer receive guidance in the churches, the clergy no longer know how to officiate at services and are poorly trained, and the commandments of Christ are neither preached nor obeyed. He offers witness to a moment of deep cultural, educational and religious impoverishment that was a direct result of the conquest of the city.[58] Nevertheless, he observes that Ottoman rulers are not motivated by religious hatred in their subjugation of Christians, but actually that Christians enjoy almost unrestricted freedom of religion in Ottoman society. The Ottomans are always willing to cooperate with and work with Christians, so long as it strengthens their imperial rule.

In spite of these mixed sentiments, Gennadios followed an eventful career as patriarch, serving for a total of three terms, all the while trying to extricate himself from the position and to retire to the Prodromos Monastery near Serres, which he finally did in 1465. Yet, even after that, he continued to write theological treatises, including a dialogue with two Turks about the divinity of Jesus Christ, *Erōtēseis kai apokriseis peri tēs theotētos tou Kyriou hēmōn Iēsou Christou*.[59]

While Mehmed II was credited with rebuilding an imperial Istanbul marked by an air of cosmopolitanism and cultural pluralism, his son and successor, Bayezid II (r. 1481-1512), moved towards a more definite

---

57 D. Thomas, '*Ḥujaj al-milla l-Ḥanīfiyya wa-jawāb kull su'āl*', in *CMR* 5, 419-20.

58 Todt, 'Gennadius II Scholarius', pp. 514-15.

59 Anastasios Yannoulatos, 'Byzantine approaches to Islam', in G.C. Papademetriou (ed.), *Two traditions, one space. Orthodox Christians and Muslims in dialogue*, Boston MA, 2011, 147-78, pp. 157-8; Todt, 'Gennadius II Scholarius', pp. 516-18.

Islamic identity for his state and his capital city. Critics of Mehmed's lenient treatment of Christians and his embracing of non-Islamic principles in order to govern his multi-religious polity, were troublesome to Bayezid, who did his best to increase the power of Muslims. As a result, he was responsible for the construction of significant imperial mosques, and also increased the power of the Sufi sects. In particular, he fostered the building of dervish lodges (*zâviyyes*) in densely populated Christian districts of Turkish cities in the hope of converting the largely Christian quarters to Islam. Actions such as these, and continued pressure on the church hierarchs to collect financial offerings for the state, had an adverse impact on Greek Christians and on the social institution of the church.

Conclusion: a new emphasis on Islamic principles

Heath Lowry identifies the 'key fault line in Ottoman history' as occurring in 1516-17 during the reign of Sultan Selim I (r. 1512-20), who turned Ottoman attention away from western conquests in the Balkans to Muslim neighbours towards the east. His first challenge was against the Safavid Empire, whose boundaries he pushed back into Persia, though in the process he was required to prove his true Islamic beliefs and Sunnī *bona fides* in order to make a distinction between the Ottomans and the Persians, who were seeing a rise of Shīʿism under the inspired leadership of Shah Ismaʿil (r. 1501-24). The result was the deliberate massacre of thousands of Kizilbash, who were considered to be heretical Alawites and confederates of the Shīʿī Safavids. After conquering the Mamluks and taking control of Egypt and Syria, Selim expanded his control over Arabia to be master of the three holy cities of Mecca, Medina and Jerusalem. It was at this time that the Ottoman sultans took the title 'Servant and protector of the holy cities of Mecca and Medina', and later 'caliph', the successor of the Prophet Muḥammad.

The Ottomans had always identified themselves culturally as Muslims, though the practice of their faith varied in time and place, and they were strongly influenced by the practicalities of ruling as a minority over a larger Christian majority. The overwhelming need to adjust to this reality led to the latitudinarian policies of *istimalet* and legal adjustments to reflect political realities. When faced with competition from a Shīʿī state, however, and when they took over the Islamic heartlands, they were faced with the challenge of establishing new norms for dealing with Christian subjects.

Sultan Süleyman, 'the Lawgiver' (r. 1520-66), was keenly aware of this challenge. Seeing the massive expansion of his empire over the traditional Islamic heartlands and the hostility of the Safavid state, he turned his attention to reforming Ottoman laws. The greatest challenge was to reconcile the principles of *istimalet*, which had been practised since the inception of the Ottoman state in north-west Anatolia, with traditional Sunnī Islamic legal codes. An immediate impact of this process was felt in 1521, when the Patriarch Theoleptos was challenged about Christian ownership of churches, especially in Istanbul, a city that had been conquered and had not capitulated. An account of this survives in the patriarchal chronicles that date from the middle of the 16th century, and are also confirmed by one of the *fetvas* of Ebussuud Efendi. The question was raised that, if Christians had actually been conquered by Muslims, why had all their churches not been forfeited to the conquerors, as Islamic law prescribed, but remained in their possession? In a creative solution, the Christian community came to the defence of Patriarch Theoleptos and proceeded to show that Constantinople had, in fact, surrendered. They brought forward three aged Janissaries, who with their own eyes had actually seen the Emperor Constantine XI offer Sultan Mehmed II the keys to the city. This fabricated story was somehow accepted, and the crisis was averted.[60]

While this was perhaps enough to stave off the immediate challenge, the Ottoman state, especially under Süleyman, sought to reform administrative practice and to bring it into line with proper Islamic norms. This was also true about the way in which the Ottomans related to Christians and legislated for them. In the end, the Ottomans favoured Islamic principles and jettisoned previous accommodationist practices, thus shaping the way in which Christians would be treated for the next three centuries.

60 Papademetriou, *Render unto the sultan*, pp. 107-8. See also M. Philippides, 'Patriarchal chronicles of the sixteenth century', *Greek, Roman, and Byzantine Studies* 25 (1984) 87-94.

Chapter 15
Muslim rulers, Christian subjects

Luke Yarbrough*

Introduction

Surveys of pre-modern Christian and other non-Muslim life under Muslim rulers have generally stressed two themes: the *dhimma* system – recently and tendentiously labelled 'dhimmitude' – and, though to a lesser extent, demographic decline.[1] The term '*dhimma* system' refers to the body of legal theory that Muslim jurists devised in order to rationalise and regulate the permanent presence of non-Muslim populations in Muslim-ruled territories, and which Muslim rulers enforced to varying degrees. It was based upon a 'pact' (*dhimma*) that non-Muslim communities were believed to have made with Muslim leaders at the time of the conquests. 'Demographic decline', meanwhile, refers to the eventual reduction of Christians and other non-Muslims to a position of demographic minority in Muslim-ruled lands, including some regions in which they had once constituted a substantial majority, such as Egypt, Syria and Anatolia.

These two themes have resonated with modern audiences for several reasons. The '*dhimma* system' heavily colours many of our sources because it was a lens through which many pre-modern Muslim historians, most of them trained in Islamic law, viewed their non-Muslim neighbours. It is also frequently treated as though it were a set of rules that

* I would like to thank Thomas Carlson, Claire Gilbert, Chris PreJean, Christian Sahner and Lev Weitz for their assistance in the preparation of this study. Any remaining errors are mine.

[1] In addition to studies cited below, general treatments include A. Tritton, *The caliphs and their non-Muslim subjects*, London, 1930; A. Fattal, *Le statut légal des non-musulmans en pays d'islam*, Beirut, 1958, 1995^2; A.-M. Eddé, F. Michea and C. Picard, *Communautés chrétiennes en pays d'islam*, Paris, 1997; W. Kallfelz, *Nichtmuslimische Untertanen im Islam*, Wiesbaden, 1995; Y. Courbage and P. Fargues, *Chrétiens et Juifs dans l'Islam arabe et turc*, Paris, 1997; D. Wasserstein, 'Conversion and the *ahl al-dhimma*', in R. Irwin (ed.), *The new Cambridge history of Islam*, vol. 4, Cambridge, 2010, 184-208; 'Dhimmitude' is a polemical neologism popularised by Gisèle Littman, *nom de plume* Bat Ye'or; see Bat Ye'or, *Le dhimmi. Profil de l'opprimé en orient et en Afrique du nord depuis la conquête arabe*, Paris, 1980.

structured patterns of Christian life uniformly wherever Muslims held political authority. By knowing this system, the reader may feel enabled to grasp the supposedly stable, constant framework within which that life was lived at all times and places, and thus to regard historical departures from the system as anomalies. The framework of the *dhimma* system makes especially good sense to citizens of modern nation-states, where public life is, in theory, regulated by state legislation, which is in turn enforced by complex state bureaucracies and regulates the actions of political leaders as well as citizens.

The minority status of Christians in modern Muslim-majority countries, for its part, has long interested European and North American publics. The reasons for this interest go beyond curiosity about its historical causes. Muslim persecution of Christians has been a staple motif of Western discourse concerning Islam since the medieval era, animating such racially-charged tropes as that of the 'cruel Saracen'.[2] The motif of Muslim persecution doubles as a convenient aetiology for Christian decline 'under Islam'. It is intuitively attractive, for example, as an explanation for why Christians converted to Islam in substantial numbers and in numerous milieus. Indeed, the supposed cause and its result are mutually reinforcing; by bearing in mind Christians' subordination, one can readily understand how allegedly perennial oppression by Muslims has been historically feasible.

Although it may appear true to the sources, didactically efficient, and intuitively persuasive to foreground the *dhimma* system and demographic decline in studying the history of Christian life in Muslim-ruled lands, this approach has certain drawbacks. Focusing on the *dhimma* system, for example, downplays not only the importance of other, non-legal normative orders, but also the ways in which pre-modern Islamic jurisprudence (*fiqh*) differed from modern legal systems. Systematic *fiqh* was constructed chiefly by private individuals, the jurists, or *fuqahāʾ*, who also wrote many of the narrative sources on which modern historians depend. Jurists disagreed sharply amongst themselves regarding the particulars of the law, and their relations with Muslim state authorities were frequently strained or even antagonistic. Not surprisingly, Muslim rulers enforced the prescriptions of Islamic law unevenly. While they were usually keen to tout their own Muslim credentials, rulers also made appeals

---

[2] See J. Tolan, *Saracens. Islam in the medieval European imagination*, New York, 2002, as well as, e.g., J. Tolan, 'Guibert of Nogent', in *CMR* 3, 329-34; T.E. Burman, 'William of Tripoli', in *CMR* 4, 515-20; E. Frunzeanu, 'Vincent of Beauvais', in *CMR* 4, 405-15.

to other power bases, including non-Muslims, and resisted attempts by the jurists to guide and restrain their actions. What is more, treating the *dhimma* system as a fixed rule governing non-Muslim life contributes to a confirmation bias, whereby historical evidence that accords with the supposed rule is taken to prove that it was continuously in force, while evidence that deviates from it is *ipso facto* exceptional.

Keeping long-term Christian demographic outcomes in focus, meanwhile, encourages teleological history, in which all manner of historical data is pressed into service to explain the central fact: the slow but inevitable 'eclipse of Christianity in Asia' or 'decline of Eastern Christianity', as two well-known modern studies express the notion in their titles.[3] Evidence of conflict and Christian suffering is especially congenial to this project; the historical Christian penchant for martyrology has thus been helpful in shaping the dominant narrative.

In an effort to avoid the drawbacks of this paradigm, this chapter will take a different approach in surveying Christian life under Muslim rulers during the first millennium of Christian-Muslim encounter. This approach denies neither the considerable salience of Islamic law in many settings, nor the legitimacy of seeking historical explanations for the growth of Islam and the concomitant demographic contraction of Christianity as a proportion of the general population in multiple regions. Yet it is equally important to recognise that the '*dhimma* system' underwent as much development and variation as any other historical aspect of Christian-Muslim relations. It was not uniform in its content, or universally acknowledged, or reliably enforced in all its particulars. Instead, it was a variegated theoretical ideal that was constructed, invoked and ignored in complex, highly contingent ways. Demographic decline, meanwhile, was undeniably a significant long-term process, but was not inevitable, unidirectional, monocausal or driven by conversion alone. Thus, those histories of Christians under Muslim rule that are haunted by the spectre of their modern, often difficult circumstances – dire as these may be – do something of a disservice to the immense complexity of their history and the agency of its participants, Christian and Muslim alike.

---

3 L.E. Browne, *The eclipse of Christianity in Asia. From the time of Muhammad till the fourteenth century*, Cambridge, 1933; Bat Ye'or, *The decline of Eastern Christianity under Islam. From jihad to dhimmitude, seventh-twentieth century*, trans. M. Kochan and D. Littman, Madison NJ, 1996.

Of the four heuristic themes that underlie this volume – accommodation, affinity, antipathy, and appeal – all but the last are clearly visible in the ways that Muslims have interacted with Christians in Muslim-ruled societies. Since 'appeal' (e.g. apologetics) implies an invitation that is both highly self-conscious and linguistically encoded, and is amply treated elsewhere in the book, it is set aside in this chapter. The three remaining themes are traced through a survey of Christians under Muslim rule in four periods of Islamic history: 1. The Prophet and the first caliphs (c. 610-61); 2. The early Islamic empires of the Umayyads and 'Abbasids (661-945); 3. Islamic societies in the middle period, when the 'Abbasid caliphs lost political control and the empire fragmented (945-1250); 4. Crises and reconsolidation, when the Islamic world was split into regional states, with no central symbol of political unity (1250-1600). In addition to noting the subtle ways in which the three themes emerge from the rich sources that survive from these periods, this survey will stress two additional features of the story: the contingent, historical development of Muslim normative thought regarding non-Muslims residing among them, and the effects of inter- and intra-religious competition upon the relative prominence of accommodation, affinity and antipathy at particular historical moments.

The Prophet and the first caliphs (c. 610-61)

Several verses of the Qur'an appear to instruct the Prophet's followers on how to treat Christians – usually called *al-Naṣārā* – and Jews.[4] Most of these are thought to be products of the later, politically oriented Medinan sections of the text rather than the earlier Meccan ones, which emphasise piety and eschatological vigilance. The verses in question tend to temper strong antipathy towards non-Muslims with a spirit of accommodation. The best-known of them is Q 9:29. In the rendering of A.J. Arberry, it reads: 'Fight those who believe not in God and the Last Day and do not forbid what God and His Messenger have forbidden – such men as practise not the religion of truth, being of those who have been given the Book – until they pay the tribute out of hand and have been humbled.' Whereas certain other verses, which classical Muslim

[4] On Christians in the Qur'an more generally, see J. Hämeen-Anttila, 'Christians and Christianity in the Qur'ān', in *CMR* 1, 21-30, and C. Gilliot, 'Christians and Christianity in Islamic exegesis', in *CMR* 1, 31-56, and studies cited there, particularly J. McAuliffe, *Qur'ānic Christians. An analysis of classical and modern exegesis*, Cambridge, 1991.

exegetes understood to have been revealed earlier, express cautious affinity with 'People of the Book', Christians included (e.g. Q 2:62, 5:82, 57:27), this verse, Q 9:29, sanctions limited warfare against them (compare, for example, Q 2:190-1, 2:194, 9:5, which do not specify People of the Book). However, it also instructs its audience to accommodate People of the Book once they have offered tribute (*jizya*) and acknowledged their subordination. While the verse's original context is difficult to pinpoint – it may connect to the Prophet's open conflict with Jewish tribes in Medina or his military expeditions against Jewish oasis towns – many later interpreters took it to abrogate earlier, more amicable passages and to establish a lasting sanction for offensive warfare and tribute-taking. Other important verses dissuade the Qur'an's audience from consorting with Christians. Q 5:51, for instance, addresses 'believers' directly: 'O believers, take not Jews and Christians as friends; they are friends of each other. Whoso of you makes them his friends is one of them.'

This and similar if more general warnings (e.g. Q 3:118, 60:1) may well be the products of a process by which the Prophet's followers fashioned for themselves a separate socio-political community, distinct not only from Arabian polytheists but also from Jews and Christians. The Prophet's own encounters with Christians, according to the semi-legendary accounts narrated in the earliest surviving Muslim sources, were largely individual, informal and peaceful.[5] They include meetings with monks and other pious men who recognised Muḥammad's prophethood; correspondence with Christian rulers of Ethiopia and Rome, some of whom were similarly impressed and converted, or wished to; and delegations of Ethiopian and South Arabian Christians who visited him, in some cases concluding treaties. Within the Prophet's lifetime, however, the state he established in Medina had turned its energies towards expansionist warfare in Arabia, against both polytheist Meccans and local Jewish tribes. At the time of his death, his followers were busy opening a new front on the fringes of Byzantine-ruled, heavily Christian Palestine.

In the wake of the vast conquests that ensued, some of the ways in which the Prophet had reportedly treated Christians assumed signal importance. A prominent example is the treaty he reportedly made with the Christians of Najrān, a town in northern Yemen that had a substantial miaphysite Christian population. This document, which echoes the

---

[5] These sources were written decades or centuries later, and modern scholars disagree about their historical accuracy. See S.A. Mourad, 'Christians and Christianity in the *Sīra* of Muḥammad', in *CMR* 1, 57-71.

language of surrender agreements from the ancient Near East, deals with the regular payments that the Christians of Najrān commit to make and the perpetual guarantees they receive in return. The Christians agree, among other things, to supply 'cloaks' or 'weapons' (*ḥulal*, sing. *ḥulla*), shields and animals at specified times, and to shelter the Prophet's emissaries. In exchange, they have 'God's protection and the pact of Muḥammad the Prophet, Messenger of God' (*jiwār Allāh wa-dhimmat Muḥammad al-nabī rasūl Allāh*) for their persons, possessions, land, religious practices and so forth. No bishop, monk, or deacon (*wāqih* or *wāfih*) will be harassed, and they will not be impressed into military campaigns. They must not, however, take usury or oppress others. This treaty was reportedly confirmed and revised by the first two caliphs, successors to the Prophet's political leadership: Abū Bakr al-Ṣiddīq and 'Umar ibn al-Khaṭṭāb.[6] While many of the purported conquest-era treaties that are found in the sources were undoubtedly composed long after the fact – including those that circulated among early-modern Christian churches and claim to record the Prophet's agreements with Najrān and other Christian communities – the archaic language in this Najrān document lends it verisimilitude.[7] Similar uncertainties surround the vast body of Hadiths that ostensibly record the Prophet's words and deeds. Several of these pertain to the treatment of Christians and other non-Muslims, as we shall see, but they are best regarded as evidence of Muslim normative views in a somewhat later period.

There is less doubt regarding the general ways in which Christians, Jews and other non-Muslims were affected by the conquests that Muḥammad initiated, and that his successors, the first caliphs, prosecuted on a much larger scale.[8] The Prophet's political movement was a militant one that claimed a divine mandate to fight non-members, where membership was predicated in part upon the adoption of distinctive dogmas and practices. Thus, the largely Christian populations of Syria

---

[6] Al-Shaybānī, *al-Aṣl*, ed. M. Buynūkālin, Beirut, 1433 [2012], vol. 7, pp. 550-7. Cf. al-Balādhurī, *Futūḥ al-buldān*, ed. 'A.-A. al-Ṭabbā', Beirut, 1307 [1987], pp. 86-92; Ibn Sa'd, *Kitāb al-ṭabaqāt al-kubrā*, ed. 'A.M. 'Umar, Cairo, 2001, vol. 1, p. 249.

[7] For informed arguments concerning the origins and historicity of this and similar treaties, see M. Levy-Rubin, *Non-Muslims in the early Islamic empire*, Cambridge, 2011, pp. 8-57, esp. 53-5. For credulous and tendentious discussions of the early modern Christian versions of such treaties, see Ahmed El-Wakil, 'The Prophet's treaty with the Christians of Najran. An analytical study to determine the authenticity of the covenants', *Journal of Islamic Studies* 27 (2016) 273-354; J.A. Morrow, *The covenants of the Prophet Muhammad with the Christians of the world*, Kettering OH, 2013.

[8] R. Hoyland, *In God's path. The Arab conquests and the creation of an Islamic empire*, Oxford, 2014.

and Iraq were subjected to military invasion by members of that movement. This experience included sieges, requisitioning, impressment, enslavement and the endemic violence that accompanies all large-scale warfare. Christians writing in Greek and Syriac presented the events as a catastrophe.[9] Yet the sources also point to factors that mitigated the severity of the early conquests for some Christians, tempering antipathy, that is, with accommodation. One is that the proto-Muslim community may have been rather more inclusive than it would later become. Some sources indicate that Syriac-speaking Christians joined the Arabian conquerors, as did certain powerful Arab tribes, such as the Banū Taghlib and Banū Tanūkh, who kept their Christian faith for decades or centuries. Here Christian-Muslim affinity can be glimpsed even amid military conquest. Another such factor was that the militant ideology that helped to inspire the conquerors also inspired a certain respect for Christianity, which they could regard as legitimate if obsolescent. Thus one Christian cleric of Iraq, writing in 647-8, remarks that the invaders 'not only do not fight Christianity, they even commend our religion, show honour to the priests and monasteries and saints of our Lord, and make gifts to the monasteries and churches'.[10] There was finally the conquerors' established practice of making treaties with communities that surrendered. Like the Najrān document, these typically specified that the conquered people would render tribute and allegiance in exchange for security and a dispensation to continue their religious practices. The treaties were minimally invasive and presume a high degree of social separation between the Arabian conquerors and their new subjects. All of these factors – in addition to the relative infrequency of extended sieges in the period of the conquests – help to explain why there is scant archaeological evidence of major social or economic disruption.[11] Yet, although the treaties set parameters for a stable post-conquest political arrangement, they could hardly have specified how Muslims were to deal with Christians and other non-Muslims as a stratified, regional post-conquest society evolved into an increasingly integrated world empire.

---

[9] M. Penn, *Envisioning Islam. Syriac Christians and the early Muslim world*, Philadelphia PA, 2015, pp. 15-52; J. Howard-Johnston, *Witnesses to a world crisis. Historians and histories of the Middle East in the seventh century*, Oxford, 2010.

[10] F. Donner, *Muhammad and the believers*, Cambridge MA, 2010, pp. 112-14; H.G.B. Teule, 'Ishoʿyahb III of Adiabene', in *CMR* 1, 133-6; L. Greisiger, 'John bar Penkāyē', in *CMR* 1, 176-81.

[11] R. Schick, *The Christian communities of Palestine from Byzantine to Islamic rule*, Princeton NJ, 1995; G. Avni, *The Byzantine-Islamic transition in Palestine*, Oxford, 2014.

Early Islamic empires (661-945)

The conquests continued for nearly a century after the rule of the Prophet and the early caliphs gave way to the patrimonial dynasty of the Umayyads following the death of the caliph ʿAlī ibn Abī Ṭālib in 661. Treaties like those described above continued nominally to structure relations between Christians and Muslims in the expanding Umayyad empire. At the same time, the tenor of those relations changed palpably as inter-communal social contacts intensified under imperial rule, as Muslims solidified and elaborated their identities and dogmas, and as Christians began converting to Islam in increasing numbers. These changes accelerated after 750, when the Umayyad caliphs were toppled by a revolt that ushered in the new caliphal dynasty of the ʿAbbasids. By about 945, when the ʿAbbasid caliphs lost the last vestiges of their own political power and were reduced to communal figureheads, Muslims had established the prescriptive discourses through which some among their descendants would aspire to regulate interactions with Christians for the rest of the pre-modern period. Certain basic historical patterns of those interactions – such as that of general comity, punctured by episodes of violence when Christians were seen to advertise their faith or power too publicly – had also emerged by 945.

The Umayyad caliphs ruled over a large proportion of the world's Christians – perhaps a majority. These Christians belonged to several competing churches and used many languages, most notably Arabic, Armenian, Coptic, Georgian, Greek, Latin, Persian, Sogdian and Syriac as well as other dialects of Aramaic. The internal social structure of the huge empire at this time may be envisioned as vertically partitioned and horizontally stratified: imperfectly partitioned among myriad, overlapping ethnic and religious identity-groups, and stratified between the largely Arab, Muslim political-military elite and their vastly more numerous non-Arab, non-Muslim subjects. Subjects paid taxes, the nature of which varied widely within and among regions, and had considerable *de facto* leeway to regulate their own affairs. The ruling Arab military class were paid stipends for service, and in some regions lived apart from their subjects in designated 'garrison cities' (*amṣār*, sing. *miṣr*), such as Basra and Kufa in Iraq. The primary way in which a non-Arab might join the ruling elite was by becoming a 'client' (*mawlā*, pl. *mawālī*) of an Arab patron, whereupon he or she was affiliated to the patron's tribe. Many *mawālī* were manumitted slaves, and most were converts to Islam. In the course of the 8th and 9th centuries, as more non-Arabs converted and as the descendants of the conquerors underwent acculturation in their new environs, distinctions between the Arab Muslim rulers and non-Arab, non-Muslim subjects gradually lost what clarity and salience they had originally possessed. The blurring of Arab Muslims and non-Arab, non-Muslim subjects also reconfigured the vertical partitions among the subject peoples, as more of them acquired elements of an empire-wide, multi-religious culture, especially at elite levels.

It was against this historical backdrop that the first sustained, intensive interactions between Muslims and Christians took place, setting precedents for Muslim dealings with non-Muslims. The first decades of the Umayyad period, in the late 7th and early 8th centuries, saw much continuity with pre-Islamic Late Antiquity. Although the conquerors displaced some Christian Roman and Zoroastrian Persian elites, non-Muslim administrators, merchants and local headmen retained positions of influence for several generations. The forebears of the theologian John of Damascus oversaw the Umayyad tax administration in Syria; their counterpart in Iraq was the Zoroastrian high official Zādhānfarrūkh.[12] The Arab Christian al-Akhṭal, a giant among the poets of the early Islamic period, consorted with Umayyad caliphs.[13] For most of the Umayyad period, Arab Muslims seem to have raised few explicit objections to the prominence of Christians and other non-Muslims in the administration and economy.

Church life was not radically altered by the conquests, either. Christians initially retained most of their church buildings and worshipped much as they had done before, if somewhat more discreetly. The nature of inter- and intra-church conflict changed more perceptibly, as the new rulers were less inclined to intervene in doctrinal disputes than the Eastern Roman state had been, but were more inclined to consolidate their dealings with the leadership of particular churches for the sake of administrative efficacy. Even in Sasanian Iraq, Christians had grown used to a degree of state involvement in their internal affairs, but only after several decades were their new Muslim rulers induced to assume analogous roles.[14] In Syria, according to the 7th-century Syriac *Maronite chronicle*, the first Umayyad caliph, Muʿāwiya ibn Abī Sufyān (r. c. 661-80), umpired a doctrinal disputation between Christian denominations,

---

[12] R.F. Glei, 'John of Damascus', in *CMR* 1, 295-301.

[13] S. Stetkevych, 'Al-Akhṭal at the court of ʿAbd al-Malik. The *qaṣīda* and the construction of Umayyad authority', in A. Borrut and F. Donner (eds), *Christians and others in the Umayyad state*, Chicago IL, 2016, 140-55.

[14] M. Morony, *Iraq after the Muslim conquest*, Princeton NJ, 1984, pp. 346-54.

fining the losers a substantial sum. He then proceeded to tour Golgotha and Gethsemane, and prayed at Mary's tomb. This was a sign of the indeterminacy that still characterised Muslim identity and imperial optics in these early days.[15]

There were noteworthy exceptions to this atmosphere of *laissez-faire*, however, and in the 8th century they grew less exceptional. Beginning with Caliph ʿAbd al-Malik ibn Marwān (r. c. 685-705), Arabic gradually became the official language of government administration, a policy that may have arisen partly from a desire to exclude Christians from influence.[16] According to the principal chronicle of the Coptic Church in Egypt, certain Umayyad governors there took *ad hoc* actions against Christians, such as destroying crosses, forcing conversions, cashiering church leaders and harassing monks.[17] Caliph Yazīd II (r. 720-4) issued an iconoclastic edict that in some areas had a detrimental impact on public Christian symbols, including churches.[18] Several sources ascribe other such policies to the pious Caliph ʿUmar II (r. 718-20), who is said to have required non-Muslims to wear distinguishing clothing and to have dismissed them from official employment.[19] He is also reported to have firmly established the principle that converts to Islam were to be exempt from the poll tax (*jizya*), thereby encouraging conversion. The late-8th century Syriac *Chronicle of Zuqnīn* bewails mass conversions, which resulted, in part, from heavy taxation.[20] The remaining Arab Christian tribes were pressured to convert by early ʿAbbasid caliphs. While there is considerable uncertainty regarding the historical details and dates of such policies, there is little doubt that measures detrimental to Christians and their churches became increasingly common during

---

15 A. Papaconstantinou, 'Between *umma* and *dhimma*. The Christians of the Middle East under the Umayyads', *Annales Islamologiques* 42 (2008) 127-56, pp. 136-7; H.G.B. Teule, '*The Maronite Chronicle*', in *CMR* 1, 145-7.

16 ʿAlī ibn al-Ḥasan ibn ʿAsākir, *Taʾrīkh madīnat Dimashq*, ed. ʿU. al-ʿAmrawī, Beirut, 1995, vol. 22, pp. 320-2. On source and author, see S.A. Mourad, 'Ibn ʿAsākir', in *CMR* 3, 683-9.

17 B. Evetts (ed. and trans.), 'History of the patriarchs of the Coptic Church of Alexandria, III: Agathon to Michael II', *Patrologia Orientalis* 5 (1910) 257-469, e.g. pp. 279, 306, 311-15, 322, 332-3. On the compilation of the Arabic *Siyar al-bīʿa al-muqaddasa* ('Biographies of the holy church') from earlier, largely Coptic sources in the 11th century, see M.N. Swanson, 'Mawhūb ibn Manṣūr ibn Mufarrij al-Iskandarānī', in *CMR* 3, 217-22; for the passages referenced here, see M.N. Swanson, 'John the Deacon', in *CMR* 1, 317-21.

18 C. Sahner, 'The first iconoclasm in Islam. A new history of the edict of Yazīd II (AH 104/AD 723)', *Der Islam* 94 (2017) 5-56.

19 On the historicity of measures ascribed to ʿUmar II, see L. Yarbrough, 'Origins of the *ghiyār*', *Journal of the American Oriental Society* 134 (2014) 113-21, and studies cited there.

20 A. Harrak, 'Joshua the Stylite of Zuqnīn', in *CMR* 1, 322-6.

the course of the 8th century. An underlying driver of such measures may have been the faltering of the territorial conquests in the late Umayyad period; this forced the ruling Arab Muslims to extract additional material and symbolic resources from their mainly non-Muslim subjects, who in the process had to be set apart and unequivocally demoted. Whatever their causes, such policies wore at the edges of the mild and independent subordination that characterised Christian life under Muslim rule in this period.

These slow changes accompanied the crystallisation of Muslim identity and of Islamic doctrine and law under the vast, multi-ethnic and multi-confessional early Islamic empires. Recent studies have argued that the reign of ʿAbd al-Malik was pivotal in solidifying Islam as a discrete body of dogmas and rituals, and its adherents – who were by then divided among several antagonistic sub-groups – as fully distinct from Jews and Christians.[21] The Umayyad and early ʿAbbasid caliphs had considerable authority to shape the content of Islam.[22] Their decrees concerning non-Muslim subjects, such as the ones attributed to ʿUmar II, as well as the decisions of the governors and judges (*qāḍīs*) they appointed, were thus substantially constitutive of 'Islamic law' in their own day.[23]

Measures taken by the state, however, increasingly coexisted with the normative visions of the earliest Muslim scholars, or *ʿulamāʾ*. Some early *ʿulamāʾ* collaborated with the state, but many were wary of it. It was in *ʿulamāʾ* circles of the 8th and 9th centuries that many of the earliest surviving Muslim views concerning proper treatment of non-Muslims were cast in durable forms. One body of such texts was the Hadith – putative sayings of the Prophet Muḥammad, or about him by his contemporaries – which would become the most authoritative source of Islamic teaching apart from the Qur'an.[24] A subset of the *ʿulamāʾ* were Hadith specialists, who composed, studied and transmitted the fast-growing corpus of Hadith literature. Many of the same men and women also dealt in

[21] C. Robinson, *ʿAbd al-Malik*, Oxford, 2005; Donner, *Muhammad and the believers*, pp. 194-224; R. Hoyland, 'New documentary texts and the early Islamic state', *BSOAS* 69 (2006) 395-416. For a view that such a 'parting of the ways' took place later, see Penn, *Envisioning Islam*, pp. 142-82.

[22] P. Crone and M. Hinds, *God's caliph. Religious authority in the first centuries of Islam*, Cambridge, 1986.

[23] M. Tillier, 'Califes, émirs et cadis. Le droit califal et l'articulation de l'autorité judiciaire à l'époque umayyade', *Bulletin d'Etudes Orientales* 63 (2014) 147-90.

[24] For a brief treatment of certain aspects, see D. Cook, 'Christians and Christianity in *ḥadīth* works before 900', in *CMR* 1, 73-82. More extensive is R.M. Speight, 'Christians in the Hadith literature', in L. Ridgeon (ed.), *Islamic interpretations of Christianity*, New York, 2001, pp. 30-53.

similar stories about the Prophet's Companions or, among Shīʿī Muslims, the ʿAlid imams (linear descendants of the Prophet's cousin and son-in-law ʿAlī ibn Abī Ṭālib). The Hadiths that were attributed to the Prophet himself are rather reticent on how Muslims should treat Christians. A few relate his encounters with the Christians of Najrān or with foreign Christian kings; a few more urge Muslims not to imitate Christians and Jews. These last seem to betray fear lest Muslims should lose their distinctive identity in the conquered territories.[25] One well-known Hadith was understood as instructing Muslims to avoid initiating greetings with non-Muslims and, when passing in the street, to crowd them to the gutter. A similar spirit is discerned in the Prophet's blanket statement that Islam must always enjoy the superior position.[26] In other Hadiths, however, the Prophet is observed permitting the imitation of Jews and Christians in certain matters, commanding that they should be treated justly, and rise to honour the passage of their funeral cortèges.[27]

Reports concerning the early caliphs, particularly ʿUmar ibn al-Khaṭṭāb, have more to say about how Muslims should deal with Christians and Jews. By the mid-8th century, reports of ʿUmar's paradigmatic policies circulated widely. These reputed policies tended to separate Muslims from non-Muslims and to demote the latter, for instance by requiring them to dress differently from Muslims, by forbidding Muslim officials to employ them, and by expelling them from Arabia. ʿUmar's authority is also invoked, however, for views that non-Muslims should be protected and treated equitably. If the historicity of these policies is questionable, the later popularity of reports about them is not.[28] By the end of the 8th century, the prominent Muslim jurist Abū Yūsuf could cite them liberally in advising the ʿAbbasid Caliph Hārūn al-Rashīd about how his government should regulate non-Muslims, their sanctuaries, and their public symbols.[29]

---

[25] M.J. Kister, '"Do not assimilate yourselves…". *lā tashabbahū…*', *Jerusalem Studies in Arabic and Islam* 12 (1989) 321-71; A. Noth, 'Abgrenzungsprobleme zwischen Muslimen und Nicht-Muslimen. Die "Bedingungen ʿUmars" (*aš-šurūṭ al-ʿumariyya*) unter einem andere Aspekt gelesen', *Jerusalem Studies in Arabic and Islam* 9 (1987) 290-315.

[26] A.J. Wensinck et al. (eds), *Concordance et indices de la tradition musulmane*, Leiden, 1936-88, vol. 1, p. 149; vol. 4, p. 341.

[27] Speight, 'Christians in Hadith literature', pp. 34-5.

[28] Yarbrough, 'Origins of the *ghiyār*'; L. Yarbrough, 'Upholding God's rule. Early Muslim juristic opposition to the state employment of non-Muslims', *Islamic Law and Society* 19 (2012) 11-85; H. Munt, '"No two religions". Non-Muslims in the early Islamic Ḥijāz', *BSOAS* 78 (2015) 249-69.

[29] D. Thomas, 'Abū Yūsuf Yaʿqūb', in *CMR* 1, 354-9.

Perhaps the most consequential legacy of this period was Muslim scholars' gradual application of the umbrella concept of *dhimma* to a matrix of issues related to the legal status and treatment of Christians and other non-Muslims. In the pre- and early-Islamic periods, the notion of *dhimma* seems to have referred not to pacts with unbelievers, but to a customary contract of security and confederation between distinct socio-political groups of any religious confession, a contract concluded most commonly among the towns and sanctuary precincts of Arabia.[30] In the conquest period, this language was adapted and applied inconsistently in the numerous local surrender treaties, which were themselves invoked in an *ad hoc* manner to assert rights and obligations during the early decades of Muslim rule.[31] In the first ʿAbbasid century, however, Muslim jurists in Iraq created more systematic legal theories of imperial rule. In these theories, an original surrender pact ([*ʿahd*] *dhimma*) between Muslim conquerors and non-Muslim subjects guaranteed the latter – who were styled 'people of the *dhimma*' (*ahl al-dhimma*) – perpetual security for their persons and possessions. In return, the Muslims were to collect an annual head tax (*jizya*) – a qur'anic term that had hitherto been employed unsystematically – and to enjoy social deference. The specific terms of local conquest treaties were recognised within this body of theory. Indeed, some jurists used them as patterns for future treaties of the same kind. A spurious treaty, the infamous 'Pact of ʿUmar', was redacted using earlier materials and circulated among ʿAbbasid jurists; in later centuries it would gain considerable authority in many regions.[32] The early local treaties, however, were increasingly subsumed within generic, empire-wide intercommunal arrangements that Muslim jurists sought to regulate. This was, in fact, the very period in which formal, coherent 'schools' (*madhāhib*, sing. *madhhab*) of Islamic law, such as those of Abū Ḥanīfa (d. 767), Mālik ibn Anas (d. 795), and al-Shāfiʿī (d. 820), were forming, and it was their followers who devised detailed rulings (*aḥkām*) concerning the resident non-Muslim, or *dhimmī*, in the jurists' parlance. These rulings presumed that Christian, Jewish and other *dhimmī* communal leaders would retain extensive authority in their communities, but they also included specific regulations for the conduct and treatment of non-Muslims in their interactions with Muslims, notably in the areas

30 S. Mirza, '*Dhimma* agreements and sanctuary systems at Islamic origins', *Journal of Near Eastern Studies* 77 (2018) 99-117, esp. pp. 102, 107-8, 112.

31 C. Robinson, *Empire and elites after the Muslim conquest*, Cambridge, 2000, pp. 1-32; Levy-Rubin, *Non-Muslims*, pp. 8-57.

32 M. Levy-Rubin, '*The Pact of ʿUmar*', in *CMR* 1, 360-4.

of family life, commerce, taxation, inheritance and torts. Jurists justified these rules by reference to the sources of Islamic law, such as the Qur'an, Hadith and reports about the practice of revered early Muslims, and analogy to other, better-established rules.[33]

The newly developed category of *dhimmī* proved to be a durable one, shaping the normative lens through which pre-modern Muslims viewed their relations with non-Muslims. Equally persistent, however, was the imperfect adoption of the jurists' law by Muslims, notably rulers, who continued to consort with elite non-Muslim officials and physicians. The jurists were influential and respected, but their political power was always limited, and so their normative programmes for regulating matters pertaining to non-Muslims were enacted only intermittently by state authorities. The ʿAbbasid caliphs al-Manṣūr and Hārūn al-Rashīd experimented with limited discriminatory measures targeting *dhimmīs*, but it was under al-Mutawakkil (r. 847-61), who sought *ʿulamāʾ* support to revive the caliph's embattled authority, that extensive measures were first implemented that compelled non-Muslims to dress in particular ways and to vacate their positions as state officials.[34] The effect of these measures was real but brief, and similar edicts had to be issued periodically according to political circumstances. These could be elicited by pressure from influential *ʿulamāʾ* and urban crowds, or by the fallout from court rivalries that involved Christians. Something like this occurred in Baghdad, for example, under the caliph al-Muqtadir (r. 908-32), and in al-Andalus under the Umayyad emir Muḥammad I (r. 852-86), who sought to end the voluntary martyrdoms of Christians in Córdoba.[35] In many regions, however, notably on the imperial periphery, contacts

---

[33] For numerous examples of such rulings, see Abū Bakr al-Khallāl, *Aḥkām ahl al-milal wa-l-ridda* [...], ed. I. ibn Sulṭān, Riyadh, 1996; Y. Friedmann, *Tolerance and coercion in Islam. Interfaith relations in the Muslim tradition*, Cambridge, 2003.

[34] On the earlier two caliphs, see Theophanes Confessor, *The Chronicle of Theophanes*, trans. C. Mango and R. Scott, Oxford, 1997, p. 596 (on author and work, see M. Vaiou, 'Theophanes the Confessor', in *CMR* 1, 426-36); Yarbrough, 'Origins of the *ghiyār*', p. 121, n. 39. On al-Mutawakkil, see Levy-Rubin, *Non-Muslims*, pp. 103-11 (arguing that the measures were enforced for a longer time); Ibn Zabr al-Rabaʿī, *Juzʾ fīhi shurūṭ al-Naṣārā*, ed. A. al-ʿAqīl, Beirut, 2006, pp. 34-41.

[35] For the incident under al-Muqtadir, see ʿArīb ibn Saʿd al-Qurṭubī, *Ṣilat tārīkh al-Ṭabarī*, ed. M.J. de Goeje, Leiden, 1898, p. 30 (on author and work, see D. Serrano Ruano, "Arīb ibn Saʿīd', in *CMR* 2, 451-5). For that under Muḥammad I, see Eulogius of Cordoba, *Memoriale sanctorum*, in *Corpus scriptorum Muzarabicorum*, ed. J. Gil, Madrid, 1973, vol. 2, 362-459, pp. 436-41 (on author and work, see J. Tolan, 'Eulogius of Cordova', in *CMR* 1, 679-83), and further the chapter by C.C. Sahner in this volume; Ch. 16, 'Martyrdom and conversion', 389-412.

with Christians and other non-Muslims were governed by quite different, locally specific factors.[36]

The rulings of Islamic law were implemented more consistently in areas over which Muslim scholars and courts had greater control, such as property transactions and family disputes that were taken before *qāḍīs*.[37] In this and all later periods, however, the story of how Muslims dealt with Christians and other non-Muslims was far more than that of how Islamic law was applied, or not, however much the jurist-historians who wrote many of the Arabic sources focused on this aspect. Most historical interactions between Muslims and Christians will have been informal, and thus widely distributed across the spectrum of accommodation, affinity and antipathy. Warfare was common; the ʿAbbasid armies campaigned against Byzantine Christians, notably in the regular summer campaign (*ṣāʾifa*), and Muslim-ruled border regions were subject to attack by Christians in their turn.[38] Muslim rulers also made truces and alliances with their Christian counterparts.[39] Christian populations occasionally revolted against Muslim rulers, and were duly suppressed.[40] Economic transactions among Muslims and Christians, both within Muslim-ruled territory and across its borders, were so routine as to be utterly unremarkable, though foreign Christian merchants might have to pay special taxes. One documentary witness to economic cooperation is a friendly letter preserved on papyrus of the late 8thcentury from an Egyptian woman named Umm al-Ḥakam, a Muslim, to her Christian business agent, Mīnā Bajūsh, instructing him to buy olives, onions, grapes, grain and oranges.[41] Muslims and Christians fell in love, though marriage between Muslim women and Christian men was rare. The reverse

---

[36] E.g. A. Vacca, *Non-Muslim provinces under early Islam. Islamic rule and Iranian legitimacy in Armenia and Caucasian Albania*, Cambridge, 2017.

[37] U.I. Simonsohn, *A common justice. The legal allegiances of Christians and Jews under early Islam*, Philadelphia PA, 2011.

[38] See, e.g. B. Roggema, 'Ibn al-Layth', in *CMR* 1, 347-53; D. Arnold, 'Pope John VIII', in *CMR* 1, 804-9; E. McGeer, 'Leo VI "the Wise"', in *CMR* 2, 89-97.

[39] N. Drocourt, 'Christian-Muslim diplomatic relations. An overview of the main sources and themes of encounter, 600-1000', in *CMR* 2, 29-72; J. Spaulding, 'Medieval Christian Nubia and the Islamic world. A reconsideration of the baqt treaty', *International Journal of African Historical Studies* 28 (1995) 577-94.

[40] F. Feder, 'The Bashmurite revolts in the Delta and the "Bashmuric dialect"', in G. Gabra and H. Takla (eds), *Christianity and monasticism in northern Egypt*, Cairo, 2017, 33-6.

[41] MS Vienna, Österreichische Nationalbibliothek – P. Vindob. 15106; see R.G. Khoury, *Chrestomathie de papyrologie arabe*, Leiden, 1993, pp. 169-71.

was not, promoting the proportional increase of Muslim populations.[42] Caliphs and their underlings continued to employ Christian officials in significant numbers, from Baghdad to Córdoba. One such official, Isḥāq ibn Nuṣayr al-ʿIbādī, headed the chancery of Egypt around the year 890. He sent funds to support renowned Muslim grammarians in his native Iraq, and relished panegyrics dedicated to him by the eminent Muslim poet al-Buḥturī.[43] Islamic law and theology had little directly to do with any of this.

The wealth that Isḥāq amassed as an official in Egypt, however, was a sign of changing times. He served a Turkic prince called Khumārawayh, whose father, Ibn Ṭūlūn, had wrested Egypt from ʿAbbasid rule. Decentralisation was also afoot in Iran, while al-Andalus and the Maghreb had long lain beyond ʿAbbasid control. In 945, Baghdad itself came under the control of the Būyids, Shīʿī mercenary warlords from the east, and the fainéant ʿAbbasid caliph was reduced to a figurehead. The empire forged by the Prophet's followers had disintegrated, even as new Islamic cultural syntheses had suffused the territories they had conquered. The many Christians who inhabited what might by now justly be called the 'Islamic world', and who increasingly spoke Arabic in their daily lives, faced challenges quite unlike those with which their forebears had contended in Umayyad and ʿAbbasid times.

Islamic societies in the middle periods (945-1250)

After the ʿAbbasid collapse, the power the caliphs had formerly wielded was assumed by two principal kinds of Muslim sovereigns: counter-caliphs and military rulers, or sultans. These two modes of rule had different effects on Muslim dealings with Christian subjects at the state level, even as Muslim and Christian populations continued the trend towards cultural integration and consistently maintained certain practices, such as the *jizya*. Although Christians continued to convert to Islam in many settings, the middle periods also saw successful military campaigns by Christian rulers against Muslim-held territories, such as the Byzantine invasion of northern Syria in the 10th century and the Latin Christian

---

42 For one legendary love story, see Abū l-Faraj al-Iṣbahānī, *Kitāb al-diyārāt*, compiled by J. al-ʿAṭiyya, London, 1991, pp. 48-52 (on author and work, see H. Kilpatrick, 'Abū l-Faraj al-Iṣbahānī', in *CMR* 2, 386-9). I owe this reference to David Cook.

43 On Isḥāq, see Yāqūt al-Ḥamawī, *Muʿjam al-udabāʾ*, ed. I. ʿAbbās, Beirut, 1993, vol. 2, pp. 628-9.

crusading movement throughout the Mediterranean in the 12th century and beyond. The cumulative effect of these conflicts for the Christians of the Islamic world was not salutary, and the concomitant advent of Sunnī Turkic and Berber dynasties applied additional pressures.

The most noteworthy counter-caliphs of the middle periods were the Fāṭimids in North Africa and Egypt (909-1171); a branch of the Umayyad family in Iberia (929-1009); and the Almohads in the Maghreb and Iberia (1130-1269). The Fāṭimids and Almohads both swept to power amid waves – very different ones, to be sure – of apocalyptic expectation and doctrinal experimentation. Within their respective doctrinal systems, their caliphs were accorded a high degree of interpretive and legislative authority. In these new orders, caliphal dictates, relatively unencumbered by the prior rulings of Muslim jurists, could have momentous consequences for the legal and political status of Christians and Jews. The early Almohads, for example, saw fit to abolish the *dhimma* arrangement altogether, thus removing the legal justification for a continued non-Muslim presence in their domains. As a result, thousands of Jews were compelled to convert.[44] While the measure proved ephemeral and affected relatively few Christians, it signalled an antipathetic stance that did not bode well for the remaining Christians in al-Andalus, over which the Almohads gained control c. 1165.[45] However, the circumstances of the later Almohads were quite different, as signalled by their use of European Christian troops in trusted roles.[46]

The Fāṭimid caliphs, too, regarded themselves as divinely sanctioned lawgivers. During their rule in Egypt – as well as North Africa and Syria for shorter periods – they made use of this latitude to treat their Christian and Jewish subjects in a range of ways. The early Fāṭimids in Egypt, such as al-Muʿizz (r. 946-53) and al-ʿAzīz (r. 953-75), elevated Christians and Jews to high office in the government. Christian officials such as ʿĪsā ibn Nasṭūrus, appointed to the powerful post of *wāsiṭa* in 995, could act as intercessors on behalf of their churches and coreligionists. Conversely, the Fāṭimid caliph al-Ḥākim (r. 996-1021) vacillated between empowering Christians and Jews and issuing harsh measures against them, these

44 See special issue of the *Journal of Medieval Iberian Studies* 2 (2010), dedicated to 'Religious minorities under the Almohads'.

45 J.P. Molénat, 'Sur le rôle des almohades dans la fin du christianisme local au Maghreb et en al-Andalus', *Al-Qanṭara* 18 (1997) 389-413; M.D. Rodríguez-Gómez, 'Ibn Ṣāḥib al-Ṣalāt', in *CMR* 4, 176-8.

46 E. Lapiedra Gutiérrez, 'Christian participation in Almohad armies and personal guards', *Journal of Medieval Iberian Studies* 2 (2010) 235-50.

last including a decree that led to the destruction of the Church of the Holy Sepulchre in Jerusalem in 1009.[47] That it was his quasi-messianic status that authorised him to deviate from Islamic norms, both towards accommodation and towards antipathy, is indicated by the posthumous reverence accorded to him by his followers, whose descendants, the Druze, live throughout the Levant today. After the late 11th century, however, Fāṭimid power passed to military viziers of Armenian origin – at least one of whom remained Christian – and caliphal authority became less significant to the lives of Christians. Instead, the viziers, now often the effective rulers of Egypt, slowly gravitated to Sunnī *ʿulamāʾ* and their teachings. Still, the Fāṭimid Caliph al-Ḥāfiẓ (d. 1149), when he was challenged about his Armenian Christian vizier, who, as it happened, bore the title 'Sword of Islam', could ask rhetorically, 'If *we* approve, who is going to contradict us?' (*idhā raḍaynā naḥnu fa-man yukhālifunā*).[48]

Among the counter-caliphs in the middle periods, the Umayyads of al-Andalus were the least inclined to use their personal religious authority to justify radical policy changes. The Umayyad ʿAbd al-Raḥmān III (r. 912-61) adopted the title of caliph largely to counter Fāṭimid pretensions, and it held no great doctrinal significance for the handful of his descendants who inherited it. ʿAbd al-Raḥmān fought Christian opponents to the north and dealt with the stubborn rebellion of Ibn Ḥafsūn, which adopted Christian ideology, but he also elevated Christian officials, such as Rabīʿ ibn Zayd, and generally seems to have maintained policies towards his Christian subjects that both they and Sunnī *ʿulamāʾ* could live with, much as his forebears, the Umayyad emirs of al-Andalus, had done for nearly two centuries.[49] When Umayyad rule collapsed in the early 11th century, its place was taken by a constellation of minor statelets ruled by Muslim strongmen, the 'party kings' (*mulūk al-ṭawāʾif*). These rulers seldom laid claim to religious authority of their own and were thus led to patronise Sunnī *ʿulamāʾ* of diverse inclinations. At one extreme was the firebrand Ibn Ḥazm, who advocated relatively strict treatment of Christians and Jews. At another, perhaps, was Ṣāʿid al-Andalusī, whose encyclopedic *Ṭabaqāt al-umam*, like the literary explorations of his

---

[47] P. Walker, *Caliph of Cairo. Al-Hakim bi-Amr Allāh, 996-1021*, Cairo, 2009. See also D. Thomas, '*Khabar al-Yahūd wa-l-Naṣārā*', in *CMR* 2, 640-2.

[48] Taqī l-Dīn al-Maqrīzī, *Ittiʿāẓ al-ḥunafāʾ*, ed. J. Shayyāl and M.Ḥ.M. Aḥmad, Cairo, 1967-73, vol. 3, p. 156. This the 'royal we'. For the state of current research on non-Muslims under the Fāṭimids, see *Medieval Encounters* 21/4-5 (2015), on 'Non-Muslim communities in Fatimid Egypt (10th-12th centuries CE)'.

[49] J.P. Monferrer Sala, 'Rabīʿ ibn Zayd', in *CMR* 2, 347-50; M. Fierro, *ʿAbd al-Raḥmān III. The first Cordoban caliph*, Oxford, 2005.

Sunnī-jurist contemporary Ibn ʿAbd al-Barr, reflects an ambiguous but broadly accommodating or even affinitive stance toward non-Muslims.[50] Broadly speaking, the 'party kings' balanced their need for Islamic legitimacy, for which they relied on *ʿulamāʾ*, who sometimes insisted on the rigorous application of Islamic law, with their need for pragmatic accommodation with their Christian subjects and the powerful Christian kings of the peninsula.

This pattern, whereby nominally Muslim, frequently foreign warlords patronised Sunnī *ʿulamāʾ* but curbed their influence on the pretext of *raison d'état*, while also waging war against external Christian rivals, was to prove a dominant theme in the middle periods of Islamic history, with significant consequences for Christian subjects. In al-Andalus, for example, the Berber Almoravid armies crossed from the Maghreb and consolidated power in 1086. Their ideologues were Sunnī jurists of the Mālikī school, who advocated more rigorous application of restrictions on Jews and Christians than had generally been implemented under the 'party kings'.[51] Such stances owed something to the ongoing, increasingly desperate wars with the Christian kingdoms of the peninsula.

The Almoravids have often been compared to their contemporaries in the eastern Islamic lands, the Seljuq Turks, who were recently converted, warlike tribesmen, and who had won control of important Islamic urban centres, paid formal allegiance to the ʿAbbasid caliph and patronised Sunnī *ʿulamāʾ*. The mildly Shīʿī Būyid dynasty, which had preceded the Seljuqs in Baghdad, had pursued relatively accommodating policies towards Christians and Jews, notwithstanding occasional episodes of violent suppression.[52] Seljuq rule, however, saw more extensive empowerment of Sunnī *ʿulamāʾ* as state administrators and ideologues. A key proponent of this change was the vizier Niẓām al-Mulk, a scholar-official from Khurāsān, who virtually ruled the Seljuq empire in the late 11th

50 J.P. Monferrer Sala and D. Thomas, 'Ibn Ḥazm', in *CMR* 3, 137-45; D. Thomas, 'Ṣāʿid al-Andalusī', in *CMR* 3, 146-9; L. Yarbrough, 'A Christian Shīʿī, and other curious confreres. Ibn ʿAbd al-Barr of Cordoba on getting along with unbelievers', *Al-Masāq* 30 (2018) 284-303.

51 V. Lagardère, 'Communautés mozarabes et pouvoir almoravide en 519H/1125 en el-Andalus', *Studia Islamica* 67 (1988) 99-120. See also, e.g. D. Serrano Ruano, 'Ibn Sahl', in *CMR* 3, 210-13; M. Meouak, 'Ibn Bassām', in *CMR* 3, 318-22; M. Fierro, 'al-Ṭurṭūshī', *CMR* 3, 387-96; C. de la Puente, 'Ibn ʿAbdūn al-Ishbīlī', in *CMR* 3, 397-400; R. El Hour, 'Abū Bakr ibn al-ʿArabī', in *CMR* 3, 520-3; D. Serrano Ruano, 'al-Qāḍī ʿIyāḍ', in *CMR* 3, 542-8; I. Ferrando, 'Ibn Quzmān', in *CMR* 3, 620-4.

52 For this period as well as the history of Baghdad's Christians more generally, see J.-M. Fiey, *Chrétiens syriaques sous les Abbassides surtout à Bagdad, 749-1258*, Louvain, 1980.

century. In his Persian mirror for princes, the *Siyāsat nāmah*, Niẓām al-Mulk counsels the ruler to delegate administrative authority to Sunnīs from Khurāsān, while dissociating from both Iraqi Muslims, whom he accuses of pro-Ismāʿīlī sympathies, and Jews and Christians. The ethos of the new Turkic rulers and their Sunnī supporters marked a shift towards antipathy.[53] It contrasted with such earlier cases as that of the renowned jurist Abū l-Ḥasan al-Māwardī (d. 1058), whose patron was a weak ʿAbbasid caliph under Shīʿī Būyid tutelage. In his famous book *al-Aḥkām al-sulṭāniyya*, al-Māwardī had advanced a relatively accommodating vision of non-Muslim life within an Islamic state.[54]

Sunnī jurists flocked to the *madrasas* established by the Seljuqs on a wide scale to teach Islamic law. Niẓām al-Mulk patronised jurists such as al-Juwaynī (d. 1085), who castigated al-Māwardī for his accommodating stance.[55] The great Sufi jurist al-Ghazālī (d. 1111) lamented this patronage in his *magnum opus*, *Iḥyāʾ ʿulūm al-dīn*, arguing that it corrupted Islamic learning by entangling it with wealth and power.[56] By the time the Seljuqs took control of the state, Islamic jurisprudence had developed extensive, highly detailed rulings relating to non-Muslims, though these varied considerably from school to school and among the different Muslim sects. In any given legal manual, such rulings might be found in many different sections, since Muslims constantly interacted with Christians and Jews as business partners, employees and slaves; wives, mothers and siblings; enemies and allies; merchants and customers; neighbours and correspondents; and as plaintiffs and defendants in court cases – all relationships that Muslim jurists aspired to regulate in their rulings.

However, by the Seljuq era several works had also been composed that dealt exclusively with laws pertaining to non-Muslim issues. The early Ḥanbalī al-Khallāl (d. 923) had collected the views of Ibn Ḥanbal (d. 855) on these matters in a discrete section of a longer work. A Shāfiʿī jurist of Iran called Abū l-Shaykh al-Iṣbahānī (d. 979) devoted an independent book to them several decades later, as did the famous Ḥanbalī Abū Yaʿlā ibn al-Farrāʾ of Baghdad in the mid-11th century.[57] Just a few years after this, a zealous Sunnī jurist of Seljuq Iraq, Ibn Badrān al-Ḥulwānī (d. 1113),

---

53 O. Turan, 'Les souverains seldjoukides et leurs sujets non-musulmans', *Studia Islamica* 1 (1953) 65-100.

54 W. Haddad, '*Ahl al-dhimma* in an Islamic state. The teaching of Abū al-Ḥasan al-Māwardī's *al-aḥkām al-sulṭāniyya*', *ICMR* 7 (1996) 169-80.

55 D. Thomas, 'al-Juwaynī', in *CMR* 3, 121-6; al-Juwaynī, *Ghiyāth al-umam*, ed. F.ʿA. Aḥmad, Alexandria, 1979, pp. 114-16.

56 M. El Kaisy-Friemuth, 'al-Ghazālī', in *CMR* 3, 363-9.

57 L. Yarbrough, 'Abū Yaʿlā ibn al-Farrāʾ', in *CMR* 5, 651-4.

presented the ʿAbbasid caliph with a yet another such work, remarking bitterly that Muslim rulers were improperly empowering non-Muslims.[58] None of these books was especially popular or influential, but they did signal that Sunnī jurists had developed a distinct body of thought on how non-Muslims should be regulated in a Muslim-dominated society. As they gained influence under the Seljuqs and in the following decades, Sunnī jurists drew on this material when counselling the rough-hewn Turkic military rulers who by the 12th century controlled most of the Islamic world. Even under the late Fāṭimids, the itinerant Iberian jurist al-Ṭurṭūshī (d. 1126) drew extensively on Islamic law in his mirror for princes, *Sirāj al-mulūk*, which was written for a Fāṭimid vizier whom he upbraided personally for employing a Christian.[59] It is crucial to note, however, that restrictive legal doctrines in themselves did not drive these developments. No less important was that Sunnī jurists were increasingly coming into direct competition with Christian literate elites for positions and prestige. For those jurists, emphasising the subordinate place of Christians and Jews in Islamic jurisprudence doubled as a way of undercutting personal rivals.[60]

Even as the Seljuq empire fragmented in the early 12th century, its customs of military rule and patronage of Sunnī jurists were carried on in successor states, not only in Iraq and Iran but also in Egypt, Syria and Anatolia, areas that were home to large Christian populations. In Syria and Egypt, Sunnī Turkic or Kurdish dynasties, notably the Zangids and Ayyūbids, filled the vacuum left by the waning of Fāṭimid power. These upstart military dynasties patronised Sunnī mosques, *madrasa*s and Sufi lodges and issued edicts unfavourable to Christians and Jews, often at the behest of Muslim advisors who competed with Christian elites for positions and prestige. Equally significant was that the Zangids and Ayyūbids waged intensive warfare against the Frankish crusaders who had invaded the Levantine coast at the turn of the 12th century. One effect of the Muslim 'counter-crusade' ideology set down in this era was to pave the way for antipathy towards indigenous Christians and to create suspicions of their disloyalty, notwithstanding that they, too, often

---

58 Al-Wansharīsī, *Al-miʿyār al-muʿrib*, ed. Muḥammad Ḥajjī et al., Rabat, 1981-3, vol. 2, pp. 257-8. On author and work, see F. Vidal-Castro, 'al-Wansharīsī', in *CMR* 7, 576-81.

59 Fierro, 'al-Ṭurṭūshī'.

60 L. Yarbrough, 'The *madrasa* and the non-Muslims of thirteenth-century Egypt. A reassessment', in E. Baumgarten, R. Karras and K. Mesler (eds), *Entangled histories*, Philadelphia PA, 2017, 93-112.

suffered from Frankish depredations.[61] Similar suspicions had arisen earlier during the Byzantine military resurgence in northern Syria in the 10th century. The Seljuqs, too, had fought Christian foes, famously defeating the Byzantine field army at Manzikert in 1071 and thus further opening the Christian Caucasus and Anatolia to the incursions of Turkic tribesmen.[62] In this setting, even such a figure as the Iberian mystic Ibn ʿArabī (d. 1240) – whose thought echoes Christian theological concepts – can be found urging an Anatolian sultan to enforce legal restrictions on non-Muslims.[63] These conflicts in the East, like contemporary ones between Muslim and Christian rulers in the western Mediterranean, heightened Muslim anxieties about Christian enmity, overt and secret, and eroded intercommunal social trust, quite apart from the physical violence they visited upon populations. They were only a prelude, however, to storms that were gathering in the East.

Crises and reconsolidation (1250-1600)

The Mongol invasions of the 13th century affected virtually all regions of Eurasia, but none more than the eastern reaches of the Islamic world. Thriving cities and towns in Islamic Central Asia – notably Bukhārā and Samarqand – were devastated and depopulated. The effect of these invasions for Christians in these regions, though largely negative, was complex. As the Mongol armies moved westwards, they pushed before them other warlike peoples, one of which, the Khwarāzmshāhs, is known to have done considerable violence to Levantine Christians in the early 13th century.[64] At first, the new Mongol rulers did not grant most-favoured status to any religion, least of all Islam, which was the creed of their enemies the Mamlūks, Turkic slave-soldiers who supplanted the last Ayyūbids in Egypt and Syria around 1250. Furthermore, some Mongol generals and the influential wives of Mongol khans were themselves Christians, and were thus inclined to show favour to Christian subjects.[65]

---

[61] C. MacEvitt, *The Crusades and the Christian world of the East. Rough tolerance*, Philadelphia PA, 2007.

[62] C. Hillenbrand, *Turkish myth and Muslim symbol*, Edinburgh, 2007. See also M.D. Abashidze, '*Life of David, King of kings*', in *CMR* 3, 567-72.

[63] S. Hirtenstein, 'Ibn ʿArabī', in *CMR* 4, 145-9.

[64] J. Pahlitzsch, 'Athanasius II, Patriarch of Jerusalem', in *CMR* 4, 325-30; S.P. Cowe, 'Dawitʿ erēcʿ Baluecʿi', in *CMR* 4, 620-3.

[65] J. Ryan, 'Christian wives of Mongol khans', *Journal of the Royal Asiatic Society* 8 (1998) 411-21.

In some instances, there are reports of Christian gloating and vengeful reprisals against local Muslims under Mongol rule; in others Christians and Muslims collaborated against the common foreign enemy.[66] The situation would change after the conversion to Islam of the Mongol ruler Ghāzān in 1295.[67] Even before this time, however, warfare between Mongols and local Muslim (and, in the Caucasus, Christian) rulers negatively affected civilian populations, including Christian churches, in Iraq, Syria, the Caucasus and Anatolia.[68] Much the same was true for the later incursions of the Muslim Turko-Mongol warlord Timur-i Leng around 1400.[69]

When the Mongols arrived in the Middle East, Christians formed large proportions of the population, if not outright majorities, in several areas: northern Mesopotamia, Armenia, Georgia, Syria, Egypt and Anatolia, where Turkic frontier fighters (*ghāzī*s) had been making uneven advances against Byzantine and Armenian kingdoms for nearly two centuries. This era has become notorious in modern historiography as one in which Muslims were especially active in persecuting Christians. The reasons for this 'persecution' as well as its notoriety are complex, and only the former can be discussed here. The Mongol, Timurid and Turkmen incursions and the aggregate harm they did to Christian (and non-Christian) populations have been noted. A portion of those populations and their churches nonetheless survived, if often in weakened forms. Yet even where local rulers were able to stave off the invaders – notably in Mamlūk Syria and Egypt – the circumstances of life for Christians were significantly altered. Christians living in parts of Syria that the early Mamlūk sultans wrested from the Mongols and Franks frequently suffered harsh treatment.[70] In Egypt and the parts of Syria that had remained under Egyptian control in the 13th and 14th centuries, the early Mamlūks adopted inconsistent policies towards Christians. On the one hand, they continued the long-standing practice of employing Christian officials as secretaries and administrators. Such individuals, even when they had converted more or less willingly to Islam, were able

66 See e.g. A. Mallett, 'Ghāzī ibn al-Wāsiṭī', in *CMR* 4, 627-9; L. Demiri, '*Al-sayf al-murhaf fī l-radd ʿalā l-muṣḥaf*', in *CMR* 4, 662-5; H.G.B. Teule, 'Barhebraeus', in *CMR* 4, 588-609.

67 E.g. S.P. Cowe, '*Martyrology of Bishop Grigor of Karin* (*Erzerum*)', in *CMR* 4, 794-7.

68 E.g. J. van Lent, '*Testament of our Lord* (*on the invasions of the Mongols*)', in *CMR* 4, 743-9.

69 E.g. C. Casali, 'John of Sulṭāniyya', in *CMR* 5, 291-7.

70 A.-M. Eddé, 'Chrétiens d'Alep et de Syrie du Nord à l'époque des croisades. Crises et mutations', in P. Canivet and J.-P. Rey-Coquais (eds), *Mélanges Monseigneur Joseph Nasrallah*, Damascus, 2006, 153-80.

to intercede on behalf of their churches and coreligionists, sometimes impeding the strict application of Islamic law and obstructing avaricious taxation of Christians. In addition, protecting Christians and Jews was a symbolic way for the foreign Mamlūk military elite to demonstrate their supremacy over native Muslims when the latter called for restrictions upon churches, monasteries and non-Muslim elites.

However, it was not unusual for the Mamlūk sultans to extort large sums from Christian officials and clergy, often under threat of violence.[71] Sultans also patronised Muslim scholars and Sufis on a large scale, out of both sincere piety and the need for legitimacy, notably after their Ilkhanid Mongol adversaries also became Muslims. These scholars, as well as the local Muslim populations whom they influenced as judges, preachers and intercessors, regularly decried what they saw as undue Christian influence and affluence, as well as perfidy.[72] They composed fiery sermons and hortatory pamphlets for Mamlūk rulers that urged the demotion and dispossession of Christians. Even their formal juristic and historical works evince heightened antipathy.[73] The well-known case of Ibn Taymiyya (d. 1328) bears out these trends. Raised in Syria amid the turmoil and uncertainty of the Mongol invasions, this brilliant scholar was a fierce critic of the Muslim impiety, Christian insubordination and Ilkhanid deviancy that he perceived around him.[74] Anti-Christian sentiment and popular action, often suppressed by Muslim authorities, became fevered at points during the late 13th and 14th centuries. In 1301, 1324 and 1354, for example, there were waves of church destruction, riots, physical attacks on Christians and their property, and coerced conversions of Christian officials. In many cases, popular pressure all but compelled the Mamlūk rulers to issue decrees that required Christians and Jews to abide strictly by the letter and spirit of the Pact of ʿUmar and other such regulations, often confiscating Christian properties in the

---

[71] See, e.g. J. van Lent, 'The prophecies and exhortations of Pseudo-Shenute', in *CMR* 5, 278-86.

[72] E.g. D. Gril, 'Une émeute anti-chrétienne à Qūṣ au début du viiie/xive siècle', *Annales Islamologiques* 16 (1980) 241-74.

[73] D. Thomas, 'Muḥammad ibn ʿAbd al-Raḥmān', in *CMR* 3, 783-4; L. Yarbrough, 'al-Nābulusī', in *CMR* 4, 310-16; D. Thomas, 'Ibn al-Rifʿa', in *CMR* 4, 692-4; A. Mallett, 'Ghāzī ibn al- Wāsiṭī', in *CMR* 4, 627-9; L. Yarbrough, '*Al-qawl al-mukhtār fī l-manʿ ʿan takhyīr al-kuffār*', in *CMR* 4, 924-7; J. Hoover, 'Ibn Qayyim al-Jawziyya', in *CMR* 4, 989-1002; L. Yarbrough, 'Ibn al-Naqqāsh', in *CMR* 5, 123-9; L. Yarbrough, 'Ibn al-Durayhim', in *CMR* 5, 138-44; A. Mallett, 'Jamāl al-Dīn al-Asnawī', in *CMR* 5, 130-2; D. Thomas, ''Imād al-Dīn al-Asnawī', in *CMR* 5, 187-8; S. Burge, 'Jalāl al-Dīn al-Suyūṭī', in *CMR* 7, 557-64.

[74] J. Hoover, 'Ibn Taymiyya', in *CMR* 4, 824-78. See also F. Bauden, 'al-Maqrīzī', in *CMR* 5, 380-95.

process.[75] It has been much noted that the very frequency of these measures points to their ephemerality. Yet their cumulative negative effect on the Christians of Egypt and Syria was considerable. A complicating factor was the growing economic and military importance of the European Christian states and their agents in the Mamlūk, Ilkhanid, Timurid and eventually Ottoman domains. Thus Ibn Taymiyya, while taking a strong position against the preservation and repair of churches, felt compelled to address the objection that cracking down on Christians could lead to painful reprisals against Muslims and the loss of lucrative trade.[76]

To the north and west, in Anatolia, the Caucasus and the western Mediterranean, local circumstances were quite different.[77] Yet the general trend in those regions, too – though it admitted of numerous exceptions – was towards the erosion of accommodation and affinity between Muslims and the Christians living under Muslim rule, even as intensive contact and conversion often led to greater assimilation. In Anatolia, the large-scale infiltration of Turkic *ghāzī*s and tribesmen since the late 11th century resulted in a patchwork of shifting Turkic statelets in which Greek, Armenian and Syriac Christians lived under uneven conditions. Some scholars have understood this era, for which the sources are relatively thin, as one of widespread suffering, ill-treatment and decline for Christians in the former Byzantine territories; others have stressed religious syncretism and creative accommodation, while still others have offered focused case-studies that complicate any broad characterisations.[78] It is far from clear than any definite pattern describes Muslim-Christian

---

75 See, e.g. U. Vermeulen, 'The rescript of al-Malik aṣ-Ṣāliḥ Ṣāliḥ against the dhimmīs (755 A.H./1354 A.D.)', *Orientalia Lovaniensia Periodica* 9 (1978) 175-84; D. Little, 'Coptic conversion to Islam under the Baḥrī Mamlūks, 692-755/1293-1354', *BSOAS* 39 (1976) 552-69; T. el-Leithy, 'Sufis, Copts, and the politics of piety. Moral regulation in fourteenth-century Upper Egypt', in R. McGregor and A. Sabra (eds), *La développement du soufisme en Égypte à l'époque mamelouke*, Cairo, 2006, 75-119.

76 Ibn Taymiyya, *Mas'ala fī l-kanā'is*, ed. 'A. al-Shibl, Riyadh, 1995, pp. 124-6. The idea that Christian and Muslim sovereigns might act as defenders of their respective coreligionists under foreign rule is sporadically attested throughout the period treated in this book. See, e.g. A. Konopacki, '*Leh kralına nâme-i hümâyun*', in *CMR* 7, 732-4.

77 For an overview with special attention to Christian-Muslim relations, see H.G.B. Teule, 'Introduction. Constantinople and Granada', in *CMR* 5, 1-16.

78 S. Vryonis, *The decline of medieval Hellenism in Asia Minor*, Berkeley CA, 1986; F.W. Hasluck, *Christianity and Islam under the sultans*, Oxford, 1929; H. Lowry, *The nature of the early Ottoman state*, Albany NY, 2003. See also A. Peacock, B. de Nicola and S. Nur Yıldız (eds), *Christianity and Islam in Medieval Anatolia*, Farnham, 2015. For Armenian and Georgian Christians in particular, see, e.g. S.P. Cowe, 'Patterns of Armeno-Muslim interchange on the Armenian plateau in the interstice between Byzantine and Ottoman hegemony', in Peacock et al. (eds), *Christianity and Islam*, 77-105, pp. 100-1, and studies cited there. On Iraq and northern Mesopotamia, see H.G.B. Teule, *Les Assyro-Chaldéens.*

encounter in this setting. What is clear, however, is that, by the end of Islam's first millennium, the Christian Greek and Armenian cast of Anatolian culture was far less prevalent than it had been a few centuries earlier, while Turkic and Muslim features had become far more prominent.[79] The ascendant religion was an Islam in which Sufi and Shīʿī elements were endemic. Armenian and Georgian Christian aristocracies in the east found themselves on the defensive within much-reduced or vassal domains, particularly after the Timurid invasions and the ensuing consolidation of Ottoman power. During the 14th and 15th centuries, the advancing Ottoman forces – often in alliance with Christian rulers, including the Byzantine emperor on occasion – brought the Balkans, too, under Ottoman rule. In this era, the Ottoman authorities treated Christians in the *ad hoc* manner characteristic of a post-conquest society. This gave way gradually to a formal arrangement that took some inspiration from the rulings of Islamic jurisprudence but was nevertheless peculiarly Ottoman.[80] One of its distinctive features, the *devshirme*, was a regular, compulsory levy of Christian boys in the Balkans to be converted to Islam and trained as elite officers and bureaucrats, even though the *devshirme* was formally in tension with Islamic law, which forbade the enslavement of Jewish and Christian subjects.[81] Ottoman power in the region was cemented in 1453 by the capture of Constantinople and the plundering of its mainly Christian population. As the Ottomans extended their control eastwards, to the Arab provinces of Syria and Egypt under Selim I around 1517, the position of Christians in these places changed only gradually. Under Ottoman and neo-Mamlūk regimes, *ʿulamāʾ* there continued to write about Christians with the combination of suspicion and disdain that had become common in the preceding Mamlūk era, if in more muted tones.[82]

Chrétiens d'Irak, d'Iran et de Turquie, Turnhout, 2008, and T. Carlson, *Christianity in fifteenth-century Iraq*, Cambridge, 2018.

[79] For the early Ottoman period, see T. Krstić, *Contested conversions to Islam. Narratives of religious change in the early modern Ottoman Empire*, Stanford CA, 2011. See also C. Norton, 'Serrâc ibn Abdullah', in *CMR* 7, 673-5; T. Krstić, 'Murad ibn Abdullah', in *CMR* 7, 698-704.

[80] On the well-known Ottoman '*millet* system', see K. Barkey and G. Gavrilis, 'The Ottoman millet system. Non-territorial autonomy and its contemporary legacy', *Ethnopolitics* 15 (2016) 24-42. See also L. Demiri and M. Kuzey, 'Ibn Kemal', in *CMR* 7, 622-38; E. Kermeli, 'Ebussuud Efendi', in *CMR* 7, 715-23.

[81] P. Wittek, 'Devshirme and Sharīʿa', *BSOAS* 17 (1955) 271-8.

[82] For a survey, see F. Armanios, *Coptic Christianity in Ottoman Egypt*, New York, 2011. See also, e.g. U. Ryad, 'Ibn Nujaym al-Miṣrī', in *CMR* 7, 688-92.

As Muslim rulers in and around late medieval Anatolia made steady gains, to the general detriment of Christianity in these areas, in the western Mediterranean the reverse was more nearly the case. In the early medieval period, Iberia, Sicily and other Mediterranean islands had hosted thriving societies ruled by Muslim sovereigns. By 1500, however, the military campaigns of European Christians had all but completely eliminated Muslim rule north of the African coast, and even in some strategic African coastal towns. As a result, the relevant issue in these regions was increasingly not Christians under Muslim power, but the reverse. Nevertheless, the former issue maintained some importance. Although the native Christian populations of North Africa were minuscule, European Christian traders, mercenaries and clerics established enclaves there for a variety of reasons. They were sometimes permitted to have churches, and were granted other dispensations from Muslim authorities.[83] In Iberia, most Christians now increasingly lived under Christian sovereigns, marking a gradual end to the sometimes uneasy accommodation that had characterised the life of Iberian Christians under Muslim rule for centuries.[84] The concomitant subjugation and expulsion of Muslims in parts of Iberia, along with European coastal raiding, helped to heighten antipathy towards Christians on the part of *ʿulamāʾ* and rulers alike in the Muslim-majority societies of the Maghreb.

Conclusion

There are good reasons as to why this volume does not include a comparable chapter on Muslim subjects of Christian rulers.[85] Although there are many historical cases in which the topic could be explored, including, among others, those of medieval and early-modern Iberia (albeit some of which are addressed by Monferrer Sala in chapter 13), Norman

83 H. Fancy, *The mercenary Mediterranean. Sovereignty, religion, and violence in the medieval Crown of Aragon*, Chicago IL, 2016; M. Lower, 'The Papacy and Christian mercenaries of thirteenth-century North Africa', *Speculum* 89 (2014) 601-31. See also, e.g. T.E. Burman, 'Ramon Martí', in *CMR* 4, 381-90; H. Hames, 'Ramon Llull', in *CMR* 4, 703-17.

84 M. de Epalza, 'Mozarabs. An emblematic Christian minority in al-Andalus', in S. Jayyusi and M. Marín (eds), *The legacy of Muslim Spain*, Leiden, 1992, 149-70; T.E. Burman, *Religious polemic and the intellectual history of the Mozarabs, c. 1050-1200*, Leiden, 1994; N. Al-Jallad, 'Ibn al-Khaṭīb', in *CMR* 5, 182-6.

85 In part this is because such interactions do not form a dominant theme in the period covered by this volume; Muslims under Christian rule becomes a distinct feature of the modern (post-1600) period, and will be addressed in the second volume of thematic essays.

Sicily, Arpad Hungary and the Latin East (Morton addresses some of these in chapter 12), they are all of relatively limited duration.[86] Whereas Christians have lived in the shadow of Muslim power for virtually the entire Islamic history of Egypt, Syria and Iraq, amongst other places, no substantial Muslim population lived so long under continuous Christian rule. The reasons for this asymmetry are, of course, complex. One difference is that, until the 18th century, there was no Christian-led military expansion into large parts of the Islamic world that compares with the 7th-century Arab conquests in the Christian world. When early-modern Europe did extend its imperial venture south-eastwards between the 16th and 20th centuries, it was a less overtly religious project than the pre-modern Muslim conquests had been. In addition, during the pre-modern age there was considerable Muslim ambivalence about the lawfulness of living under non-Muslim rule. In fact, many jurists forbade it, enjoining emigration, though with mixed success.[87] In addition, whereas the circumstances of the early Arab Muslims had obliged them to formalise and even sacralise the permanent accommodation of Christian and Jewish populations, pre-modern Christians lacked a comparably robust and stable precedent for accommodating large, permanent and subordinate Muslim populations. It is telling that when they did accommodate Muslim subjects, they often appropriated Islamic institutions such as the *jizya* for the purpose, in a curious example of Christian-Muslim affinity.[88] Such expedients, however, did not typically strike deep roots. The usual end-result was the more or less forcible conversion of Muslims to Christianity, or their physical expulsion. The subject Muslims of what is now Spain, famously, were required to convert between 1499 and about

---

[86] See, e.g. J. Powell (ed.), *Muslims under Latin rule*, Princeton NJ, 1990; B. Catlos, *Muslims of medieval Latin Christendom, c. 1050-1614*, Cambridge, 2014; J. Johns, *The Arabic administration of Norman Sicily*, Cambridge, 2002; N. Berend, *At the gate of Christendom*, Cambridge, 2001; A. Metcalfe, *Muslims of medieval Italy*, Edinburgh, 2014; A. Zimo, 'Muslims in the landscape. A social map of the Kingdom of Jerusalem in the thirteenth century', Minneapolis MN, 2017 (PhD Diss. University of Minnesota); J. Trimingham, *Islam in Ethiopia*, London, 1952, e.g. pp. 63-5, 71-6. Note also, in this connection, A. Mallett, 'Ibn Jubayr', in *CMR* 4, 159-65.

[87] A. Verskin, *Islamic law and the crisis of the Reconquista. The debate on the status of Muslim communities in Christendom*, Leiden, 2015; Vidal-Castro, 'al-Wansharīsī'; L. Bernabé Pons, 'The Mufti of Oran', in *CMR* 6, 67-72.

[88] E.g. A. Metcalfe, 'The Muslims of Sicily under Christian rule', in G. Loud and A. Metcalfe (eds), *The society of Norman Italy*, Leiden, 2002, 289-317; A. Echevarría, *La minoría islámica de los reinos cristianos medievales. Moros, sarracenos, mudéjares*, Málaga, 2004. Cf. D. Abulafia, 'The servitude of Jews and Muslims in the medieval Mediterranean. Origins and diffusion', *Mélanges de l'École Française de Rome* 112 (2000) 687-714.

1520; their descendants were expelled in 1609-14.[89] No event in the premodern history of Christians under Muslim rule presents a very good parallel. By the 16th century, one of the most portentous new aspects of that history was the growing accommodation of foreign Christian representatives, largely from western Europe, in the courts and ports of the Muslim 'gunpowder empires': the Ottomans, Safavids and Mughals. Their connections to the increasingly powerful Christian states of Europe would eventually have a profound effect upon the circumstances of Christian life in Muslim-ruled territories.[90]

[89] See O. Zwartjes, 'Pedro de Alcalá', in *CMR* 6, 73-8.

[90] E.g. M. Frederiks, 'Introduction: Christians, Muslims and empires in the 16th century', in *CMR* 6, 1-10, and *CMR* 7, 1-14; A. Guenther, 'The arrival of European Christians in India during the 16th century', in *CMR* 7, 15-25; R. Matthee, 'Jesuits in Safavid Persia', in *EIr*; S. Aslanian, *From the Indian Ocean to the Mediterranean. The global trade networks of Armenian merchants from New Julfa*, Berkeley CA, 2014. See also R. Loureiro, 'Gaspar da Cruz', in *CMR* 6, 369-75.

Chapter 16
Martyrdom and conversion

Christian C. Sahner

Introduction

At the time of the Arab conquest in the 7th century, much of the greater Middle East was predominantly Christian, including areas such as North Africa, Egypt, Syria, Mesopotamia and Anatolia.[1] By the early modern period, however, many of these regions had become majority Muslim, in the process, abandoning traditionally Christian languages such as Latin, Coptic, Syriac and Greek for Arabic, Persian and Turkish. There were regional variations in the process, of course, as well as moments when the pace of conversion sped up and slowed down. But the broad arc of religious change in the medieval period is indisputable: Islam waxed as Christianity waned.[2]

Despite the steady pace of Islamisation, the conversion of the Christian population was not inevitable, especially at the beginning of the Islamic period. Indeed, history furnishes numerous examples of the process unfolding in reverse, in which instead of conversion to Islam, we find Muslim conversion to Christianity. Along with this, we also find examples of Christians challenging the Islamic social and political order through acts of blasphemy. Christians sometimes recorded these episodes in the form of martyrdom narratives, that is, stylised hagiographical accounts of violence, often but not exclusively at the hands of Muslim

1 This essay draws and expands upon C.C. Sahner, *Christian martyrs under Islam. Religious violence and the making of the Muslim world*, Princeton NJ, 2018.

2 For the most important studies, see T.W. Arnold, *The preaching of Islam. A history of the propagation of the Muslim faith*, London, 1896; D.C. Dennett, *Conversion and the poll tax in early Islam*, Cambridge MA, 1950; R.W. Bulliet, *Conversion to Islam in the medieval period. An essay in quantitative history*, Cambridge MA, 1979; M. Gervers and R.J. Bikhazi (eds), *Conversion and continuity. Indigenous Christian communities in Islamic lands*, Toronto, 1990; J.-M. Fiey, 'Conversions à l'islam de juifs et chrétiens sous les Abbasides d'après les sources arabes et syriaques', in J. Irmscher (ed.), *Rapports entre juifs, chrétiens et musulmans*, Amsterdam, 1995, 13-28; D.J. Wasserstein, 'Conversion and the *ahl al-dhimma*', in R. Irwin (ed.), *The new Cambridge history of Islam*, vol. 4. *Islamic cultures and societies to the end of the eighteenth century*, Cambridge, 2010, 184-208; A.C.S. Peacock (ed.), *Islamisation. Comparative perspectives from history*, Edinburgh, 2017.

officials. The subjects of these narratives were revered as saints, with annual feasts and pilgrimages held and churches built in their honour.[3]

The concept of martyrdom is as old as Christianity itself. For the martyrs of later generations, Jesus himself served as the prototype of finding strength through weakness and achieving victory through defeat. Many of his earliest followers – including all but one of the Apostles – were martyred. These were followed by large numbers of martyrs killed during bouts of persecution in the Roman Empire, when many Christians refused to sacrifice to pagan gods or take part in the imperial cult. Martyrdom largely came to an end after Constantine's (r. 306-37) conversion to Christianity in the early 4th century, but it carried on outside Rome's borders in the Zoroastrian Sasanian Empire. Along with these, there were martyrs killed amidst intra-Christian disputes, including Donatist martyrs in North Africa and Miaphysite martyrs in the Levant and Mesopotamia.

The rise of Islam in the 7th century provided Christians with new occasions for martyrdom. Often called 'neomartyrs', or 'new martyrs', these saints and the cults that grew up around them emphasised a sense of continuity between the sufferings of the early Church and those of the present. Instead of pagans persecuting Christians, however, it was Muslims who were now portrayed as forcing Christians to choose between life and death; between converting to Islam – for Christians, effectively a form of 'heathenism' – and preserving their Christian faith. The earliest recorded examples of martyrdom under Islam come from the 7th century, and they continued to be recorded through to the early modern period. Indeed, Christians across the greater Middle East still commemorate the victims of inter-religious violence as saints in the modern day.[4] Accounts of martyrdom come from nearly every corner of the medieval Middle East where Christians and Muslims lived side-by-side, including

[3] Along with Sahner, *Christian martyrs under Islam*, see especially Ḥ. Zayyāt, 'Shuhadā' al-naṣrāniyya fī l-islām', *Al-Machreq* 36 (1938) 459-65; R.G. Hoyland, *Seeing Islam as others saw it. A survey and evaluation of Christian, Jewish, and Zoroastrian writings on early Islam*, Princeton NJ, 1997, pp. 336-86; S.H. Griffith, 'Christians, Muslims, and neo-martyrs. Saints' lives and Holy Land history', in A. Kofsky and G.G. Stroumsa (eds), *Sharing the sacred. Religious contacts and conflicts in the Holy Land, first to fifteenth centuries CE*, Jerusalem, 1998, 163-207; D.H. Vila, 'Christian martyrs in the first Abbasid century and the development of an apologetic against Islam', St. Louis MO, 1999 (PhD Diss. Saint Louis University); C. Foss, 'Byzantine saints in early Islamic Syria', *Analecta Bollandiana* 125 (2007) 93-119; and most recently, S.J. Shoemaker (trans.), *Three Christian martyrdoms from early Islamic Palestine*, Provo UT, 2016.

[4] See M. Mosebach, *The 21. A journey into the land of the Coptic martyrs*, Walden NY, 2019.

al-Andalus, Egypt, Syria, Mesopotamia, Armenia and Georgia. They survive in a kaleidoscope of languages, reflecting the wide geographical area in which they occurred.

This essay explores the history of Christian martyrdom in the medieval Middle East, as both a historical and a literary phenomenon. It investigates the legal and historical context of the violence; some key martyrs of the early period (7th-10th centuries); the development of the tradition in the later Middle Ages; the characteristics of the genre of martyrology, or narratives of martyrdom; and finally, the apologetic purposes of the written accounts of martyrdom.

Apostasy and blasphemy in Islamic history

Apostasy was not considered a capital offence during the Prophet's lifetime. The Qur'an, for example, makes no provision for the execution of apostates, and in fact, urges forgiveness of those who leave Islam (see Q 2:109). It took until after Muḥammad's death for this to change, particularly as a consequence of the Ridda Wars (c. 632-3), when numerous Arab tribes 'apostatised' from Islam by refusing to pay taxes to the Prophet's successor, Abū Bakr. In the wake of this tumult, a strong consensus emerged that abandoning Islam was forbidden and should be punished by death.[5]

Despite this, apostasy did occur from time to time. In the early period, at least, it seems to have happened most frequently among recently converted populations, whose attachment to Islam could be described as contingent or tentative. The early legal sources bear this out through the anecdotes they use to describe the phenomenon of apostasy. These anecdotes almost never focus on individuals from longstanding Muslim families or tribes, but instead on Christian or pagan converts who experienced a change of heart and wished to return to their natal faiths.[6] The legal texts focus on the circumstances in which such individuals might

[5] For overviews of apostasy in Islamic law and theology, see Y. Friedmann, *Tolerance and coercion in Islam. Interfaith relations in the Muslim tradition*, Cambridge, 2003, pp. 121-59; W. Heffening, art. 'Murtadd', in *EI2*; W. Hallaq, art. 'Apostasy', in *EQ*; F. Griffel, art. 'Apostasy', *EI3*; R. Peter and G.J.J. de Vries, 'Apostasy in Islam', *Die Welt des Islams* 17 (1976) 1-25; J.L. Kraemer, 'Apostates, rebels and brigands', *Israel Oriental Studies* 10 (1980) 34-73; F. Griffel, *Apostasie und Toleranz im Islam*, Leiden, 2000; D. Cook, 'Apostasy from Islam. A historical perspective', *Jerusalem Studies in Arabic and Islam* 31 (2006) 248-88.

[6] E.g. the Christian apostate al-Mustawrid al-ʿIjlī, discussed in Sahner, *Christian martyrs under Islam*, pp. 256-63.

re-join the Muslim community – usually after making an act of repentance. Most jurists believed the authorities had to offer the chance to repent three times. If an apostate refused, he or she could be killed.[7]

Across the medieval period, most converts remained committed to Islam, presumably due to a combination of 'carrots' and 'sticks'. That is, they were incentivised to remain Muslim by the social, economic and political benefits that came from practising the faith of the ruling class. At the same time, they were discouraged from leaving by the threat of the punishment that awaited them if they were ever caught. Still, as we shall see in the case of the neomartyrs, flip-flopping to and away from Islam happened to a far greater extent than many historians have generally acknowledged.[8] In many ways, this was a symptom of a much wider culture of porosity between religious groups, especially in the early period: as the first Muslims settled on certain core doctrines and practices, they intermarried with non-Muslims, adopted their cultures and social customs, and held to many of the same religious beliefs.[9] In rare instances in this mixed-up world, Muslims could be tempted to go back to Christianity or adopt it anew.

The largest group of neomartyrs in the medieval Middle East was apostates of one kind or another, but a second important group included blasphemers, who were executed after verbally attacking the Prophet Muḥammad. Attitudes about blasphemy in Islam were much slower to crystallise than those about apostasy.[10] For example, the Qur'an says nothing specific about blasphemy, though it condemns those who dare to challenge the Prophet's mission and reputation. We also know from later biographical sources that Muḥammad executed individuals who had insulted him, and such behaviours seem to have fed into later legal texts, which urge fierce punishments for blasphemers, including execution. Blasphemy was often treated as a subcategory of apostasy in Islamic

---

[7] F.M. Denny, art. 'Tawba', in *EI2*; Sahner, *Christian martyrs under Islam*, pp. 168-70.

[8] U.I. Simonsohn, 'Halting between two opinions. Conversion and apostasy in early Islam', *Medieval Encounters* 19 (2013) 344-72. Sahner, *Christian martyrs under Islam*, esp. pp. 33-8.

[9] On the porosity of the early Muslim community more broadly, see F.M. Donner, *Muhammad and the believers. At the origins of Islam*, Cambridge MA, 2012; M.P. Penn, *Envisioning Islam. Syriac Christians and the early Muslim world*, Philadelphia PA, 2015, pp. 142-82; J. Tannous, *The making of the medieval Middle East: Religion, society, and simple believers*, Princeton NJ, 2018, especially pp. 225-504.

[10] For overviews of blasphemy in Islamic law and thought, see L. Wiederhold, art. 'Shatm', in *EI2*; Friedmann, *Tolerance and coercion*, pp. 149-52; M.H. Kamali, *Freedom of expression in Islam*, Cambridge, 1997, pp. 212-58; Sahner, *Christian martyrs under Islam*, pp. 120-5.

law and so does not figure prominently as a topic for deliberation in early legal sources. Yet many of the leading lights of early Islamic jurisprudence, including Aḥmad ibn Ḥanbal (d. 855) and numerous Mālikīs from North Africa and al-Andalus, treated the matter in detail. Several, for example, were keen to distinguish between different tiers of blasphemous speech, such that non-Muslims were free to state points of disagreement between themselves and Muslims, but were not free to 'weaponise' these disagreements in the form of blasphemous speech. Interestingly, our earliest stand-alone treatises on blasphemy date to the later Middle Ages, written by jurists such as Ibn Taymiyya (d. 1328) and Tāqī l-Dīn al-Subkī (d. 1355).[11] As with apostasy, another rich source of evidence about blasphemy laws comes from Christian hagiographical texts of the early medieval period, particularly as it pertains to the implementation and perception of these laws in daily life.

Converting and returning

The single largest group of martyrs from the early Islamic period consisted of Christian converts to Islam who then returned to Christianity.[12] As we have seen, this behaviour is well attested in Islamic legal sources, along with Islamic and Christian chronicles. The very earliest neomartyr of all falls into this category: George the Black, who died in Damascus sometime in the mid-7th century. A profile of him is given by the Greek-speaking churchman Anastasius of Sinai (d. c.700) in *The edifying and supportive tales*.[13] George was born to a Christian family, possibly in Syria or across the frontier in Byzantium, before being captured and sold into slavery among Muslims. He reportedly converted to Islam at the age of eight, but returned to his original religion as an adult, worshipping in secret for fear that his Muslim master might discover him. He was eventually betrayed by another slave who had converted to Islam and was killed. George's experience mirrors that of other martyrs from the period who also converted to Islam and returned to Christianity in the

[11] Ibn Taymiyya, *Al-ṣārim al-maslūl ʿ alā shātim al-rasūl*, ed. I. Shams al-Dīn, Beirut, 2009; Tāqī l-Dīn al-Subkī, *Al-sayf al-maslūl ʿalā man sabba l-rasūl*, ed. I.A. al-Ghawj, Amman, 2000.

[12] Sahner, *Christian martyrs under Islam*, pp. 29-79.

[13] A. Binggeli, 'Anastate le Sinaïte. *Récits sur le Sinaï* et *Récits utiles à l'âme*. Édition, traduction, commentaire', Paris, 2001 (PhD Diss. Université Paris–IV) p. 252 (Greek), p. 567 (French); Sahner, *Christian martyrs under Islam*, pp. 40-1; also on this work, see A. Binggeli, 'Anatasius of Sinai', in *CMR* 1, 193-202, pp. 198-200.

context of captivity. These include Vahan of Gołt'n (d. 737) and the Martyrs of Syracuse (d. c. 875-86).[14] Slavery was a major engine of Islamisation in the post-conquest period, and most slaves who converted in this way remained Muslims. But the martyrs demonstrate how, on occasion, slaves could resist the pressure to join the faith of the ruling class and cling to their Christianity instead.

Another category of martyrs who converted and then returned did so in highly contested circumstances. These martyrs shed light on the process of conversion more broadly, especially the way it could be instantiated through certain ambiguous symbols and gestures. A good example is Elias of Helioupolis, who was killed in Damascus in 779 and whose biography was written in a Greek text.[15] According to this text, Elias was around ten when he and his family set out from Helioupolis (Baalbek) for Damascus. Upon arriving in the former Umayyad capital, Elias found work making camel saddles in the shop of a Syrian Christian who had recently converted to Islam. This man was attached – possibly as a client (Greek *parasitos*, from Arabic *mawlā*?) – to a wealthy Arab Muslim, whose son, in turn, enlisted the Syrian and his workers to serve at the birthday party of his own infant child. In the course of the evening, the Muslims heckled Elias, asking why he was not a Muslim and inviting him to convert and join them as an equal. Elias deflected their taunts, and the guests soon relented, allowing him to celebrate with them regardless of his religion. One of the Muslims, however, coaxed the Christian onto the dance floor, furtively loosening the boy's belt in the process. This was allegedly to allow him freer movement as he danced, but in the process of stripping away the belt, the Muslim removed what was also a key marker of Elias's Christian faith – in effect, converting him to Islam without his realising it. The next morning, Elias went to pray at a local church. One party-goer noticed him leaving and asked where he was going. When he replied, the man asked, 'Did you not deny your faith last night?' Denying that he was a Muslim, Elias rushed out in fear: the accidental convert to Islam was now the accidental apostate to Christianity. He was eventually charged for renouncing Islam and was executed.

---

[14] For Vahan, see R.W. Thomson, '*The Martyrdom of Vahan*', in *CMR* 1, 281-3; for the Martyrs of Syracuse, see B. Flusin, '*Synaxarion of the Great Church*', in *CMR* 3, 574-85, p. 576. For discussion, see Sahner, *Christian martyrs under Islam*, pp. 41-5.

[15] S. Efthymiadis, '*The martyrdom of Elias of Helioupolis* (Elias of Damascus)', in *CMR* 1, 916-18; Sahner, *Christian martyrs under Islam*, pp. 53-9. Since the publication of the entry in *CMR* 1, a new publication on Elias has appeared: T. Sizgorich, 'The dancing martyr. Violence, identity, and the Abbasid postcolonial', *History of Religions* 57 (2017) 2-27.

The central scene in the story is the removal of Elias' belt. This was one of a variety of garments Christians were required to wear to distinguish them from Muslims in mixed settings.[16] As a result, medieval sources sometimes describe the process of conversion to Islam as culminating in the removal of the belt, and indeed, the decision to return to Christianity was often signalled by the decision to refasten this belt.[17] Such articles of clothing took on great importance at a time when Muslims and Christians might look the same, speak the same languages, inhabit the same cities, and even share the same marital beds. To emphasise difference in this way was to fight against the prevailing culture of resemblance.[18] That Elias could be understood to convert by removing and donning such a garment suggests the central importance of symbols such as the *zunnār* (belt). It also suggests the ways in which they could be interpreted ambiguously. We see something similar in the Syriac *Life* of Cyrus of Ḥarrān (d. 769), in which the martyr is accused of converting after registering himself as a Muslim in the public tax rolls; or the Arabic *Life* of ʿAbd al-Masīḥ al-Ghassānī (d. mid-8th century), in which the martyr is represented as converting almost passively while fighting alongside Muslims on the frontiers between the caliphate and Byzantium.[19]

A third group of convert martyrs were born into religiously mixed families.[20] Such unions were relatively common in the medieval Middle East and al-Andalus, facilitated by Islamic law which allowed Muslim men to marry up to four women from the People of the Book (*ahl al-kitāb*, meaning Christians and Jews) without these women having to convert.

---

16 On this theme more broadly, see Ḥ. Zayyāt, 'Simāt al-naṣārā wa-l-yahūd fī l-islām', *Al-Machreq* 43 (1949) 161-252; A. Noth, 'Problems of differentiation between Muslims and non-Muslims. Re-reading the "Ordinances of 'Umar" (*al-Shurūṭ al-ʿUmariyya*)', in R.G. Hoyland (ed.), *Muslims and others in early Islamic society*, Farnham, 2004, 103-24; M. Levy-Rubin, *Non-Muslims in the early Islamic empire. From surrender to coexistence*, Cambridge, 2011, pp. 58-98; L.B. Yarbrough, 'Origins of the *ghiyār*', *Journal of the American Oriental Society* 134 (2014) 113-21.

17 Sahner, *Christian martyrs under Islam*, p. 58, with further references.

18 M.J. Kister, '"Do not assimilate yourselves ..." *Lā tashabbahū*', *Jerusalem Studies in Arabic and Islam* 12 (1989) 33-52.

19 For Cyrus, see A. Harrak, 'Piecing together the fragmentary account of the martyrdom of Cyrus of Ḥarrān', *Analecta Bollandiana* 121 (2003) 297-328; and the text from which it comes, A. Harrak, 'Joshua the Stylite of Zuqnīn', in *CMR* 1, 322-6. For ʿAbd al-Masīḥ, see D.H. Vila, '*The Martyrdom of ʿAbd al-Masīḥ*', in *CMR* 1, 684-7. For discussion of both, see Sahner, *Christian martyrs under Islam*, pp. 45-53.

20 For general comment on interreligious marriage, see A. Fattal, *Le statut légal des non-musulmans en pays d'islam*, Beirut, 1958, pp. 129-37; Friedmann, *Tolerance and coercion*, pp. 160-93; J.M. Safran, *Defining boundaries in al-Andalus. Muslims, Christians, and Jews in Islamic Iberia*, Ithaca NY, 2013, pp. 103-6, 125-67; Sahner, *Christian martyrs under Islam*, pp. 59-62; Tannous, *Making of the medieval Middle East*, pp. 437-56.

Muslim women, however, were forbidden from marrying non-Muslim men. Jurists explained this ban by appealing to the principle of *kafāʾa*, that is, the need for parity between a husband and a wife, whereby a woman could only marry a man of equal or higher social, tribal or religious standing, and hence, only a Muslim. One example of martyrdom occurring in the context of a religiously mixed family is the *Life* of the Egyptian saint George the New (d. 978), written in Arabic.[21] Muzāḥim, as the martyr was known at birth, was the son of a Muslim man and a Christian woman from the Nile Delta. As such, he was considered a Muslim under the law. That being said, he used to accompany his mother to church and was reportedly so impressed by the piety of the Christians that he would beseech God to permit him to convert. His mother would not allow this, however, for fear of his father's reaction, though she did allow him to take the unconsecrated bread at the end of the liturgy. Eventually discovering his son's interest in Christianity, the father flew into a rage, and George fled. He was baptised, taking the name 'George', and he married the daughter of a local priest. He was eventually killed for his apostasy. There were other martyrs whose conversions away from Islam were nurtured by Christian relatives, especially Christian mothers and sisters, as we see in the case of the Palestinian saint Bacchus (d. 787-8), several of the Córdoba martyrs (d. 850-9), and in a slightly later period, the Egyptian saint, Dioscorus (d. 1279-90).[22] These stories underscore the possibility of a residual Christianity surviving in mixed families – as we see especially in the case of the 'crypto-Christians' of Córdoba. One assumes, however, that these dilemmas mostly disappeared over time, as family trees in which one parent had once been a Christian became thoroughly Muslim in later generations.

---

21 M.N. Swanson, 'The monk Mīnā', in *CMR* 2, 460-3; Sahner, *Christian martyrs under Islam*, pp. 68-70.

22 For Bacchus, see S. Efthymiadis, *'The Life of Bacchus the younger'*, in *CMR* 1, 597-9. For the Córdoba martyrs, see J. Tolan, 'Eulogius of Cordova', in *CMR* 1, 679-83. For Dioscorus, see M.N. Swanson, 'The Copto-Arabic Synaxarion', in *CMR* 4, 937-45, p. 940. For general comment, see Sahner, *Christian martyrs under Islam*, pp. 62-77. For the dating of the martyrdom of Dioscorus, see A. Khater, 'Nouveaux fragments du Synaxaire arabe', *Bulletin de la Société d'Archéologie Copte* 17 (1963-64) 75-100, esp. pp. 94-6.

True apostasy

Although the majority of convert-martyrs were born as Christians, a small but fascinating group were born into Muslim families and converted without any prior knowledge of their new religion. We might label these individuals 'true apostates', to borrow the words of David Cook.[23] Such figures are extremely difficult to detect in historical sources, presumably because true apostasy was rare, given the stiff disincentives against it. Furthermore, most Muslims who converted to Christianity and got away with it probably wished to be discreet and disguise their actions, and thus, are less visible to the eyes of history. Martyrdom narratives, however, provide an unparalleled window onto this phenomenon.

A fascinating case of true apostasy comes from Georgia, the northernmost limit of Muslim expansion during the conquest period, where Abo of Tiflīs was killed in 786 (see his *Life*, written in Georgian).[24] Abo was reportedly an Arab Muslim from Baghdad who worked as a perfumer. Somehow he became attached to the Georgian duke, Nerse, who was released from prison in 775 on the accession of the new ʿAbbasid caliph, al-Mahdī (r. 775-85). Nerse then made his way back to Georgia with Abo in tow, presumably to serve as a purveyor of perfumes at his reconstituted court. In Georgia, Abo came into contact with Christianity and even learned to speak and write the local language. Since the region was under Muslim control, he could not convert publicly, but his chance arose when Nerse was forced to flee north to the land of the Khazars, and Abo was baptised there. Eventually, Abo returned to the ʿAbbasid capital at Tiflīs (Georgian, Tbilisi), where he felt compelled to announce his conversion and to convert other Muslims like him. He was eventually captured and executed.

The most famous neomartyr of the early Islamic period was also a true apostate: Anthony al-Qurashī (d. 799), an alleged descendant of the Prophet Muḥammad who converted to Christianity in Damascus and was killed by Hārūn al-Rashīd.[25] Along with his original Arabic biography, mentions of him are found in Syriac chronicles, an Ethiopic translation of his *Life*, and even a notice about him in the work of a Muslim

23 Cook, 'Apostasy from Islam', pp. 260-6; more broadly, Sahner, *Christian martyrs under Islam*, pp. 80-117.

24 G. Shurgaia, 'Ioane Sabanisdze', in *CMR* 1, 334-7; Sahner, *Christian martyrs under Islam*, pp. 96-100.

25 D.H. Vila, '*The Martyrdom of Anthony* (*Rawḥ al-Qurashī*)', in *CMR* 1, 498-501; Sahner, *Christian martyrs under Islam*, pp. 84-92.

writer, the famous Iranian polymath al-Bīrūnī (d. 1050). His conversion was precipitated by two miracles he allegedly witnessed in a church near his home in Damascus, the first connected to an icon of St Theodore, and the second connected to the Eucharist, which he saw transformed into a lamb. Convinced by these experiences that Christianity was true, he headed south and was baptised in the River Jordan. Thereafter, he became a monk and returned to Damascus, where he disputed with his Muslim relatives and various state officials. He was eventually tried by the caliph and killed at al-Raqqa.

The *Life* of Anthony has many elements that seem to reflect a real historical environment, though it also contains numerous elements of fantasy, as befitting the *Life* of a Christian martyr who hailed from the tribe of Quraysh (to which Muḥammad and the early caliphs also traced their ancestry). Perhaps not surprisingly, many elements in the story started circulating in other texts, in which we also find accounts of aristocratic Muslims (often described as members of the Umayyad and ʿAbbasid royal families) who converted to Islam after witnessing miracles connected to icons and the Eucharist.[26] These fictional stories of apostasy and martyrdom expressed a widespread desire among Christians for a second 'Constantinian moment', that is, the conversion of a non-Christian sovereign who would bring about the conversion of a pagan empire. The boldest example of this genre is found in a lengthy hagiographical novel known as the *Life of Theodore of Edessa* (in Greek and Arabic).[27] Among other things, it tells the story of how a Melkite bishop named Theodore baptised a caliph – modelled on the figure of al-Maʾmūn (r. 813-33) – who then suffered a martyr's death after announcing his Christian faith in public.

Blasphemy

The third major group of martyrs comprised those killed for blasphemy.[28] Although they did not undergo conversions like members of the other two groups, their outbursts may be interpreted as reactions to many of

---

[26] See especially A. Binggeli, 'Converting the caliph. A legendary motif in Christian hagiography and historiography of the early Islamic period', in A. Papaconstantinou, with M. Debié and H. Kennedy (eds), *Writing 'true stories'. Historians and hagiographers in the late antique and medieval Near East*, Turnhout, 2010, 77-103 (published subsequently to the relevant entry in *CMR*); Sahner, *Christian martyrs under Islam*, pp. 105-13.

[27] K.-P. Todt and M.N. Swanson, '*Life of Theodore, Bishop of Edessa*', in *CMR* 2, 585-93.

[28] Sahner, *Christian martyrs under Islam*, pp. 118-59.

the same social pressures. These include the mounting pace of conversion to Islam, along with the widespread embrace of Arabic language and culture. Our richest information about Christian blasphemy comes from Córdoba, the capital of the independent Umayyad emirate of al-Andalus, where 48 Christians were executed between 850 and 859. Their deeds were recorded in a large body of Latin biographical and apologetic texts written by the priest Eulogius (who was himself executed in 859) and his friend, the layman Paulus Alvarus.[29] Although some of the martyrs were killed for apostasy, the vast majority were executed for blasphemy.

A good example is Perfectus, a priest who was the very first martyr to die in 850.[30] According to Eulogius, Perfectus was on the road one day when he encountered a group of Muslims, who peppered him with questions about Christianity, specifically his opinion about the Prophet Muḥammad. Knowing the risks of speaking too frankly in such a setting, Perfectus initially demurred. But the Muslims pressed him, promising that they would not harm him in exchange for expressing his views very frankly. Per their agreement, Perfectus explained in Arabic how Muḥammad had been a false prophet consumed with lust. The Muslims departed, at first leaving him alone. But the next day, fuming with rage at his blasphemous speech, they captured and handed him over to the authorities, who had him killed.

Despite their evident hatred of Islam, several of the Córdoba martyrs were deeply embedded in Islamic culture and society. Isaac, for instance, who was killed in 851, hailed from one of the noble Christian families of Córdoba[31] and so had acquired a powerful position at the Umayyad court, serving as the *exceptor rei publicae* (probably corresponding to the Arabic *mustakhrij*), responsible for the affairs of the Christian community with the state, especially the collection of taxes. For unclear reasons, he left his post to become a monk at the neighbouring monastery of Tabanos, where several other martyrs are known to have lived. He spent three years there, only to return suddenly to Córdoba, where he confronted the chief *qāḍī* – probably Saʿīd ibn Sulaymān al-Ghāfiqī, who may have been a former colleague at court. He proceeded to disparage

[29] K.B. Wolf, 'Paul Alvarus', in *CMR* 1, 645-8; Tolan, 'Eulogius of Cordova'. See also K.B. Wolf (trans.), *The Eulogius corpus*, Liverpool, 2019. (This is the first complete English translation of Eulogius's writings, published subsequently to the entry on Eulogius in CMR).

[30] I. Gil (ed.), *Corpus scriptorum Muzarabicorum*, Madrid, 1973, vol. 2, pp. 369, 377-8, 397-401; Sahner, *Christian martyrs under Islam*, pp. 145-9.

[31] Gil, *Corpus scriptorum Muzarabicorum*, vol. 2, pp. 367-9, 402; Sahner, *Christian martyrs under Islam*, pp. 149-52.

the Prophet and various Muslim doctrines, which led to his being thrown in prison and eventually executed. Isaac is emblematic of many of the 9th century Andalusī martyrs, who in an earlier phase of life profited from professional contacts with Muslims, mastered Arabic language and literature, and often belonged to religiously mixed families. Yet for some reason, their attitudes towards the surrounding culture suddenly soured, and they expressed this dissatisfaction through acts of blasphemy.

There are many theories as to why this episode occurred, some wilder than others. What seems clear is that the mid-9thcentury was a time of rapid Islamisation and Arabisation in the Iberian Peninsula, at least in the eyes of its Christian population. There are hints in the Islamic sources that this may have been true. For example, at precisely this moment we find new markers of a distinctively Islamic society emerging, including rising numbers of Muslim scholars, mosques and religious texts, and a new determination to structure Andalusī society around Islamic norms. This process also seems to have manifested itself in new anxieties about mixing between Muslims and non-Muslims, which had been relatively common in the century or so after the conquest (c. 711). The increasing segregation and stratification of society along religious lines, in turn, may have prompted the martyrs to protest about their situation through vicious outbursts in public.[32]

As a cause of martyrdom, blasphemy is relatively poorly attested outside al-Andalus. That being said, we do have interesting examples of the phenomenon from the eastern reaches of the caliphate, most prominently in the *Life* of Peter of Capitolias (d. 715).[33] Peter was a village priest from Capitolias (Arabic, Bayt Rās) in north-western Transjordan, who witnessed large numbers of his fellow Christians converting to Islam under duress. Determined to provide them with an example of courage and resistance, he publically disparaged the Islamic faith before the city's Muslims. The authorities initially believed Peter was sick or mad, but when he repeated his blasphemous tirades, he was sent to Damascus for trial. There, the Caliph al-Walīd (r. 705-15) interrogated him and sentenced him to death. He was returned to Capitolias and executed. As with the martyrs of Córdoba, the *Life* of Peter demonstrates the close connection between the perceived erosion of Christianity and the

---

32 Sahner, *Christian martyrs under Islam*, pp. 154-9.

33 Peter's *Life* is in Georgian, but was probably based on a Greek original. See S. Efthymiadis, *'The martyrdom of Peter of Capitolias'*, in *CMR* 1, 419-22; Sahner, *Christian martyrs under Islam*, pp. 130-40. After the publication of the entry in *CMR*, the first complete translation of the text appeared in Shoemaker, *Three Christian martyrdoms*, pp. 1-65.

impulse to blaspheme. If it has any basis in reality, the text also testifies to the crystallisation of blasphemy laws at this relatively early point in Islamic history.

Other forms of martyrdom

Not all martyrs died for explicitly religious reasons. Even as hagiographers strove to demonise Muslims as bloodthirsty and cruel, it is obvious that some martyrs died in the context of what were mainly political disputes, military operations or random non-religious violence. Two exemplary martyrdoms of this kind are the *Passions* of the Sixty Martyrs of Gaza (d. c. late 630s)[34] and the Sixty Martyrs of Jerusalem (d. 725).[35] The Gaza martyrs were a group of Byzantine soldiers captured by the Arabs at the time of the conquest.[36] After being thrown in prison, they were told they could convert to Islam or die. The famous patriarch of Jerusalem, Sophronius (d. 638), reportedly ministered to them, encouraging them to remain steadfast in their faith. Indeed, not a single one of the soldiers apostatised, and they were all eventually killed. A similar story unfolds almost a century later, when we read about an otherwise unattested battle between the Caliph Sulaymān ibn ʿAbd al-Malik (r. 715-17) and the Byzantine Emperor Leo III (r. 717-41), which resulted in a seven-year truce between the two powers.[37] Among other things, this truce guaranteed the safe passage of Christian pilgrims from Byzantium to the Holy Land. The story resumes in the seventh year of the treaty, as a group of heavily armed Byzantine archons visited Jerusalem. Not realising that the truce had expired, the group was captured, imprisoned and offered the choice of conversion or death. Some of the soldiers apostatised, but the vast majority of them held fast to their religion and were killed. In both instances, martyrdom occurred as a result of political and military disputes, to which hagiographers later added thick layers of religious significance.

The same applies to the Forty-Two Martyrs of Amorion – rare examples of neomartyrs who were commemorated on both sides of the Islamic-Byzantine frontier – a group of soldiers who were captured during a

34 The texts are in Latin, based on a Greek original.

35 The accounts of these are in Greek but possibly based on a Syriac-Aramaic original.

36 D. Woods, *'The passion of the sixty martyrs of Gaza'*, in *CMR* 1, 190-2.

37 S. Efthymiadis, *'The Sixty martyrs of Jerusalem'*, in *CMR* 1, 327-9; Sahner, *Christian martyrs under Islam*, p. 18, on the language of the text.

Muslim raid on the fortress of Amorion in Anatolia in 838. They became the subjects of numerous hagiographical works in Greek.[38] Another group martyrdom in this vein is that of the *Passion* of the Twenty Martyrs of Mar Saba (d. 788/797).[39] Written by the Sabaite monk Stephen Manṣūr – who was also responsible for the *Passion* of the martyr Romanus (d. 780)[40] – it tells the story of a Bedouin raid on the famous monastery of Mar Saba near Bethlehem. The attackers seem to have been Muslims, but there was nothing about the violence to suggest it was motivated by religious concerns. Indeed, it seems that the raiders were driven by a desire to plunder what was simply a wealthy and vulnerable institution (which had experienced sometimes difficult relations with the local nomads since Late Antiquity).

A good example of a martyrdom arising in the midst of a political dispute comes from the *Passion* of Christopher, the Melkite bishop of Antioch (d. 967).[41] Born near Baghdad, Christopher rose through the church hierarchy and was eventually appointed patriarch through the help of his ally, the Ḥamdānid emir, Sayf al-Dawla (d. 967). Christopher engaged in charitable works, especially efforts to gain relief from the *jizya* for individual Christians. In the background of the story, swirl two key factors: the threat of Byzantine invasion (which would eventually occur in 969) and a local Muslim rebellion against Sayf al-Dawla. Through this tumult, Christopher remained loyal to the emir, which the emir's enemies used as a premise to conspire against the bishop. In a *fatwā*, they accused Christopher of plotting against the city by helping the Byzantine emperor capture it. The conspiracy succeeded, and Christopher was eventually beheaded. The text is anomalous for its lack of interest in confessional or theological issues; indeed, Christopher's death is presented

---

[38] There are several recensions of the story: A. Kolia-Dermitzaki, 'Michael the Synkellos', in *CMR* 1, 627-32; A. Kolia-Dermitzaki, '*The forty-two martyrs of Amorion* (BHG 1212)', in *CMR* 1, 636-8; A. Kolia-Dermitzaki, '*The forty-two martyrs of Amorion* (BHG 1214c)', in *CMR* 1, 639-41; A. Kolia-Dermitzaki, 'Euodius the monk', in *CMR* 1, 844-7.

[39] D.H. Vila, 'The Martyrdom of the twenty martyrs of Mār Saba', in *CMR* 1, 393-6; Sahner, *Christian martyrs under Islam*, pp. 100-1, 204-5. After the publication of the entry in *CMR*, the first complete translation of the text appeared in Shoemaker, *Three Christian martyrdoms*, pp. 67-147.

[40] The text of this is in Georgian, but based on a Greek original. See M. Nanobashvili, 'The Martyrdom of Romanus the Younger', in *CMR* 1, 390-3; Sahner, *Christian martyrs under Islam*, 206-8. After the publication of the entry in *CMR*, the first complete translation of the text has appeared in Shoemaker, *Three Christian martyrdoms*, pp. 149-97.

[41] J.C. Lamoreaux, 'Ibrāhīm ibn Yuḥannā al-Anṭākī', in *CMR* 2, 611-16. See also J. Mugler, 'A Martyr with too many causes: Christopher of Antioch (d. 967) and local collective memory', Washington DC, 2019 (PhD Diss. Georgetown University).

within the matrix of high power politics in northern Syria during the mid-10th century, not of rivalry between Christianity and Islam as such.

Later developments

The golden era of martyrdom writing in the medieval Middle East lasted from the late 7th to the 10th century. Thereafter, Christians continued writing hagiographical accounts of apostasy and blasphemy, but generally in areas far away from the Arabic-speaking heartlands where the genre was pioneered.

The most prolific writers of martyrdom narratives in the late medieval period were Armenian Christians. Peter Cowe has identified more than 20 examples of such texts, mostly dating from the early 13th to the mid-16th century.[42] They were written across a wide geographical area, from eastern Anatolia to Armenia itself, and Iran. What is striking about these sources is that, although the identity of the Muslim opponents is changed from the hagiographical narratives of the early period – no longer Umayyads and ʿAbbasids, but now Seljuks, Kipchaks, Turkmen and Mongols – the general arc of the narratives does not change. This is a testament to the conservatism of the genre and also the fairly consistent ways in which social conflict could erupt between Muslims and Christians in different times and places. These, in turn, were shaped by common demographic realities and legal norms.

An interesting case is the martyrdom of the leatherworker Awag (d. 1390), who originally came from Salmas in what is today Iranian Azerbaijan.[43] Apprenticed to a Muslim master as a youth, Awag later moved to Bitlis in what is today eastern Turkey near Lake Van. In his new home, a Muslim from Salmas accused him of apostatising from Islam. He was

[42] In addition to the texts discussed below, see S.P. Cowe, 'Martyrology of Tʿēodoros Kesaracʿi', in *CMR* 4, 94-7; S.P. Cowe, 'Kirakos Ganjakecʿi or Arewelcʿi', in *CMR* 4, 438-42; S.P. Cowe, 'Dawitʿ erēcʿ Baluecʿi', in *CMR* 4, 620-23; S.P. Cowe, *'Martyrology of Bishop Grigor of Karin'*, in *CMR* 4, 794-7; S.P. Cowe, 'Yovhannēs vardapet', in *CMR* 4, 911-13; S.P. Cowe, 'Martyrology of Archbishop Stepʿanos Sebastacʿi', in *CMR* 5, 199-202; S.P. Cowe, 'Martyrology of Zakʿaria, catholicos of Ałtʿamar', in *CMR* 5, 216-19; S.P. Cowe, 'Martyrology of Tʿamar Mokacʿi', in *CMR* 5, 250-3; S.P. Cowe, 'The martyrology of Vardan Bałišecʿi', in *CMR* 5, 339-41; S.P. Cowe, 'Aṙakʿel Bałišecʿi', in *CMR* 5, 346-50; S.P. Cowe, 'Martyrology of the Confessor Stepʿannos', in *CMR* 5, 549-52; S.P. Cowe, 'Priest Yovhannēs', in *CMR* 7, 572-5; S.P. Cowe, 'Martyrology of Xačʿatur Kołbecʿi in 1517', in *CMR* 7, 588-91; S.P. Cowe, 'Grigoris Ałtʿamarcʿi', in *CMR* 7, 599-607; S.P. Cowe, 'Mkrtičʿ Abełay', in *CMR* 7, 608-14; S.P. Cowe, 'Yovasapʿ Sebastacʿi', in *CMR* 7, 644-9; S.P. Cowe, 'Mec Paron', in *CMR* 7, 668-72.

[43] S.P. Cowe, 'Martyrology of Awag Salmastecʿi', in *CMR* 5, 207-9.

brought before the local Kurdish emir, who referred the case to the *qāḍī*. Before he could reach the judge, however, the saint was attacked and killed by a Muslim mob. The description of the mixed workplace and the disputed conversion calls to mind the life of Elias of Helioupolis and other hagiographical texts set centuries earlier, which hinge on related concerns about ambiguity, identity and belief. Similar themes surface in the *Life* of the martyr Yovhannēs Xlatʿecʿi (d. 1438).[44] According to the text, Yovhannēs was a young bard from the western shore of Lake Van, revered by both Christians and Muslims for his skill in singing. Local Kurds, however, resented his abilities and falsely accused him of having sexual relations with a Muslim dancer and singer. They offered him the choice of converting to Islam and going free, or remaining Christian and facing death. He initially accepted their offer and was paraded through the city in celebration. That same day, however, he regretted this choice and called on several Armenian priests to bring him communion. The priests refused, doubting his sincerity. Eventually, the *qāḍī* and the emir demanded that he formally renounce Christianity and undergo circumcision. Yovhannēs refused and was stoned to death by a mob. Once again, disputed conversion, promiscuous social interactions and a perilous workplace feature prominently in accounts of Christian martyrdom under Islam.

We gain a completely different view of the phenomenon of martyrdom from the *Life* of Yovhannēs, bishop of Tarōn (d. 1463), in what is today eastern Turkey.[45] As bishop, he began restoring old monastic churches throughout the region, and this provoked the ire of the Kurds (who were presumably upset by this resurgence of Christian building, which technically violated the dictates of Islamic law). Arrested, Yovhannēs refused their offer to convert, then condemned Islam and was killed. Quite clearly, there were limits to how active a Christian leader could be in such an environment, especially when it came to expanding the footprint of Christian institutions in a mixed area. A final example is the martyrdom of Mirakʿ Tawrizecʿi, a Christian magnate in the Iranian city of Tabriz, who often interceded with the local Qara Quyunlu and Aq Quyunlu rulers to help other Christians in need.[46] A Muslim courtier, however, became upset with his political influence, especially his efforts to protect a church that was slated for destruction. Instructed to convert

44 S.P. Cowe, 'Martyrology of the youth Yovhannēs Xlatʿecʿi', in *CMR* 5, 370-4.
45 S.P. Cowe, 'Martyrology of Yovhannēs bishop of Tarōn', in *CMR* 5, 478-80.
46 S.P. Cowe, 'Martyrology of Mirakʿ Tawrizecʿi', in *CMR* 5, 553-6.

to Islam or face death, Mirak' nonetheless held fast to his beliefs and was killed. In this and the previous example, we witness how martyrdom narratives, far from revealing the passivity of Christian communities under Islamic rule, sheds light on their agency and ability to exercise power in a Muslim-dominated society.

Another region that generated martyrologies in the later Middle Ages was Egypt.[47] In fact, one of the latest surviving prose compositions in Coptic (the Coptic language was later eclipsed by Arabic) was a martyrology, namely, the *Life* of John of Phanijōit, who died at the beginning of the 13th century.[48] It tells the story of a Christian flax merchant and deacon who entered into a relationship with a Muslim woman in Cairo, assimilating into Islamic culture. He eventually returned to Christianity and publically professed his faith, which led to his execution. The Copts commemorate a number of martyrs in the Mamlūk period, too, though one of our most vivid accounts of violence in this context actually comes from the Byzantine statesman, scholar and litterateur Theodore Metochites, not from an Egyptian. He describes the death of a saint named Michael the New, who was born near Smyrna in coastal Anatolia. He was captured by Turks and sold into slavery in Egypt.[49] Michael was converted to Islam while still a youth and assigned to the Mamlūk forces, where he enjoyed great success and rose through the ranks. Said to have realised the error of his ways, Michael resolved to return to Christianity and flee from Egypt. He heard of a Byzantine embassy departing for Constantinople from Alexandria. Dressed as a monk, he attempted to board the vessel but was discovered and handed over to the authorities. He was eventually killed after refusing to renounce his Christian faith.

The final large group of martyrs in Islamic lands falls outside the chronological scope of this volume, and these are the Ottoman neomartyrs.[50] Nevertheless, they bear mentioning here, given their close geographical

---

47 For later Egyptian martyrs, see T. el-Leithy, 'Coptic culture and conversion in medieval Cairo, 1293-1524 A.D.', Princeton NJ, 2005 (PhD Diss. Princeton University), pp. 101-39; M.M. Shenoda, 'Lamenting Islam, imagining persecution. Copto-Arabic opposition to Islamization and Arabization in Fatimid Egypt', Cambridge MA, 2010 (PhD Diss. Harvard University), pp. 121-71; F. Armanios, *Coptic Christianity in Ottoman Egypt*, New York, 2011, pp. 41-90.

48 J.R. Zaborowski, 'The Martyrdom of John of Phanijōit', in *CMR* 4, 128-31.

49 J. Pahlitzsch, 'Theodore Metochites', in *CMR* 4, 808-14.

50 N. Vaporis, *Witnesses for Christ. Orthodox Christian neomartyrs of the Ottoman period*, Crestwood NY, 2000; T. Krstić, *Contested conversions to Islam. Narratives of religious change in the early modern Ottoman empire*, Stanford CA, 2011; M. Greene, *The Edinburgh history of the Greeks, 1453 to 1768. The Ottoman Empire*, Edinburgh, 2015, pp. 74, 146-51.

and thematic connections to the earlier generations of saints. These texts were written primarily in Greek, along with Old Russian and other languages from the Balkans. They have been the subject of extensive research, but by and large have not been compared with older martyrological traditions from other areas under Islamic control.

The texts

As we have seen throughout this essay, most of our information about the Christian martyrs of the first millennium of Islamic history comes from the genre of *Lives*, or *Vitae*, to use the common Latin term.[51] These are stand-alone biographies written independently of larger historical or literary works. Some of these biographies run for as much as 40 pages in modern printed editions (such as the *Passion of the Twenty Martyrs of Mar Saba*), others for as little as four pages – as with the *Passion of the Sixty Martyrs of Gaza*. Most of the early martyrdom narratives have been edited, but not necessarily translated into modern European languages. Many of the later narratives, especially those in Armenian, remain in manuscript form or are untranslated from the original.

Another important source of information about the martyrs is liturgical calendars. Known as *synaxaria* in Greek (and cognate languages), they detail the feasts celebrated in the course of the church year. In some instances, they identify a saint with a single line of information, though in others they contain longer biographies, which may be based on now-missing independent works. Chronicles are another source of insight into martyrdom. Unlike hagiographical texts, however, chronicles do not always make clear whether a given Christian who was killed by Muslims was also venerated as a saint. Some pseudo-hagiographical works actually come from this genre, including the *Life of Cyrus of Ḥarrān*, which appears as the epilogue of a longer historical work known as *The chronicle of Zuqnīn*. We sometimes have information about martyrs in the form of edifying tales, sermons and orations, which cannot be called strictly biographical or hagiographical.

The languages of the martyrdom narratives are as diverse as the places in which they are set. In the post-conquest period, Greek was an extremely important language of martyrdom-writing, especially in the

---

[51] This and the following paragraphs draw on Sahner, *Christian martyrs under Islam*, pp. 14-22.

monasteries of southern Palestine and the Sinai. Here and throughout the Middle East, Arabic eventually became the dominant language of Christian life, and indeed, some of the earliest original compositions in Christian Arabic are martyrdom texts (see, for example, the *Lives* of ʿAbd al-Masīḥ al-Ghassānī and Anthony al-Qurashī). On the periphery of the caliphate, ancient Christian languages continued to be used, including for hagiography, as we see with Latin texts from al-Andalus, along with Armenian and Georgian texts from the south Caucasus. Interestingly, Syriac – one of the most important Christian languages of the Middle East in Late Antiquity and the Middle Ages – furnishes almost no records of martyrdoms under Islam.

Because of the strong theological, political and economic ties among Christian communities in the greater Middle East, martyrdom narratives were frequently translated from one language to another. In some instances, we have multiple recensions of the same text (e.g. the *Life* of Anthony al-Qurashī, which was originally written in Arabic, but also exists in Georgian and Ethiopic). In other instances, the original version of a saint's *Life* has disappeared, but translations into other languages survive, such as the *Life* of Peter of Capitolias, originally written in Greek but surviving only in Georgian, or the *Life* of Romanus, probably written in Arabic but also surviving only in Georgian. Thus, Georgian emerges as an extremely important language with respect to the preservation of these texts. This was a function of the close ties between the Georgian Orthodox Church and its Melkite counterpart in the Levant, where many Georgian monks were dispatched to copy and translate texts, especially at sites such as the Black Mountain near Antioch, the Holy Cross Monastery in Jerusalem, and St Catherine's Monastery at Mount Sinai.[52]

There is no hard and fast rule about the date of the texts. In many but not all instances, it seems that the lives of the martyrs were written in relatively close chronological proximity to the events that they describe. Some texts show great knowledge of local topography, and can therefore be trusted as products of the immediate worlds they describe (e.g.

---

[52] On the role of Georgian in the transmission and preservation of Oriental Christian literature, see P. Peeters, *Orient et Byzance. Le tréfonds oriental de l'hagiographie byzantine*, Brussels, 1950, pp. 155-64; T. Mgaloblishvili, 'The Georgian Sabaite (Sabatsminduri) literary school and the Sabatsmindian version of the Georgian *Mravaltavi* (Polykephalon)', in J. Patrich (ed.), *The Sabaite heritage in the Orthodox Church from the fifth century to the present*, Leuven, 2001, 229-33; S.F. Johnson, 'Introduction. The social presence of Greek in Eastern Christianity, 200-1200 CE', in S.F Johnson (ed.), *Languages and cultures of Eastern Christianity. Greek*, Farnham, 2014, 1-222, especially pp. 81-4. On Georgian in the martyrologies, see Sahner, *Christian martyrs under Islam*, pp. 17-18, 237.

the *Life* of Peter of Capitolias, the Córdoba martyr texts; and so forth). Other texts were composed in one place but rewritten later far away from their original context, and thus may have lost much of their original colour (e.g. the *Life* of Bacchus, the surviving version of which comes from Constantinople, not Palestine where the saint lived and where a prior recension must have been written). In some instances, we know the names of the hagiographers, such as those of the *Lives* of Abo of Tiflīs and Christopher of Antioch, but in other cases the authors are completely anonymous.

The question of authorship bears directly on the question of reliability: are most martyrdom narratives accurate descriptions of real events, or are they pious fantasies with little grounding in fact?[53] It would be imprudent to generalise about a body of texts spanning nearly a millennium of history and many thousands of miles. Suffice it to say, while some *Lives* are plainly fictional (e.g. the *Lives* of Michael of Mar Saba and Theodore of Edessa), many seem to reflect real events, though stylised to meet the expectations of the genre. We can often contextualise our sources using Islamic texts in a range of languages, which provide information about characters, events and places described in the course of the Christian narratives. We can also contextualise them by exploring the legal context for the violence, especially Islamic norms about conversion, apostasy and blasphemy. Very often, Islamic legal principles are clearly and precisely reflected in Christian accounts of violence. While many martyrs are otherwise unattested in medieval sources – as one would expect of such a wide array of sub-elites, including farmers, soldiers, traders and minor clergy – more often than not the stories strike the reader as plausible. Their original audiences must have responded similarly, with the result that they merited copying and studying, and the martyrs were venerated in their own time. This is not to deny that, like all hagiographical narratives, these texts trade on a significant element of fantasy, often encased in literary tropes. But it is also to say that a judicious reading of the sources can help us glimpse worlds that are otherwise invisible from more conventional kinds of evidence.

---

53 For a methodological exercise regarding this question, see Sahner, *Christian martyrs under Islam*, pp. 253-63.

The purposes of martyrdom narratives

A final question to consider is why Christians bothered writing martyrdom narratives after the rise of Islam. What were readers supposed to get out of these vivid accounts of religious violence? As with hagiography of any period, the saints' *Lives* were composed to encourage imitation. The martyrs were models of the Christian life, mirrors of Christ himself, exemplifying the virtues of forbearance, courage and devotion to God. Not all martyrs were the same, of course, and each biography conveyed a slightly different message.[54] The *Lives* of the martyrs who converted to Islam and returned to Christianity were probably designed to encourage other recent converts to abandon Islam. In the process, they conveyed a message of unconditional forgiveness to those who were also contemplating returning to the church, especially given the risks involved. Far from facing stigmatisation or rejection, returnees could expect to be absolved of their sins and celebrated as heroes of the faith.

As for biographies of Muslim converts to Christianity, especially those written in Arabic, such as the *Life of Anthony al-Qurashī*, some have gone so far as to argue that they were written with Muslim audiences in mind.[55] By drawing on motifs, themes and key words familiar to Muslims, they may have aimed to provide support and succour to individuals considering this difficult leap from the mosque to the church. We cannot rule out this possibility, but what is even more likely is that these biographies were meant to assert the superiority of Christianity over Islam, specifically by showcasing high-status Muslims debasing themselves and embracing the church. Finally, the *Lives* of blasphemers were composed to articulate the perceived falsehoods of Islam and to encourage Christians to stick up for their beliefs at a time when they felt besieged by conversion and assimilation.

The *Lives* of the martyrs offered models to emulate, but they also highlighted models to avoid. The most important was a recurring character found in numerous texts: 'the unrepentant apostate', who began life as a Christian and converted to Islam.[56] Unlike the martyr, however, this figure refused to admit his or her error and remained a Muslim. The unrepentant apostate appears in a variety of hagiographical texts from

---

54 Sahner, *Christian martyrs under Islam*, pp. 200-2.

55 T. Sizgorich, 'For Christian eyes only? The intended audience of the martyrdom of Antony Rawḥ', *ICMR* 20 (2009) 119-35, esp. p. 121.

56 Sahner, *Christian martyrs under Islam*, pp. 202-8.

the medieval period, often serving as a narrative foil for the martyr, even precipitating the martyrdom itself, as we see in the *Lives* of George the Black, Elias of Helioupolis and Romanus. An interesting variation on the character of the unrepentant apostate is the unrepentant aristocratic apostate, an especially prominent figure in hagiographical texts from al-Andalus and the Caucasus.[57] There, as throughout the Middle East, lay nobles played an important intermediary role between local churches and the Muslim authorities, and so there was often extra pressure on them to convert, and in so doing preserve their elite status in the new Islamic order. Hagiographers demonised aristocrats who chose this path, portraying them as traitors to their communities and their faiths. Without the leadership of such individuals, churches were more vulnerable to the whims of the authorities and susceptible to conversion. Thus, hagiographers strove to demonise elites who opted for Islam over their natal faith.

When it comes to the first three centuries after the Arab conquests, martyrdom narratives seem to highlight an emergent split between Christians who wished to accommodate Islamic rule and Arab culture, and those who wished to resist these forces.[58] The *Lives* of the saints seem to emanate from the latter group. This chasm is not evident in every setting in which narratives were written, and indeed, one suspects there were many shades of grey between these two positions. But we can see the divide clearly in Umayyad Córdoba, where Eulogius and Paulus Alvarus – the authors of biographical and apologetic texts about the martyrs of the 850s – spoke bitterly about Christians who wished to paper over disagreements with and alleged abuses by their Muslim rulers.[59] Even if Christian communities elsewhere in the greater Middle East were not as polarised as their counterparts in al-Andalus, it is easy to see how churches could have become divided over such disagreements. The accounts of martyrs represent the literary residue of those factions that urged resistance.

The most prolific writers of martyrdom narratives in the early Islamic period were Melkites, the Chalcedonian Christians who remained in communion with Constantinople after the conquest (also known as

---

57 Sahner, *Christian martyrs under Islam*, pp. 208-12.

58 Sahner, *Christian martyrs under Islam*, pp. 212-25.

59 My thinking draws on I. de las Cagigas, *Los mozárabes*, Madrid, 1947-48, pp. 179-209; J.A. Coope, *The martyrs of Córdoba. Community and family conflict in an age of mass conversion*, Lincoln NE, 1995, pp. 55-69; C.L. Tieszen, *Christian identity amid Islam in medieval Spain*, Leiden, 2013, pp. 45-97.

Arab Orthodox or *Rūm*).[60] Their greater affinity for martyrdom-writing, at least in contrast to other communities (e.g. the West Syrians, Copts and East Syrians), might be explained by reference to certain social and ideological factors. There is limited but important evidence that Melkites sometimes faced a higher degree of scrutiny by Muslim officials because of their putative loyalties to the Byzantine emperors, who remained the sworn enemies of the caliphs. Indeed, there are a number of Melkite saints' *Lives* in which violence is triggered by accusations of spying or collusion with the Byzantines. What is more certain is that the Melkites seem to have been jarred by the Arab conquests to a greater extent than their counterparts in other Christian groups. After all, they had enjoyed the patronage of the Byzantine Empire for centuries before the advent of Islam. But with the arrival of Arab armies, they were demoted to merely one of a variety of Christian sects under the thumb of Islamic rule, all equals as second-class citizens. This experience of triumph and fall must have been especially disorienting for the Melkites, in contrast to other Christian sects, all of whom had experience of living outside the mainstream of imperial power, whether in the staunchly Chalcedonian Byzantine Empire (West Syrians and Copts) or in the Zoroastrian Sasanian Empire (East Syrians). If this is true, it is easy to imagine why tales of protest and resistance may have been especially appealing for Melkites.

Conclusion

For the social historian, one of the most exciting payoffs of studying martyrdom narratives is the possibility of tracking the ebb and flow of Islamisation in the greater Middle East across the medieval period. This is not the appropriate forum to speculate on this complex process in detail. Suffice it to say, it seems that the conversion of the region happened not gradually – like a tap that slowly fills a sink with steady drops of water. Instead, it probably happened in fits and spurts, with short periods of intense violence giving rise to floods of converts, filling the sink, as it were, all at once.[61] In Egypt, for example, scholars speculate that the predominantly Christian population became Muslim over the course of the Middle Ages during several periods of heightened tension. These include the tax revolts of the 8th and 9th centuries, the persecutions

60 Sahner, *Christian martyrs under Islam*, pp. 225-39.

61 Sahner, *Christian martyrs under Islam*, pp. 191-8 (especially the non-Muslim rebellions discussed here), 248.

under the Fatimids, especially al-Ḥākim (r. 996-1021), and the economic and bureaucratic pressures of the Mamluk period, from the end of the 13th until the middle of the 14th century.[62]

If this is true, one suspects that the martyr accounts – as records of actual violence and as literary works that resonated among Christians in the wake of the tumult – can help us understand the fits and spurts of conversion more broadly. This was a process that varied by region and time, such that a truly comprehensive history of Christian martyrdom in the medieval Middle East would need to compare and contrast settings as varied as Syria in the 8th century and Armenia in the 16th. It would also entail embedding the martyrdom narratives in a broader matrix of texts written by Christians and Muslims across a range of different languages. If this can be achieved – probably as the work of an entire team of scholars, not a single individual – we may come closer to understanding the process whereby the majority of the population of the Middle East ceased to be Christian and eventually became Muslim.

[62] I.M. Lapidus, 'The conversion of Egypt to Islam', *Israel Oriental Studies* 2 (1972) 248-62; G. Frantz-Murphy, 'Conversion in early Islamic Egypt. The economic factor', in Y. Rāġib (ed.), *Documents de l'islam médiéval. Nouvelles perspectives de recherche*, Cairo, 1991, 11-17; Y. Lev, 'Persecutions and conversion to Islam in eleventh-century Egypt', *Asian and African Studies* 22 (1988) 37-50, 73-91; D.P. Little, 'Coptic conversion to Islam under the Bahrī Mamlūks, 692-755/1293-1354', *BSOAS* 39 (1976), 552-69; El-Leithy, 'Coptic culture and conversion', pp. 34-65, 457-79; Y. Rapoport, *Rural economy and tribal society in Islamic Egypt. A study of al-Nābulusī's 'Villages of the Fayyum'*, Turnhout, 2018.

Chapter 17
Muslim and Christian apocalypticism. Playing off each other

David Bryan Cook

Throughout the history of Christian-Muslim relations the genre of apocalyptic literature has been important for the communication of group fears, the creation of group solidarity and the promulgation of polemics against the other religious group. The tendency to utilise it is present from the earliest phases of Christian-Muslim encounters. This chapter will provide an overview of Muslim apocalyptic tendencies, together with some Christian responses down to the middle of the Ottoman period.

Islamic apocalyptic traditions and movements

Muslim apocalyptic beliefs are an outgrowth of the early development of Hadith and the failure of the cataclysmic apocalypse that is foreseen in the Qur'an (see Q 54:1; 87:1-2, etc.) to appear. Almost all the apocalyptic material in both Sunnī and Shīʿī Islam is related in the form of a Hadith, purporting to be from the Prophet Muḥammad, his cousin and son-in-law ʿAlī ibn Abī Ṭālib, or one of their close companions. These Hadiths have the form of conversations in which Muḥammad will be asked about the signs of the Hour of Judgement, and will give some such formulation such as 'the Hour will not arise until [...]' the following events, usually of a horrifying or cataclysmic nature, will be fulfilled. Unlike the Christian and Jewish literary apocalypses of Late Antiquity, Hadiths are not literary documents, but atomistic and random sayings that usually lack any context.

Apocalyptic Hadiths are arranged for convenience sake into two basic groups, the 'Lesser Signs of the Hour' and the 'Greater Signs of the Hour'. The Lesser Signs are those dozens of preconditions that must be fulfilled prior to the appearance of the more obviously apocalyptic Greater Signs. These Lesser Signs may be political events, evidence of moral or social decay, economic disparity, natural catastrophes (volcanic eruptions, famines, plagues, locusts), celestial spectacles (the appearance of comets, unusual conjunctions of stars or a series of eclipses in a row) or other random events. There are several hundreds of them in total. The Lesser Signs are sufficiently general that they occur at almost any time in history and have a great deal of relevance for the appearance of apocalyptic or messianic movements because they are frequently used by instigators of these movements as proof that the End is nigh.

In contradistinction, the Greater Signs are those incontrovertibly apocalyptic events that herald the End. They include, in no particular order, the appearance of the Dajjāl (the Muslim Antichrist), the return of Jesus to fight and kill him, the appearance of the Mahdī (the Sunnī messianic figure), the appearance of the beast from the earth (Q 27:82), the rising of the sun from the west, the appearance of Gog and Magog (Q 18:94; 21:96), and the final destruction of the world. These events herald the Day of Judgement. However, Muslim apocalypses or more properly apocalyptic fragments do not take the reader all the way from the end of the world into the next. Most probably the cataclysmic scenery from the Qur'an is sufficient.

The qur'anic material is focused mostly on the graphic end of the world. Mountains move, the skies are rolled back, the moon is split, stars fall, and many other similar portents occur. In general, the sense one gets from reading the Qur'an is that the events of the end of the world are so blindingly obvious that the world has no future, no time-line leading up to the apocalypse: 'Do they, then, only expect that the Hour should come upon them suddenly? In fact, its signs have already come' (Q 47:18).[1] In the text of the Qur'an, observers are frequently said to ask when the Hour of Judgement will come:

> They ask you about the Hour, when will it strike. Say: 'The knowledge thereof is with my Lord; none but He will disclose it at the right time. It will be fateful in the heavens and on earth and will not come upon you except suddenly.' They ask you, as though you know about it. Say: 'The knowledge thereof is with Allah, but most people do not know.' (Q 7:187)

It is not difficult to understand why Muḥammad's early audience was curious about the Hour. After all, nearly seven centuries had passed since the time of Jesus – seven being one of the key numbers of apocalypse – and the world of Late Antiquity was in the process of self-destruction.

[1] Unless otherwise specified, all English quotations from the Qur'an are from M. Fakhry, *An interpretation of the Qur'an. English translation of the meanings*, New York, 2002.

Throughout Muḥammad's career, the two great empires of the day, the Byzantine (successor to the Roman Empire in the east, centred on Constantinople) and the Sasanian (Persian, centred upon Ctesiphon, present-day Baghdad), were at war. Q 30:1-2 reflects this reality, saying 'The Greeks (lit. Romans) have been vanquished in the nearest part of the land; but after being vanquished they shall vanquish [...] and the believers shall rejoice.' The Byzantine Empire that had seemed to the Arabs to be the pillar of stability for centuries was overcome and reduced down just to the city of Constantinople itself. Even though the Byzantines did make a comeback in 628, this was just a brief interlude before the Muslim conquest in the 630s and 640s.

When we leave the Qur'an, the Hadith literature becomes the most important source for apocalyptic prophecies. The apocalyptic scenarios after this speak of wars between the newly Muslim Arabs and their most intractable opponents, the Byzantines. These wars usually took place in the region of northern Syria where the border between the two empires was located. For this reason, much of the apocalyptic landscape is Syrian – Muslim control over this area was tenuous during the early period of Islam.

The messianic figure is the most problematic one in classical Islam. Not only is there a sharp divide between Sunnī and Shīʿī messianic figures, but there are a large number of local messiahs as well as claimants, who hark back to traditions older than Islam. In early Islam (before the sharp divide between Sunnism and Shīʿism), the figure of Jesus was probably the original messianic hero. However, possibly because of the polemics between Christianity and Islam, most especially those found in the 7th-century *Apocalypse of Pseudo Methodius*,[2] by the end of the 7th century messianic hopes began to be centred on the figure of the Mahdī. Traditions about this figure apparently first developed in southern Iraq among proto-Shīʿites, but they quickly spread into most Islamic sects. The central tradition about the Mahdī is that 'he will fill the earth with justice and righteousness just as it has been filled with injustice and unrighteousness'.[3]

In his Sunnī form, the Mahdī appears from one of two alternative locations: Khurāsān (today in eastern Iran and Afghanistan) or the holy cities of Mecca and Medina. Both of these Mahdī narratives have their

[2] See P. Ubierna, '*The Apocalypse of Pseudo-Methodius* (*Greek*)', in *CMR* 1, 245-8, and J.P. Monferrer Sala, '*The Apocalypse of Pseudo-Methodius* (*Latin*)', in *CMR* 1, 249-52.

[3] D. Cook, *Studies in Muslim apocalyptic*, Princeton NJ, 2002, p. 137.

basis in historical messianic movements – the one from Khurāsān with the ʿAbbasid dynasty, and the one from Mecca and Medina with the failed messianic movement of Muḥammad al-Nafs al-Zakiyya (d. 762). In general, the Sunnī Mahdī will gather an army, punish evil Arab rulers (usually the figure of the Sufyānī), and establish a messianic kingdom in Jerusalem. However, the millennial impulse in Sunnī Islam is weak, and the messianic kingdom is usually said to last only five, seven or nine years. In some cases, the Mahdī will establish a dynasty; in others he remains an isolated figure. Usually, he continues with the conquests of the first Muslim century and conquers those areas that were too difficult for the early Muslims (the Byzantines, the rest of Europe, Afghanistan, India, the Turks).

The Shīʿī Mahdi, who is also known as the Qāʾim (the one who rises), is a considerably different figure. In Shīʿī beliefs prior to 874, this title could be taken by any of the descendants of the Prophet Muḥammad through his daughter Fāṭima and son-in-law ʿAlī. Many did take the title at one time or another and led the (usually) small, futile revolts that characterised early Shīʿism. But the normative branch of Shīʿism, called the Twelver Shīʿa because of their belief in the position and role of 12 descendants of Muḥammad, adheres to the Last Imam or the Mahdī, who disappeared and went into occultation in 874. He will reappear at the end of the world and establish the messianic kingdom, and inaugurate a dynasty that will rule for hundreds of years.

There are many strains of apocalyptic and messianic practice in Islam. This chapter will examine several of the most popular and enduring that have influenced Muslim history. Side-by-side with the popular movements, there existed a whole body of apocalyptic and messianic literature with which the movements interacted.

Apocalyptic and messianic literature in Hadith and history

Apocalyptic and messianic beliefs are backed up by a substantial literature that takes a number of forms. The first and most important for the larger Muslim community, both Sunnī and Shīʿī, is the Hadith literature. Most of the prominent Hadith collections in Sunnī Islam were compiled during the 9th and 10th centuries, although some date to earlier or later. Six collections in particular are known as canonical, of which the most important are those of al-Bukhārī (d. 870) and Muslim ibn al-Ḥajjāj (d. 875). Both of these collections, all of the other canonical collections and many of the less authoritative Hadith compilations have sections devoted to apocalyptic traditions. These include sections on the signs of the Hour, the appearance of the Dajjāl, the return of Jesus to kill him, the appearance of Gog and Magog, and other minor apocalyptic sequences. It is interesting to note, however, that most of the authoritative collections avoid detailed descriptions of the available traditions on the Mahdī and in general are weak in their accounts of the messianic age. This is probably due to the politically explosive nature of these traditions.

The earliest of the works devoted specifically to apocalyptic or messianic topics is the *Kitāb al-fitan* ('The book of tribulations') by Nuʿaym ibn Ḥammād al-Marwazī (d. 844), who collected a great deal of the apocalyptic heritage of Syria.[4] His book is unique in that it includes a wide range of traditions, mainly originating from the north Syrian town of Ḥimṣ,[5] that were not accepted by the canonical collections. These traditions enable us to see the background to the Muslim apocalyptic scenario described above, which is alluded to but not fleshed out in the accepted materials.

A major characteristic of Nu`aym is the wars against the Byzantines that it is said will occur at the end of the world. Sometimes, these wars will take place within the context of an alliance between the Byzantines and the Syrian Muslims to fight the Iraqi Muslims. When the former are victorious over the latter then the question of who won the victory divides the two allies:

> The Byzantines will say: 'You have only prevailed over them [the Iraqi Muslims] through the cross', and the Muslims will say: 'Nay, by Allah and His Messenger we have prevailed over them.' The issue will go back and forth between them, and the Byzantines will be enraged. A man of the Muslims will rise up and break their cross, and the two [armies] will separate, the Byzantines taking cover so that a river will divide between the two forces. Thus the Byzantines will break the peace (*ṣulḥ*), and they will kill the Muslims in Constantinople.[6]

There are many versions of these battles. The attitude towards Jews and Christians in Nuʿaym is one of suspicion, as there is the constant fear that the numerically superior Christians will betray the Muslims to the Byzantines.[7]

---

[4] See now D. Cook, *'The Book of Tribulations'. The Syrian Muslim apocalyptic tradition*, Edinburgh, 2017.

[5] See W. Madelung, 'Apocalyptic prophecies in Ḥimṣ', *Journal of Semitic Studies* 31 (1986) 141-85.

[6] Nuʿaym ibn Ḥammād al-Marwazī, *Kitāb al-fitan*, Beirut, 1993, p. 273.

[7] D. Cook, 'Christians and Christianity in *ḥadīth* works before 900', in *CMR* 1, 73-82, p. 75.

Another early collector was the Iraqi Ibn al-Munādī (d. 947-8), who in his *Kitāb al-malāḥim* ('The book of apocalyptic wars') preserved an equally large number of non-canonical eastern Muslim traditions. Like most Iraqi pro-ʿAlīds, he did not include very much polemical material against Christianity. In general, Iraqi apocalypses concern intra-Muslim conflicts rather than focusing upon the Byzantine Christians. Both Nuʿaym and Ibn al-Munādī, however, remained on the fringes because of the problematic nature of their materials (from the point of view of the Sunnī mainstream).

The two most popular apocalyptic books ever published among Sunnīs, those by al-Qurṭubī (d. 1272) and Ibn Kathīr (d. 1372-3), were both from the middle Islamic period. Al-Qurṭubī, who lived in Muslim Spain, witnessed the devastation of his homeland by the Spanish Christian *Reconquista* as well as from afar the Mongol destruction of Baghdad in 1258. For him, therefore, it was self-evident that the end of the world was near and, in his *Al-tadhkira fī aḥwāl al-mawtā wa-l-umūr al-ākhira* ('A note on the status of the dead and final matters'), he included a lengthy description of the events that were to take place before that happened. There is little specifically Spanish or anti-Christian material in it, however. His presentation has been widely accepted among Sunnī Muslims.

A century later, Ibn Kathīr, student of the famous iconoclast Ibn Taymiyya (d. 1328), produced as the final section to his world history, *Al-bidāya wa-l-nihāya* ('The beginning and the end'), an epitome of all the important apocalyptic and messianic traditions that he considered to be authentic. Following in the footsteps of a wide range of Muslim historians who had frequently speculated as to the length of the world's duration in their works, Ibn Kathīr apparently believed that the end was near. In his epitome, he notes that, despite the many traditions that indicate a short time-span between the revelation of Islam and the end of the world,[8] God had given the community a respite of 500 years,[9] apparently pointing to the idea that the end of the world would happen around the year 1000 AH (1591-2 CE). Although this calculation did not hold up, Ibn Kathīr's compilation is still considered to be authoritative by Sunnīs today. Ibn Kathīr, throughout all his works, was very polemical against Christians and frequently cited the apocalyptic traditions concerning warfare against the Byzantines in Syria. This is not surprising as he lived in the immediate wake of the crusades. However, his most interesting

8 S. Bashear, 'Muslim apocalypses', *Israel Oriental Studies* 13 (1993) 75-93.

9 Ibn Kathīr, *Al-fitan wa-l-malāḥim*, Cairo, [n.d.], vol. 1, p. 25.

interpretations have to do with the widely accepted idea that the Mongol invasions were those of Gog and Magog that were predicted in the apocalyptic sources.

During the Mamluk period, dating the end of the world continued to be important and a catalyst for apocalyptic writings. In 1492, about a century before 1000/1591-2, an unidentified author wrote to the famous Egyptian religious scholar Jalāl al-Dīn al-Suyūṭī (d. 1505) saying that the Prophet Muḥammad's bones would not remain in their grave for more than a thousand years, and therefore the events of the end of the world were due to take place immediately. Al-Suyūṭī answered him in his tract *Al-kashf ʿan mujāwazat hādhihi al-umma al-alf* ('An exposé that this community will pass a thousand years'), and stated that God had given the community another respite of 500 years since not everybody had received a chance to repent of their sins.[10] Similar calculations and refutations of other calculations are strewn throughout the history books.

Later apocalyptic literature has been mostly reactive to various cataclysmic events or designed to refute the claims of messianic pretenders. The most popular writer from the middle Ottoman period was al-Barzanjī (d. 1691), who wrote his *Al-ishāʿa li-ashrāt al-sāʿa* ('The propagation of the portents of the Hour') in response to the Jewish messianic movement of Shabbetai Zvi in 1665-6. The literary apocalyptic and messianic manifestation of Islam is quite large, and throughout its history has consistently influenced, and in some cases sparked, active movements.

Christian responses to Muslim apocalyptic

In the face of this vast apocalyptic output, the Christian communities of the Middle East and the eastern Mediterranean basin rose to the challenge. We have already noted the *Apocalypse of Pseudo Methodius* (c. 680) as a response to the early Muslim conquests,[11] a grand rewrite of history, which places the responsibility for Christian political and military failure squarely upon Christians' moral failings. This analysis of the causes for God's allowing the Muslims to rise up so suddenly and dominate Christians in some of their most venerable holy cities (Jerusalem,

[10] Al-Suyūṭī, *Ḥāwī*, Beirut, [n.d.], vol. 2, pp. 86-9.

[11] G. Reinink (ed.), *Die Syrischen Apokalypse des Pseudo-Methodius*, 2 vols (Corpus Scriptorum Christianorum Orientalium, vols 540-1), Louvain, 1993; for the Latin, W.J. Aerts and G.A.A. Kortekaas (eds), *Die Apokalypse des Pseudo-Methodius. Die ältesten Griechischen und Lateinischen übersetzungen*, Louvain, 1998.

Antioch and Alexandria) proved to be extremely popular throughout the Mediterranean basin, and was quickly translated from Syriac into Greek, and then into Latin. *Pseudo-Methodius*, as an apocalyptic framework for interpreting the appearance of Islam and the place of Muslims in the divine plan, proved to be enduring and influential.

One of the most unexpected ways in which *Pseudo-Methodius* influenced Christian apocalyptic was the introduction of Christian Ethiopia into the apocalyptic scenario through a unique exegesis of Psalm 68:31 'Envoys will come from Egypt; Cush [Ethiopia] will submit herself to God'. Here, the word 'submit' is understood in the Syriac version to mean 'hand over',[12] and was interpreted by the author of *Pseudo-Methodius* as meaning 'will hand over rule' (to God) – quite a remarkable leap. However weak this interpretation was linguistically, it set the stage for a major theme in Christian-Muslim relations, which turned out to be the European impulse to cross the Islamic world in order to find a Christian king or kingdom on the other side. Eventually, this impulse was focused upon the figure of Prester John.[13]

For the Byzantines, the Christian empire that survived the initial Arab Muslim conquests, apocalyptic was not a prominent theme. We noted above that, while the Syrian Muslims, as documented by Nuʿaym ibn Ḥammād, focused a great deal of their apocalyptic energies upon the future (projected) conquest of Constantinople, there is no equivalent fixation by the Byzantines upon Syria. Probably the best-known example of post-conquest Byzantine apocalyptic, the *Life and conduct of our holy father Andrew, the fool for the sake of Christ*,[14] is more focused on divine judgement upon the sinning city of Constantinople than upon regaining lost territories in either Syria or Egypt.

Like the Muslims, as demonstrated by Nuʿaym and Ibn al-Munādī, Christians under Muslim rule tended to utilise the biblical Daniel frameworks for predicting the downfall of the Islamic empire.[15] However, other pre-Christian oracles and Sibylline frameworks also remained popular.[16] These predictions were usually so encoded or sufficiently vague that they did not attract the negative attention of the Muslim authorities, but

---

[12] Reinink, *Die Syrischen Apokalypse des Pseudo-Methodius*, vol. 1, p. 44 (original); vol. 2, p. 73 (trans.).

[13] J. Tolan, 'Alexander III', in *CMR* 3, 695-6, p. 696; P. Jackson, '*The letter of Prester John*', in *CMR* 4, 118-23.

[14] C. Ludwig, 'Nicephorus', in *CMR* 2, 550-3.

[15] See. J. van Lent, '*The fourteenth vision of Daniel*', in *CMR* 3, 697-703.

[16] J. van Lent, 'The Copto-Arabic Sibylline prophecy', in *CMR* 3, 270-3; W. Brandes, '*Oracula Leonis*', in *CMR* 4, 124-7.

could still function to give hope to the down-trodden Christians. Just like the Christians (and Jews), there were some Muslim communities who also had to resort to esoteric interpretations.

Shīʿīs and messianism

Esotericism in Islam is virtually synonymous with Shīʿism. As the major non-Sunnī group, Shīʿīs were frequently compelled to dissimulate their beliefs with respect to bringing about the eventual rule of the rightful descendant of Muḥammad – a process that, from their perspective, took some 300 years. One of the basic problems for Islam is the fact that Muḥammad left no obvious successor. While most of the early Muslim community accepted the first Caliph Abū Bakr (r. 632-4) as Muḥammad's successor, there were many who could not because he had no blood relationship with the Prophet. These people believed that the charismatic authority of Muḥammad – although not his prophetic office – should and must devolve upon his genealogical descendants. However, there was a problem with this idea as well: Muḥammad left no male progeny at his death, and only one of his four daughters bore male children who came to maturity. Arab custom had not seen descent through a female line as significant, but it seems that the need to continue venerating the Prophet through his descendants was sufficiently strong to override that prejudice.

Even within the lifetime of ʿAlī ibn Abī Ṭālib (r. 656-61), Muḥammad's son-in-law and the father of his two grandchildren al-Ḥasan and al-Ḥusayn, certain extremist factions worshipped the Prophet's family. (ʿAlī had one of his supporters burned for proclaiming him to be a manifestation of God.) At first, this veneration was diffuse, and included ʿAlī's children not from Fāṭima, Muḥammad's daughter. The best example of this tendency was the messianic claim of Muḥammad ibn al-Ḥanafiyya, who was the first person in Islam to have been accorded the title of Mahdī, in the 680s. But he himself did not make this claim; his supporters in Iraq made it on his behalf.

As the veneration of Muḥammad's descendants spread, and especially after the rise of the ʿAbbasid dynasty in the mid-8th century, who used Shīʿī slogans to gain power, messianic claims were made by the descendants of both al-Ḥasan and al-Ḥusayn. The descendants of al-Ḥusayn had a very powerful point in their favour: their ancestor was murdered tragically by an Umayyad armed detail at Karbalāʾ in southern Iraq. The

Ḥusaynids gained a huge level of prestige from this event, and most Shīʿīs tended to support claimants from this branch of the ʿAlid family. In contrast, the Ḥasanids had no such history of sacrifice. By the middle of the 8th century, they were restive in Medina – probably as a result of seeing the success of the ʿAbbasids – and proclaimed one of their own, Muḥammad al-Nafs al-Zakiyya, to be the Mahdī. Muḥammad al-Nafs al-Zakiyya had gained a large following throughout the Arabian Peninsula, among both scholars in Medina and Arab tribesmen in the surrounding regions. In 762, he revolted against the ʿAbbasids and proclaimed himself the Mahdī. However, because of the indefensibility of the oasis city of Medina, the ʿAbbasids quickly crushed this revolt.

The entire incident would be unremarkable were it not for the fact that the messianic traditions propagated by Muḥammad al-Nafs al-Zakiyya became normative within Sunnism (ironically) as one of the two messianic narratives, the ʿAbbasids themselves having contributed the other (below). Virtually all Shīʿī risings during the first three centuries of Islam suffered the same fate as Muḥammad al-Nafs al-Zakiyya. They were usually supported by a significant number of the religious leadership, used apocalyptic and messianic slogans, appealed to the emotional loyalty of the populace towards the Prophet Muḥammad's family, and failed to gather the necessary military support needed to overthrow the regime. Almost always, the populace turned against the Shīʿī claimants at some particular key moment or remained passive when armed force was desperately needed. The claims of the family of Muḥammad were always tacitly recognised, but the force needed to make them good almost always melted away in the face of opposition. The one exception to this rule during the first three hundred years of Islam was the family of al-ʿAbbās, the uncle of the Prophet Muḥammad (and ancestor of the ʿAbbasid caliphs), who took the slogans of the Shīʿa and used their emotive force to create a mass movement.

The ʿAbbasids and realised messianism

During the early centuries of Islam, messianism was usually associated with the Prophet Muḥammad's family in the broadest sense. This meant that, for most Muslims, the family of Muḥammad comprised the descendants of his great-grandfather, Hāshim. Most claimants to messianic titles had to come from this group. While Shīʿīs eventually managed to whittle down the number of possible claimants to just the immediate genealogical descendants of Muḥammad, they did this only after the ʿAbbasid family had succeeded in pulling off a bait-and-switch operation that used Shīʿī slogans to come to power to the benefit of the descendants of al-ʿAbbās. Messianic claims had a major part in making this a reality.

The ʿAbbasid family were not prominent in the early Islamic period and played little part in the attempts of their cousins – either of the Ḥasanid or the Ḥusaynid line – to come to power. Instead, they focused their efforts on a distant location, the region of Khurāsān, where many Arab tribesmen had settled and intermingled with the local Persian population. To this region they sent their agent Abū Muslim, who, over a number of years preached loyalty to 'the agreed-upon one of the Family [of Muḥammad]'. This slogan, which was kept deliberately ambiguous, proved to be attractive to many tribesmen, and Abū Muslim wove a web of clandestine operations throughout the province in support of the ʿAbbasid family. Many Shīʿīs and Shīʿa sympathisers were taken in by this slogan, and supported the ʿAbbasid revolution, which began in 744 and continued for the following several years.

Abū Muslim promoted a large number of messianic prophecies, and it is probably due to his propaganda network that there is so much material on the Mahdī or the supporters of the Mahdī appearing from the east, from Khurāsān. A typical tradition is the following:

> [...] then the black banners will rise from the east, and they will kill a number of you the like of which has never been seen previously [...] when you see him [coming] swear allegiance to him, even if you have to crawl on the snow, for he is the caliph of God, the Mahdī.[17]

This propaganda was directed against the then ruling Umayyad dynasty in Syria (661-747), and sought to delegitimise its claims to authority. The ʿAbbasid armies advanced until they defeated the Umayyad armies in 747 and in Kūfa (southern Iraq) they proclaimed Abū l-ʿAbbās al-Saffāḥ caliph. All of the first seven of the ʿAbbasids – al-Saffāḥ (749-54), al-Manṣūr (754-75), al-Mahdī (775-85), Mūsā al-Hādī (785-6), Hārūn al-Rāshid (786-809), Muḥammad al-Amīn (809-13) and al-Māʾmūn (813-33) – took messianic titles (though not all are easily understood and some are associated with

[17] Ibn Mājah, *Sunan*, Beirut: Dār al-Fikr, [n.d.], vol. 2, p. 1367 (no. 4084).

minor or local messianic figures).[18] The message that this dynasty sought to convey was that the messianic era was realised under them.

Gradually, under al-Manṣūr and especially under al-Mahdī, the dynasty moved away from its Shīʿī and revolutionary roots. One of the first things al-Manṣūr did was to murder Abū Muslim, who later became an important messianic figure in his own right in Persia, and he spent much of his time combating Shīʿīs such as Muḥammad al-Nafs al-Zakiyya. The dynasty for the most part – al-Māʾmūn excepted – preached that the messianic rights devolved upon their ancestor al-ʿAbbas from the Prophet Muḥammad and that they would give the caliphate over to Jesus when he appeared to kill the Dajjāl at the end of time. By this tactic, the ʿAbbasid family sought to create the impression that they would remain in power indefinitely. By the time of al-Mutawakkil (r. 847-61), the ʿAbbasids were firmly Sunnī and, although they were to a large extent deprived of power by their Turkish slave-soldiers in the middle of the 9th century, they continued to rule until the last of them was exterminated by the Mongols in 1258. Although their realised messianic phase was only a part of their 500 years in power, it took them through a most rocky period of seeking political and religious legitimacy.

While the ʿAbbasids' deadliest ideological enemies were obviously the Shīʿīs, who supported the claims of the genealogical descendants of Muḥammad – and the ʿAbbasids as a dynasty persecuted the family of Muḥammad more ruthlessly than did any other group in history – there were a wide range of other apocalyptic movements and messianic claimants in the early Muslim period, of whom the ʿAbbasids also needed to beware. These were the tribal and local messiahs.

The Qaḥṭānī and the Sufyānī: local traditions

Messianism in Islam is far broader than one sees in the strictly religious literature, and it also has pre-Islamic roots. Thus, it is not surprising that some messianic claimants were local or tribal. Prior to the rise of Islam, the Arab tribes had been divided into northern and southern groups, although by the 7th century these had no geographical meaning. Culturally, the southern tribes were originally associated with the region of Yemen, while the northern tribes were associated with the desert

---

18 B. Lewis, 'The regnal titles of the first ʿAbbāsid Caliphs', in *Dr. Zakir Husain presentation volume*, New Delhi: Matba' Jami'a, 1968, 13-22.

cultures of north Arabia. But because of migration (even prior to the conquests), the various groupings of tribes were to be found all over the peninsula. After the conquests, each tribe took with them their affiliation to either the northern or southern groupings, and the often fought each other because of this rivalry. For the first two centuries of Islam, whole provinces were torn apart because of the northern-southern division. (One should note that the Prophet Muḥammad's tribe, the Quraysh, was a northern tribe.)

The oldest tribal messianic traditions are connected with the Qaḥṭānī, the messianic figure associated with the southern Yemenī tribes. He is described thus in the tradition: 'a man from Qaḥṭān will appear having pierced ears and [will rule] according to the manner of the Mahdī.'[19] There are few classical examples of Qaḥṭānī claimants, but it is worth noting that the messianic revolt of Juhaymān al-ʿUtaybī in November 1979 (in the *hijrī* year 1400) was in the name of one Muḥammad al-Qaḥṭānī. Apparently, al-ʿUtaybī believed the prophecies that said the Qaḥṭānī was to appear 20 years before the Mahdī and usher in the latter.

Beyond the tribal messianic figures, there were those apocalyptic or messianic figures whose appeal was to a particular locality. The principle example of this tendency is the Sufyānī in the region of Syria. This figure stems from the family of Abū Sufyān, the most determined opponent of the Prophet Muḥammad in the early years of his ministry, who led the Meccan pagans against him for six years (624-30). However, Abū Sufyān became a Muslim at the end of his life and his son, Muʿāwiya, became the fifth caliph (r. 661-80). Muʿāwiya came to prominence after his close relative, the third caliph ʿUthmān (r. 644-56), was assassinated by a group of Muslim malcontents. Although his immediate successor ʿAlī – the same man who was also the father of the Prophet Muḥammad's grandchildren – was not actually involved in the assassination, Muʿāwiya was able to tarnish his reputation because of his willingness to pardon the assassins and ultimately to cause his downfall (although ʿAlī was assassinated in 661 by another group, the Khārijites, a radical, egalitarian, puritanical sect of early Islam who opposed ʿAlī and Shīʿism as a whole because of its focus upon genealogical affiliation as a basis for rule).

For Shīʿīs, therefore, Muʿāwiya was an opponent of Islam, since he opposed the rights of Muḥammad's family to rule; if that was not enough, he was also the father of Yazīd (r. 680-3), under whose orders al-Ḥusayn was killed at Karbala. But for the Muslims of Syria, the rule of

19 Al-Suyūṭī, *Ḥāwī*, vol. 2, p. 80.

Muʿāwiya and Yazīd, the family of Abū Sufyān, was a golden age and it was remembered as such in popular legend. Muʿāwiya was a brilliant and cultured ruler and, during his reign, there was a continuation of the great conquests, which brought tremendous wealth to the people of Syria. In general, Muʿāwiya enjoyed close relations with the majority Christian population as well (his wife and a number of close advisors were Christians), and so he was remembered as a tolerant and broad-minded ruler. For all these reasons, according to local Syrian apocalyptic narratives, the figure of the Sufyānī was supposed to appear to recreate this golden age. Shīʿīs, however, propagated numerous counter-traditions in which the Sufyānī is presented as an evil and arbitrary ruler, who hates Islam and slaughters large numbers of people, especially Muslims, without just cause.

These counter-traditions had little effect upon the historical appearances of Sufyānīs in Syria. There are at least nine documented appearances of Sufyānī claimants between 749 and 1413, all in the region of Syria. The first was apparently an actual descendant of the family of Abū Sufyān; concerning the others it is difficult to know. This figure, Ziyād ibn ʿAbd Allāh ibn Yazīd ibn Muʿāwiya, who revolted in 749 against the victorious ʿAbbasids, clearly sought to focus discontent with the new regime upon himself and called for rule to return to the descendants of Muʿāwiya.[20] Later, in 754, the appearance of a comet heralded another Sufyānī revolt and, 100 years later, a figure called Abū Ḥarb al-Muburqaʿ ('the veiled one') was hailed as the Sufyānī in Syria:

> Abū Ḥarb used to appear openly during the daytime and sit out, veiled, on the mountain in which he had taken refuge, and people would see him and come to him. He would exhort them and enjoin upon them good behaviour and the prohibition of evil actions, and he would mention the central government and how it oppressed the people and would speak scathingly of it. He persisted in doing this habitually until a group of peasant cultivators from that region and also the villagers responded to his call. He used to assert that he was an Umayyad, with the result that those who responded to him said: 'This man is the Sufyānī!' When his adherents and followers from this class of people grew numerous, he summoned the members of the leading families and notables of the region. Out of these a good number of the leaders of the Yemenīs [southern Arab tribes] responded to his call [...].[21]

---

[20] Al-Balādhūrī, *Ansāb al-ashrāf*, Wiesbaden, 1978, vol. 3, pp. 169-70.

[21] C.E. Bosworth (trans.), *The history of al-Ṭabarī*, vol. 33. *Storm and stress along the northern frontiers of the ʿAbbāsid Caliphate*, Albany NY, 1991, pp. 203-4.

By the time of Abū Ḥarb, there was no longer any way to prove one was a descendant of Muʿāwiya, so it was apparently sufficient that he was pious and known as an opponent of the ʿAbbasids.

Most of the other Sufyānī appearances are very poorly documented, but one in 1413 is interesting because the claimant made a major effort to fulfil exactly the prophecies written in the books about the Sufyānī. For example, this claimant, whose name was ʿUthmān, appeared in the region of ʿAjlūn (today in northern Jordan), which is exactly the region associated with the Sufyānī in the traditions related in Nuʿaym. He took care to make sure that his appearance was in accord with the classical Sufyānī and that the numbers of his followers were the same as those listed for the Sufyānī. After a time, this Sufyānī claimant made a public proclamation of the foundation of a messianic state, and many are said to have responded to his call. However, the regime of the Mamluks, then ruling in Syria and Egypt, quickly suppressed this revolt, taking its leader captive and eventually killing him.[22]

For Christians, the local apocalypse was represented by those trends that expressed frustration and dismay at the continuing dissolution of their communities through conversion to Islam and loss of cultural pre-eminence. This trend can be seen with the Coptic (and Arabic) *Apocalypse of Samuel*, Abbot of Dayr al-Qalamūn,[23] which describes in poignant terms the gradual abandonment of the Coptic language in favour of Arabic.

> Woe and woe again, O my beloved children – what can I say about these times, and the great sloth that will come over the Christians? During this time many will tend away from standing straight, and will look like the *hijra* in their actions. They will name their children by their names and abandon the names of the angels, the prophets, the messengers and the martyrs. They will perform another action of which I will inform you – the heart is pained to hear of it – they will abandon the beautiful language of Coptic in which the Holy Spirit spoke many times through the mouths of our spiritual fathers. They will teach their children from their youth to speak in the language of the Arabs, and boast concerning it. Even the priests and the monks – even they! – will dare to speak in Arabic and boast concerning it, and this inside the basilica![24]

---

[22] Ibn Ḥajar al-ʿAsqalānī, *Inbāʾ al-ghumr bī anbāʾ al-ʿumr*, Hyderabad: Dar al-Maʿārif al-ʿUthmaniyya, 1974, vol. 7, pp. 106-7.

[23] J. van Lent, '*The Apocalypse of Samuel*', in *CMR* 2, 742-52.

[24] J. Ziadeh (ed.), 'L'Apocalypse de Samuel, Supérieur de Deir-el-Qalamoun', *Revue de l'Orient Chrétien* 10 (1917) 374-404, p. 387.

As van Lent states, this is more a sermon than a strictly formed apocalypse; nonetheless it has a strong apocalyptic flavour of doom. Local apocalyptic figures such as the Sufyānī, like the Qaḥṭānī, never gained religious legitimacy; as we have seen, even the figure of the Mahdī was dubious from the point of view of the strict Hadith collectors. However, there was one revivalist apocalypse figure who gained full Muslim legitimacy.

Renewal and religious restoration

One of the most prevalent traditions concerning religious revival is to be found in the early collection of Abū Dā'ūd al-Sijistānī (d. 888-9): 'God will send to this community [Muslims] at the turn of every century someone who will renew the religion for it.'[25] This tradition is the basis for the idea that there is (or in some cases needs to be) a renewer (*mujaddid*) of Islam every one hundred years, usually at the 100-year mark (of the *hijrī* calendar). The idea that the religion needs to be 'renewed' is quite remarkable, given the extreme abhorrence in Sunnī Islam of anything connected with innovation (bidʿa). And it is unclear from the tradition what form the renewal would take or what the authority of the 'renewer' would be.

In general, the title of 'renewer' was accorded in retrospect, with the exception of certain very egotistical scholars such as the great theologian, jurisprudent and Sufi al-Ghazālī (d. 505/1111), the Egyptian Jalāl al-Dīn al-Suyūṭī (d. 911/1505) or the Indian Ahmad Sirhindi (d. 1034/1624), who arrogated it to themselves. Nor is there any consensus as to who exactly is the 'renewer' of a given century; the Arabic is ambiguous enough to support the idea that there might be multiple 'renewers'. Other prominent 'renewers' who have gained general acceptance are the Umayyad Caliph ʿUmar II (r. 99-101/717-20), who is usually seen as the one righteous member of that dynasty, and the great jurisprudent al-Shāfiʿī (d. 205/820), the founder of one of the four Sunnī schools of law. For the most part, indeed, the title 'renewer' was not given an extraordinary level of apocalyptic or messianic significance, since, with the exception of ʿUmar II, none of the people listed in the sources had or aspired to political rule.[26] Probably the most significant effect of the 'renewer' tradition upon Christians (and

---

[25] Abū Dā'ūd, *Sunan*, Beirut: Dār al-Jīl, 1988, vol. 4, pp. 106-7 (no. 4291).

[26] E. Landau-Tessaron, 'Cyclical reform. A study of the *mujaddid* tradition', *Studia Islamica* 70 (1989) 79-113.

Jews) has been the occasional Muslim desire to see them converted *en masse* at these given 100-year intervals. It appears that the Fatimid ruler al-Ḥākim (d. 412/1021) began this trend, as he summoned the Jewish and Christian leaders in Egypt around the year 400/1009-10, and demanded to know when they would convert.[27]

In later centuries, especially after the decline of Muslim power and the coming of European colonialism, the idea of renewal has acquired a certain amount of messianic or political significance. In those cases, the renewal is seen as a restoration of Muslim power or domination either in a given area or in the world as a whole. During the century cycles of 1882 (1300 AH) and 1979 (1400 AH), prominent Muslim opponents of Western interests, such as Muḥammad Aḥmad al-Mahdī in the Sudan, Ghulam Ahmad in British India, and then later, in 1979, Ayatullah Ruhullah Khumayni in Iran, gained considerable messianic prominence. Because of the change in the circumstances of Islam, an originally non-apocalyptic tradition has acquired during the recent past a more messianic function.

Gunpowder empires and messianic justice

In the course of the 16th century, five great Muslim empires came to prominence. These were the Ottomans in the Middle East and south-eastern Europe, the Shīʿī Safavids in Iran, the Shaybānids in Central Asia, the Saʿdids in Morocco, and the Mughals in India. All of these 'gunpowder' empires – called this because the foundation of their domination over such vast territories was the use of gunpowder – used messianic themes in different ways to legitimise their rule. Muslim apocalyptic and messianic traditions and beliefs are not merely destructive, but as in the case of the ʿAbbasids and the Fatimids can be used to legitimise dynasties.

The Ottomans are the best case in point. Starting as a warrior band in the 13th century, the Ottomans had come by the 14th and especially the 15th century to dominate the territory of the former Byzantine Empire in Anatolia and south-eastern Europe. During a remarkable series of conquests in the 16th century, they came to rule most of the Middle East, and continued to do so until World War I. Many of the early Ottoman rulers apparently used the apocalyptic aspect of jihad to justify their rule – although the extent to which this use should be taken seriously remains

[27] D. Thomas, '*Khabar al-Yahūd wa-l-Naṣara*', in *CMR* 2, 640-2, p. 641.

an open question – but later rulers especially, starting with Süleyman the Magnificent (or the Law Giver) (r. 1520-66), used realised Messianism as the basis for their rule. Through the giving of and establishment of law, and the construction of monumental buildings (in Constantinople and throughout its close environs), Süleyman sought to create the sense that the ideal or perfect time had come.[28] However, he never took deliberate messianic titles as had the ʿAbbasids and the Fatimids before him. Later Ottomans continued to follow in his footsteps in avoiding outright messianism.

Both the Saʿdids and the Shaybānids in Morocco and Central Asia used messianic themes of dynasty to legitimise their rule. The Saʿdids claimed descent from the Prophet Muḥammad, while the Shaybānids claimed descent from Ghenghis Khan and the Mongol royal family (though they also emphasised their propagation of and defence of Islam among the Turks). Both dynasties, at opposite ends of the Islamic world, sought to realise grander visions of expansion. (On a smaller scale, so did the great Ethiopian conqueror Ahmad Grañ, who sought to conquer the Ethiopian highlands for Muslims during the 1530s and 1540s and was inspired by apocalyptic motifs.)[29]

The Safavid dynasty in Iran was truly an apocalyptic dynasty from the beginning. Shah Ismāʿīl I (r. 1501-24), the founder of the dynasty, made messianic claims (and possibly even claims of divinity). Prior to the appearance of the Safavids, Iran had been majority Sunnī, but through the use of a charismatic blend of Sufism and Shīʿism, in some cases making extreme claims about the authority of the dynasty, the Safavids managed to convert most of the country by the middle of the 17th century. A key moment happened under the young Shah ʿAbbās I (r. 1588-1629) at the turn of the Islamic millennium in 1591-2, when he suppressed the hitherto powerful Kizilbash group that had been the backbone of messianic beliefs and the most fervent supporters of the Safavids. Thereafter, like the Ottomans, the Safavids moved away from reliance on apocalyptic and messianic themes.

In India, the foundation of the Mughal dynasty was not accompanied by any apocalyptic ideals. Bābur (r. 1526-30), the founder of the dynasty, was a refugee from Central Asia, who managed to gain control over most

---

[28] C.H. Fleischer, 'The lawgiver as Messiah. The making of the imperial image in the reign of Süleimân', in G. Veinstein (ed.), *Suleyman the Magnificent and his time*, Paris, 1992, 159-77.

[29] P. Stenhouse (trans.), *ʿArab Faqīh, Futūḥ al-Ḥabasha. The conquest of Abyssinia*, Hollywood CA, 2003.

of northern India and ruled the mixed population of Hindus and Muslims through the Turkish military aristocracy. However, his descendants, especially the great Akbar (r. 1558-1605), either used messianic themes of justice or had to react to mass movements that were messianic in nature. Given the fact that Akbar, who was ecumenical enough to have actually founded his own belief-system (called the *Din-i ilahi*, 'religion of God'), was ruling as the Muslim millennium approached, it is not surprising that there were those who thought him to be the Mahdī, though the title they gave him was *ṣāḥb al-zamān* ('lord of time', a messianic title). 'Abd al-Qadir Badaouni writes about this as follows:

> In this year [1581] low and mean fellows, who pretended to be learned but in reality were fools, collected evidence that his Majesty was the *Sahib al-zaman*, who would remove all the differences of opinion among the seventy-two sects of Islam and the Hindus. Sharif brought proofs from the writings of Mahmud of Basakhwan that he had said that in the year 990 [1582] a certain person would abolish lies, and how he has specified all sorts of interpretations of the expression 'professor of the true religion', which came to the sum-total of 990. And Khawaja Mowlana of Shiraz, the heretic of Jafrdan, came with a pamphlet by some of the Sharifs [rulers] of Mecca, in which a tradition was quoted to the effect that the earth would exist for 7,000 years, and as that time was now over, the promised appearance of the Mahdi would immediately take place. The Moulana also brought a pamphlet written by himself on the subject [...] All of this made the Emperor the more inclined to claim the dignity of a prophet, perhaps I should say, the dignity of something else.[30]

The 'something else' to which Badaouni refers in the last sentence is the fact that most probably Akbar entertained claims of divinity. This selection demonstrates the numerous different ways in which an apocalyptic moment can be triggered. For example, there was strong feeling that the *hijrī* year 1000 (1591-2) must mean something, thus there were geometrical calculations made by Mahmud of Basakhwan; the proffering of chronological 'proofs' based upon the notion of a 7000-year life-span for the current epoch, in which Muḥammad was supposedly sent at the year 6000 from creation and therefore the world would come to an end in the year 1000 *hijri*; and there was already a strong sentiment of Mahdism in India which also expressed strong apocalyptic motifs.

---

[30] 'Abd al-Qādir Badā'ūnī, *Muntakhab al-tawārīkh*, trans. G. Ranking, Delhi: Munshiram Manoharlal, 1973, vol. 2, p. 275.

This sense of Mahdism was cultivated by the Mahdawi movement, which had already been propagated by Sayyid Muḥammad Jaunpuri, who had proclaimed himself to be the Mahdī while on the annual pilgrimage in Mecca in 901 AH (1496). Later, Jaunpuri proclaimed himself again in Gujarat (India) and gained many followers. Eventually, he wandered still further to Kandahar in Afghanistan, where he died in 1505. However, one of his celebrated followers, Mustafa Gujarati, gained some prominence in debating before Akbar and this no doubt aided in spreading the teachings of the Mahdawi movement (which is still extant in India).[31] The imperialist aspect of Muslim messianism was strong and useful to the rulers of powerful dynasties, and messianism at the popular level was equally present and sometimes served to drive the rulers to use further messianic themes themselves.

Conclusion

The apocalyptic and messianic heritage of Islam, in both its Sunnī and Shīʿī versions, is considerable. This apocalyptic heritage is represented by both religious and historical literary works, as well as the attestations of movements of would-be prophets, Mahdīs, Sufyānīs and a wide range of other claimants to various titles. Many of the prominent and less-known dynasties and rulers in Islam in fact legitimised their rule by using messianic themes after having achieved power through apocalyptic movements. When one considers the number of failed Mahdīs throughout the Muslim world – those attested run into the hundreds – it is easy to see the broad popularity of the title and the ideal of justice that stands behind it. One assumes that the number of Mahdīs etc. that are listed in the sources are only the tip of the iceberg and that in actuality there were, on a local scale, a great number who did not make it into the history books.

Apocalyptic and messianic movements in Islam after the earliest period were traditionally focused against the other, often Christians and Jews. It is not at all unusual for an outbreak of messianism to coincide with a push to convert non-Muslims or to degrade them socially, usually by implementing the Pact of ʿUmar and its attendant strictures upon

[31] M. Qamaruddin, *The Mahdawi movement in India*, Delhi: Idarat-i Asabiyat, 1985; D.N. MacLean, 'La sociologie de l'engagement politique. Le Mahdawiya indien et l'état', *Revue des Mondes Musulmans et de la Méditeranée* 91-94 (2000) 239-56.

minorities. Apocalyptic predictions are full of polemical themes against Christianity, and to a lesser extent, against Judaism.

The relationship of the religious elite of Islam to the apocalyptic and messianic traditions and movements is problematic. On the one hand, this elite in fact preserved the materials concerning the Mahdī, and in a number of cases either supported or even participated in apocalyptic or messianic risings. But given the conservative nature of the religious elite, it is not surprising to find that the figure of the Mahdī is a problem, and that they might not want the messianic age to appear. The reasons might be some hesitation as to the religious authority of the Mahdī, because no Muslim would want a figure that would call into question the finality of Muḥammad's prophethood, and the question about the end of the possibility of repentance that the proximity of the apocalypse might seem to imply.

Despite these problems it is easy to see the popularity of the materials and the universality of the sentiments they proclaim. Issues such as justice, plenty, universal peace and goodwill between humanity and even between species are common throughout Muslim apocalyptic literature. But most of the universal peace between religions will, according to the apocalyptic predictions, be achieved by conversion to Islam.

Chapter 18
Conflict, conquest & reconquest. Arabian and Iberian experience

James Harry Morris

Introduction

Hugh Goddard writes that encounter and interchange between Christians and Muslims has in many situations 'led not to the growth of mutual understanding and sympathy but to conflict'.[1] The advent of Islam and subsequent territorial expansion brought Christians and Muslims into direct contact through military conquest and conflict. Under the Prophet Muḥammad (570-632), the Rashidūn caliphs (632-61) and the Umayyad Caliphate (661-750), the new empire expanded throughout the Middle East, North Africa and the Iberian Peninsula.[2] In turn, Christian powers later sought to reconquer historically Christian areas that had been forfeited to Muslim conquest. Such attempts at re-conquest included, for example, the *Reconquista* in Iberia and the crusades in the Middle East,[3] resulting in a cycle of conflict. As a consequence of such conquests and reconquests, Christians and Muslims became residents in empires ruled by their religious counterparts. At times, they converted and apostatised, intermarried, entered commercial dealings and debates;[4] at other times they rejected the new status quo through deviant behaviour, the acceptance of martyrdom or by composing polemical and apologetical texts.

Conflict was certainly not the only form of encounter in historical Christian-Muslim relations, but it has played an important role in the history of the interaction of the two religions. Such past instances of conflict continue to influence Christian-Muslim relations today. It is this conflictual aspect of Christian-Muslim interactions, both within and outside the Iberian Peninsula, that will be our focus here. Accordingly, this chapter introduces texts pertaining to conflictual and hostile relations reflecting Christian-Muslim antipathy during the first millennium of encounter,

1 H. Goddard, *A history of Christian-Muslim relations*, Chicago IL, 2000, p. 2.
2 Goddard, *History of Christian-Muslim relations*, p. 79.
3 T.F. Madden, *The new concise history of the crusades*, Lanham MD, 2014^3, pp. 4-7.
4 R.G. Hoyland, *Seeing Islam as others saw it. A survey and evaluation of Christian, Jewish and Zoroastrian writings on early Islam*, Princeton NJ, 1997, p. 12.

with a focus on the Arab conquests and conquest and reconquest in Iberia. The primary concern is Christian and Muslim responses to violence, and explanations and justifications of it, as these are encapsulated in writings from both sides, as well as in the authors' practices of 'othering' their religious counterparts through polemical and apologetic texts.

The first part explores the reactions of Christians to the early Arab conquests. It introduces some of the primary themes present in early Eastern Christian textual responses to Muslim advance and conquest, arguing that texts of the period can be loosely categorised according to themes of divine retribution, apocalypse and apology. The reactions of Eastern Christians to the Arab conquests bear a thematic similarity to later Western Christian responses to the Muslim conquest of the Iberian Peninsula, and this suggests that some overarching trends may be perceived by exploring both period and geographic dimensions.

The second and more substantive part focuses on conflict in Iberia, allied issues, and relevant texts. These texts pertain not only to Muslim and Christian conquest of the region, but also to attitudes of antipathy towards religious 'others' encapsulated in the work of some contemporary commentators. This section thus seeks to illustrate the employment and development of thematic tropes in Christian texts that first appeared in the context of the Arab conquests. It argues that, whereas Christian writers tended to take an uncompromisingly anti-Muslim view, Muslim writers provided more 'balanced' visions of Christian-Muslim relations by focusing on Christian-Muslim cooperation and coexistence, even within texts that focused on conflict. Nevertheless, it also suggests that Muslim texts became increasingly anti-Christian following the waning of Muslim power in Iberia.

I. Arab conquests and Christian reactions

The earliest examples of texts referring to Christian-Muslim conflict emerged shortly after the foundation of Islam, and are essential for understanding similar texts from the Andalusian context. After unifying the majority of the Arab tribes within the Arabian Peninsula, the Prophet Muḥammad turned his attention to territorial expansion during the early 630s.[5] Following his death in 632, the empire expanded further

[5] W.M. Watt, 'Muḥammad', in P.M. Holt, A.K.S. Lambton, and B. Lewis (eds), *The Cambridge history of Islam*, vol. 1A. *The central Islamic lands from pre-Islamic times to the First World War*, Cambridge, 2008, 30-56, pp. 51-4.

under Abū Bakr (r. 632-4) and then ʿUmar (r. 634-44), bringing Byzantine, Syrian and North African territory into *dār al-Islām*.[6] This brought Muslims into direct contact with Middle Eastern Christians, who began to comment upon the new religion and to reflect in their writings on the conquests and Muslim rule. Many early Christian references to Muslims and Islam composed in this context illustrate that, while knowledge of the new religion was limited and references to it were incidental, Islam and its followers were generally understood to be the bringers of war and violence. In the late 7th century, however, Christian sources displayed an increasing knowledge of Islam and sought to explain and remedy the issues that Muslim expansion and Muslim rule brought to the fore.

Some early sources

Most early Christian sources from the 630s to the 660s viewed Islam and its invasions with disdain. But they did not illustrate, or give evidence of, particularly complex understandings of the religion. Rather, early commentators probably viewed the conquests as 'little more than incursions by Arab tribesmen from the desert',[7] which had historically tended to flare up in times of Byzantine and Persian weakness. For instance, Sophronius of Jerusalem's (560-638) *Christmas sermon* of 634[8] refers to the capture of Bethlehem by the Saracens and alludes to the siege of Jerusalem, which he complains has rendered the Christians unable to visit the place of Christ's birth.[9] Sophronius makes no reference to the invaders' religion; he simply labels them 'godless'.[10] Other contemporaneous

6 L.V. Vaglieri, 'The Patriarchal and Umayyad caliphates', in Holt, Lambton, and Lewis, *Cambridge history of Islam*, vol. 1A, 57-103, pp. 58-66.

7 S.H. Griffith, *The church in the shadow of the mosque. Christians and Muslims in the world of Islam*, Princeton NJ, 2008, p. 23.

8 The text is described in D.J. Sahas, 'Sophronius, Patriarch of Jerusalem', in *CMR* 1, 120-7, pp. 126-7 ('Tou en hagiois patros hēmōn Sōphroniou archiepiskopou Hierosolymōn logos eis to hagion baptisma'); Sophronius's earlier *Synodical Letter* (634) also refers to the Saracen invasions, 'Ta Synodika tou autou en hosia tē mnēmē Sōphroniou', pp. 123-5.

9 D.J. Sahas, 'The face to face encounter between Patriarch Sophronius of Jerusalem and the Caliph ʿUmar ibn al-Khaṭṭāb. Friends or foes?', in E. Grypeou, M.N. Swanson, and D. Thomas (eds), *The encounter of Eastern Christianity with early Islam*, Leiden, 2006, 33-44, pp. 33-5.

10 W.E. Kaegi, 'Initial Byzantine reactions to the Arab conquest', *Church History* 38 (1969) 139-49, p. 140. Benevich notes that, unlike some other contemporaneous sources that focus only on the Arabs' barbarity and cruelty, Sophronius's descriptions of the Arabs, which note their opposition to God and alliance with the devil, characterises the invaders as anti-Christian; see G.I. Benevich, 'Christological polemics of Maximus the Confessor and the emergence of Islam onto the world stage', *Theological Studies* 72 (2011) 335-44.

sources, such as *Doctrina Iacobi nuper baptizati* ('Teachings of Jacob, the newly baptised'), an African text probably composed in the 630s or 640s,[11] indicate the acquisition of some basic knowledge regarding the religion, namely that there was a new prophet. In reported speech referring to this figure, the document states: 'He is deceiving. For do prophets come with swords and chariot? [...] I, Abraham [...] heard from the followers of the prophet that you will discover nothing true from the said prophet except human bloodshed.'[12] Similarly, the Coptic source, *The panegyric of the three holy children of Babylon*,[13] written in the early 640s, notes that the Saracens fast and pray, but labels them as oppressors who massacre and lead men into captivity.[14] This pattern of describing Christian tribulations at the hands of the Saracens with only limited descriptions of Islam and Muslims remained a prominent form of Christian commentary on the religion throughout the mid-7th century.[15] Early Christian assessments of Islam and Muslims were overwhelmingly negative, highlighting themes of cruelty and bloodshed, and this reappears in later texts.[16] However, such sources were not concerned only with describing Muslim expansion and violence; they also sought to explain these events and address them.

Christian responses to Muslim expansion

A comparison of early Christian sources shows that there were three primary responses to Muslim expansion. The same types of response appear to have also been prevalent in the Andalusian context. The first and seemingly most popular was to blame Christian sin for the conquests, which were thus understood to be acts of divine retribution. Sophronius makes this point in both his *Christmas sermon* and his later *Epiphany sermon* (637),[17] and compares the situation that Christians faced to Adam's experiences following the Fall.[18] In his *Christmas sermon*, moreover, he

---

11 J. Pahlitzsch, *'Doctrina Iacobi nuper baptizati'*, in *CMR* 1, 117-19.

12 Kaegi, 'Initial Byzantine reactions', p. 141-2.

13 It is described in H. Suermann, *'The Panegyric of the three holy children of Babylon'*, in *CMR* 1, 128-9.

14 Hoyland, *Seeing Islam as others saw it*, p. 121.

15 Refer, for instance, to the *Chronicle of Fredegar* (660), which describes the Arab conquests but displays no knowledge of Islam as such; see R. Collins, 'Fredegar', in *CMR* 1, 137-8; Hoyland, *Seeing Islam as others saw it*, p. 219.

16 Griffith, *The church in the shadow of the mosque*, p. 25.

17 The text is described in Sahas, 'Sophronius, Patriarch of Jerusalem', pp. 126-7.

18 Kaegi, 'Initial Byzantine reactions', pp. 139-40; Hoyland, *Seeing Islam as others saw it*, pp. 71-3; see also Sahas, 'Sophronius, Patriarch of Jerusalem', pp. 126-7.

argues that defeat of the Arabs will follow a strengthening of Christian faith.[19] Sophronius's contemporary, Maximus the Confessor (580-662), also understood the conquests to be the result of Christian sin.[20] Grigory Benevich argues that, in the case of both these authors, these sins were linked to what they perceived to be compromises in faith, namely the acceptance of Monophysite teachings amongst high ranking Orthodox Christians in Alexandria.[21]

In the late 7th century, this sort of explanation remained prominent. Contrary to Sophronius's and Maximus's texts, the *Mädäbbär chronicle* (alternatively the *Chronicle of John*), produced at the turn of the century (700),[22] attributes the invasions to divine punishment brought about by the Chalcedonians and the anti-Monophysite persecutions. The text is vehemently anti-Muslim and at the same time notes that numerous 'false' Egyptian Christians had embraced Islam and persecuted Christianity.[23] The *Ktābā d-rēsh mellē* ('The book of main points'),[24] written in the late 680s or early 690s, provides a more extensive and nuanced version of this sort of response. It argues that the conquests and Muslim rule 'formed a part of the divine plan and were designed to punish both the Byzantines for their teaching and their attempt to impose the theopaschite heresy on Orthodox Christians, and the Sassanids for persecuting Christians'.[25]

The *Ktābā d-rēsh mellē* provides both positive and negative assessments of Islam. On the one hand, Muslims had been called to act as God's vengeance against the persecutors of Christians, to care for the Christians, and importantly were monotheistic.[26] On the other, they too were to be punished because they were cruel, and because their religious policy, which guaranteed Christian freedom, had resulted in the growth of heretical groups.[27] The attribution of the conquests to Christian conduct was a popular position linked in many cases to the concerns of commentators regarding debates between Chalcedonian and Monophysite

---

19 Sahas, 'Face to face encounter', p. 35.

20 Benevich, 'Christological polemics of Maximus the Confessor', pp. 339-40; Hoyland, *Seeing Islam as others saw it*, p. 78.

21 Benevich, 'Christological polemics of Maximus the Confessor', p. 340.

22 It is described in G. Fiaccadori, 'John of Nikiou', in *CMR* 1, 209-18, pp. 211-18.

23 R.H. Charles, trans., *The Chronicle of John, Bishop of Nikiu, translated from Zotenberg's Ethiopic text*, London, 1916, p. 201.

24 See L. Greisiger, 'John bar Penkāyē', in *CMR* 1, 176-81.

25 Greisiger, 'John bar Penkāyē'.

26 Greisiger, 'John bar Penkāyē'.

27 Greisiger, 'John bar Penkāyē'.

theologians, which they believed were the cause of the issues facing Christendom. Moreover, the position was potentially grounded (at least initially) in the belief that the conquests were temporary incursions upon a weak empire by Arab tribes.

A second response to the conquests was to understand the events as part of the eschaton.[28] This concept surfaced in some of the works explored above. For example, Benevich notes the eschatological element present in the work of Maximus the Confessor.[29] The *Ktābā d-rēsh mellē* also contains apocalyptic material, arguing in its final section that plagues and famines in the late 680s brought by God in response to ongoing Christian sin were signs of the coming eschaton.[30] *The history of Sebeos*,[31] written in the late 650s, provides an apocalyptic contemplation of Islam, arguing that the last days had arrived.[32] These texts made way for more strictly apocalyptic literature such as *The apocalypse of Pseudo-Methodius* (691/2)[33] and *The apocalypse of Pseudo-Shenute* (695).[34] *The apocalypse of Pseudo-Methodius* became a highly influential work that was rapidly translated from Syriac into Greek and Latin.[35] It links Muslim rule to that of the Midianites in the 5th millennium BCE, identifying both groups as descendants of Ishmael, in order to suggest that, like the Midianites, the Muslims will be vanquished.[36] The author predicts that the Muslims will confiscate land, impose the poll tax on all, chastise the entire population, kill members of the priesthood, fornicate in churches, cause Christians and priests to apostatise, and eventually destroy the population.[37] Thereafter, the King of the Greeks will attack and defeat them, the remaining Christians will return to their native lands, and apostates will be punished.[38] Following the subsequent appearance of

---

28 Robert Hoyland notes the prevalence and importance of apocalypticism in the Middle East from the late 6th century to the 8th century. Hoyland, *Seeing Islam as others saw it*, pp. 26-31.

29 Benevich, 'Christological polemics of Maximus the Confessor', pp. 340-1.

30 Greisiger, 'John bar Penkāyē'.

31 See T. Greenwood, '*The History of Sebeos*', in *CMR* 1, 139-44.

32 Greenwood, '*History of Sebeos*'.

33 It is described in L. Greisiger, '*The Apocalypse of Pseudo-Methodius (Syriac)*', in *CMR* 1, 163-71.

34 See J. van Lent, '*The Apocalypse of Shenute*', in *CMR* 1, 182-5.

35 B. Garstad (trans.), *Apocalypse of pseudo-Methodius. An Alexandrian world chronicle*, Cambridge MA, 2012, pp. ix-x; M.P. Penn, *When Christians first met Muslims. A sourcebook of the earliest Syriac writings on Islam*, Oakland CA, 2015, pp. 108, 115.

36 Greisiger, '*Apocalypse of Pseudo-Methodius (Syriac)*'; P.J. Alexander, *The Byzantine apocalyptic tradition*, Berkeley CA, 1985, p. 18.

37 Alexander, *Byzantine apocalyptic tradition*, pp. 20-1.

38 Alexander, *Byzantine apocalyptic tradition*, pp. 21-2.

the Antichrist, the King of the Greeks will hand over his kingship to God, and the Second Coming will commence.[39] Lutz Greisiger writes that the *Apocalypse* is designed to refute Muslim claims of political and religious primacy by seeking to convince Christians that the success of the conquests and subsequent rule 'was not a sign of its predestined victory and that conversion to Islam would mean leaving behind the only true faith'.[40] Michael W. Twomey concurs, noting that the text is a piece of anti-Islamic propaganda designed to terrify Christians into action.[41] *The apocalypse of Pseudo-Shenute*, on the other hand, was written, according to Jos van Lent, to counter the threat of conversion to Islam by encouraging and promising eternal reward to those who do not apostatise.[42] The text compares the Muslim rulers to the Antichrist, portrays the Muslims as evil, and denies Islam's religious claims.[43] These texts, as well as acting as pieces of apocalyptic literature, therefore also sought to remedy issues that faced contemporary Christian communities as a result of Muslim expansion and rule, most notably apostasy.

The third response to the Arab conquests was that of Christian apology. Apologetic motifs aimed at strengthening Christian faith are to be found in the work of Sophronius who, as noted, argued that Arab defeat would follow the strengthening of Christian faith.[44] However, it was later authors who placed these motifs at the centre of their work. *Edifying and supportive tales which occurred in various places in our times* (690) by Anastasius of Sinai (630-701) is one such text.[45] It contains stories that aimed to bring comfort to readers living under Muslim rule and particularly to Christian prisoners of war.[46] This text sought to defend Christianity and the power of its symbols, and sway readers from potential apostasy whilst simultaneously attacking Islam and its 'demonic' followers.[47]

In summary, early Christian commentary on Islam written in the context of the Arab conquests and early Muslim rule were dominated by

---

39 Alexander, *Byzantine apocalyptic tradition*, p. 22.

40 Greisiger, '*Apocalypse of Pseudo-Methodius* (*Syriac*)'.

41 M.W. Twomey, 'The *Revelationes* of Pseudo-Methodius and scriptural study at Salisbury in the eleventh century', in C.D. Wright, F.M. Biggs and T.N. Hall (eds), *Source of wisdom. Old English and early medieval Latin studies in honour of Thomas D. Hill*, Toronto, 2007, 370-86, p. 370.

42 van Lent, '*Apocalypse of Shenute*'.

43 van Lent, '*Apocalypse of Shenute*'.

44 Sahas, 'Face to face encounter', p. 35.

45 It is described in A. Binggeli, 'Anastasius of Sinai', in *CMR* 1, 193-202, pp. 198-200.

46 Hoyland, *Seeing Islam as others saw it*, pp. 99-100.

47 Hoyland, *Seeing Islam as others saw it*, pp. 100-2; Binggeli, 'Anastasius of Sinai'.

a negative assessment of the religion of Islam. Initially, these negative assessments had little to do with Islam's content; rather the Arab invaders were defined by their godlessness, violence, and cruelty. Such elements remained prominent as rhetorical devices in later texts, although under Muslim rule, as knowledge of the religion increased, texts began to attack specific Muslim truth claims.[48] Such texts encapsulate three sorts of responses to Arab expansion and Muslim rule that seek to explain contemporaneous events or provide a real or hoped for remedy. Texts of one position often encapsulated ideas and concepts from other positions. The above categories are therefore fluid; they are heuristic devices to aid our understanding and interpretation, not in themselves representative of hard and fixed perspectives. Thus texts could, and do, include multiple responses to the Arab conquests.

While these texts are important for exploring early reactions to Islam and the conflictual aspects present in early Christian-Muslim relations, a focus on texts composed by Christian authors who viewed Islam in overwhelmingly negative terms may skew historical reality. As Michael Phillip Penn wryly notes, early Christian-Muslim relations 'were not characterized by unmitigated conflict'.[49] In the case of Syriac Christianity, for instance, Muslim rule tolerated religious expansion, involvement in politics, cooperative academic work and intermarriage. Furthermore, following the ʿAbbāsid revolution (747-50), Christians became increasingly able 'to accommodate themselves to Islamic culture'.[50] Given all this, some early texts such as the *Tashʿītā awkīt neṣḥānē d-qaddīshā mār(i) t'wdwṭ' epīsqupā d-āmīd mdī(n)tā* ('The story or heroic deeds of the holy one, my lord Theoduṭe, bishop of the city of Āmīd')[51] are indifferent towards Muslims and Islam. The sorts of responses that emerged in Christian texts in relation to the Arab conquests in the 7th and 8th centuries reappeared and were developed in the Andalusian context, where Christians once more met Muslims in the context of conflict.

---

48 Some later texts, whilst using anti-Muslim rhetoric, do not indicate the acquisition of greater knowledge of Islam. An example is *Historia vel gesta Francorum* ('The History of the Franks') from 751. See R. Collins, *'Historia vel Gesta Francorum'*, in *CMR* 1, 293-4.

49 M.P. Penn, *Envisioning Islam. Syriac Christians and the early Muslim world*, Philadelphia PA, 2015, p. 3.

50 S.H. Griffith, 'Christians under Muslim rule', in T.F.X. Noble and J.M.H. Smith (eds), *The Cambridge history of Christianity*, vol. 3. *Early medieval Christianities, c. 600-c. 1100*. Cambridge, 2010, 197-212, p. 200.

51 See A. Palmer, 'Symeon of Samosota', in *CMR* 1, 186-9.

II. Conflict in Al-Andalus. Conquest and *Reconquista*

Continuing to expand during the early 8th century in what has been termed the second wave of Islamic conquests, Arab and Berber forces invaded the Iberian Peninsula (Hispania) in 711.[52] They had been invited initially by the sons of the Visigoth King Witiza (687-710), to aid them in their struggle against King Ruderic (d. 711/12), whose succession Witiza's sons disputed. However, following initial successes, and realising that conquest was possible, the governor of Ifrīqiya (North Africa), Mūsā ibn Nuṣayr (640-716), decided to press the advantage and started to bring the region under Muslim control.[53] This led to the rapid replacement of a social order that embraced Christianity under the rule of the Romano-Gothic elite with another that was marked by new governance and religion.[54] By 716, large numbers of converts to Islam had been gained amongst those desiring to attain the rights of citizenship.[55] Members of the former elite who supported and collaborated with the conquerors, such as Witiza's sons, benefited from their association with the Arabs through land rights, promises of safety, intermarriage, wealth, and in some cases freedom of religion.[56] Muslim rule went through numerous stages of political organisation, including the Emirate of Córdoba (756-929), the Caliphate of Córdoba (929-1031), and the *ṭāʾifa* or Party Kingdoms.[57] After centuries of intermittent ('re-') conquest by Castilian, Aragonian, Portuguese and various other forces, Muslim rule came to an end with the fall of Granada to Castile and Aragon on 2 January 1492.[58] Like the early Arab conquests, the Muslim conquest of the Iberian Peninsula and the Christian *Reconquista*, an ambiguous term in itself,[59]

---

52 W.M. Watt and P. Cachia, *A history of Islamic Spain*, New Brunswick NJ, 2007, p. 1; N. Clarke, *The Muslim conquest of Iberia. Medieval Arabic narratives*, Abingdon, 2012, p. 6; E. Moreno, 'The Iberian Peninsula and North Africa', in M. Cook et al. (eds), *The new Cambridge history of Islam*, vol. 1. *The formation of the Islamic world, sixth to eleventh centuries*, Cambridge, 2010, 581-622, p. 584.

53 Moreno, 'Iberian Peninsula and North Africa', p. 585.

54 R. Collins, *Caliphs and kings. Spain, 796-1031*, Chichester, 2012, p. 5.

55 A.H. Miranda, 'The Iberian Peninsula and Sicily', in P.M. Holt, A.K.S. Lambton, and B. Lewis (eds), *The Cambridge history of Islam*, vol. 2A. *The Indian sub-continent, South-East Asia, Africa and the Muslim West*, Cambridge, 2008, 406-39, p. 407.

56 Moreno, 'Iberian Peninsula and North Africa', pp. 586-7.

57 Miranda, 'Iberian Peninsula and Sicily', pp. 409-32; Watt and Cachia, *History of Islamic Spain*, pp. 12-96.

58 Miranda, 'Iberian Peninsula and Sicily', pp. 413-32.

59 Whilst the ideology of reconquest was present within Iberia, it was appropriated by others outside the peninsula. The term *Reconquista* is part of this external appropriation, as it occurs for the first time in France. See D. Wasserstein, *The rise and fall of the*

brought Muslims and Christians into direct contact through warfare, and created dominions in which Muslims ruled over Christians and Christians ruled over Muslims. Such contexts spurred the composition of texts that both described and justified conflictual Christian-Muslim relations, and sought to address issues that arose from being in close proximity to the religious 'other'. Authors took a number of positions describing the conquest of Iberia and subsequent Muslim governance 'variously as a dreadful calamity, an act of God, high adventure, or the careful foundation of later administration'.[60] Indeed, many of the themes present in works that grew out of the Arab conquests also became prevalent in works written in the evolving contexts of the Iberian Peninsula.

Christian-Muslim relations during the period remain important today. Formulated in the 19th and 20th centuries, popular and academic narratives on Muslim rule over the Iberian Peninsula and the subsequent Christian conquest of the region have 'served as a unifying symbol of national identity.'[61] Understood as a formative period in the history of the peninsula, the *Reconquista* remains central to the study of medieval Iberian history. Narratives about it have not only been formative for national identity, but have also fed into modern narratives about Christian-Muslim conflict. As Alan G. Jamieson notes, in the aftermath of 9/11, some Muslims referred to events in medieval and early modern Spain in order to justify their theo-political positions.[62] Modern scholarship on this period of history has tended to focus on the coexistence and cooperation of members of the Abrahamic faiths, a trend that reflects academic responses to popular narratives on Islam in the post-9/11 world more generally. Nevertheless, the events of conquest and *Reconquista* were conflictual, marked by warfare and changes in governance as well as to the political and legal statuses of all citizens.[63]

Party-Kings. Politics and society in Islamic Spain, 1002-1086, Princeton NJ, 1985, pp. 268-73; and R.A. Fletcher, 'Reconquest and Crusade in Spain, c. 1050–1150', *Transactions of the Royal Historical Society* 37 (1987) 31-47.

60 Clarke, *Muslim conquest of Iberia*, p. 1.

61 J. Ray, *The Sephardic frontier. The Reconquista and the Jewish community in medieval Iberia,* Ithaca NY, 2006, p. 1. See also J. Stearns, 'Representing and remembering al-Andalus. Some historical considerations regarding the end of time and the making of nostalgia', *Medieval Encounters* 15 (2009) 355-74.

62 A.G. Jamieson, *Faith and the sword. A short history of Christian-Muslim conflict*, London, 2016², pp. 12-13.

63 Lucy Pick notes that the term *convivencia* has been used to describe the coexistence of religious groups in medieval Iberia. The context of *convivencia,* she notes, is one in which 'potential cooperation and interdependence in economic, social, cultural, and intellectual spheres coexist with the continual threat of conflict and violence'. See

Texts regarding conflict in Iberia

Texts composed in Iberia during the first half or so of the 8th century are few. They include the *Continuatio Hispana* (754)[64] and the earlier *Chronica Hispana-Orientalia ad annum 724*, both written by unknown Christian authors.[65] *Chronica Hispana-Orientalia* provides details of Muslim military expansion across Africa and the Iberian Peninsula.[66] It notes little about the new religion.[67] *Continuatio Hispana* provides an account of the history of the peninsula from the arrival of the Muslims, whose religious affiliation is not noted, until 754, detailing the military and political endeavours of various Muslim rulers.[68] Like early texts written in the context of the Middle Eastern Arab conquests, these two works are more concerned with describing the circumstances of the invasion than with the nature of Islam, as is illustrated by their disregard for the religious identity of the invaders. Nevertheless, whereas a genuine lack of knowledge of Islam and a belief that the invasions were only temporary probably influenced the lack of content about the religion in early texts pertaining to the Arab conquests in the Middle East, it seems unlikely that the same factors influenced Andalusian authors.

The author of *Continuatio Hispana* views the conquest of Spain as a calamity. However, although the invaders are portrayed negatively, his account of Andalusian history is relatively neutral.[69] While the text records Christian-Muslim conflict principally through its description of the invasions, it also demonstrates that collaboration took place, including joint Muslim-Christian raids on Frankish territory.[70] Daniel G. König notes that Muslim measures to ingratiate themselves with the conquered population were effective, even at this early stage, and are identified in

L.K. Pick, *Conflict and coexistence. Archbishop Rodrigo and the Muslims and Jews of medieval Spain*, Ann Arbor MI, 2004, p. 1.

64 See K.B. Wolf, '*The Chronicle of 754*', in *CMR* 1, 302-4. See also H. Daiber, 'Orosius' *Historiae adversus paganos* in arabischer Überlieferung', in J.W.W. van Rooden, H.J. de Jonge and J.W. van Henten (eds), *Tradition and re-interpretation in Jewish and early Christian literature. Essays in honour of Jürgen C.H. Lebram*, Leiden, 1986, 202-49, p. 207.

65 See C. Aillet, '*The Chronicle of 741*', in *CMR* 1, 284-9.

66 Aillet, '*Chronicle of 741*'. See also K.B. Wolf, 'Christian views of Islam in early medieval Spain', in J.V. Tolan (ed.), *Medieval Christian perceptions of Islam*, Abingdon, 2000, 85-108, p. 87; Hoyland, *Seeing Islam as others saw it*, p. 423.

67 Wolf, 'Christian views of Islam', p. 87.

68 Wolf, '*Chronicle of 754*'.

69 Wolf, '*Chronicle of 754*'; J.V. Tolan, *Saracens. Islam in the medieval European imagination*, New York, 2002, pp. 79-80.

70 D.G. König, *Arabic-Islamic views of the Latin West. Tracing the emergence of medieval Europe*, Oxford, 2015, p. 47.

the text through its records of intermarriage, for example.[71] Kenneth B. Wolf similarly notes that favourable terms of surrender, the low number of Muslims initially present in al-Andalus and their segregation, and Christian religious freedom, all aided in the forestalling of the composition of markedly anti-Muslim texts.[72] These factors, as well as the fact that al-Andalus was under established Muslim rule, may have influenced the lack of treatment of the religion of the invaders and current leadership in contemporaneous accounts.

Despite the initial lack of religious commentary, the reactions of the Christian educated classes to Muslim rule seem to have become hostile, with numerous polemical and apologetic texts being composed from the early 9th century onwards. This was potentially the result of the Muslims' consolidation of power and their associated importation of Islamic culture.[73] However, as is noted by Juan Pedro Monferrer Sala, such positions were also influenced by Eastern Christian responses to Islam, such as those that arose following the Arab conquests.[74]

The first theological attacks on Islam were made by Speraindeo (d. 853), Paul Alvarus (d. c.861) and Eulogius (d. 859).[75] Speraindeo composed a polemic in the 830s or 840s, which foreshadowed and influenced later texts in decrying Muslim sexual immorality and Islam's brothel-like image of Paradise.[76] In 854, Paul Alvarus composed *Indiculus luminosus* ('A shining declaration')[77] and *Vita Eulogii* ('Life of Eulogius'),[78] both of which were apologies that defended the Córdoban martyrs movement.[79] *Indiculus luminosus* also includes polemical elements that employ biblical exegesis to attack Islam and Muḥammad.[80] Like the work of Alvarus, Eulogius's *Memoriale sanctorum* ('In memory of the saints'),[81] *Liber apologeticus martyrum* ('Book in defence of the martyrs'),[82] and

---

71 König, *Arabic-Islamic views of the Latin West*, p. 48.

72 Wolf, 'Christian views of Islam', pp. 90-1.

73 Tolan, *Saracens*, p. 85.

74 See J.P. Monferrer Sala, Chapter 13 above, 'Conduits of interaction. The Andalusi experience', 307-29.

75 Tolan, *Saracens*, p. 78.

76 It is described in J.A. Coope, 'Speraindeo', in *CMR* 1, 633-5.

77 See K.B. Wolf, 'Paul Alvarus', in *CMR* 1, 645-8, pp. 647-8.

78 See Wolf, 'Paul Alvarus', pp. 646-7.

79 On these persecutions, see O.R. Constable with D. Zurro (eds), *Medieval Iberia. Readings from Christian, Muslim, and Jewish sources*, Philadelphia PA, 2012², p. 61; Tolan, *Saracens*, pp. 78, 87-95.

80 Wolf, 'Paul Alvarus', pp. 647-8; Wolf, 'Christian views of Islam', pp. 98-9.

81 See J. Tolan, 'Eulogius of Cordova', in *CMR* 1, 679-83, pp. 680-2.

82 See Tolan, 'Eulogius of Cordova', p. 683.

Documenta martyriale ('Martyrial document'),[83] all written in the 850s, offer apologetic and hagiographical descriptions of the Córdoban martyrs movement, and polemical attacks on Islam.[84] The Córdoban martyrs deliberately sought martyrdom by insulting Islam and its prophet, or, in the case of the descendants of mixed marriages who were legally classified as Muslims, by illegally practising Christianity, and they sought to break Christian-Muslim alliances in Córdoba.[85] Many Christians, including bishops, opposed these actions and *Liber apologeticus martyrum* suggests that ordinary Christians recognised Muslims as worshipping 'the same God [...] on the basis of a distinct, revealed law'.[86] Nevertheless, these early apologetical and polemical pieces sought to convince Christians 'of the sanctity of the martyrs and the evilness of the Muslim authorities'.[87] Following the subsiding of the martyrdoms, these early polemical and apologetical texts paved the way for writings in subsequent centuries as Christians sought to defend their position by questioning or attacking Islam.[88] Indeed, as noted by Monferrer Sala, the themes that emerged in these works are also prevalent in texts from much later periods of Andalusian history.[89]

The *Reconquista* was a series of sporadic conflicts and conquests against the Muslims on the Iberian Peninsula and in North Africa that continued from the 720s up until the end of the 15th century.[90] Muslim supremacy went unquestioned until the collapse of the Caliphate of Córdoba in 1031, following which Christian forces were slowly able to capture the peninsula.[91] The *Reconquista* spurred the composition of numerous texts, particularly historical chronicles. Alfonso III's (r. 866-910) *Chronica Visegothorum* is a series of royal biographies covering the reigns of the Visigothic and Asturian kings that describes the events of the Muslim conquest, as well as Asturian conflict against the Muslims,

83 See Tolan, 'Eulogius of Cordova', p. 682.
84 Such attacks in the works of both Alvarus and Eulogius sought to portray Muslims as violent and lustful; see Tolan, *Saracens*, p. 94.
85 Tolan, *Saracens*, p. 88.
86 Wolf, 'Christian views of Islam', p. 96.
87 Wolf, 'Christian views of Islam', p. 96.
88 Tolan, *Saracens*, p. 97.
89 See Monferrer Sala, Chapter 13 above, 'Conduits of interaction. The Andalusi experience', 307-29.
90 Miranda, 'Iberian Peninsula and Sicily', p. 408; A. Verskin, *Islamic law and the crisis of the Reconquista. The debate on the status of Muslim communities in Christendom*, Leiden, 2015, pp. 3-6.
91 J.F. O'Callaghan, *Reconquest and crusade in medieval Spain*, Philadelphia PA, 2003, pp. 1-3.

their dealings with conquered territories, and collaboration with Muslim rebels.[92] *Chronica Visegothorum* views the Muslim conquest of Iberia as 'a scourge designed to punish the Goths for transgressing divine law [...] God had raised up the Muslims to punish the sinful Goths and would restore their kingdom once they had paid the price for their sins.'[93] Therefore, notable accounts, such as Alfonso I's (r. 739-57) conquering of villages and his slaughter of the Muslims living there, were viewed by the author as progress towards the recovery of the 'promised land' by a 'chosen people'.[94]

This treatment of Muslims and their invasion, which is seen as simultaneously a punishment from God and something which Christians will overcome through divine providence, is similar to the treatment given in texts written in the context of the Middle Eastern Arab conquests such as the *Ktābā d-rēsh mellē* mentioned above. Despite this, the *Chronica Visegothorum*, by giving Hispania the status of a Christian 'promised land', develops a new trope that is absent from earlier sources. Other contemporaneous texts also affirm that the Muslim conquests were a punishment for sins and describe the Asturian dynasty as the 'anointed successors of the Goths of old, destined to drive the Saracen invader from Spain'.[95] These texts include the anonymous, late-9th-century texts *Chronica Albendensia* and *The prophetic chronicle*.[96] Like *Chronica Visegothorum*, the *Chronica Albendensia* includes military accounts of the Asturian monarchs' conquests over the Muslims. *The prophetic chronicle*, an addendum to the *Chronica Albendensia*, also includes accounts of the Muslim conquest, and contains an anti-Muslim polemic focusing on Muḥammad. Later chronicles often use a similar structure, combining historical accounts and descriptions with polemical and apologetic material. The *Chronica Visegothorum*, *Chronica Albendensia* and *The prophetic chronicle* were the first texts to introduce the idea of reconquest.[97]

92 See T. Deswarte, '*Chronica Visegothorum*', in *CMR* 1, 883-8.

93 K.B. Wolf (ed.), *Conquerors and chroniclers of early medieval Spain*, Liverpool, 1999², p. 45.

94 Wolf, *Conquerors and chroniclers*, pp. 45, 52; see also Deswarte, '*Chronica Visegothorum*'; T.F. Glick, *Islamic and Christian Spain in the early Middle Ages*, Leiden, 2005², p. 35.

95 Tolan, *Saracens*, p. 98. Jerrilynn Dodds argues that the formation of this identity was partially the result of opposition to and the rejection of Islam. See J.D. Dodds, *Architecture and ideology in early medieval Spain*, Pennsylvania PA, 1990, pp. 79-80.

96 For details on both *Chronica Albendensia* and *The Prophetic Chronicle*, see T. Deswarte, '*The Chronicle of Albelda and the Prophetic Chronicle*', in *CMR* 1, 810-15.

97 O'Callaghan, *Reconquest and crusade*, p. 4.

One example of a historical account that also employs polemical, apologetic and even apocalyptic material is Adémar of Chabannes's (988-1034) *Chronicon*, a history of the Frankish kingdoms from the 5th to the early 11th century that includes accounts of Muslim raids from Spain into Frankish territory, Italy and the Belearic Islands, as well as Frankish-Moorish conflicts in Corsica and Sardinia.[98] This work also contains passages linked to the *Reconquista*. For example, it includes an account of the actions of Roger I of Tosny (d. 1040) in capturing Muslim towns and killing Muslims, as well as his alleged killing and cannibalistic serving up of his Muslim captives as food to other prisoners.[99] Although these accounts highlight the violent clashes experienced by Muslims and Christians in the period, it is the text's description of the destruction of the Holy Sepulchre by the Fāṭimid Caliph al-Ḥākim bi-Amr Allāh (r. 996-1021) in 1009 that is most pertinent for understanding contemporary Christian-Muslim relations, since this passage introduces a new polemical theme into Christian interpretations of Muslim action. According to Adémar, the Holy Sepulchre's destruction was the result of a Jewish-Muslim conspiracy; Jews had warned al-Ḥākim that Christian armies were preparing to attack the Muslims, and so he ordered the persecution of Christianity.

Such events are viewed eschatologically. Al-Ḥākim is portrayed as an Antichrist-like figure whose persecutions of Christians foreshadowed the return of Christ. This is reinforced by his connection to the Jews, who were central in contemporary literature pertaining to the Antichrist.[100] This linking of Muslim leaders to the Antichrist also reflects texts written during the Arab conquests. Like other texts at that time, Adémar refers to Muslims in derogatory terms,[101] identifying them as heretical Christians, which 'reinforces their eschatological status'.[102] In his sermons, he also sought to portray Islam negatively and grouped Muslims with other non-Christian religious groups.[103] These anti-Muslim attitudes and

98 See M. Frassetto, 'Ademar of Chabannes', in *CMR* 2, 648-56, pp. 650-3.

99 Frassetto, 'Ademar of Chabannes', pp. 650-3.

100 M. Frassetto, 'Heretics, Antichrists, and the year 1000. Apocalyptic expectations in the writings of Ademar of Chabannes', in M. Frassetto (ed.), *The year 1000. Religious and social response to the turning of the first Millennium*, New York, 2002, 73-84, pp. 74-5; see also M. Frassetto, 'The image of the Saracen as heretic in the sermons of Ademar of Chabannes', in D.R. Blanks and M. Frassetto (eds), *Western views of Islam in medieval and early modern Europe. Perception of other*, New York, 1999, 83-96.

101 Frassetto, 'Ademar of Chabannes', pp. 650-3.

102 Frassetto, 'Image of the Saracen', p. 85.

103 Frassetto, 'Ademar of Chabannes', pp. 654-6.

the portrayal of Christian persecution resulting from a Jewish-Muslim conspiracy foreshadow later texts regarding the First Crusade.[104] However, they also point to contemporary fears that evil in the world is blossoming as the eschaton draws near.[105] The text is interesting for its combination of historical descriptions, polemics and apocalyptic material, which shows a development in anti-Muslim thought since the Arab conquests during which authors gave an array of responses to Muslim expansion, but tended each to centre on one.

Martyrdom. The case of Pelagius

Accounts of martyrdom also emerged in this period. One example is *Pelagius* written by Hrotsvit of Gandersheim (935-1002) around 955.[106] This describes the martyrdom in 925 of Pelagius, a Christian in Córdoba who was condemned by the Caliph ʿAbd al-Raḥmān III (r. 929-61). The text begins with a history of the Islamic conquest of Spain, and gives information on Islamic culture and Christian life under Muslim rule, before beginning the story of Pelagius.[107] In this, the history of Islamic Spain and Christian life under Muslim rule is portrayed with some accuracy, including information on taxation and Christians' freedom to practise their religion.[108] However, it also contains anti-Muslim material, portraying Muslims as barbaric, pagan idolaters and as given over to sodomy.[109] This focus on sexual immorality mirrors the earlier works of Alvarus and Eulogius.[110] Pelagius was the caliph's hostage, held through his own will as a substitute for his father.[111] Due to his beauty and eloquence, the caliph sought to begin a sexual relationship with him. However, Pelagius resisted and eventually struck the caliph following the latter's attempts

---

104 Frassetto, 'Ademar of Chabannes', pp. 650-3.

105 D.F. Callahan, *Jerusalem and the Cross in the life and writings of Ademar of Chabannes*, Leiden, 2016, p. 183.

106 See L.A. McMillin, 'Hrotsvit of Gandersheim', in *CMR* 2, 293-7, pp. 295-7. See also on martyrdom C.C. Sahner in Ch. 16, 'Martyrdom and conversion', 389-412, above.

107 McMillin, 'Hrotsvit of Gandersheim', pp. 295-7. See also S.L. Wailes, *Spirituality and politics in the works of Hrotsvit of Gandersheim*, Selinsgrove PA, 2006, pp. 68-9.

108 McMillin, 'Hrotsvit of Gandersheim', pp. 295-7.

109 McMillin, 'Hrotsvit of Gandersheim', pp. 295-7. See also M.D. Jordan, 'Saint Pelagius, ephebe and martyr', in J. Blackmore and G.S. Hucheson (eds), *Queer Iberia. Sexualities, cultures, and crossings from the Middle Ages to the Renaissance*, Durham NC, 1999, 23-47, p. 34; J.C. Frakes, *Vernacular and Latin literary discourses of the Muslim other in medieval Germany*, New York, 2011, p. 49.

110 Tolan, *Saracens*, p. 94.

111 McMillin, 'Hrotsvit of Gandersheim', pp. 295-7; Jordan, 'Saint Pelagius, ephebe and martyr', p. 32.

to kiss him.[112] The caliph then condemned him to death. Although several methods of slaying Pelagius proved ineffective, he was eventually killed by decapitation.[113] The story serves to humiliate the caliph, attributing corruption to him alone, and also to illustrate that, while rebellions and border skirmishes were rife at the time, God was protecting and vindicating his people through the blood of chaste martyrs.[114] This theme illustrates that martyrdom could take the form of a singular event, unrelated to warfare or conflict, at the whim of corrupt rulers, since the narrative takes place outside the context of warfare or wide-scale persecution. Moreover, the negative portrayal of Muslim leaders would become prominent in later texts from Iberia.

Crusade advocacy

Numerous accounts sought to persuade their readership of the virtues of anti-Islamic war on the Iberian Peninsula, or at least to describe those who had historically engaged in such conflicts in a positive light. The early 12th-century text, *Historia Silense* ('The history of [the town of] Silos'),[115] for example, describes the prototypically virtuous monarch as a capable warrior who captures Muslim territory and converts the inhabitants to Christianity.[116] Alfonso VI (1040-1109) is one such monarch who embraces this prototype and is celebrated in the text for his capture of Muslim territory.[117] The text also records events relating to the *Reconquista*, including military endeavours, the enslavement of Muslim women and children by Christians, and the Muslim destruction of churches.[118]

The late 12th-century *Chronica Naierensis* ('Chronicle of Najera') covers the conquest of the peninsula and the *Reconquista*, devoting large passages to describing the oppression of Christians by Muslims and

112 Jordan, 'Saint Pelagius', p. 32; S.L. Wailes, 'The sacred stories in verse', in P.R. Brown and S.L. Wailes (eds), *A companion to Hrotsvit of Grandersheim (fl. 960). Contextual and interpretive approaches*, Leiden, 2012, 85-119, p. 107-8.

113 McMillin, 'Hrotsvit of Gandersheim', pp. 295-7.

114 McMillin, 'Hrotsvit of Gandersheim', pp. 295-7. See also Jordan, 'Saint Pelagius', p. 33.

115 See P. Henriet, *'Historia Silense'*, in *CMR* 3, 370-4.

116 Henriet, *'Historia Silense'*. The text shares themes present in *Chronica Visegothorum*, *Chronica Albendensia*, and *The Prophetic Chronicle*, such as the chosen status of the Asturian line; see C.F. Fraker, *The scope of history. Studies in the historiography of Alfonso el Sabio*, Ann Arbor MI, 1996, p. 39.

117 Henriet, *'Historia Silense'*.

118 Henriet, *'Historia Silense'*; see also A. Lappin, *The medieval cult of Saint Dominic of Silos*, Leeds, 2002, p. 182.

Muslim plots against Christians.[119] The text depicts Iberian history as a succession of Christian-Muslim struggles in which Muslim domination, the destruction of churches and Christian oppression are seen as divine punishment for Christian sins. Nevertheless, God sends Castilian figures such as Sancho García to bring salvation to Iberia. Such themes, which would become prominent in other texts following the start of the crusades, sought to portray war against the Muslims as divinely justified. These texts further develop the tropes present in earlier works, which view Islam as a scourge against Christian sin and predict a future Christian victory over Islam. These themes are developed through descriptions of ideal monarchs and, like the *Chronica Visegothorum*, through linking victory over Islam to historical figures chosen by God.

Fictional narratives

Accounts containing fictional matter came into vogue during the mid-12th century, including *The chronicle of Pseudo-Turpin*,[120] written around 1140, and *La chanson de Roland*,[121] written in the late 12th century. Both provide legendary accounts of Charlemagne's expeditions against al-Andalus. As well as including fictitious records of Christian-Muslim conflict, both accounts also offer justification for, and seek to glorify, Holy War against the Muslims on the Iberian Peninsula, a theme which had become popular since the start of the crusades. In *The chronicle of Pseudo-Turpin*, Charlemagne's expeditions result in the providential conquest of Spain, the conversion of the Muslims there, and the killing of those who refused to convert, as well as the destruction of idols and the building of churches. However, shortly after Charlemagne's return to France, the fictional African Muslim King Agolant invades the peninsula and massacres the Christians.[122] Agolant is defeated, and, following a betrayal that risks overturning Charlemagne's plans, the Muslims are finally overcome.[123] Magali Cheynet argues that the text reads like 'a call

[119] See P. Henriet, *'Chronica Naierensis'*, in *CMR* 3, 778-82.

[120] See M. Cheynet, *'The Chronicle of Pseudo-Turpin'*, in *CMR* 3, 455-77.

[121] See S. Kinoshita, *'La Chanson de Roland'*, in *CMR* 3, 648-52.

[122] Kinoshita, *'Chanson de Roland'*; see also C. Lowney, *A vanished world. Muslims, Christians, and Jews in medieval Spain*, Oxford, 2005, pp. 50-1; K.V. Jensen, 'Creating a crusader saint. Canute Lavard and others of that ilk', in J. Bergsagel, D. Hiley, and T. Riss (eds), *Of chronicles and kings. National saints and the emergence of nation states in the High Middle Ages*, Copenhagen, 2015, 51-72, p. 58.

[123] Cheynet, *'Chronicle of Pseudo-Turpin'*; Lowney, *Vanished world*, p. 51.

to crusade in the context of *Reconquista*'.[124] Moreover, it provides a stereotypically positive image of Holy War, views the conquest of Spain in terms of liberation and, drawing on an ideology reminiscent of *Chronica Visegothorum* and later texts, provides the Christian rule of Spain with divine sanction and establishes the region as a new Holy Land.[125]

La chanson de Roland is a text that transforms Charlemagne's historical defeat into 'a heroic tale of his betrayal and loss, followed by his ultimate victory [...] against the "pagan" king of Saragossa and his overlord, the "emir of Babylon"'.[126] Aiding in formulating what would become a popular trope, the text depicts the Muslims as polytheistic pagans who worship a demonic trinity of ineffectual deities: Mahumet, Apollin and Tervagant.[127] The text notes that, following Charlemagne's conquest, the Franks took control of synagogues and mosques, destroying their idols and forcibly converting the population.[128] Nevertheless, the text frames Christian-Muslim relations in such a way that, in spite of Charlemagne's victory, conflict must continue until Islam is utterly destroyed and all Muslims are converted to Christianity.[129] The text, therefore, seeks to justify further divinely ordained war against the Muslims and, like *Historia Silense*, *Chronica Naierensis* and *The chronicle of Pseudo-Turpin*, offers the example of a virtuous and pious monarch who seeks to take Muslim territory and convert its inhabitants. Although both *The chronicle of Pseudo-Turpin* and *La chanson de Roland* are fictional accounts with little bearing on the historical reality of Christian-Muslim relations and conflict, they portray popular images of Islam that help us to understand how Christians viewed the religious 'other' and sought to justify interreligious conflict. Indeed, at the centre of these texts is the othering and demonising of Muslims, who had unjustly captured a Christian Holy Land. While Christian-Muslim conflict occurred through the conquest and re-conquest of the Iberian Peninsula, taking Christian accounts of conflict and

124 Cheynet, '*Chronicle of Pseudo-Turpin*'. Lowney similarly notes that the text served the Crusader movement and its ideology (*Vanished world*, p. 52).

125 Cheynet, '*Chronicle of Pseudo-Turpin*'; J. Stuckey, 'Charlemagne as crusader? Memory, propaganda, and the many uses of Charlemagne's legendary expedition to Spain', in M. Gabriele and J. Stuckey (eds), *The legend of Charlemagne in the Middle Ages. Power, faith and crusade*, New York, 2008, 137-52, p. 142.

126 Kinoshita, '*Chanson de Roland*'; D.L. Lewis, *God's crucible. Islam and the making of Europe, 570-1215*, New York, 2008, pp. 255-62.

127 Kinoshita, '*Chanson de Roland*'. For a detailed exploration of the text's portrayal of Muslims, see B.P. Edmonds, 'Le portrait des Sarrasins dans "La Chanson de Roland"', *The French Review* 44 (1971) 870-80.

128 Kinoshita, '*Chanson de Roland*'.

129 Lewis, *God's crucible*, p. 261.

the oppression of Christians at face value would risk espousing historical fantasy, propaganda and polemics as fact. Indeed, the primary purposes of many of the texts discussed above was not to record historical realities but to justify and glorify war and anti-Muslim sentiment.

Christian-Muslim coexistence

The conquest of Iberia, as Ann Christys notes, placed Christians 'on one side or the other of a geographical and ideological frontier between Christianity and Islam which has dominated the historiography of the peninsula'.[130] However, Christians and Muslims were not at constant war, and the conquest of the peninsula did not result in the complete expiry of Christianity or Christians. Rather, Muslim rule was 'defined by coexistence with Christians and Jews and the concept of *dhimma* (protection)'.[131] Thus, unlike Christian texts, which tended to provide an uncompromisingly negative assessment of Muslims and justification for war against them, Muslim texts, whilst including military accounts and anti-Christian material, tend also to include extensive references to coexistence and cooperative Christian-Muslim relations.[132] For example, the *Akhbār mulūk al-Andalus* ('Reports on the kings of al-Andalus'),[133] written by Aḥmad al-Rāzī before 955, details the Arab conquest of Hispania and records details about Christian-Muslim relations in the peninsula, both peaceful and conflictual. It records Christian support of the Muslim conquest by Julian, Count of Ceuta, for instance. This indicates that

---

130 A. Christys, *Christians in al-Andalus (711-1000)*, Abingdon, 2002, p. 1.

131 J.M. Safran, *Defining boundaries in al-Andalus. Muslims, Christians, and Jews in Islamic Iberia*, Ithaca NY, 2013, p. 9. Some have even theorised that al-Andalus is best understood not as Islamic in nature but as 'a multi-confessional entity wherein an "Andalusian" cultural identity transcended religious difference'. See J.P. Decter, *Iberian Jewish literature. Between al-Andalus and Christian Europe*, Bloomington IN, 2007, p. 5.

132 It is interesting to note that some Christian texts from the context of the crusades took a similar approach, encapsulating hostile attitudes towards Islam whilst simultaneously describing coexistence and cooperation. Examples include Walter the Chancellor's *Bella Antiochena* (1119), Fulcher of Chartres's *Historia Hiersolymitana* (12th century), and Ambroise's *L'Estorie de la guerre sainte* (12th century). See S.B. Edgington, 'Walter the Chancellor', in *CMR* 3, 379-82; M. Bull, 'Fulcher of Chartres', in *CMR* 3, 401-8; C. Croizy-Naquet, 'Ambroise', in *CMR* 4, 182-92, pp. 185-92. See also T.S. Asbridge, *The creation of the principality of Antioch, 1098-1130*, Woodbridge, Suffolk, 2000, pp. 6-7; M.J. Ailes, 'Heroes of war. Ambroise's heroes of the Third Crusade', in C. Saunders, F. le Saux and N. Thomas (eds), *Writing war. Medieval literary responses to warfare*, Cambridge, 2004, 29-48; J. Tolan, 'Mirror of chivalry. Salah al-Din in the medieval European imagination', in D. Blanks (ed.), *Images of the Other. Europe and the Muslim world before 1700*, Cairo, 1996, 7-38.

133 See M. Penelas, 'Aḥmad al-Rāzī', in *CMR* 2, 288-92.

conflict was not solely related to religious affiliation and that Muslims and Christians cooperated for their own, as well as mutual, political and military ends. Related to this, *Akhbār mulūk al-Andalus* also argues that the conquest was the result of the immorality and treachery of the Visigoth rulers, who were willing to betray their leaders to further their personal goals.

The extant fragments of *Tarṣīʿ al-akhbār wa-tanwīʿ al-āthār wa-l-bustān fī gharāʾib al-buldān wa-l-masālik ilā jamīʿ al-mamālik*[134] ('The adornment of reports and the classification of monuments and gardens') by al-ʿUdhrī (1003-85), written in the second half of the 11th century, provide a similar image of Christian-Muslim relations, recording instances of both conflict and coexistence. Its descriptions of interactions between al-Andalus and the Christian kingdoms to its north include accounts of governmental relations, Muslim raids and campaigns against the Christians, and reports of intermarriage. An account of al-Andalus's history, *Taʾrīkh iftitāḥ al-Andalus* ('The history of the conquest of al-Andalus') by Ibn al-Qūṭiyya (d. 977),[135] refers to Christians holding high ranking positions such as legal offices. It indicates that the Muslim author was proud of his royal Christian heritage. This suggests that Christians were hardly subjected to an all-encompassing anti-Christian ideology, but rather in some cases held status that, in this instance, bestowed prestige upon a Muslim descendant.

A final example is the *Dhikr bilād al-Andalus* ('Description of the country of al-Andalus), written between the mid-14th and late 15th centuries.[136] It provides details of both peaceful and hostile relations, including military campaigns and embassies. It also records early Muslim treatment of Iberian Christians, namely sharing of churches, the infrequent destruction of churches, legal and social restrictions, taxes, etc. Later, as the Christian kingdoms advanced, the story is reversed and the Muslim rulers agree to pay an annual tribute in return for peace and survival.

---

134 See M. Penelas, 'Al-ʿUdhrī', in *CMR* 3, 176-81.
135 See J.P. Monferrer Sala, 'Ibn al-Qūṭiyya', in *CMR* 2, 456-9.
136 See M. Penelas, '*Dhikr bilād al-Andalus*', in *CMR* 5, 593-4.

Polemical texts

There are, of course, numerous texts that embody overtly anti-Christian positions. As Monferrer Sala notes, a negative attitude towards Christians is present from the very first Islamic sources.[137] Many of these texts were the product of the context of *Reconquista*, which spurred an intellectual crisis in which Muslims were transported into a context where Islam's religious and legal institutions lacked a Muslim political leader capable of reflecting upon their religious, legal and political position within Christendom.[138] Nevertheless, even anti-Christian texts provide insights into the multiple layers of Christian-Muslim relations to be found in al-Andalus. Ibn Bashkuwāl's (1101-83) biographical dictionary, the *Kitāb al-ṣila fī ta'rīkh a'immat al-Andalus* ('The continuation of the history of the sages of al-Andalus'), written in 1139, includes in its history of al-Andalus references to Muslim figures who took part in *jihād* against the Christians and those 'who carried out *ribāṭ* on the Christian-Muslim frontier'.[139] It thereby frames Christian-Muslim conflict in terms of Holy War and as part of the defence of Islam. It also refers to Christian-Muslim coexistence through references to Christian servants and slaves in Muslim households.[140] Although such references create a dynamic of power in which Christians are lower than Muslims in terms of social standing, they simultaneously illustrate that Christian-Muslim relations were not singularly conflictual. However, Ibn Ḥayyān's (987-1076) late 1060s text, the *Kitāb al-muqtabis fī taʾrīkh rijāl al-Andalus* in the *Al-taʾrīkh al-kabīr* ('The great history'), describes Christianity in negative terms, referring to Christians as infidels, enemies of God and polytheists.[141] Although the text contains accounts of conquests and raids, it also details Christian-Muslim diplomatic relations, and the involvement and cooperation of Christian kingdoms with al-Andalus. *Fatḥ al-Andalus*,[142] a history of al-Andalus from the Arab conquest to the early 12th century, written in the early 1100s, includes legendary accounts that depict Christian rulers in a negative light, attributing the conquests to, for example, the greed and underhandedness of the last Visigoth King of Hispania, Ruderic. The text illustrates the complexity of contemporary Christian-Muslim relations in

---

137 See Monferrer Sala, Chapter 13 above, 307-29.

138 Verskin, *Islamic law and the crisis of the* Reconquista, p. 1.

139 See A.M. Carballeira Debasa, 'Ibn Bashkuwāl', in *CMR* 3, 451-4, pp. 453-4.

140 T. Ladjal, 'The Christian presence in North Africa under Almoravids rule (1040-1147CE). Coexistence or eradication?' *Cogent Arts and Humanities* 4 (2017) 1-17.

141 See M. Meouak, 'Ibn Ḥayyān', in *CMR* 3, 165-71, pp. 166-70.

142 See M. Penelas, '*The conquest of Iberia. Fatḥ al-Andalus*', in *CMR* 3, 335-7.

its description of the differences in treatment meted out to Christians in towns taken by force and who therefore had their property confiscated, and those in towns that surrendered and therefore kept their property.

These accounts provide further multifaceted images of Christian-Muslim relations in al-Andalus. Again, while there were times of conflict, there were also times of coexistence, intermarriage and cooperation. Christians and Christianity were on occasion depicted negatively, but at other times the Christian heritage became a badge of honour to wear with pride. Such texts illustrate that, although conflict was an important form of Christian-Muslim interaction, it was not the sole defining factor in the Andalusian Christian-Muslim context.

It would be disingenuous to suggest that all anti-Christian texts composed by Muslims also contain materials pertaining to peaceful coexistence. As with Christian compositions, numerous Islamic texts take an uncompromisingly anti-Christian stance and present an uncompromising conflictual view of Christian-Muslim relations. For example, although it refers to Christian concubines who mothered Cordóban rulers, and was written at a time when the fortunes of the *Reconquista* had begun to turn in favour of the Christian powers,[143] the *Al-bayān al-mughrib fī [ikhtiṣār] akhbār mulūk al-Andalus wa-l-Maghrib* of Ibn ʿIdhārī al-Marrākushī (1312 or 1313)[144] takes a thoroughly anti-Christian stance. Christians feature as enemies, and are described as polytheists, tyrants, 'infidels and hypocrites who must be resisted in order to protect Islam'.[145] Military victory against them is highlighted and glorified, whereas those who employ Christian soldiers, a new practice 'that provoked shock and fear',[146] are criticised.[147] This is but one amongst a number of uncompromisingly anti-Christian polemical works that had begun to be composed when the *Reconquista* was achieving successes. But they are relatively rare in the Andalusian context.[148] Among such texts, *Maqāmiʿ al-ṣulbān wa-marātiʿ (rawātiʿ) riyāḍ (rawḍat) ahl al-īmān* ('Mallets for crosses and provender in the meadows of the faithful') by al-Khazrajī (d. 1187), written in the 1140s, is a refutation of Christian beliefs and a defence of the

143 For details on this period and the decline of al-Andalus, see for example, Miranda, 'Iberian Peninsula and Sicily', pp. 418-32.

144 See D. Serrano Ruano, 'Ibn ʿIdhārī al-Marrākushī', in *CMR* 4, 737-42.

145 Serrano Ruano, 'Ibn ʿIdhārī al-Marrākushī'.

146 M. Fierro, 'Violence against women in Andalusi historical sources (third/ninth-seventh/thirteenth centuries)', in R. Gleave and I.T. Kristó-Nagy (eds), *Violence in Islamic thought from the Qur'an to the Mongols*, Edinburgh, 2015, 155-74, p. 167.

147 Serrano Ruano, 'Ibn ʿIdhārī al-Marrākushī'.

148 D. Thomas, 'Al-Qaysī', in *CMR* 4, 732-6.

Qur'an.[149] It seeks to illustrate the corruption of the Bible and the falsehood of Christian miracles, and to provide a defence of *jihād* and polygamy. Another is the *Kitāb miftāḥ al-dīn wa-l-mujādala bayna l-Naṣārā wa-l-Muslimīn min qawl al-anbiyāʾ wa-l-mursalīn wa-l-ʿulamāʾ al-rāshidīn alladhīna qaraʾū l-Anājīl* ('The key of religion or the disputation between the Christians and the Muslims'), written by al-Qaysī in the early 14th century. It provides a scriptural defence of Muḥammad and seeks to illustrate that Christianity 'has lost its original purity'.[150] It also provides accounts of the *Reconquista*. These texts illustrate that in times of *Reconquista* success, Muslim scholars found it necessary to defend Islam and attack Christianity, resulting in the formulation of anti-Christian polemics and chronicles containing anti-Christian material that ignored, or were silent on, matters of non-conflictual Christian-Muslim interaction. Contrariwise, it is arguable that Muslim authors tended to provide more balanced accounts of Christian-Muslim relations when Muslim power on the peninsula was strong. It may also be the case that the actual experiences of Muslim authors with their Christian counterparts allowed them to write more nuanced accounts of contemporaneous Christian-Muslim relations than Christian authors confined to churches, monasteries and political offices.[151]

Summary

This section has sought to describe Christian and Muslim texts referring to interactions between the two religions in the context of the conquest of the Iberian Peninsula and the subsequent *Reconquista.* Christian authors employed and developed tropes present in textual responses to the Arab conquests, but also developed new responses to Muslim rule and conquest based on changes in the context of European Christian-Muslim relations such as the advent of the crusades. Whereas Christian texts tend to take a principally anti-Muslim stance, dichotomising Christians and Muslims[152] and seek to justify and glorify resistance to Muslims, many Muslim texts generally provide a more nuanced vision of Christian-Muslim relations in the period by referring to instances of

---

149 See J.P. Monferrer Sala, 'Al-Khazrajī', in *CMR* 3, 526-8.

150 See Thomas, 'Al-Qaysī', pp. 734-6.

151 Here, I build on the thought of Alex Mallett, who makes a similar argument in relation to the contents of *La vie de Saint Louis* written by Jean de Joinville in 1309. See A. Mallett, 'John de Joinville', in *CMR* 4, 718-23.

152 Glick, *Islamic and Christian Spain*, p. 185.

conflict, cooperation and coexistence. Despite this, there are Muslim texts that take an anti-Christian position, seeking to justify Muslim political and religious claims, the defence of Islam and Holy War. As illustrated by the sudden emergence of Muslim polemical and apologetic texts following the waning of Muslim power, these more 'balanced' accounts are probably linked to Muslim control of the peninsula, written at times when Christianity did not pose a viable threat to Muslim rule. It is also important to note that the complex image of Christian-Muslim interactions presented in Muslim texts does not indicate that Christians and Muslims had equal status. As Wolf notes: 'Although from the beginning Christians were given virtual autonomy to govern the affairs of their own religious communities, their subordinate position theoretically restricted their access to government positions [...].'[153] Christians were, in fact, subjected to numerous restrictions – religious, social and political. Such laws did not mean that 'the actual situation of Christians living under Islam deteriorated to any appreciable degree',[154] but we cannot assume that references to cooperation and coexistence indicated the equality of the people of the *dhimma* with Muslims. Moreover, such references should not diminish the importance we attribute to the very real and violent Christian-Muslim conflicts that took place on the Iberian Peninsula.

Conclusion

The authors examined in this chapter reflected on the respective contexts in which they found themselves, composing texts that sought to explain, describe and theologise Christian-Muslim conflict. They also composed polemical and apologetic texts that fed into narratives that opposed their religious counterparts. Christian texts written in the context of the Arab conquests have in common a lack of sophisticated knowledge of Islam and Muslims. These can be loosely categorised according to the following themes: the conquests were viewed as divine retribution, the sign of the coming eschaton, or the starting point of a state of affairs that needed remedy. In many senses, there was a continuity between earlier texts dating from the Arab conquests and those that emerged in other contexts such as al-Andalus and the *Reconquista*. The identification of

153 K.B. Wolf, *Christian martyrs in Muslim Spain*, Cambridge, 1988, p. 10.
154 Wolf, *Christian martyrs*, p. 10.

Christian sin as the cause of Muslim victory, for example, is a theme that time and time again appears in Christian texts.

A comparison of Christian texts from the Middle Eastern Arab conquests and the Iberian Peninsula illustrates that there was a propensity to attribute conflict to the sinful behaviour of Christians, but that there was hope for providential victory over Muslims spurred by reformations in behaviour or (in the case of Hispania) idealised Christian figureheads. Conflict in Iberia spanned several centuries, and therefore texts from the region illustrate an increasing complexity in responses to and commentary on Christian-Muslim conflict. Authors introduced new themes and reflections into their works, providing Hispania with the status of a Holy Land and describing prototypical Christian monarchs. Such texts foreshadowed those written in the context of the crusades, which would draw upon similar ideologies and imagery.

Both Christian and Muslim authors had a propensity to describe the religious other in negative terms, viewing the other as violent, pagan and heretical. However, positions of relative power and actual direct interactions with the 'other' often resulted in the composition of texts that simultaneously demonised religious opponents whilst noting the redeemable qualities of the other and registering relatively positive forms of Christian-Muslim coexistence. Historical instances of Christian-Muslim marriage, rule over citizens of other religions, trade and diplomacy referred to in some texts illustrate that many accounts provide a skewed vision of Christian-Muslim relations by highlighting Holy War, its justification, glorification and theological rationale above instances of cooperation.

In sum, this chapter has argued that Muslim texts written in the Iberian context tend to offer multifaceted visions of Christian-Muslim relations that refer to both conflict and coexistence. Nevertheless, it has also sought to suggest that, following the wane of Muslim power, Muslim texts lost their multifaceted explorations in favour of unilateral anti-Christian rhetoric. Christian-Muslim conflict, though it certainly does not characterise the totality of relationships, is an important element in the history of Christian-Muslim interaction, and one that can even frame Christian-Muslim relations in the modern world. The story of Christian-Muslim conflict is one that has been painted as an illegitimate picture of interreligious interaction marred by warfare, an interaction that in reality consisted of multiple layers of interaction, both cooperative and conflictual in nature.

Chapter 19
Christian missions to Muslims

Martha T. Frederiks

> I tell them [the Saracens] the prophets,
> What they taught us about God
> I proclaim them the Holy Christ,
> – Perhaps it may be of use? –
> The Holy Gospel.
> What can you do better?
> If somebody taught them,
> Maybe they would convert?
> Priest Konrad's Song of Roland (c. 1170)[1]

Introduction

Benjamin Kedar opens his book, *Crusade and mission. European approaches toward the Muslims*, with the intriguing observation that Christian missions to Muslims appear to be a relatively recent phenomenon.[2] While the Church of the East through mission and migration established churches as far east as China and Tibet, and while the Byzantine Church sent missionaries to Eastern Europe and the southern borders of the Arabian peninsula, and the Latin Church directed an ever-expanding Christianisation of northern Europe, sources suggest that during the first five centuries of Islam's existence few, if any, systematic missions were conducted to Muslims. Christians responded to the rise of Islam in a variety of ways, such as with apocalyptic, apologetic and polemical works, public debates, internal reforms and military expeditions. But if texts are a window into the reality on the ground, systematic missionary initiatives towards Muslims were first organised only during the early decades of the 13th century, when the Latin Church encountered

---

[1] B.Z. Kedar, *Crusade and mission. European approaches toward the Muslims*, Oxford, 1984, p. 122. See also M.G. Cammarota, *'Rolandslied'*, in *CMR* 3, 656-64.

[2] Kedar, *Crusade and mission*, pp. 3-9.

substantial communities of Muslims in the reconquered territories on the Iberian Peninsula and in the Crusader states.[3]

The accuracy of Kedar's observation of mission to Muslims as a relatively late development depends to a large extent on one's definition of mission. Kedar himself regards mission as 'peaceful efforts to cause the infidel to convert'.[4] His description is helpful in that it highlights the aim of mission activities as conversion.[5] However, his stipulation that mission consists solely of peaceful endeavours precludes the possibility of understanding apocalyptic movements such as the martyrs of Córdoba,[6] apologetic works such as the *Disputation* of Patriarch Timothy I,[7] or polemical texts such as *The Apology of al-Kindī*,[8] as part of a larger Christian project in the context of Islam that consisted of efforts to convert Muslims as well as to avert Christian conversion to Islam. Also, works by people such as Peter of Cluny (d. 1156),[9] Jacques de Vitry (d. 1240),[10] and Ramon Llull (d. 1315-16),[11] seem to suggest that irenic and militant methods were not necessarily considered to be mutually exclusive; many deemed enforced conversion, or military intervention to ensure missionary access, acceptable strategies.

This chapter uses the term 'mission' to denote all intentional efforts aimed at conversion, and situates the rise of mission to Muslims as part of a larger project in the context of Islam and part of a larger reform movement that simultaneously promoted the spiritual renewal of Western Europe's Christianity and the evangelisation of non-Christians. I begin by briefly charting how, via apologetics, polemics, debates and martyrologies, the idea of Christian mission towards Muslims gradually

[3] See e.g. B. Bombi, 'The Fifth Crusade and the conversion of Muslims', in E.J. Mylod et al. (eds), *The Fifth Crusade in context. The crusading movement in the early thirteenth century*, London, 2017, 68-91, p. 68; A. Mallett, *Popular Muslim reactions to the Franks in the Levant, 1079-1291*, Farnham, 2014, pp. 106-20.

[4] Kedar, *Crusade and mission*, p. xii.

[5] In missiological circles, there is an ongoing debate as to 'what is mission'. For an overview, see for example D. Bosch, *Transforming mission. Paradigm shifts in the theology of mission*, Maryknoll NY, 1991. Considering the period under discussion, a definition of mission in terms of conversion seems appropriate.

[6] J. Tolan, 'Eulogius of Cordova', in *CMR* 1, 679-83.

[7] M. Heimgartner, 'Disputation with the Caliph al-Mahdī', in *CMR* 1, 522-6.

[8] L. Bottini, *'The Apology of al-Kindi'*, in *CMR* 1, 585-94.

[9] D. Iogna-Prat and J. Tolan, 'Peter of Cluny', in *CMR* 3, 604-10. Kedar points out that Peter of Cluny's famous words 'I love you; loving you I write to you, writing to you I invite you to salvation', are spoken by a man who also lauds the Templars for their continuous crusading work; Kedar, *Crusade and mission*, pp. 99-100.

[10] J. Tolan, 'Jacques de Vitry', in *CMR* 4, 295-306.

[11] H. Hames, 'Ramon Llull', in *CMR* 4, 703-17.

began to emerge. I then explore key movements, figures and texts that played a crucial role in shaping the reflection and implementation of Christian mission to Muslims, highlighting the differences between them in motivation and the diversity in approaches to mission.

Explaining Islam

The oldest Christian sources referencing Islam are texts that comment on the Arab conquests.[12] Archbishop Sophronius of Jerusalem in his Christmas sermon of 634 laments: 'As once that of the Philistines, so now the army of the godless Saracens has captured the divine Bethlehem and bars our passage there, threatening slaughter and destruction if we leave this holy city and dare to approach our beloved and sacred Bethlehem'.[13] It is only in retrospect, after it had become apparent that with the invaders there came a new religious persuasion, later conceptualised as Islam, that these texts gain a significance beyond the merely political.

Many of these early texts make use of apocalyptic imagery, depicting the Arab-Muslim conquest as a time of trial and tribulation.[14] The Syriac *Apocalypse of Pseudo-Methodius* (c. 691), for example, describes the Arab-Muslim invasions as 'a merciless chastisement' and 'a testing furnace', during which

> [m]any, who were sons of the Church will deny the Christians' true faith, the holy cross, and the glorious mysteries. Without compulsion, lashings, or blows, they will deny Christ and make themselves the equivalent of unbelievers. [...] In the end times, men will leave the faith and go after defiled spirits and the teachings of demons. [...] All who are fraudulent and weak in faith will be tested in this chastisement and become known.

The author urges the believers to remain steadfast, for 'God will remain patient while his worshipers are persecuted so that through chastisement the sons might be known'.[15] The Coptic *Apocalypse of Shenute* (c. 695) uses

---

12 See for example H. Suermann, '*The Panegyric of the three holy children of Babylon*', in *CMR* 1, 127-9; H. Teule, '*The Chronicle of Khuzistan*', in *CMR* 1, 130-2.

13 R.G. Hoyland, *Seeing Islam as others saw it. A survey and evaluation of Christian, Jewish and Zoroastrian writings on early Islam*, Princeton NJ, 1997, p. 71; D. Sahas, 'Sophronius, Patriarch of Jerusalem', in *CMR* 1, 120-7.

14 Later authors (e.g. Joachim of Fiore) also make use of apocalyptic imagery; see B. McGinn, 'Joachim of Fiore', in *CMR* 4, 83-91.

15 L. Greisiger, '*The Apocalypse of Pseudo-Methodius* (*Syriac*)', in *CMR* 1, 163-71. Quotations from M.P. Penn, *When Christians first met Muslims. A sourcebook of the earliest Syriac writings on Islam*, Oakland CA, 2015, pp. 116, 120-1.

even stronger language and seems to suggest that the harassments and confiscation of property under Muslim rule, and subsequent apostasy of Christians, signal the imminent reign of the Antichrist. The opening passage therefore insists: 'Tell your children of them [i.e. the hardships and miseries], and write them for them so that they may all be vigilant and be guided and be on their guard, so that they will not be negligent and surrender their souls to the devil.'[16]

The pastoral concerns that inform these apocalyptic writings are also expressed in other genres. The *Arabic homily of Pseudo-Theophilus of Alexandria* (late 7th or early 8th century) cautions believers against assimilation to Islam, stressing that Muslims, despite their seemingly pious lifestyle of fasting and prayer, will not enter the Kingdom of Heaven.[17] Concern for religious accommodation is also the subject of a letter by the Syrian Orthodox Patriarch Athanasius of Balad (c. 684), which instructs the clergy to ensure that their parishioners refrain from interfaith marriages and ritually slaughtered meat. About a century later, Pope Hadrian (r. 772-95) sent similar directives to his emissary Egila in Spain, instructing him to denounce matrimonial alliances and other forms of socialising with Muslims and Jews in order to avoid 'contamination' by their 'various errors'.[18] Kindred sentiments are expressed in later works, as is evidenced, for example, by the canonical collections of the Coptic Metropolitan Michael of Damietta and the Dominican canon law expert Raymond of Penyafort (1175-1275).[19]

Texts such as these seem to suggest that, during the first centuries of Islam, church leaders living under Muslim rule understood their first and foremost 'mission' as being to ensure the preservation of the Christian community. Rather than seeking Muslim conversion to Christianity, their prime concern was the flagging allegiance of the faithful. Social pressure, intermarriage, cultural assimilation, harassment and even financial incentives, all strained Christian allegiance, resulting in

---

[16] Hoyland, *Seeing Islam as others saw it*, p. 279; J. van Lent, '*The Apocalypse of Shenute*', in *CMR* 1, 182-5.

[17] J. van Lent, '*The Arabic homily of Pseudo-Theophilus of Alexandria*', in *CMR* 1, 256-60.

[18] H. Teule, 'Athanasius of Balad', in *CMR* 1, 157-9; C. Aillet, 'Pope Hadrian's epistles to bishop Egila', in *CMR* 1, 338-42. Raymond of Penyafort in his *Summa de casibus poenitentiae* makes mention of Christians under Muslim rule who venerate Muḥammad as a messenger and saint; see Kedar, *Crusade and mission*, p. 103.

[19] M.N. Swanson, 'Michael of Damietta', in *CMR* 4, 109-14; J. Tolan, 'Raymond of Penyafort', in *CMR* 4, 252-8.

large-scale conversion to Islam.[20] By framing Muslim political rule in apocalyptic and eschatological terms, they attempted to dissuade religious accommodation and avert Christian conversion to Islam. The rise of Christian apologetic works can also be understood as part of this quest for self-preservation. Though seemingly addressed to Muslims, these apologetic texts were primarily written for Christian audiences. They served as manuals on how to respond to Muslim queries of the Christian faith and may also have had an educational function; examples of such texts included *Fī tathlīth Allāh al-wāḥid* (mid-8th century), *The dialogue between a Saracen and a Christian* (second half of the 8th century), the *Disputation* (c. 782) of Patriarch Timothy I with the Caliph al-Mahdī and the vast corpus of Theodore Abū Qurra.[21] John Tolan describes their purpose as 'to immunize the faithful against the theological errors of the other and to convince new converts to reject the vestiges of their old religion'.[22]

These texts reflect attempts by church leaders to come to terms, theologically as well as pastorally, with drastic political changes and subsequent social and religious ramifications. *The legend of Sergius Baḥīrā*, an early 9th-century Syriac text, for example, 'seeks to explain the rise of Islam from a Christian perspective', by 'revealing' that Muḥammad was influenced by a Christian monk called Baḥīrā.[23] The text exemplifies how genres such as polemics, apologetics and apocalyptic texts were entangled. The legend frames Islam as a 'simplified version of Christianity suitable for pagan Arabs' and is part of an apocalyptic vision about

---

20 The metropolitan of Erbil Isho'yahb III of Adiabene writes in the mid-7th century: 'As for the Arabs, to whom God has at this time given rule (*shūlṭānā*) over the world, you know well how they act towards us. Not only do they not oppose Christianity, but they praise our faith, honour the priests and saints of our Lord, and give aid to the churches and the monasteries. Why then do your *Mrwnaye* reject their faith on a pretext of theirs? And this when the *Mrwnaye* themselves admit that the Arabs have not compelled them to abandon their faith, but only asked them to give up half of their possessions in order to keep their faith. Yet they forsook their faith, which is forever, and retained half of their wealth, which is for a short time' (Hoyland, *Seeing Islam as others saw it*, p. 181; H. Teule, 'Isho'yahb III of Adiabene', in *CMR* 1, 133-6). John Tolan writes that, after three centuries, the 'majority' of Christians in the Near East had converted to Islam; J.V. Tolan, *Saracens. Islam in the medieval European imagination*, New York, 2002, p. 55.

21 M.N. Swanson, '*Fī tathlīth Allāh al-wāḥid*', in *CMR* 1, 330-3; P. Schadler, '*The dialogue between a Saracen and a Christian*', in *CMR* 1, 367-70. Other well-known apologetics include the *Disputation* by Patriarch Timothy I (see M. Heimgartner, 'Letter 59 (Disputation with the Caliph al-Mahdī)', in *CMR* 1, 522-6), and the works of Theodore Abū Qurra (see J.C. Lamoreaux, 'Theodore Abū Qurra', in *CMR* 1, 439-91).

22 Tolan, *Saracens*, p. 36.

23 B. Roggema, '*The legend of Sergius Baḥīrā*', in *CMR* 1, 600-3.

the rise of the 'Sons of Ishmael', while seeking to underscore the truth of the Christian faith.

Reflecting on the first centuries of Christian life under Muslim rule, Kedar observes that Christians 'had no choice but to engage in apologetics and polemics, since their self-preservation depended to a considerable extent on their ability to defend their faith against the pressure of the Muslim surrounding'.[24] Therefore, rather than entertaining plans for a mission to Muslims, most energy was channelled into discouraging Christians from converting to Islam. Aspirations of missions to Muslims may have been further curbed by the knowledge that in some settings there was an interdiction against converting from Islam (apostasy). Documents such as *The martyrdom of Anthony* (early 9th century), a sermon by *Gregory Dekapolis* and the *Documentum martyriale* (c. 857) by Eulogius of Cordova,[25] testify to this. However, as the *Ritual of abjuration*, *Tomos*, and other texts demonstrate, conversions from Islam to Christianity did occur.[26] Especially in contact zones such as the Iberian Peninsula, Crete and Sicily, religious identities seem to have been more transient, with conversions primarily perceived as problematic in times of interreligious tensions.[27] Further, the prevailing Christian conceptualisation of Islam was that it was a Christian heresy rather than an independent religious tradition. In his *Summa totius haeresis ac diabolicae sectae Saracenorum siue* (c. 1143) Peter of Cluny, for example, depicts Islam as 'the sum of all heresies previously known to Christendom'.[28] This may also to some extent explain why large-scale Christian mission to Muslims did not occur; heresies required correction rather than mission.[29]

24 Kedar, *Crusade and mission*, p. 36.

25 D.H. Vila, '*The martyrdom of Anthony* (*rawḥ al-Qurashī*)', in *CMR* 1, 498-501; D. Sahas, 'Gregory Dekapolites', in *CMR* 1, 614-17; Tolan, 'Eulogius of Cordova'.

26 A. Rigo, '*Ritual of abjuration*', in *CMR* 1, 821-4; N. Zorzi, '*Tomos*', in *CMR* 3, 759-63. See also Tolan, 'Jacques de Vitry', p. 301; Mallett, *Popular Muslim reactions*, p. 115.

27 R.W. Southern, *Western views of Islam in the Middle Ages*, Cambridge, 1962, p. 39; J. Coope, *The martyrs of Córdoba. Community and family conflict in an age of mass conversion*, Lincoln NE, 1995, pp. 16-17; R.J. Burns, 'Muslims in the thirteenth-century realms of Aragon. Interaction and reaction', in J.M. Powell (ed.), *Muslims under Latin rule, 1100-1300*, Princeton NJ, 1990, 57-102, p. 81; Mallett, *Popular Muslim reactions*, pp. 108-9.

28 Iogna-Prat and Tolan, 'Peter of Cluny', p. 607.

29 Tolan observes that in medieval Europe conceptualisations of Islam as paganism were also popular. He writes: 'This portrayal placed the Crusades firmly in an old and familiar place in Christian history, as part of the age-old struggle against pagan demon worship', and adds: 'The image is so common that writers on Islam who know better – from the twelfth century on – go to great pains to explain that the Saracens *are not* pagans' (Tolan, *Saracens*, p. 128).

Muslim conversion

By the 11th century, the theme of Muslim conversion begins to appear in texts with some frequency, often in the context of the Spanish *reconquista* or the crusades.[30] An early reference to what may have been a mission to Muslims is a passage in the *Life of Saint Nicon.*[31] This Greek text, probably written in Sparta in the mid-11th century, recounts that, after the fall of the Emirate of Crete in 961, the Byzantine monk Nikon Metanoeite travelled to Crete to preach.

> Now he reached the island just when it had been snatched from the hands of the Agarenes. [...] The island still bore traces of the vile superstition of the Agarenes, since its inhabitants, by time and long fellowship with the Saracens, alas! were led astray to their customs and foul and unhallowed rites. Therefore, when the great one began to cry 'Repent' according to his custom, they cried out against this strange and foreign preaching. And inflamed with passion, they violently opposed the just man, wishing to destroy him. The strangeness and unusualness of the thing inflamed them to obvious madness; for they were already converted, as our story has made clear, to the superstitious error of the Saracens. And so the blessed one saw their harshness and wildness, and realized that he would never prevail against their resistance without a wise plan. So he used, as they say, the next best tack, putting aside the first, and, in the manner of wise doctors, he wisely contrived their salvation. [...] Then he somehow gently seized upon their hearts[...] And so the blessed one, if not through the power of his word, but through that of virtue, was a wise fisherman and skilled in hunting souls of men.[32]

Whether or not Nicon's sojourn in Crete can be understood as an attempt to convert Muslims is a matter of conjecture. While some scholars maintain that he preached to Muslims, others presume that the author of Nicon's *Vita* embellished Nicon's achievements in Crete; they suggest that his main audience consisted of Muslims of Christian ancestry, whose families had only recently converted to Islam, or of Christians whose faith had been 'contaminated' by Islam.[33] Another early missionary

---

30 According to Kedar, two groups were most prone to conversion: members of the nobility who wanted to safeguard their social status, and slaves who considered conversion a means of emancipation (Kedar, *Crusade and mission*, p. 83; cf. Mallett, *Popular Muslim reactions*, pp. 109-10, 113, 116).

31 T. Pratsch, '*Life of Saint Nicon*', in *CMR* 2, 643-5.

32 D.F. Sullivan (ed. and trans., *The life of Saint Nikon*, Brookline MA, 1987, pp. 83-7.

33 Thomas Pratsch believes Nikon preached to Muslims; see 'Life of Saint Nicon', p. 644. Others disagree; see e.g. E. Voulgarakis, 'Nikon Metanoeite und die

expedition seems to have been undertaken by the hermit Anastasius of Cluny, who is said to have been sent to Spain on the instructions of Pope Gregory VII (r. 1073-85) around 1074. Transmitted only in *Vita S Anastasii auctore Galtero*, opinions vary as to whether Anastasius's work was among Muslims in the recently reconquered territories or in areas under Muslim rule.[34] The *Vita* relates that Anastasius's mission was unproductive and that he eventually returned to France.

The conversion of Muslims in reconquered territories is also a concern expressed by Pope Urban II (r. 1088-99), best known for summoning the First Crusade. Urban instructed the archbishop of Toledo 'to endeavour by word and example to convert, with God's grace, the infidels to the faith'.[35] However, there is little evidence that his instructions resulted in systematic missionary endeavours, though in reconquered Spain and Sicily occasional conversions from Islam to Christianity did occur.[36] Joseph O'Callaghan, discussing the position of *mudejars* in the reconquered territories in Castile and Portugal, attributes this partly to the accommodative attitude of the Spanish conquerers, and partly to the fact that many Muslims chose to leave the conquered territories, hoping for a turn of events with the Almoravid ascendency.[37] He writes: 'The impetus for mission among Muslims came from outside the peninsula',

Rechristianisierung der Kreter von Islam', *Zeitschrift für Missionswissenschaft und Religionswissenschaft* 47 (1963) 192-204, 258-69, p. 199; A. Louth, *Greek East and Latin West. The church 681-1071*, New York, 2007, p. 261; Sullivan, *Life of Saint Nikon*, pp. 278-9; A. Kaldellis, *Streams of gold, rivers of blood. The rise and fall of Byzantium, 955 AD to the First Crusade*, Oxford, 2017, pp. 37, 310. Ibn Jubayr claims that Crete's Muslims were forcibly converted after the conquest by the Byzantine Emperor Nicephoros II (r. 963-69). Ibn Jubayr, who describes the conversion of Muslims in Crete in a passage on Sicily, writes: 'The most clear-sighted of them fear that it shall chance to them as it did in earlier times to the Muslim inhabitants of Crete. There a Christian despotism so long visited them with one (painful) circumstance after another that they were all constrained to turn Christian, only those escaping whom God so decreed'; Ibn Jubayr, *The travels of Ibn Jubayr*, trans. and intro. R.J.C. Broadhurst, London, 1952, p. 259.

34 Kedar, *Crusade and mission*, p. 45.

35 Kedar, *Crusade and mission*, p. 46; T. Mastnak, 'Urban II', in *CMR* 3, 229-48.

36 For the way the various kingdoms related to their religious minorities, see e.g. J.M. Powell (ed.), *Muslims under Latin rule, 1100-1300*, Princeton NJ, 2014; B.A. Catlos, *The victors and the vanquished. Christians and Muslims of Catalonia and Aragon, 1050-1300*, Cambridge, 2004; H.J. Hames (ed.), *Jews, Muslims and Christians in and around the Crown of Aragon*, Leiden, 2004.

37 J.F. O'Callaghan, 'The Mudejars of Castile and Portugal in the twelfth and thirteenth centuries', in J.M. Powell (ed.), *Muslims under Latin rule 1100-1300*, Princeton NJ, 1990, 1-56, p. 14.

and 'Hispanic Christians seem not to have made any concerted effort to convert the subject Moors'.[38]

Texts written in 11th and 12th centuries appear to indicate that the theme of enforced conversion of Muslims raised fewer qualms in other parts of Europe. By the mid-12th century, conversion (including enforced conversion) of Muslims seems to have become widely accepted as a central goal of the crusades. Hugh of Flavigny's account of the pilgrimage of Richard, Abbott of St-Vanne, for example, expresses the need for Muslim conversion in connection with pilgrimage and the crusades.[39] Similar sentiments are expressed in the Latin hagiography *Martyrdom of Bishop Thiemo* (early 12th century),[40] the account or the siege and conquest of Lisbon in *De expugnatione Lyxbonensi* (c. 1147) and the *Instruction in the Catholic faith to the sultan* (c. 1177) by Pope Alexander III (r. 1159-81).[41] Also, Peter of Cluny, in his preface to *Contra sectam Saracenorum* (c. 1155), mentions Muslim conversion, though he seems to have had few illusions that his Latin refutation would actually produce tangible results.[42] The opening chapter of Pfaffe Konrad's *Rolandslied*, written around 1170, also takes up the theme. It describes the crusader ideals, the readiness to become a martyr at the hands of Muslims, the rumours of Muslim leaders willing to convert, and the necessity of evangelisation and baptism. In the opening pages, Pfaffe Konrad has Bishop St Johannes exclaim:

> 'Should my lord be willing – and I hope for his support,' he said, 'I would like to cross the Guadalquivir River to the city of Almeria and there proclaim God's word. I do not fear death in any form. If I were worthy of

---

38 O'Callaghan, 'Mudejars of Castile', pp. 46, 48. O'Callaghan supports his argument with a reference to Alfonso X of Castile's *Siete partidas* (mid-13th century), which approved of mission by example but rejected all forms of enforced conversion. The text instructs Christians 'to labor by good words and suitable preaching to convert the Moors and cause them to believe in our faith and to lead them to it not by force nor by pressure . . . for (the Lord) is not pleased by service that men give him through fear, but with that that they do willingly and without any pressure' (O'Callaghan, 'Mudejars of Castile', p. 50).

39 P. Healy, 'Hugh of Flavigny', in *CMR* 3, 301-6. A. Cutler, 'The First Crusade and the idea of conversion', *The Muslim World* 58 (1968) 57-71, 155-64; see also A. Cutler, *Catholic missions to Muslims at the end of the First Crusade*, Los Angeles CA, 1963 (PhD Diss. University of Southern California); http://digitallibrary.usc.edu/cdm/ref/collection/p15799coll17/id/154281.

40 J. Tolan, *'Martyrdom of Bishop Thiemo'*, in *CMR* 3, 555-7.

41 J. Tolan, 'Alexander III', in *CMR* 3, 695-6.

42 Peter of Cluny writes: 'If the Moslems cannot be converted by it, at least it is right for the learned to support the weaker brethren in the Church, who are so easily scandalized by small things', cited in Southern, *Western views of Islam*, p. 39.

> having fire or sword purify my body and God so willed, then I could be certain that He wanted me.'[43]

Likewise, Byzantine texts of the period also refer to Muslim conversion. *The Alexiad* (c. 1148) by Anna Comnena speaks about the ambitions of her father, Emperor Alexius I Comnenus (r. 1081-1118), 'to bring into the fold of our church not only the Scythian nomads, but also the whole of Persia, as well as the barbarians who inhabit Libya and Egypt and follow the rites of Mohammed'. Muslim subjects in lands reconquered by the Byzantine crown were either enforced or more often enticed to embrace Christianity, it seems.[44] However, in most of these works, mission to Muslims remains a literary imaginary. Substantial and tangible missionary work among Muslims only began to emerge in the second decade of the 13th century, and it would take the mendicant orders to transform the ideas, and the ideals, into action.

The mendicant missions to Muslims

Jessica Bird situates the origins of mission (in the strict sense of the word) to Muslims within the Parisian reform circles around Peter the Chanter (d. 1197). Bird states that the Parisian group, which included men such as Jacques de Vitry (d. 1240) and Oliver of Paderborn (d. 1227),[45] was strongly influenced by the apocalyptic writings of Joachim of Fiore (d. 1202);[46] they interpreted the crises that afflicted Europe (e.g. wars, heresy, 'pagans' in the Baltics, Muslims in Spain and the eastern Mediterranean) as signs of the Apocalypse. Attributing these crises to a lack of religious commitment, they aspired to spiritual renewal and ecclesial reform, concerns that were also at the centre of the Fourth Lateran Council (1215). By demonstrating that people like De Vitry and Oliver de Paderborn were also associated with the Albigensian and Baltic crusades, Bird argues that mission to Muslims was part of a much larger movement of renewal, which included spiritual renewal of churches in Europe and the Orient and the suppression of heresy (Abigensians and Muslims), a

---

[43] J.W. Thomas (ed. and trans.), *Priest Konrad's Song of Roland*, Columbia SC, 1994, p. 27.

[44] Anna Comnena, *The Alexiad*, trans., E.A.W. Dawes, Cambridge, Ontario, 2000, p. 116.

[45] J. Bird, 'Oliver of Paderborn', in *CMR* 4, 212-29.

[46] McGinn, 'Joachim of Fiore'.

view also advanced by John Tolan.[47] Several names are linked to these beginnings of systematised missions; most prominent among them are Jacques de Vitry,[48] Oliver of Paderborn, Francis of Assisi (d. 1226)[49] and the founder of the Dominican order, Dominic Guzmán (1170-1221).[50]

Jacques de Vitry, bishop of Acre between 1216 and 1229, had already gained a reputation as a popular preacher before he was appointed bishop of Acre, promoting spiritual renewal and crusader ideals. On arrival in the crusader kingdom, he was shocked by the life-style of its residents and the melée of Christian traditions in the Holy Land, and he took to preaching tours to try to remedy the situation. It seems that the first Muslim conversions occurred as a by-product of this itinerant Christian ministry. According to Tolan, de Vitry had a basic knowledge of Islam and was probably familiar with some of the popular polemical writings on Islam of his time, such as the works of William of Tyre (d. c. 1185)[51] and Petrus Alfonsi (d. after 1116).[52] Tolan also writes that de Vitry, in his *Historia orientalis*, concludes 'that it is not difficult to convert Muslims to Christianity through preaching and example, and that many learned Muslims realize the falseness of their faith and are ready to abandon it'.[53]

Not averse to enforced baptism, de Vitry took up work among Muslim captives, and among enslaved children in particular. His letters, written during his participation in the Fifth Crusade, describe how Muslims fleeing the beleaguered city of Damietta offered themselves or their children for baptism in order to escape enslavement or death. They also document that, after the fall of Damietta in 1219, de Vitry bought some 500 children from among the captives, baptised them and had them raised as Christians by friends or nuns.[54] Though an avid supporter of

---

47 J. Bird, 'Crusade and conversion after the Fourth Lateran Council (1215). Oliver of Paderborn's and James of Vitry's mission to Muslims reconsidered', *Essays in Medieval Studies* 21 (2004) 23-47, pp. 24-5; Tolan, *Saracens*, pp. 199-201, 216-18.

48 Tolan, 'Jacques de Vitry'.

49 J. Tolan, *Saint Francis and the sultan. The curious history of a Christian-Muslim encounter*, Oxford, 2009; R. Armour, *Islam, Christianity and the West. A troubled history*, Maryknoll NY, 2004, p. 88.

50 Kedar, *Crusade and mission*, pp. 120-1.

51 A. Mallett, 'William of Tyre', in *CMR* 3, 769-77.

52 J. Tolan, 'Petrus Alfonsi', in *CMR* 3, 356-62. There are interesting similarities between de Vitry's work among enslaved children and those of e.g. the Spiritans in East Africa in the 19th century; see P. Kollmann, *The evangelisation of slaves and Catholic origins in East Africa*, Maryknoll NY, 2005.

53 Tolan, 'Jacques de Vitry', pp. 298, 301.

54 See also Bombi, 'Fifth Crusade'.

the crusades, de Vitry believed in the two-tier strategy of military campaigns and preaching.[55] His *Epistola* 6 and *Historia occidentalis*, possibly the earliest sources on Francis of Assisi's renowned encounter with the Egyptian Sultan Malik al-Kāmil, laud the Franciscan missions to the Saracens because of their public preaching and exemplary lifestyle of humility and simplicity, but are also somewhat sceptical about what this approach would accomplish.[56]

The Paris-trained cleric Oliver of Paderborn, who recruited for and participated in the Fifth Crusade, also witnessed Francis's attempt to evangelise the sultan. Emboldened by Malik al-Kāmil's honourable treatment of both Francis and Christian prisoners of war, Oliver wrote two letters, a *Letter to al-Kāmil of Egypt*, and a *Letter to the learned men of Egypt*, inviting them to convert to Christianity and allow Christian missionary work in their realm. Oliver can be considered a representative of the time-honoured approach that sought to convert sovereigns, as being gatekeepers to the evangelisation of a people, while his letters are indicative of the persistent rumours in medieval Christendom that some Muslim rulers were willing to convert. His missionary tactic hinged on rational argumentation,[57] a strategy that would be honed to perfection by the Dominicans.[58]

Another key figure in the development of mission to Muslims (theoretically as well as actually) is Francis of Assisi. While Francis's encounter with the Ayyubid sultan in 1219 is probably the best-known episode in Francis's attempts at Muslim conversion,[59] possibly the earlier of his

---

55 Tolan, 'Jacques de Vitry', p. 298.

56 Bombi, 'Fifth Crusade', p. 74; Tolan, 'Jacques de Vitry', p. 305.

57 In his letter, Oliver of Paderborn links mission and crusade by maintaining that the military intervention is the result of the rejection of mission. He states: 'If your people had publicly granted admittance to the teaching of Christ and his preachers, God's church would gladly have sent them the sword of God's word, and joyfully invited them to the community of faith. But because it does not find any other remedy against the Saracen might, the law of the Catholic princes licitly makes use of the material sword for the defense of Christianity and the recovery of its right. For assuredly all laws and all rights permit the repulsion of force by force' (Kedar, *Crusade and mission*, p. 132).

58 Bird, 'Oliver of Paderborn', pp. 218-22. It is uncertain whether the letters were actually sent or were a mere literary exercise.

59 Studies on Francis's encounter with Sultan Malik al-Kāmil are numerous. See e.g. J. Hoeberichts, *Franciscus en de Islam*, Utrecht, 1991, English trans. *Francis and Islam*, Quincy IL, 1997; Tolan, *Saint Francis and the sultan*; P. Moses, *The saint and the sultan. The crusades, Islam and Francis of Assisi's mission of peace*, New York, 2009; G. Dardess and M.L. Krier Mich, *In the spirit of St Francis and the sultan. Catholics and Muslims working together for the common good*, Maryknoll NY, 2011; K. Warren, *Daring to cross the threshold. Francis of Assisi encounters Sultan Malek al Kamil*, Eugene OR, 2012; J. Hoeberichts, *Franciscus en de Sultan. Mannen van vrede*, Nijmegen, 2012; Bombi, 'Fifth Crusade'.

two rules, the *Regula non bullata* (1221), gives more insight into how he envisioned this. Chapter 16, entitled *Those who are going among Saracens and other non-believers*, states:

> The Lord says: Behold, I am sending you as lambs in the midst of wolves. Therefore, be prudent as serpents and simple as doves (Mt. 10:16). [...] As for the brothers who go, they can live spiritually among [the Saracens and nonbelievers] in two ways. One way is not to engage in arguments or disputes, but to be subject to every human creature for God's sake (1 Pet. 2:13) and to acknowledge that they are Christians. Another way is to proclaim the word of God when they see that it pleases the Lord, so that they believe in the all-powerful God – Father, and Son, and Holy Spirit – the Creator of all, in the Son Who is the Redeemer and Saviour, and that they be baptized and become Christians.[60]

For Francis, mission was an integral aspect of the re-enactment of the *vita apostolica* that he envisioned, and mission to Muslims was part of an all-encompassing mission project that would eventually bring Franciscans to Karakorum (William of Rubroeck / Rubruck), China, India, New Spain, West Africa and Mozambique.[61] Following in Christ's Apostles' footsteps of mission by preaching and example, martyrdom was one of the possible – and at times inevitable – consequences of this venture, and considered the ultimate witness to the Gospel.[62]

Apart from his encounter with Sultan Malik al-Kāmil, Francis was never personally involved in mission to Muslims. His call for mission among the Saracens and the suggestion of a possible martyrdom in

60 *Francis and Clare. The complete works*, ed. and trans. R.J. Armstrong and I.C. Braidy, New York, 1982, p. 121. For a discussion, see L. Gallant, 'Francis of Assisi forerunner of interreligious dialogue. Chapter 16 of the Earlier Rule revisited', *Franciscan Studies* 64 (2006) 53-82.

61 J. Moorman, *History of the Franciscan order. From its origins to the year 1517*, Oxford, 1968; C. Dawson (ed.), *The Mongol mission. Narratives and letters to the Franciscan missionaries in Mongolia and China in the thirteenth and fourteenth centuries*, New York, 1955; A. Camps, *The Friars Minor in China (1294-1955)*, Hong Kong, 2000; A. Camps, 'Franciscan missions to the Mogul Court', in A. Camps, *Studies in Asian mission history 1958-1996*, Leiden, 2014, 60-74; S.E. Turley, *Franciscan spirituality and mission in New Spain 1524-1599. Conflict beneath the sycamore tree*, Burlington VT, 2013; C. Racheado, 'Alexis de St. Lô', in *CMR* 11, 556-60; C. Racheado, 'Gaspar de Seville', in *CMR* 11, 573-7; N. Vila-Santa, 'Francisco Coutinho', in *CMR* 7, 849-52. See also J. Richard, *La Paupeté et les missions d'orient au moyen age (XIIIe-XVe siècle)*, Rome, 1977, and A. Müller, *Bettelmönche in islamischer Fremde. Institutionelle Rahmenbedingungen franziskanischer und dominikanischer Mission in muslimischen Räumen des 13. Jahrhunderts*, Münster, 2002.

62 Bombi, Kedar and Tolan differ over the extent to which martyrdom was part of Francis's aims in mission among Muslims, or whether the emphasis on martyrdom was introduced his Franciscan biographers; see Bombi, 'Fifth Crusade', p. 71; Tolan, *Saracens*, p. 215; Kedar, *Crusade and mission*, pp. 124-5.

the process, however, found ample response among his friars, many of whom, according to Tolan, were characterised more by a zeal for preaching and martyrdom than by knowledge of Islam. As early as 1220, six friars were martyred after attacking Islam in Muslim Seville and Morocco. They were the first of a long list of Franciscan martyrs who died at the hands of (often reluctant) Muslim authorities: six Franciscans were put to death in Ceuta in 1224, two in Valencia in 1228, five in Marrakesh in 1232, one in Fez in 1246, ten in the Near East in the period 1265-9 and seven in Tripoli in 1289.[63] Kedar pointedly observes:

> But since it soon transpired that Mendicant missionizing in Muslim countries was much more conducive to filling heaven with Christian martyrs than the earth with Muslim converts, and that preaching stood a chance of success only among Muslims subjected to Christian rule, practical men could not regard this Mendicant activity as a viable solution to the Muslim threat.[64]

Tolan interprets the fact that most of these martyrs were not canonised until 1442 as an indication that the Vatican was ambivalent towards this mission-by-martyrdom strategy.[65] Francis's rule of 1223, the *Regula Bullata*, may possibly reflect this ambivalence; it restricts mission among 'the Saracens' to those who are considered suitable by their superiors. Furthermore, contemporaries criticised the Franciscan quest for martyrdom. Thomas of Chantom wrote:

> It therefore seems that preachers should not hesitate to go and preach where they know they will be killed as long as it is the authority of the church that sends them. But to this some say that things are different with the Saracens than they once were with the Gentiles. For the Gentiles listened to the preaching of the apostles and others and argued with them, and many of them were converted by them. They did not kill the preachers as long as any hope remained that they might pervert them to their idolatry. But now it has been decreed among the Saracens that if anyone comes as a preacher, as soon as he names Christ, he should immediately be killed without being heard out. And so they say that to go to such people is not

---

63 Tolan, *Saracens*, p. 218. Kedar also hypothesises that the friars' bold attacks on Islam were not merely instigated by a desire for Muslim converts or attempts to gain the martyr's palm, but were also a tactic to ensure Muslims' eternal condemnation: 'Moreover, it is plausible to assume that among the friars who adopted this stance, there were some who [...] believed that by openly attacking the religion of the Saracens and calling upon them to convert, they would ensure eternal punishment for their unrepentant listeners' (Kedar, *Crusade and mission*, p. 126).

64 Kedar, *Crusade and mission*, p. 155.

65 Tolan, *Saracens*, p. 218.

> to go to preaching, but rather to go to death without preaching. Nor are they certain that God will produce miracles through them when they die.[66]

The Franciscan strategy of preaching without knowledge of Arabic and Islam was criticised even within the Franciscan order itself. Roger Bacon (d. after 1292) for example, in his *Opus maius*, writes that 'no one knows the necessary languages; the types of unbelief have not been studied and distinguished; and there has been no study of the arguments by which each can be refuted';[67] therefore he 'proposed preaching, rational arguments and study of languages as the most effective means to convert the infidel'.[68] Much of the content of Bacon's criticism of the Franciscan missionary strategy had already been taken up by the other mendicant order with missionary ambitions: the Dominicans. From the mid-13th century onwards most of the Iberian Peninsula had been reconquered, leading to more and more Muslims and Jews living under Christian rule.

The Dominican order aspired to conversion in the newly conquered territories. Initially founded by Dominic Guzmán to combat the Cathars, the Dominicans soon directed their energy to Jews and Muslims under Christian rule. But where the Franciscans opted for public preaching and martyrdom, often openly vilifying Islam and its prophet, the Dominicans opted for an intellectual approach.[69] According to Tolan, the 'Dominican friars studied Arabic, pored over Koran and Hadith, engaged Muslim scholars in theological debate, and preached to captive Muslim audiences in the mosques of the Crown of Aragon' in the hope of proving Christianity's superiority.[70] Dominicans like Raymond de Peynafort (d. 1275)[71] and Ramon Martí (c. 1220-c. 1284)[72] established Arabic schools in Valencia to teach its Arabic-speaking Muslim population the rudiments of the Christian faith. De Peynaforte claimed that, through the schools he founded, tens of thousands of (often upper-class) Muslims were converted.[73]

---

66 Cited as in Tolan, *Saracens*, pp. 230-1.

67 Southern, *Western views of Islam*, p. 57. For a discussion of Bacon by Southern, see pp. 56-61; see also A. Power, 'Roger Bacon', in *CMR* 4, 457-70.

68 A. Klemeshov, 'The conversion and destruction of the infidels in the works of Roger Bacon', in J. Carvalho (ed.), *Religion and power in Europe. Conflict and convergence*, Pisa, 2007, 15-27.

69 The Gregorian report, summarised in Matthew Paris's *Chronica majora*, gives some insight in the lines of argumentation of the Dominicans; see L. Giamalva, 'The Gregorian report', in *CMR* 4, 259-63.

70 Tolan, *Saracens*, p. 172.

71 Tolan, 'Raymond de Penyafort', pp. 253-8.

72 T.E. Burman, 'Ramon Marti', in *CMR* 4, 381-90.

73 Burns, 'Muslims in the thirteenth-century', p. 83. Burns points to a difference of the treatment of the Muslim population in Aragon and Castile (who were typically banned,

The Dominican approach, as espoused by men like Ramon Martí (Spain), Thomas Aquinas (Italy),[74] Alfonso Buenhombre (Marrakesh),[75] William of Tripoli (Acre)[76] and Riccoldo da Monte di Croce (Baghdad),[77] hinged on persuasion by rational arguments. In-depth knowledge of Jewish and Muslim sources, however, did not make the Dominican representations of Islam and Muḥammad any more sympathetic. Rather, public debates with representatives from the Jewish and Muslim elite, with their rational but vehement attacks on Jewish and Muslim sacred scriptures as contradictory, confusing and irrational, proved counter-productive and hardened Jewish and Muslim resistance to conversion. Despite de Peynaforte's claims of Muslim conversions, by the end of the 13th century the hope that Muslims would willingly convert in large numbers had begun to dwindle. The fall of Acre (1291), the enslavement of large numbers of Christians, the conversion of the Mongol Ilkhan Ghazan (r. 1295-1304) to Islam, and the subsequent destruction of churches, synagogues and Buddhist temples, seemed to signal Muslim advance rather than defeat.

The letters of Riccoldo da Monte di Croce (d. 1320) reflect his disillusionment and despondency at this turn of events; he writes: '[...] the people of the East now openly say that you [God] are powerless to help us', and: 'If it pleases you that Muḥammad rules, make this known to us so that we might venerate him.'[78] Bird, reflecting on these early Franciscan and Dominican missions among Muslims, writes that '(a)lthough hopes for the conversion of Muslim rulers persisted, most missionaries from both the Franciscan and Dominican orders soon focused their efforts on preventing apostasy among Latin Christians living in proximity with suspect groups and on Christian captives, who it was feared would convert to Islam or eastern Christian sects'.[79]

---

enslaved or given the choice to migrate with only their portable belongings) from that accorded to Valencia's substantial Muslim population. The Valencian Muslims were allowed to continue practising their religion. As most of them were only literate in Arabic, the Dominicans established Arabic schools to persuade them to convert to Christianity.

74 D. Burrell and J. Tolan, 'Thomas Aquinas', in *CMR* 4, 521-9.

75 Tolan, *Saracens*, pp. 281-2.

76 T.E. Burman, 'William of Tripoli', in *CMR* 4, 515-20.

77 T.E. Burman, 'Riccoldo da Monte di Croce', in *CMR* 4, 678-91.

78 Burman, 'Riccoldo da Monte di Croce', p. 681.

79 Bird, 'Crusade and conversion', p. 30.

The Muslim in our midst

By the mid-13th century, the Reconquista had brought most of the Iberian Peninsula under Christian rule, but its on-going impact on social and societal interactions in the reconquered territories sparked a yearning for a new, more peaceful order among some intellectuals. One such person was Raymond (Ramon / Raimundo) Llull (d. c. 1315). Born into a noble family on Mallorca just after the island had been reconquered by James I of Aragon (r. 1213-76), Llull grew up in a predominantly Muslim society, but was also a first-hand witness of the rapid impoverishment and marginalisation of Mallorca's Muslim population.[80] A series of visions (c. 1263) signalled a turning point in his life. Having witnessed the discord brought about by religious and linguistic diversity, he decided to abandon his life as a courtier, become a Franciscan tertiary and dedicate himself to the pursuit of a world in which these diversities were surmounted. In Llull's view, this new order could only be attained by purging it of diversity; the conversion of Muslims (and Jews) played a central role in this project. This evokes from Gregory Stone the remark that 'Llull's effort to replace physical combat with the verbal construction of a new world is an infliction on others of a discursive power ultimately more destructive of alterity and more pernicious than military action.'[81]

Llull spent the remainder of his life in quest of this new order. He studied Arabic and preached to Muslims, tried to write the best possible book to explain Christianity to Muslims (the *Ars major*) and lobbied for missionary training schools where aspiring missionaries could study Islam and Arabic.[82] To bring about Muslim conversion, he conceived of a method of preaching that replicated the Dominican approach in its emphasis on knowledge of Islam, but differed from the Dominicans by its positive argumentation.[83] Though Llull continued to hold onto Christianity as the only true religion, his writings demonstrate regard for Islam and contend that missionaries could and should build on what Muslims already believed.[84] Llull made several unsuccessful missionary journeys

80 G.B. Stone, 'Ramon Llull', in M.R. Menocal, R.P Schneidlin and M. Sells (eds), *The literature of al-Andalus*, Cambridge, 2012, 345-57.

81 Stone, 'Ramon Llull', p. 348.

82 With the financial backing of King James of Mallorca, Llull was able to open such a school in a monastery in Miramar, Mallorca, in about 1276. It was frequented by Franciscan missionaries who wanted to study Arabic; Hames, 'Ramon Llull', p. 705.

83 Hames, 'Ramon Llull'.

84 Tolan, *Saracens*, pp. 256-8.

to North Africa (to Tunis in 1293 and 1314, and to Bougie in 1307), leaving him somewhat disillusioned regarding the feasibility of his project.

Llull's project is best illustrated in *The gentile and the three wise men* (1274),[85] which presents 'a cordial debate between a Jew, a Christian and a Muslim before a Gentile who seeks the truth'.[86] Llull has each of the discussants explain his faith to the Gentile, after which the men depart, leaving it to the Gentile to decide which religion is best. In the course of the discussion one of the characters exclaims:

> Ah! What a great good fortune it would be if [...] we could all – every man on earth – be under one religion and belief, so that there would be no more rancour or ill will among men, who hate each other because of diversity and contrariness of beliefs and sects! And just as there is only one God, Father, Creator and Lord of everything that exists, so all peoples could unite and become one people. (Prologue, *Selected works*, vol. 1, p. 116)[87]

The book stands out among contemporary publications because of its fair and informed representation of the three religions and its lack of polemics. Though it is open-ended and the reader is left in the dark as to the Gentile's preference, close reading reveals that the Gentile critically interrogates the Muslim position repeatedly, thus displaying a bias towards Christianity.[88]

Though the older Llull continued to advocate the importance of preaching and prayer, he also endorsed a more confrontational approach. Realising that mere preaching would not achieve Muslim conversion and the envisioned new order, Llull validated the idea of military expeditions (e.g. a crusade to recover Acre) that would compel Muslim rulers to admit Christian preachers. Highly educated preachers trained in Arabic were to accompany these crusading armies to preach to prisoners of war. Llull believed that these prisoners, once subjected to enforced Christian education, would convert to Christianity without much resistance. Thus, by the end of his life, Llull was convinced that his dream of a new order would only be realised by the wielding of the Church's 'two swords (intellectual and corporeal power)'.[89] In the grand Franciscan

---

[85] Hames, 'Ramon Llull', pp. 709-12.

[86] Hames, 'Ramon Llull', p. 709.

[87] Cited in Stone, 'Ramon Llull', p. 346.

[88] Tolan describes the book as an 'irenic island' in a 'sea of tempestuous disputation and polemic', but also states that closer scrutiny of the text reveals a distinct bias towards the ideas brought forward by the Christian (Tolan, *Saracens*, p. 266).

[89] Stone, 'Ramon Llull', p. 247.

tradition of martyrdom, legend has it that Llull was stoned by an angry mob of Muslims in Tunis or Bougie whilst on a missionary expedition and died of his injuries (1315 or 1316), either in North Africa or on the journey home to Mallorca.

Llull was not the only scholar in late medieval times who pursued peace amidst religious and cultural diversity. The quest for peace and unity also features prominently in the work of Nicholas of Cusa (1401-64)[90] and Juan de Segovia (c. 1390-1458),[91] though both lived in a time of Ottoman advance, iconically embodied in the fall of Constantinople. Both men had attended the Council of Basel (1431) and were influenced by its achievement of reconciling with the majority of the Hussites through cautious, respectful negotiation. The optimism that followed the Council – based on the belief that it was possible to heal the major schisms in the Church – is evident in Nicholas of Cusa's *De pace fide* (1453).[92] The book presents a fictive setting in which wise men from various religious traditions engage in a conversation, only to conclude that 'their faith and religion is one, under a diversity of rites (*una religio in rituum varietate*)'.[93] In a later day and age, Theodor Bibliander's *De monarchia* (1533) made a similar case for the universal nature of religion.[94] And Nicholas of Cusa's *Cribratio Alkorani* (1461) also testifies to a genuine interest in Islam's sacred text and reflects his serious consideration of the possibility that nuggets of truth can be found in the Qur'an.

Where Nicholas of Cusa's work seems to promote dialogue and interreligious reconciliation rather than mission, his contemporary and friend Juan de Segovia considered Muslim conversion non-negotiable. Influenced like Nicholas by the Council of Basel, Juan de Segovia maintained that, before Muslims could be receptive to Christian mission, their misconceptions about Christianity needed to be redressed. Once this was

---

90 J. Tolan, 'Nicholas of Cusa', in *CMR* 5, 421-8. See also I.A. Levy, D.F. Duclow and R. George-Tvrtković (eds), *Nicholas of Cusa and Islam. Polemic and dialogue in the late Middle Ages*, Leiden, 2014.

91 A.M. Wolf, 'Juan de Segovia', in *CMR* 5, 429-42; A.M. Wolf, *Juan de Segovia and the fight for peace. Christians and Muslims in the fifteenth century*, Notre Dame IN, 2014.

92 For the text, see *Nicolas of Cusa's De pace fidei and cribratio alkorani. Translation and analysis*, trans. J. Hopkins, Minneapolis MN, 1994, pp. 33-71.

93 Tolan, 'Nicholas of Cusa', p. 423.

94 B. Gordon, 'Theodor Bibliander', in *CMR* 6, 673-85. Because Bibliander believed that the second coming of Christ was imminent, he considered it a Christian duty to evangelise Muslims. His three-volume *Machumetis Saracenorum pricipis, eiusque successorum vitae, ac doctrina, ipseque Alcoran* (1543) was intended to serve as a preparation for missionaries to Muslims. He considered knowledge of the Qur'an essential for the success of missions.

accomplished, the Christian message could be preached by means of a *via pacis et doctrinae* in a terminology comprehensible and inoffensive to Muslims. Missionary access to territories under Muslim rule, in Juan de Segovia's opinion, would have to be achieved via diplomatic negotiations rather than by military means. Anne Marie Wolf writes: 'Any contemporaries who had hoped for a quick solution would have been frustrated by his long-range approach to their problem.'[95]

Few contemporaries, it seems, seriously engaged with the ideas of Nicholas of Cusa and Juan de Segovia, with one noted exception: Hernando de Talavera (d. 1507).[96] In post-1492 Spain, the two dominant approaches to Muslim conversion, persuasion or force, are personified in the iconic figures of Hernando de Talavera and Francisco Jiménez de Cisneros (1436-1517). De Talavera had been trained at the University of Salamanca; influenced by the ideas of Juan de Segovia and Nicholas de Cusa he seems to have conceived of Islam as both a religion and a culture.[97] When after the fall of Granada (1492) he was appointed its archbishop, de Talavera implemented a missionary strategy that he had developed in Seville and described in his *Católica impugnación* (1479). The strategy hinged on the dual approach of acculturation and evangelisation of the newly converted. De Talavera argued that observance of everyday religious practice (e.g. making the sign of the cross), and the accommodation of Christian identity markers in terms of dress code and language, would diminish the distinctions between 'old' and 'new' Christians and would facilitate the integration of the newly converted. He also believed that outward practice would serve as a preparation for inward conversion.

Alongside attention to performative religion, de Talavera recognised that effective religious instruction of Muslims required teachers, who were familiar with Arabic as well as with Muslim beliefs and practices, to have a conviction reminiscent of what Ramon de Penyaforte and Ramon Martí had underscored with regard to the Valencian *mudejars*. Isabella Iannuzzi writes:

> Talavera perceived the importance of the everyday as a normalising factor for both the newly converted and the host community. This is the great novelty of his approach. Only by carefully preparing the clergy in Christian

---

95 Wolf, *Juan de Segovia and the fight for peace*, p. 175. For an elaborate discussion of Juan de Segovia's views on Muslim conversion, see pp. 175-222.

96 I. Iannuzzi, 'Hernando de Talavera', in *CMR* 6, 59-66.

97 Iannuzzi, 'Hernando de Talavera', p. 65.

> teachings and in the culture of those who are to be converted is effective evangelisation possible. Thus, he was eager for his priests in Granada to learn Arabic [...] In the cultural *milieu* of the University of Salamanca, Talavera had absorbed the ideas of Juan de Segovia and Nicolas de Cusa about the conversion of Muslims by addressing cultural differences as well as difference in belief.[98]

De Talavera personifies a pastoral approach to Muslim conversion, advocating the gradual initiation of Muslims into the Christian faith. Likewise, there are indications that contemporaries, such as Gómez García and his *Carro de dos vidas* (1500),[99] Juan Bautista de Jerónimo Anyés (1480-1553)[100] and Pedro de Alcalá (d. after 1508) 'regarded Muslims as lost rather than recalcitrant and they thought that patient preaching of the Christian Gospel in the Muslims' own language, using terms that they would recognize (such as *miḥrāb* for altar, *ṣalāt* for the mass), would secure true conversions'.[101] To facilitate Christian education of Muslims, de Alcalá composed an Arabic grammar. The tone of his introduction to this is respectful towards Muslims, and in the religious texts he included in the grammar itself he adopted Muslim terms (e.g. *Allāh, miḥrāb* and *ṣalāt*) to describe Christian beliefs and practices.[102] Similarly, Pedro Ramirez de Alba's *Doctrina Christiana* (c. 1526), which aimed to explain Christianity and Christian practices to newly baptised Moriscos, shows no disdain for Islam, but rather represents a genuine invitation to the newly converted to inwardly embrace the Christian faith after outward baptism. It also pleads with the *Cristianos viejos* to willingly receive the new converts into their community and provide them with good examples.[103] In Valencia, whose sizable Muslim population had been forced to convert in the aftermath of the revolt of the Germanías (1519-22), Bernando Pérez

---

98 Iannuzzi, 'Hernando de Talavera', p. 65.

99 R. Perez, 'Gómez García', in *CMR* 6, 54-9. García's book presents an entreaty for a peaceful evangelisation of Muslims and was published just after the Mudéjar revolt in Granada. This signalled the beginning of the politics of enforced conversion, spearheaded by Archbishop Francisco Jiménez de Cisneros.

100 For the instruction of Moriscos in Valencia, see also B.F. Llopis, 'Juan Bautista de Jerónimo Anyés', in *CMR* 6, 144-9. Anyés favours an irenic approach to evangelise Valencia's Moriscos. Standing in the humanist tradition, he considers Muslims to be 'innocents' who are born in the wrong religion and need guidance and education to come to the true faith.

101 M.T. Frederiks, 'Introduction: Christians, Muslims and empires in the sixteenth century', in *CMR* 6, 1-10, p. 5.

102 O. Zwartjes, 'Pedro de Alcalá', *CMR* 6, 73-8; M.J. Framiñán de Miguel, 'Martín Pérez de Alaya', in *CMR* 7, 207-14.

103 L. Resines, 'Pedro Ramírez de Alba', in *CMR* 6, 93-5.

de Chinchón (d. 1548) composed a series of sermons that in simple but respectful words reject Muslim beliefs and teach Christianity.[104]

While throughout the 16th century there was support in Spain for the method of conversion by persuasion, the more hardline approach of enforced conversion, as advocated and implemented by Cardinal Francisco Jiménez de Cisneros, found more widespread patronage. From 1499 onwards, he ordered the burning of Islamic books and the transformation of mosques into churches in Granada, and forced its Muslims to submit to baptism. His close companion, Antonio García de Villalpando (d. 1513), supported his campaign against Islam and argued that it was legal for the monarchs to confiscate Muslim and Jewish property.[105] In Zaragoza, Joan Martí Figuerola's aggressive missionary tactics of entering the mosque to preach and refute Islam (1519) caused such commotion among Muslims, as well as the civil authorities, that he was asked to leave the town.[106] In Aragón, the Augustinian friar Alonso de Orozco (1500-91) wrote a popular, polemical catechism, which depicted Islam as the work of the devil and propagated Christianity as the only and absolute truth. The fact that the catechism saw three editions between 1568 and 1575 indicates the widespread support for his views.[107] Also, Pedro Guerra de Lorca's *Catecheses mysagogicae* (1586)[108] and the *Catecismo del Sacromonte* (1588)[109] were strongly polemical, condemning Islam as well as Moriscos who retained their former cultural and linguistic habits. Yet despite these aggressive missionary techniques, the continued resistance of Moriscos to embrace Christianity is evident from the numerous documents (royal laws, edicts, *pragmáticas*, as well as Church documents) issued throughout the 16th century, instructing Moriscos to convert and/or change their lifestyle. During the course of the century, the tone of these documents became increasingly harsh, ultimately culminating in the expulsion of the Moriscos in 1608.[110]

---

104 F. Pons Fuster, 'Bernardo Pérez de Chinchón', in *CMR* 6, 119-24.
105 A.I. Carrasco Manchado, 'Antonio García de Villalpando', in *CMR* 6, 49-53.
106 E. Ruiz García, 'Joan Martí Figuerola', in *CMR* 6, 88-92.
107 L. Resines, 'Alonso de Orozco', in *CMR* 7, 219-23.
108 J. Busic, 'Pedro Guerra de Lorca', in *CMR* 7, 250-8.
109 L. Resines, 'Catechismo del Sacromonte', in *CMR* 7, 265-7.
110 Frederiks, 'Introduction: Christians, Muslims', pp. 2-7.

Mission beyond Latin Christendom

As Christian missions to Muslims in Spain, Italy, North Africa and the Crusader states had demonstrated, neither exemplary lifestyle, persuasion or intellectual engagement nor force had been able to secure large numbers of Muslim converts; disenchantment over this fact gradually turned into bitterness, animosity and repression, with the expulsion of the Moriscos from Spain in 1608 as its all-time low.[111] Yet, despite the surrender of the last Islamic dynasty on the Iberian Peninsula in 1492 and the unremitting marginalisation of Moriscos, Islam seemed on the rise. Rather than the imagined ultimate victory over Muslim empires, 16th-century Ottoman control over the Mediterranean, Asia and large parts of Europe signalled Muslim expansion rather than decline.

Sixteenth-century political achievements of Muslim empires gave rise to a new wave of apocalyptic, apologetic and polemical literature (e.g. *Türkenbüchlein*), expressing concern over the inroads Islam was making into Christian communities.[112] In Georgia and Armenia, where Ottoman-Safavid clashes had resulted in numerous casualties, martyrologies were composed to buoy the faithful.[113] In Russia, Archbishop Feodosil of Novgorod (1491-1563) hailed Grand Prince Ivan IV (r. 1547-84) for his campaigns against Kazan, lauding him as 'defender of the orthodox faith', and meanwhile he reminded him of his duty to convert the 'pagans' (Muslims) of Kazan.[114] Maximus the Greek (1475-1556), an Orthodox monk from Athos who spent most of his working life in Russia, wrote *Answers of the Christians to the Hagarenes who revile our Orthodox faith* (c. 1525), which evidences that, in early 16th-century Russia, Christians felt compelled to defend their faith.[115]

Meanwhile, Christians were converting to Islam in large numbers in central and eastern Europe. Abbot Macarie's *The Chronicle of Moldova from 1504 to 1551* describes in bitter terms how the Ottomans persuaded Prince Iliaş Rareş to convert to Islam. The prince, Macarie writes,

---

111 Nearly a century earlier, in 1497, also under Spanish influence, King Manuel I of Portugal had ordered the entire non-Christian population to convert or go into exile; R.L. de Jesus, 'King Manuel I of Portugal', in *CMR* 7, 745-8.

112 S. Küçükhyüseyin, 'Benedict Curipeschitz', in *CMR* 7, 168-73.

113 S.P. Cowe, 'Martyrology of Xač'atur Kołbec'i in 1517, in *CMR* 7, 588-91; S.P. Cowe, 'Grigoris Ałt'amarc'i', in *CMR* 7, 599-607; S.P. Cowe, 'Mec Peron', in *CMR* 7, 668-72. The Kazan campaigns against the Tartars also produced martyrs; see C. Soldat, 'Nifont Kormilitsin', in *CMR* 7, 372-8.

114 C. Soldat, 'Feodosil, archbishop of Novgorod', in *CMR* 7, 308-12.

115 D. Savelyev, 'Maximus the Greek', in *CMR* 7, 135-40.

subsequently 'surrounded himself with the sons and daughters of Hagar and even with "Turkish whores" and followed their malicious advice until the Devil settled in his soul. He abjured the faith of his ancestors, embraced Islam and took the name of the "damned Muhammad", which was synonymous with Satan.'[116]

Anton Vrančić (1503-1573), historiographer and later archbishop of Esztergom, also signalled how, under Ottoman rule, Christianity had increasingly come under siege. In his *Journey from Buda to Hadrianopolis in 1553*, Vrančić recorded a number of oral traditions about the decline of Christianity in parts of present-day Bulgaria; Christian monasteries has been destroyed, the older generation of Christians had gradually died and young people preferred to embrace Islam in order to have better prospects.[117]

With Christian communities once again under Muslim control in parts of Europe, the hope of better prospects in the newly-discovered parts of the world were high. However, though some Roman Catholic missions in Africa, Asia and Latin America met with positive responses, Muslim conversion proved difficult beyond Europe and the Mediterranean world. A Jesuit mission to the Moghul court in India initially seemed promising but, despite a courteous reception, the anticipated conversions never materialised.[118] In Bijapur (South India), the only person who converted was the daughter of a Muslim aristocrat.[119] To assist missionary work among Muslims (and others), Jesuits and other missionary orders began the production of missionary material that consisted of both translations of core theological texts and newly written materials for evangelisation purposes. An example of the latter is a text entitled *Muṣaḥaba rūḥāniyya* ('The spiritual conversation'), which seeks to counter the Muslim accusation of *taḥrīf*. The story recounts conversations between two shaykhs, who together discover mistakes in the Qur'an and conclude that only Christians possess authentic scriptures. Whether books like this were

---

116 R.G. Păun, 'Abbot Macarie', in *CMR* 7, 311-20, p. 317.

117 E. Gyulai, 'Antonius Verantius', in *CMR* 7, 362-71; for similar observations about Croatia, see F. Posset, B. Lucin and B. Jozić, 'Marcus Marulus', in *CMR* 7, 91-125, esp. *Evangelistarium*, pp. 111-15. The circulation of polemical materials and conversion narratives by converts to Islam may also have reinforced the feelings of disheartenment; C. Norton, 'Serrâc ibn Abdullah', in *CMR* 7, 673-5; T. Krstić, 'Murad ibn Abdullah', in *CMR* 7, 698-704.

118 G. Nickel, 'Rodolfo Acquaviva', in *CMR* 7, 889-96.

119 G. Nickel, 'Luís Fróis', in *CMR* 7, 858-65; G. Nickel, 'Gonçalo Rodrigues', in *CMR* 7, 837-41.

actually distributed and, if so, what impact they had on Muslims, is uncertain.[120]

In Africa, mission proved no easy task. When in the 1560s the Jesuit Dom Gonçalo da Silva succeeded in converting and baptising the king of Monomotapa (in south-east Africa), some members of his nobility, resident Muslims, convinced the king that da Silva's sprinkling with water indicated that he was a *moroo*, a wizard, who would bring hunger and death to the country. Persuaded by their arguments, the king had da Silva put to death. In Mozambique, a Franciscan monk caused an uproar among the Muslim population when he ordered a mosque to be demolished (c. 1561); during the retaliations, property was destroyed, crosses were burned and a number of Christians were killed, indicating the tensions between Christians and Muslims in the country in the mid-16th-century.[121] Gradually, the words of the old-hand Jesuit missionary Baltasar Barreira (1531-1612) came to represent the missionary stance towards mission to Muslims. Writing from his mission station in 1606, in present-day Sierra Leone, he observed: '[I]t does not appear that there is any cure for those who have already received the sect of Mohammed but one may have more hope for others who have only sniffed at this sect or still have idols they worship.'[122] The disenchantment over the results of Christian mission to Muslims gradually inaugurated an era in Christian mission in which priority was given to the conversion of 'the heathen' over that of 'the infidel'. It was in this mission that, in many parts of the world, Christians and Muslims would once again become rivals, now as competitors for the soul of the 'heathen'.

Conclusion

This chapter has positioned Christian missions to Muslims as part of a larger Christian project in the context of Islam, and has located the development of systematic mission to Muslims in the 13th-century reform movement in western Europe. In areas under Muslim rule, the churches' main 'mission' during the period under discussion seems to have consisted of the safeguarding of the Christian community. Apocalyptic, apologetic and polemical treatises, as well as martyrologies and

120 A. Girard, 'Giovanni Battista Eliano', in *CMR* 7, 724-31.
121 N. Vila-Santa, 'Francisco Coutinho'.
122 M. Frederiks, 'Baltasar Barreira', in *CMR* 11, 492-8, p. 496.

pastoral decrees, were primarily materials that addressed the Christian community, and they seem to have served the theological (and often teleological) project of understanding and explaining the rise of Islam as well as the pastoral project of ensuring Christianity's survival in terms of numbers, content and distinctiveness.

In Latin Christendom, the notion of mission work among Muslims began to emerge from the 11th century onwards. Systematic missionary endeavours, however, first occurred as an offshoot of the 13th-century reform movement in western Europe; this movement called for the spiritual renewal of Christianity in Europe and the East, the suppression of heresy (Albigensians and Muslims), and the evangelisation of non-Christians. The movement was characterised by a strong apocalyptic awareness; spurred on by the imminent arrival of the end of time, its adepts took to conquering the Holy Land with renewed energy and stressed the urgency of the conversion of 'pagans', Eastern Christians, Jews and Muslims, who it was thought would all play a crucial role in the pending Apocalypse. The spirit that gave rise to the reform movement also brought about the mendicant orders. Franciscans and Dominicans alike aspired towards spiritual renewal through the emulation of apostolic life, and considered mission (and martyrdom) an intrinsic part of this apostolic vocation. The significant advance of the Reconquista in the Iberian Peninsula during the 13th century, resulting in large numbers of Muslims under Christian rule, brought Muslim conversion into prominence on the theological agenda. Voices that seem to prefer a nascent form of interreligious dialogue over mission (e.g. Nicholas of Cusa) were rare in Europe before 1600.

Mission to Muslims proved an uphill task. Neither preaching, exemplary life or martyrdom (e.g. Franciscans), nor intellectual reasoning (Oliver of Paderborn, the Dominicans), acculturation (Llull, Juan de Segovia, de Talavera and others) or enforced conversion (de Vitry, Jiménez de Cisneros) succeeded in engendering large-scale Muslim conversion. Missionaries to Africa, Asia and the Middle East, as well as clergy pursuing Muslim/Morisco conversion on the Iberian Peninsula, tended to underestimate Muslim commitment to their religion. To cite Benjamin Kedar once more:

> [...] when in 1326 Andrea of Perugia, the Franciscan bishop of Zaitun in Mongol China, observed that 'we can preach [here] freely and safety, yet none of the Jews and the Saracens does convert', he must have realized that the Islamic prohibition against Christian missionizing was

> not the only reason for the missionaries' lack of success among the Saracens.[123]

Gradually, missionary congregations directed their attention to the evangelisation of groups other than Muslims. It would take many more years before Christians began to reflect on the soteriological implications of the fact that Islam seemed to offer its adherents a worldview that could compete with Christianity.

123 Kedar, *Crusade and mission*, p. 202.

Chapter 20
Discussing religious practices

Charles Tieszen

When Theodore Abū Qurra, Melkite bishop of Ḥarrān (c.755-c.830),[1] wrote his treatise defending the necessity of venerating icons and the cross in an Islamic context, he did so on the basis of an already long tradition of explaining religious practices. Before Theodore's *Treatise on the veneration of holy icons*,[2] pagans wrote to defend their use of images in worship. They also accused Christians of praying to idols when they prostrated before them. As a result, we have texts written by Christians that include defences of their religious devotion.[3]

Similarly, Jewish communities also distrusted Christian religious practices. In particular, the Christian devotion to icons and the cross brought their monotheism, in the Jewish mind, under suspicion. In turn, Christians wrote texts in what became the *adversus Judaeos* tradition that attempted to defend and explain the use of icons and crosses in worship. Christian authors deployed numerous strategies in order to make their case. They used logic and metaphor in an attempt to explain veneration. They mined the Hebrew Bible, showing through typological exegesis how such practices could have ancient precedent. And they also shot accusations back at Jews, claiming that if they themselves were guilty of idolatry in some of their practices, then surely Jews could also be guilty of the same.[4]

Another contributor was John of Damascus (c.675-c.754).[5] In the 8th century, John wrote his *Orations against the calumniators of the icons* in an effort to explain and defend the Christian use of images (icons and crosses) in their worship.[6] In the process of doing so, he preserved and

---

[1] J.C. Lamoreaux, 'Theodore Abū Qurra', in *CMR* 1, 439-91, pp. 439-48.

[2] J.C. Lamoreaux, '*Maymar qālahu Anbā Thāwudhūrūs …*', in *CMR* 1, pp. 463-6. Theodore's treatise focuses almost exclusively on icon veneration, but he also mentions cross veneration. See also S.H. Griffith, *A treatise on the veneration of holy icons written in Arabic by Theodore Abū Qurrah, Bishop of Harrān (c. 755-c. 830 A.D.)*, Louvain, 1997, p. 45.

[3] On the pagan context, see C.L. Tieszen, *Cross veneration in the medieval Islamic world*, London, 2017, pp. 18-22.

[4] On the Jewish context and *Adversus Judaeos* literature, see Tieszen, *Cross veneration*, pp. 22-6.

[5] R.F. Glei, 'John of Damascus', in *CMR* 1, 295-301, pp. 295-7.

[6] For more on John's *Orations*, see Tieszen, *Cross veneration*, pp. 26-41.

transmitted material in *florilegia* from the Church Fathers, such as Basil the Great (d. 379), whose treatise *On the Spirit* (*Tou hagiou Basileiou peri tou Pneumatos biblion*) included passages devoted to justifying a list of Christian religious practices,[7] and the *adversus Judaeos* tradition. Taking his cues from these sources, John also included in *testimonia* lengthy proof-texts culled from the Christian Old Testament. Through these means, John not only defended the use of images in worship as a part of monotheistic devotion, but also explained why they were necessary to what he saw as Christian orthopraxy.

Significantly, Theodore Abū Qurra's *Treatise on the veneration of holy icons* is heavily dependent upon John's *Orations* and contains much of the same argumentation. Likewise, both texts probably functioned as defences of Christian religious practices in contexts influenced by Islam and Muslims. This is not made explicit in John's *Orations*. His references to Emperor Leo III (r. 717-41) and Patriarch Germanus I (deposed by Leo in 730) could suggest that he wrote in light of Byzantine iconomachy debates, but many other features of the *Orations* point to an Islamic context where Melkite Christian communities needed encouragement to preserve the practices that marked them out as distinctly Christian.[8] Theodore is more explicit about the context in which he was writing. Though he does not mention Muslims by name, he does write about 'anti-Christians, especially ones claiming to have in hand a scripture sent down from God' who were accusing Christians of idolatry and mocking their prostration before icons.[9]

In this light, the encounter between Muslims and Christians was not only one between politicians, soldiers, shopkeepers or theological interlocutors discussing dogma. Clearly, Muslims and Christians were observing the ways in which each worshipped God, commenting and even making accusations based on their observations. In turn, treatises were written in order to defend and explain what, exactly, each was doing in worship. Beyond mere explanation, however, it also becomes apparent that authors were using their discussions of religious practice in order to solidify the commitment their readers had to their religion in environments of competing religious claims. This means that discussions about

---

[7] See Basil the Great, 'On the Spirit', in *Nicene and Post-Nicene Fathers*, vol. 8, ed. P. Schaff and H. Wace, Peabody MA, 1999, 41-2 (27.66).

[8] On the Islamic context of John's *Orations* and its likely Melkite audience, see Tieszen, *Cross veneration*, pp. 31-9.

[9] Griffith, *Treatise on the veneration of holy icons*, p. 29.

why Christians and Muslims worshipped in the ways they did were as much about identity formation as they were matters of disputation.

In what follows, attention is drawn to the topics concerning religious practice that appear in Christian-Muslim disputation and interaction. A wide variety of practices appears in the relevant literature. These include prayer and the direction one faces in prayer, fasting, almsgiving, monasticism and asceticism, the use of holy oil, the use or experience of violence (e.g. jihad or martyrdom), marriage (celibacy, monogamy or polygyny), and specified days for corporate worship. Also, circumcision, pilgrimage and related rites, propagation of or invitation to faith, ritual purification (e.g., *wuḍūʾ*, *ghusl*, or *tayammum*), dietary restrictions, baptism, the Eucharist, confession or absolution, and veneration of objects (icons, relics, crosses, the Qur'an, or the Kaʿba) were addressed. My concern in this chapter, and indeed within the smaller group of religious practices that constitute a thematic issue in Christian-Muslim relations, will be icon veneration, cross veneration (veneration of the Qur'an and the Kaʿba appears in discussions of icons and crosses), the Eucharist, baptism and prayer, particularly the direction one faces in prayer. Narrowing the list of religious practices like this is important, for while many authors commented on any number of practices they observed, it is really only this shorter list of five practices that consistently and frequently receive attention as a point of discussion and debate. In fact, more often than not, authors will take up these particular practices as a special grouping of practices. In this way, they can be viewed as topoi of Christian-Muslim disputational and apologetic literature.

A surprising feature of this topic, and one that *CMR* helps to bear out, is not only that discussions of religious practice were a common theme authors returned to, but also that so many authors chose or felt the need to make comment on the topic. Indeed, topics related to religious practices appear with nearly as much frequency and in nearly as many authors' texts as other, more common discussions related to doctrines, beliefs or jurisprudence. This frequency and range suggest that debates about certain religious practices not only had a powerful identity-shaping effect, but could also be as much about catechism as apologetics, polemics or simple explanation for the inquiring observer.

With this in mind, it is not possible to address every author who includes a discussion of icon veneration, cross veneration, the Eucharist, baptism or prayer. Instead, a few authors have been selected that can be representative of the kinds of arguments and presentations that appear in discussions of each these five religious practices. The main features of the arguments presented are summarised, and an attempt to highlight the apparent continuities and unique developments in nearly a millennium of textual evidence is given.

Whilst a number of Muslim texts will be highlighted, another interesting feature of this topic is that it is Christian authors who more frequently bring up the subject of religious practices. As a result, most of the texts touched on below are written by Christians, and in most cases it is Christian practices that are being discussed.[10] Nevertheless, many of these texts preserve Muslim questions and accusations about Christian practices or reconstitute Muslim arguments about their own practices.

Icon veneration

Introducing our discussion with Abū Qurra's defence of icons, as done above, is important because it shows that one of the earliest defences of Arabophone Christian practices – and mentions of Muslim critiques – is connected to a long history and tradition of defending and explaining religious practices stretching back before the Islamic era. Whilst Abū Qurra is an important author marking the trajectory of this tradition, there were other Christian authors, some even before him, who also took up the project of explaining and defending veneration of images in contexts that were influenced by Islam. These texts come to us from the East-Syrian and West-Syrian traditions. A few were written in Arabic, but many of them were composed in Syriac. They, too, preserve earlier strategies developed in Patristic and *adversus Judaeos* literature, but also develop their own lines of argumentation.

Among these texts, and certainly one of the earliest, is an account of an early 8th-century disputation between an Arab notable and an

[10] For Muslims, the Five Pillars – *shahāda, ṣalāt, zakāt, ṣawm* and *ḥajj* – usually mark the main Islamic religious practices. Christian authors often note these Pillars, frequently in order to attack them, as Petrus Alfonsi did in the chapter he devoted to Islam in his 12th-century *Dialogi contra Iudeos* (J. Tolan, 'Petrus Alfonsi', in *CMR* 3, 356-62). However, many authors use these pillars as a structure on which to model their own Christian practices and explain them to their readers. Such was the case in the late 10th-century, when Sāwīrus ibn al-Muqaffaʿ wrote his *Kitāb miṣbāḥ al-ʿaql* (M.N. Swanson, 'Sāwīrus ibn al-Muqaffaʿ', in *CMR* 2, 491-509, pp. 491-4, 501-3), addressing Christian practices in ways that were analogous to the Pillars of Islam. See also Muṭrān Dāʾūd in his *Kitāb al-kamāl* (M.N. Swanson, 'Muṭrān Dāʾūd', in *CMR* 3, 130-2), and Ibn Sabbāʿ in his *Al-jawhara l-nafisa* (M.N. Swanson, 'Ibn Sabbāʿ', in *CMR* 4, 918-23). The redactor of the long Arabic version of the *Legend of Sergius Baḥīrā* (B. Roggema, '*The legend of Sergius Baḥīrā*', in *CMR* 1, 600-3), offers an extensive discussion of Muslim practices, particularly the direction Muslims face in prayer; see B. Roggema, *The legend of Sergius Baḥīrā*, Leiden, 2009, pp. 474-7.

East-Syrian monk.[11] As with many other disputations, the essential function of this account was to help its readers discern the true religion between Christianity and Islam.[12] Early on in the debate, the Arab declares that Muslims, not Christians, 'are vigilant concerning the commandments of Muḥammad and the sacrifices of Abraham'. In other words, Muslims do not stray from God's commandments by inventing new (idolatrous) practices such as 'worship[ing] the cross, or the bones of martyrs, or images'.[13] A lengthy discussion follows, covering both doctrine – Christology, the Trinity – and other practices like circumcision, baptism and the Eucharist. However, the conversation eventually shifts back when the Muslim shares his confusion over the notion that God might replace pre-Islamic idolatry in Arabia with the 'worship of created things', i.e. the Christian invention of venerating images, the cross and the bones of martyrs.[14] The monk sets out to prove the inherent monotheism of Christian veneration of images, beginning with typological exegesis of the Old Testament, a common strategy particularly in Syriac theology but more generally in *adversus Judaeos* literature as well.

The monk's first reference to the Old Testament is to Exodus and the pillar of fire that guided the Israelites out of Egypt (Exodus 13:21, 14:19-20; Joshua 24:7). However, the monk describes the pillar not as being made of fire but as a 'pillar of light' (*nuhrā*). This suggests, as Gerrit Reinink points out, that the author of the account is referring back to an East-Syrian exegetical tradition.[15] The monk's other references are to Moses and the bronze serpent in the desert (Numbers 21:8-9) and the Ark of the Covenant (Joshua 7:6). Each of these examples is meant to show that the Israelites venerated created objects and were rescued by them. In turn, the monk uses them to demonstrate typologically the Christian

11 See B. Roggema, '*The disputation between a monk of Bēt Ḥālē and an Arab notable*', in *CMR* 1, 268-73.

12 On the function of these texts, especially the Syriac tradition, see S.H. Griffith, 'Disputes with Muslims in Syriac Christian texts. From Patriarch John (d. 648) to Bar Hebraeus (d. 1286)', in B. Lewis and F. Niewöhner (eds), *Religionsgespräche im Mittelalter*, Wiesbaden, 1992, 173-96.

13 D.G.K. Taylor, 'The disputation between a Muslim and a monk of Bēt Ḥālē. Syriac text and annotated English translation', in S.H. Griffith and S. Grebenstein (eds), *Christsein in der islamischen Welt: Festschrift für Martinn Tamcke zum 60. Geburstag*, Wiesbaden, 2015, 187-242, p. 208.

14 Taylor, 'Disputation between a Muslim and a monk', pp. 224-5.

15 G.J. Reinink, 'The veneration of icons, the cross, and the bones of the martyrs in an early East-Syrian apology against Islam', in D. Bumazhnov et al. (eds), *Bibel, Byzanz und Christlicher Orient. Festschrift für Stephen Gerö zum 65. Geburstag*, Leuven, 2011, 329-42, p. 332.

fulfilment of some aspect of Jewish (or, for Muslims, Abrahamic) cultic practice: the pillar of light, Christ's eschatological judgement; Moses and the serpent, the cross of Christ and his power; the Ark of the Covenant, a Christian altar.[16]

The argument closes with the monk saying, 'And we worship and honour [Christ's] image because He impressed (it) with His face and delivered it to us, and whenever we look at his icon it is Him we see. And we honour the image of the king because of the king.' The first part of the statement alludes to the image of Christ, the *Mandylion*, made when, according to tradition, Christ pressed his face upon a cloth and sent it to King Abgar of Edessa (d. c. 40).[17] The reference to the king is an abbreviated form of a metaphor that is nearly ubiquitous in explanations for image veneration. In it, the Christian practice is compared to kissing a king's ring or reverencing his image, each action a way to pay the king an honour that is certainly short of worship. Likewise, Christians honour Christ in his image, but do not worship the image. After this argument, the Muslim concedes, 'it is right that all who believe in Christ should honour his image as (Christ in) his entirety'.[18]

Hence, Christians venerate images because Christ commanded it, because such veneration has an ancient, biblical precedent and because, through images, they worship Christ himself. Each of these elements was either firmly fixed in the Syriac exegetical tradition or in Patristic and *adversus Judaeos* literature. And, importantly, these elements are also employed again and again in later texts used to defend images.

In the early 12th century, East-Syrian Patriarch Elias II (d. 1133)[19] made a number of comments on the veneration of icons in his *Kitāb uṣūl al-dīn*.[20] He remarked that icons in churches may function as *biblia pauperum*. 'We depict images in the churches, which take the place of writing for those who cannot write nor read, such as youngsters or illiterate people.' He goes on, 'If one sees and contemplates the image, one no longer needs to ask questions about it, such as a person who does not know to read asks someone else to read (something) for him. In this respect, images of this matter are better than anything.'[21]

---

16 Taylor, 'Disputation between a Muslim and a monk', pp. 226-7.

17 On this story in the Syriac tradition, see Reinink, 'Veneration of icons', pp. 335-6.

18 Taylor, 'Disputation between a Muslim and a monk', p. 228.

19 See H.G.B. Teule, 'Elias II, Ibn al Muqlī', in *CMR* 3, 418-21, pp. 418-19.

20 See Teule, 'Elias II, Ibn al Muqlī', pp. 419-21.

21 Translated in H.G.B. Teule, 'The veneration of images in the East Syriac tradition', in B. Groneberg and H. Spieckermann (eds), *Der Welt der Götterbilder*, Berlin, 2007, 324-46, p. 338.

After explaining this function of icons, Elias provides an intriguing comparison. 'That we venerate, kiss, and honour them', he explains, 'comes in the place of the honour, paid by our friends, the Muslims, to the copies (of their Holy Scriptures).'[22] His remark is meant to counter the accusation that Christians practise idolatry. In fact, they do not worship icons, but merely honour them in the same way that Muslims honour the Qur'an. In this way, Elias's comparison has an explanatory function, but it also reveals that Muslims in his setting took issue with the Christian use of icons. These concerns could have come from Muslims known to Elias, or it may be that Elias was simply aware of the general Muslim distaste for the way Christians used religious images. In this light, Elias's comparison further shows that Christians' explanations of religious practices had to take into account the Islamic element of their environment.

A story that was popular among both Christians and Muslims helps to introduce another important text. The story concerns Ḥunayn ibn Isḥāq (809-73),[23] scholar and personal physician to the Abbasid Caliph al-Mutawakkil (822-61), and comes to us via several sources including Ḥunayn's autobiography.[24] According to Ḥunayn's retelling, a fellow Christian physician named Bukhtīshūʿ ibn Jibrāʾīl hatched a devious plot against him. Bukhtīshūʿ acquired an expensive icon of the Theotokos and Christ-child and had it brought into the court, where al-Mutawakkil saw it and was rather impressed with the image. Before presenting it to him, Bukhtīshūʿ kissed it reverently. When the caliph asked him why he did this, he replied that this was the Christian practice and asked, 'If I do not kiss the image of the Mistress of Heaven and Earth [...] then whose image should I kiss?'[25] As part of his plot, Bukhtīshūʿ went on to explain that, despite this common Christian practice, there was a pseudo-Christian (Ḥunayn) who enjoyed the favour of the caliph and the generous treatment he granted to Christians. Nevertheless, he denounced God and even spat on the icon. Al-Mutawakkil was incensed and sent for Ḥunayn. But before Ḥunayn had reached the court, Bukhtīshūʿ met him and convinced him that the caliph was using the icon to torment Christians, ridiculing their practice of icon veneration. In order to put an end to the

[22] Teule, 'Veneration of images', p. 338.

[23] See J.P. Monferrer Sala, 'Ḥunayn ibn Isḥāq', in *CMR* 1, 768-71.

[24] For commentary, see Teule, 'Veneration of images', pp. 335-6, and S. Griffith, *The church in the shadow of the mosque*, Princeton NJ, 2008, pp. 142-3.

[25] Translated in D.F. Reynolds (ed.), *Interpreting the self. Autobiography in the Arabic literary tradition*, Berkeley CA, 2001, p. 112.

mockery, Bukhtīshūʿ told Ḥunayn that he had spat on the icon and suggested that Ḥunayn should do the same, simply so that the caliph might move on to other matters.

Ḥunayn fell for the trick. Al-Mutawakkil sent for him, showed him the icon, and asked what he thought of it. 'Isn't it the image of your god and his mother?' al-Mutawakkil wondered. 'God forbid, your Majesty! Is God Almighty an image', Ḥunayn replied, 'can he be depicted? This is a picture like any other.'[26] Ḥunayn went on to agree that the image had no special power at all and, as proof, he spat on it. For this, he was thrown in prison.

Bukhtīshūʿ had got rid of Ḥunayn, for the time being anyway, but the caliph's curiosity about Christian images was all the more piqued. As a result, he sent for the East-Syrian Patriarch Theodosius I (r. 853-8). 'The moment he saw the icon', Ḥunayn reported, 'he fell upon it without even saluting the caliph and held it close, kissing it and weeping at length.'[27] Al-Mutawakkil eventually gave Theodosius the icon and ordered the patriarch to tell him 'how you deal with someone who spits on it'.[28] Theodosius replied that there would no punishment for a Muslim or uneducated Christian, though both should be reprimanded and made aware of the proper behaviours towards a sacred object. 'But', the patriarch added, 'should someone in full command of his own mind spit on this image, he spits on Mary the Mother of God and on Our Lord Jesus Christ.'[29] In another account of the story, Theodosius's reply is more explicit: anyone being cognizant of their actions 'does not spit on the image, but on Christ and Mary'.[30] Ḥunayn was subsequently imprisoned and tortured, though the caliph eventually retracted the sentence and restored him to his former position.[31]

Ḥunayn's story tells us several things about icons in Islamic contexts. To begin with, the Muslim attitude towards images was not statically iconophobic.[32] It shows that in some East-Syrian communities, often

---

26 Reynolds, *Interpreting the self*, p. 113.

27 Reynolds, *Interpreting the self*, p. 113.

28 Reynolds, *Interpreting the self*, p. 113.

29 Reynolds, *Interpreting the self*, p. 114.

30 Teule, 'Veneration of images', p. 336.

31 The story is similar to one in Mēna of Nikiou's early 8th-century biography of Isaac, the Coptic Patriarch of Alexandria (d. c. 692) (H. Suermann, 'Mēna of Nikiou', in *CMR* 1, 219-21). In this story, a trap is set for Isaac that he craftily overcomes to win the favour of the Muslim emir. See Mēna of Nikiou, *The Life of Isaac of Alexandria and the martyrdom of Saint Macrobius*, trans. D.N. Bell, Kalamazoo MI, 1988, pp. 71-2.

32 For more on Muslim views about images, see J.J. Elias, *Aisha's cushion. Religious art, perception, and practice in Islam*, Cambridge MA, 2012.

thought not to favour icons, religious images could be widely accepted.[33] Further, images and the practice of venerating them could become a flashpoint between Christians and Muslims, serving to mark out religious identity. However, most intriguing here is Theodosius's remark attributing a kind of sacramental real presence to icons in much the same way that the bread and wine of the Eucharist are Christ's body and blood.

The argument that there was a relationship between an image and its prototype – either that the two could be equated in some way or, at least, that the presence of the prototype could somehow be present in the image – was developed and made more explicit by a later East-Syrian author, Isho'yahb bar Malkon (d. 1246),[34] in an early 13th-century text on venerating images.[35] In fact, whilst John of Damascus and Theodore the Studite (d. 826) discuss this idea,[36] its specific contours among East Syrian Christians living in Islamic milieus seem to reveal another interpretive tradition. Touching on the same *biblia pauperum* theme as Elias II, Isho'yahb remarks, 'Images in the churches take the place of writing for those who do not know how to write or read [...] When they see the images, there is no need for them to ask for information from the experts.'[37] It may be that Isho'yahb is making a subtle comparison with the calligraphy that adorned mosques, which would not be legible or readable to all Muslims. Isho'yahb devotes a number of passages in this same text to explaining cross veneration; in doing so, he draws a comparison with the way in which Muslims venerate the Black Stone of the Ka'ba.[38] This comparison is offered without invective, though one could read a quick jab in his comparison between Christian icons and qur'anic Arabic calligraphy.

Isho'yahb goes on to explain the nature of Christian icon veneration and its purpose, incorporating many of the same explanations and metaphors as other authors had before him. Intriguingly, however, he

---

33 On the varying views of icon and cross veneration in Christian communities, see Tieszen, *Cross veneration*, p. 11; H.G.B. Teule, 'Isho'yahb bar Malkon's treatise on the veneration of the holy icons', in M. Tamcke (ed.), *Christians and Muslims in dialogue in the Islamic Orient of the Middle Ages*, Beirut, 2007, 157-69, pp. 168-9. Cf. B. Landron, *Chrétiens et musulmans en Irak. Attitudes nestoriennes vis-à-vis de l'islam*, Paris, 1994, where, in the discussion about venerating images (pp. 238-9), he comments on a general Semitic repugnance for images that increased along with contact with Muslims (p. 239). This assessment, however, does not square well with the evidence.

34 See H.G.B. Teule, 'Isho'yab bar Malkon', in *CMR* 4, 331-8, pp. 331-3.

35 See H.G.B. Teule, '*Al-radd ʿalā l-Yahūd wa l-Muslimīn* [...]', in *CMR* 4, 333-5.

36 See Tieszen, *Cross veneration*, pp. 12-13.

37 Translated in Teule, 'Isho'yahb bar Malkon's treatise', p. 165.

38 Teule, 'Isho'yahb bar Malkon's treatise', p. 164-5.

remarks that 'the images of the friends of God [take the place] of their persons and kissing them resembles greeting them; performing liturgy before them and their altars and the remembrance of their virtues are as if we are speaking and conversing with them'.[39] For Ishoʿyahb, religious images of saints, the Theotokos or Christ carried with them a kind of real presence such that venerating an icon was to venerate the person depicted therein.[40]

There are also texts that mention veneration of icons, but do so disapprovingly. For example, Elias of Nisibis (975-1046),[41] writing in his *Kitāb al-burhān*,[42] condemns the use of icons in worship by West-Syrian Christians and Melkites:

> In their churches, they have images in great numbers and they hold the opinion that all of them are to be venerated equally. Moreover, they despise the images of Christ and of the Virgin. They put them in their bathhouses in the most despicable and dirty places where they show their nakedness. Is it not foolish to maintain – incorrectly – that the Virgin is the Mother of God and yet to leave her image in the most squalid of places?[43]

Elias's comment is best understood as an attempt to portray his East-Syrian community as more coherent in light of Islam than these other Christian traditions.[44] As we have seen, his remarks clearly do not fully represent the general attitude towards icons held by East Syrian Christians. What comes to light once again, then, is that a discussion of religious practices could be used to mark a community out as authentic.

Cross veneration

In most texts that discuss religious practices, the topic of cross veneration is the main focus and it becomes clear that devotion to the cross is the pre-eminent practice that distinguishes Christians. It is also the one that seems to garner the most attention from Muslims. Caliph ʿUmar II (r. 717-20) allegedly wrote to Leo III and accused Christians as follows:

---

39 Teule, 'Veneration of images', p. 342 (see Teule's comment on this passage, p. 343).

40 These remarks are similar to those made in the 7th century by Isaac of Nineveh, who equates the cross with the actual body of Christ and even claims that God's Shekhinah glory is present in it. See Tieszen, *Cross veneration*, pp. 190 n. 51, and 199 n. 50.

41 See J.P. Monferrer Sala, 'Elias of Nisibis', in *CMR* 2, 727-41, pp. 727-8.

42 See Monferrer Sala, 'Elias of Nisibis', pp. 737-9.

43 Translated in Teule, 'Veneration of images', p. 337.

44 Cf. Teule's remarks in 'Ishoʿyahb bar Malkon's treatise', p. 162.

> You worship the cross and the image [of Christ], kiss them, and bow before them, even though they are only the product of human work which can neither hear nor see, which can neither help nor harm, and the ones you esteem the most are the images made of gold and silver. In fact, it is in this way that the people of Abraham behaved with their images and idols.[45]

'Alī al-Ṭabarī (d. c. 860),[46] the East-Syrian Christian who converted to Islam in the mid-9th century, mocked his former co-religionists: 'You work a piece of wood with your hands and then you hang it around your necks!'[47] The implications were that, like the pagans of antiquity, Christians worshipped a wooden idol when they venerated the cross. It was a powerless object of their own creation that made them look rather senseless and silly.

Christians responded with texts designed to address these accusations and some of them made accusations of their own against Muslims. They also tried to inform Christian readers about the importance and function of cross veneration in their Islamic contexts. In order to do so, they drew from the same body of literature that was used to defend icon veneration. They employed much of the same typological exegesis, attempting to demonstrate that the cross was a powerful symbol worthy of honour. Four examples introduce some of the more unusual arguments.[48] To begin with, Abū Rā'iṭa,[49] a West-Syrian theologian writing in the early-9th century, explains that Christians venerate the cross because 'it has become for us a *qibla*, and something particular apart from all other things'.[50] In this explanation, he takes a typically Islamic term that

45 J. Gaudeul, 'The correspondence between Leo and 'Umar. 'Umar's letter re-discovered?', *Islamochristiana* 10 (1984) 109-57, p. 149. For a new study of the alleged exchange between 'Umar and Leo, see S. Kim, 'The Arabic letters of the Byzantine Emperor Leo III to the Caliph 'Umar Ibn 'Abd al-'Aziz. An edition, translation, and commentary', Washington DC, 2017 (PhD Diss. Catholic University of America). See also, T. Greenwood, '*The letter of Leo III* in Ghewond', in *CMR* 1, 203-8; B. Roggema, '*Pseudo-Leo III's first letter to 'Umar II*', in *CMR* 1, 375-6; B. Roggema, '*Pseudo-'Umar II's letter to Leo III*', in *CMR* 1, 381-5.

46 D. Thomas, ''Alī l-Ṭabarī', in *CMR* 1, 669-74, p. 669-71.

47 R. Ebied and D. Thomas (ed. and trans.), *The polemical works of 'Alī al-Ṭabarī*, Leiden, 2016, p. 169. See also, D. Thomas, '*Al-radd 'alā l-Naṣārā*', in *CMR* 1, 671-2. The 13th-century Copt al-Ṣafī ibn al-'Assāl preserves some parts of the lost last section of this refutation; see M. Jirjis (ed.), *Kitāb al-ṣaḥā'iḥ fī jawāb al-naṣā'iḥ*, Cairo, 1926, pp. 121-2. See also, W. Awad, 'Al-Ṣafī ibn al-'Assāl', in *CMR* 4, 538-51, pp. 538-44.

48 I have written extensively on this topic in my book *Cross veneration in the medieval Islamic world*, situating the practice in its literary, social, historical and political contexts, as well as examining the ways it was discussed by Muslims and Christians.

49 S.T. Keating, 'Abū Rā'iṭa l-Takrītī', in *CMR* 1, 567-81, pp. 567-71.

50 Abū Rā'iṭa, 'Fī ithbāt dīn al-naṣrāniyya wa-ithbāt al-Thālūth al-maqaddas', in S.T. Keating, *Defending the 'People of Truth' in the early Islamic period. The Christian*

indicates the Muslim direction of prayer and infuses it with Christian meaning. Abū Rā'iṭa goes on to explain that the Christian *qibla* protects those who turn towards it from idolatry:

> For how is it possible that the one who turns his face towards worship of his Lord should be oriented to a *qibla* other than His *qibla*? Now the cross is for us a *qibla* and a glorious [thing], deserving of exaltation and honour and devotion (*wa-l-ikhlāṣ*), and who takes up [this] *qibla*, apart from [all] other things, is saved (*khalaṣa*).[51]

With this explanation, Abū Rā'iṭa not only elaborates on the cross as a *qibla*, but also draws upon another word typically associated with Islam. In the Qur'an, Sura 112 is given the title *Al-Ikhlāṣ* and is a summary statement of the belief in God's absolute oneness (*tawḥīd*). It also functions as a warning to Christians who, so Muslims believe, have committed an egregious error in their belief in a divine Christ. Sura 112 argues, in essence, that pure belief (*ikhlāṣ*) means confessing that God is one and does not have partners.[52] Intriguingly, it is not just a credal summary of Islamic belief, but may also be a response to earlier, non-Muslim creeds. Its first statement – *Qul huwa llāhu aḥad* ('Say, "He is God, one"') – is both a thematic and auditory echo of the Jewish creed – *Shema Yisrael, adonai elohenu adonai ehad* ('Hear, Israel, the Lord our God is One'). This first statement, as well as the remaining three in the sura, also echoes the Nicene Creed.[53] The Qur'an takes these credal statements and turns them on their head, emphasising the strict oneness of God. However, Abū Rā'iṭa turns this manoeuvre back on itself again, arguing that *Christians* worship the One God, manifest in the person of Christ and marked out by the symbol of the cross. Those who point themselves in *this* direction find pure belief and salvation.

Of course, besides the notion that the cross might be a metaphorical *qibla*, it often functioned as a literal marker of the direction in which Christians faced in prayer. More generally, the cross was painted on

---

apologies of Abū Rā'iṭah, Leiden, 2006, 73-146, pp. 132-3. See also, S.T. Keating, '*Risāla li-Abī Rā'iṭa l-Takrītī fī ithbāt dīn al-naṣrāniyya wa-ithbāt al-Thālūth al-muqaddas*', in *CMR* 1, 571-2.

[51] Abū Rā'iṭa, 'Fī ithbāt dīn al-naṣrāniyya', pp. 132-5.

[52] I am grateful to Ida Glaser for drawing my attention to this similarity. Her reflections appear in I. Glaser, 'Cross, qiblah and glory. What should direct Christian responses to Islam?', *Muslim-Christian Encounter* 10 (2017) 9-53.

[53] A. Neuwirth, 'Two faces of the Qur'ān. *Qur'ān* and *muṣḥaf*', *Oral Tradition* 25 (2010) 150-3.

the eastern walls of homes in order to mark the direction of prayer.[54] Hence, in the 12th century, a Christian convert to Islam named Naṣr ibn Yaḥyā[55] recalls that Christians 'worship a cross of metal or wood like [they] worship the Messiah; [they] put it on an elevated stand (*minbar*) in the direction of [their] prayer (*qibla*), on fine cloth, and have a group of priests serve it'.[56] In many cases, then, the accent is placed on the direction of prayer, a topic we address below, not necessarily on facing the cross. Even so, the cross becomes a marker for worship – or even pure worship as in Abū Rā'iṭa's argument – and as such it is worthy of veneration.

As with icons, there is a tendency among some authors to sacramentalise the cross, making of it an object in which Christ is truly present. For example, the anonymous Melkite author of the 9th-century *Al-jāmiʿ wujūh al-īmān*[57] – who also identifies the cross as the Christian *qibla* comparable to the Kaʿba[58] – writes that Christ, before he ascended, left behind the cross as a substitute for himself. 'The cross is Christ our Lord in his body', the author submits, and therefore 'prostration before the cross is like our prostration to Christ our Lord.'[59] For the author, the cross is not unlike the elements of the Eucharist: it faces the congregation and embodies the real presence of Christ. As such, it demands the prostration of worshippers.[60]

Other authors make a similar sacramental connection. It appears as early as the disputation between the Christian monk and the Arab notable discussed above. In his explanation for cross veneration, the monk concludes that Christians do not worship the material of the cross, but rather, 'we are worshipping our Lord, God the word, who dwelt in the temple (received) from us, and (dwells) in this sign of victory'.[61] The

54 See J. Daniélou, *The theology of Jewish Christianity. The development of Christian doctrine before the Council of Nicaea*, vol. 1, trans. and ed. J.A. Baker, London, 1964, pp. 268-9.

55 L. Demiri, 'Naṣr ibn Yaḥyā', in *CMR* 3, 750-4, pp. 750-1.

56 Quoted in H. Lazarus-Yafeh, 'Some neglected aspects of medieval Muslim polemics against Christianity', *Harvard Theological Review* 89 (January 1996) 61-84, p. 78. See also, L. Demiri, '*Al-naṣīḥa l-imāniyya fī faḍīḥat al-milla l-Naṣrāniyya*', in *CMR* 3, 751-4.

57 M.N. Swanson, '*Al-jāmiʿ wujūh al-īmān*', in *CMR* 1, 791-8.

58 See Griffith's description in S.H. Griffith, 'Islam and the *Summa theologiae rabica*', *Jerusalem Studies in Arabic and Islam* 13 (1990) 225-64, p. 250.

59 As quoted in M.N. Swanson, 'The cross of Christ in the earliest Arabic Melkite apologies', in S.K. Samir and J.S. Nielsen (eds), *Christian Arabic apologetics during the Abbasid period (750-1258)*, Leiden, 1994, 115-45, p. 141.

60 Swanson, 'Cross of Christ', p. 141.

61 Taylor, 'Disputation between a Muslim and a monk', p. 232. See also n. 40 above.

East-Syrian ʿAbdishoʿ of Nisibis (d. 1318) makes a similar connection.[62] In his *Kitāb uṣūl al-dīn*,[63] he justifies his designation of the cross as a *qibla* by noting that the Arabic word for cross, *ṣalīb*, expresses the same meaning as the Syriac word for both cross and crucified one, *ṣlibā*. It is Christ himself, then, not simply the object of the cross, that guides the direction of Christian worship, and therefore Christians venerate it.[64]

Making these sacramental connections helped the authors convince their readers of the necessity of venerating the cross. In contexts where Christians were not only absorbing Arabic language, but were also tempted to syncretise bits of Islam into their faith – and this is especially the case for the Melkite community to whom the author of the *Jāmiʿ wujūh al-īmān* writes – it was important to maintain the actions that marked them out as distinctly Christian.

Eucharist

In a letter dated 2 December 1454, Juan de Segovia (d. 1458)[65] wrote to Nicholas of Cusa (d. 1464)[66] to discuss strategies by which Muslims might be converted to Christianity.[67] In the letter, Juan shares some of his previous experiences in dialogue with Muslims, noting what he perceived to be Muslim confusion over various Christian doctrines and practices. In doing so, he mentions the Muslim objection 'that Christians ate their God' (*quod Chistiani comederent Deum suum*),[68] referring of course to the Eucharist. It is not clear whether the objection represents a critique or a misunderstanding. ʿAbd al-Jabbār in the late 10th century refers to the Eucharist (*qurbān*) several times in his 'Critique of Christian origins' and does so with remarkable specificity.[69] Many other Muslim authors critique the sacrament, some even quoting biblical passages, and are deeply suspicious of the illogical notion that the elements become Christ's body

62 H.G.B. Teule, "Abdishoʿ of Nisibis', in *CMR* 4, 750-61, pp. 750-3.

63 Teule, "Abdishoʿ of Nisibis', pp. 759-61.

64 See Teule, "Abdishoʿ of Nisibis', p. 760; Landron, *Chrétiens et musulmans en Irak*, p. 238.

65 A.M. Wolf, 'Juan de Segovia', in *CMR* 5, 429-42, pp. 429-31.

66 J. Tolan, 'Nicholas of Cusa', in *CMR* 5, 421-8, pp. 421-2.

67 A.M. Wolf, '*Epistola ad cardinelem Sancti Petri*', in *CMR* 5, 432-5.

68 This appears in the conclusion to Juan's letter, which D.C. Rodríguez includes in his *Juan de Segovia y el problema islámico*, Madrid, 1952, p. 309.

69 For instance, see ʿAbd al-Jabbār, *Critique of Christian origins*, ed. and trans. G.S. Reynolds and S.K. Samir, Provo UT, 2010, p. 113. See also, G.S. Reynolds and D. Thomas, "Abd al-Jabbār', in *CMR* 2, 594-610, pp. 594-7, 604-9.

and blood or that Christians insist on performing this sacrifice as frequently as possible.[70]

One of the most biting critiques comes from Shihāb al-Dīn al-Qarāfī (1228-85).[71] His *Al-ajwiba l-fākhira* is a lengthy polemic that is, in part, a refutation of a Christian letter (the *Letter to a Muslim friend* by the 12th-century Melkite Bishop Paul of Antioch),[72] and a response to issues raised by Christians or presented by Christianity.[73] His discussion of the Eucharist reveals his extensive knowledge not only of Christian scripture, but of other Christian and Muslim sources as well.[74] Al-Qarāfī's main concerns are the inconsistences he perceives between the Torah's prescriptions for animal sacrifices and the Christian Eucharist (*qurbān*) that replaces these with bread and wine. Nowhere did Jesus abrogate the animal sacrifices, but the Apostles instituted the use of bread and wine out of lazy thriftiness and their enjoyment of wine.[75] The commands to eat Christ's flesh and blood in the New Testament were taken too literally, according to al-Qarāfī, and he argues that the Christian Eucharist lacks a scriptural basis. It amounts to an abandonment of the Torah based on the Apostles' own arbitrariness.[76] The Muslim rejection of the Eucharist was not, then, merely confusion over what it entailed, but an outright rejection of its basis in scripture and logic.

Christian remarks on the Eucharist were not always a direct response to Muslim objections. But their consistent presence in texts suggests the Eucharist was another subject of controversy for which Christian communities would benefit from a reminder of the importance of the practice to Christian worship and to marking out Christians as distinct in Islamic milieus. For example, Anastasius of Sinai (d. c. 700)[77] wrote his

---

70 Lazarus-Yafeh, 'Some neglected aspects', pp. 78-9.

71 M. El Kaisy-Friemuth, 'Al-Qarāfī', in *CMR* 4, 582-7, pp. 582-3.

72 See D. Thomas, 'Paul of Antioch', in *CMR* 4, 78-82. Paul discusses the Eucharist in his letter, comparing the 'table' mentioned in Q 5:112-15 to the Eucharist. See S. Griffith's translation, 'Paul of Antioch', in S. Noble and A. Treiger (eds), *The Orthodox Church in the Arab world, 700-1700. An anthology of sources*, DeKalb IL, 2014, 224-5. Al-Qarāfī considers the comparison 'blindness and error'. See D.R. Sarrió Cucarella, *Muslim-Christian polemics across the Mediterranean. The splendid r eplies of Shihāb al-Dīn al-Qarāfī (d. 684/1285)*, Leiden, 2015, p. 126.

73 M. El Kaisy-Friemuth, *'Al-ajwiba'*, in *CMR* 4, 585-7. Al-Qarāfī's discussion also includes Jews and Judaism.

74 He incorporates the 9th-century Ḥafṣ ibn Albar al-Qūṭī (J.P. Monferrer Sala, 'Ibn Albar al-Qūṭī', in *CMR* 2, 281-4), by way of al-Imām al-Qurṭubī (1182-1258) and his *Al-iʿlām* (J.P. Monferrer Sala, 'Al-Imām al-Qurṭubī', in *CMR* 4, 391-4, pp. 392-4).

75 Sarrío Cucarella, *Muslim-Christian polemics*, p. 190.

76 Sarrío Cucarella, *Muslim-Christian polemics*, pp. 191-2.

77 A. Binggeli, 'Anastasius of Sinai', in *CMR* 1, 193-202, pp. 193-6.

Narrationes[78] as a series of stories meant to defend Christianity from the growing influence of Islam. Achieving this goal meant using the stories to demonstrate 'the power of the external signs of Christian faith'.[79] Among these external signs were, of course, the cross and icons, but also the Eucharist.

Many other texts give standard explanations of the Eucharist: Christ's institution of it at the Last Supper, his designation of the elements as his body and blood, and his instructions to the Apostles that they should continue to partake of the Eucharistic meal until his return. Many of these explanations incorporate Jesus' words in the New Testament (e.g. Matthew 26:26-8, Mark 14:22-4, Luke 2:17-20) or reflect liturgical language based on these words. For example, Theodore Abū Qurra discusses the Eucharist in debate with a Muslim who finds the prospect of bread becoming Christ's body a mockery.[80] Theodore argues that human bodies grow larger by virtue of eating bread. He adds a biological proof, demonstrating how the body digests food, turning it into blood 'so that it is converted into each of the [body] parts. [...] This is how an infant grows into an adult: when bread becomes, for that infant, body; and drink, blood.' In a very similar process, he explains, bread and wine become, by virtue of the Holy Spirit and the Eucharistic prayer, Christ's body and blood. 'Or don't you concede', he taunts the Muslim, 'that the Holy Spirit can do what the liver can do?' The Muslim concedes.[81]

ʿAmmār al-Baṣrī,[82] an East-Syrian Christian writing in the 9th century, devoted his *Kitāb al-burhān*[83] to defending Christian theology, particularly those topics that Muslims found most disagreeable, and structured his treatise around 12 sections that represent an economy of Christian salvation. He discusses the main elements of Christian theology and practice and devotes chapters to baptism, the Eucharist and veneration of the cross. In his section on the Union (*al-ittiḥād*) of the two natures of Christ, he writes that Muslims oppose Christians when they mention baptism and receiving the Eucharist as the body and blood of Christ.[84]

---

78 Binggeli, 'Anastasius of Sinai', pp. 198-200.

79 Binggeli, 'Anastasius of Sinai', p. 198.

80 See J.C. Lamoreaux, '*Ek tōn pros tous Sarakēnous antirrhēseōn tou episkopou Theodōrou Charran...*', in *CMR* 1, 474-7.

81 Theodore Abū Qurra, 'Refutations of the Saracens by Theodore Abū Qurrah, the Bishop of Haran, as reported by John the Deacon', in *Theodore Abū Qurrah*, trans. J.C. Lamoreaux, Provo UT, 2005, 211-27, pp. 219-20.

82 M. Beaumont, "Ammār al-Baṣrī', in *CMR* 1, 604-10, p. 604.

83 Beaumont, "Ammār al-Baṣrī', pp. 607-10.

84 M. Hayek, *ʿAmmār al-Baṣrī, Apologie et controverses*, Beirut, 1977, pp. 56-7.

'Ammār's statement not only acknowledges the Muslim objections, but it reveals the interconnectedness of the topics he addresses. In this way, 'Ammār's discussion of the Incarnation supports the way he addresses Christian practices.

With this in mind, 'Ammār notes that Christians refer to the Word of God as Son in keeping with the Gospel. 'We do not say', he clarifies, 'that the Word of God is a body' (*wa-lā naqūlu anna kalimat Allāh jism*).[85] This is an important clarification in keeping with East-Syrian Christology, whereby a distinction is maintained between the two natures of Christ: his divine nature and his human nature. In this case, it was the human nature of Christ that had a body, not the Word, i.e. not his divine nature. This distinction undergirds the rest of 'Ammār's discussion of the union of the two natures, the Incarnation, the crucifixion, baptism and Eucharist.

In his section on the Eucharist, 'Ammār explains that Christ gave the Eucharist as a physical means by which his followers might remember him. Just as baptism is the symbol (*mithāl*) of his death and resurrection, so he offered in the body and blood of the Eucharist a means by which to remember and participate in his victorious life.[86] In the elements of the Eucharist, Christ's victorious life is made to appear, or his followers can remember his victory as they receive the elements. Thus far, the discussion closely follows Theodore of Mopsuestia (d. c. 428). Theodore, of course, was the leading theologian of the Antiochene theological school and, effectively, the main proponent of what became East-Syrian (Nestorian) Christology. In one of Theodore's explanations of the Eucharist, he remarks that Christ called himself the bread because it is by this means that humanity sustains itself. In this way, his body becomes bread, for by consuming the bread in the Eucharist they participate in his victory over death.[87] Theodore also argues that Christ did not say that the bread was a symbol of his body or that the wine was a symbol of his blood. Instead, Christ said simply, 'This is my body' and 'This is my blood.'[88] By this, Theodore is able to maintain the sacramental nature of the Eucharist

85 Hayek, *'Ammār al-Baṣrī*, p. 57.

86 Hayek, *'Ammār al-Baṣrī*, p. 85. See also, S. Griffith, "Ammār al-Baṣrī's *Kitāb al-burhān*. Christian *kalām* in the first Abbasid century', *Le Muséon* 96 (1983) 145-81, p. 179.

87 A. Mingana, *Commentary of Theodore of Mopsuestia on the Lord's Prayer and on the sacraments of baptism and the Eucharist*, Cambridge, 1933, pp. 74-5.

88 Mingana, *Commentary of Theodore of Mopsuestia*, p. 75.

and his Christology, which affirms that the consecrated bread and wine become Christ's human body and blood (not the divine Word).[89]

ʿAmmār follows much of this argument, and one would expect him to affirm, like Theodore, that the bread and the wine are Christ's (human) body and blood. Even his fellow East-Syrian, the monk from Bēt Ḥālē, explains that the 'bread is of wheat, and the wine is of the vine, and by the mediation of priests and through the Holy Spirit (i.e. the epiclesis) it becomes that body and blood of Christ'.[90] Curiously, ʿAmmār does not give this explanation, but instead clarifies that in offering his body and blood in the bread and the wine Christ did *not* mean to indicate 'that bread and that wine was his body and blood' (*dhālika al-khubz wa-dhālika al-sharāb huwa jasadih wa-damah*).[91] The bread and wine are only Christ's body and blood insofar as they reveal the meaning of his resurrected life.[92] Neither does ʿAmmār mention, as do Theodore of Mopsuestia and the monk of Bēt Ḥālē, the Holy Spirit's central role in the transformation of bread and wine to body and blood.[93]

These small ways in which ʿAmmār seemingly steps to the side of East-Syrian tradition are puzzling. In addition, they are notable, largely because they are unexpected in light of other East-Syrian explanations of the Eucharist. One suspects, therefore, that ʿAmmār's explanation is designed to serve an apologetic function, elucidating the Christian practice of the Eucharist but in such a way as to avoid further Muslim objections to the figure of the Holy Spirit and the mystical and sacramental elements of the epiclesis.[94]

Finally, there is the hagiographical account from Gregory Dekapolites (d. 842)[95] about a Muslim who observes the preparation of the Eucharistic gifts during a Divine Liturgy. What the Muslim saw, however, was not the mere preparation of bread and wine, but 'that the priest took

---

89 F. McLeod, 'The Christological ramifications of Theodore of Mopsuestia's understanding of baptism and the Eucharist', *Journal of Early Christian Studies* 10 (2002) 37-75, p. 67 n. 134, and H. Chadwick, 'Eucharist and Christology in the Nestorian controversy', *The Journal of Theological Studies* 2 (Oct 1951) 145-64, pp. 156-7. See also, J. Quasten, 'The liturgical mysticism of Theodore of Mopsuestia', *Theological Studies* 15 (1954) 431-9.

90 Taylor, 'Disputation between a Muslim and a monk', p. 218.

91 Hayek, *ʿAmmār al-Baṣrī*, p. 85.

92 Hayek, *ʿAmmār al-Baṣrī*, pp. 85-6.

93 P.K. Chalfoun, 'Baptême et eucharistie chez ʿAmmār al-Baṣrī', *Parole de l'Orient* 27 (2002) 321-34, p. 330.

94 Chalfoun, 'Baptême et eucharistie', p. 330. Cf. W.Y.F. Mikhail, "Ammār al-Baṣrī's *Kitāb al-burhān*. A topical and theological analysis of Arabic Christian theology in the ninth century', Birmingham, 2013 (PhD Diss. University of Birmingham), pp. 294-5.

95 D.J. Sahas, 'Gregory Dekapolites', in *CMR* 1, 614-17.

in his hand a child which he slaughtered, drained the blood inside the cup, cut the body into pieces, and placed them on the tray!'. The Muslim confronted the priest after the liturgy and described the horror he had seen. The priest explained the miracle the Muslim had witnessed and the Christian views of the Eucharist. In turn, the Muslim was baptised. In this case, the author does not push back against common Muslim objections to the Eucharist, but instead turns them into a miraculous vision by which the practice is explained and, in common hagiographical fashion, used to bring about conversion.[96]

Baptism

When the monk from Bēt Ḥālē spoke with the Arab notable, the topic of baptism arose. In the first instance, the monk likens the practice to circumcision. For the monk, Christian baptism replaces Abrahamic circumcision and is a type of Christ's death and resurrection. Anyone who was not circumcised was not a 'son of Abraham'; similarly, anyone not baptised 'is not called a Christian'.[97]

Towards the end of their discussion, the Muslim asks, 'Will the sons of Hagar (Muslims) enter the kingdom, or not?'[98] The monk drew his reply from the New Testament; John chaps 3 and 14 – Christ's conversation with Nicodemus about the second birth, and Christ's description of heavenly mansions – and the Syriac exegetical tradition. In light of this tradition, the monk answers that anyone who has performed good deeds may, by grace, live in the 'mansions which are far removed from the torment, but he shall be considered as a hired hand and not as a son'.[99] Anyone who is baptised, however, will enter the kingdom of God.[100] By this, the monk presumably implies that moral Muslims may reside near the kingdom, but only as second-class citizens. Baptised residents will be heirs living fully within the kingdom.[101]

---

96 D.J. Sahas, 'What an infidel saw that a faithful did not. Gregory Dekapolites (d. 842) and Islam', *Greek Orthodox Theological Review* 31 (1986) 47-67.

97 Taylor, 'Disputation between a Muslim and a monk', p. 214.

98 Taylor, 'Disputation between a Muslim and a monk', p. 240.

99 Taylor, 'Disputation between a Muslim and a monk', p. 241.

100 Taylor, 'Disputation between a Muslim and a monk', p. 240.

101 See Taylor's commentary in his, 'Disputation between a Muslim and a monk', p. 241 n. 209, with reference to Ephrem the Syrian, who discusses 'mansions which are at the fences (of Paradise) / do the souls of the just and righteous reside'.

In one of the earliest Arabic apologetic texts, the 8th-century *Fī tathlīth Allāh al-wāḥid*,[102] the Melkite author compares baptism to the cleansing of water, the second birth that forgave sins. Further, Christ used baptism to destroy Satan and the worship of idols.[103] What bath or washing', the author asks, 'puts away the sins of men from before the Lord save the [...] immersion of baptism in the name of Christ?'[104] The wide-ranging theological topics addressed in the text strongly suggest that it served a catechetical function for a Christian community using Arabic and considering their faith in a context of growing Islamic influence. At several points, the author even directly addresses Muslims. In this light, one suspects the author is comparing Christian baptism with Muslim ritual cleansing and indirectly suggesting that the former was uniquely powerful.[105] In this way, baptism could be for the author a boundary marker between those who worship correctly and those who worship incorrectly.

In the 'Arabic homily in honour of Peter and Paul',[106] possibly dating to the late-7th century, the Coptic author explains that baptism is the salvific, second birth and given in place of circumcision.[107] Without this second birth, the author claims, no one can enter the kingdom of God. This eventually leads to a similar discussion to the one between the monk from Bēt Ḥālē and the Arab notable. The question is posed, 'Tell me whether the nations who worship God, but do not accept the Son or the Holy Spirit and are not baptised in his name nor do they receive the holy mysteries – may they enter into the kingdom of heaven [...]?'[108] In response, the same passages from John 3 and 14 are cited, but the conclusion is much less magnanimous in this text, where there is no mention

---

[102] M.N. Swanson, '*Fī tathlīth Allāh al-wāḥid*', in *CMR* 1, 330-3.

[103] M.D. Gibson (ed.), *An Arabic version of the Acts of the Apostles and* [...] *a treatise on the Triune nature of God with translation, from the same codex*, London, 1899, pp. 35-6.

[104] Gibson, *Arabic version of the Acts of the Apostles*, p. 36.

[105] In *Kitāb al-burhān*, 'Ammār al-Baṣrī compares Christian baptism to Muslim ritual ablutions, mocking the incoherence of the latter (Hayek, *'Ammār al-Baṣrī*, pp. 81-2). In the 'Disputation of Jirjī the monk', the monk proposes a trial whereby he, who only rarely washes, and a Muslim, who washes daily, wash themselves to see who is cleaner. This prompts a discussion on Christian baptism and the Muslim practices of ablution and circumcision. See C. Bacha, *Mujādalat al-anbā Jirjī l-rāhib al-Sim'ānī ma'a thalāthat shuyūkh min fuqahā' al-Muslimīn bi-ḥaḍrat al-amīr Mushammar al-Ayyūbī*, Beirut, 1932, pp. 102-6.

[106] J. van Lent, '*The Arabic homily of Pseudo-Theophilus of Alexandria*', in *CMR* 1, 256-60.

[107] H. Fleisch, 'Une homélie de Théophile d'Alexandrie en l'honneur de St Pierre et de St Paul', *Revue de l'Orient Chrétien* 30 (1935-6) 371-419, pp. 376-81.

[108] Fleisch, 'Homélie de Théophile d'Alexandrie', pp. 392-5. Translation from R.G. Hoyland, *Seeing Islam as others saw it*, Princeton NJ, 1997, p. 469 n. 47.

of mansions for the unbaptised – no matter how moral or just they may be – on the perimeter of the kingdom.[109]

The discussion perhaps hints at a context in which there may be some confusion over baptism as a holy mystery or even a pastoral concern over Christians converting to Islam or smoothing out the distinctions between Islam and Christianity. In this light, the practice of baptism is made a marker distinguishing between those who will enter heaven and those who will not.

Prayer

The subject of prayer was repeatedly commented on and debated among Christians and Muslims. Sometimes these discussions consist of deriding commentary on Christian bells or clappers (*nāqūs*), or the Muslim call to prayer.[110] At other times there is evident concern for how prayers from one tradition begin to mimic those of another. For example, we find Shīʿī statements about Sunnīs who complete their recitation of the *Fātiḥa* by saying '*amīn*', thereby improperly mimicking Christian (or Jewish) prayer.[111] Ibn Taymiyya (d. 1328)[112] repeatedly issued statements in response to the perceived influence of Christianity on Muslim practice. These include his *Iqtiḍāʾ*,[113] where he proscribes Muslim imitation (*tashabbuh*) of unbelievers; participating in Christian festivals or praying at graves, for example, could quickly descend into imitating their polytheistic beliefs.[114] Other texts, such as a *fatwā* from the mufti of Oran,[115] discuss the ways in which Muslims (Moriscos) living in 16th-century Spain might participate in Christian practices, such as prayer, but maintain their Islamic identities.[116]

Christian authors express similar laments, and offer instructions for Christian prayer that will help to distinguish religious communities.

---

109 Fleisch, 'Homélie de Théophile d'Alexandrie', pp. 394-7.

110 See J. Tolan, 'A dreadful racket. The clanging of bells and the yowling of muezzins in Iberian interconfessional polemics', in J. Tolan (ed.), *Sons of Ishmael. Muslims through European eyes in the Middle Ages*, Gainesville FL, 2008, 147-60.

111 See D.M. Freidenreich's comments in his 'Christians in early and classical Shīʿī law', in *CMR* 3, 27-40, p. 35.

112 J. Hoover, 'Ibn Taymiyya', in *CMR* 4, 824-78, pp. 824-33.

113 Hoover, 'Ibn Taymiyya', pp. 865-73.

114 Hoover, 'Ibn Taymiyya', p. 869. See also, J. Hoover, '*Masʾala fī man yusammī l-khamīs ʿīd*', in *CMR* 4, 874-5.

115 L. Bernabé Pons, 'The Mufti of Oran', in *CMR* 6, 67-72, pp. 67-8.

116 Bernabé Pons, 'Mufti of Oran', pp. 68-72.

The author of *Al-jāmiʿ wujūh al-īmān* insisted that his Christian readers should make the sign of the cross whenever they prayed, whether they were in a church or in any other location.[117] Such an instruction was an important means for marking prayer out as distinctly Christian in nature in a context where multiple faith communities prayed and where Islam and Arabic were having an increasing influence upon Christians.[118]

There are also examples where the nature and sound of prayer among Christians and Muslims was similar enough that one could be mistaken for the other and lead, in the end, to conversion. There is, for example, the 9th-century hagiographical account of ʿAbd al-Masīḥ al-Najrānī and his martyrdom.[119] ʿAbd al-Masīḥ was a Christian who wished to go to Jerusalem in order to pray. During his journey to the holy city, he fell in with a band of Muslim raiders and joined them in their battles and prayers, and he eventually converted to Islam. He later repented, returned to Christianity, and publicised his apostasy from Islam, and he was martyred.[120] One of the functions of this text was to demonstrate that conversions were not unknown and could take place in contexts where the absence of distinctive marks meant that the lines distinguishing religious traditions became blurred.[121]

In many other cases, the discussion of prayer focused on the direction one faced whilst praying. For Ibn Taymiyya, the unbelievers were those who were baptised, venerated the cross, and prayed towards the east.[122] For ʿAbd al-Jabbār, Christians prayed toward the east even though Christ prayed to the west, towards Jerusalem – more evidence in his mind that Christians had invented religious rites.[123] Similarly, the 16th-century *Burbetnâme-i-Sultan cem*[124] argues that Christians had abandoned the

---

117 See Tieszen, *Cross veneration*, p. 110.

118 Swanson, 'Cross of Christ', p. 140. Pedro Ramírez de Alba offers similar comments in his *Doctrina christiana* and Hernando de Talavera instructs Morisco communities on the sign of the cross in his *Instrucción del Arzobispo de Granada* (L. Resines, 'Pedro Ramírez de Alba', in *CMR* 6, 93-5, pp. 94-5; I. Iannuzzi, 'Hernando de Talavera', in *CMR* 6, 60-6).

119 D. Vila, '*The martyrdom of ʿAbd al-Masīḥ*', in *CMR* 1, 684-7.

120 See the account in S.H. Griffith, 'The Arabic account of ʿAbd al-Masīḥ an-Najrānī al-Ghassānī', *Le Muséon* 98 (1985) 331-74.

121 M.N. Swanson, 'The martyrdom of ʿAbd al-Masīḥ, Superior of Mount Sinai (Qays al-Ghassānī)', in D. Thomas (ed.), *Syrian Christians under Islam. The first thousand years*, Leiden, 2001, 107-29, pp. 121-4. See also D.H. Vila, '*The martydom of Anthony* (*Rawḥ al-Qurashī*), in *CMR* 1, 498-501, where 'Anthony repents of his having participated in Muslim worship (sacrifice on ʿĪd al-aḍḥā and prayer facing Mecca)', pp. 499-500.

122 Hoover, '*Masʾala fī man yusammī l-khamīs ʿīd*', in *CMR* 4, 874-5.

123 ʿAbd al-Jabbār, *Critique of Christian origins*, p. 87.

124 L. Demiri, 'Gurbetnâme-i Sultan Cem', in *CMR* 7, 676-87.

religion of Jesus; among the evidence is that they face east in prayer even though their *qibla* used to be Jerusalem. The likely culprit in making such changes was the Apostle Paul.[125]

Some responses to the dilemma of the direction of prayer were rather objective. Jacob of Edessa (d. 708)[126] observed in a letter:[127]

> [...] it is not to the south that the Jews pray, nor either do the Muslims. The Jews who live in Egypt, and also the Muslims there, as I saw with my own eyes [...] prayed to the east, and still do, both peoples – the Jews towards Jerusalem and the Muslims towards the Kaʿba. And those Jews who are to the south of Jerusalem pray to the north; and those in the land of Babel, in Ḥira and in Baṣra, pray to the west. And also the Muslims who are there pray to the west, towards the Kaʿba; and those who are to the south of the Kaʿba pray to the north.[128]

However, many other texts follow the lines of traditional apologetic and polemic. For example, the early 7th-century *Testimonies of the prophets about the Dispensation of Christ*[129] explains that Christians face east in prayer towards Paradise, but also assert that they have done so from the time of Adam. Further, their religion is more excellent than any other as a result.[130] In the disputation of the monk from Bēt Ḥālē, the Muslim asks why Christians only face east in prayer since God can be found everywhere. The monk responds that Christians face east because the Garden of Eden was in the east and Christ prayed in this direction, teaching his followers to do so as well. Further, according to the monk, this is the 'chief' direction.[131]

We have already seen that Abū Rā'iṭa calls the cross the Christian *qibla*. He does this in order to explain why Christians venerate the cross, but it also allows him to explain why Christians face east in prayer. He also addresses the Muslim accusation that the Jews faced toward Jerusalem, and 'did not take the east as their *qibla*'.[132] For Abū Rā'iṭa, this was a *mysterion* connected to the fact that Jerusalem was the location of

125 Demiri, 'Gurbetnâme-i Sultan Cem', pp. 680, 681.

126 H.G. Teule, 'Jacob of Edessa', in *CMR* 1, 226-33, pp. 226-7.

127 Teule, 'Jacob of Edessa', pp. 227-30.

128 Quoted in Hoyland, *Seeing Islam as others saw it*, pp. 565-6.

129 M. Debié, '*Testimonies of the prophets about the dispensation of Christ*', in *CMR* 1, 242-4.

130 M. Debié, 'Muslim-Christian controversy in an unedited Syriac text', in E. Grypeou, M.N. Swanson, and D. Thomas (eds), *The encounter of Eastern Christianity with early Islam*, Leiden, 2006, 225-35, p. 232.

131 Taylor, 'Disputation between a Muslim and a monk', pp. 235-7.

132 Abū Rā'iṭa, 'Fī ithbāt dīn al-naṣrāniyya', pp. 134-5.

Christ's Incarnation, crucifixion and, significantly, his affirmation that he would return again one day, presumably from the east.[133] All this informs the reasons why Christians designate the cross as their *qibla* and use it to mark the direction they face in prayer. Whoever 'takes up [this] *qibla*, apart from [all] other things, is saved'.[134]

Finally, in a passage heavily dependent on Jacob of Edessa, Dionysius bar Ṣalībī (d. 1171) explains why Christians face east in prayer. He adds the traditional explanations for the Christian practice, but also includes references to the Qur'an.[135] He writes, 'Christ also worshipped toward the east after being baptized, and the apostles learned from him. Before baptism, Christ and the prophets worshipped in the direction of Jerusalem. But', he says to Muslims, 'you abandoned (worship toward) Jerusalem, and you now worship toward Makka.'[136] He concludes, 'God is light, and he should be worshipped in the direction of the light.'[137]

Conclusion

The prominent place of these five practices – icon and cross veneration, celebration of the Eucharist, baptism, and prayer – in disputational and apologetic literature indicates that they were an important theme to discuss for Muslims and Christians. In doing so, authors were surely able to shed light on their practices and respond to rebuffs. Nevertheless, so they might also have worked to speak to their communities by reminding them why they incorporated these practices in worship and how clinging to them was a necessary part of bearing witness to the distinct truth of their faith in multi-religious milieus.[138] In many instances, these discussions reflect a reality of Christian-Muslim relations whereby Muslims are witnessing Christian practices and asking about them, or Christians are attempting to discuss practices in environments that are increasingly and continually being shaped by Islam. In other cases, the discussions reflect attempts to claim space for one religion or another. As records of discussions continued in later centuries, they seem to grow

133 Abū Rā'iṭa, 'Fī ithbāt dīn al-naṣrāniyya', pp. 136-7.

134 Abū Rā'iṭa, 'Fī ithbāt dīn al-naṣrāniyya', pp. 134-5.

135 Dionysius bar Ṣalībī, *A response to the Arabs*, trans. J.P. Amar (Corpus Scriptorum Christianorum Orientalium 614/15), Louvain, 2005, pp. 88-90/81-2. See also H.G. Teule, 'Dionysius bar Ṣalibi', in *CMR* 3, 665-70.

136 Dionysius bar Ṣalībī, *Response to the Arabs*, pp. 89/82.

137 Dionysius bar Ṣalībī, *Response to the Arabs*, pp. 89/82.

138 Griffith, *Church in the shadow of the mosque*, p. 145.

distant from lived concerns and do more to reflect the need to address literary topoi and deploy a stock set of arguments, examples, and strategies. In each case, however, it becomes clear that, beyond just what worshippers believed, the way they practised their faith was an integral means by which to control Christian-Muslim encounters.

Bibliography

A. Abel, art. 'Baḥīrā', in *EI2*

D. Abulafia, 'The servitude of Jews and Muslims in the medieval Mediterranean. Origins and diffusion', *Mélanges de l'École Française de Rome* 112 (2000) 687-714

M. Accad, 'The ultimate proof-text. The interpretation of John 20:17 in Muslim-Christian dialogue (second/eighth-eighth/fourteenth centuries)', in Thomas, *Christians at the heart of Islamic rule*, 2003, 199-214

M. Accad, *Sacred Misinterpretation. Reaching across the Christian-Muslim divide*, Grand Rapids MI, 2019

M. Acién Almansa, 'La herencia del protofeudalismo visigodo frente a la imposición del estado islámico', in Caballero Zoreda and Mateos Cruz, *Visigodos y Omeyas*, 2000, 429-41

C. Adang, *Muslim writers on Judaism and the Hebrew Bible. From Ibn Rabban to Ibn Hazm*, Leiden, 1996

C. Adang, 'Islam as the inborn religion of mankind. The concept of *fiṭra* in the works of Ibn Ḥazm', *Al-Qanṭara* 21 (2000) 391-410

C. Adang, art. 'Belief and unbelief', in *EQ*

C. Addas, *Quest for the red sulphur*, trans. P. Kingsley, Cambridge, 1993

Yaḥyā ibn 'Adī, *The reformation of morals*, trans. S.H. Griffith, Provo UT, 2002

W.J. Aerts and G.A.A. Kortekaas (eds), *Die Apokalypse des Pseudo-Methodius. Die ältesten Griechischen und Lateinischen übersetzungen*, Louvain, 1998

A. Afsaruddin, *The first Muslims. History and memory*, Oxford, 2008

J. Aguadé, 'Some remarks about sectarian movements in al-Andalus', *Studia Islamica* 64 (1986) 53-77

Raymond of Aguilers, *Le 'Liber' de Raymond d'Aguilers*, ed. J. Hill and L. Hill, Paris, 1969

M.J. Ailes, 'Heroes of war. Ambroise's heroes of the Third Crusade', in Saunders, et al., *Writing war*, 2004, 29-48

M. Ailes and M. Barber (eds), *The history of the holy war. Ambroise's Estoire de la Guerre Sainte*, vol. 1, Woodbridge, 2003

C. Aillet, *Les mozarabs. Christianisme, islamisation et arabisation en péninsule Ibérique (IXᵉ-XIIᵉ siècle)*, Madrid, 2010

Al-Nāshi' al-Akbar, 'Refutation of the Christians', in Thomas, *Christian doctrines in Islamic theology*, 2008, 35-77

M. Akyol, *The Islamic Jesus. How the king of the Jews became a prophet of the Muslims*, New York, 2017

Paulus Albarus, 'Indiculus luminosus', in Gil, *Corpus scriptorum muzarabicorum*, vol. 1, 1973

Albert of Aachen, *Historia Ierosolimitana. History of the journey to Jerusalem*, ed. S. Edgington, Oxford, 2007

M.C. Albl, *'And scripture cannot be broken'. The form and function of the early Christian testimonia collections*, Leiden, 1999

J.C. Alexander, *Toward a history of post-Byzantine Greece. The Ottoman* kanunnames *for the Greek lands, circa 1500-circa 1600*, Athens, 1985

J.C. Alexander, 'The Lord giveth and the Lord taketh away. Athos and the confiscation affair of 1568-9', in Komine-Dialete, *Athos in the 14th-16th centuries*, 1997, 149-200

P.J. Alexander, *The Byzantine apocalyptic tradition*, Berkeley CA, 1985

C. Alvar et al. (eds), *Studia in honorem prof. M. de Riquer*, Barcelona, 1986

H. Amirav, E. Grypeou, and G. Stroumsa (eds), *Apocalypticism and eschatology in late antiquity: encounters in the Abrahamic religions, 6th-8th centuries*, Leuven, 2017

R. Amitai-Preiss, *Mongols and Mamluks. The Mamluk Īlkhānid war, 1260-1281*, Cambridge, 1995

Malik ibn Anas, *Al-Muwaṭṭa'*, *K. Ṣifat al-nabī*, 'Bāb mā jā' fī ṣifat 'Īsā ibn Maryam wa-l-Dajjāl', vol. 2, ed. M.F.'A. al-Bāqī, Beirut, 1985

G.C. Anawati, 'Factors and effects of Arabization and of Islamization in medieval Egypt and Syria', in Vryonis, *Islam and cultural change*, 1975, 17-41

G.C. Anawati, art. ''Isā', in *EI2*

C. D'Ancona, art. 'Greek into Arabic', in *EI3*

T. Andrae, *Die Person Muhammeds in Lehre und Glaube seiner Gemeinde*, Stockholm, 1917

T. Andrae, *In the garden of myrtles. Studies in early Islamic mysticism*, trans. A. Schimmel, Albany NY, 1987

T.L. Andrews, *Matt'ēos Uṙhayec'i and his Chronicle. History as apocalypse in a crossroads of cultures*, Leiden, 2017

D.G. Angelov (ed.), *Church and society in late Byzantium*, Kalamazoo MI, 2009

S. Anthony, 'The composition of S. b. 'Umar's "Account of King Paul and his corruption of ancient Christianity"', *Der Islam* 85 (2010) 164-202

Thomas Aquinas, *Summa contra gentiles*, 1:2, trans. A.C. Pegis, Notre Dame IN, 1975

Thomas Aquinas, *Summa contra gentiles*, 4:1, trans. C.J. O'Neil, Notre Dame IN, 1975

Ibn 'Arabī, *Al-Futuḥāt al-makkiyya*, ed. 'U. Yahya, Cairo, 1972-92

Ibn 'Arabī, *The ringstones of wisdom*, trans. C.K. Dagli, Chicago IL, 2004

A.J. Arberry, *The Koran interpreted. A translation*, London, 1955
F. Armanios, *Coptic Christianity in Ottoman Egypt*, New York, 2011
R. Armour, *Islam, Christianity and the West. A troubled history*, Maryknoll NY, 2004
R.J. Armstrong and I.C. Braidy (ed. and trans.), *Francis and Clare. The complete works*, New York, 1982
G. Arnakis, *Oi protoi Othomanoi* [The first Ottomans], Athens, 1947
T.W. Arnold, *The preaching of Islam. A history of the propagation of the Muslim faith*, London, 1896
T.W. Arnold and R.A. Nicholson (eds), *A volume of Oriental studies presented to Professor Edward G. Browne* [...] *on his 60th birthday*, Cambridge, 1922
M. Asad, *The message of the Quran*, London, 2003
ʿAlī ibn al-Ḥasan ibn ʿAsākir, *Tàrīkh madīnat Dimashq*, vol. 22, ed. ʿU. al-ʿAmrawī, Beirut, 1995
ʿAlī ibn al-Ḥasan ibn ʿAsākir, *Tārīkh madīnat Dimashq*, vol. 47, ed. M. al-ʿAmrawī, Beirut, 1995
T.S. Asbridge, *The creation of the principality of Antioch, 1098-1130*, Woodbridge, Suffolk, 2000
M. Asín Palacios, 'Logia et agrapha Domini Jesu', in Nau et al., *Patrologia orientalis*, 1919, vol. 13, fasc. 3, 335-431
M. Asín Palacios, 'Influencias evangélicas en la literatura religiosa del Islam', in Arnold and Nicholson, *A volume of Oriental studies*, 1922, 8-27
M. Asín Palacios, 'Logia et agrapha Domini Jesu', in Nau et al., *Patrologia orientalis*, 1926, vol. 19, fasc. 4, 531-624
A. Aslan, *Religious pluralism in Christian and Islamic philosophy. The thought of John Hick and Seyyed Hossein Nasr*, London, 1994
S. Aslanian, *From the Indian Ocean to the Mediterranean. The global trade networks of Armenian merchants from New Julfa*, Berkeley CA, 2014
al-ʿAsqalānī, *Fatḥ al-bārī bi-sharḥ Ṣaḥīḥ al-imām Abī ʿAbd Allāh Muḥammad b. Ismāʿīl al-Bukhārī*, vol. 6, ed. M.F. ʿAbd al-Bāqī and M. al-D. al-Khaṭīb, Beirut, 1959
Ibn Ḥajar al-ʿAsqalānī, *Inbāʾ al-ghumr bī anbāʾ al-ʿumr*, Hyderabad: Dar al-Maʿārif al-ʿUthmaniyya, 1974, vol. 7
Ibn al-Athīr, *Al-Nihāya fī gharīb al-ḥadīth wa-l-athar*, vol. 4, ed. Ṭ.A. al-Zāwī and M.M. al-Ṭanāḥī, Cairo, 1963
Ibn al-Athīr, *The chronicle of Ibn al-Athir for the crusading period from* al-Kamil fi'l-ta'rikh, part 1, trans. D.S. Richards, Aldershot, 2006
G. Avni, *The Byzantine-Islamic transition in Palestine*, Oxford, 2014
N.G. Awad, *Orthodoxy in Arabic terms. A study of Theodore Abu Qurrah's theology in its Islamic context*, Berlin, 2015
Al-ʿAyyāshī, *Tafsīr al-ʿAyyāshī*, vol. 1, ed. H.al-R. al-Maḥallātī, Beirut, 1991

C. Bacha (ed.), *Les oeuvres arabes de Theodore Aboucara*, Beirut, 1904

C. Bacha, *Mujādalat al-anbā Jirjī l-rāhib al-Simʿānī maʿa thalāthat shuyūkh min fuqahāʾ al-Muslimīn bi-ḥaḍrat al-amīr Mushammar al-Ayyūbī*, Beirut, 1932

ʿAbd al-Qādir Badāʾūnī, *Muntakhab al-tawārīkh*, vol. 2, trans. G. Ranking, Delhi: Munshiram Manoharlal, 1973

A. Bakhou, *Defending Christian faith. The fifth part of the Christian apology of Gerasimus*, Warsaw, 2014

al-Balādhūrī, *Ansāb al-ashrāf*, vol. 3, Wiesbaden, 1978

al-Balādhurī, *Futūḥ al-buldān*, ed. ʿA.-A. al-Ṭabbāʿ, Beirut, 1307 [1987]

A. Ballestín, 'El Islam en los *Dialogi* de Pedro Alfonso', *Revista Española de Filosofía Medieval* 10 (2003) 59-66

Bar Hebraeus, *The Chronography of Gregory Abû'l Faraj, the son of Aaron, the Hebrew physician commonly known as Bar Hebraeus*, ed. E.W. Wallis Budge, vol. 1, Oxford, 1932

R. Barkai, *Cristianos y musulmanes en la España medieval (El enemigo en el espejo)*, Madrid, 1991

K. Barkey and G. Gavrilis, 'The Ottoman millet system. Non-territorial autonomy and its contemporary legacy', *Ethnopolitics* 15 (2016) 24-42

Ibn ʿAbd al-Barr, *Al-Tamhīd li-mā fī l-Muwaṭṭāʾ min al-maʿānī wa-l-asānīd*, vol. 14, ed. M. b. A. al-ʿAlawī and M.ʿA. al-K. al-Bakrī, Rabat, 1967

Al-Bāqillānī, 'Refutation of the Christians from the Book of the introduction', in Thomas, *Christian doctrines in Islamic theology*, 2008, 152-3

M. Barber and K. Bate (trans.), *Letters from the East. Crusaders, pilgrims and settlers in the 12th-13th centuries*, Farnham, 2010

Qusṭanṭīn al-Bāshā [Bacha], *Mayāmir Thāwudūrus Abī Qurra usquf Ḥarrān*, Beirut: Maṭbaʿat al-Fawāʾid, 1904

S. Bashear, 'Muslim apocalypses', *Israel Oriental Studies* 13 (1993) 75-93

ʿAmmār al-Baṣrī, *Kitāb al-masāʾil wa-l-ajwiba*, in Hayek, *ʿAmmār al-Baṣrī. Apologie et controverses*, 1977, 92-265

F.V. Bauerschmidt, *Holy teaching. Introducing the Summa theologiae of St. Thomas Aquinas*, Grand Rapids MI, 2005

E. Baumgarten, R. Karras and K. Mesler (eds), *Entangled histories*, Philadelphia PA, 2017

I.M. Beaumont, 'Early Christian interpretation of the Qur'an', *Transformation* 22 (2005) 195-203

I.M. Beaumont, ''Ammār al-Baṣrī on the alleged corruption of the gospels', in Thomas, *The Bible in Arab Christianity*, 2007, 241-55

I.M. Beaumont, *Christology in dialogue with Muslims. A critical analysis of Christian presentations of Christ for Muslims from the ninth and twentieth centuries*, Eugene OR, 2011

I.M. Beaumont, 'Speaking of the Triune God. Christian defence of the Trinity in the early Islamic period', *Transformation* 29 (2012) 111-27

I.M. Beaumont (ed.), *Arab Christians and the Qur'an from the origins of Islam to the medieval period*, Leiden, 2018

I.M. Beaumont, "Ammār al-Baṣrī. Ninth century Christian theology and qur'anic presuppositions', in Beaumont, *Arab Christians and the Qur'an*, 2018, 83-105

I.M. Beaumont and M. El Kaisy-Friemuth (ed. and trans.), Al-radd al-jamīl. *A fitting refutation of the divinity of Jesus, attributed to Abū Ḥamid al-Ghazālī*, Leiden, 2016

T. Beg, *The history of Mehmed the Conqueror*, Minneapolis MN, 1978

A.D. Beihammer, *Byzantium and the emergence of Muslim-Turkish Anatolia, ca. 1040-1130*, Abingdon, 2017

G.I. Benevich, 'Christological polemics of Maximus the Confessor and the emergence of Islam onto the world stage', *Theological Studies* 72 (2011) 335-44

N. Berend, *At the gate of Christendom*, Cambridge, 2001

J. Bergsagel, D. Hiley, and T. Riss (eds), *Of chronicles and kings. National saints and the emergence of nation states in the High Middle Ages*, Copenhagen, 2015

M. Bernand and G. Troupeau, art. 'Ḳiyās', in *EI2*

D. Bertaina, 'Early Muslim attitudes towards the Bible', in Thomas, *Routledge handbook on Christian-Muslim Relations*, 2018, 98-106

D. Bertaina, 'An Arabic Christian perspective on monotheism in the Qur'an. Elias of Nisibis' *Kitab al-majalis*', in Bertaina et al., *Heirs of the Apostles*, 2019, 3-21

D. Bertaina et al. (eds), *Heirs of the Apostles. Studies on Arabic Christianity in honor of Sidney H. Griffith*, Leiden, 2019

S. Binay and S. Leder (eds), *Translating the Bible into Arabic. Historical, text-critical and literary aspects*, Beirut, 2012

A. Binggeli, 'Anastate le Sinaïte. *Récits sur le Sinaï* et *Récits utiles à l'âme*. Édition, traduction, commentaire', Paris, 2001 (PhD Diss. Université Paris–IV)

A. Binggeli, 'Converting the caliph. A legendary motif in Christian hagiography and historiography of the early Islamic period', in Papaconstantinou, et al., *Writing 'true stories'*, Turnhout, 2010, 77-103

Al-Biqāʿī, *Naẓm al-durar fī tan āsub al-āyāt wa al-suwar*, Hyderbad, 1978

J. Bird, 'Crusade and conversion after the Fourth Lateran Council (1215). Oliver of Paderborn's and James of Vitry's mission to Muslims reconsidered', *Essays in Medieval Studies* 21 (2004) 23-47

J. Blackmore and G.S. Hucheson (eds), *Queer Iberia. Sexualities, cultures, and crossings from the Middle Ages to the Renaissance*, Durham NC, 1999

D. Blanks (ed.), *Images of the Other. Europe and the Muslim world before 1700*, Cairo, 1996

D.R. Blanks and M. Frassetto (eds), *Western views of Islam in medieval and early modern Europe. Perception of other*, New York, 1999

P. Blessing and R. Goshgarian (eds), *Architecture and landscape in medieval Anatolia, 1100-1500*, Edinburgh, 2017

A.J. Boas (ed.), *The crusader world*, Abingdon, 2016

H. Bobzin, *Der Koran im Zeitalter der Reformation*, Beirut, 2008

H. Bobzin, 'Guglielmo Raimondo Moncada e la sua traduzione della sura 21 ('dei profeti')', in Perani, *Guglielmo Raimondo Moncada* alias *Flavio Mitridate*, 2008, 173-83

B. Bombi, 'The Fifth Crusade and the conversion of Muslims', in Mylod et al., *The Fifth Crusade in context*, 2017, 68-91

A. Bonner (ed.), *Selected works of Ramon Llull (1232-1316)*, vol. 1, Princeton NJ, 1985

A. Borrut, 'La circulation de l'information historique entre les sources arabo-musulmanes et syriaques. Élie de Nisibe et ses sources', in Debié, *L'historiographie syriaque*, 2009, 137-59

A. Borrut and F. Donner (eds), *Christians and others in the Umayyad state*, Chicago IL, 2016

D. Bosch, *Transforming mission. Paradigm shifts in the theology of mission*, Maryknoll NY, 1991

C.E. Bosworth (trans.), *The history of al-Ṭabarī*, vol. 33. *Storm and stress along the northern frontiers of the ʿAbbāsid Caliphate*, Albany NY, 1991

G. Böwering, art. 'Chronology and the Qurʾān', in *EQ*

G. Böwering, art. 'God and his attributes', in *EQ*

R. Brann (ed.), *Languages of power in Islamic Spain*, Bethesda MD, 1997

M. Breydy, *Das Annalenwerk des Eutychios von Alexandrien. Ausgewählte Geschichten und Legenden kompiliert von Saʿīd ibn Baṭrīq um 935 AD*, 2 vols (*CSCO* 471-2), Louvain, 1985

J.S. Bridger, *Christian exegesis of the Qurʾān*, Eugene OR, 2015

R. Broadhurst (trans.), *The travels of Ibn Jubayr. A mediaeval Spanish Muslim visits Makkah, Madinah, Egypt, cities of the Middle East and Sicily*, London, 1952

P.R. Brown and S.L. Wailes (eds), *A companion to Hrotsvit of Grandersheim (fl. 960). Contextual and interpretive approaches*, Leiden, 2012

L.E. Browne, *The eclipse of Christianity in Asia. From the time of Muhammad till the fourteenth century*, Cambridge, 1933

S.G. Bruce, *Cluny and the Muslims of La Garde-Freinet. Hagiography and the problem of Islam in medieval Europe*, Ithaca NY, 2015

E.A.W. Budge, *The Chronography of Gregory Abû 'l Faraj, the son of Aaron, the Hebrew physician commonly known as Bar Hebraeus. Being the first part of his political history of the world*, London, 1932

F. Buhl, art. 'Taḥrīf', in *EI1*

F. Buhl et al., art. 'Muḥammad', in *EI2*

al-Bukhārī, *K. Aḥādīth al-anbiyāʾ*, Damascus, 2002

R.W. Bulliet, *Conversion to Islam in the medieval period. An essay in quantitative history*, Cambridge MA, 1979

R.W. Bulliet, *The case for Islamo-Christian civilisation*, New York, 2004

D. Bumazhnov et al. (eds), *Bibel, Byzanz und Christlicher Orient. Festschrift für Stephen Gerö zum 65. Geburstag*, Leuven, 2011

A. Bundgens et al. (eds), 'Die *Errores legis Mahumeti* des Johannes von Segovia', *Neulateinisches Jahrbuch* 15 (2013) 27-60

T.E. Burman, 'The influence of the *Apology of al-Kindī* and *Contrarietas alfolica* on Ramon Llull's late religious polemics, 1305-1313', *Mediaeval Studies* 53 (1991) 197-208

T.E. Burman, *Religious polemic and the intellectual history of the Mozarabs, c. 1050-1200*, Leiden, 1994

T.E. Burman, *Reading the Qur'ān in Latin Christendom, 1140-1560*, Philadelphia PA, 2007

T.E. Burman, 'How an Italian friar read his Arabic Qur'an', *Dante Studies* 125 (2007) 93-109

R.J. Burns, 'Muslims in the thirteenth-century realms of Aragon. Interaction and reaction', in Powell, *Muslims under Latin rule*, 1990, 57-102

J. Burton, art. 'Muṣḥaf', in *EI2*

L. Caballero Zoreda and P. Mateos Cruz (eds), *Visigodos y Omeyas. Un debate entre la Antigüedad Tardía y la Alta Edad Media*, Madrid, 2000

I. de las Cagigas, *Los mozárabes*, Madrid, 1947-48

D.F. Callahan, *Jerusalem and the Cross in the life and writings of Ademar of Chabannes*, Leiden, 2016

A. Camps, *The Friars Minor in China (1294-1955)*, Hong Kong, 2000

A. Camps, *Studies in Asian mission history 1958-1996*, Leiden, 2014

S.R. Canby et al. (eds), *Court and cosmos. The great age of the Seljuqs*, New York, 2016

P. Canivet and J.-P. Rey-Coquais (eds), *Mélanges Monseigneur Joseph Nasrallah*, Damascus, 2006

T. Carlson, *Christianity in fifteenth-century Iraq*, Cambridge, 2018

J. Carvalho (ed.), *Religion and power in Europe. Conflict and convergence*, Pisa, 2007

Y. Casewit, 'A Muslim scholar of the Bible. Prooftexts from Genesis and Mattew in the Qur'an commentary of Ibn Barrajān of Seville (d. 536/1141)', *Journal of Qur'anic Studies* 18 (2016) 1–48

Y. Casewit, *The mystics of al-Andalus. Ibn Barrajan and Islamic thought in the twelfth century*, Cambridge, 2017

D. Catalán and M. Soledad de Andrés (eds), *Crónica del moro Rasis*, Madrid, 1975

B.A. Catlos, *The victors and the vanquished. Christians and Muslims of Catalonia and Aragon, 1050-1300*, Cambridge, 2004

B.A. Catlos, *Muslims of medieval Latin Christendom, c. 1050-1614*, Cambridge, 2014

U. Cecini, *Alcoranus Latinus*, Berlin, 2012

M. Di Cesare, *The pseudo-historical image of the Prophet Muḥammad in medieval Latin literature. A repertory*, Berlin, 2011

H. Chadwick, 'Eucharist and Christology in the Nestorian controversy', *The Journal of Theological Studies* 2 (Oct 1951) 145-64

P.K. Chalfoun, 'Baptême et eucharistie chez 'Ammār al-Baṣrī', *Parole de l'Orient* 27 (2002) 321-34

P. Charanis, 'On the date of the occupation of Gallipoli by the Turks', *Byzantinoslavica* 15 (1955) 113-16

R.H. Charles (trans.), *The Chronicle of John, Bishop of Nikiu, translated from Zotenberg's Ethiopic text*, London, 1916

F.H. Chase (trans.), *Saint John of Damascus. Writings* [The Fathers of the Church 37], Washington DC, 1958

Chronicle of 741, in J. Gil (ed.), *Corpus scriptorium muzarabicorum*, vol. 1, Madrid, 1973

N. Clarke, *The Muslim conquest of Iberia. Medieval Arabic narratives*, Abingdon, 2012

L. Cheikho, 'Majālis Īliyyā muṭrān Naṣībīn', *Al-Mashriq* 20 (1922) 267–70

N. Christie, *Muslims and crusaders. Christianity's wars in the Middle East from 1095-1382, from the Islamic sources*, London, 2014

A. Christys, *Christians in al-Andalus, 711-1000*, Abingdon, 2002

P. Cobb, *Usama ibn Munqidh, warrior poet of the age of the crusades*, Oxford, 2005

P. Cobb, *The race for paradise. An Islamic history of the crusades*, Oxford, 2016

J.J. Collins (ed.), *The Oxford handbook of apocalyptic literature*, New York, 2014

R. Collins, *Caliphs and kings. Spain, 796-1031*, Chichester, 2012

A. Comnena, *The Alexiad*, trans. E.A.W. Dawes, Cambridge, Ontario, 2000

A. Comnena, *Alexias*, ed. D.R. Reinsch et al., 2 vols, Berlin, 2001

L.I. Conrad, 'Qur'ānic studies. A historian's perspective', in Kropp, *Results of contemporary research on the Qur'an*, 2007, 9-15

O.R. Constable with D. Zurro (eds), *Medieval Iberia. Readings from Christian, Muslim, and Jewish sources*, Philadelphia PA, 1997, 2012[2]

D. Cook, *Studies in Muslim apocalyptic*, Princeton NJ, 2002

D. Cook, 'Apostasy from Islam. A historical perspective', *Jerusalem Studies in Arabic and Islam* 31 (2006) 248-88

D. Cook, 'New Testament citations in the ḥadīth literature and the question of early Gospel translations into Arabic', in Grypeou et al., *The encounter of Eastern Christianity with early Islam*, 2006, 185-223

D. Cook, *'The Book of Tribulations'. The Syrian Muslim apocalyptic tradition*, Edinburgh, 2017

M. Cook et al. (eds), *The new Cambridge history of Islam*, vol. 1. *The formation of the Islamic world, sixth to eleventh centuries*, Cambridge, 2010

J.A. Coope, *The martyrs of Córdoba. Community and family conflict in an age of mass conversion*, Lincoln NB, 1995

C. Cornille (ed.), *The Wiley-Blackwell companion to inter-religious dialogue*, Oxford, 2013

F. Corriente, 'Tres mitos contemporáneos frente a la realidad de Alandalús: romanticismo filoárabe, "cultura Mozárabe" y "cultura Sefardí"', in Parrilla and García, *Orientalismo, exotismo y traducción*, 2000, 39-47

M. Cortés Arrese (ed.), *Toledo y Bizancio*, Cuenca, 2002

Y. Courbage and P. Fargues, *Chrétiens et Juifs dans l'Islam arabe et turc*, Paris, 1997

S.P. Cowe, 'Patterns of Armeno-Muslim interchange on the Armenian plateau in the interstice between Byzantine and Ottoman hegemony', in Peacock et al., *Christianity and Islam in Medieval Anatolia*, 2015, 77-105

K. Cragg, *Jesus and the Muslim*, Oxford, 1999

P. Crone and M. Hinds, *God's caliph. Religious authority in the first centuries of Islam*, Cambridge, 1986

M. Crusius, *Turco-Graeciae, libri octo*, Basle, 1584

D.S. Cucarella, *Muslim-Christian polemics across the Mediterranean. The splendid replies of Shihāb al-Dīn al-Qarāfī (d. 684/1285)*, Leiden, 2015

A. Cutler, *Catholic missions to Muslims at the end of the First Crusade*, Los Angeles CA, 1963 (PhD Diss. University of Southern California)

A. Cutler, 'The First Crusade and the idea of conversion', *The Muslim World* 58 (1968) 57-71, 155-64

H. Daiber, 'Orosius' *Historiae Adversus paganos* in arabischer Überlieferung', in van Rooden et al., *Tradition and re-interpretation in Jewish and early Christian literature*, 1986, 202–49

M. Daneshgar and W.A. Saleh (eds), *Islamic studies today. Essays in honor of Andrew Rippin*, Leiden, 2017

J. Daniélou, *The theology of Jewish Christianity. The development of Christian doctrine before the Council of Nicaea*, vol. 1, trans. and ed. J.A. Baker, London, 1964

G. Dardess and M.L. Krier Mich, *In the spirit of St Francis and the sultan. Catholics and Muslims working together for the common good*, Maryknoll NY, 2011

C. Dawson (ed.), *The Mongol mission. Narratives and letters to the Franciscan missionaries in Mongolia and China in the thirteenth and fourteenth centuries*, New York, 1955

Abū Dā'ūd, *Sunan*, Beirut: Dār al-Jīl, 1988, vol. 4

M. Debié, 'Muslim-Christian controversy in an unedited Syriac text', in Grypeou et al., *The encounter of Eastern Christianity with early Islam*, 2006, 225-35

M. Debié (ed.), *L'historiographie syriaque*, Paris, 2009

J.P. Decter, *Iberian Jewish literature. Between al-Andalus and Christian Europe*, Bloomington IN, 2007

A.-M. Delcambre and R. Arnaldez (eds), *Enquêtes sur l'Islam. En homage à Antoine Moussali*, Paris, 2004

F. Delgado León, *Álvaro de Córdoba y la polémica contra el islam. El Indiculus luminosus*, Córdoba, 1996

G.L. Della Vida, art. 'Sīra', in *EI1*

D.C. Dennett, *Conversion and the poll tax in early Islam*, Cambridge MA, 1950

F.M. Denny, art. 'Tawba', in *EI2*

F. Déroche, *Qur'ans of the Umayyads*, Leiden, 2014

I. Dick, *Maymar fī wujūd al-Khāliq wa-dīn al-qawīm*, Jounieh: al-Maktaba al-Būlusiyya, 1982

Kamāl al-Dīn, 'Extraits de la Chronique d'Alep', *Recueil des historiens des croisades. Historiens orientaux*, vol. 3, Paris, 1884

M. Dimmock, *Mythologies of the Prophet Muhammad in early modern English culture*, Cambridge, 2013

Dionysius bar Ṣalībī, *A response to the Arabs*, trans. J.P. Amar (Corpus Scriptorum Christianorum Orientalium 614/15), Louvain, 2005

J.D. Dodds, *Architecture and ideology in early medieval Spain*, Pennsylvania PA, 1990

B. Dodge (trans.), *The Fihrist of al-Nadīm, a tenth century survey of Muslim culture*, New York, 1970

F.M. Donner, *Muhammad and the believers. At the origins of Islam*, Cambridge MA, 2012

C.E. Dubler, 'Sobre la Crónica arábigo-bizantina de 741 y la influencia bizantina en la Península Ibérica', *Al-Andalus* 11 (1946) 283-349

A. Duderija and H. Rane, *Islam and Muslims in the West*, Cham, Switzerland, 2019

R. Ebied and D. Thomas (eds), *Muslim-Christian polemic during the crusades. The letter from the people of Cyprus and Ibn Abī Ṭālib al-Dimashqī's response*, Leiden, 2005

R. Ebied and D. Thomas (ed. and trans.), *The polemical works of 'Alī al-Ṭabarī*, Leiden, 2016

A. Echevarría, *La minoría islámica de los reinos cristianos medievales. Moros, sarracenos, mudéjares*, Málaga, 2004

A. Echevarría, 'Los marcos legales de la islamización. El procedimiento judicial entre los cristianos arabizados y mozárabes', *Studia Historica. Historia Medieval* 27 (2009) 37-52

A.-M. Eddé, 'Chrétiens d'Alep et de Syrie du Nord à l'époque des croisades. Crises et mutations', in Canivet and Rey-Coquais, *Mélanges Monseigneur Joseph Nasrallah*, 2006, 153-80

A.-M. Eddé, F. Michea and C. Picard, *Communautés chrétiennes en pays d'islam du début du VIIe siècle au milieu du XIe siècle*, Paris, 1997

S.B. Edgington and H.J. Nicholson (eds), *Deeds done beyond the sea. Essays on William of Tyre, Cyprus and the military orders presented to Peter Edbury*, Farnham, 2014

B.P. Edmonds, 'Le portrait des Sarrasins dans "La Chanson de Roland"', *The French Review* 44 (1971) 870-80

J.J. Elias, *Aisha's cushion. Religious art, perception, and practice in Islam*, Cambridge MA, 2012

R. Ellenblum, *Crusader castles and modern histories*, Cambridge, 2007

M. de Epalza, 'Mozarabs. An emblematic Christian minority in al-Andalus', in Jayyusi and Marín, *The legacy of Muslim Spain*, 1992, 149-70

M. de Epalza, 'Influences islamiques dans la théologie chrétienne médiévale. L'adoptionisme hispanique', *Islamochristiana* 18 (1992) 55-72

Eulogius of Cordoba, *Memoriale sanctorum*, in Gil, *Corpus scriptorum Muzarabicorum*, vol. 2, 1973

B. Evetts (ed. and trans.), 'History of the patriarchs of the Coptic Church of Alexandria, III: Agathon to Michael II', *Patrologia Orientalis* 5 (1910) 257-469

M. Fakhry, *An interpretation of the Qur'an. English translation of the meanings*, New York, 2002

H. Fancy, *The mercenary Mediterranean. Sovereignty, religion, and violence in the medieval Crown of Aragon*, Chicago IL, 2016

A. Fattal, *Le statut légal des non-musulmans en pays d'islam*, Beirut, 1958, 1995[2]

F. Feder, 'The Bashmurite revolts in the Delta and the "Bashmuric dialect"', in Gabra and Takla, *Christianity and monasticism in northern Egypt*, 2017, 33-6

J.M. Fernández Catón (ed.), *Monarquía y sociedad en el reino de León, de Alfonso III a Alfonso VII*, vol. 2, León, 2007

A. Fernández Félix, *Cuestiones legales del Islam temprano. La 'Utbiyya y el proceso de formación de la sociedad islámica andalusí*, Madrid, 2003

A. Fernández Félix and M. Fierro, 'Cristianos y conversos al Islam en al-Andalus bajo los omeyas. Una aproximación al proceso de islamización a través de una fuente legal andalusí del s. III/IX', in Caballero Zoreda and Mateos Cruz, *Visigodos y Omeyas*, 2000, 415-27

M.I. Fierro, *La heterodoxia en al-Andalus durante el periodo omeya*, Madrid, 1987

M.I. Fierro, *'Abd al-Raḥmān III. The first Cordoban caliph*, Oxford, 2005

M.I. Fierro, *Abderramán III y el califato omeya de Córdoba*, Donostia-San Sebastián, 2011

M.I. Fierro, 'A Muslim land without Jews or Christians. Almohad policies regarding the "protected people"', in Tischler and Fidora, *Christlicher Norden – Muslimischer Süden*, 2011, 231-47

M.I. Fierro, 'Violence against women in Andalusi historical sources (third/ninth-seventh/thirteenth centuries)', in Gleave and Kristó-Nagy, *Violence in Islamic thought*, 2015, 155-74

J.-M. Fiey, *Chrétiens syriaques sous les Abbassides surtout à Bagdad, 749-1258*, Louvain, 1980

J.-M. Fiey, 'Conversions à l'islam de juifs et chrétiens sous les Abbasides d'après les sources arabes et syriaques', in Irmscher, *Rapports entre juifs, chrétiens et musulmans*, 1995, 13-28

B. Fischer, 'Zur Liturgie der lateinischen Handschriften vom Sinai', *Revue Bénédictine* 74 (1964) 284-97

H. Fleisch, 'Une homélie de Théophile d'Alexandrie en l'honneur de St Pierre et de St Paul', *Revue de l'Orient Chrétien* 30 (1935-6) 371-419

C.H. Fleischer, 'The lawgiver as Messiah. The making of the imperial image in the reign of Süleimân', in Veinstein, *Suleyman the Magnificent and his time*, 1992, 159-77

R.A. Fletcher, 'Reconquest and Crusade in Spain, c. 1050–1150', *Transactions of the Royal Historical Society* 37 (1987) 31-47

E. Flórez, *España sagrada*, Madrid, 1754

J. Flori, *L'islam et la fin des temps. L'interprétation prophétique des invasions musulmanes dans la chrétienté médiévale*, Paris, 2007

J. Folda, *Crusader art in the Holy Land. From the Third Crusade to the fall of Acre, 1187-1291*, Cambridge, 2005

C. Foss, 'Byzantine saints in early Islamic Syria', *Analecta Bollandiana* 125 (2007) 93-119

C.F. Fraker, *The scope of history. Studies in the historiography of Alfonso el Sabio*, Ann Arbor MI, 1996

J.C. Frakes, *Vernacular and Latin literary discourses of the Muslim other in medieval Germany*, New York, 2011

J. France (ed.), *Warfare, crusade and conquest in the Middle Ages*, Aldershot, 2014

R.M. Frank, *Beings and their attributes. The teaching of the Basrian school of the Muʿtazila in the classical period*, Albany NY, 1978

P. Frankopan, *The First Crusade. The call from the east*, London, 2012

G. Frantz-Murphy, 'Conversion in early Islamic Egypt. The economic factor', in Rāġib, *Documents de l'islam médiéval*, 1991, 11-17

M. Frassetto, 'The image of the Saracen as heretic in the sermons of Ademar of Chabannes', in Blanks and Frassetto, *Western views of Islam in medieval and early modern Europe. Perception of other*, 1999, 83-96

M. Frassetto, 'Heretics, Antichrists, and the year 1000. Apocalyptic expectations in the writings of Ademar of Chabannes', in Frassetto, *The year 1000. Religious and social response to the turning of the first Millennium*, 2002, 73-84

M. Frassetto (ed.), *The year 1000. Religious and social response to the turning of the first Millennium*, New York, 2002

Y. Friedmann, *Tolerance and coercion in Islam. Interfaith relations in the Muslim tradition*, Cambridge, 2003

Ibn al-Furāt, *Ayyubids, Mamlukes and Crusaders. Selections from the* Tārīkh al-duwal wa'l-mulūk, trans. U. Lyons and M.C. Lyons, Cambridge, 1971

G. Gabra and H.N. Takla (eds), *Christianity and monasticism in Middle Egypt: al-Minya and Asyut*, Cairo, 2015

M. Gabriele and J. Stuckey (eds), *The legend of Charlemagne in the Middle Ages. Power, faith and crusade*, New York, 2008

L. Gallant, 'Francis of Assisi forerunner of interreligious dialogue. Chapter 16 of the Earlier Rule revisited', *Franciscan Studies* 64 (2006) 53-82

L.A. García Moreno, 'Elementos de tradición bizantina en dos *Vidas de Mahoma* mozárabes', in Pérez Martín and Bádenas de la Peña, *Bizancio y la Península Ibérica*, 2004, 250-60

L. Gardet, art. 'Al-Burhān', in *EI2*

L. Gardet, art. ''Ilm al-Kalām', in *EI2*

L. Gardet, art. 'Kalām', in *EI2*

B. Garstad (trans.), *Apocalypse of pseudo-Methodius. An Alexandrian world chronicle*, Cambridge MA, 2012

J. Gaudeul, 'The correspondence between Leo and 'Umar. 'Umar's letter rediscovered?' *Islamochristiana* 10 (1984) 109-57

C. Geffré, 'La portée théologique du dialogue islamo-chrétien', *Islamochristiana* 18 (1992) 1-23

M. Gervers and R.J. Bikhazi (eds), *Conversion and continuity. Indigenous Christian communities in Islamic lands*, Toronto, 1990

Al-Ghazālī, *Iḥyā' ʿulūm al-dīn*, vol. 3, ed. A. al-Khālidī, Beirut, 1998

G. Gianazza, 'Lettre de Makkīḫā († 1109), sur la vérité de la religion chrétienne', *Parole de l'Orient* 25 (2000) 493-555

M.D. Gibson, *An Arabic version of the Acts of the Apostles and the seven Catholic Epistles from an eighth or ninth century ms. in the Convent of St. Katherine on Mount Sinai, with a treatise On the Triune nature of God with translation, from the same codex*, Cambridge, 1899 (repr. Piscataway NJ, 2003)

J. Gil (ed.), *Corpus Scriptorum Muzarabicorum*, 2 vols, Madrid, 1973

D. Gimaret, art. 'Shirk', in *EI2*

J. van Ginkel, 'Michael the Syrian and his sources. Reflections on the methodology of Michael the Great as a historiographer and its implications for modern historians', *Journal of the Canadian Society for Syriac Studies* 6 (2006) 53-60

I. Glaser, 'Cross, qiblah and glory. What should direct Christian responses to Islam?', *Muslim-Christian Encounter* 10 (2017) 9-53

R. Gleave and I.T. Kristó-Nagy (eds), *Violence in Islamic thought from the Qur'an to the Mongols*, Edinburgh, 2015

R. Glei (ed.), *Petrus Venerabilis. Schriften zum Islam*, Altenberge, 1985

R. Glei and A.T. Khoury (eds), *Johannes Damaskenos und Theodor Abū Qurra. Schriften zum Islam*, Würzburg, 1995

T.F. Glick, *Islamic and Christian Spain in the early Middle Ages*, Leiden, 2005[2]

H. Goddard, *A history of Christian-Muslim relations*, Chicago IL, 2000

I. Goldziher, 'Influences chrétiennes dans la littérature religieuse de l'Islam', *Revue de l'Histoire des Religions* 18 (1888) 180-99

H. Goussen, *Die christlich-arabische Literatur der Mozaraber*, Leipzig, 1909

O. Grabar, *The shape of the holy. Early Islamic Jerusalem*, Princeton NJ, 1996

F. de la Granja, 'Fiestas cristianas en al-Andalus (materiales para su estudio). I: *Al-durr al-munaẓẓam* de al-ʿAzafī', *Al-Andalus* 34 (1969) 39-46

M. Greene, *The Edinburgh history of the Greeks, 1453 to 1768. The Ottoman Empire*, Edinburgh, 2015

J. Gribomont, 'Le mystérieux calendrier latin du Sinai. Édition et commentaire', *Analecta Bollandiana* 75 (1957) 105-34

F. Griffel, *Apostasie und Toleranz im Islam*, Leiden, 2000

F. Griffel, art. 'Apostasy', *EI3*

S.H. Griffith, 'Comparative religion in the apologetics of the first Christian Arabic theologians', *Proceedings of the PMR [Patristic, Mediaeval and Renaissance] conference* 4 (1979) 63–87

S.H. Griffith, 'Ḥabīb ibn Ḫidmah Abū Rā'iṭah, a Christian *mutakallim* of the first Abbasid century', *Oriens Christianus* 64 (1980) 161-201

S.H. Griffith, 'The concept of *al-uqnūm* in ʿAmmār al-Baṣrī's Apology for the doctrine of the Trinity', in Samir, *Actes du premier congrès international d'études arabes chrétiennes*, 1982, 169-91

S.H. Griffith, 'ʿAmmār al-Baṣrī's *Kitāb al-burhān*. Christian Kalām in the first Abbasid century', *Le Museon* 96 (1983) 145-81

S.H. Griffith, 'The Prophet Muḥammad, his scripture and his message according to Christian apologies in Arabic and Syriac from the first Abbasid century', in Monnot, *La vie du Prophète Mahomet. Colloque de Strasbourg (octobre 1980)*, 1983, 99-146

S.H. Griffith, 'The Arabic account of ʿAbd al-Masīḥ an-Najrānī al-Ghassānī', *Le Muséon* 98 (1985) 331-74

S.H. Griffith, 'Free will in Christian kalām. Moshe Bar Kepha against the teachings of the Muslims', *Le Museon* 100 (1987) 143-59

S.H. Griffith, 'Islam and the *Summa theologiae Arabica*', *Jerusalem Studies in Arabic and Islam* 13 (1990) 225-64

S.H. Griffith, 'Disputes with Muslims in Syriac Christian texts. From Patriarch John (d. 648) to Bar Hebraeus (d. 1286)', in Lewis and Niewöhner (eds), *Religionsgespräche im Mittelalter*, 1992, 173-96

S.H. Griffith, 'Faith and reason in Christian *kalam*. Theodore Abū Qurrah on discerning the true religion', in Samir and Nielsen, *Christian Arabic apologetics during the Abbasid period (750-1258)*, 1994, 1-43

S.H. Griffith, *A treatise on the veneration of holy icons written in Arabic by Theodore Abū Qurrah, Bishop of Harrān (c. 755-c. 830 A.D.)*, Louvain, 1997

S.H. Griffith, 'Christians, Muslims, and neo-martyrs. Saints' lives and Holy Land history', in Kofsky and Stroumsa, *Sharing the sacred. Religious contacts and conflicts in the Holy Land, first to fifteenth centuries CE*, 1998, 163-207

S.H. Griffith, art. 'Gospel', in *EQ*

S.H. Griffith, 'The Gospel, the Qur'ān, and the presentation of Jesus in al-Ya'qūbī's *Tảrīkh*', in Reeves, *Bible and Qur'ān*, 2003, 133-60

S.H. Griffith, *The church in the shadow of the mosque. Christians and Muslims in the world of Islam*, Princeton NJ, 2008

S.H. Griffith, 'Christians under Muslim rule', in Noble and Smith, *The Cambridge history of Christianity*, vol. 3, 2010, 197-212

S.H. Griffith, *The Bible in Arabic. The scriptures of the 'People of the Book' in the language of Islam*, Princeton NJ, 2013

S.H. Griffith, 'The Manṣūr family and Saint John of Damascus. Christians and Muslims in Umayyad times', in Borrut and Donner, *Christians and others in the Umayyad state*, 2016, 29-51

S. Griffith, 'The Qur'an in Christian Arabic literature. A cursory overview', in Beaumont, *Arab Christians and the Qur'an*, 2018, 1-19

S.H. Griffith and S. Grebenstein (eds), *Christsein in der islamischen Welt. Festschrift für Martinn Tamcke zum 60. Geburstag*, Wiesbaden, 2015

D. Gril, 'Une émeute anti-chrétienne à Qūṣ au début du viiie/xive siècle', *Annales Islamologiques* 16 (1980) 241-74

B. Groneberg and H. Spieckermann (eds), *Der Welt der Götterbilder*, Berlin, 2007

A. Guillaume, *The life of Muhammad. A translation of Isḥāq 's Sīrat rasūl Allāh*, Oxford, 1955

S. Günther (ed.), *Ideas, images, and methods of portrayal. Insight into classical Arabic literature and Islam*, Leiden, 2005

J. Guráieb, 'Al-Muqtabis de Ibn Ḥayyān', *Cuadernos de Historia de España* 20 (1953) 155-64

D. Gutas, *Greek thought, Arabic culture*, London, 1998

E. Grypeou, '"A people will emerge from the desert": apocalyptic perceptions of early Muslim conquests in contemporary Eastern Christian literature', in H. Amira, et al., *Apocalypticism and eschatology in late antiquity*, 2017, 291–309

E. Grypeou, M.N. Swanson and D. Thomas (eds), *The encounter of Eastern Christianity with early Islam*, Leiden, 2006

R. Haddad, *La Trinité divine chez les théologiens arabes 750-1050*, Paris, 1985

W. Haddad, '*Ahl al-dhimma* in an Islamic state. The teaching of Abū al-Ḥasan al-Māwardī's *al-aḥkām al-sulṭāniyya*', *ICMR* 7 (1996) 169-80

Y.Y. Haddad and W.Z. Haddad (eds), *Christian-Muslim encounters*, Gainesville FL, 1995

M. José Hagerty, *Los cuervos de San Vicente. Escatología mozárabe*, Madrid, 1978

Muslim ibn al-Ḥajjāj. *Ṣaḥīḥ Muslim*, ed. A.Ṣ. al-Karmī, Riyadh, 1998

W. Hallaq, art. 'Apostasy', in *EQ*

Yāqūt al-Ḥamawī, *Muʿjam al-udabāʾ*, vol. 2, ed. I. ʿAbbās, Beirut, 1993

O. Hamdan, 'The second maṣāḥif project. A step towards the canonization of the qur'anic text', in Neuwirth et al., *The Qurʾān in context*, 2010, 794-835

H.J. Hames (ed.), *Jews, Muslims and Christians in and around the Crown of Aragon*, Leiden, 2004

B. Hamilton, *The Latin Church in the Crusader states. The secular church*, London, 1980

M. Hammam (ed.), *L'Occident musulman et l'Occident chrétienne au moyen âge*, Rabat, 1995

Ibn Ḥanbal, *K. al-Zuhd*, ed. M.ʿA. al-Salām Shāhīn, Beirut, 1983

Aḥmad ibn Ḥanbal, *Musnad*, vol. 3, ed. A.M. Shākir, Cairo, 1995

B. Harakat, 'La communauté chrétienne et celle d'origine chrétienne en Espagne musulmane, vues par les sources arabes', in Hammam, *L'Occident musulman*, 1995, 197-205

A. Harrak, *The Chronicle of Zuqnin*, Toronto, 1999

A. Harrak, 'Piecing together the fragmentary account of the martyrdom of Cyrus of Ḥarrān', *Analecta Bollandiana* 121 (2003) 297-328

R. Harris, 'Introduction', *Woodbrooke Studies* 2 (1928) 1-10

F.W. Hasluck, *Christianity and Islam under the sultans*, Oxford, 1929

H.L.-Y. Hava, *Intertwined worlds. Medieval Islam and Bible criticism*, Princeton NJ, 1992

G. Hawting, art. 'Idolatry and idolaters', in *EQ*

M. Hayek (ed.), *ʿAmmār al-Baṣrī. Apologie et controverses*, Beirut, 1977

Ibn Ḥayyān, *Crónica de los emires Alḥakam I y ʿAbdarraḥmān II entre los años 796 y 847* [*Almuqabis II-1*], trans. Maḥmūd ʿAlī Makkī and F. Corriente, Zaragoza, 2001

Ibn Ḥazm, *Kitāb al-fiṣal fī l-milal wa-l-ahwāʾ wa-l-niḥal*, Cairo, 1899

Ibn Ḥazm, *Al-fiṣal fī l-milal wa-l-ahwāʾ wa-l-niḥal*, vol. 2, ed. Muḥammad Ibrāhīm Naṣr and ʿAbd al-Raḥmān ʿUmayr, Beirut, 1996

W. Heffening, art. 'Murtadd', in *EI2*

J. den Heijer, 'Coptic historiography in the Fāṭimid, Ayyūbid and early Mamlūk periods', *Medieval Encounters* 2 (1996) 67-98

R.M.T. Hill (ed.), *Gesta Francorum. The deeds of the Franks and other pilgrims to Jerusalem*, Oxford, 1962

W.J. Hill, *The three-personed God*, Washington DC, 1982

C. Hillenbrand, *A Muslim principality in crusader times*, Leiden, 1990

C. Hillenbrand, *The crusades. Islamic perspectives*, Edinburgh, 2006

C. Hillenbrand, *Turkish myth and Muslim symbol*, Edinburgh, 2007

Ibn Hishām, *Al-Sīra l-nabawiyya*, vol. 1, ed. 'U.'A. al-S. Tadmurī, Beirut, 1990

R. Hitchcock, *Mozarabs in medieval and early modern Spain. Identities and influences*, London, 2008

J. Hoeberichts, *Franciscus en de Islam*, Utrecht, 1991

J. Hoeberichts, *Francis and Islam*, Quincy IL, 1997

J. Hoeberichts, *Franciscus en de Sultan. Mannen van vrede*, Nijmegen, 2012

P.M. Holt, A.K.S. Lambton, and B. Lewis (eds), *The Cambridge history of Islam*, vol. 1A. *The central Islamic lands from pre-Islamic times to the First World War*, Cambridge, 2008

P.M. Holt, A.K.S. Lambton, and B. Lewis (eds), *The Cambridge history of Islam*, vol. 2A. *The Indian sub-continent, South-East Asia, Africa and the Muslim West*, Cambridge, 2008

J. Hopkins, *Nicolas of Cusa's De pace fidei and cribratio alkorani. Translation and analysis*, Minneapolis MN, 1994

J. Horrent, 'L'invasion de l'Espagne par les musulmans selon l'*Historia Silense*, le *Chronicon Mundi* et l'*Historia de rebus Hispaniae*', in Alvar et al., *Studia in honorem prof. M. de Riquer*, 1986, vol. 2, 373-93

J. Howard-Johnston, *Witnesses to a world crisis. Historians and histories of the Middle East in the seventh century*, Oxford, 2010

R. Hoyland, 'The correspondence of Leo III (717-41) and 'Umar II (717-20)', *Aram* 6 (1994) 165-77

R.G. Hoyland, *Seeing Islam as others saw it. A survey and evaluation of Christian, Jewish and Zoroastrian writings on early Islam*, Princeton NJ, 1997

R. Hoyland, 'Jacob of Edessa on Islam', in Reinink and Klugkist, *After Bardaisan*, 1999, 149-60

R. Hoyland, 'New documentary texts and the early Islamic state', *BSOAS* 69 (2006) 395-416

R.G. Hoyland, *In God's path. The Arab conquests and the creation of an Islamic empire*, Oxford, 2014

R.G. Hoyland (ed.), *Muslims and others in early Islamic society*, Farnham, 2004

Pedro Alfonso de Huesca, *Diálogo contra los Judíos*, ed. K.P. Mieth, Huesca, 1996

S.L. Husseini, *Early Christian-Muslim debate on the unity of God. Three Christian scholars and their engagement with Islamic thought*, Leiden, 2014

Al-Qāsim ibn Ibrāhīm, 'Refutation of the Christians', ed. I. di Matteo, 'Confutazione contro i Cristiani dello zaydita al-Qāsim b. Ibrāhīm', *Rivista degli Studi Orientali* 9 (1921-2) 301-64

H. Inalcik, *Suret-i Defter-i Sancak-i Arvanid*, Ankara, 1954

H. Inalcik, 'Ottoman methods of conquest', *Studia Islamica* 2 (1954) 104-29

H. Inalcik, 'The policy of Mehmed II toward the Greek population of Istanbul and the Byzantine buildings of the city', *Dumbarton Oaks Papers* 23-4 (1969/1970) 229-49

H. Inalcik, 'The status of the Greek Orthodox Patriarchate under the Ottomans', *Turcica* 21-3 (1991) 407-36

O. Ioan, 'Arabien und die Araber im kirchenleitenden Handeln des Katholikos Patriarchen Ischo'jahb III. (649-659)', in Tamcke and Heinz, *Die Suryoye und ihre Umwelt*, 2005, 43-58

Ireneus of Lyon, *Contra haereses*, ed. J.P. Migne, *Patrologia Graeca*, vol. 7, Paris, 1857

J. Irmscher (ed.), *Rapports entre juifs, chrétiens et musulmans*, Amsterdam, 1995

R. Irwin (ed.), *The new Cambridge history of Islam*, vol. 4. *Islamic cultures and societies to the end of the eighteenth century*, Cambridge, 2010

R. Izquierdo Benito, 'Toledo en época visigoda', in Cortés Arrese, *Toledo y Bizancio*, 2002, 43-74

Abū l-Faraj al-Iṣbahānī, *Kitāb al-diyārāt*, compiled by J. al-'Aṭiyya, London, 1991

'Abd al-Jabbār, *Critique of Christian origins*, ed. and trans. G.S. Reynolds and S.K. Samir, Provo UT, 2010

P. Jackson, *The Mongols and the west, 1221-1410*, Harlow, 2005

P. Jackson, *The Mongols and the Islamic world. From conquest to conversion*, New Haven CT, 2017

P. Jaffé, *Bibliotheca rerum germanicarum*, vol. 4, Paris, 1867

A.G. Jamieson, *Faith and the sword. A short history of Christian-Muslim conflict*, London, 2016[2]

D. Janosik, *John of Damascus*, Eugene OR, 2016

S. Jayyusi and M. Marín (eds), *The legacy of Muslim Spain*, Leiden, 1992

Ibn Qayyim al-Jawziyya, *Hidāyat al-ḥayārā fī ajwibat al-Yahūd wa-l-Naṣārā*, ed. M.A. al-Ḥājj, Damascus, 1996

A. Jeffery, 'Ghevond's text of the correspondence between 'Umar II and Leo III', *Harvard Theological Review* 37 (1944) 269-332

A. Jeffery, art. 'Āya', in *EI2*

K.V. Jensen, 'Creating a crusader saint. Canute Lavard and others of that ilk', in Bergsagel et al., *Of chronicles and kings*, 2015, 51-72

Jerome, *Hieronymi Commentariorum in Esaiam libri XII-XVIII*, ed. M. Adriaen, Turnhout, 1963
R. Jiménez Pedrajas, *Historia de los mozárabes en Al Ándalus*, Córdoba, 2013
M. Jirjis (ed.), *Kitāb al-ṣaḥā'iḥ fī jawāb al-naṣā'iḥ*, Cairo, 1926
John of Damascus, 'The heresy of the Ishmaelites', trans. D.J. Sahas, in Sahas, *John of Damascus on Islam*, 1972, 132-41
J. Johns, *The Arabic administration of Norman Sicily*, Cambridge, 2002
S.F Johnson (ed.), *Languages and cultures of Eastern Christianity. Greek*, Farnham, 2014
M.D. Jordan, 'Saint Pelagius, ephebe and martyr', in Blackmore and Hucheson, *Queer Iberia*, 1999, 23-47
Ibn Jubayr, *The travels of Ibn Jubayr*, trans. and intro. R.J.C. Broadhurst, London, 1952
Ibn Ḥārith al-Jushanī, *Kitāb al-quḍāt bi-Qurṭuba. Historia de los Jueces de Córdoba por Aljoxani*, ed. and trans. J. Ribera, Madrid, 1914 (repr. Seville, 2005)
al-Juwaynī, *Ghiyāth al-umam*, ed. F.ʿA. Aḥmad, Alexandria, 1979
G.H.A. Juynboll, art. 'Tawātur', in *EI2*
W.E. Kaegi, 'Initial Byzantine reactions to the Arab conquest', *Church History* 38 (1969) 139-49
W.E. Kaegi, *Byzantium and the early Islamic conquests*, Cambridge, 1992
A. Kaldellis, *Streams of gold, rivers of blood. The rise and fall of Byzantium, 955 AD to the First Crusade*, Oxford, 2017
W. Kallfelz, *Nichtmuslimische Untertanen im Islam*, Wiesbaden, 1995
J. Kaltner and Y. Mirza, *The Bible and the Qur'an. Biblical figures in the Islamic tradition*, London, 2018
M.H. Kamali, *Freedom of expression in Islam*, Cambridge, 1997
H.E. Kassis, 'Arabicization and Islamization of the Christians of al-Andalus. Evidence of their scriptures', in Brann, *Languages of power*, 1997, 136-55
H.E. Kassis, 'Some aspects of the legal position of Christians under Mālikī jurisprudence in al-Andalus', *Parole de l'Orient* 24 (1999) 113-28
Ibn Kathīr, *Al-fitan wa-l-malāḥim*, Cairo, [n.d.], vol. 1
Ibn Kathīr, *Al-Bidāya wa-l-nihāya*, vol. 2, Beirut, 1990
Ibn Kathīr, *Qiṣaṣ al-anbīyā'*, ed. I. Ramaḍān, Beirut, 1996
Ismāʿīl ibn 'Umar ibn Kathīr, *Stories of the prophets*, trans. R.A. Azami, Riyadh, 2003
S.T. Keating, 'Refuting the charge of *taḥrīf*. Abū Rā'iṭah (d. c. 835 CE) and his first *risāla* on the Holy Trinity', in Günther, *Ideas, images, and methods of portrayal*, Leiden, 2005, 41-57
S.T. Keating (ed. and trans.), *Defending the 'People of truth' in the early Islamic period. The Christian apologies of Abū Rā'iṭah*, Leiden, 2006

S.T. Keating, 'Manipulation of the Qur'an in the epistolary exchange between al-Hāshimī and al-Kindī', in Beaumont, *Arab Christians and the Qur'an*, 2018, 5-65

S.T. Keating, 'The Paraclete and the integrity of scripture', in Tieszen, *Theological issues in Christian-Muslim dialogue*, 2018, 15-25

B.Z. Kedar, *Crusade and mission. European approaches toward the Muslims*, Oxford, 1984

B.Z. Kedar, 'The subjected Muslims of the Frankish Levant', in Madden, *The crusades*, 2002, 233-64

B.Z. Kedar, 'The Jerusalem massacre of July 1099 in the western historiography of the crusades', *Crusades* 3 (2004) 15-75

D. Kempf and M. Bull (eds), *The Historia Iherosolimitana of Robert the Monk*, Woodbridge, 2013

N. Kenaan-Kedar, 'Decorative architectural sculpture in crusader Jerusalem. The eastern, western and Armenian sources of a local visual culture', in Boas, *The crusader world*, 2016, 609-23

D.A. Kerr, '"He walked in the path of the prophets". Toward Christian theological recognition of the prophethood of Muhammad', in Haddad and Haddad, *Christian-Muslim encounters*, 1995, 426-46

Ibn Khaldūn, *Tārīkh Ibn Khaldūn al-musammā dīwān al-mubtadaʾ wa-l-khabar fī tārīkh al-ʿarab wa-l-barbar wa-man ʿāṣarahum min dhawī al-shaʾn al-akbar*, vol. 2, ed. K. Shiḥāda and S. Zakkār, Beirut, 2001

T. Khalidi, *The Muslim Jesus. Sayings and stories in Islamic literature*, Cambridge MA, 2001

Abū Bakr al-Khallāl, *Aḥkām ahl al-milal wa-l-ridda ...*, ed. I. ibn Sulṭān, Riyadh, 1996

N. Khan, *Perceptions of Islam in the Christendoms. A historical survey*, Oslo, 2005

A. Khater, 'Nouveaux fragments du Synaxaire arabe', *Bulletin de la Société d'Archéologie Copte* 17 (1963-64) 75-100

R.G. Khoury, *Chrestomathie de papyrologie arabe*, Leiden, 1993

A.A. al-Khowayter, 'A critical edition of an unknown source for the life of al-Malik al-Zahir Baibars. With introduction, translation, and notes', London, 1960 (PhD Diss. SOAS)

H. Kilpatrick, 'Monasteries through Muslim eyes. The diyārāt books', in Thomas, *Christians at the heart of Islamic rule*, 2003, 19-37

S. Kim, 'The Arabic letters of the Byzantine Emperor Leo III to the Caliph 'Umar Ibn 'Abd al-'Aziz. An edition, translation, and commentary', Washington DC, 2017 (PhD Diss. Catholic University of America)

C. Kimball, *Striving together: a way forward in Christian-Muslim relations*, Maryknoll, NY, 1991

Al-Kisāʾī, *Qiṣaṣ al-anbīyāʾ*, ed. I. Eisenberg, Leiden, 1922

M.J. Kister, '"Do not assimilate yourselves...". *lā tashabbahū...*', *Jerusalem Studies in Arabic and Islam* 12 (1989) 321-71

A. Klemeshov, 'The conversion and destruction of the infidels in the works of Roger Bacon', in Carvalho, *Religion and power in Europe*, 2007, 15-27

A. Kofsky and G.G. Stroumsa (eds), *Sharing the sacred. Religious contacts and conflicts in the Holy Land, first to fifteenth centuries CE*, Jerusalem, 1998

P. Kollmann, *The evangelisation of slaves and Catholic origins in East Africa*, Maryknoll NY, 2005

D. Komine-Dialete (ed.), *Athos in the 14th-16th centuries*, Athens, 1997

D.G. König, *Arabic-Islamic views of the Latin West. Tracing the emergence of medieval Europe*, Oxford, 2015

P.S. Van Koningsveld, *The Latin-Arabic glossary of the Leiden University Library. A contribution to the study of Mozarabic manuscripts and literature*, Leiden, 1977

P.S. Van Koningsveld, 'Christian Arabic literature from medieval Spain. An attempt at periodization', in Samir and Nielsen, *Christian Arabic apologetics*, 1994, 203-24

P.S. van Koningsveld, *The Arabic Psalter of Ḥafṣ ibn Albar al-Qûṭî. Prolegomena for a critical edition*, Leiden, 2016

P.S. van Koningsveld, *An Arabic source of Ramon Martí*, Leiden, 2018

J.L. Kraemer, 'Apostates, rebels and brigands', *Israel Oriental Studies* 10 (1980) 34-73

I. Kratchkovsky (ed.), F. Micheau and G. Troupeau (trans.), *Histoire de Yaḥyā ibn Saʿīd d'Antioche*, Turnhout, 1997

Kritovoulos of Imvros, *History of Mehmed the Conqueror*, trans. C.T. Riggs, Princeton NJ, 1954

J. Kritzeck, *Peter the Venerable and Islam*, Princeton NJ, 1964

M. Kropp (ed.), *Results of contemporary research on the Qurʾan. The question of a historico-critical text*, Würzburg, 2007

T. Krstić, *Contested conversions to Islam. Narratives of religious change in the early modern Ottoman Empire*, Stanford CA, 2011

T. Ladjal, 'The Christian presence in North Africa under Almoravids rule (1040-1147 CE). Coexistence or eradication?' *Cogent Arts and Humanities* 4 (2017) 1-17

V. Lagardère, 'Communautés mozarabes et pouvoir almoravide en 519H/1125 en el-Andalus', *Studia Islamica* 67 (1988) 99-120

J.C. Lamoreaux, *Theodore Abu Qurrah*, Provo UT, 2005

E. Landau-Tessaron, 'Cyclical reform. A study of the *mujaddid* tradition', *Studia Islamica* 70 (1989) 79-113

B. Landron, *Chrétiens et musulmans en Irak. Attitudes nestoriennes vis-à-vis de l'islam*, Paris, 1994

I.M. Lapidus, 'The conversion of Egypt to Islam', *Israel Oriental Studies* 2 (1972) 248-62

E. Lapiedra, '*Ulūǧ, rūm, muzarabes* y mozárabes. Imágenes encontradas de los cristianos de al-Andalus', *Collectanea Christiana Orientalia* 3 (2006) 105-42

E. Lapiedra Gutiérrez, 'Christian participation in Almohad armies and personal guards', *Journal of Medieval Iberian Studies* 2 (2010) 235-50

A. Lappin, *The medieval cult of Saint Dominic of Silos*, Leeds, 2002

O. Latiff, *The cutting edge of the poet's sword. Muslim poetic responses to the crusades*, Leiden, 2018

J.C. Laurent (ed.), *Peregrinatores medii aevi quatuor*, Leipzig, 1864

B. Lawrence, *The Qur'an. A biography*, New York, 2007

T. Lawson, *The crucifixion and the Qur'an. A study in the history of Muslim thought*, Oxford, 2009

S. Lay, *The Reconquest kings of Portugal. Political and cultural reorientation on the medieval frontier*, Basingstoke, 2009

H. Lazarus-Yafeh, art. 'Taḥrīf', in *EI2*

H. Lazarus-Yafeh, 'Some neglected aspects of medieval Muslim polemics against Christianity', *Harvard Theological Review* 89 (January 1996) 61-84

T. el-Leithy, 'Coptic culture and conversion in medieval Cairo, 1293-1524 A.D.', Princeton NJ (PhD Diss. Princeton University), 2005

T. el-Leithy, 'Sufis, Copts, and the politics of piety. Moral regulation in fourteenth-century Upper Egypt', in McGregor and Sabra, *La développement du soufisme en Égypte*, 2006, 75-119

F.D. León, *Álvaro de Córdoba y la polémica contra el islam. El Indiculus luminosus*, Córdoba, 1996

Y. Lev, 'Persecutions and conversion to Islam in eleventh-century Egypt', *Asian and African Studies* 22 (1988) 37-50, 73-91

E. Lévi-Provençal and E. García Gómez (eds), *Una crónica anónima de 'Abd al-Raḥmān III al-Nāṣir*, Madrid, 1950

É. Lévi-Provençal (ed.), *Thalātha rasāʾil andalusiyya fī ādāb al-ḥiṣba wa-l-muḥtasib*, Cairo 1955

I.A. Levy, D.F. Duclow and R. George-Tvrtković (eds), *Nicholas of Cusa and Islam. Polemic and dialogue in the late Middle Ages*, Leiden, 2014

M. Levy-Rubin, 'Arabization versus Islamization in the Palestinian Melkite community during the early Muslim period', in Kofsky and Stroumsa, *Sharing the sacred*, 1998, 149-6

M. Levy-Rubin, *Non-Muslims in the early Islamic empire. From surrender to coexistence*, Cambridge, 2011

D.L. Lewis, *God's crucible. Islam and the making of Europe, 570-1215*, New York, 2008

B. Lewis and M. Holt (eds), *Historical writings of the peoples of Asia*, vol. 4. *Historians of the Middle East*, London, 1962

B. Lewis, 'The regnal titles of the first 'Abbāsid Caliphs', in *Dr. Zakir Husain presentation volume*, 1968, 13-22

B. Lewis and F. Niewöhner (eds), *Religionsgespräche im Mittelalter*, Wiesbaden, 1992

O. Lieberknecht, 'Zur Rezeption der arabischen Apologie des Pseudo-Kindi in der lateinischen Mohammedliteratur des Mittelalters', in Schönberger and Zimmermann, *De orbis Hispani linguis litteris historia moribus*, 1994, vol. 1, 523-38

W.M. Lindsay (ed.), *Isidori Hispalensis Etymologiarum sive originum libri*, Oxford, 1966

D.P. Little, 'Coptic conversion to Islam under the Baḥrī Mamlūks, 692-755/1293-1354', *BSOAS* 39 (1976) 552-69

Ramon Llull, *Liber de gentili et tribus sapientibus*, ed. O. de la Cruz Palma, Turnhout, 2015

Ramon Lull, *Blanquerna*, trans. E.A. Peters, ed. R. Irwin, London, 1987

Á.C. López, 'El conde de los cristianos Rabīʿ ben Teodulfo. Exactor y jefe de la guardia palatina del emir al-Ḥakam I', *Al-Andalus-Magreb* 7 (1999) 169-84

G. Loud and A. Metcalfe (eds), *The society of Norman Italy*, Leiden, 2002

A. Louth (trans.), *Three treatises on the divine images*, Crestwood NY, 2003

A. Louth, *Greek East and Latin West. The church 681-1071*, New York, 2007

A. Louth, *St John Damascene*, Oxford, 2009

E.A. Lowe, 'An unknown Latin Psalter on Mount Sinai', *Scriptorium* 9 (1955) 177-99

E.A. Lowe, 'Two new Latin liturgical fragments on Mount Sinai', *Revue Bénédictine* 74 (1964) 252-83

E.A. Lowe, 'Two other unknown Latin liturgical fragments on Mount Sinai', *Scriptorium* 19 (1965) 3-29

M. Lower, 'The Papacy and Christian mercenaries of thirteenth-century North Africa', *Speculum* 89 (2014) 601-31

C. Lowney, *A vanished world. Muslims, Christians, and Jews in medieval Spain*, Oxford, 2005

H. Lowry, *The nature of the early Ottoman state*, Albany NY, 2003

Martin Luther, *Martin Luthers Werke, Weimarer Gesamtausgabe*, vol. 1, Weimar, 1912

D.N. MacLean, 'La sociologie de l'engagement politique. Le Mahdawiya indien et l'état', *Revue des Mondes Musulmans et de la Méditeranée* 91-94 (2000) 239-56

C. MacEvitt, *The crusades and the Christian world of the East. Rough tolerance*, Philadelphia PA, 2008

T. Madden (ed.), *The crusades. The essential readings*, Oxford, 2002

T.F. Madden, *The new concise history of the crusades*, Lanham MD, 2014[3]

W. Madelung, 'Apocalyptic prophecies in Ḥimṣ', *Journal of Semitic Studies* 31 (1986) 141-85

D. Madigan, 'Christian—Muslim Dialogue', in Cornille, *The Wiley-Blackwell companion to inter-religious dialogue*, 2013, 244-60

H.J. Magoulias (ed. and trans.), *Decline and fall of Byzantium to the Ottoman Turks by Doukas. An annotated translation of 'Historia Turco-Byzantina'*, Detroit MI, 1975

C.T. Maier, *Crusade propaganda and ideology. Model sermons for the preaching of the cross*, Cambridge, 2000

Ibn Mājah, *Sunan*, Beirut: Dār al-Fikr, [n.d.], vol. 2

Ibn Mājah, *Sunan Ibn Mājah, K. al-Fitan*, 'Bāb fitnat al-Dajjāl', vol. 4, ed. M.M.H. Naṣṣār, Beirut, 2012

Maʿānī ibn Abī l-Makārim, *History of the patriarchs of the Egyptian Church*, vol. 3, pt 1. *Macarius II - John V*, ed. S. ibn al-Muqaffa', Cairo, 1968

A. Mallett, *Popular Muslim reactions to the Franks in the Levant, 1079-1291*, Farnham, 2014

G. Malaterra and E. Pontieri (eds), *De rebus gestis Rogerii Calabriae et Sicilae Comitis et Roberti Guiscardi Ducis fratris eius*, Bologna, 1927

C. Mango and R. Scott, *The Chronicle of Theophanes Confessor. Byzantine and Near-Eastern history AD 284-813*, Oxford, 1997

E. Manzano Moreno, *Conquistadores, emires y califas*, Barcelona, 2006

Taqī l-Dīn al-Maqrīzī, *Ittiʿāẓ al-ḥunafā'*, vol. 3, ed. J. Shayyāl and M.Ḥ.M. Aḥmad, Cairo, 1967-73

Al-Maqrīzī, *A history of the Ayyūbid sultans of Egypt*, trans. R.J.C. Broadhurst, Boston MA, 1980

J.M. March, (ed.), 'En Ramon Marti y la seva "Explanatio Simboli Apostolorum"', *Anuari de l'Institut d'Estudis Catalans* (1908 [1909]) 443-96

Y. Marquet, 'Les Iḫwān al-Ṣafā' et le Christianisme', *Islamochristiana* 8 (1982) 129-58

R.C. Martin (ed.), *Approaches to Islam in religious studies*, Tucson AZ, 1985

R.C. Martin, art. 'Inimitability', in *EQ*

J. Martinez Gazquez (ed.), 'El prologo de Juan de Segobia al Coran (*Qur'ān*) trilingue (1456)', *Mittellateinisches Jahrbuch* 38 (2003) 389-410

Nuʿaym ibn Ḥammād al-Marwazī, *Kitāb al-fitan*, Beirut, 1993

L. Massington et al., art. 'Taṣawwuf', in *EI2*

I. di Matteo, 'Le pretese contraddizioni della S. Scrittura secondo Ibn Ḥazm', *Bessarione* 39 (1923) 77-127

R. Matthee, 'Jesuits in Safavid Persia', in *EI2*

Matthew of Edessa, *Armenia and the crusades, tenth to twelfth centuries. The Chronicle of Matthew of Edessa*, trans. A.E. Dostourian, New York, 1993

Al-mawsūʿa l-lāhūtiyya al-shahīra bi-l-ḥāwī l-Ibn al-Makīn, 4 vols, Cairo, 1999–2001

J. McAuliffe, *Qur'ānic Christians. An analysis of classical and modern exegesis*, Cambridge, 1991

R. McClary, 'Craftsmen in medieval Anatolia. Methods and mobility', in Blessing and Goshgarian, *Architecture and landscape in medieval Anatolia, 1100-1500*, 2017, 27-58

F. McLeod, 'The Christological ramifications of Theodore of Mopsuestia's understanding of baptism and the Eucharist', *Journal of Early Christian Studies* 10 (2002) 37-75

R. McGregor and A. Sabra (eds), *La développement du soufisme en Égypte à l'époque mamelouke*, Cairo, 2006

M. Meerson, P. Schäfer and Y. Deutsch, *Toledot Yeshu. The life story of Jesus*, Tübingen, 2014

I. Melikoff, 'L'origine sociale des premiers Ottomans', in Zachariadou, *The Ottoman Emirate (1300-1389)*, 1993, 135-44

Mēna of Nikiou, *The Life of Isaac of Alexandria and the martyrdom of Saint Macrobius*, trans. D.N. Bell, Kalamazoo MI, 1988

M.R. Menocal, R.P Schneidlin and M. Sells (eds), *The literature of al-Andalus*, Cambridge, 2012

M. Meouak, *Pouvoir souverain, administration centrale et élites politiques dans l'Espagne umayyade (IIe-IVe/VIIIe-Xe siècles)*, Helsinki, 1999

M. Meserve, *Empires of Islam in Renaissance historical thought*, Cambridge MA, 2008

A. Metcalfe, 'The Muslims of Sicily under Christian rule', in Loud and Metcalfe, *The society of Norman Italy*, 2002, 289-317

A. Metcalfe, *Muslims of medieval Italy*, Edinburgh, 2014

R. Menéndez Pidal, *Orígenes del español. Estado lingüístico de la Península Ibérica hasta el siglo XI*, Madrid, 1980

T. Mgaloblishvili, 'The Georgian Sabaite (Sabatsminduri) literary school and the Sabatsmindian version of the Georgian *Mravaltavi* (Polykephalon)', in Patrich, *The Sabaite heritage in the Orthodox Church*, 2001, 229-33

T. Michel (trans.), *A Muslim theologian's response to Christianity. Ibn Taymiyya's* al-Jawab al-sahih, Delmar NY, 1984

W.Y.F. Mikhail, "Ammār al-Baṣrī's *Kitāb al-burhān*. A topical and theological analysis of Arabic Christian theology in the ninth century', Birmingham, 2013 (PhD Diss. University of Birmingham)

F. Miklosich and J. Müller (eds), *Acta et diplomata medii aevi sacra et profana*, 6 vols, Vienna, 1860-90

D. Millet-Gérard, *Chrétiens mozarabes et culture islamique dans l'Espagne des VIIIe-IXe siècles*, Paris, 1984

M. Milwright, *The Dome of the Rock and its Umayyad mosaic inscriptions*, Edinburgh, 2016

A.K. Min (ed.), *Rethinking the medieval legacy for contemporary theology*, South Bend IN, 2014

L. Minervini (ed.), *Cronica del Templare di Tiro (1243-1314)*, Naples, 2000

A. Mingana, 'Timothy's Apology', *Woodbrooke Studies* 2 (1928) 11-162

A. Mingana (trans.), 'The apology of Timothy the Patriarch before the Caliph Mahdi', *Bulletin of the John Rylands Library* 12 (1929) 137-226

A. Mingana, *Commentary of Theodore of Mopsuestia on the Lord's Prayer and on the sacraments of baptism and the Eucharist*, Cambridge, 1933

A.H. Miranda, 'The Iberian Peninsula and Sicily', in Holt et al., *The Cambridge history of Islam*, vol. 2A, 2008, 406-39

S. Mirza, '*Dhimma* agreements and sanctuary systems at Islamic origins', *Journal of Near Eastern Studies* 77 (2018) 99-117

V. Mistrīḥ (ed.), *Jûḥannâ ibn Abî Zakarîâ ibn Sibâʿ, Pretiosa margarita de scientiis ecclesiasticis*, Cairo, 1966

J.P. Molénat, 'Sur le rôle des almohades dans la fin du christianisme local au Maghreb et en al-Andalus', *Al-Qanṭara* 18 (1997) 389-413

J.P. Monferrer Sala, *La literature árabe cristiana de los mozárabes*, Córdoba, 1999

J.P. Monferrer Sala, *Scripta theologica Arabica Christiana. Andalusi Christian Arabic fragments preserved in Ms. 83 (al-Maktabah al-Malikiyyah, Rabat)*, Porto, 2016

J.P. Monferrer Sala, 'Christians and Muslims in the Iberian Peninsula, 1000-1600', in Thomas, *Routledge handbook on Christian-Muslim relations*, 2018, 149-57

J.P. Monferrer Sala and U. Cecini, 'Once again on Arabic "alkaufeit" (Alb. Ind. 23,14). Between polemics and inculturation', *Mittellateinisches Jahrbuch* 49 (2014) 201-10

J.P. Monferrer Sala and P. Mantas-España, *De Toledo a Córdoba. Tathlīth al-waḥdāniyyah ('La Trinidad de la Unidad'), fragmentos teológicos de un judeo-converso arabizado*, Madrid, 2018

G. Monnot, 'Les citations coraniques dans le "Dialogus" de Pierre Alfonse', in *Islam et chrétiens du Midi, XIIe–XIVe s.*, Toulouse, 1983, 261-77

G. Monnot (ed.), *La vie du Prophète Mahomet. Colloque de Strasbourg (octobre 1980)*, Paris, 1983

Ricoldus de Monte Crucis, *Tractatus seu disputatio contra Saracenos et Alchoranum*, ed. D. Pachurka, Wiesbaden, 2016

J. Moorman, *History of the Franciscan order. From its origins to the year 1517*, Oxford, 1968

E. Moreno, 'The Iberian Peninsula and North Africa', in Cook et al., *The new Cambridge history of Islam*, vol. 1, 2010, 581-622

M. Morony, *Iraq after the Muslim conquest*, Princeton NJ, 1984

J.A. Morrow, *The covenants of the Prophet Muhammad with the Christians of the world*, Kettering OH, 2013

N. Morton, 'William of Tyre's attitude towards Islam. Some historiographical reflections', in Edgington and Nicholson, *Deeds done beyond the sea*, 2014, 13-24

N. Morton, *Encountering Islam on the First Crusade*, Cambridge, 2016

N. Morton, 'Walter the Chancellor on Ilghazi and Tughtakin. A prisoner's perspective', *Journal of Medieval History* 44 (2018) 170-86

N. Morton and France, 'Arab Muslim reactions to Turkish authority in northern Syria, 1085-1128', in J. France, *Warfare, crusade and conquest in the Middle Ages*, 2014, 1-38

M. Mosebach, *The 21. A journey into the land of the Coptic martyrs*, Walden NY 2019

P. Moses, *The saint and the sultan. The crusades, Islam and Francis of Assisi's mission of peace*, New York, 2009

S.A. Mourad, 'A twelfth-century Muslim biography of Jesus', *ICMR* 7 (1996) 39-45

S. Mourad, 'On the qur'anic stories about Mary and Jesus', *Bulletin of the Royal Institute for Inter-Faith Studies* 1 (1999) 13-24

S. Mourad, 'Christian monks in Islamic literature. A preliminary report on some Arabic *Apophthegmata Patrum*', *Bulletin of the Royal Institute for Inter-Faith Studies* 6 (2004) 81-98

MS Konya, Koyunoğlu Museum Library – 10812, *Bir râhib ile bir pîr-i Müslim arasında İsa (a.s.) hakkında Mükâleme* fols 1r-v, 2v-3r, 3v-4r, 7r, 10

MS Paris, BnF – Ms. Fr. 226, Giovanni Boccaccio, *Le cas de nobles*, fol. 243r

MS Paris, BnF – Ms. Lat. 3394, *Liber denudationis*, fol. 244v

MS Rampur, Uttar Pradesh, Raza Library – *al-Muntaqā min Kitāb al-ruhbān*, fols. 190b-192a

MS Vienna, Österreichische Nationalbibliothek – P. Vondob. 15106

Ibn al-Mubārak, *K. al-Zuhd wa-yalīh K. al-Raqā'iq*, ed. Ḥ. al-R. al-Aʿẓamī, Beirut, 2004

J. Mugler, 'A Martyr with too many causes. Christopher of Antioch (d. 967) and local collective memory', Washington DC (PhD Diss. Georgetown University) 2019

W. Muir, *Life of Mahomet*, London, 1858

W. Muir, *The Apology of al Kindy. Written at the court of al Mâmûn (circa A.H. 215, A.D. 830), in defence of Christianity against Islam. With an essay on its age and authorship*, London, 1882

A. Müller, *Bettelmönche in islamischer Fremde. Institutionelle Rahmenbedingungen franziskanischer und dominikanischer Mission in muslimischen Räumen des 13. Jahrhunderts*, Münster, 2002

Hammām ibn Munabbih, *Ṣaḥīfat Hammām ibn Munabbih ʿan Abī Hurayra raḍī Allāh ʿanhu*, no. 134, ed. R.F. ʿAbd al-Muṭṭalib, Cairo, 1985

F. González Muñoz, *Latinidad mozárabe. Estudios sobre el latín de Álbaro de Córdoba*, Corunna, 1996

F. Gonzalez Muñoz, 'El conocimiento del Coran entre los mozarabes del siglo IX', in M. Dominguez Garcia et al. (eds), *Sub luce florentis calami. Homenaje a Manuel C. Díaz y Diaz*, Santiago de Compostela, 2002, 390-409

F. Gonzalez Muñoz, 'Liber Nycholay. La leyenda de Mahoma y el cardenal Nicolas', *Al-Qanṭara* 25 (2004) 5-43

F. González Muñoz, *Exposición y refutación del Islam. La versión latina de las epístolas de al-Hāšimī y al-Kindī*, Corunna, 2005

F. González Muñoz, *Pseudo Pedro Pascual. Sobre la se[c]ta mahometana*, Valencia, 2011

Usāma ibn Munqidh, *The book of contemplation. Islam and the crusades*, trans. P.M. Cobb, London, 2008

H. Munt, '"No two religions". Non-Muslims in the early Islamic Ḥijāz', *BSOAS* 78 (2015) 249-69

E.J. Mylod et al. (eds), *The Fifth Crusade in context. The crusading movement in the early thirteenth century*, London, 2017

T. Nagel, art. 'al-Kisāʾī', in *EI2*

J. Nasrallah, 'Deux auteurs melchites inconnus du Xe siècle', *Oriens Christianus* 63 (1979), 75-86

W. Nasry, *The caliph and the bishop*, Beirut, 2008

F. Nau, 'Littérature canonique syriaque inédite', *Revue de l'Orient Chrétien* 14 (1909) 113-30

F. Nau et al. (eds), *Patrologia orientalis*, Paris, 1919

N. Nazlar, 'Re-reading Glabas in terms of the question of the origin of the Devshirme', *International Journal of Turkish Studies* 22 (2016) 1-15

Synaxaristēs Neomartyrōn, *Ergon psychōphelestaton kai sōtēriōdestaton, periechon martyria 150 kai pleon Neophanōn Hagiōn Martyrōn tēs Orthodoxou tou Christou Ekklēsias mas tōn etōn 1400 eōs 1900 meta Christou*, Thessalonika, 1984

I. Netton, *Muslim Neoplatonists. An introduction to the thought of the Brethren of Purity*, Edinburgh, 1991

G.D. Newby, art. 'Forgery', in *EQ*

N.A. Newman (ed.), *The early Christian-Muslim dialogue. A collection of documents from the first three Islamic centuries (632-900 AD)*, Hatfield PA, 1993

A. Neuwirth, 'Two faces of the Qur'ān. *Qur'ān* and *m uṣḥaf*', *Oral Tradition* 25 (2010) 150-3

A. Neuwirth, N. Sinai and M. Marx (eds), *The Qurʾān in context. Historical and literary investigations into the qurʾānic milieu*, Leiden, 2010

Y. Nevo, Z. Cohen, and D. Heftman, *Ancient Arabic inscriptions from the Negev*, vol. 1, Midreshet Ben-Gurion, 1993

G. Nickel, *Narratives of tampering in the earliest commentaries on the Qurʾān*, Leiden, 2011

G. Nickel, '"Self-evident truths of reason". Challenges to clear thinking in the *Tafsīr al-kabīr* of Fakhr al-Dīn al-Rāzī', *IMCR* 22 (2011) 161-72

G. Nickel, *The gentle answer to the Muslim accusation of biblical falsification*, Calgary, 2015

G. Nickel, 'Scholarly reception of Alphonse Mingana's "The transmission of the Ḳur'ān". A centenary perspective', in Pratt et al., *The character of Christian-Muslim encounter*, 2015, 343-64

G. Nickel, 'Muqātil on Zayd and Zaynab. "The *sunna* of Allāh concerning those who passed away before" (Q 33:38)', in Daneshgar and Saleh, *Islamic studies today*, 2017, 43-61

G. Nickel, 'Jesus', in Rippin and Mojaddedi, *The Wiley Blackwell companion to the Qurʾān*, 2017, 288-302

G. Nickel, '"They find him written with them". The impact of Q 7:157 on Muslim interaction with Arab Christianity', in Beaumont, *Arab Christians and the Qur'an*, 2018, 106-30

S. Noble and A. Treiger, 'Christian Arabic theology in Byzantine Antioch', *Le Muséon* 124 (2011) 371-417

S. Noble and A. Treiger (eds), *The Orthodox Church in the Arab world 700-1700, An anthology of sources*, De Kalb IL, 2014

T.F.X. Noble and J.M.H. Smith (eds), *The Cambridge history of Christianity*, vol. 3. *Early medieval Christianities, c. 600-c. 1100*. Cambridge, 2010

Guibert de Nogent, *Dei Gesta per Francos*, ed. R. Huygens, Turnhout, 1996

D. Norberg, *An introduction to the study of medieval Latin versification*, trans. G.C. Roti and J. de La Chapelle Skubly, ed. J. Ziolkowski, Washington DC, 2004

A. Noth, 'Abgrenzungsprobleme zwischen Muslimen und Nicht-Muslimen. Die "Bedingungen ʿUmars" (*aš-šurūṭ al-ʿumariyya*) unter einem andere Aspekt gelesen', *Jerusalem Studies in Arabic and Islam* 9 (1987) 290-315

A. Noth, 'Problems of differentiation between Muslims and non-Muslims. Re-reading the "Ordinances of ʿUmar" (*al-Shurūṭ al-ʿUmariyya*)', in Hoyland, *Muslims and others in early Islamic society*, 2004, 103-24

J.F. O'Callaghan, 'The Mudejars of Castile and Portugal in the twelfth and thirteenth centuries', in Powell, *Muslims under Latin rule 1100-1300*, 1990, 1-56

J.F. O'Callaghan, *Reconquest and crusade in medieval Spain*, Philadelphia PA, 2003

Odo of Deuil, *De profectione Ludovici in Orientem. The journey of Louis VII to the east*, ed. V.G. Berry, New York, 1948

K.-H. Ohlig and G.-R. Puin (eds), *Die dunklen Anfänge*, Berlin, 2007

J. Orlandis, *Estudios visigóticos*, Madrid, 1956

A. Papaconstantinou, 'Between *umma* and *dhimma*. The Christians of the Middle East under the Umayyads', *Annales Islamologiques* 42 (2008) 127-56

A. Papaconstantinou, with M. Debié and H. Kennedy (eds), *Writing 'true stories'. Historians and hagiographers in the late antique and medieval Near East*, Turnhout, 2010

D. Papademetriou and A.J. Sopko (eds), *The church and the library*, Boston MA, 2005

G.C. Papademetriou (ed.), *Two traditions, one space. Orthodox Christians and Muslims in dialogue*, Boston MA, 2011

T. Papademetriou, 'The continuity of the holy man. Orthodox hesychasm and dervish mysticism in the late Byzantine and early Ottoman period', in Papademetriou and Sopko, *The church and the library*, 2005, 32-74

T. Papademetriou, 'The Turkish conquests and decline of the church reconsidered', in Angelov, *Church and society in late Byzantium*, 2009, 183-200

T. Papademetriou, *Render unto the sultan. Power, authority, and the Greek Orthodox Church in the early Ottoman centuries*, Oxford, 2015

G.F. Parrilla and M.C. Feria García (eds), *Orientalismo, exotismo y traducción*, Cuenca, 2000

J. Patrich (ed.), *The Sabaite heritage in the Orthodox Church from the fifth century to the present*, Leuven, 2001

A.C.S. Peacock (ed.), *Islamisation. Comparative perspectives from history*, Edinburgh, 2017

A. Peacock, B. de Nicola and S. Nur Yıldız (eds), *Christianity and Islam in Medieval Anatolia*, Farnham, 2015

P. Peeters, *Orient et Byzance. Le tréfonds oriental de l'hagiographie byzantine*, Brussels, 1950

C. Pellat (ed.), *Le calendrier de Cordoue*, Leiden, 1961

M.T. Penelas, 'A possible author of the Arabic translation of Orosius' *Historiae*', *Al-Masāq* 13 (2001) 113-35

M.T. Penelas (ed.), *Kitāb Hurūšiyūš* (*Traducción árabe de las Historiæ adversus paganos de Orosio*), Madrid, 2001

M. Penelas, 'Some remarks on conversion to Islam in al-Andalus', *Al-Qanṭara* 23 (2002) 193-200

M.P. Penn, *When Christians first met Muslims. A sourcebook of the earliest Syriac writings on Islam*, Oakland CA, 2015

M.P. Penn, *Envisioning Islam. Syriac Christians and the early Muslim world*, Philadelphia PA, 2015

M. Perani (ed.), *Guglielmo Raimondo Moncada* alias *Flavio Mitridate. Un ebreo converso siciliano*, Palermo, 2008

I. Pérez Martín and P. Bádenas de la Peña (eds), *Bizancio y la Península Ibérica. De la antigüedad tardía a la edad moderna*, Madrid, 2004

M. Perlmann (trans.), *Ibn Kammūna's examination of the three faiths. A thirteenth-century essay in the comparative study of religion*, Berkeley CA, 1971

R. Peter and G.J.J. de Vries, 'Apostasy in Islam', *Die Welt des Islams* 17 (1976) 1-25

F.E. Peters, *The voice, the word, the books. The sacred scriptures of the Jews, Christians and Muslims*, Princeton NJ, 2007

M. Philippides, 'Patriarchal chronicles of the sixteenth century', *Greek, Roman, and Byzantine Studies* 25 (1984) 87-94

L.K. Pick, *Conflict and coexistence. Archbishop Rodrigo and the Muslims and Jews of medieval Spain*, Ann Arbor MI, 2004

D. Pinault, 'Images of Christ in Arabic literature', *Die Welt des Islams* 27 (1987) 103-25

E. Platti, 'Abd al-Masīḥ al-Kindī on the Qur'an', in Beaumont, *Arab Christians and the Qur'an*, 2018, 66-82

Z. Pogossian, 'The frontier existence of the Paulician heretics', K. Szende and M. Sebők (eds), *Annual of medieval studies at CEU*, vol. 6, Budapest, 2000, 203-6

N. Petrus Pons (ed.), *Alchoranus Latinus quem transtulit Marcus canonicus Toletanus*, Madrid, 2016

J. Powell (ed.), *Muslims under Latin rule, 1100-1300*, Princeton NJ, 1990

D.S. Powers, *Muḥammad is not the father of any of your men. The making of the last prophet*, Philadelphia PA, 2009

D. Pratt, *The challenge of Islam. Encounters in interfaith dialogue*, Farnham 2005 (Abingdon, 2017)

D. Pratt et al. (eds), *The character of Christian-Muslim encounter*, Leiden, 2015

D. Pratt, *Christian engagement with Islam. Ecumenical journeys since 1910*, Leiden, 2017

J. Prawer, *The history of the Jews in the Latin Kingdom of Jerusalem*, Oxford, 1988

A.-L. de Prémare, "Abd al-Malik b. Marwān et le processus de constitution du Coran', in Ohlig and Puin, *Die dunklen Anfänge*, 2007, 178-210

D. Pringle, *The churches of the Crusader Kingdom of Jerusalem. A corpus*, vol. 2, Cambridge, 1998

M. Qamaruddin, *The Mahdawi movement in India*, Delhi: Idarat-i Asabiyat, 1985

Al-Qarāfī, *Al-Ajwiba l-fākhira 'an al-as'ila l-fājira fī l-radd 'alā l-milla l-kāfira*, ed. M.M. al-Shahāwī, Beirut, 2005

J. Quasten, 'The liturgical mysticism of Theodore of Mopsuestia', *Theological Studies* 15 (1954) 431-9

Abū Qurra, 'Treatise on the Trinity', in Bacha, *Les oeuvres arabes de Theodore Aboucara*, 1904, 23-47

'Arīb ibn Sa'd al-Qurṭubī, *Ṣilat tārīkh al-Ṭabarī*, ed. M.J. de Goeje, Leiden, 1898

Ḥafṣ Ibn-Albar al-Qūṭī, *Le Psautier de Hafs le Goth*, ed. trans. and introduction M.-T. Urvoy, Toulouse, 1994

Ibn Zabr al-Rabaʿī, *Juz' fīhi shurūṭ al-Naṣārā*, ed. A. al-ʿAqīl, Beirut, 2006

Y. Rāġib (ed.), *Documents de l'islam médiéval. Nouvelles perspectives de recherche*, Cairo, 1991

Abū Rā'iṭa, 'Fī ithbāt dīn al-naṣrāniyya wa-ithbāt al-Thālūth al-maqaddas', in Keating, *Defending the 'People of truth' in the early Islamic period*, 2006, 73-146

Abū Rā'iṭa, 'Letter on the Incarnation', in Keating, *Defending the 'People of truth' in the early Islamic period*, 2006, 268-71

Y. Rapoport, *Rural economy and tribal society in Islamic Egypt. A study of al-Nābulusī's 'Villages of the Fayyum'*, Turnhout, 2018

W. Raven, art. 'Sīra', in *EI2*

J. Ray, *The Sephardic frontier. The Reconquista and the Jewish community in medieval Iberia*, Ithaca NY, 2006

J. Reeves (ed.), *Bible and Qur'ān. Essays in scriptural intertextuality*, Atlanta GA, 2003

G. Reinink (ed.), *Die Syrischen Apokalypse des Pseudo-Methodius*, 2 vols (Corpus Scriptorum Christianorum Orientalium, vols 540-1), Louvain, 1993

G.J. Reinink, 'The veneration of icons, the cross, and the bones of the martyrs in an early East-Syrian apology against Islam', in Bumazhnov et al., *Bibel, Byzanz und Christlicher Orient*, 2011, 329-42

G.J. Reinink and A.C. Klugkist (eds), *After Bardaisan. Studies on continuity and change in Syriac Christianity*, Louvain, 1999

D.F. Reynolds (ed.), *Interpreting the self. Autobiography in the Arabic literary tradition*, Berkeley CA, 2001

G.S. Reynolds (ed.), *New perspectives on the Qur'ān. The Qur'ān in its historical context 2*, London, 2012

G.S. Reynolds, 'The Quran and the Apostles of Jesus', *BSOAS* 76 (2013) 209-27

G.S. Reynolds, *The Qur'ān & the Bible. Text and commentary*, New Haven CT, 2018, 1-25

J. Richard, *La Paupeté et les missions d'orient au moyen age (XIIIe-XVe siècle)*, Rome, 1977

D.S. Richards (trans.), *The rare and excellent history of Saladin. Or al-Nawādir al-Sulṭāniyya wa'l-Maḥāsin al-Yūsufiyya by Bahā' al-Dīn Ibn Shaddād*, Aldershot, 2002

L. Ridgeon (ed.), *Islamic interpretations of Christianity*, New York, 2001

A.F. al-Rifāʿī, *ʿAṣr al-Mamūn*, vol. 2, Cairo, 1927

A. Rippin, 'Literary analysis of *Qur'ān*, *tafsīr*, and *sīra*. The methodologies of John Wansbrough', in Martin, *Approaches to Islam in religious studies*, 1985, 151-63

A. Rippin, *Muslims. Their religious beliefs and practices*, London, 2001[2]

A. Rippin and J. Mojaddedi (eds), *The Wiley Blackwell companion to the Qurʾān*, Oxford, 2017

J.F. Rivera Recio, *El adopcionismo en España, siglo VIII: historia y doctrina*, Toledo, 1980

C.F. Robinson, *Empire and elites after the Muslim conquest*, Cambridge, 2000

C.F. Robinson, 'The conquest of Khuzistan. A historiographical reassessment', *BSOAS* 67 (2004) 14-40

C.F. Robinson, *ʿAbd al-Malik*, Oxford, 2005

P. Robinson (ed.), *The writings of Saint Francis of Assisi*, Philadelphia PA, 1905

D.C. Rodríguez, *Juan de Segovia y el problema islámico*, Madrid, 1952

B. Roggema, 'A Christian reading of the Qur'an. The legend of Sergius-Baḥīrā and its use of Qur'an and Sīra', in Thomas, *Syrian Christians under Islam*, 2001, 57-74

B. Roggema, 'Muslims as crypto-idolaters. A theme in the Christian portrayal of Islam in the Near East', in Thomas, *Christians at the heart of Islamic rule*, 2003, 1–18

B. Roggema, *The legend of Sergius Baḥīrā. Eastern Christian apologetics and apocalyptic in response to Islam*, Leiden, 2009

J.W.W. van Rooden, J.J. de Jonge and J.W. van Henten (eds), *Tradition and reinterpretation in Jewish and early Christian literature. Essays in honour of Jürgen C.H. Lebram*, Leiden, 1986

M. Root and J.J. Buckley (eds), *Christian theology and Islam*, Eugene OR, 2013

F. Rosenthal, 'The influence of the biblical tradition on Muslim historiography', in Lewis and Holt, *Historical writings of the peoples of Asia*, vol. 4, 1962, 35-45

U. Roth and R. Glei, 'Die Spuren der lateinischen Koranubersetzung des Juan de Segovia. Alte Probleme und ein neuer Fund', *Neulateinisches Jahrbuch* 11 (2009) 109-54

U. Roth and R. Glei, 'Eine weitere Spur der lateinische Koranubersetzung des Juan von Segovia', *Neulateinisches Jahrbuch* 13 (2011) 221-8

José Palacios Royán (ed.), *Apologético del Abad Sansón*, Madrid, 1988

Mawlānā Jalāl al-Dīn Rūmī, *The Mathnawī of Jalālu'ddīn Rūmī*, ed and trans R.A. Nicholson, London, 1926

J. Ryan, 'Christian wives of Mongol khans', *Journal of the Royal Asiatic Society* 8 (1998) 411-21

Ibn Saʿd, *Kitāb al-ṭabaqāt al-kubrā*, vol. 1, ed. ʿA.M. ʿUmar, Cairo, 2001

Y. Ṣādir, *Ruhbān ʿarab fī baʿḍ siyar al-mutaṣawwifīn al-muslimīn*, Beirut, 2009

O. Safi, *The politics of knowledge in premodern Islam. Negotiating ideology and religious inquiry*, Chapel Hill NC, 2006

J.M. Safran, *Defining boundaries in al-Andalus. Muslims, Christians, and Jews in Islamic Iberia*, Ithaca NY, 2013

D.H. Sahas, '"Holosphyros"? A Byzantine perception of "The God of Muḥammad"', in Haddad and Haddad, *Christian-Muslim encounters*, 1995, 109-25

D.J. Sahas, *John of Damascus on Islam. The 'heresy of the Ishmaelites'*, Leiden, 1972

D.J. Sahas, 'Captivity and dialogue. Gregory Palamas (1296-1360) and the Muslims', *Greek Orthodox Theological Review* 25 (1981) 409-36

D.J. Sahas, 'What an infidel saw that a faithful did not. Gregory Dekapolites (d. 842) and Islam', *Greek Orthodox Theological Review* 31 (1986) 47-67

D.J. Sahas, 'The face to face encounter between Patriarch Sophronius of Jerusalem and the Caliph ʿUmar ibn al-Khaṭṭāb. Friends or foes?', in Grypeou et al., *The encounter of Eastern Christianity with early Islam*, 2006, 33-44

Ibn Sahl, *Dīwān al-aḥkām al-kubrā, al-nawāzil wa-l-iʿlām*, vol. 2, ed. R.H. al-Nuʿaymī, Riyadh, 1997

C.C. Sahner, 'The first iconoclasm in Islam. A new history of the edict of Yazīd II (AH 104/AD 723)', *Der Islam* 94 (2017) 5-56

C.C. Sahner, *Christian martyrs under Islam. Religious violence and the making of the Muslim world*, Princeton NJ, 2018

Jean de Saint-Arnoul, *La vie de Jean, abbé de Gorze*, ed. and trans. M. Parisse, Paris, 1999

F. Sáinz Robles, *Elipando y San Beato de Liébana, siglo VIII*, Madrid, 1934

W.A. Saleh, *In defense of the Bible. A critical edition and an introduction to al-Biqāʿī's Bible treatise*, Leiden, 2008

W.A. Saleh and K.C. Waled, 'An Islamic Diatessaron. Al-Biqāʿī's harmony of the four Gospels', in Binay and Leder, *Translating the Bible into Arabic*, 2012, 89-115

S.K. Samir (ed.), *Actes du premier congrès international d'études arabes chrétiennes*, Rome, 1982

S.K. Samir (ed.), *Maqāla fī l-tathlīth wa-l-tajassud wa-ṣiḥḥat al-masīḥiyya li-Būlus al-Būshī*, Dayr al-Malāk Mīkhāʾīl: al-Turāth al-ʿArabī l-Masīḥī, 1983

S.K. Samir, 'The earliest Arab apology for Christianity', in Samir and Nielsen, *Christian Arabic apologetics*, 1994, 57-114

S.K. Samir, 'The Prophet Muḥammad as seen by Timothy I and other Arab Christian authors', in Thomas, *Syrian Christians under Islam*, 2001, 75-106

S.K. Samir and W. Nasry, *The patriarch and the caliph. An eighth-century dialogue between Timothy I and al-Mahdī*, Provo UT, 2018

S.K. Samir and J.S. Nielsen (eds), *Christian Arabic apologetics during the Abbasid period (750-1258)*, Leiden, 1994

S.K. Samir and P. Nwyia (eds), *Une correspondence islamo-chrétienne entre Ibn al-Munağğim, Ḥunayn ibn Isḥāq et Qusṭa ibn Lūqā*, Turnhout, 1981

al-Ṣanʿānī, *Al-muṣannaf*, vol. 11, ed. Ḥ. al-R. al-Aʿẓamī, Beirut, 1983

Hannād al-Sarī, *K. al-Zuhd*, ed. ʿA. al-R. al-Faryawāʾī, Kuwait, 1985

D.R. Sarrió Cucarella, *Muslim-Christian polemics across the Mediterranean. The splendid replies of Shihāb al-Dīn al-Qarāfī (d. 684/1285)*, Leiden, 2015

D.R. Sarrió Cucarella, 'Corresponding across religious borders. The *Letter of al-Qūṭī*', *Islamochristiana* 43 (2017) 149-171

C. Saunders, F. le Saux and N. Thomas (eds), *Writing war. Medieval literary responses to warfare*, Cambridge, 2004

J. Schacht, art. 'Aḥmad', in *EI2*

P. Schadler, *John of Damascus and Islam. Christian heresiology and the intellectual background to earliest Christian-Muslim relations*, Leiden, 2018

P. Schaff and H. Wace, *Nicene and Post-Nicene Fathers*, vol. 8, Peabody MA, 1999

R. Schaffner, 'The Bible through a Qur'ānic filter. Scripture falsification (*Taḥrīf*) in 8th and 9th-Century Muslim Disputational Literature', Columbus OH, 2016 (PhD Diss. The Ohio State University)

R. Schick, *The Christian communities of Palestine from Byzantine to Islamic rule. A historical and archaeological study*, Princeton NJ, 1995

A. Schimmel, *And Muhammad is his Messenger. The veneration of the Prophet in Islamic piety*, Chapel Hill NC, 1985

S. Schmidtke, 'The Muslim reception of biblical materials. Ibn Qutayba and his *Aʿlām al-nubuwwa*', *ICMR* 22 (2011) 249–74

A. Schönberger and K. Zimmermann (eds), *De orbis Hispani linguis litteris historia moribus*, Frankfurt am Main, 1994

R. Schwinges, *Kreuzzugsideologie und Toleranz. Studien zu Wilhelm von Tyrus*, Stuttgart, 1977

Johannes von Segovia, *De gladio divini spiritus in corda mittendo Sarracenorum*, ed. U. Roth, 2 vols, Wiesbaden, 2012

B. Septimus, 'Petrus Alfonsi on the cult at Mecca', *Speculum* 56 (1981) 517-33

E.R.A. Sewter, trans., *The Alexiad of Anna Comnena*, Harmondsworth, 1969

C.F. Seybold (ed.), *Glossarium latino-arabicum*, Berlin, 1900

Al-Shahrastānī, *Al-Milal wa-l-niḥal*, vol. 2, ed. A.F. Muḥammad, Beirut, 1992

A. Shalem et al., *Constructing the image of Muhammad in Europe*, Berlin, 2013

M. Sharon, art. 'People of the Book', in *EQ*

Ibn Abī Shayba, *Al-Muṣannaf*, Cairo, 2007

Al-Shaybānī, *al-Aṣl*, vol. 7, ed. M. Buynūkālin, Beirut, 1433 [2012]

M.M. Shenoda, 'Lamenting Islam, imagining persecution. Copto-Arabic opposition to Islamization and Arabization in Fatimid Egypt', Cambridge MA (PhD Diss. Harvard University), 2010

ʿAbdallāh Maḥmūd Shiḥāta (ed.), *Tafsīr Muqātil ibn Sulaymān*, vol. 3, Beirut, 2002

ʿAbdallāh Maḥmūd Shiḥāta (ed.), *Tafsīr al-Ṭabarī musamma Jāmiʿ al-bayān fī taʾwīl al-qurʾān*, vol. 10, Beirut, 2005

S.J. Shoemaker (trans.), *Three Christian martyrdoms from early Islamic Palestine*, Provo UT, 2016

M. Siddiqui (ed.), *The Routledge reader in Christian-Muslim Relations*, London, 2013

F.J. Simonet, *Historia de los mozárabes de España, deducida de los mejores y más auténticos testimonios de los escritores cristianos y árabes*, 4 vols Madrid, 1897-1903 (repr. 1983), vol. II

U.I. Simonsohn, *A common justice. The legal allegiances of Christians and Jews under early Islam*, Philadelphia PA, 2011

U.I. Simonsohn, 'Halting between two opinions. Conversion and apostasy in early Islam', *Medieval Encounters* 19 (2013) 344-72

H. Sirantoine, 'Le discours monarchique des "Chroniques asturiennes", fin IXe siècle. Trois modes de légitimation pour les rois des Asturies', in Fernández Catón, *Monarquía y sociedad en el reino de León*, 2007, 793-819

G.D. Sixdenier, 'A propos de l'origine du Psautier latin du Sinaï: Une piste?', *Scriptorium* 41 (1987) 129

T. Sizgorich, 'For Christian eyes only? The intended audience of the martyrdom of Antony Rawḥ', *ICMR* 20 (2009) 119-35

T. Sizgorich, 'The dancing martyr. Violence, identity, and the Abbasid postcolonial', *History of Religions* 57 (2017) 2-27

H. Smith, *God's Arrow against atheists*, London, 1617

R.W. Southern, *Western views of Islam in the Middle Ages*, Cambridge MA, 1962

T. Spandounes, *On the origin of the Ottoman emperors*, ed. and trans. D.M. Nicol, Cambridge, 1997

J. Spaulding, 'Medieval Christian Nubia and the Islamic world. A reconsideration of the baqt treaty', *International Journal of African Historical Studies* 28 (1995) 577-94

R.M. Speight, 'Christians in the Hadith literature', in Ridgeon, *Islamic interpretations of Christianity*, 2001, 30-53

A. Sprenger, *The life of Mohammad from original sources*, Allahabad, 1851

K.K. Starczewska (ed.), *Latin translation of the Qurʾān (1518/1621)*, Wiesbaden, 2018

J. Stearns, 'Representing and remembering al-Andalus. Some historical considerations regarding the end of time and the making of nostalgia', *Medieval Encounters* 15 (2009) 355-74

P. Stenhouse (trans.), *ʿArab Faqīh, Futūḥ al-Ḥabasha. The conquest of Abyssinia*, Hollywood CA, 2003

S. Stetkevych, 'Al-Akhṭal at the court of 'Abd al-Malik. The *qaṣīda* and the construction of Umayyad authority', in Borrut and Donner, *Christians and others in the Umayyad state*, 2016, 140-55

G.B. Stone, 'Ramon Llull', in Menocal et al., *The literature of al-Andalus*, 2012, 345-57

S. Stroumsa, 'The signs of prophecy. The emergence and early development of a theme in Arabic theological literature', *Harvard Theological Review* 78 (1985) 101-14

J. Stuckey, 'Charlemagne as crusader? Memory, propaganda, and the many uses of Charlemagne's legendary expedition to Spain', in Gabriele and Stuckey, *The legend of Charlemagne in the Middle Ages*, 2008, 137-52

Tāqī l-Dīn al-Subkī, *Al-sayf al-maslūl 'alā man sabba l-rasūl*, ed. I.A. al-Ghawj, Amman, 2000

H. Suermann, 'The use of biblical quotations in Christian apocalyptic writings of the Umayyad period', in Thomas, *The Bible in Arab Christianity*, 2007, 69-90

D.F. Sullivan (ed. and trans.), *The life of Saint Nikon*, Brookline MA, 1987

Al-Suyūṭī, *Ḥāwī*, Beirut, [n.d.], vol. 2

M.N. Swanson, 'The cross of Christ in the earliest Arabic Melkite apologies', in Samir and Nielsen, *Christian Arabic apologetics*, 1994, 115-45

M.N. Swanson, 'Beyond prooftexting. Approaches to the Qur'ān in some early Arabic Christian apologies', *The Muslim World* 88 (1998) 297-319

M.N. Swanson, 'The martyrdom of 'Abd al-Masīḥ, Superior of Mount Sinai (Qays al-Ghassānī)', in Thomas, *Syrian Christians under Islam*, 2001, 107-29

M.N. Swanson, art. 'Proof', in *EQ*

M.N. Swanson, 'The Trinity in Christian-Muslim conversation', *Dialog. A Journal of Theology* 44 (2005) 256-63

M.N. Swanson, 'Folly to the *ḥunafā'*. The crucifixion in early Christian-Muslim controversy', in Grypeou et al., *The encounter of Eastern Christianity with early Islam*, 2006, 237-56

M.N. Swanson, 'Beyond prooftexting (2). The use of the Bible in some early Arabic Christian apologies', in Thomas, *The Bible in Arab Christianity*, 2007, 91-112

M.N. Swanson, 'A curious and delicate correspondence. The *Burhān* of Ibn al-Munajjim and the *Jawāb* of Ḥunayn ibn Isḥāq', *ICMR* 22 (2011) 173-83

M.N. Swanson, 'Apology or its evasion? Some ninth-century Arabic Christian texts on discerning the true religion', in Root and Buckley, *Christian theology and Islam*, 2013, 45–63

M.N. Swanson, 'Discerning the true religion in late-fourteenth-century Egypt', in Gabra and Takla, *Christianity and monasticism in Middle Egypt*, 2015, 133–44

K. Szende and M. Sebők (eds), *Annual of medieval studies at CEU*, vol. 6, Budapest, 2000

K. Szilágyi, 'The disputation of the monk Abraham of Tiberias', in Noble and Treiger, *The Orthodox Church in the Arab world*, 2014, 90-111

R. Szpiech, 'Citas arabes en caracteres hebreos en el *pugio fidei* del dominico Ramon Marti: Entre la autenticidad y la autoridad', *Al-Qanṭara* 22 (2011) 71-107

'Alī ibn Rabban al-Ṭabarī, *The book of religion and empire*, trans. A. Mingana, London, 1922

Al-Ṭabarī, *Ta'rīkh al-rusul wa-l-mulūk*, vol. 2, Cairo, 1967

Al-Ṭabarī, *Jāmi' al-bayān fī taʾwīl al-Qur'ān*, vol. 6, ed. M.A. Bayḍūn, Beirut, 1988

Al-Ṭabarī, *The history of al-Ṭabarī*, trans. F. Rosenthal, vol. 1, Albany, NY, 1989

'Alī ibn Rabban al-Ṭabarī, *Refutation of the Christians*, in Ebied and Thomas, *The polemical works of 'Alī al-Ṭabarī*, 2016, 84-163

H. Takahashi, *Barhebraeus. A bio-bibliography*, Piscataway NJ, 2013

M. Tamcke (ed.), *Christians and Muslims in dialogue in the Islamic Orient of the Middle Ages*, Beirut, 2007

M. Tamcke and A. Heinz (eds), *Die Suryoye und ihre Umwelt*, Münster, 2005

J. Tannous, *The making of the medieval Middle East. Religion, society, and simple believers*, Princeton NJ, 2018

G. Tartar, 'Dialogue islamo-chrétien sous le calife al-Ma'mun (813-834). Les épîtres d'al-Hâsimî et d'al-Kindî', Strasbourg, 1977 (PhD Diss. Université des Sciences Humaines de Strasbourg)

D.G.K. Taylor, 'The disputation between a Muslim and a monk of Bēt Ḥālē. Syriac text and annotated English translation', in Griffith and Grebenstein, *Christsein in der islamischen Welt*, 2015, 187-242

Ibn Taymiyya, 'The correct answer to those who have changed the religion of Christ, *Al-jawāb al-ṣaḥīḥ li-man baddala dīn al-Masīḥ*', in Michel, *A Muslim theologian's response to Christianity*, 1984, 1-369

Ibn Taymiyya, *Mas'ala fī l-kanā'is*, ed. 'A. al-Shibl, Riyadh, 1995

Ibn Taymiyya, *Al-Jawāb al-ṣaḥīḥ li-man baddaladīn al-Masīh*, vol. 3, ed. 'A. b. Ḥ. b. Nāṣīr, 'A. al-'A. b. I. al-'Askar and Ḥ. b. M. al-Ḥamdān, Riyadh, 1999

Ibn Taymiyya, *Al-ṣārim al-maslūl ' alā shātim al-rasūl*, ed. I. Shams al-Dīn, Beirut, 2009

H.G.B. Teule, 'Gregory Barhebraeus and his time. The Syriac Renaissance', *Journal of the Canadian Society for Syriac Studies* 3 (2003) 21-43

H.G.B. Teule, 'The veneration of images in the East Syriac tradition', in Groneberg and Spieckermann, *Der Welt der Götterbilder*, 2007, 324-46

H.G.B. Teule, 'Isho'yahb bar Malkon's treatise on the veneration of the holy icons', in Tamcke, *Christians and Muslims in dialogue*, 2007, 157-69

H.G.B. Teule, *Les Assyro-Chaldéens. Chrétiens d'Irak, d'Iran et de Turquie*, Turnhout, 2008

Al-Thaʿlabī, *Qiṣaṣ al-anbiyāʾ al-musammā ʿarāʾis al-majālis*, ed. ʿA. al-L. al-Raḥmān, Beirut, 2004

Theophanes Confessor, *The Chronicle of Theophanes*, trans. C. Mango and R. Scott, Oxford, 1997

D. Thomas, art. 'Tathlīth', in *EI2*

D. Thomas (ed. and trans.), *Anti-Christian polemic in early Islam. Abū ʿĪsā al-Warrāq's 'Against the Trinity'*, Cambridge, 1992

D. Thomas (ed.), *Syrian Christians under Islam. The first thousand years*, Leiden, 2001

D. Thomas, 'Paul of Antioch's *Letter to a Muslim Friend* and *The Letter from Cyprus*', in Thomas, *Syrian Christians under Islam*, 2001, 203-21

D. Thomas, *Early Muslim polemic against Christianity. Abū ʿĪsā al-Warrāq's 'Against the Incarnation'*, Cambridge, 2002

D. Thomas (ed.), *Christians at the heart of Islamic rule*, Leiden, 2003

D. Thomas (ed. and trans.), *The Bible in Arab Christianity*, Leiden, 2007

D. Thomas (ed. and trans.), *Christian doctrines in Islamic theology*, Leiden, 2008

D. Thomas (ed.), *Routledge handbook on Christian-Muslim relations*, Abingdon, 2018

J.W. Thomas (ed. and trans.), *Priest Konrad's Song of Roland*, Columbia SC, 1994

P. Thorau, *The Lion of Egypt. Sultan Baybars I & the Near East in the thirteenth century*, trans. P.M. Holt, Harlow, 1992

A. Tien (trans.), 'The Apology of al-Kindi', in Newman, *The early Christian-Muslim dialogue*, 1993, 365-545

C.L. Tieszen, *Christian identity amid Islam in medieval Spain*, Leiden, 2013

C.L. Tieszen, *A Textual History of Christian-Muslim Relations, seventh – fifteenth centuries*, Minneapolis, MN, 2015

C.L. Tieszen, *Cross veneration in the medieval Islamic world*, London, 2017

C.L. Tieszen (ed.), *Theological issues in Christian-Muslim dialogue*, Eugene OR, 2018

C.L. Tieszen, 'Christians under Muslim rule, 650-1200', in Thomas, *Routledge handbook on Christian-Muslim relations*, 2018, 75-9

M. Tillier, 'Dalifes, émirs et cadis. Le droit caliphal et l'articulation de l'autorité judiciaire à l'époque umayyade', *Bulletin d'Etudes Orientales* 63 (2014) 147–90

M.M. Tischler and A. Fidora (eds), *Christlicher Norden – Muslimischer Süden. Ansprüche und Wirklichkeiten von Christen, Juden und Muslimen auf der Iberischen Halbinsel im Hoch- und Spätmittelalter*, Achendorff, 2011

J. Tolan, 'Mirror of chivalry. Salah al-Din in the medieval European imagination', in Blanks, *Images of the Other*, 1996, 7-38

J.V. Tolan (ed.), *Medieval Christian perceptions of Islam*, Abingdon, 2000

J.V. Tolan, *Saracens. Islam in the medieval European imagination*, New York, 2002

J. Tolan (ed.), *Sons of Ishmael. Muslims through European eyes in the Middle Ages*, Gainesville FL, 2008

J. Tolan, *Saint Francis and the sultan. The curious history of a Christian-Muslim encounter*, Oxford, 2009

J. Tolan, G. Veinstein and H. Laurens, *Europe and the Islamic world. A history*, Princeton NJ, 2013

M. Sanudo Torsello, *The book of the secrets of the faithful of the cross. Liber secretorum fidelium crucis*, trans. P. Lock, Farnham, 2011

A. Treiger, 'New works of Theodore Abū Qurra preserved under the name of Thaddeus of Edessa', *Journal of Eastern Christian Studies* 68 (2016) 1-51

A. Treiger, 'Mutual influences and borrowings', in Thomas, *Routledge handbook on Christian-Muslim relations*, 2018, 194-206

J. Trimingham, *Islam in Ethiopia*, London, 1952

A. Tritton, *The caliphs and their non-Muslim subjects*, London, 1930

G. Troupeau, 'Un traité sur les principes des êtres attribué à Abū Sulaymān al-Siğistānī, *Pensamiento* 25 (1969) 259-70

G. Troupeau, 'Présentation et réfutation des croyances des chrétiens chez Ibn Hazm de Cordoue', in Delcambre and Arnaldez, *Enquêtes sur l'Islam*, 2004, 193-210

Al-Ṭūfi, *Muslim exegesis of the Bible in medieval Cairo. A critical edition and annotated translation with an introduction*, ed. and trans. L. Demiri, Leiden, 2013

O. Turan, 'Les souverains seldjoukides et leurs sujets non-musulmans', *Studia Islamica* 1 (1953) 65-100

A.M. Turki, 'La lettre du "Moine de France" à al-Muqtadir billāh, roi de Saragosse, et la résponse d'al-Bāŷī, faqīh andalou', *Al-Andalus* 31 (1966) 73-153

S.E. Turley, *Franciscan spirituality and mission in New Spain 1524-1599. Conflict beneath the sycamore tree*, Burlington VT, 2013

H. Turtledove (ed. and trans.), *The Chronicle of Theophanes. Anni mundi 6095-6305 (A.D. 602-813)*, Philadelphia PA, 1982

M.W. Twomey, 'The *Revelationes* of Pseudo-Methodius and scriptural study at Salisbury in the eleventh century', in Wright et al., *Source of wisdom*, 2007, 370-86

Y. Tzvi Langermann and J. Stern (eds), *Adaptations and innovations. Studies on the interaction between Jewish and Islamic thought and literature from the Early Middle ages to late Twentieth century*, Paris, 2007

Sayf ibn 'Umar, *Kitāb al-ridda wa-al-futūḥ wa-kitāb al-jamal wa-maṣīr 'Ā'isha wa-'Alī*, no. 133, ed. Q. al-Samarrai, Leiden, 1995

D. Urvoy, 'Les aspects symboliques du vocable "mozarabe". Essai de réinterprétation', *Studia Islamica* 78 (1993) 117-53

M.-T. Urvoy, 'Influence islamique sur le vocabulaire d'un Psautier arabe d'al-Andalus', *Al-Qanṭara* 15 (1994) 509-17

A. Vacca, *Non-Muslim provinces under early Islam. Islamic rule and Iranian legitimacy in Armenia and Caucasian Albania*, Cambridge, 2017

L.V. Vaglieri, 'The Patriarchal and Umayyad caliphates', in Holt et al., *The Cambridge history of Islam*, vol. 1A, 2008, 57-103

P. Valkenberg, 'Can we talk theologically? Thomas Aquinas and Nicholas of Cusa on the possibility of a theological understanding of Islam', in Min, *Rethinking the medieval legacy for contemporary theology*, 2014, 131-66

N. Vaporis, *Witnesses for Christ. Orthodox Christian neomartyrs of the Ottoman period*, Crestwood NY, 2000

G. Veinstein (ed.), *Suleyman the Magnificent and his time*, Paris, 1992

U. Vermeulen, 'The rescript of al-Malik aṣ-Ṣāliḥ against the dhimmīs (755 A.H./1354 A.D.)', *Orientalia Lovaniensia Periodica* 9 (1978) 175-84

A. Verskin, *Islamic law and the crisis of the Reconquista. The debate on the status of Muslim communities in Christendom*, Leiden, 2015

D.H. Vila, 'Christian martyrs in the first Abbasid century and the development of an apologetic against Islam', St. Louis MO (PhD Diss. Saint Louis University), 1999

K. Vollers, 'Das Religionsgespräch von Jerusalem (um 800 D); aus dem arabischen übersetzt', *Zeitschrift für Kirchengeschichte* 29 (1908) 29-71

R.E. Van Voorst, *Jesus outside the New Testament. An introduction to the ancient evidence*, Grand Rapids MI, 2000

E. Voulgarakis, 'Nikon Metanoeite und die Rechristianisierung der Kreter von Islam', *Zeitschrift für Missionswissenschaft und Religionswissenschaft* 47 (1963) 192-204, 258-69

S. Vryonis (ed.), *Islam and cultural change in the Middle Ages*, Wiesbaden, 1975

S. Vryonis, *The decline of medieval Hellenism in Asia Minor*, Berkeley CA, 1986

Yūḥannā ibn Wahb, *History of the patriarchs of the Egyptian Church*, vol. 4, pt. 2. *Cyril III, Ibn Laklak*, ed. A. Khater and O.H.E. Burmester, Cairo, 1974

S.L. Wailes, *Spirituality and politics in the works of Hrotsvit of Gandersheim*, Selinsgrove PA, 2006

S.L. Wailes, 'The sacred stories in verse', in Brown and Wailes, *A companion to Hrotsvit of Grandersheim (fl. 960)*, 2012, 85-119

Ahmed El-Wakil, 'The Prophet's treaty with the Christians of Najran. An analytical study to determine the authenticity of the covenants', *Journal of Islamic Studies* 27 (2016) 273-354

P. Walker (ed.), *The wellsprings of wisdom. A study of Abū Ya'qūb al-Sijistānī's* Kitāb al-yanābī', Salt Lake City UT, 1994

P. Walker, *Caliph of Cairo. Al-Hakim bi-Amr Allāh, 996-1021*, Cairo, 2009

Walter the Chancellor, *Bella Antiochena*, ed. H. Hagenmeyer, Innsbruck, 1896

J. Wansbrough, *Quranic studies. Sources and methods of scriptural interpretation*, Oxford, 1977

J. Wansbrough, *The sectarian milieu. Content and composition of Islamic salvation history*, Oxford, 1978

Al-Wansharīsī, *Al-miʿyār al-muʿrib*, vol. 2, ed. Muḥammad Ḥajjī et al., Rabat, 1981-3

Abū ʿĪsā l-Warrāq, 'Refutation of the Trinity. The first part of the Refutation of the three Christian sects', in Thomas, *Anti-Christian polemic in early Islam*, 1992, 66-181

K. Warren, *Daring to cross the threshold. Francis of Assisi encounters Sultan Malek al Kamil*, Eugene OR, 2012

D. Wasserstein, *The rise and fall of the Party-Kings. Politics and society in Islamic Spain, 1002-1086*, Princeton NJ, 1985

D. Wasserstein, 'Conversion and the *ahl al-dhimma*', in Irwin, *The new Cambridge history of Islam*, vol. 4, 2010, 184-208

W.M. Watt, *Muslim-Christian encounters. Perceptions and misperceptions*, London, 1991

W.M. Watt, 'Muḥammad', in Holt et al., *The Cambridge history of Islam*, vol. 1A, 2008, 30-56

W.M. Watt and P. Cachia, *A history of Islamic Spain*, New Brunswick NJ, 2007

L. Weitz, *Between Christ and caliph. Law, marriage, and Christian community in early Islam*, Philadelphia PA, 2018

A.J. Wensinck, art. 'Muʿdjiza', in *EI2*

A.J. Wensinck, et al. (eds), *Concordance et indices de la tradition musulmane*, Leiden, 1936-88

M. Whittingham, 'The value of *taḥrīf maʿnawī* (corrupt interpretation) as a category for analysing Muslim views of the Bible. Evidence from *Al-radd al-jamīl* and Ibn Khaldūn', *ICMR* 22 (2011) 209-22

L. Wiederhold, art. 'Shatm', in *EI2*

C. Wilde, 'Is there room for corruption in the "books" of God?', in Thomas, *The Bible in Arab Christianity*, 2007, 225-40

C. Wilde, 'Early Christian Arabic texts. Evidence for non-ʿUthmānic Qurʾān codices, or early approaches to the Qurʾān?', in Reynolds, *New perspectives on the Qurʾān*, 2012, 358-71

C. Wilde, *Approaches to the Qur'an in early Christian Arabic texts (750-1258 CE)*, Palo Alto CA, 2014

William of Malmesbury, *Gesta regum Anglorum*, trans. R.A.B. Mynors, R.M. Thomson and M. Winterbottom, Oxford, 1998

William of Tyre, *Chronique*, ed. R.B.C Huygens, H.E. Mayer and G. Rösch, Turnhout, 1986

F. Williams (trans.), *The Panarion of Epiphanius of Salamis*, Leiden, 2009-13[2]
P. Wittek, *The rise of the Ottoman Empire*, London, 1938
P. Wittek, 'Devshirme and Sharīʿa', *BSOAS* 17 (1955) 271-8
A.M. Wolf, *Juan de Segovia and Western perspectives on Islam in the fifteenth century*, Minneapolis MN, 2003
A.M. Wolf, *Juan de Segovia and the fight for peace. Christians and Muslims in the fifteenth century*, Notre Dame IN, 2014
K.B. Wolf, *Christian martyrs in Muslim Spain*, Cambridge, 1988
K.B. Wolf, *Conquerors and chroniclers of early medieval Spain*, Liverpool, 1990, 1999[2]
K.B. Wolf (trans.), 'Eulogius, A Christian account of the life of Muhammad', in Constable and Zurro, *Medieval Iberia*, 1997, 2012[2], 48-50
K.B. Wolf (trans.), *The Eulogius corpus*, Liverpool, 2019
K.B. Wolf, 'Christian views of Islam in early medieval Spain', in Tolan, *Medieval Christian perceptions of Islam*, 85-108
C.D. Wright, F.M. Biggs and T.N. Hall (eds), *Source of wisdom. Old English and early medieval Latin studies in honour of Thomas D. Hill*, Toronto, 2007
Anastasios Yannoulatos, 'Byzantine approaches to Islam', in Papademetriou, *Two traditions, one space*, 2011, 147-78
L. Yarbrough, 'Upholding God's rule. Early Muslim juristic opposition to the state employment of non-Muslims', *Islamic Law and Society* 19 (2012) 11-85
L. Yarbrough, 'Origins of the *ghiyār*', *Journal of the American Oriental Society* 134 (2014) 113-21
L. Yarbrough, 'Did ʿUmar b. ʿAbd al-ʿAzīz issue an edict concerning non-Muslim officials?' in Borrut and Donner, *Christians and others in the Umayyad state*, 2016, 173-216
L. Yarbrough, 'The *madrasa* and the non-Muslims of thirteenth-century Egypt. A reassessment', in Baumgarten et al., *Entangled histories*, 2017, 93-112
L. Yarbrough, 'A Christian Shīʿī, and other curious confreres. Ibn ʿAbd al-Barr of Cordoba on getting along with unbelievers', *Al-Masāq* 30 (2018) 284-303
Bat Ye'or, *Le dhimmi. Profil de l'opprimé en orient et en Afrique du nord depuis la conquête arabe*, Paris, 1980
Bat Ye'or, *The decline of Eastern Christianity under Islam. From jihad to dhimmitude, seventh-twentieth century*, trans. M. Kochan and D. Littman, Madison NJ, 1996
E. Zachariadou, 'Early Ottoman documents of the Prodromos Monastery', *Südost Forshungen* 28 (1969) 1-12
E. Zachariadou (ed.), *The Ottoman Emirate (1300-1389)*, Rethymnon, Crete, 1993
A.P. Zāde, *Vom hirtenzelt zur hohen pforte*, Graz, 1959
Zakir Hussain Presentation Volume Committee, *Dr. M. Zakir Husain presentation volume*, New Delhi: Matba' Jami'a, 1968

Ḥ. Zayyāt, 'Shuhadā' al-naṣrāniyya fī l-islām', *Al-Machreq* 36 (1938) 459-65

Ḥ. Zayyāt, 'Simāt al-naṣārā wa-l-yahūd fī l-islām', *Al-Machreq* 43 (1949) 161-252

K. Zebiri, art. 'Polemic and polemical Language', in *EQ*

J. Ziadeh (ed.), 'L'Apocalypse de Samuel, Supérieur de Deir-el-Qalamoun', *Revue de l'Orient Chrétien* 10 (1917) 374-404

A. Zimo, 'Muslims in the landscape. A social map of the Kingdom of Jerusalem in the thirteenth century', Minneapolis MN, 2017 (PhD Diss. University of Minnesota)

S.M. Zwemer, *Raymond Lull. First missionary to the Moslems*, New York, 1902

Index of *CMR* References

References to entries appearing in *Christian-Muslim Relations, a Bibliographical History*

Abbot Macarie (R.G. Păun) *CMR* 7, 311-20 484
Abbot Samson (J.A. Coope) *CMR* 1, 691-4 316
ʿAbd al-Jabbār (G.S. Reynolds and D. Thomas) *CMR* 2, 594-610 502
ʿAbdallāh ibn al-Faḍl al-Anṭākī (A. Treiger) *CMR* 3, 89-113 39, 63
ʿAbdishoʿ of Nisibis (H.G.B. Teule) *CMR* 4, 750-61 502
Abū Bakr ibn al-ʿArabī (R. El Hour) *CMR* 3, 520-3 377
Abū Ḥātim al-Rāzī (S. Nomoto and D. Thomas) *CMR* 2, 200-9 40, 60
Abū ʿIsā l-Warrāq (D. Thomas) *CMR* 1, 695-701 34, 59, 130, 193,
Abū l-Faraj al-Iṣbahānī (H. Kilpatrick) *CMR* 2, 386-9 61, 374
Abū l-Ḥasan ibn al-Munajjim (D. Thomas) *CMR* 2, 234-6 46
Abū l-Hudhayl al-ʿAllāf (D. Thomas) *CMR* 1, 544-9 130
Abu l-Husayn al-Basri (D. Thomas) *CMR* 2, 698-702 63
Abū l-Ḥusayn al-Miṣrī (D. Thomas) *CMR* 2, 373-6 40
Abū l-Maʿālī (A. Mallett) *CMR* 3, 214-16 41, 66
Abū Rāʾiṭa l-Takrītī (S.T. Keating) *CMR* 1, 567-81 80, 84, 185, 200, 260, 499
Abū Sulaymān al-Sijistānī (D. Thomas) *CMR* 2, 480-4 63
Abu Yaʾqub al-Sijistani (D. Thomas) *CMR* 2, 381-5 37, 61, 213
Abū Yaʿlā ibn al-Farrāʾ (L. Yarbrough) *CMR* 5, 651-4 378
Abū Yūsuf Yaʿqūb (D. Thomas) *CMR* 1, 354-9 49, 370
Adelphus, *Vita Machometi* (J. Tolan) *CMR* 3, 572-3 29, 169
Ademar of Chabannes (M. Frassetto) *CMR* 2, 648-56 29, 235, 449
Adillat al-waḥdāniyya fī l-radd ʿalā l-milla l-Naṣrāniyya (D. Thomas) *CMR* 4, 265-6 201
Aghushtīn (T.E. Burman) *CMR* 3, 745-7 326
Aḥmad al-Rāzī (M. Penelas) *CMR* 2, 288-92 454
Al-ajwiba (M. El Kaisy-Friemuth) *CMR* 4, 585-7 503
Alexander III (J. Tolan) *CMR* 3, 695-6 420, 469
Alexis de St. Lô (C. Racheado) *CMR* 11, 556-60 473
ʿAlī al-Ṭabarī (D. Thomas) *CMR* 1, 669-74 91, 130, 208, 499
ʿAlī ibn Yaḥyā ibn al-Munajjim (B. Roggema) *CMR* 1, 762-7 38, 90
Alonso de Espina (A. Echevarría) *CMR* 5, 451-5 247
Alonso de Orozco (L. Resines) *CMR* 7, 219-23 482
Ambroise (C. Croizy-Naquet) *CMR* 4, 182-92 454
Al-ʿĀmirī (E.K. Rowson) *CMR* 2, 485-90 41
ʿAmmār al-Baṣrī (M. Beaumont) *CMR* 1, 604-10 44, 84, 186, 196, 260, 504
Anastasius of Sinai (A. Binggeli) *CMR* 1, 193-202 83, 393, 441, 503
Anasthasius Bibliothecarius (B. Neil) *CMR* 1, 786-90 234
Antonio García de Villalpando (A.I. Carrasco Manchado) *CMR* 6, 49-53 482
Antonius Verantius (E. Gyulai) *CMR* 7, 362-71 484
The apocalypse of Pseudo-Athanasius (B. Witte) *CMR* 1, 274-80 75
The apocalypse of Pseudo-Ephrem (H. Suermann) *CMR* 1, 160-2 55, 75, 181
The apocalypse of Pseudo-Methodius (Greek) (P. Ubierna) *CMR* 1, 245-8 76, 311, 415
The apocalypse of Pseudo-Methodius (Latin) (J.P. Monferrer Sala) *CMR* 1, 249-52 76, 311, 415
The apocalypse of Pseudo-Methodius (Syriac) (L. Greisiger) *CMR* 1, 163-71 75, 76, 181, 440, 463
The apocalypse of Samuel (J. van Lent) *CMR* 2, 742-52 427

The apocalypse of Shenute (J. van Lent) *CMR* 1, 182-5 76, 440, 464
Apologetic commentary on the Creed (P. Masri and M.N. Swanson) *CMR* 3, 671-5 45
The apology of al-Kindī (L. Bottini) *CMR* 1, 585-94 44, 184, 190, 232, 257, 324, 462
The Arabic homily of Pseudo-Theophilus of Alexandria (J. van Lent) *CMR* 1, 256-60 464, 508
The Arabic letter of Leo III to ʿUmar II (M.N. Swanson) *CMR* 1, 377-80 131, 267
The Arabic Sibylline prophecy (M.N. Swanson) *CMR* 1, 492-7 76
Aṙakʿel Bałišecʿi (S.P. Cowe) *CMR* 5, 346-50 403
ʿArīb ibn Saʿīd (D. Serrano Ruano) *CMR* 2, 451-5 372
The arrival of European Christians in India during the 16th century (A. Guenther) *CMR* 7, 15-25 387
al-Ashʿarī (D. Thomas) *CMR* 2, 210-16 65
Athanasius II, Patriarch of Jerusalem (J. Pahlitzsch) *CMR* 4, 325-30 380
Athanasius of Balad (H.G.B. Teule) *CMR* 1, 157-9 56, 64, 464
al-awsaṭ fī l-maqālāt, Kitāb (D. Thomas) *CMR* 2, 86-8 205

Al-Bājī (A. Zomeño) *CMR* 3, 172-5 327
Baltasar Barreira (M. Frederiks) *CMR* 11, 492-8 485
Al-Bāqillānī (D. Thomas) *CMR* 2, 446-50 34, 91, 130
Barāhīn ʿalā ṣiḥḥat al-Injīl (H.G.B. Teule) *CMR* 4, 335-6 192
Barhebraeus (H.G.B. Teule) *CMR* 4, 588-609 68, 173-4, 381
Bartholomew of Edessa (J. Niehoff-Panagiotidis) *CMR* 3, 715-19 172
Benedict Curipeschitz (S. Küçükhyüseyin) *CMR* 7, 168-73 483
Bernardo Pérez de Chinchón (F. Pons Fuster) *CMR* 6, 119-24 482
Bertrandon de la Broquière (J. Tolan) *CMR* 5, 443-6 70
al-Biqāʾī (D. Thomas) *CMR* 5, 537-43 69, 221
Birgivi Mehmed Efendi (J. Allen) *CMR* 7, 705-14 47
Al-Bīrūnī (G. Strohmaier) *CMR* 3, 73-80 66, 93
Būlus al-Bushī (M.N. Swanson) *CMR* 4, 280-7 92, 167
Burchard of Strasbourg (J. Tolan) *CMR* 3, 679-82 40, 67
al-burhān ʿalā siyāqat al-tadbīr al-ilāhī, Kitāb (M. Beaumont) *CMR* 1, 607-10 186, 196

Carmen in victoriam Pisanorum (J. Tolan) *CMR* 3, 223-5 33
Catechismo del Sacromonte (L. Resines) *CMR* 7, 265-7 482
Chanson d'Antioche (C. Sweetenham) *CMR* 3, 422-6 157
La Chanson de Roland (S. Kinoshita) *CMR* 3, 648-52 29, 78, 157, 289, 452
A Christian Arabic Disputation (PSR 438) (M.N. Swanson) *CMR* 1, 386-87 83
Christian-Muslim diplomatic relations. An overview of the main sources and themes of encounter, 600-1000 (N. Drocourt) *CMR* 2, 29-72 373
Christians and Christianity in Islamic exegesis (C. Gilliot) *CMR* 1, 31-56 362
Christians and Christianity in the Qurʾān (J. Hämeen-Anttila) *CMR* 1, 21-30 154, 362
Christians and Christianity in the *Sīra* of Muḥammad (S.A. Mourad) *CMR* 1, 57-71 194, 363
Christians and Christianity in *ḥadīth* works before 900 (D. Cook) *CMR* 1, 73-82 135, 369, 417
Christians in early and classical *Shīʿī* law (D.M. Freidenreich) *CMR* 3, 27-40 509
A Christological discussion (S.T. Keating) *CMR* 1, 553-5 184
Chronica Naierensis (P. Henriet) *CMR* 3, 778-82 452
Chronica Visegothorum (T. Deswarte) *CMR* 1, 883-8 448
Chronicle of Pseudo-Turpin (M. Cheynet) *CMR* 3, 455-77 78, 252
The chronicle of 741 (C. Aillet) *CMR* 1, 284-9 166, 228, 321, 445
The chronicle of 754 (A.M. Wolf) *CMR* 1, 302-4 166, 228, 321, 445
The chronicle of Albelda and the prophetic chronicle (T. Deswarte) *CMR* 1, 810-15 321, 448
The chronicle of Alfonso III (T. Deswarte) *CMR* 1, 882-8 321
The Chronicle of Khuzistan (H.G.B. Teule) *CMR* 1, 130-2 36, 55, 463

The Confession which Kaʿb al-Aḥbār handed down to the Ishmaelites (B. Roggema) *CMR* 1, 403-5 29
The conquest of Iberia. Fatḥ al-Andalus (M. Penelas) *CMR* 3, 335-7 456
The Copto-Arabic Sibylline prophecy (J. van Lent) *CMR* 3, 270-3 76, 420
The Copto-Arabic Synaxarion (M.N. Swanson) *CMR* 4, 937-45 396
Cribratio Alchorani (J. Tolan) *CMR* 5, 425-7 82, 121

David of Damascus (J.C. Lamoreaux) *CMR* 2, 79-82 56
Dawitʿ erēcʿ Baluecʿi (S.P. Cowe) *CMR* 4, 620-3 403
Al-Dāwudī (J.P. Monferrer Sala) *CMR* 2, 637-9 49, 320
The debate of Theodore Abū Qurra (D. Bertaina) *CMR* 1, 556-64 57
Demetrius Cydones (F. Tinnefeld) *CMR* 5, 239-49 350
denudationis, Liber (T.E. Burman) *CMR* 3, 414-17 30, 241, 325
Destruction of the Cathedral of Our Lady Mart Maryam in Damascus (Sāliḥ ibn Saʿīd al-Masīḥī) *CMR* 5, 698-704 93
Dhikr Bilād al-Andalus (M. Penelas) *CMR* 5, 593-5 328, 455
A dialogue between a monk and a Muslim elder about Jesus (peace be upon him) (M. Kahveci) *CMR* 7, 740–2 233
The dialogue between a Saracen and a Christian (P. Schadler) *CMR* 1, 367-70 158, 465
aldīn wa-l-dawla, Kitāb (D. Thomas) *CMR* 1, 672-4 84
Dionysius bar Ṣalibi (H.G.B. Teule) *CMR* 3, 665-70 31, 512
Dionysius of Tell-Maḥrē (H.G.B. Teule) *CMR* 1, 621-6 31
Dionysius the Carthusian (A. Mallett) *CMR* 5, 522-5 247
Ḍirār b. ʿAmr (D. Thomas) *CMR* 1, 371-4 130
The disputation between a monk of Bēt Ḥālē and an Arab notable (B. Roggema) *CMR* 1, 268-73 44, 100, 187, 493
The disputation of Jirjī the monk (M.N. Swanson) *CMR* 4, 166-72 93
The disputation of John and the Emir (B. Roggema) *CMR* 1, 782-5 79
The disputation of the monk Ibrāhīm al Ṭabarānī (M.N. Swanson) *CMR* 1, 876-81 37, 93, 267
Doctrina Iacobi nuper baptizati (J. Pahlitzsch) *CMR* 1, 117-19 75, 438
Doucas (G. Prinzing) *CMR* 5, 469-77 351
Al-durr al-thamīn (M.N. Swanson) *CMR* 2, 508-9 200

Ebussuud Efendi (E. Kermeli) *CMR* 7, 715-23 384
The Edessene Apocalypse (L. Greisiger) *CMR* 1, 172-5 75, 181
Edward Pococke (N. Matar) *CMR* 8, 445-58 175
Ek tōn pros tous Sarakēnous antirrhēseōn tou episkopou Theodōrou Charran ... (J.C. Lamoreaux) *CMR* 1, 474-7 504
Elias II, Ibn al Muqlī (H.G.B. Teule) *CMR* 3, 418-21 494
Elias of Nisibis (J.P. Monferrer Sala) *CMR* 2, 727-41 60, 88, 498
ʿEltā d-Quran (B. Roggema) *CMR* 1, 595-6 194
Embrico of Mainz (J. Tolan) *CMR* 3, 592-5 29
Epistola ad cardinelem Sancti Petri (A.M. Wolf) *CMR* 5, 432-5 502
Epistula Saraceni [et] rescriptum Christiani (F. González Muñoz) *CMR* 3, 479-82 165
Eulogius of Cordova (J. Tolan) *CMR* 1, 679-83 32, 229, 309, 372, 396, 446, 462
Euodius the monk (A. Kolia-Dermitzaki) *CMR* 1, 844-7 402
European Qur'an translations, 1500-1700 (T.E. Burman) *CMR* 6, 25-38 249

Fakhr al-Dīn al-Rāzī (M. Iskenderoglu) *CMR* 4, 61-5 27, 94
Felix of Urgell (J. Tolan) *CMR* 1, 365-6 314-5
Feodosil, archbishop of Novgorod (C. Soldat) *CMR* 7, 308-12 483
al-fisal fi l-milal wa-l-ahwa wa-l-nihal, Kitab (J.P. Monferrer Sala) *CMR* 3, 141-3 27, 377
Fī tathlīth Allāh al-wāhid (M.N. Swanson) *CMR* 1, 330-3 57, 79, 101, 184, 259, 465, 508
The forty-two martyrs of Amorion (BHG 1212) (A. Kolia-Dermitzaki) *CMR* 1, 636-8 402

The forty-two martyrs of Amorion (BHG 1214c) (A. Kolia-Dermitzaki) *CMR* 1, 639-41 402
The fourteenth vision of Daniel (J. van Lent) *CMR* 3, 697-703 420
Francisco Countinho (N. Vila-Santa) *CMR* 7, 849-52 473, 485
Fredegar (R. Collins) *CMR* 1, 137-8 438
Fulcher of Chartres (M. Bull) *CMR* 3, 401-8 454

Gabriel, Superior of Mount Athos (R.G. Păun) *CMR* 7, 76-84 50
Gaspar da Cruz (R. Loureiro) *CMR* 6, 369-75 387
Gaspar de Seville (C. Racheado) *CMR* 11, 573-7 473
Gautier de Compiègne (J. Tolan) *CMR* 3, 601-3 29, 169
Gennadius II Scholarius (K.-P. Todt) *CMR* 5, 503-18 355
George the Archdeacon (M.N. Swanson) *CMR* 1, 234-8 48
George the Monk (S. Efthymiadis) *CMR* 1, 729-33 29
Gerasimos (A. Bakhou and J. Lamoreaux) *CMR* 4, 666-71 89
Gesta Francorum (M. Bull) *CMR* 3, 249-56 78, 284
al-Ghazālī (M. El Kaisy-Friemuth) *CMR* 3, 363-9 41, 78
Ghāzī ibn al-Wāsiṭī (A. Mallett) *CMR* 4, 627-9 381, 382
Ghewond (T. Greenwood) *CMR* 1, 866-71 184
Ghiwarghis I (H.G.B. Teule) *CMR* 1, 151-3 56
Al-ghunya fī l-kalām (D. Thomas) *CMR* 5, 666-7 205
Giovanni Antonio Menavino (P. Schwarz Lausten) *CMR* 6, 512-22 70
Giovanni Battista Eliano (A. Girard) *CMR* 7, 724-31 485
Glossarium latino-arabicum (T.E. Burman) *CMR* 3, 724-4 311
Gómez García (R. Perez) *CMR* 6, 54-9 481
Gonçalo Rodrigues (G. Nickel) *CMR* 7, 837-41 484
The Gregorian report (L. Gimalva) *CMR* 4, 259-63 47, 475
Gregory Dekapolites (D.J. Sahas) *CMR* 1, 614-17 466, 506
Gregory Palamas (J. Pahlitzsch) *CMR* 5, 101-8 342
Grigoris Ałtámarcʿi (S.P. Cowe) *CMR* 7, 599-607 403, 483
Guibert of Nogent (J. Tolan) *CMR* 3, 329-34 78, 169, 284, 360
Guillaume Postel (C. Isom-Verhaaren) *CMR* 6, 712-25 250
Gurbetnâme-i Sultan Cem (L. Demiri) *CMR* 7, 676-87 510

Al-Hādī ilā l-Ḥaqq (G.S. Reynolds) *CMR* 2, 125-9 45
ḥaqīqat al-dīn al-Masīḥī, Kitāb fī (H.G.B. Teule) *CMR* 3, 324-6 197
Al-ḥāwī l-mustafād min badīhat al-ijtihād (A. Sidarus and M.N. Swanson) *CMR* 5, 256-61 192, 201
Henry Smith (C. Bennett) *CMR* 6, 826-32 170
Hermann of Carinthia (O. de la Cruz Palma and C. Ferrero Hernandez) *CMR* 3, 497-507 239
Hernando de Talavera (I. Iannuzzi) *CMR* 6, 59-66 480, 481, 510
Historia Silense (P. Henriet) *CMR* 3, 370-4 322, 451
Historia vel Gesta Francorum (R. Collins) *CMR* 1, 293-4 442
Historians of Tʿamar Queen of Queens (M.D. Abashidze) *CMR* 4, 1003-7 48
The History of Sebeos (T. Greenwood) *CMR* 1, 139-44 55, 75, 440
History of the churches and monasteries of Egypt (J. Den Heijer with P. Pilette) *CMR* 4, 983-8 303
Hodegos (A. Binggeli) *CMR* 1, 196-7 188
Hrotsvit of Gandersheim (L.A. McMillin) *CMR* 2, 291-7 32, 235, 320, 450
Hugh of Flavigny (P. Healy) *CMR* 3, 301-6 39, 469
Hugh of Fleury (E. Mégier and M. de Ruiter) *CMR* 3, 341-50 67
Ḥujaj al-milla l-Ḥanīfiyya wa-jawāb kull su'āl (D. Thomas) *CMR* 5, 419-20 356
al-ḥujja fī tathbīt al-nubuwwa, Kitāb (D. Thomas) *CMR* 1, 707-8 195
Humbert of Romans (T.E. Burman) *CMR* 4, 509-14 246
Ḥunayn ibn Isḥāq (J.P. Monferrer Sala) *CMR* 1, 768-74 62, 495

Ibn ʿAbdūn al-Ishbīlī (C. de la Puente) *CMR* 3, 397-400 36, 323, 377
Ibn Abī l-Dunyā (D. Thomas) *CMR* 1, 829-31 53, 62

Ibn Abī Ṭālib al-Dimashqī (D. Thomas) *CMR* 4, 798-801 277
Ibn Abī Zar (M.D. Rodríguez-Gómez) *CMR* 4, 815-19 322
Ibn Albar al-Qūṭī (J.P. Monferrer Sala) *CMR* 2, 281-4 38, 315, 503
Ibn ʿArabī (S. Hirtenstein) *CMR* 4, 145-9 146, 380
Ibn ʿAsākir (S.A. Mourad) *CMR* 3, 683-9 35, 66, 139, 368
Ibn al-Azraq (A. Mallett) *CMR* 3, 690-4 66
Ibn Bābawayh (D. Thomas) *CMR* 2, 514-18 34
Ibn Barrajān (J.P. Monferrer Sala) *CMR* 3, 488-9 38, 216
Ibn Bashkuwāl (A.M. Carballeira Debasa) *CMR* 3, 451-4 322, 456
Ibn Bassām (M. Meouak) *CMR* 3, 318-22 308, 377
Ibn al-Durayhim (L. Yarbrough) *CMR* 5, 138-44 382
Ibn Ḥabīb (J.P. Monferrer Sala) *CMR* 1, 825-8 322
Ibn Ḥayyān (M. Meouak) *CMR* 3, 165-71 308, 456
Ibn Ḥazm (J.P. Monferrer Sala and D. Thomas) *CMR* 3, 137-45 214, 326
Ibn ʿIdhārī al-Marrākushī (D. Serrano Ruano) *CMR* 4, 737-42 457
Ibn Jubayr (A. Mallett) *CMR* 4, 159-65 293, 386
Ibn al-Kalbī (D. Thomas) *CMR* 1, 510-14 61
Ibn Kemal (L. Demiri and M. Kuzey) *CMR* 7, 622-38 47, 384
Ibn Khaldūn (M. Whittingham) *CMR* 5, 300-8 69, 150, 211
Ibn al-Khaṭīb (N. Al-Jallad) *CMR* 5, 182-6 385
Ibn al-Layth (B. Roggema) *CMR* 1, 347-53 104, 131, 190, 373
Ibn al-Naqqāsh (L. Yarbrough) *CMR* 5, 123-9 382
Ibn Nujaym al-Miṣrī (U. Ryad) *CMR* 7, 688-92 384
Ibn Qayyim al-Jawziyya (J. Hoover) *CMR* 4, 989-1002 27, 134, 382
Ibn Qutayba (D. Thomas) *CMR* 1, 816-18 59, 209
Ibn al-Qūṭiyya (J.P. Monferrer Sala) *CMR* 2, 456-9 319, 455
Ibn Quzmān (I. Ferrando) *CMR* 3, 620-4 377
Ibn al-Rifʿa (D. Thomas) *CMR* 4, 692-4 382
Ibn Sabbāʿ (M.N. Swanson) *CMR* 4, 918-23 94, 492
Ibn Ṣāḥib al-Ṣalāt (M.D. Rodríguez-Gómez) *CMR* 4, 176-8 375
Ibn Sahl (D. Serrano Ruano) *CMR* 3, 210-13 322, 377
Ibn Saʿīd al-Maghribī (J.P. Monferrer Sala) *CMR* 4, 361-4 322
Ibn Taymiyya (J. Hoover) *CMR* 4, 824-78 69, 94, 133, 176, 277, 382, 509
Ibn al-Ṭayyib (J. Faultless) *CMR* 2, 667-97 193
Ibn Waḍḍāḥ (M. Fierro) *CMR* 1, 834-9 63, 323
Ibn Ẓafar (L. Demiri) *CMR* 3, 625-31 46
Ibrāhīm ibn Yūḥannā al-Anṭākī (J.C. Lamoreaux) *CMR* 2, 611-16 64, 402
Ice de Gebir (G. Wiegers) *CMR* 5, 462-8 248
Ikhwān al-Ṣafāʾ (O. Ali-de-Unzaga) *CMR* 2, 306-11 41, 61, 212
ʿImād al-Dīn al-Asnawī (D. Thomas) *CMR* 5, 187-8 382
Al-Imām al-Qurṭubī (J.P. Monferrer Sala) *CMR* 4, 391-4 327, 503
Iniquus Mahometus (J. Tolan) *CMR* 4, 654-6 169
Al-intiṣārāt al-Islāmiyya fī kashf shubah al-Naṣrāniyya (L. Demiri) *CMR* 4, 729-31 191
Introduction: Constantinople and Granada (H.G.B. Teule) *CMR* 5, 1-16 383
Introduction: Christians, Muslims and empires in the 16th century (M. Frederiks) *CMR* 6, 1-10 387, 481, 482
Introduction: Christians, Muslims and empires in the 16th century (M. Frederiks) *CMR* 7, 1-14 387
Ioane Sabanisdze (G. Shurgaia) *CMR* 1, 334-7 32, 397
Al-Īrānshahrī (D. Thomas) *CMR* 1, 889-91 65
Isḥāq ibn Ḥunayn (M.N. Swanson) *CMR* 2, 121-24 62
Ishoʿyab bar Malkon (H.G.B. Teule) *CMR* 4, 331-8 497
Ishoʿyahb III of Adiabene (H.G.B. Teule) *CMR* 1, 133-6 37, 55, 83, 365, 465
Isidore Glabas (M.St. Popovic) *CMR* 5, 220-5 339

Islam and Muslims in Byzantine historiography of the 10th-15th centuries (K.-P. Todt) *CMR* 5, 35-46 333
Islamic "Psalms of David" (D.R. Vishanoff) *CMR* 3, 724-30 28
Istoria de Mahomet (J. Tolan) *CMR* 1, 721-2 229, 325
ithbāt nubuwwat al-nabī, Kitāb (D. Thomas) *CMR* 2, 235-6 195

Jacob of Edessa (H.G.B. Teule) *CMR* 1, 226-33 56, 511
Jacques de Vitry (J. Tolan) *CMR* 4, 295-306 93, 305, 462, 471
Al-Jāḥiẓ (D. Thomas) *CMR* 1, 706-12 45, 91, 130
Jalāl al-Dīn al-Suyūṭī (S. Burge) *CMR* 7, 557-64 46, 382
Jamāl al-Dīn al-Asnawī (A. Mallett) *CMR* 5, 130-2 382
Al-jāmiʿ wujūh al-īmān (M.N. Swanson) *CMR* 1, 791-8 43, 80, 501
Al-jawāb al-ṣaḥīḥ li-man baddala dīn al-Masīḥ (J. Hoover) *CMR* 4, 834-44 191
Joachim of Fiore (B. McGinn) *CMR* 4, 83-91 75, 463, 470
Joan Martí Figuerola (E. Ruiz García) *CMR* 6, 88-92 482
Job of Edessa (B. Roggema) *CMR* 1, 502-9 42
Johann Albrecht Widmanstetter (U. Cecini) *CMR* 7, 235-45 250
John Anagnostes (E. Mitsiou) *CMR* 5, 353-7 351
John Bale (K.S. Brokaw) *CMR* 6, 689-98 75
John bar Penkāyē (L. Greisiger) *CMR* 1, 176-81 37, 365, 439-40
John Calvin (J. Balserak) *CMR* 6, 732-45 75
John Cananus (S. Kolditz) *CMR* 5, 342-5 333, 351
John de Joinville (A. Mallett) *CMR* 4, 718-23 458
John Mandeville (I.M. Higgins) *CMR* 5, 147-64 161
John of Damascus (R.F. Glei) *CMR* 1, 295-301 77, 155, 231, 260, 367, 489
John of Nikiou (G. Fiaccadori) *CMR* 1, 209-18 439
John of St Arnoul (M. Frassetto) *CMR* 2, 475-9 235, 320
John of Sulṭāniyya (C. Casali) *CMR* 5, 291-7 381
John the Deacon (M.N. Swanson) *CMR* 1, 317-21 368
John VI Cantacuzenus (K.-P. Todt) *CMR* 5, 165-78 350
John VIII, pope (D. Arnold) *CMR* 1, 804-9 373
Joshua the Stylite of Zuqnīn (A. Harrak) *CMR* 1, 322-6 56, 368, 395
Juan Andres (Z. Zuwiyya) *CMR* 6, 79-84 249
Juan Bautista de Jerónimo Anyés (B.F. Llopis) *CMR* 6, 144-9 481
Juan de Segovia (A.M. Wolf) *CMR* 5, 429-42 177, 479, 502
Justus Jonas (J. Hund) *CMR* 7, 161-7 75
Al-Juwaynī (D. Thomas) *CMR* 3, 121-6 28, 378

Kalām fī l-ʿaql wa-l-ʿāqil wa-l-maʿqūl (H.G.B. Teule) *CMR* 3, 757-8 117
Kalām fī l-Thālūth al-muqaddas (A. Treiger) *CMR* 3, 98-100 201, 205
Kayfiyyat idrāk ḥaqīqat al-diyāna (B. Roggema) *CMR* 1, 775-9 90
Khabar al-Yahūd wa-l-Naṣārā (D. Thomas) *CMR* 2, 640-2 376, 429
Al-Khazrajī (J.P. Monferrer Sala) *CMR* 3, 526-8 30, 327, 458
Al-Khushanī (D. Serrano Ruano) *CMR* 2, 342-6 313
Al-Kindī (D. Thomas) *CMR* 1, 746-50 34, 63, 90
Al-Kindī, ʿAbd al-Masīḥ ibn Isḥāq (pseudonym) (L. Bottini) *CMR* 1, 587-94 161
King Manuel I of Portugal (R.L. de Jesus) *CMR* 7, 745-8 483
Kirakos Ganjakecʿi or Arewelcʿi (S.P. Cowe) *CMR* 4, 438-42 403
Kitāb al-awsaṭ fī l-maqālāt (D. Thomas) *CMR* 2, 86-8 205
Kitāb al-burhān ʿalā siyāqat al-tadbīr al-ilāhī (M. Beaumont) *CMR* 1, 607-10 186, 196
Kitāb aldīn wa-l-dawla (D. Thomas) *CMR* 1, 672-4 84
Kitab al-fisal fi l-milal wa-l-ahwa wa-l-nihal (J.P. Monferrer Sala) *CMR* 3, 141-3 27, 377
Kitāb al-ḥujja fī tathbīt al-nubuwwa (D. Thomas) *CMR* 1, 707-8 195

Kitāb al-milal wa-l-niḥal (D. Thomas) *CMR* 3, 550-2 196
Kitāb al-murshid (H.G.B. Teule and M.N. Swanson) *CMR* 3, 282-6 201
Kitāb al-radd ʿalā l-Naṣārā, al-Jaʿfarī (L. Demiri) *CMR* 4, 485 191, 197
Kitāb al-radd ʿalā l-Naṣārā, al-Qāsim ibn Ibrāhīm (W. Madelung) *CMR* 1, 542-3 190
Kitāb al-Shāmil fī uṣūl al-dīn (D. Thomas) *CMR* 3, 124-6 35, 196
Kitāb fī ḥaqīqat al-dīn al-Masīḥī (H.G.B. Teule) *CMR* 3, 324-6 197
Kitāb ithbāt nubuwwat al-nabī (D. Thomas) *CMR* 2, 235-6 195
Kitāb Usṭāth (*al-rāhib*) (E. Salah and M.N. Swanson) *CMR* 1, 908-10 202

Landolfus Sangax (J. Tolan) *CMR* 2, 524-5 234
Laonicus Chalcocondyles (J. Preiser-Kapeller) *CMR* 5, 481-9 70, 352
The legend of Sergius Baḥīrā (B. Roggema) *CMR* 1, 600-3 55, 81, 194, 258, 465, 492
Leh kralına nâme-i hümâyun (A. Konopacki) *CMR* 7, 732-4 383
Leo VI "the Wise" (E. McGeer) *CMR* 2, 89-97 373
Leontius of Damascus (J.C. Lamoreaux) *CMR* 1, 406-10 56
The letter from the People of Cyprus (D. Thomas) *CMR* 4, 769-72 69, 176, 191, 259
The Letter of Leo III, in Ghewond (T. Greenwood) *CMR* 1, 203-8 184, 190, 267, 499
The letter of Prester John (P. Jackson) *CMR* 4, 118-23 420
Liber de veritate catholicae fidei contra errores infidelium qui dicitur Summa contra gentiles (J. Tolan) *CMR* 4, 523-7 163
Liber denudationis (T.E. Burman) *CMR* 3, 414-17 30, 241, 325
Liber Nycholay (F. González Muñoz) *CMR* 4, 650-3 234
The Life of Bacchus the younger (S. Efthymiadis) *CMR* 1, 597-9 396
Life of David, King of kings (M.D. Abashidze) *CMR* 3, 567-72 380
The Life of Elias the Younger (B. Krönung) *CMR* 2, 246-50 26
Life of George the Younger (K. Sokolov) *CMR* 5, 375-8 337
Life of Saint Nicon (T. Pratsch) *CMR* 2, 643-5 467
Life of Theodore, bishop of Edessa (K.-P. Todt and M.N. Swanson) *CMR* 2, 585-93 398
The life of Timothy of Kākhushtā (J.C. Lamoreaux) *CMR* 1, 919-22 93
The life and miracles of Anbā Ruways (M.N. Swanson) *CMR* 5, 287-90 93
The life and miracles of Barṣawmā al-ʿUryān (M.N. Swanson) *CMR* 5, 114-18 93
The life and miracles of Marqus al-Anṭūnī (M.N. Swanson) *CMR* 5, 203-6 93
Ludovico de Varthema (A. Fuess) *CMR* 6, 405-9 70
Luigi Bassano (P. Madsen) *CMR* 6, 501-5 70
Luís Fróis (G. Nickel) *CMR* 7, 858-65 484

Machumetis Saracenorum principis, eiusque successorum vitae, ac doctrina, ipseque Alcoran (B. Gordon) *CMR* 6, 680-5 165
Maḥbūb ibn Qusṭantīn al-Manbijī (M.N. Swanson) *CMR* 2, 241-5 39, 60
Al-Makīn Jirjis ibn al-ʿAmīd (A. Sidarus and M.N. Swanson) *CMR* 5, 254-61 95
Makkīkhā ibn Sulaymān al-Qankāni (H.G.B. Teule) *CMR* 3, 323-38 93
Manuel II Palaeologus (F. Tinnefeld) *CMR* 5, 314-25 350
Al-maqāla al-ūlā min qawl al-qiddīs Būlus al-Būshī (M.N. Swanson) *CMR* 4, 283-6 197
Maqāla fī l-tathlīth (J. Faultless) *CMR* 2, 690-1 116, 193
Maqāla fī l-tathlīth wa-l-tawḥīd (J. Faultless) *CMR* 2, 692-3 193
Maqāla fī l-uṣūl al-dīniyya (J. Faultless) *CMR* 2, 683-4 193
Maqāla mawsūma bi-l-ʿaql wa-l-ʿāqil wa-l-maʿqūl (E. Platti) *CMR* 2, 419-21 204
Maqāla mukhtaṣara fī l-aqānīm wa-l-jawhar, wa-anna l-fiʿl li-l-jawhar (J. Faultless) *CMR* 2, 694 193
al-Maqrīzī (F. Bauden) *CMR* 5, 380-95 382
Marcus Marulus (F. Posset, B. Lucin and B. Jozić) *CMR* 7, 91-125 484
Mark of Toledo (T.E. Burman) *CMR* 4, 150-6 240

The Maronite Chronicle (H.G.B. Teule) *CMR* 1, 145-7 368
Martin Luther (A.S. Francisco) *CMR* 7, 225-34 74, 250
Martín Pérez de Alaya (M.J. Framiñán de Miguel) *CMR* 7, 207-14 481
The martyrdom of ʿAbd al-Masīḥ (D.H. Vila) *CMR* 1, 684-7 395, 510
The martyrdom of Anthony (rawḥ al-Qurashī) (C. Vila) *CMR* 1, 498-501 397, 466, 510
Martyrdom of Bishop Thiemo (J. Tolan) *CMR* 3, 555-7 33, 469
The martyrdom of Elias of Helioupolis (Elias of Damascus) (S. Efthymiadis) *CMR* 1, 916-18 32, 394
The martyrdom of John of Phanijōit (J.R. Zaborowski) *CMR* 4, 128-31 405
The martyrdom of Peter of Capitolias (S. Efthymiadis) *CMR* 1, 419-22 400
The martyrdom of Romanus the Younger (M. Nanobashvili) *CMR* 1, 390-3 402
The martyrdom of the twenty martyrs of Mār Saba (D.H. Vila) *CMR* 1, 393-6 402
The martyrdom of Vahan (R.W. Thomson) *CMR* 1, 281-3 394
Martyrology of Archbishop Stepʿanos Sebastacʿi (S.P. Cowe) *CMR* 5, 199-202 403
Martyrology of Awag Salmastecʿi (S.P. Cowe) *CMR* 5, 207-9 403
Martyrology of Bishop Grigor of Karin (Erzerum) (S.P. Cowe) *CMR* 4, 794-7 381, 403
Martyrology of Mirakʿ Tawrizecʿi (S.P. Cowe) *CMR* 5, 553-6 404
Martyrology of Tʿamar Mokacʿi (S.P. Cowe) *CMR* 5, 250-3 403
Martyrology of Tʿēodoros Kesaracʿi (S.P. Cowe) *CMR* 4, 94-7 403
Martyrology of the Confessor Stepʿannos (S.P. Cowe) *CMR* 5, 549-52 403
The martyrology of Vardan Bałišecʿi (S.P. Cowe) *CMR* 5, 339-41 403
Martyrology of the youth Yovhannēs Xlatʿecʿi (S.P. Cowe) *CMR* 5, 370-4 404
Martyrology of Xačʿatur Kołbecʿi in 1517 (S.P. Cowe) *CMR* 7, 588-91 403, 483
Martyrology of Yovhannēs bishop of Tarōn (S.P. Cowe) *CMR* 5, 478-80 404
Martyrology of Zakʿaria, catholicos of Altʿamar (S.P. Cowe) *CMR* 5, 216-19 403
Masʾala fī man yusammī l-khamīs ʿīd (J. Hoover) *CMR* 4, 874-5 509, 510
al-Masʿūdī (D. Thomas) *CMR* 2, 298-305 129
Matthew of Edessa (T.L. Andrews) *CMR* 3, 444-50 285
Al-Māturīdī (D. Thomas) *CMR* 2, 251-4 34
Mawhūb ibn Manṣūr ibn Mufarrij al-Iskandarānī (M.N. Swanson) *CMR* 3, 217-22 368
Mawlānā Jalāl al-Dīn Rūmī (L. Lewisohn) *CMR* 4, 491-508 217, 341
Maximus the Greek (D. Savelyev) *CMR* 7, 135-40 483
Maymar fī mawt al-Masīḥ (J.C. Lamoreaux) *CMR* I, 454-6 199
Maymar fī wujūd al-Khāliq wa-l-dīn al-qawīm (J.C. Lamoreaux) *CMR* 1, 448-50 196
Maymar qālahu Anbā Thāwudhūrūs usquf Ḥarrān al-muqaddas wa-huwa Abū Qurra [...] (J.C. Lamoreaux) *CMR* 1, 463-6 202, 489
Maymar yuḥaqqiqu anna dīn Allāh (J.C. Lamoreaux) *CMR* 1, 467-8 196
Mec Peron (S.P. Cowe) *CMR* 7, 668-72 403, 483
Mēna of Nikiou (H. Suermann) *CMR* 1, 219-21 48, 496
Michael of Damietta (M.N. Swanson) *CMR* 4, 109-14 464
Michael of Damrū (M.N. Swanson) *CMR* 3, 84-8 92
Michael the Synkellos (A. Kolia-Dermitzaki) *CMR* 1, 627-32 402
Michael the Syrian (H.G.B. Teule) *CMR* 3, 736-41 67
al-milal wa-l-niḥal, Kitāb (D. Thomas) *CMR* 3, 550-2 196
Min qawl Abī Rāʾiṭa l-Takrītī al-Suryānī usquf Nasībīn mustadillan bihi ʿalā ṣiḥḥat al-Naṣrāniyya [...] (S.T. Keating) *CMR* 1, 578-80 195
Mkrtičʿ Abełay (S.P. Cowe) *CMR* 7, 608-14 403
The monk Mīnā (M.N. Swanson) *CMR* 2, 460-3 396
Moses bar Kephā (H.G.B. Teule) *CMR* 2, 98-101 37, 61
The Mufti of Oran (L. Bernabé Pons) *CMR* 6, 67-72 386, 509
Muḥammad ibn ʿAbd al-Raḥmān (D. Thomas) *CMR* 3, 783-4 382

Al-mughnī fī abwāb al-tawḥīd wa-l-ʿadl (G.S. Reynolds) *CMR* 2, 597-602 34
Munāzara fī l-radd ʿalā l-Naṣārā (M. Iskenderoglu) *CMR* 4, 63-5 195
Murad ibn Abdullah (T. Krstić) *CMR* 7, 698-704 384, 484
al-murshid, Kitāb (H.G.B. Teule and M.N. Swanson) *CMR* 3, 282-6 201
Muslim regard for Christians and Christianity (D. Thomas) *CMR* 2, 15-27 60
Muslims in Eastern Canon Law, 1000-1500 (D.M. Freidenreich) *CMR* 4, 45-59 174
Muṭrān Dā'ūd (M.N. Swanson) *CMR* 3, 130-2 492

al-Nābulusī (L. Yarbrough) *CMR* 4, 310-16 382
Al-Nāshi' al-Akbar (D. Thomas) *CMR* 2, 85-8 34
Al-naṣīḥa l-imāniyya fī faḍīḥat al-milla l-Naṣrāniyya (L. Demiri) *CMR* 3, 751-4 202, 501
Naṣr ibn Yaḥyā (L. Demiri) *CMR* 3, 750-4 35
Nicephoras Gregoras (D. Manolova) *CMR* 5, 133-7 335
Nicephorus (C. Ludwig) *CMR* 2, 550-3 420
Nicetas of Byzantium (A. Rigo) *CMR* 1, 751-6 77
Nicetus Clericus (T. Pratsch) *CMR* 2, 263-5 93
Nicholas of Cusa (J. Tolan) *CMR* 5, 421-8 177, 249-50, 479, 502
Nicolas Mysticus (M. Vaiou) *CMR* 2, 169-83 31, 49
Nifont Kormilitsin (C. Soldat) *CMR* 7, 372-8 32, 483
Nonnus of Nisibis (H.G.B. Teule) *CMR* 1, 743-5 42
Nycholay, Liber (F. González Muñoz) *CMR* 4, 650-3 234

Oliver of Paderborn (J. Bird) *CMR* 4, 212-29 47, 470
On the Trinity (S.T. Keating) *CMR* 1, 572-4 265
Oracula Leonis (W. Brandes) *CMR* 4, 124-7 420
Orderic Vitalis (A. Mallett) *CMR* 3, 490-6 33

The Pact of ʿUmar (M. Levy-Rubin) *CMR* 1, 360-4 49, 371
The panegyric of the three holy children of Babylon (H. Suermann) *CMR* 1, 127-9 438, 463
The passion of the sixty martyrs of Gaza (D. Woods) *CMR* 1, 190-2 401
Paul Alvarus (A.M. Wolf) *CMR* 1, 645-8 75, 309, 399, 446
Paul of Antioch (D. Thomas) *CMR* 4, 78-82 133, 176, 258, 277, 503
Pedro de Alcalá (O. Zwartjes) *CMR* 6, 73-8 387, 481
Pedro Guerra de Lorca (J. Busic) *CMR* 7, 250-8 482
Pedro Pascual (J. Tolan) *CMR* 4, 673-7 320
Pedro Ramírez de Alba (L. Resines) *CMR* 6, 93-5 481, 510
Peri haireseōn (R.F. Glei) *CMR* 1, 297-301 100, 187
Peter of Bayt Rås (M.N. Swanson) *CMR* 1, 902-6 80
Peter of Cluny (D. Iogna-Prat and J. Tolan) *CMR* 3, 604-10 30, 81, 165, 238, 290, 325, 462
Peter of Toledo (F. González Muñoz) *CMR* 3, 478-82 238-9, 325
Petrus Alfonsi (J. Tolan) *CMR* 3, 356-62 236, 325, 471, 492
Philipp Melanchthon (J. Balserak) *CMR* 7, 246-52 75
Pierre Belon (A. Merle) *CMR* 6, 703-11 70
Pope Hadrian's epistles to Bishop Egila (C. Aillet) *CMR* 1, 338-42 312, 464
Priest Yovhannēs (S.P. Cowe) *CMR* 5, 572-5 403
The prophecies and exhortations of Pseudo-Shenute (J. van Lent) *CMR* 5, 278-86 382
Pseudo-Leo III's first letter to ʿUmar II (B. Roggema) *CMR* 1, 375-6 131, 267, 499
Pseudo-ʿUmar II's letter to Leo III (B. Roggema) *CMR* 1, 381-5 26, 94, 131, 190, 499

al-Qāḍī ʿIyāḍ (D. Serrano Ruano) *CMR* 3, 542-8 377
Al-Qarāfī (M. El Kaisy-Friemuth) *CMR* 4, 582-7 132, 277, 503
Al-Qāsim ibn Ibrāhīm (W. Madelung) *CMR* 1, 540-3 105, 130

Al-qawl al-mukhtār fī l-manʿ ʿan takhyīr al-kuffār (L. Yarbrough) *CMR* 4, 924-7 382
Al-Qaysī (D. Thomas) *CMR* 4, 732-6 458
Qusṭa ibn Lūqā (M.N. Swanson) *CMR* 2, 147-53 65
Al-Qūṭī (J.P. Monferrer Sala) *CMR* 3, 524-5 327

Rabīʿ ibn Zayd (J.P. Monferrer Sala) *CMR* 2, 347-50 376
Al-Radd ʿalā l-Naṣārā, ʿAlī al-Ṭabarī (D. Thomas) *CMR* 1, 671-2 89, 499
al-radd ʿalā l-Naṣārā, Kitāb, al-Jaʿfarī (L. Demiri) *CMR* 4, 485 191, 197
al-radd ʿalā l-Naṣārā, Kitāb, al-Qāsim ibn Ibrāhīm (W. Madelung) *CMR* 1, 542-3 190
Al-radd ʿalā l-thalāth firaq min al-Naṣārā (longer version) (D. Thomas) *CMR* 1, 698-9 115
Al-radd ʿalā l-Yahūd wa l-Muslimīn [...] (H.G.B. Teule) *CMR* 4, 333-5 202, 497
Raguel (P. Henriet) *CMR* 2, 377-80 235
Ralph of Caen (B. Packard) *CMR* 3, 375-8 78
Ramon Llull (H. Hames) *CMR* 4, 703-17 47, 172, 246, 305, 324, 385, 462
Ramon Martí (T.E. Burman) *CMR* 4, 381-90 243, 385, 475
De rationibus fidei contra Saracenos, Graecos et Armenos ad cantorem Antiochenum (J. Tolan) *CMR* 4, 527-9 163
Raymond of Aguilers (B. Packard) *CMR* 3, 297-300 33, 78, 285
Raymond of Penyafort (J. Tolan) *CMR* 4, 252-8 464
Representative of Nicephorus Phocas (D. Thomas) *CMR* 2, 367-9 28
Riccoldo da Monte di Croce (T.E. Burman) *CMR* 4, 678-91 244, 476
Risāla fī tathbīt waḥdāniyyat al-bāriʾ wa-tathlīth khawāṣṣihi (B. Holmberg) *CMR* 1, 759-61 204
Risāla ilā baʿḍ aṣdiqāʾihi alladhīna bi-Ṣaydā min al-Muslimīn (D. Thomas) *CMR* 4, 79-82 191
Risāla li-Abī Rāʾiṭa l-Takrītī fī ithbāt dīn al-Naṣrāniyya wa-ithbāt al-Thālūth al-muqaddas (S.T. Keating) *CMR* 1, 571-2 196, 500
Al-risāla l-thāniya li-Abī Rāʾiṭa l-Takrītī fī l-tajassud (S.T. Keating) *CMR* 1, 574-5 191, 200
Al-risāla l-ūlā fī l-Thālūth al-muqaddas (S.T. Keating) *CMR* 1, 572-4 191, 204
Risālat Abī l-Rabīʿ Muḥammad ibn al-Layth allatī katabahā li-l-Rashīd ilā Qusṭanṭīn malik al-Rūm (B. Roggema) *CMR* 1, 349-53 195
Ritual of abjuration (A. Rigo) *CMR* 1, 821-4 78, 466
Robert of Ketton (O. de la Cruz Palma and C. Ferrero Hernandez) *CMR* 3, 508-19 28, 170, 238-9
Robert the Monk (M. Bull) *CMR* 3, 312-17 78, 284
Rodolfo Acquaviva (G. Nickel) *CMR* 7, 889-96 484
Rodolfus Glaber (M. Frassetto) *CMR* 2, 721-6 39
Rodrigo Jimenez de Rada (M. Maser) *CMR* 4, 343-55 240
Roger Bacon (A. Power) *CMR* 4, 457-70 475
Roger II of Sicily (A. Mallett) *CMR* 5, 671-4 50
Rolandslied (M.G. Cammarota) *CMR* 3, 656-64 461

Al-Ṣafī ibn al-ʿAssāl (W. Awad) *CMR* 4, 538-51 499
Ṣāʿid al-Andalusī (D. Thomas) *CMR* 3, 146-9 377
Saʿīd ibn Baṭrīq (U. Simonsohn) *CMR* 2, 224-33 60
Ṣalībā ibn Yuḥannā (M.N. Swanson) *CMR* 4, 900-5 93
Sāliḥ ibn Saʿīd al-Masīḥī (A. Treiger) *CMR* 5, 644-50 65
Sāwīrus ibn al-Muqaffaʿ (M.N. Swanson) *CMR* 2, 491-509 45, 492
Al-sayf al-murhaf fī l-radd ʿalā l-muṣḥaf (L. Demiri) *CMR* 4, 662-5 244, 381
Sayf ibn ʿUmar (D. Thomas) *CMR* 1, 437-8 129
To Sergius, *Letter 40* (B. Roggema) *CMR* 1, 519-22 192
Serrâc ibn Abdullah (C. Norton) *CMR* 7, 673-5 384, 484
Al-Shābushtī (H. Kilpatrick) *CMR* 2, 565-9 36, 62
Shahādāt min qawl al-Tawrāt wa-l-anbiyāʾ wa-l-qiddīsīn (S.T. Keating) *CMR* 1, 576-7 80, 191, 200

Al-Shahrastānī (D. Thomas) *CMR* 3, 549-54 35, 65, 138
al-Shāmil fī uṣūl al-dīn, Kitāb (D. Thomas) *CMR* 3, 124-6 35, 196
The sixty martyrs of Jerusalem (S. Efthymiadis) *CMR* 1, 327-9 401
Sophronius, Patriarch of Jerusalem (D.J. Sahas) *CMR* 1, 120-7 437, 463
Speraindeo (J.A. Coope) *CMR* 1, 633-5 324, 446
Stepane of Tbeti (M.D. Abashidze) *CMR* 2, 141-4 32
Su'ila Abū Qurra Anbā Thādhurus usquf Ḥarrān 'an al-Masīḥ bi-hawāhi ṣuliba am bi-ghayr hawāhi (J.C. Lamoreaux) *CMR* I, 468-9 199
Symeon of Samosota (A. Palmer) *CMR* 1, 186-9 442
Synaxarion of the Great Church (B. Flusin) *CMR* 3, 574-85 394

Al-Ṭabarī (D. Thomas) *CMR* 2, 184-7 210
Tabyīn ghalaṭ Muḥammad ibn Hārūn al-ma'rūf bi-Abī 'Īsā l-Warrāq (E. Platti) *CMR* 2, 413-15 193
Takhjīl man ḥarrafa l-Tawrāh wa-l-Injīl (L. Demiri) *CMR* 4, 481-3 191
Taronites (M. Vucetic) *CMR* 5, 109-13 343
Tathbīt dalā'il al-nubuwwa (G.S. Reynolds) *CMR* 2, 604-9 34, 102, 132
Tathbīt nubuwwat Muḥammad (G.S. Reynolds) *CMR* 2, 127-9 195
Tathlīth al-waḥdāniyya (T.E. Burman) *CMR* 4, 115-17 318
Testament of our Lord (on the invasions of the Mongols) (J. van Lent) *CMR* 4, 743-9 381
Testimonies of the prophets about the dispensation of Christ (M. Debié) *CMR* 1, 242-4 43, 511
Theodor Bibliander (B. Gordon) *CMR* 6, 673-85 250, 479
Theodore Abū Qurra (J.C. Lamoreaux) *CMR* 1, 439-91 43, 80, 84, 158, 185, 195, 465, 489
Theodore Metochites (J. Pahlitzsch) *CMR* 4, 808-14 405
Theophanes of Nicea (K.-P. Todt) *CMR* 5, 189-93 345
Theophanes the Confessor (M. Vaiou) *CMR* 1, 426-36 56, 160, 372
Thomas Aquinas (D. Burrell and J. Tolan) *CMR* 4, 521-9 476
Timothy I (M. Heimgartner and B. Roggema) *CMR* 1, 515-31 79, 161, 261
Timothy I, *Letter 59* (M. Heimgartner) *CMR* 1, 522-6 58, 83, 184, 200, 462, 465
Tomos (N. Zorzi) *CMR* 3, 759-63 78, 466
Treatise on the Unity (of God) (E. Platti) *CMR* 2, 123-4 116
Al-Ṭūfī (L. Demiri) *CMR* 4, 724-31 69, 219
Tultusceptru de libro domni Metobii (J. Tolan) *CMR* 2, 83-4 28
al-Ṭurṭūshī (M. Fierro) *CMR* 3, 387-96 377

Al-'Udhrī (M. Penelas) *CMR* 3, 176-81 455
Untitled appendix to Ḥunayn ibn Isḥāq, *Kayfiyyat idrāk ḥaqīqat al-diyāna* (M.N. Swanson) *CMR* 3, 721-3 197
Urban II (T. Mastnak) *CMR* 3, 229-48 468
Usāma ibn Munqidh (A. Mallett) *CMR* 3, 764-8 66, 82
Usṭāth, Kitāb (E. Salah and M.N. Swanson) *CMR* 1, 908-10 202
Al-'Utbī l-Qurṭubī (J.P. Monferrer Sala) *CMR* 1, 734-7 313

de veritate catholicae fidei contra errores infidelium qui dicitur Summa contra gentiles, Liber (J. Tolan) *CMR* 4, 523-7 163
Vicentius (A. Echevarría) *CMR* 3, 81-3 315
Vincent of Beauvais (E. Frunzeanu) *CMR* 4, 405-15 360
Vita Mahometi (V. Valcarcel) *CMR* 4, 207-11 169

Walter the Chancellor (S.B. Edgington) *CMR* 3, 379-82 284, 454
al-Wansharīsī (F. Vidal-Castro) *CMR* 7, 576-81 379
Al-Wāsiṭī (D. Thomas) *CMR* 2, 145-6 46
William of Malmesbury (J. Tolan) *CMR* 3, 483-7 31, 38, 67, 157, 289
William of Tripoli (T.E. Burman) *CMR* 4, 515-20 171, 360, 476
William of Tyre (A. Mallett) *CMR* 3, 769-77 40, 67, 165, 289, 471

Yaḥyā ibn 'Adī (E. Platti) *CMR* 2, 390-438 38, 63, 90, 116, 192
Yaḥyā ibn Sa'īd al-Anṭākī (M.N. Swanson) *CMR* 2, 657-61 64
Al-Ya'qūbī (D. Thomas) *CMR* 2, 75-8 40, 59, 209

Yovasap‘ Sebastac‘i (S.P. Cowe) *CMR* 7, 644-9 403
Yovhannēs vardapet (S.P. Cowe) *CMR* 4, 911-13 403
The young man of Arevalo (J. Chesworth and L.F. Bernabe Pons) *CMR* 6, 159-68 46
Yūḥannā ibn al-Ṣalt (B. Roggema) *CMR* 1, 849-51 186
Yuḥannā ibn Mīnā (M.N. Swanson) *CMR* 3, 720-3 91
Yūḥannā ibn Wahb (S. Moawad) *CMR* 4, 316-19 281

Al-Zāhidī (D. Thomas) *CMR* 4, 397-9 42
Al-Zuhayrī (D. Thomas) *CMR* 2, 522-3 46

Index

Abashidze, Medea D. 32 n. 52, 48 n. 126, 380 n. 62
'Abbās I, Shah of Persia 430
al-'Abbas 422, 423, 424
'Abbasid(s) 38, 76, 90, 130, 131, 148, 161, 175, 182, 185, 192, 196, 257, 260, 339, 362, 366, 368, 369, 370, 371, 372, 373, 374, 377, 378, 379, 390, 397, 398, 416, 421, 422, 423, 424, 442, 495
'Abd Allāh ibn al-Faḍl al-Anṭākī 39, 62, 201, 205
'Abd al-Jabbār 102, 132, 502, 510
'Abd al-Malik 128, 186, 231, 255, 274, 313, 368, 369
'Abd al-Malik ibn Marwān 128, 368
'Abd al-Masīḥ al-Ghassānī 395, 407
'Abd al-Masīḥ ibn Isḥāq al-Kindī 57, 157, 183 n. 4, 186 n. 17, 204, 257, 324
'Abd al-Mu'min 323
'Abd al-Raḥmān II 232
'Abd al-Raḥmān III 320, 321, 376, 450
'Abdallāh ibn Salām 238
'Abdisho' of Nisibis 502
Abo (perfumer) 32, 397, 408
Abbot Gerasimos 89 n. 73, 92 n. 90, 94
Abbot Macarie 483, 484 n. 116
Abbott Samson 316
Abgar of Edessa, king 494
Abraham, Patriarch 36, 37, 43, 108, 123, 136, 163, 177, 215, 217, 231, 237, 438, 493, 499, 507
Abraham, Monk of Tiberias 101, 102 n. 12 & n. 13
abrogation 189, 270, 356
Abū l- 'Abbbās al-Saffāḥ 423
Abū l- 'Abbās Aḥmad al-Ya'qūbī 40, 59, 129, 130, 209, 210
Abū l-'Alā l-Ma'arrī 62
Abū Bakr 115, 160, 161, 166, 172, 274, 391, 421, 437
Abū Bakr al-Bāqillāni 115, 130
Abū Bakr al-Ṣiddīq 364
Abū Bishr Mattā 63
Abū Ḥāmid al-Ghazālī 41, 68, 102, 117, 142, 143, 174, 216, 244, 378, 428
Abū Ḥanīfa 371
Abū Ḥarb al-Muburqa' 426
Abū l-ḥasan al-'Āmirī 41
Abū l-Ḥasan al-Ash'arī 65
Abū l-Ḥasan al-Māwardī 378
Abū l-Hudhayl al-'Allāf 109, 112, 113, 130
Abū 'Īsā Muḥammad ibn Hārūn al-Warrāq 58, 113, 115, 116, 130, 193
Abū Ja'far Muḥammad ibn Jarīr al-Ṭabarī 130, 131, 147, 209, 210, 211, 212, 216, 267
Abū l-Ma'ālī 66
Abū Muḥammad 'Alī ibn Ḥazm 27, 214, 215, 216, 217, 225, 326, 376
Abū Muslim 423, 424
Abū l-Qāsim al-Anṣārī 205
Abū Qurra, Theodore, *see also* Theodore Abū Qurra 43, 57, 80, 84, 85, 86, 88, 91, 92, 94, 95, 109, 110, 113, 158, 165, 185, 194, 195, 196, 199, 200, 202, 272, 465, 489, 490, 492, 504
Abū l-Rabī' ibn al-Layth 104, 131, 189, 195
Abū Rā'iṭa l-Takrītī 80, 84, 87, 88, 90 n. 76, 107, 109, 110, 111, 113, 185, 191, 195, 196, 199, 200, 203, 204, 260, 499, 500, 501, 511
Abū l-Faraj al-Iṣbahānī 61, 374 n. 42
Abū l-Shaykh al-Iṣbahānī 378
Abū Sufyān 425, 426
Abū l-Walīd al-Bājī 327
Abū Ya'lā ibn al-Farrā' 378
Abū Dā'ūd al-Sijistānī 428
Abū Sulaymān al-Sijistānī 63
Abū Ya'qūb al-Sijistānī 37, 61, 213, 214
Accad, Martin 3 n. 7, 107-8
Accommodation 5, 15-16, 24, 35, 43, 48, 50, 51, 164, 175, 176, 306, 331, 338, 358, 362, 365, 373, 376, 377, 383, 385, 386-7, 464, 465, 480

Acculturation 14, 174, 307, 313-19, 329, 367, 480, 486
Acre 244, 245, 247, 282, 295, 297-99, 300 n. 62, 301, 302, 471, 476
Adam 124, 130, 135, 141, 209-10, 217, 237, 511
Adang, Camilla 211
Adelphus 29 n. 26, 169
Adémar of Chabannes 29, 235, 449-50
al-ʿĀdil 301
Adnotatio Mammetis Arabum principis 232
adversus Judaeos 489, 490, 492, 493, 494
Affinity 5, 9, 16, 24, 36, 38, 50, 143, 153, 158, 159, 174, 362, 363, 365, 373, 383, 386, 411
Afghanistan 217, 415, 416, 432
Africa 4, 445, 471 n. 52, 473, 484, 485-6
Afsaruddin, Asma 2
Afterlife, the 2, 44, 85, 87, 89, 135
Agapius of Menbij 131
Agolant, fictional African king 452
aḥkām 371
Al-aḥkām al-kubrā 322
Al-aḥkām al-sulṭāniyya 378
ahl al-dhimma 371
ahl al-kitāb, see also People of the Book 135 n. 48, 189, 308, 353, 395
Ahl al-Sunna 191
Aḥmad 194, 218, 264
Ahmad Grañ 430
Aḥmad ibn ʿAbd al-Ṣamad al-Khazrajī 327, 457
Aḥmad al-Rāzī 322, 454
ʿĀʾisha 129 n. 12, 267
al-ʿajamiyya 314
ʿAjlūn 427
Al-ajwiba l-fākhira 133 n. 34, 503
Akapnios, monastery of 345
Akbar, The Great 431, 432
Akhbār mulūk al-Andalus 322, 454, 455
Akhluqu 263
al-Akhṭal 367
ʿalā ʿAmmār al-Naṣrānī fī l-radd ʿalā l-Naṣārā, Kitāb 112
al-ʿālam, Kitāb 318
Aʿlām al-nubuwwa 40, 209 n. 11
ʿAlawīs 68
Albarus of Cordova, *also* Cordubensis 12, 232-3, 309
Alcorani seu legis Mahometi et Evangelistarum concordiae liber 251, 252
Alexander III, pope 469
Alexandria 221, 405, 420, 439
Alexius I Comnenus, Emperor 283, 470
Aleppo 297
Alfonso I 448
Alfonso III 447
Alfonso VI 322, 451
Alfonsi, Petrus 12, 236-8, 240, 243, 325, 471, 492 n. 10
ʿAlī 129, n. 12, 274, 416, 425
ʿAlī ibn Abī Ṭālib 366, 370, 413, 421
ʿAlī ibn Rabban al-Ṭabarī 11, 59, 84 n. 53, 89 n. 75, 91, 105, 106, 131, 208, 209, 216, 225, 499
ʿAlid 370, 418, 422
Allāh 128, 138, 143, 148, 150, 207, 242, 256, 257, 261-4, 267, 269, 271-2, 339, 364, 414, 417, 481, 505
Almohad(s) 322, 375
Almoravid(s) 216, 377, 456 n. 140, 468
Alonso de Espina 247
Alonso de Orozco 482
Alp Arslen 332
Alphonsus of Aragon 236
Alvar, Paul, *also* Paulus Alvarus, Albarus 12, 75 n. 9, 232-3, 235, 309 n. 7, 313, 315, 399, 410, 446, 447 n. 84, 450
al-ʿĀmirī, Abū l-Ḥasan 41
ʿAmmār al-Baṣrī 44, 45 n. 125, 84, 87, 88, 92, 109, 112, 113, 114, 186 n. 16, 196, 260, 504, 508 n. 105
amṣār 366
al-amwāl, Kitāb 320
Anagnostes, John 351
Analogy 109, 116, 117, 188, 203-5, 372
Anastasius of Cluny 468
Anastasius of Sinai 66, 83 n. 51, 188, 393, 441, 503
Anatolia 15, 16, 217, 283, 286, 300 n. 59, 331, 332, 333, 341, 351, 354, 358, 359,

379, 380, 381, 383, 385, 389, 402, 403, 405, 429
Anawati, Georges 124, 143, 146, 313
al-Andalus 14, 225, 236, 293, 307, 308, 309, 310, 311, 313, 314, 315, 316, 319, 322, 323, 326, 328, 329, 372, 374, 375, 376, 377, 391, 393, 395, 399, 400, 407, 410, 443, 446, 452, 454, 455, 456, 457, 457 n. 143, 459
Andalusī 309, 311, 312, 314, 315, 317, 319, 323, 400
Andalusia 14, 38, 436, 438, 442, 445, 447, 457
al-Andalusī, Ṣāʿid 376
Andres, Juan 249
Ankara 350, 351
Annunciation, Church of the 281
Annunciation, to Mary 124
ʿanṣara 323
al-Anṣārī, Abū l-Qāsim 205
Anthony al-Qurashī 397, 407, 409
Antichrist, the 10, 167, 168, 181, 229, 232, 233, 235, 324, 352, 414, 441, 449, 464
Antioch 39, 62, 64, 67, 68, 133, 176, 191, 283, 284, 285, 286, 291, 297, 302, 402, 407, 408, 420, 503
Antipathy 5, 9, 14, 16, 18, 19, 23, 24-31, 33, 35-6, 51, 153, 154, 294, 344, 352, 362, 365, 373, 376, 378, 379, 382, 385, 435, 436
Antonio Garcia de Villalpando 482
Anton Vrančić 484
Apocalypse(s) viii, 18, 76, 413-15, 418, 427-8, 433, 436, 441, 470, 486
Apocalyptic 4, 10, 18, 31, 75-6, 123, 126, 136, 147, 148, 149, 153, 290, 375, 413-20, 422, 424-6, 428-33, 440-1, 449, 450, 461-5, 470, 483, 485-6
Apocalypse of Pseudo-Methodius 76, 415, 419, 440, 463
Apocalypse of Pseudo-Shenoute 440, 441
Apocalypse of Samuel 427
Apocalypse of Shenoute 76, 463
Apollin 78, 157, 453
Apologetic commentary on the Creed 45
Apologetics 6, 10, 14, 24, 41-6, 51, 71, 87, 132, 185-8, 190, 192, 194, 204, 246, 271, 362, 462, 465, 466, 491
apologeticus martyrum, Liber 229, 233, 446, 447
The apology of al-Kindī 44, 161, 184, 190, 232, 238, 240, 462
Apostasy 32, 56, 74, 309, 350, 391-3, 396, 397-9, 403, 408, 441, 464, 466, 476, 510
Apostles 17, 86, 87, 143, 224, 225, 271, 272, 390, 473, 474, 503-4, 512
Apostles' Creed 244
Appeal 5, 24, 41-2, 46, 47, 99, 102-4, 108, 153, 165, 170-1, 179, 362
Aqānīm 109, 113-14
Aquinas, St Thomas 118, 119, 163, 164, 476
Al-aqwāl al-qawīma fī ḥukm al-naql min al-kutub al-qadīma 223
Arabia x, 70, 228, 357, 363, 370, 371, 425, 493
Arabic (language) 7, 13, 28, 30, 31, 36, 38, 42, 43, 44, 45, 46, 56, 57, 62, 67, 73, 76, 79, 80, 81, 82, 84, 87, 90, 93, 96, 101, 109, 110, 118, 119, 132, 134, 139, 153, 155, 158, 161, 165, 173, 174, 183, 184, 185, 187, 192, 193, 199, 200, 203, 204, 212, 216, 231, 232, 238, 239, 240, 241, 243, 244, 245, 248, 249, 253, 255, 256, 257, 258, 261, 262, 263, 273, 277, 309, 310, 311, 314, 315, 316, 317, 318, 319, 324, 329, 339, 355, 366, 368, 373, 374, 389, 394, 395, 396, 397, 398, 399, 400, 403, 405, 407, 409, 427, 428, 475, 477, 478, 480, 481, 492, 497, 502, 508, 510
Arabic Sibylline prophecy 76
Arabisation 14, 307-9, 313-19, 328, 400
ʿaraḍ 113, 223
Aragon 236, 443, 475, 477, 482
Aramaic (language) xv, 211 n. 19, 243, 366, 401 n. 34
Arberry, A.J. 362
Arian / Arianism 157, 159, 231, 308, 311-12
Aristotle / Aristotelianism 63, 90 n. 76, 110-11, 113, 192, 193
Armenian (language) 13, 184, 257, 366, 406-7

Armenian Christians /Christianity 4, 6, 31, 66, 184, 198, 284, 285, 300, 354, 376, 381, 383-4, 403, 404
Arnakis, George 333, 334 n. 3
ʿarūḍ 317
Asad, Muhammad 124
Aṣbagh ibn Nabīl 318
asceticism 8, 61, 123, 127, 142-6, 148, 218, 491
Asfār al-asrār 93
Ashʿarī 27, 115, 130, 196
al-Ashʿarī, Abū l-Ḥasan 65
Ashraka 263
Asia Minor 15, 69, 298, 331-2, 340, 342, 344, 345
al-asmāʾ al-ḥusnā 203
al-ʿAsqalānī 135 n. 49, 221
Assassins 286, 294, 304, 425
Assimilation 50, 233, 314-15, 383, 409, 464
Assizes of Roger 50
Asturian dynasty 448
Athanasius of Balad 56, 64, 464
Augustine, St 119
Avicenna, *see also* Ibn Sīnā 68
Awad, Najib 110
Awag 403
āyāt 91, 195, 266
Ayatullah Ruhullah Khumayni 429
ʿAyn Jālūt 297
Ayyūbid(s) 93, 282, 295, 296, 297, 303, 379, 380, 472
Azerbaijan 173, 403
al-ʿAzīz 62, 375

Bābur 430
Baddala 264
Bacon, Roger 475
Baetica 309
Baghdad 32, 38, 53, 58, 63, 67, 68, 106, 173, 197, 219, 244, 283, 297, 325, 372, 374, 377, 378, 397, 402, 415, 418, 476
l-Baghdādī, Saʾd al-Dīn Masʿūd al-Ḥārithī 219
Bahāʾ al-Dīn 291
Baḥīrā, *see also* Sergius Baḥīrā 81, 154, 164, 171, 172, 178, 194, 258, 465
al-Bājī, Abū l-Walīd 327
Balkans, the 50, 331, 334, 335, 337, 339, 341, 348, 354, 357, 384, 406
Balkh 217
al-Balkhī, Ḥīwī 215
Banū l-Qasī 316
Banū Qaynuqāʿ 164
Banū Taghlib 365
Banū Tanūkh 365
Banū l-Ṭawī 316
baptism 21, 44, 78, 80, 182, 347, 469, 471, 481, 482, 491, 493, 504-5, 507-9, 512
Barhebraeus, Gregory 68, 155, 173-76, 381 n. 66
bar Malkon, Ishoʿyahb 191, 202, 497, 497 n. 33
bar Ṣalībī, Dionysius 31, 512
al-Bāqillāni, Abū Bakr 91 n. 86, 115, 130
Barreira, Baltasar 485
Bartholomew of Edessa 172
al-Barzanjī 419
Basel, Council of 479
Basil the Great 490
Basra 286, 366, 511
al-Baṣrī, Abū l-Ḥusayn 63
al-Baṣrī, ʿAmmār 44, 45 n. 125, 84, 87, 88, 92, 109, 112, 113, 114, 186 n. 16, 196, 260, 504, 508 n. 105
Bassano, Luigi 70
Bautista de Jeronimo Anyes, Juan 481
Al-bayān al-mughrib fī [ikhtiṣār] akhbār mujlūk al-Andalus wa-l-Maghrib 457
Baybars, Mamlūk Sultan 67, 281, 294
Bayezid I, Ottoman sultan 345-6, 350-1
Bayezid II, Ottoman sultan 70, 356-7
Bayt Rās 400
Beaumont, I. Mark xv, xvii, 7
Bektash-i Veli, Haji 341, 342
Bektashi, the 341
Bella Antiochena 67, 284 n. 9, 454 n. 132
Belon, Pierre 70
Benevich, Grigory 437 n. 10, 439, 440
Bennett, Clinton xv, 9
Berber 308, 375, 377, 443
Bertaina, David xv, 5, 6
Bertrandon de la Broquière 70
Bible, Hebrew 207, 221, 229, 231, 489

Bible, the vii, ix, x, xi, 7, 10-11, 13, 26, 27-8, 39, 58, 59, 61, 69, 73, 74, 75, 77, 78, 83, 84, 121, 163, 188, 191, 198, 200, 205, 207-26, 245, 253, 259, 264-5, 271, 326, 327, 328, 458
Bibliander, Theodor 165, 239, 250, 251, 478 n. 94
Bibliothecarius, Anastasius 234, 240
bida' 428
Al-bidāya wa-l-nihāya 137 n. 54, 418
al-Biqā'ī, Abū l-Ḥasan Ibrāhīm ibn 'Umar 69, 221, 222, 223, 225
bird *from* clay 142, 263
Bird, Jessalyn 470, 476
Bir rāhib ile bir pîr-I Müslim arasinda İsa (a.s.) hakkinda mükâleme 223
al-Bīrūnī, Abū Rayḥān Muḥammad 65 n. 58, 66, 93 n. 98, 398
Bithynia 332, 333, 335
Black Sea 297, 298
Black Stone 77, 156, 210, 497
blasphemers 392, 409
blasphemy 17, 268, 389, 391-3, 398-401, 403, 408
Boccaccio, Giovanni 170
Bologna 70
Boniface of Molini 286
Bosporus 298
Breve compendio de nuestra ley y sunna 46
Brockelmann, Carl 132
al-Buḥturī 374
Bukhārā 380
al-Bukhārī 124 n. 1, 135, 135 n. 48, 136, 139, 416
Bukhtīshū' ibn Jibrā'īl 495, 496
Bulgaria 484
Bulliet, Richard 3, 308
Būlus al-Būshī 92, 197
Būluṣ ibn Rajā' 325
Būlus al-Rāhib 108
Burchard of Strasbourg 40, 67
burhān 90, 91, 186, 187
al-burhān, Kitāb 44, 45 n. 125, 80, 112, 498, 504, 508 n. 105
Burman, Thomas E. 245
Bursa 334, 338, 341, 343
Būyid(s) 374, 377, 378
Byzantine Empire 160, 228, 332, 411, 415, 429

Cairo 69, 219, 221, 405
Caliph al-Mahdī 58, 83, 161-2, 184, 200, 260, 264, 272, 276, 397, 423-4, 465
Caliph al-Walīd 400
caliphate, 'Abbasid 182, 196
Caliphate of Córdoba 313, 443, 447
caliphate, Shi'a 304
caliphate, the 15, 160, 395, 400, 407, 424
caliphate, Umayyad 184, 435
Cananus, John 333, 351
Cantacuzenus, John, emperor 333-4, 349, 350
Casanova, Paul 275
Castile 443, 468
Catalan (language) 47, 119, 246
catechesis 90, 186
Cathars 475
Catholic Church 309-12
Catholic faith 308, 309, 469
Caucasus 380, 381, 383, 407, 410
Cave of treasures 59
Cecini, Ulisse xv, 11-12
Central Asia 65, 332, 380, 429, 430
Chalcedon, Council of 10, 181, 198
Chalcedon, Metropolitan of 345, 346
Chalcedonian Christians /Christianity 6, 26, 31, 53, 82, 101, 149, 150, 198-9, 410, 411, 439
Chanson de Roland 29, 78, 157, 289, 452, 453
Chansons d'Antioche 157
Charles V 250
Charlemagne 452-3
Charles the Bald 316
Cheynet, Magali 452
China 298, 461, 473, 486
Chiones, the 343-4
Christ, *see also* Jesus x, 26, 37, 43, 54, 58, 69, 80, 86, 94, 99, 100, 102, 103, 104, 105, 106, 108, 121, 123, 124, 125, 130, 132, 136, 137, 140, 141, 143, 147, 148, 150-1, 160, 163-4, 171, 190, 195, 200, 201, 213, 220, 260, 264, 305, 309, 323, 346,

351-2, 355, 356, 409, 449, 461, 463, 474, 494, 495, 496, 498-9, 501-2, 505-6, 508, 510-11, 512
Christ, ascension of 125, 126, 147, 149
Christ, circumcision of 64, 132
Christ, crucifixion of 2, 41, 44, 60, 76, 82, 89, 92, 147, 156, 198, 199-202, 213, 222, 260, 261, 327, 343, 505, 512
Christ, death of 261, 507
Christ, devotion to 202
Christ, divinity / nature of 26, 34, 43, 55, 100, 102, 103, 104, 108, 124, 125, 126, 197, 198, 220, 264, 327, 337, 356, 500, 504-5
Christ, Incarnation vii, 2, 34, 43-4, 58, 65, 82, 90, 116, 120, 133, 158, 163, 184, 185-7, 189-90, 193, 197-8, 200-5, 213, 223, 326-7, 355, 505, 512
Christ, resurrection of 163, 175, 198, 213, 260-1, 505, 507
Christ, temptation of 142, 145, 220
Christ, virgin birth of 124, 126
Christ, worship of 94, 494
Christendom 32, 74, 223, 281, 298, 299, 301, 320, 440, 456, 466, 472, 483-5, 486
Christian missions to Muslims 20, 41, 47, 305, 461-87
Christmas Sermon 437, 438, 463
Christology 37, 42-5, 55, 124, 197-202, 493, 505-6
Christopher of Antioch 408
Chronica Albendensia 321, 448
Chronica Hispana-Orientalia ad annum 724 445
Chronica Naierensis 451, 453
Chronica Visegothorum 447, 448, 452, 453
Chronicle of 741 166, 228, 321
Chronicle of 754 166, 228, 321
Chronicle of Albelda 321, 448
Chronicle of Alfonso III 321
Chronicle of John, see also *Mädābbār chronicle* 439
Chronicle of Khuzistan 36, 55
Chronicle of Moldova from 1504 to 1551 483
Chronicle of Pseudo-Turpin 78, 452, 453
Chronicle of Zuqnīn 56, 368, 406
Chronicon 29, 67, 234, 449
Chronographia 56, 160, 161, 234
Chronographia tripertita 234
Chronographikon syntomon 234
Christys, Ann 454
Church of the East 6, 37, 42, 53, 55, 56, 61, 65, 93, 149, 150, 161, 198, 199, 311, 461
Cilicia 54
coexistence 3, 15, 19, 24, 48, 50, 153, 307, 328-9, 436, 444, 454-8, 459, 460
Comnena, Anna 333, 470 n. 44
Companions of Muḥammad 138, 143, 219, 370, 413
Confrontation 2, 170, 171, 233, 250, 297
Confusión de la secta mahometana 249
Coptic Christians /Christianity 6, 45, 48, 53, 117, 197, 198, 281, 302, 368, 464, 508
Constantine VI, Byzantine emperor 104, 131
Constantine XI / XII, Byzantine emperor 352, 353, 358, 340
Constantinople 15, 69, 178, 247, 250, 295, 331-3, 334, 335, 344, 345, 346, 350, 351, 352-7, 358, 384, 405, 408, 415, 417, 420, 430, 479
Constantinople, Patriarchate 162, 344-5, 346, 347, 410
Continuatio Hispana 445
Contra legem Sarracenorum 245, 249, 350
contra sectam sive hearesim Saracenorum, Liber 30
Contrarietas Alfolica 241-6
Contra sectam Sarracenorum 240
Conversion / converts, issues of vii-viii, 17-18, 46, 187, 196-7, 202, 225, 247, 284, 289, 302-4, 306, 340, 361, 363, 389-91, 409-11, 435, 462, 466, 484-6, 510
Conversion / converts to Christianity 17, 20, 30, 32, 47, 78, 129, 149, 183, 195, 201, 236, 241, 246, 248, 251, 253, 305, 310, 318, 322, 386, 389-90, 393, 396-8, 409, 451-3, 461-2, 464-72, 474-86, 502, 507

Conversion / converts to Islam 16, 11, 17, 30, 32, 37, 57, 59, 90, 124, 160, 162, 182-3, 196, 202, 208, 223, 237-8, 242, 248, 249, 257, 304, 308-9, 315, 319, 322-3, 335, 337, 339, 343, 357, 360, 366, 368, 374-5, 377, 381-4, 389, 385, 390, 393-5, 398-9, 400-1, 404-5, 409, 411, 427, 429-30, 432-3, 441, 443, 462, 465-7, 476, 483, 499, 501, 509-10
Cook, David Brian xvi, 18, 397
Coptic (language) 13, 184, 197, 257, 366, 389, 405, 427, 438
Cordoba / Cordova 12, 32, 167, 229, 232-3, 235, 309, 310, 312-13, 315, 319, 321, 372, 374, 396, 399, 400, 408, 410, 443, 447, 450, 462, 466
Cordubensis, Albarus 309
Corsica 70, 449
Cowe, Peter S. 403
Crete 466-8
Cribratio Alchorani 81, 120, 121 n. 98
Cross, the 40, 44, 60, 61, 79, 80, 132, 150, 199, 213, 222, 224, 296, 352, 417, 463, 480, 494, 504, 510, 511
Cross, the veneration of 21, 489, 491, 493, 497, 498-502, 504, 510, 511-12
Crusaders 245, 281-306, 332, 379, 471
Crusader states 20, 33, 281-2, 286-8, 291, 293-5, 297, 299, 302, 462, 464, 483
Crusades, Albigensian *and* Baltic 470
Crusades, the 13, 20, 26, 33, 40, 66, 69, 78, 170, 221, 239, 259, 281-306, 418, 435, 452, 458, 460, 467, 469, 472, 478
Crusade, the Baron's 296
Crusade, the Fifth 167, 303, 471-2
Crusade, the First 29, 32, 33, 283-4, 301, 304, 450, 468
Crusade, the Fourth 295, 332
Crusade, the German 295
Crusade, the Second 300
Crusade, the Third 295, 299, 301
Cydones, Demetrius 350
Cyprus 103, 140
Cyrus of Ḥarrān 395, 406

Dajjāl 136, 137, 148, 414, 417, 424
Dalā'il al-nubuwwa 46, 209
Dalīl 186
Damietta 219, 471
Damascus 53, 66, 69, 70, 100, 148, 219, 221, 287, 288, 295, 296, 297, 299, 308, 313, 393, 394, 397, 398, 400
Daniel, book of 75, 167, 220
Daniel, prophet 222, 420
dār al-Islām 12, 13, 24, 49, 92, 94, 149, 437
David, king 28, 79, 215
David, house of 138
David of Damascus 56
al-Dawla, Sayf 64, 402
al-Dāwūdi, Abū Jaʿfar 49, 320
Day of Resurrection 126, 147, 149, 198
Debate of Theodore Abū Qurra 57
De gladio divini spiritus in corda mittendo Sarracenorum 248
Dei gesta per Francos 169
De haeresibus 100, 155
De orbis terrae Concordia 252
denudationis sive ostensionis aut patefaciens, Liber 30, 241, 325
Deroche, F. 275
Dervish 341, 357
De seta Machometi 244
De statu Sarracenorum 246
Devil, the xi, 23, 39, 142, 157, 170, 178, 220, 223, 235, 236, 237, 464, 482, 484
Devshirme 15, 331, 339-40, 384
Devotion 21, 70, 127, 202, 245, 246, 291, 341, 409, 489, 490, 498, 500
dhāt 110, 111
dhimma 16, 66, 162, 308, 315, 359, 360, 361, 371, 375, 454, 459
dhimmī(s) 12, 15, 16, 24, 48, 49, 265, 308, 315, 331, 371, 372
dhimmī communities 48, 49
dhikr 126, 202
Dhikr bilād al-Andalus 455
Dialogi contra Iudaeos 236, 325
Dialogos meta tinos Persou 350
Dialogue between a Saracen and a Christian 158, 465
dīn 7, 73, 82, 83, 84, 96
Din-i ilahi 431
al-dīn wa-l-dawla, Kitāb 208
Dionysius bar Ṣalibi 31, 512

Dionysius of Tell-Maḥrē 31
Diplomacy 48, 49, 69, 287, 460
Disciples, of Jesus, other 91, 132, 149, 150
Disciples, of Jesus, the x, 35, 61, 104, 105, 106, 107, 108, 126, 144, 146, 147, 150, 194, 208, 213, 220
Disciples, of Ibn Taymiyya 102, 134
Disputation between a monk of Bēt Ḥālē and an Arab notable 43, 100 n. 1, 187, 199, 493 n. 11
Disputation of the monk Ibrāhīm al-Ṭabarānī 37 n. 80 & n. 81, 267
Disputation of John and the Emir 79
Dionysius the Carthusian 247
Divine retribution 351, 436, 438, 459
Divine Plan, Islam part of the 18, 420, 439
Divine Providence 37, 448
Divorce 156, 164, 175, 237, 266, 312
al-diyārāt, Kitāb 35, 61, 374 n. 42
Dmitri, Georgian king 66
Doctrina Iacobi nuper baptizati 75 n. 9, 438
Doctrina pueril 173, 324
Documenta martyriale 447
Dome of the Rock 8, 12, 78, 128, 157, 255-6, 262, 278
Dom Goncalo da Silva 485
Dominic Guzman 471, 475
Dominican Order, the 20, 118, 471, 475, 476
Donatism 17
Druze, the 68, 286, 376
l-Dunyā, Ibn Abī 53, 62

East Syrians, *see also* Nestorian Christians / Christianity 6, 36, 37, 53, 79, 87, 109, 192, 200, 204, 411, 493, 494, 496-8, 499, 502, 504, 506
Eastern Christians / Christianity (includes Middle Eastern) 12, 13, 19, 43, 68, 99, 104, 108, 119, 121, 255-7, 284, 287, 300, 303, 311, 324, 325, 361, 436, 437, 446, 476, 486
Ebussuud Efendi 349, 358
Ecclesiology 45
Edessa 286, 302
Edifying and supportive tales which occurred in various places in our times 441
Egidio da Viterbo, cardinal 249, 250, 252
Egila, bishop 312, 464
Egypt 16, 29, 47, 48, 54, 60, 64, 67, 69, 70, 94, 104, 139, 140, 201, 219, 225, 287, 295-9, 301, 352, 357, 359, 368, 374-6, 379, 380-1, 383, 384, 386, 389, 391, 405, 411, 420, 427, 429, 470, 493, 511
Elias II, Patriarch 494-5, 497
Elias of Helioupolis 32, 394-5, 404, 410
Elias of Nisibis 60, 88, 498
Elias the Younger, The Life of 26
Elipandus of Toledo 311
Embrico of Mainz 169
Emir Muḥammad I 316, 372
End of Time, *see also* eschaton 46, 178, 424, 486
Epiphanius of Salamis 81
Epiphany sermon 438
epistemology 41, 43, 262
Epistolae de prosperitate Sarracenorum 245
Epistula Saraceni 165, 325
Epistola salutaris doctoribus Egipti transmissa 47
Errores legis Mahometi 247
Ertoghrul 332, 333
Eschaton 148, 440, 450, 459
Ethiopia 363, 420
Eucharist 21, 44, 398, 491, 493, 497, 501, 502-7, 512
Eulogius of Cordova / Córdoba 12, 167, 168, 229, 232-3, 235, 309, 310, 313, 315, 399, 410, 446, 450, 466
Europe ix, xii, 74, 161, 166, 176, 178, 204, 301, 329, 334, 386, 387, 416, 429, 461, 469, 470, 483-6
Eurasia 298, 380
Eutychius of Alexandria 60
Evangelisation 20, 462, 469, 472, 480, 481, 484, 486, 487
Evangelism 304
Ezekiel, book of 75, 220
Ezekiel, prophet 141
Ezra 140, 190, 215

Exodus, book of 211, 269, 493
Explanatio simboli apostolorum 244

Fakhr al-Dīn al-Rāzī 68, 94 n. 103, 195, 261, 265
Fall, The 159, 201, 438
Faqīh 248
al-Fārābī, Abū Naṣr᾿ 63
Faraklit 223
farḍ al-kifāya 219
Fatḥ al-Andalus 456
Fātiḥa 509
Fāṭima 416, 421
Fāṭimid(s) 285, 287, 304, 375, 376 n. 48, 379, 412, 429, 430
Fatwā 402, 509
Faultless, Julian 116
Federigo da Montefeltro 249
Feodosil of Novgorod 483
Festivals 6, 56, 62, 64, 71, 323, 509
Fī tathlīth Allāh al-wāḥid 57, 79, 80, 82, 83 n. 52, 84, 259, 263, 271, 465, 508
Fīl-maqālāt 58
Fiqh 360
al-fiṣal fī l-milal wa-l-ahwā᾿ wa-l-niḥal, Kitāb 326
al-fitan, Kitāb 417
Flavius Mithridates 249
Florence, Council of 352
food 53, 56, 77, 125, 140, 149, 213, 301, 342, 449, 504
Forty-Two Martyrs of Amorion 401
Francis of Assisi 20, 93, 171, 172, 173, 177, 201, 305, 471-3
Francisco Jimenez de Cisneros 480, 482, 486
Franks, the 66, 78, 88, 281, 283-94, 297, 299, 301, 302-4, 316, 381, 453
Frederick II, emperor 295
Frederiks, Martha T. xvi, 20
Free will 37, 38, 63, 201
French (language) 29, 119, 157, 289
fuqahā᾿ 241, 323, 360

Gabriel, Archangel 39, 138 n. 61, 160, 161, 167, 175, 229
Gabriel of Mt Athos 50
Galicia 316
Gallipoli 334, 340, 342, 350
Gautier de Compiegne 169
Gazi Evrenos 334, 339
Genesis, book of 79, 84, 204, 208, 210, 214, 217, 220
Gennadius II Scholarius, patriarch 352, 354
Genoa 299
Gentile(s) 47, 119, 120, 324, 474, 478
de gentili et tribus sapientibus, Liber 246
Geoffrey of Donjon 305
George Gemistos Plethon 352
George of Trebizond 354
George the Archdeacon 48
George the Black 393, 410
George the Martyr 337
George the Monk 310
George the Synkellos 234
George the New 396
Georgia 32, 48, 381, 391, 397, 483
Georgian Christians / Christianity 32, 66, 384, 387, 407
Georgian (language) 32, 184, 366, 387, 407
Germanus I, patriarch 490
Gesta Francorum 78, 284, 288
Gesta Tancredi 78
Geyikli Baba 341
al-Ghāfiqī, Saʿīd ibn Sulaymān 399
al-Ghazālī, Abū Ḥāmid 41, 68, 102, 117, 142, 143, 174, 216, 244, 378, 428
Ghāzān, Mongol ruler 381, 476
ghāzīs 338, 381, 383
ghusl 491
Gibson, Margaret D. 271
Gidelli, Yca 177, 248
Glaber, Rodulfus 39
Glei, Reinhold F. 100, 232 n. 27, 239 n. 55
Glossary of Leiden 311
God vii, viii, ix, xi, 2, 8, 18, 21, 28, 30, 31, 32, 33, 36, 37, 38, 41, 44, 45, 53, 55, 58, 60, 61, 63, 65, 74, 76, 77, 78, 79, 82-4, 85, 87, 89, 99-121, 123-7, 129, 131, 135, 137-9, 140-1, 142, 144, 145, 147, 150, 156-7, 160-1, 162, 163, 167, 169, 171-2, 174, 188, 193, 194, 195, 196, 197, 198,

199, 200, 202, 203-5, 210-11, 214-15, 217, 220, 224-5, 228, 230, 232, 236-8, 242-3, 245, 258, 259, 260, 261, 264, 267-8, 270, 272-3, 277, 288, 292, 304, 320, 342, 345, 350-1, 355, 362, 364, 396, 409, 418-19, 420-1, 423, 428, 431, 441, 444, 447, 451, 452, 456, 461, 463, 468, 470, 473, 475, 476, 490, 493, 495, 496, 498, 501, 502, 507-8, 511, 512
God, Attributes of 99-121, 159, 204, 264
God, Beautiful names of 203, 216
God, Beliefs about 25, 99-121
God, Concept of 2, 7, 99-121
God, Creator, the 92, 111, 156-7, 263, 289, 355
God, Father, the 38
Godhead 34, 202, 262
God, Holy Spirit, the 99-121, 123-4, 133, 143, 156, 158, 233, 264, 353
God, incarnation of 199, 201, 203
God, name(s) of 99-121, 215, 237
God, providence of 37
God, Son of 8, 89, 99-121, 220, 233, 262-3
God the Trinity, Triune 57, 79, 89, 90 n. 76, n. 77, 99-104, 110, 125, 158, 262, 478
God, Unity of 8, 43, 63, 99-121, 125, 128, 162-3, 173, 175, 185-7, 189, 192-3, 202-3, 241, 263-4, 500
God, Vengeance of 439-40, 448
God, Word of 99-101, 132, 145, 158, 171, 178, 233, 243, 264-5, 268, 469, 473, 505
Goddard, Hugh 435
Gospels, the vii, ix-x, 7, 8, 41, 44, 59, 60, 69, 85, 95, 99, 102, 104-8, 121, 126, 130, 132-4, 140, 142, 144-6, 150, 171, 190, 194, 208, 209, 212-13, 218, 219-22, 224-5, 261, 264, 266, 272, 461, 473, 481, 505
Gospel, of John 102, 107, 108, 117, 121, 132, 145, 166, 224, 194, 204, 208, 223-4, 507, 508
Gospel, of Luke 100, 224
Gospel, of Mark 224
Gospel, of Matthew 37, 213, 217, 224, 234
Goths 346, 448
Granada 320, 443, 480, 481, 482
Grand Vizier, the 337, 340
Greek (language *and* texts) xv, 13, 38, 43, 56, 62, 77, 100, 109, 153, 155, 158, 159, 161, 184, 192, 199, 231, 244, 245, 257, 263, 311, 355, 365, 366, 389, 394, 402, 406-7, 420, 440, 467
Greek Christians, includes Greek Orthodox 56, 335, 337, 342, 345, 354, 355, 357, 383, 393
Greek philosophy / thought 34, 106, 110, 175, 198, 200, 203
Greeks, the 283, 415, 440-1
Gregory VII, pope 468
Gregory Dekapolites 506
Gregory Palamas 331, 342-4
Greisiger, Lutz 441
The Gregorian report 47
Griffith, Sydney 111, 112, 257, 274, 276
Guibert of Nogent 78, 169, 284
Gujarati, Mustafa 432

Habakkuk, book of 220
Ḥabīb Abū Rā'iṭa 80, 84, 87, 88, 90 n. 76, 107, 109, 110, 111, 113, 185, 191, 195, 196, 199, 200, 203, 204, 260, 499, 500, 501, 511
al-Hādī ilā l-Ḥaqq 45, 195
al-Hādī, Mūsā 423
Hadith(s) 8, 18, 59, 135-6, 138, 144, 148-9, 189, 190, 195, 244, 278, 353, 364, 369-70, 372, 413, 415, 416-19, 428, 475
Hadrian I, pope 312, 464
al-Ḥāfiẓ 376
Ḥafṣ ibn Albar al-Qūṭī 503 n. 74, 315, 317, 318
Hagar 79, 333, 484, 507
Hagia Sophia 70, 353
hagiography 26, 398 n. 25, 407, 409, 469
al-ḥajar al-aswad 210
ḥajj 210, 492 n. 10
Ḥajjāj ibn Yūsuf 274, 275, 275 n. 99, 276
al-Ḥakam I 316
al-Ḥākim 64, 65, 375, 412, 429, 449
al-Ḥākim bi-Amr Allāh 449
Hamdan, Omar 275
Ḥamdānid 402
Hames, Harvey 246

Hanbalī 69, 133, 134, 219, 378
Harūshiyūsh, Kitāb 318
ḥarrafa 264
Ḥarrān 395, 490
Harris, Rendel 162
Hārūn al-Rashīd 76 n. 15, 104, 131, 370, 372, 397, 423
al-Ḥasan 421
Al-Ḥasan al-Baṣrī 149
Ḥasanid(s) 422
al-Hāshimī, ʿAbd Allāh ibn Isḥāq 162, 183 n. 4, 186, 257, 324
Hass Murad Pasha 340
Ḥaṭṭīn 295
al-ḥawārī Yaḥyā 318
Heaven 123, 125, 126, 142, 144-5, 146, 147-8, 155, 161, 231, 260, 353, 464, 474, 475, 508, 509
Hebrew (language *and* text) xv, 124, 127, 207, 221, 229, 231, 243, 244, 489
Hebron 219
Heraclius, Byzantine Emperor 155, 160, 175
Heresiarch(s) 29, 33, 167, 168
heresiography 65, 187 n. 19
heretic(s) ix, 30, 33, 81, 118, 157, 169, 192, 194, 232, 234, 238, 286, 309, 326, 357, 431, 439, 449
Heresy 29, 77, 81, 100, 155, 156, 158, 160, 165, 187 n. 19, 231, 240, 252, 289, 312, 439, 466, 470, 486
Heresy of the Ishmaelites 81, 100
Hermann of Carinthia 239
Hernando de Talavera 480, 510 n. 118
hijrī 425, 428, 431
Ḥimṣ 417
Hispania 307, 310, 316, 321, 443, 448, 454, 456, 460
Historiæ adversus paganos 318
Historia ecclesiastica 234
Historia Francorum qui ceperunt Iherusalem 33
Historia Romana 234
Historia Silense 322, 451, 453
Historion biblia tessara 349
History of Sebeos 55, 440
History of the patriarchs of Alexandria 92
Ḥīwī al-Balkhī 215
Holy Cross Monastery 407
Holy Land, the 13, 70, 401, 453, 471, 486
Holy Sepulchre, Church of 65, 128, 255, 300, 376, 449
holy war 15, 33, 287, 293, 298, 302, 306, 331, 337, 338, 452, 453, 456, 459, 460
Hosea, book of 220
Hostegesis, bishop of Malaga 309
Hour, the 126, 144, 147-9, 413-14, 417, 419
Hrotsvit of Gandersheim 32, 450
Hugh of Flavigny 39, 469
al-ḥujja fī tathbīt al-nubuwwa, Kitāb 91 n. 86, 195
ḥulal 364
Hulegu 297
ḥulla 364
Ḥunayn ibn Isḥāq 62, 90, 91, 197, 485, 496
Hungary 386
al-Ḥusayn 421
Ḥusaynid(s) 422, 423, 425
Husseini, S. 113
Hussites 479

Iannuzzi, I 480
al-ʿIbādī, Isḥāq ibn Nuṣayr 374
al-ʿibar, Kitāb 211
Iberia 166, 167, 170, 304, 375, 385, 435-6, 443 n. 59, 444, 445, 448, 451, 452, 454, 460
Iberian Peninsula viii, 14, 19, 20, 165, 238, 308, 310-11, 325, 328, 352, 400, 435-6, 443-5, 447, 451, 452, 453, 458-60, 462, 466, 475, 477, 483, 486
Ibn ʿAbbās 136, 139 n. 65, 274
Ibn ʿAbd al-Barr 137, 137 n. 55, 138, 139 n. 63, 377
ibn ʿAbd al-Malik, Sulaymān 401
Ibn ʿAbd al-Ẓāhir 209 n. 11, 293, 297
Ibn ʿAbdūn al-Ishbīlī 36, 323
Ibn Abī l-Dunyā 53, 62
Ibn Abī Ṭālib al-Dimashqī 103, 103 n. 21, 140, 141, 176, 277
ibn ʿAdī, Yaḥyā 38, 63, 90, 116, 117, 118, 192, 204
Ibn al-ʿAmīd 212
Ibn ʿAsākir 66, 139, 141, 142 n. 80

Ibn al-Athīr 68, 137 n. 55, 68 n. 57, 283, 290
Ibn al-Azraq 66
Ibn Badrān al-Ḥulwānī 378
Ibn al-Barrajān 216, 217, 217 n. 51, 225
Ibn Bashkuwāl 456
ibn Baṭrīq, Saʿīd 60
ibn al-Farrāʾ, Abū Yaʿlā 378
ibn al-Ḥajjāj, Muslim 416
ibn al-Ḥanafiyya, Muḥammad 421
ibn Ḥanbal, Aḥmad 139 n. 65, 144, 145, 378
Ibn Ḥayyān 456
Ibn Ḥazm, Abū Muḥammad ʿAlī 27, 214, 215, 216, 217, 225, 326, 376
Ibn Hishām 135 n. 49, 194
Ibn ʿIdhārī al-Marrākushī 457
Ibn Isḥāq 154, 155, 168, 194
ibn Isḥāq, Ḥunayn 62, 90, 197, 495
ibn Jarīr, Yaḥyā 201
Ibn Jubayr 293, 294, 299, 468 n. 33
ibn Kaʿb, Ubayy 274
Ibn Khaldūn, ʿAbd al-Raḥmān ibn Muḥammad 69, 150, 211, 212
Ibn Kathīr 130, 137 n. 54, 138, 140, 418
ibn al-Layth, Abū l-Rabīʿ 104, 131, 189, 195
ibn Lūqā, Qusṭā 64
Ibn Masʿūd 124, 274
ibn Mīnā, Yūḥannā 91
ibn Munqidh, ʿUsāma 66, 292, 293, 301
Ibn al-Munādī 418, 420
Ibn al-Munajjim 90
Ibn al-Nadīm 109
ibn Nuṣayr, Mūsā 307, 443
Ibn al-Qalānasī 290
Ibn Qayyim al-Jawziyya 107, 134, 150 n. 110
Ibn Qutayba 59, 209, 216, 225
Ibn al-Qūṭiyyah 319
ibn Rajāʾ, Būluṣ 325
ibn Sabbā, Yūḥannā 94
ibn Saʿīd al-Anṭākī, Yaḥyā 64
Ibn al-Shaddād 60, 292
Ibn al-Sikkīt 63
Ibn Sīnā (Avicenna) 68, 244
Ibn al-Ṭayyib 63, 116, 193
Ibn Taymiyya (of Damascus) 69, 102, 103, 103 n. 94, 104, 117, 133, 134, 176, 191, 219, 277, 382, 383, 393, 418, 509, 510
Ibn Ṭūlūn 374
ibn Yūḥannā, Ṣalībā 93
ibn Yaḥyā, Naṣr 202, 501
ibn Yūsuf, Ḥajjāj 274, 275, 276
ibn Ziyād, Ṭāriq 307
Ibn al-Zubayr 216
Ibrāhīm ibn Yūḥannā al-Anṭākī 64
Ibrāhīm al-Ṭabarānī 93, 267
Icon(s) 21, 44, 182, 187, 201-2, 204, 398, 489-92, 494-9, 501, 504, 512
Iconoclasm 201, 368, 418
İçöz, Ayşe xvi, 10, 11
Iḍāḥ al-ḥikma bi-aḥkām al-ʿibra 216
Idol(s) 42, 78, 138, 155, 157, 174, 452, 453, 485, 489, 499, 508
Idolatry 21, 29, 32, 42, 77-8, 121, 155-7, 163, 167, 175, 203-4, 235, 243, 252, 289, 322, 328, 450, 474, 485, 489-90, 493, 495, 500
Ifrīqiya, see also North Africa 307, 443
Iḥyāʾ ʿulūm al-dīn 142, 143, 378
iʿjāz al-Qurʾān 91, 278, 327
Ikhwān al-Ṣafāʾ 60, 212, 213
Iktisāb 193
Al-iʿlām bi-manāqib al-Islām 42
Ilghazi of Mardin 287
Ilkhanate, the 297
Ilkhan Ghazan 476
Ilkhanid 332, 382, 383, 418
ʿilm al-kalām 192
al-Imām al-Qurṭubī 326, 327, 503 n. 74
Inalcik, Halil 336-8
India 86, 298, 416, 429-32, 473, 484
Indiculus luminosus 233, 313, 446
Inferiority, of Christianity 35, 344
Infidels 121, 215, 247, 250, 321, 335, 338, 456, 457, 468
Iniquus Mahometus 169
Injīl vii, ix, x, 134
Innocent III, pope 167
inquiry 6, 14, 36, 38-40, 50, 53-5, 192, 344
interreligious cooperation 36, 38
Iohannes Gabriel Terrolensis 249
Iqtiḍāʾ 509

al-Īrānshahrī 65
Iraq 53, 155, 173, 274, 286-7, 365-7, 371, 374, 378, 379, 381, 383 n. 78, 386, 415, 421, 423
ʿĪsā, *see also* Jesus 8, 127, 128, 148-9, 256, 259, 261, 262
ʿĪsā ibn Nasṭūrus 375
ʿĪsā ibn Sabīh al-Murdār 109
Isaac, Coptic Archbishop 48, 496 n. 31
Isaac, martyr of Cordoba 399-400
Isaac, son of Abraham 212, 215
Isaiah, Book of 74, 77, 83 n. 53, 84, 124, 220, 230
al-Iṣbahānī, Abū l-Shaykh 378
al-Iṣbahānī, Abū l-Faraj 61, 374 n. 42
l-Iṣfahānī, Muḥyī l-Dīn al-ʿAjamī 116
Al-ishāʿa li-ashrāt al-sāʿa 419
Isḥāq ibn Nuṣayr al-ʿIbādī 374
Ishbāniya 307
al-Ishbīlī, Ibn ʿAbdūn 36, 323
Ishmael 37, 79, 208, 333, 343-4, 440, 466
Ishmaelites 77, 81, 100, 155, 263
Ishoʿyab III of Adiabene 36
Ishoʿyahb bar Malkon 191, 202, 497, 497 n. 33
Isidore Glabas 339
Isidore of Seville 230
Islamic Empire(s) viii, 53, 55, 263, 265, 266, 269, 362, 366-8, 420
Islamisation 14, 17, 283, 307, 308, 313, 389, 394, 400, 411
al-Iskandarī, Khaṭīb 201
Iṣlāḥ al-manṭiq 62
Ismāʿīl I, Shah of Persia 250
Ismāʿīlī 37, 40, 41, 60, 61, 212, 213, 378
Israel 78, 131, 212, 215, 500
Israelites / children of Israel 79, 125, 126, 132, 143, 147, 211, 215, 493
Israel of Kashkar 204
Istanbul 70, 340, 354, 356, 358
al-istiḥsān 86-8
Istimalet 15, 331, 338, 339, 357, 358
Istoria de Mahomet 12, 167, 168, 229, 232
ithbāt 186, 208
ithbāt al-nubuwwa 208
ithbāt nubuwwat al-nabī, Kitāb 195
Al-itqān fī ʿulūm al-Qurʾān 275
al-ittiḥād 504
Ivan IV, Grand Prince 483

Jacobite Christians / Christianity, *see also* West Syrians 6, 38, 53, 58, 64, 65, 150, 198, 199, 200, 238, 260, 284
Jacob of Edessa 56, 511-12
Jacques de Vitry 305, 462, 470-1
al-Jaʿfarī 191, 196
Jaffa 148, 299
al-Jāḥiẓ, Abū ʿUthmān 45, 91 n. 86, 130, 195
Jalāl al-Dīn Rūmī 217, 218, 219, 341
Jalāl al-Dīn al-Suyūṭī 46, 275, 419, 428
Al-Jallad, Nader 385 n. 84
Jāmiʿ al-bayān ʿan taʾwīl āy al-Qurʾān 211
Jamieson, Alan G. 444
Al-Jāmiʿ wujūh al-īmān 42, 50, 80, 82, 501, 502, 510
Janissaries 340, 342, 358
al-Jarrāḥ, Mufarrij ibn Daghfal ibn 65
Jaunpuri, Sayyid Muḥammad 432
Jawāb ilā risālat rāhib Faransā ilā l-Muslimīn 327
Al-jawāb al-ṣaḥīḥ li-man baddala dīn al-Masīḥ 69, 133
Jawhar 111, 112, 113, 114
Jeffery, Arthur 275, 276
Jeremiah, book of 74, 220
Jerome, St 230
Jerusalem 12, 65, 67, 70, 78, 86, 92-3, 101, 126, 129, 138, 157, 212, 215, 221, 255-6, 278, 281-2, 285-8, 294-7, 299, 300, 302, 357, 376, 401, 407, 416, 419, 437, 463, 510-12
Jesuit mission / missionary 484, 485
Jesus, *see also* ʿĪsā *and* Christ vii, 17, 27, 35, 38, 46-7, 54, 70, 78, 103, 117, 154, 156, 158, 163-4, 171, 179, 194, 197-202, 208, 212, 214, 218, 220, 222, 224-5, 233, 238, 243, 246, 256, 259, 264, 269-71, 323, 341, 343, 353, 390, 414-15, 417, 424, 496, 503, 504, 511
Jesus, crucifixion *and* death of 2, 13, 41, 44, 60, 76, 82, 86, 89, 92, 147, 156, 168, 198-202, 213, 222, 224, 260-1, 327, 343, 505, 512

Jesus, deity / divinity of vii, ix, 13, 26, 28, 34, 43, 102-4, 107-8, 110, 114, 117, 124-5, 131, 134, 142, 197-8, 200-1, 213, 221, 223-4, 259, 262-3, 327, 337, 356
Jesus, incarnation vii, 2, 34, 43-4, 54, 58, 65, 82, 89, 90, 116, 120, 133, 156, 158, 163, 182, 185-7, 189-90, 193, 197-8, 200-5, 213, 223, 326-7, 355, 505, 512
Jesus, miracles of 45, 202, 266
Jesus, Muslim perceptions of 7-9, 40-1, 58-61, 99-100, 102, 104, 106-8, 121, 123-5, 156, 198, 260-1
Jesus, son of God 89, 100, 105, 108, 220, 233, 262-3
Jesus, son of Mary / ibn Maryam 46, 100, 105, 124-5, 129, 135-7, 141, 144, 148-9, 198, 262, 269
Jew(s) 2, 11, 18, 21, 28, 30, 31, 36, 38, 43, 46-9, 54, 65, 66, 78-9, 105, 118-20, 126, 129, 131, 134, 147-8, 156, 158, 160, 164, 168-9, 174, 181, 184, 186-90, 193-5, 198, 203, 207, 211, 213, 215, 217, 220, 222, 224, 236, 246, 260, 265-6, 270, 286, 312, 318, 323, 325, 329, 343, 354, 362-4, 369-71, 375-9, 382, 384, 386, 395, 417, 421, 429, 432, 449, 454, 464, 475-8, 486, 489, 511
jihad / *jihād* 68, 149, 287, 291, 297, 298, 322, 327, 429, 456, 458, 491
Jimenez de Rada, Rodrigo 240-1
jizya 148, 149, 162, 270, 363, 368, 371, 374, 386, 402
Joachim of Fiore 75 n. 8, 463 n. 14, 470
Joan Marti Figuerola 482
Job of Edessa 42
John I Tzimisces 64
John V Palaiologos 350
John VI Cantacuzenus 333, 334, 349-50
John bar Penkāyē 37
John Cananus 333, 351
John Cinnamus 333
John of Damascus 77, 79, 81, 100-1, 114, 155-6, 158-9, 163, 168, 187, 199, 201, 231-2, 260, 263-4, 266-7, 272, 367, 489-90, 497
John of Gorze 235, 320
John of Liminata 286
John of Phanijōit 405
John of Seville 232
John of St Arnoul 235
John Philoponus 66
John, St (Apostle) 35, 117, 318
John the Baptist 64, 146, 260
Jonah 220
Jordan river 398
Jordan valley 303
Joseph 167, 231
Journey from Buda to Hadrianopolis in 1553 484
Jovaynī, ʿAlāʾ al-Dīn 68
Judah 212, 215
Judaism 18, 27, 42, 77, 78-9, 82, 187, 237, 243, 433
Juhaymān al-ʿUtaybī 425
Juwānnish 318
l-Juwaynī, Abū l-Maʿālī 27, 196, 378
Julian, Count of Ceuta 454

Kaʿb al-Aḥbār 238
Kaʿba 21, 36, 77, 210, 237, 491, 497, 501, 511
Kabbalah, the 252
kafāʾa 396
Kalām 45, 80, 80 n. 37, 84, 108, 219
Kalām fī l-ʿaql wa-l-ʿāqil wa-l-maʿqūl 117
al-Kalbī, Ibn 61
Kasb 193
Al-kashf ʿan mujāwazat hādhihi al-umma al-alf 419
Kaykhusraw II, Sultan 286
Keating, Sandra Toenies xvi, 10, 110-11, 273, 278
Kedar, Benjamin Z. 461, 462, 466, 467 n. 30, 473 n. 62, 474, 486
Kerr, David 277
Khadīja 161, 169, 174, 178
Khalaqa 263
al-Khallāl 372 n. 33, 378
Khan, Jengiz / Ghenghis 332, 330
al-kharāj, Kitāb 49
Khārijites 425
Khatam al-nabiyyīn 189, 327
Khaṭīb al-Iskandarī 201
khawāṣṣ 204
Khayr al-bishar bi-khayr al-bashar 46

al-Khazrajī, Aḥmad ibn ʿAbd al-Ṣamad 327, 457
Khorasan 332
Khwarazm, empire of 296
Khwarāzmshāhs 380
Khumārawayh 374
Khumayni, Ayatullah Ruhullah 429
Khurāsān 377-8, 415-16, 423
al-Kindī 13, 57, 161, 162, 164, 165, 170, 171, 179, 186 n. 17, 190, 204, 232, 238, 257, 265, 267, 268, 269, 270, 272, 273, 275, 276, 277, 278
al-Kindī, ʿAbd al-Masīḥ ibn Isḥāq 57, 157, 183 n. 4, 186 n. 17, 204, 257, 324
al-Kindī, Abū Yūsuf 63, 90 n. 76
Kitāb ʿalā ʿAmmār al-Naṣrānī fī l-radd ʿalā l-Naṣārā 112
Kitāb al-ʿālam 318
Kitāb al-amwāl 320
Kitāb al-burhān 44, 45 n. 125, 80, 112, 498, 504, 508 n. 105
Kitāb al-dīn wa-l-dawla 208
Kitāb al-diyārāt 35, 61, 374 n. 42
Kitāb al-fiṣal fī l-milal wa-l-ahwāʾ wa-l-niḥal 326
Kitāb al-fitan 417
Kitāb Harūshiyūsh 318
Kitāb al-ḥujja fī tathbīt al-nubuwwa 91 n. 86, 195
Kitāb al-ʿibar 211
Kitāb ithbāt nubuwwat al-nabī 195
Kitāb al-kharāj 49
Kitāb al-majālis 88
Kitāb al-malāḥim 418
Kitāb al-manfaʿa 39
Kitāb al-masāʾil wa-l-ajwiba 112
Kitāb miftāḥ al-dīn wa-l-mujādala bayna l-Naṣārā wa-l-Muslimīn min qawl al-anbiyāʾ wa-l-mursalīn wa-l-ʿulamāʾ al-rāshidīn alladhīna qaraʾū l-Anājīl 458
Kitāb al-milal wa-l-niḥal 35
Kitāb miṣbāḥ al-ʿaql 45, 492 n. 10
Kitāb al-muqtabis fī taʾrīkh rijāl al-Andalus 456
Kitāb al-radd ʿalā l-thalāth firaq min al-Naṣārā 58
Kitāb al-ruhbān 62
Kitāb al-shurūḥ 319
Kitāb al-ṣila fī tàrīkh àimmat al-Andalus 456
Kitāb al-tawḥīd 34
Kitāb uṣūl al-dīn 494, 502
Kitāb al-yanābīʿ 37, 61, 213
Kizilbash 357, 430
König, D.G. 445
Koningsveld, Pieter van 244, 318
Konya (Iconium) 332
Kormilitsin, Nifont 32
Köse Mihal 334, 339
Ktābā d-rēsh mellē 79 n. 30, 439, 440, 448
Ktōbō d-maktbōnut zabnē 68, 173, 176
Kūfa 144, 366, 423
kufr 203
Kurds 64, 68, 404

laghw 242
lāhūt 110, 213
Laonicus Chalcocondyles 70, 351
Lamoreaux, John C. 84, 85
Latakia 297
Latin (language & texts) 12, 28-30, 32, 38, 77, 119, 153, 155, 160, 165, 166-8, 169, 170, 193, 204, 227-53, 309-11, 313-14, 316-19, 324, 325, 326, 329, 366, 389, 399, 406-7, 420, 440, 469
Latin Christians / Christianity, *see also* Western 11, 12, 20, 28, 39, 66, 68, 227-9, 279, 287, 374, 386, 461, 476, 483-5
Last Supper 213, 504
Laughable stories 174
Law 24, 44, 50, 132, 167, 169, 178, 218, 230, 234, 269-72, 292, 314, 430, 447, 448, 464, 472 n. 57
Law, Islamic 50, 173, 207, 236-7, 271, 289, 315, 325, 338, 347, 352-3, 358, 359-61, 369, 371-4, 377-9, 382, 384, 392-3, 395-6, 404, 428
Lebanon 54, 221, 293
Le cas de nobles 170
Legend of Sergius Bahira 29, 81, 465
van Lent, Jos 428, 441

Leo III, emperor 26, 131, 267, 275, 401, 490, 498
Leontius of Damascus 56
Letter from the People of Cyprus 69, 133, 176, 259, 277
Letter of ʿUmar II to Leo III 94, 184, 190, 267, 275, 498
Letter on the Incarnation 107
Letter to a Muslim friend 68, 133, 176, 191, 258, 277, 503
Levant, the 69, 297, 376, 390, 407
Lex sive doctrina Mahumeti 170
Liber apologeticus martyrum 229, 233, 446, 447
Liber contra sectam sive hearesim Saracenorum 30
Liber de gentili et tribus sapientibus 246
Liber denudationis sive ostensionis aut patefaciens 30, 241, 325
Liber peregrinationis 244
Life and conduct of our holy father Andrew 420
Life of Cyrus of Ḥarrān 395, 406
Life of Theodore of Edessa 398
Llibre del gentil i dels tres savis 47, 119, 324
Llull, Ramon 12, 47, 119-20, 172-3, 177, 243, 246-7, 305, 324, 462, 477-9, 486
Lisbon 469
Louis VII, king 300
Lowry, Heath 338, 357
Ludovico de Varthema 70
Luther, Martin 74, 250-1

Maʿānī ibn Abī l-Makārim 303
Machumetis Saracenorum principis eiusque successorum vitae, ac doctrina, ipseque Alcoran 251
Mädābbār chronicle, see also *Chronicle of John* 439
madhhab, madhāhib 82, 371
madrasa(s) 378, 379
Madigan, Daniel 3
Maghreb 298, 374, 375, 377, 385
al-Maghribī, Abū l-Qāsim al-Ḥusayn ibn ʿAlī 60
Maḥbūb ibn Qusṭanṭīn al-Manbijī 39, 60
al-Mahdī, the Mahdī 148-9, 414-17, 421-3, 425, 428, 431-3
Mahmud Pasha 340
Mahometis Abdallae filii theologia *dialogo explicata* 251
Mahumet 78, 154, 157, 453
al-majālis, Kitāb 88
Majorca, *see also* Mallorca 119
l-Makārim, Ma ʿānī ibn Abī 303
al-Makīn Jirjis ibn al-ʿAmīd 91 n. 82, 95, 150, 192, 201
Makkīkhā ibn Sulayman al-Qankānī 93, 197
maktbōnut zabnē, Ktōbō d- 68, 173, 176
Malachi, book of 220
al-malāḥim, Kitāb 418
Malaterra, Geoffrey 290
Mālikī(s) 49, 132, 137, 377, 393
Mālik ibn Anas 136, 371
al-Malik al-Kāmil 93, 201, 295, 296, 305, 472, 472 n. 59, 473
al-Malik al-Nāṣir II 295
Mallorca, *see also* Majorca 477, 479
Mamluk(s) 67, 69-70, 281, 297-9, 302, 339, 352, 357, 380-4, 405, 412, 419, 427
al-Maʾmūn 76 n. 15, 398, 423, 424
al-manfaʿa, Kitāb 39
al-Manbijī, Maḥbūb ibn Qusṭanṭīn 39, 60
Manichaeism 82
Manicheans 54
al-Manṣūr 372, 423, 424
Manuel II Palaeologus 350
Mar Ghiwarghis I 56
marriage 56, 174, 178, 214, 232, 325, 335, 347, 352, 491
marriage, interreligious 55, 182, 312, 373, 395 n. 19, 442, 443, 446, 447, 455, 457, 460, 464
Mark of Ephesus 352
Mark of Toledo 240-1, 245
Mark, St (apostle) 222, 224
Maronite Christians / Christianity 6, 54, 304
Maronite chronicle 367
Mār Saba, monastery of 231, 310, 402
Mar Timothy I 199, 200

Martin Luther 74, 75 n. 10, 250, 251
martyr(s), *see also* neomartyrs 17, 31-3, 167, 232-3, 337, 352, 390-1, 393-402, 404-10, 427, 446-7, 451, 462, 469, 474, 493
martyrdom vii, viii, 4, 17-18, 26, 31, 32-3, 197, 233, 320, 337, 372, 389-412, 435, 447, 450-1, 473-5, 478, 486, 491, 510
Martyrdom of Bishop Thiemo 469
Martyrdom of Christopher 64
martyrology 361, 391, 405-6, 462, 483, 485
al-Marwazī, Nuʿaym ibn Ḥammād 417
Maqāmiʿ al-ṣulbān wa-marātiʿ (rawātiʿ) riyāḍ (rawḍat) ahl al-īmān 30, 327, 457
al-masāʾil wa-l-ajwiba, Kitāb 44, 112
al-Masīḥī, Ṣāliḥ ibn Saʿīd 65
Matthew I, Patriarch 346
Matthew of Edessa 285
al-Māturīdīʾ, Abū Manṣūr 34
Mavrozoumis 342, 344
mawālī 366
al-Māwardī, Abū l-Ḥasan 378
mawlā 366, 394
Maximus the Confessor 439-40
Maximus the Greek 483
Maymar fī wujūd al-Khāliq wa-l-dīn al-qawīm 84, 85
Mecca 55, 64, 70, 126, 166, 169, 173-4, 179, 208, 210, 237, 241, 357, 415-16, 431, 432
Medina 70, 126, 179, 211, 357, 363, 415-16, 422
Mehmed II, Ottoman sultan 334, 340, 352-3, 355-6, 358
Melkite Christians /Christianity 6, 10, 39, 43, 53, 56, 58, 60, 62, 64-6, 68, 82, 108, 133, 149-50, 155, 158, 176, 198, 199, 231, 258, 284, 310, 398, 402, 407, 410-11, 489, 490, 498, 501-3, 508
Memoriale sanctorum 233, 446
Mēna of Nikiou 48
Menavino, Giovanni Antonio 70
Mesih Pasha 340
Messiah, the 78, 105, 124, 125, 129, 197, 198, 224, 257, 259, 260, 262, 263, 264, 269, 270, 272, 501
Messianism, Islamic 18, 421, 422, 424, 430, 432
Mesopotamia 53, 158, 166, 228, 381, 389, 390, 391
Miaphysite 42, 53, 198, 363, 390
Michael VIII Palaeologus 332, 334
Michael of Damietta 464
Michael Psellus 333
Michael the New 405
Michael the Syrian 67
Michel, Thomas F. 216
Middle East viii, 54, 58, 64, 67, 70, 99, 102, 104, 109, 121, 221, 278, 282, 286-7, 296-8, 300, 303, 306, 339, 381, 389-92, 395, 403, 407, 410-12, 419, 429, 435, 437, 445, 448, 460, 486
Midianites 440
Midrashim 243
miftāḥ al-dīn wa-l-mujādala bayna l-Naṣārā wa-l-Muslimīn min qawl al-anbiyāʾ wa-l-mursalīn wa-l-ʿulamāʾ al-rāshidīn alladhīna qaraʾū l-Anājīl, Kitāb 458
Migetius 312
miḥrāb 481
mīlād 323
al-milal wa-l-niḥal, Kitāb 35
millet system 69, 354
Mīnā Bajūsh 373
Mingana, Alphonse 275
Mirakʿ Tawrizecʿi 404
miṣbāḥ al-ʿaql, Kitāb 45, 492 n. 10
al-Miṣrī, Abū l-Ḥusayn 40
mission 20, 46-7, 81, 87, 139-40, 164, 177, 193, 208, 211-12, 225, 229, 320, 327, 392
missions, evangelistic 305, 312
missions, Jesuit 484-5
mission to Muslims 20, 41, 47, 118-19, 176, 461-487
Missionaries 47, 118-19, 173, 305, 461, 477
Mithāl 505
monasteries 35, 61-2, 93, 170, 310, 341, 348-9, 352, 365, 382, 407, 458, 465 n. 20, 484
Monastery, of Akapnios 345-6
Monastery, of Bēt Ḥālē 100

Monastery, at Cluny 30
Monastery, of Mār Saba 231, 310, 402
Monastery, of Mt Athos 348-9
Monastery, of St Catherine 310, 407
Monastery, of St John Prodomos 348, 356
Monastery, of St Symeon 94
Monastery, of Tabanos 399
Monastery, of the Holy Cross 407
Monferrer Sala, Juan Pedro xvi, 14, 385, 446-7, 456
Mongol(s) 67-8, 221, 286, 296-7, 304, 305, 332, 351, 352, 380-2, 403, 418, 419, 424, 430, 476, 486
Monophysite 199, 439
monotheism x, 7, 35, 37, 38, 79, 82, 89, 101, 120, 176, 196, 237, 439, 489, 493, 490
Monotheist(s) 25, 79, 189, 293
Moriscos 14, 46, 307, 328, 481-3, 509
Morocco 173, 429, 430, 474
Morris, James Harry xvii, 18-19
Morton, Nicholas xvii, 13-14, 386
Motzki, H 275
Moses, *see also* Mūsā 79, 126, 128, 131, 132, 136, 137, 141, 208, 211-12, 215, 231, 266, 270, 493, 494
Moses bar Kephā 37, 61
Mozambique 473, 485
Mozarabs 309
Muʿāwiya 367, 425, 426, 427
al-Mu'ayyad bi-llāh 195
Mufarrij ibn Daghfal ibn al-Jarrāḥ 65
Mughals 387, 429, 430
Muḥammad I, Ummayad emir 316, 372, 372 n. 35
Muḥammad Aḥmad al-Mahdī 429
Muḥammad al-Amīn 423
Muḥammad ibn al-Ḥanafiyya 421
Muḥammad al-Nafs al-Zakiyya 416, 422, 424
Muḥammad al-Qaḥṭānī 425
Muḥammad, Prophet vii, ix, xi, 8, 28, 35, 47, 55, 59, 67, 73, 75-6, 77, 83, 91, 100, 123, 125, 126, 127, 128, 130, 134, 136, 148, 181-2, 183, 186, 187, 188-90, 193-6, 198, 203, 205, 207-9, 211, 218, 219, 223, 224, 228, 250, 258, 263, 275, 337, 350, 353, 357, 364, 369, 391-2, 397, 398, 413-16, 419, 421-5, 430-1, 435-6, 458, 465, 476, 484, 493
Muḥammad, biographies of 54, 57, 66, 232
Muḥammad, Christian perceptions of 9, 10, 26, 28-30, 33, 37-9, 78, 82, 120-1, 153-179, 194, 229-34, 238, 240-5, 250, 252, 258, 264-71, 277, 320-1, 324-5, 327-8, 356, 363-4, 399, 446, 448
Muḥammad, mission of 193, 208, 211-12, 225, 327
Muḥammad, prophethood of 2, 41, 45-6, 131-2, 135, 194-5, 197, 208, 220, 269, 273, 277, 327, 343, 356, 363, 433
Muḥyī l-Dīn al-ʿAjamī l-Iṣfahānī 116
Muir, William 165
al-Muʿizz 375
mujaddid 428
mulūk al-ṭawāʾif 376
al-Mu'min x, 150, 323
Munāzara fī l-radd ʿalā l-Naṣārā 195
Murad I 339, 348, 350
Murad II 351
Muqadimma 211
al-Muqaffaʿ, Sāwīrus ibn 45, 200, 492 n. 10
al-muqtabis fī ta'rīkh rijāl al-Andalus, Kitāb 456
al-Muqtadir 372, 372 n. 35
al-Murdār, ʿĪsā ibn Sabīh 109
Mūsā, *see also* Moses 127
Mūsā al-Hādī 423
Mūsā ibn Nuṣayr 307, 443
Muṣaḥaba rūḥāniyya 484
musālima 308
muṣḥaf 191
Muṣḥaf al-ʿālam al-kā'in 326
Mushrif 316
mushrikūn 263, 353
Muslim ibn al-Ḥajjāj 416
mutakallim, mutakallimūn 80, 109, 111, 114, 186, 326
mutawaffīka 261
al-Mutawakkil 372, 424, 495, 496
Muʿtazila 53, 309
muwalladūn 308, 313

Muzāḥim 396
mystic(s) 146, 216, 217, 380
mysticism, Christian 342
mysticism, Islamic 127, 143, 146

Nablus 281, 302
al-Nafs al-Zakiyya, Muḥammad 416, 422, 424
Najrān 154, 363, 364-5, 370
Narrationes 504
al-Naṣārā 362
al-Nāshi' al-Akbar 34, 58, 106, 204
Naṣr ibn Yaḥyā 202, 501
al-nāsūt 213
nāsūtuhu 213
Nayrūz 323
Nazareth 117, 281
Naẓm al-durar fī tanāsub al-āyāt wa-l-suwar 221
Near East 14, 283, 300, 308, 316, 364, 465 n. 20, 474
Negev, the 128
neomartyrs 337, 390, 392, 401, 405
Nēphōn, St 50
Nestorius 150, 169
Nestorian Christians / Christianity, *see also* East Syrians 6, 31, 53, 58, 116, 150, 157, 161, 162, 164, 192, 198, 199, 200, 204, 260, 311, 505
Netton, Ian 213
New Testament 27, 38, 59, 60, 77, 118, 124, 126, 129, 132, 151, 155, 194, 207, 212, 213, 217, 222, 231, 234, 243, 253, 503, 504, 507
Nicaea 332, 334, 343, 345
Nicea, Council of 312
Nicene Creed 158, 500
Nicephorus Gregoras 333, 335
Nicephorus of Constantinople 234
Nicephorus Phocas 64
Nicetas of Byzantium 77
Nicholas of Cusa 81, 120, 177, 239, 245, 247, 249-52, 479, 480, 486, 502
Nickel, Gordon xvii, 12-13
Nicolaites, the 234
Night Journey, the 136, 172, 178
Nikon Metanoeite 467
Nile Delta, the 285, 298, 305, 396
Niẓām al-Mulk 377, 378
Nizārīs, *see also* assassins 304
Nonnus of Nisibis 42
Normans, the 50
North Africa, *see also Ifrīqiya* viii, 119, 211, 221, 310, 375, 385, 389, 390, 393, 435, 437, 443, 478, 479, 483
Notitia de Machometo 246
Nuʿaym ibn Ḥammād al-Marwazī 417, 420
nuhrā 493
Nūr al-Dīn 287, 291, 292, 298, 300
Nuzūl ʿĪsā ibn Maryam ākhir al-zamān 46

O'Callaghan, Joseph F. 468, 469
Odo of Deuil 300
Old Testament 38, 59, 69, 77, 79, 80, 83, 118, 155, 201, 208, 220, 231, 234, 243, 253, 490, 493
Oliver of Paderborn 470-2, 486
On the divine images 201
On the regimen for the pilgrimage 64
Orations against the calumniators of the icons 489
Orhan, Sultan 334, 335, 341, 343, 350
Orosius, Paulus 212, 318
Osman 333-5, 337, 338, 339, 341
Osman tribal group 332-4
Otia de Machomete 169
Otto I, king 320, 321
Otto IV, Holy Roman Emperor 282
Ottomans 4, 15, 50, 69-70, 74, 223, 250, 331-58, 384, 387, 429-30, 479, 483-4

Pact of ʿUmar viii, 49, 371, 382, 432
pagan(s) 17, 21, 30, 32, 33, 78, 81, 118, 126, 192, 203, 235, 246-7, 288-9, 320, 390, 391, 398, 425, 450, 453, 465, 470, 483, 486, 489, 499
Paganism 29, 42, 157, 192, 231, 252, 263, 289, 325, 390
Palacios, Miguel Asín 143
Palestine 29, 55, 66, 160, 174, 201, 245, 363, 407, 408
Papademetriou, Tom xviii, 15

Paraclete 83 n. 53, 194, 208, 223
paradise 30, 135, 147, 160, 164, 173, 175, 178, 210, 217, 233, 234, 237, 248, 253, 353, 446, 511
Patriarchal Synod 344-6
Paul, St (apostle) ix, 45, 77, 109, 129, 133, 149-51, 190, 236, 508, 511
Paulicians 286
Paul of Antioch 68, 133, 176-7, 179, 191, 258-9, 277, 503
Paul of Sidon 258
Pedro de Alcala 481
Pedro Guerra de Lorca 482
Pedro Ramirez de Alba 481
Pēgē gnōseōs 81, 100, 231
Pelagius 32, 320, 450-1
Penelas, Mayte 318
Penn, Michael Philip 96, 442
Pentateuch 311
de Penyafort, Ramon 118, 480
People of the Book, *see also ahl al-kitāb* 24, 129, 147, 189, 255, 270, 308, 353, 363, 395
peregrinationis, Liber 244
Perez de Chinchon, Bernando 481-2
Perfectus 233, 399
Peri haeresiōn 155, 260, 263
Peri tēs monēs hodou pros tēn sōtērian tōn *anthrōpōn* 355
persecution, of Christians 16, 32, 64, 67, 222, 355, 360, 381, 390, 411, 439, 449-51
Persia 55, 163, 175, 357, 424, 470
Persian (language) 66, 339, 366, 389
Persians 88, 210, 211, 213, 283, 357, 367, 423
Peter of Bayt Ra 80
Peter of Capitolias 400, 407-8
Peter of Cluny, *see also* Peter the Venerable 30, 165, 170, 173, 177, 325, 462, 466, 469
Peter of Poitiers 239, 240, 325
Peter of Toledo 165, 238, 239, 325
Peter, Simon, St (apostle) 105, 109, 140, 236, 508
Peter the Chanter 470
Peter the Venerable, *see also* Peter of Cluny 12, 30, 81, 234, 235, 238, 240, 243, 251, 289, 304
Petrus Alfonsi 12, 236-8, 240, 243, 325, 471
Pfaffe Konrad 469
philosophy 6, 41, 47, 60, 62, 63, 68, 106, 192, 198, 200, 204, 252
Pickthall, M. 261, 263
piety 21, 28, 155, 218, 291, 362, 382, 396
pilgrim(s) 70, 143, 146, 237, 282, 292, 293, 300, 401
Pilgrimage(s) 17, 33, 70, 157, 210, 219, 237, 325, 352, 390, 432, 469, 491
Pius II, pope 120
Platti, E. 116, 117, 268, 269, 270, 278
Pococke, Edward 175
polemic(s) 1-2, 6, 12, 14, 18, 23, 25-6, 28, 29, 36, 42, 51, 57, 66, 71, 77, 81, 141, 165, 186, 219, 223, 232, 239, 240, 241, 249, 253, 264-5, 278, 306, 324-5, 344, 413, 415, 462, 465, 478, 491, 511
Polemic(s), anti-Christian 34, 45, 65, 115, 128, 132, 134, 264-5, 458, 503
polemic(s), anti-Muslim 29-30, 174, 186 n. 17, 228, 231-2, 238, 248-9, 276, 325, 446, 448, 450, 454, 466
polemicist(s) ix, 11, 121, 130, 189, 207, 234, 245, 250, 321, 324-6
politics 10, 63, 68, 298, 403, 442
polity 10, 48, 357
polygamy 327, 458
polytheism xi, 121, 163, 202
Portugal 308, 468
Postel, Guillaume 250, 251, 252
Powers, David 268
Pratt, Douglas xviii
prayer 21, 44, 65, 70, 105, 132, 133, 142, 149, 182, 187, 224, 237, 352, 464, 478, 491, 500, 501, 504, 509-12
predestination 37, 312
de Premare, Alfred-Louis 275
Prester John 420
Proofs of prophethood 26, 45-6, 102, 193-7, 209
prophecy 13, 30, 76, 80 n. 37, 83, 171, 197, 201

Prophet, *see also* Muḥammad ix, 16, 29, 73, 126, 135-6, 138, 154, 175, 179, 194, 208-9, 211-12, 218, 219-20, 223, 224, 225, 228, 231, 237-41, 253, 268-9, 288, 320, 324, 325, 353, 357, 362-4, 366, 369-70, 392, 397, 399, 400, 413, 416, 419, 421-2, 424-5, 430, 435-6, 438
prophets 8, 39, 54, 79, 103, 123, 125, 127, 128, 130, 132, 135, 137, 140-1, 160, 162-3, 176, 178, 188, 189, 194-5, 197, 209, 214-15, 218, 220, 222, 231, 237, 260, 277, 427, 432, 438, 461, 512
Protestantism 250, 252
Psalms, book of 28, 79, 209, 315, 317, 318
punishment 26, 31, 33, 74, 125, 161, 337, 351, 392, 439, 448, 452, 496
Pyrenees 308

qāḍī(s) 369, 373, 399, 404
Qaḥṭānī 424, 425, 428
al-Qaḥṭānī, Muḥammad 425
Qā'id ghilmān al'-ajam 316
Qā'im 416
al-Qankānī, Makkīkhā ibn Sulayman 93, 197
Al-Qanūn al-muqaddas 315
al-Qarāfī, Shihāb al-Dīn 132, 133, 133 n. 34, 277, 503, 503 n. 72, 503 n. 73
al-Qāsim ibn Ibrāhīm 104, 105, 130, 190
al-Qaysī 458
Qibla / *qibla* 499-502, 511-12
qiyas 203, 204
Queen T'amar 48
Qur'an, the vii, ix, 6-8, 11-13, 18, 21, 26, 45, 54, 57-9, 68, 81-3, 91, 99-101, 104-5, 119, 121, 123-7, 130, 133, 138, 140, 143, 145, 147-8, 156, 159, 165, 170-2, 177, 179, 181, 185-91, 194-5, 198, 202-3, 207, 219-21, 227-53, 255-79, 310, 326-7, 362, 392, 413-14, 484, 491, 500
Quraysh 398, 425
qurbān 502, 503
al-Qurṭubī, al-Imām 326, 327, 418, 503 n. 74
Qūs 219
al-Qūṭī, Ḥafṣ ibn Albar 503 n. 74, 315, 317, 318

Rabī' ibn Tudulf 316
Rabā' ibn Zayd 376
Radbertus, Pascasius 234
Radd 'alā l-Naṣārā 89 n. 75, 105, 130
Radd 'alā l-tathlīth 113
al-radd 'alā l-thalāth firaq min al-Naṣārā, Kitāb 58
Al-radd al-jamīl li-ilāhiyyat 'Īsā bi-ṣarīḥ al-Injīl 41, 117
râhib-i Müslim 223
rajaz mashṭūr 317
Ramon Llull 12, 47, 119-20, 172-3, 177, 243, 246-7, 305, 324, 462, 477-9, 486
Ramon Marti 242
Rasā'il Ikhwān al-Ṣafā' wa-khillān al-wafā' 212
al-Rashīd, Hārūn 76 n. 15, 104, 131, 370, 372, 397, 423
Rashidūn 435
Raymond of Aguilers 285
Raymundus de Moncada, Guillelmus 249
al-Rāzī, Abū Ḥātim 40, 60
al-Rāzī, Aḥmad 322, 454
al-Rāzī, Fakhr al-Dīn 68, 94 n. 103, 195, 261
Reconquista 20, 78, 352, 418, 435, 443-4, 447, 449, 451, 453, 456-9, 467, 477, 486
refutation, of Christianity 11, 26, 34-5, 40, 58, 102, 104-7, 109, 112-17, 130-1, 133, 191, 193, 196, 201-2, 205, 207, 277, 326-7, 458, 503
refutation, of Islam 26, 31, 44-5, 65, 68, 116, 188, 237, 239-41, 244-5, 247, 252-3, 469
relics 44, 351, 352, 491
religious diversity 7, 10, 13, 282, 310, 311, 312, 478, 479
rēsh mellē, Ktābā d- 79 n. 30, 439, 440, 448
Resurrection, Church of the 93
Resurrection, Day of 126, 147, 149, 198

Resurrection of Jesus Christ 163, 198, 213, 260, 261, 355, 505, 507
Resurrection of the dead 143, 175, 309, 327
revelation ix, 11, 25, 28, 35, 44, 54, 60, 104, 119, 121, 134, 137, 156-7, 160-2, 168-9, 181, 188-9, 193-4, 205, 209, 216, 232, 241-2, 418
Revelation, book of 75, 148, 167
Revelatio S. Methodii de temporibus nouissimis 311
Reynolds, Gabriel Said xviii, 8, 102
ribāṭ 456
Riccoldo da Monte di Croce 238-9, 241-4, 350, 476
Richard I, king 295, 301
Ridda Wars 391
Rippin, Andrew 272, 273, 276
Risāla ilā baʿḍ aṣdiqāʾihi alladhīna bi-Ṣaydā min al-Muslimīn 68, 258
Risāla fī l-firaq al-mutaʿārifa min al-Naṣārā 108
Risāla fī l-qaḍāʾwa-l-ḥisba 323
Risāla of al-Kindī, *Risālat al-Kindī* 13, 238, 241, 257, 325
Risāla min ahl jazīrat Qubruṣ 69, 259
Al-risāla l-nāṣiriyya 42
Risālat al-Qūṭī 327
Ritual of abjuration 77, 466
Robert of Ketton 12, 28, 30, 165, 170, 179, 238-40, 247-9, 251
Robinson, Chase 275
Roger I of Tosny 449
Roger II of Sicily 50
Roger Bacon 475
Roggema, Barbara 100
Roman Empire 6, 17, 77, 175, 354, 390, 415
Romanus 402, 407, 410
Romanus IV Diogenes 332
Rome 175, 304, 350, 352, 363, 390
Rosenthal, Franz 210
al-ruhbān, Kitāb 62
Ruderic, Visigothic king 308, 443, 456
Rūm 286, 332, 411
Rum, Sultanate of 286, 332, 411
Rūmī, Jalāl al-Dīn 217-19, 341
Russia 483
Sabbath 126, 132
Sa'd al-Dīn Masʿ ūd al-Ḥārithī l-Baghdādī 219
Saʿdid(s) 429, 430
Safavid(s) 357, 358, 378, 429, 430, 483
al-Saffāḥ, Abū l-ʿAbbās 423
ṣāḥb al-zamān 431
ṣāḥib al-mukūs 316
Sahner, Christian xviii, 17
Safavid Empire 357-8, 387, 429-30, 483
Sagax, Landolfus 234
Ṣāʿid al-Andalusī 376
Saʿīd ibn Sulaymān al-Ghāfiqī 399
ṣāʾifa 373
Ṣalāḥ al-Dīn / Saladin 290-2, 295, 298-302, 304
Salaka fī sabīl al-anbiyāʾ 277
ṣalāt 481, 492 n. 10
ṣalīb 502
Ṣalībā ibn Yūḥannā 93
Ṣāliḥ ibn Saʿīd al-Masīḥī 65
Ṣallā Allāhu ʿalayhiʾ 269
Salvation 54, 163, 175, 177, 199, 201, 345, 351, 355, 452, 467, 500, 504
Samaritans 286
Samir, Samir Khalil 271, 277, 278
Samuel, bishop of Elvira 309
Sancho García 452
Saracen(s) 30-2, 38, 78-9, 120, 155, 157-8, 167, 169, 171, 228, 234, 241, 246-7, 288-9, 325, 360, 437-8, 448, 461, 463, 467, 472-4, 486-7
Saragossa 78, 453
Sasanian 55, 271, 367, 390, 411, 415
Satan 138, 141-2, 145, 164-5, 178, 220, 269-70, 484, 508
Sāwīrus ibn al-Muqaffaʿ 45, 200, 492 n. 10
Sayf al-Dawla 64, 402
Al-sayf al-murhaf fī-l-radd ʿalā-l-Muṣḥaf 244
scriptures, Christian, *see also* Bible 28, 60, 69, 155-6, 182, 194, 231, 253, 484
scriptures, general 36, 59, 65, 79, 101, 189-90, 215, 217, 229, 265
scriptures, Muslim, *see also* Qur'an 60, 476, 495

Sefardi, Moses 236-7
de Segovia, Juan 177-9, 239, 247-50, 479-81, 486, 502
Selim I, Ottoman sultan 69, 70, 357, 384
Selim II, Ottoman sultan 349
Seljuqs 377-9
Sens, archbishop 312
Sergius Baḥīrā 29, 81, 157, 164, 238, 465
Serres 348-9, 356
Seville 230, 232, 323, 474, 480
al-Shābushtī, Abū l-Ḥasan 35, 62
Shāfiʿī 27, 371, 428
al-Shāfiʿī 378
al-Shahrastānī, Abū al-Fatḥ 35, 65, 137, 138, 139 n. 64, 196
Shaizar 281-2, 284
Sharḥ al-asmāʾ al-ḥusnā 216
sharīʿa 82, 95, 96, 224, 349
Sharīk 128, 263
Shaybānid(s) 429, 430
shaykh(s) 223, 224, 225, 484
Shaykh, The 223-5
Shīʿa / Shīʿi 18, 66, 191, 284-5, 304, 309, 357, 370, 374, 377, 384, 413, 415-16, 421-6, 429-30, 432, 509
Shihāb al-Dīn al-Qarāfī 132, 133, 277, 503
shirk 125, 127, 156, 203
Shīrkūh 300, 304
Shoemaker, S. 275
shubbiha 147, 198
shubh 214
al-shurūḥ, Kitāb 319
Sicily 50, 385, 386, 466, 468
al-Ṣiddīq, Abū Bakr 364
Siddiqui, M. 1
Sidon 68, 108, 176, 258, 297
Sierra Leone 485
ṣifāt, ṣifātih 111, 112, 113, 116, 150, 203, 205
al-Sijistānī, Abū Dāʾūd 428
al-Sijistānī, Abū Sulaymān 63
al-Sijistānī, Abū Yaʿqūb 37, 61, 213, 214
al-ṣila fī taʾrīkh aʾimmat al-Andalus, Kitāb 456
sin, Christian (as cause of Muslim victory) 26, 31, 125, 438-9, 440, 452, 460
Sinai, Mt 208
Sinai, Nicolai 275
al-sīra l-nabawiyya 135 n. 49
Sirāj al-mulūk 379
Sirhindi, Ahmad 428
Sixty Martyrs of Gaza 401, 406
Sixty Martyrs of Jerusalem 401
siyar 220
Siyāsat nāmah 378
slavery 315, 342, 353, 393-4, 405
ṣlibā 502
Smith, Henry 170
Smyrna 405
Sobre la seta Mahometana 320
Sophronius 401, 437-9, 441, 463
soteriology 43, 45, 197-202
Southern, R.W. 78
Spain 118, 166-8, 322, 386, 418, 444-5, 448-50, 452-3, 464, 468, 470, 473, 476, 480, 482-3, 509
Spanish (language) 119, 248, 249
Spandounes, Theodore 334
Sparta 467
Sprenger, Aloys 161, 172
St Catherine's Monastery 310, 407
St Demetrius 351
Stephen Manṣūr 402
St Mary the Virgin, Church of 282
al-Subkī, Tāqī l-Dīn 393
Sufi(s), Sufism 127, 143, 143 n. 84, 216, 217, 219, 223, 225, 304, 341, 357, 378, 379, 382, 384, 428, 430
Sufyānī(s) 416, 424, 425, 426, 427, 428, 432
Sulaymān ibn ʿAbd al-Malik 401
Süleyman (the Magnificent), Ottoman sultan 250, 358, 430
Summa contra gentiles 118
Summa totius haeresis Saracenorum 30, 81
Sunna 46, 271, 326
Sunnī Islam 18, 291, 304, 341, 357-8, 376, 413-16, 422, 428, 432
Sunnī Muslims 66, 68, 284, 304, 375-9, 418, 424, 430, 509
superiority, of Islam 41-2, 46-7, 130, 188-193, 344
sūra(s) 11, 124, 125, 126, 242, 249 n. 98, 272, 275, 500

al-Suyūṭī, Jalāl al-Dīn 46, 275, 419, 428
Swanson, Mark N. xix, 7
Syria 16, 55-6, 64, 66-7, 69, 154-5, 201, 228, 284, 287, 291, 296, 297, 304, 357, 367, 374-5, 379-84, 386, 389, 391, 393, 403, 412, 415, 417-18, 420, 423, 425-7, 437
Syriac / Syrian 13, 29-31, 36, 42-3, 59, 62, 76, 79, 81, 100, 113, 127, 161, 184, 208, 231, 244, 257, 311, 365-8, 389, 395, 397, 407, 420, 426, 440, 463, 465, 492, 494, 502, 507
Syrian(s) 6, 30, 32, 36, 37, 40, 42-3, 53, 58, 61, 64, 66-8, 87-8, 96, 107, 109, 116, 149-50, 173, 175, 192, 198, 199, 200, 204, 287, 364, 383, 394, 411, 417, 420, 425-6, 442, 464, 494, 496-9, 504-6
Szilagyi, Krisztina 101

Ṭabaqāt al-umam 376
al-Ṭabarī, Abū l-Ḥasan ʿAlī ibn Sahl Rabbān 11, 59, 84 n. 53, 89 n. 75, 91, 105, 106, 131, 208, 209, 216, 225, 499
al-Ṭabarī, Abū Jaʿfar Muḥammad ibn Jarīr 130, 131, 147, 209, 210, 211, 212, 216, 267
ṭabīʿāt al-mumkin 193
Tabriz 404
Al-tadhkira fī aḥwāl al-mawtā wa-l-umūr al-ākhira 418
taḥaddī 272
taḥrīf 11, 131, 188, 189, 190, 191, 194, 203, 207, 211, 215 n. 43, 216, 217, 225, 325, 326, 327, 484
taḥrīf al-lafẓ 216
taḥrīf al-maʿnā 216
ṭāʾifa 443
Takawi, Mourad xix, 8
Al-taʿlīq ʿalā l-anājīl al-arbaʿa wa-l-taʿlīq ʿalā l-Tawrāh waʾlā ghayrihā min kutub al-anbiyāʾ 219
Talmud 243
Tamerlane, *see also* Timur *and* Timur-I Leng 351-2, 381
Tanbīh al-afhām ilā tadabbur al-kitāb al-ḥakīm wa-taʿarruf al-āyāt wa-l-nabaʾ al-ʿaẓīm 216
Tancred 281
Tāqī l-Dīn al-Subkī 393
Tārīkh 209, 210
Taʾrīkh iftitāḥ al-Andalus 455
Al-taʾrīkh al-kabīr 456
Tārīkh al-rusul wa-l-mulūk 210
Ṭāriq ibn Ziyād 307
Taronites 343-4
Tarṣīʿ al-akhbār wa-tanwīʿ al-āthār wa-l-bustān fī gharāʾib al-buldān wa-l-masālik ilā jamīʿ al-mamālik 455
Tartus 282
tashabbuh 509
tashbīh 115
Tashʿītā awkīt neṣḥānē d-qaddīshā mār(i) tʾwdwṭʾ epīsqupā d-āmīd mdī(n)tā 442
Tathbīt dalāʾil al-nubuwwa 102, 132
Tathbīt nubuwwat Muḥammad 195
Tathlīth 110, 150, 203 n. 87
Tathlīth al-waḥdāniyya 317, 326
tawaffā 261
tawātur 190
tawḥīd 110, 113, 189, 193, 500
al-tawḥīd, Kitāb 34
Tawrāt vii, ix, 79
Tax / Taxation 49, 56, 64, 140, 160, 162, 237, 293, 295, 308, 316, 333, 336, 347-8, 354, 366-8, 371-3, 382, 391, 395, 399, 411, 440, 450, 455
Tax farming 346-7, 355
tayammum 491
Temple Mount 128, 255, 278
Testimonies of the prophets about the Dispensation of Christ 43, 511
Teule, Herman G.B. 116
Tervagant 78, 453
textual corruption 11, 35, 214, 216
The apology of Timothy the Patriarch 161
The gentile and the three wise men 47, 119, 324, 478
The martyrdom of Anthony 446
The panegyric of the three holy children of Babylon 438
The prophetic chronicle 448
Theodore Abu Qurra 43, 80, 84-9, 92, 94-5, 109, 158-60, 165, 185, 194, 196, 199, 465, 489-90, 504
Theodore bar Kōnī 8

Theodore Metochites 405
Theodore of Mopsuestia 505-6
Theodore Spandounes 334
Theodore the Studite 497
Theodore of Edessa, St 398, 408
Theodosius I, Patriarch 496-7
Theoleptos, Patriarch 358
theology 3, 34, 37-8, 45, 53, 62, 68-9, 108-9, 124, 159, 188, 192, 196, 204-5, 216, 219, 250, 252, 311, 320, 326, 374, 493, 504
Theophanes of Nicae 344
Theophanes the Confessor 56, 131, 160-2, 234
Theosophy 213
Theotokos 495, 498
Thessaloniki 31, 49, 339, 342, 351
Thomas Aquinas, St 118-19, 163, 476
Thomas, David vi-xi, xiii, 115, 176, 277
Thomas of Chantom 474
Thomas, St (apostle) 86
Tibet 461
Tieszen, Charles xiii, xix, 1-22, 51
Timar 336, 338-9
Timariots 15, 331, 336-9
Timothy I, Catholicos 58, 79, 161, 184, 192, 199-200, 260, 272, 276, 462, 465
Timur-i Leng, *see also* Tamerlane *and* Timur 351-2, 381
Timurid 334, 381, 383-4
Tolan, John 119, 250, 465, 471
Toledo 308, 318, 319, 327, 468
Toledot Yeshu 168
tolerance 14, 24, 47, 48, 67, 246, 306
Torah vii, ix, 44, 137, 200, 210-11, 214-15, 217, 219, 264-6, 269, 503
Tou hagiou Basileiou peri tou Pneumatos biblion 490
Tractatus seu disputatio contra Saracenos et Alchoranum 244
trade 13, 29, 49, 55, 69, 154, 282, 298-9, 383, 385, 408, 460
Transjordan 400
travelogues vii
Travels of John Mandeville 161, 172
Treatise on the foundations of the religion 193
Treatise on the veneration of holy icons 489, 490
Trinity, the vii, 7-8, 30, 34, 43-5, 58, 63, 65, 81, 84, 89-90, 99-104, 107-21, 150, 154, 156-8, 163, 173, 182, 186-7, 189-93, 197, 201-5, 262, 311, 326-7, 493
Tripoli 12, 286, 474
True Religion Apology 7, 84-91, 93-6
al-Ṭūfī, Najm al-Dīn Sulaymān 69, 191, 219, 220, 221
Tughtakin of Damascus 287
Tunis 118, 173, 243, 478-9
Tunisia 173
Turkic 283, 284, 342, 374, 375, 378, 379, 380, 381, 383, 384
Turkmen 297, 331-5, 340-2, 344-6, 349, 381, 403
Turks, the 31, 64, 67-8, 70, 74, 88, 157, 178, 247, 250-2, 283-8, 290-2, 302, 304, 333-4, 350-2, 356, 377, 405, 416, 430
al-Ṭurṭūshī 379
al-Ṭūsī, Nāṣir al-Dīn 68
Twenty Martyrs of Mar Saba 402, 406
Twomey, M.W. 441

Ubayy ibn Kaʿb 274
al-ʿUdhrī 455
ʿulamāʾ 369, 372, 376, 377, 384, 385
ʿUmar, ʿUmar ibn al-Khaṭṭāb viii, 255, 274, 364, 370, 437, 499 n. 45
ʿUmar II viii, 26, 131, 148, 184, 255, 267, 275, 364, 368-70, 428, 437, 498
Umayyad(s) 16, 55-7, 128-9, 131, 182, 184, 231, 255, 260, 308, 316, 321, 362, 366-9, 374-6, 394, 398-9, 403, 410, 421, 423, 426, 435
Umm al-Ḥakam 373
ʿummī 264
Umur Pasha 349
Urban II, pope 468
Urjūza 315, 315 n. 40
Usāma ibn Munqidh 66, 292, 293, 301
Usṭāth al-Rāhib 202
uṣūl al-dīn, Kitāb 494, 502

al-ʿUtaybī, Juhaymān 425
ʿUthmān 172, 274, 425, 427

vājib al-vujūd 223
Valencia 474-5, 480-1
Venice 299
Virgin Mary, the 231, 251
Visigoths 308, 311
Vita Eulogii 446
Vita Mahometi 169
Vryonis, Speros 340

Wāfih 364
wajh, wujūh 109, 110
al-Walīd 231, 400
Walter the Chancellor 67, 284
Wansbrough, John 268, 275
Wāqih 364
al-Warrāq, Abū ʿĪsā Muḥammad ibn Hārūn 58, 113, 115, 116, 130, 193
wāsiṭa 375
al-Wāṣitī, Abū ʿAbd Allāh 46
Watt, William Montgomery 25
West Africa 4, 473
West Syrians, *see also* Jacobite Christians / Christianity 53, 150, 411
West, the xii, 3, 4, 12-13, 20, 32-3, 39, 66, 70, 78, 99, 118, 228-31, 234, 236, 281, 292, 298-9, 301, 304, 311, 320, 332, 351, 357, 387, 414, 436, 462, 485-6, 510-11
Western Christians / Christianity, *see also* Latin 11, 12, 20, 28, 39, 66, 68, 227-9, 279, 287, 374, 386, 461, 476, 483-5
Widmanstetter, Johann Albrecht von 250-2
Wilbrand of Oldenburg 282
Wilde, Clare 278
William of Malmesbury 31, 37-8, 67, 157, 289
William of Rubroeck / Robruck 473
William of Tripoli 12, 171, 246, 476
William of Tyre 39, 67, 165, 288, 292, 471
Wittek, Paul 338
Witiza, Visigoth King 443
Wolf, Ann Marie 480
Wolf, Kenneth B. 166, 446, 459
Word of God, the 100, 102-3, 117, 132, 145, 171, 233, 243, 264-5, 268, 473, 505
Worship 36, 38, 42, 44, 55, 66, 68, 77, 78, 94, 105, 141-2, 157, 167, 174, 175, 188 n. 21, 203, 220, 308, 453, 466 n. 29, 485, 489-91, 493-5, 498-503, 508, 512
wrath, of God 74, 76
wuḍūʾ 491

Xlatʿecʿi Yovhannēs 404

Yaḥyā ibn ʿAdī 38, 63, 90, 116, 117, 118, 192, 204
Yaḥyā ibn Jarīr 201
Yaḥyā ibn Saʿīd al-Anṭākī 64
Yannayir 323
Yarbrough, Luke xix, 16
al-Yaʿqūbī, Abū l-ʿAbbās 40, 59, 129, 130, 209, 210
Yazīd, caliph 425-6
Yazīd II, caliph 368
Yemen 363, 424, 425
Yemenī(s) 425, 426
al-yanābīʿ, Kitāb 37, 61, 213
Yūḥannā ibn Mīnā 91, 197
Yūḥannā ibn Sabbā 94, 492 n. 10
Yūsuf, Abū 34, 49, 370

Zachariah 146, 167, 231
Zādhānfarrūkh 367
ibn Ẓafar, Abū ʿAbd Allāh 46
l-Zāhidī, Abū l-Rajā 42
Zanādiqa 309
Zayd 117-18, 164, 167-8, 232-3, 267
Zayd ibn Thābit 274
Zayd –Zaynab affair 156, 168, 178
Zaynab 164, 232, 267, 325
Ziyād ibn ʿAbd Allāh ibn Yazīd ibn Muʿāwiya 426
Zoroastrianism 42, 82
Zoroastrians 54, 367, 390, 411
zunnār 395

Printed in the United States
By Bookmasters